Concise Dictionary of Great 20th Century Biographies

GRAMERCY BOOKS

New York • Avenel

This 1997 edition is published by Gramercy Books,
a division of Random House Value Publishing, Inc.,
40 Engelhard Avenue, Avenel, New Jersey 07001.

Gramercy Books and colophon are trademarks of
Random House Value Publishing, Inc.

Random House
New York • Toronto • London • Sydney • Auckland
http: / / www.randomhouse.com/

Printed and bound in the United States of America

A CIP catalog record for this book is available from the Library of Congress.

Concise Dictionary of Great 20th Century Biographies
ISBN 0-517-18069-3
8 7 6 5 4 3 2 1

Foreword

The illustrated *Concise Dictionary of Great 20th Century Biographies* is just that: a record, in words and pictures, of 300 *great* lives—of men and women who, across many cultures, races, religions, and beliefs, and over many decades, contributed positively to their time and to our world.

The reader will find no Adolf Hitler, no Josef Stalin, no Charles Manson in this volume, however notorious these names may be. For it is not fame but the furthering of society and culture which has earned the people included here their place in this book.

In keeping, perhaps, with the moral complexity of this century, not every entry will seem uniformly non-controversial or "politically correct." Still, as Abraham Lincoln wrote, "Show me a man without vices, and I'll show you a man without virtues." History appears to bear him out.

We make neither apologies for our choices nor excuses for omissions. Instead, we encourage readers to search their own values, their own hopes and dreams, to design a list of great biographies of their own. The process, we promise, will be humbling. For indeed, to be great, this book reminds us, is no small achievement. Yet how much more difficult it is to be *good*.

KATHRYN KNOX SOMAN
New York City, 1997

Adams, Ansel

(1902–1984)

AMERICAN PHOTOGRAPHER

Ansel Adams was born in San Francisco, California on February 20, 1902, and raised in a house that overlooked the Golden Gate Bridge. He took an early interest in music and taught himself how to play the piano. In 1916 Adams obtained his first camera and took a trip to Yosemite National Park in California. From that time on, the park, nature, and especially the High Sierra Mountains became his major interests. He returned to Yosemite every year to explore and to photograph. In 1920 he decided to become a professional musician. He gave concerts and piano lessons until 1927, when the publication of his first book of photographs won wide acclaim. He decided to change careers and concentrated solely on photography. Just as he had done with the piano, Adams studied the camera diligently and quickly began taking distinct and beautiful photographs.

Adams's early pictures were in the soft-focus tradition popular at the time, in which the image is hazy, or seen through a mist in order to make it look more like a painting. After he met the photographer Paul Strand, whose style was crisp and clear in detail, his ideas about photography were changed. He set about his work with great excitement. "Now photography exists!" he said to himself.

In 1932 Ansel Adams helped start Group f/64, which rebelled against the soft-focus technique. Adams wanted sharp detail in his pictures, focused through the smallest aperture in the camera lens (f/64). His photographs caught the attention of fellow photographer Alfred Stieglitz, who exhibited Adams's work for the first time in 1936.

Adams's involvement with nature was not limited to art. In 1934 he became involved with the Sierra Club conservation society and served on its Board of Directors until 1971. He was made honorary vice president in 1978 and held that position until his death. He appeared frequently before Congress, trying to preserve and protect the landscape he photographed, and he was awarded the Presidential Medal of Freedom in 1980 for his lifelong contributions.

He helped found the photography department of the Museum of Modern Art in New York in 1940. By the mid-1960s he had stopped taking pictures and concentrated on making prints from his negatives. He also worked on more than forty books in which he described in accurate detail the techniques he used to achieve his images.

Adams helped change the public's attitude toward photography by convincing many people that photographs should be considered as art. His wilderness photography, which celebrates an ideal vision of nature and the American West, includes some of the finest photographs in history.

Adenauer, Konrad

(1876–1967)

POST–WORLD WAR II
LEADER OF GERMANY

Konrad Adenauer, who led West Germany out of its low point after losing World War II to become a major economic power in Europe, was born in Cologne, Germany, on January 5, 1876. His father was first a soldier and then worked for Cologne's local government. Adenauer, admired in his youth for his hard-working determination, went to university and earned a law degree. His first job was with a well-known legal firm in Cologne.

In 1906, Adenauer went to work for Cologne's mayor; by 1917 he had become lord mayor, representing the German Center Party, a political group formed to protect the rights of Catholics, who were in the minority in Cologne. During his sixteen years as mayor, he earned a reputation for defending the interests of his region of Germany—the Rhineland (named after the important Rhine River)—against too much government control from Berlin, Germany's capital.

In 1933, as Adolf Hitler came to power in Germany, Adenauer was forced out of politics due to his strong opposition to Nazism. Until the end of World War II he kept a low profile and spent much of his time away from public attention. He did not escape the impact of Nazism, however, and was twice arrested and imprisoned by Hitler's secret police, the Gestapo. His second wife (Adenauer's first wife had died during World War I) was so badly abused during their imprisonment in 1944 that she died, and Adenauer was scheduled to be sent to the Buchenwald concentration camp. The ending of World War II not only saved his life but gave him the opportunity to return to his position as lord mayor of Cologne.

After World War II, the control of Germany was divided among the Allied countries that had defeated Hitler. Adenauer, whose uncompromising anti-Nazi policies made him popular with the Allies, soon disagreed with the British authorities who controlled Cologne and he was fired from his post. He turned his attention to German party politics and, expanding the German Center Party to take in all religions and groups that supported traditional democratic rule, helped create the Christian Democratic Union (CDU). By 1949, he was chairman of the powerful CDU for all of West Germany (the Soviet Union controlled what came to be known as East Germany).

In 1949, Germany held its first nationwide elections since the end of the war and, as leader of the victorious CDU party, Konrad Adenauer, at the age of seventy-three, was named chancellor after a close vote among his party's leaders. As Germany's first leader since Hitler, he had the task of rebuilding the country. He did this by focusing on the development of international relationships and entrusting the economic development of Germany to his economics minister, Ludwig Erhard. His approach to economic growth was essentially to give private business as much freedom as possible to develop.

In foreign affairs, Adenauer cultivated strong ties with the United States and worked hard to win back the trust of France, Germany's neighbor immediately to the west. From 1949 until his last election victory, in 1961, he was instrumental in forging the beginnings of Western European cooperation that would not only stand up to the Soviet bloc during the Cold War years, but would make Europe an economic powerhouse rivaling the United States and Japan.

The 1960s brought a change in political mood in Europe and elsewhere in the world. Adenauer's conservative policies and hard-line approach to relations with the Soviets were seen as old-fashioned. In 1963, the CDU forced him to resign as chancellor. When he died four years later, on April 16, 1967, at the age of ninety-one, Konrad Adenauer's contributions to rebuilding Europe were recognized and honored throughout the world.

Albee, Edward

(1 9 2 8 –   )

AMERICAN PLAYWRIGHT

Born in Virginia, Edward Albee was abandoned by his parents at birth. As a two-week-old infant, he was adopted by Reed and Frances Albee, the millionaire owners of a theater chain. Albee grew up in Larchmont, New York, in a lavish home complete with horses, servants, and private tutors. Since his parents were involved in the entertainment business, their home was often visited by many theatrical people.

Although Albee seemed to have everything a boy could want, he was not a very happy child. He did not do well in school, either, and was expelled from Lawrenceville Preparatory School in New Jersey and Valley Forge Military Academy in Pennsylvania. Finally, Albee ended up at the Choate School in Connecticut, where he often spent entire days writing fiction and poetry. He graduated from Choate in 1946, and attended Trinity College in Hartford, Connecticut, from 1946 to 1947.

Albee still did not get along well with his parents, and at the age of twenty he decided to leave home. He settled in Greenwich Village, in New York. For the next ten years, he supported himself with miscellaneous jobs. While living in Greenwich Village, Albee began to meet other authors. The poet W.H. Auden advised Albee to give up poetry and write prose instead. Thornton Wilder, a playwright, suggested that Albee try writing plays.

At the age of thirty, Albee wrote his first play, *The Zoo Story*. Unfortunately, he could not spark much interest in the play from the New York theater world. Albee's roommate, a composer named William Flanagan, sent the play to a friend of his in Europe. This contact led to the production of *The Zoo Story* in Germany in September 1959. Once it had achieved success abroad, *The Zoo Story* was produced in America in 1960, double-billing with Samuel Beckett's famous play, *Krapp's Last Tape*. Beckett belonged to a school of European playwrights who wrote for what was known as the Theater of the Absurd. Since Albee's play was coproduced with Beckett's, he became linked with the absurdist playwriting genre.

In his work, Albee dramatizes the reality of humanity's condition as well as the illusions that people create to distance themselves from the truth of their condition. His characters' searches for true identity are usually portrayed within the context of family relationships.

Albee wrote five plays in two years following the production of *The Zoo Story*. They include *The Death of Bessie Smith* (1960), *The Sandbox* (1960), *Fam and Yam* (1960), *The American Dream* (1961), and his most successful and well-known play, *Who's Afraid of Virginia Woolf?* (1962). In each of these plays, characters give up the identities they derived from their family or from popular culture in order to find their own sense of identity. The earlier plays involved characters that represented certain symbolic types of people. *Who's Afraid of Virginia Woolf?*, however, portrays characters and situations that more closely resemble real life.

In 1963, he won two Tony Awards and the New York Drama Critics' Circle Award for *Who's Afraid of Virginia Woolf?* He received a Pulitzer Prize in 1966 for *A Delicate Balance* (though many critics and fans believed that *Who's Afraid of Virginia Woolf?* should have won the prestigious award). Albee was awarded a second Pulitzer Prize in 1975 for a play entitled *Seascape.*

Ali, Muhammad (born Cassius Marcellus Clay)

(1942–)

AMERICAN BOXER

"I am the boldest, the prettiest, the most superior, most scientific, most skillfullest fighter in the ring today," said Muhammad Ali. As a boxer, Ali set out to prove these words true. He charmed many people with his wit and angered some when he protested the Vietnam War and spoke out bluntly against racism.

Born in Louisville, Kentucky, Ali's birth name came from his great-great-great-grandfather, a slave. His mother was a domestic worker. His father was a sign painter who described Ali as a large baby with a big head. "I used to look at him and say, 'That's gonna be nothing but another Joe Louis.'"

Ali started boxing in junior high. Angered when someone stole his new bike, he sought help from a policeman who taught boxing at the local gym. The man told Ali he should learn how to box. Ali proved to be fast and strong for his 89 pounds. He beat opponents by fighting so tirelessly that they gave up.

In high school, Ali had some problems at the start. He sometimes fell asleep in class because he got up so early each morning to run in the park. He got into fights with other students. But, his principal said, "Cassius continually improved in schoolwork, attendance, and citizenship. He was an average student and we planned his program to help him in his career." By then Ali was seriously training to be a prizefighter. He spent hours skipping rope and hitting a punching bag, hoping to box in the Olympics.

By age 18, Ali had won 100 of 108 amateur matches. In 1959, he had won the national Golden Gloves and Amateur Athletic Union light-heavyweight championships, and his trophies and medals adorned the Clays' four-room home.

In 1960, the Olympics were held in Rome, Italy. The 6′2″ Ali was known as one of the friendliest athletes. Greeting people from many countries and posing for pictures, he called America "the greatest country in the world." In the four events he had to win, Ali used swift movements and solid punches to crush his opponents.

Now the 178-pound teenager was Olympic lightweight champion. Thrilled with his gold medal, he wore it around the clock for two days. Back home, Louisville honored him with a parade and other events. But the city still discriminated against blacks during those years. Certain restaurants and stores refused to serve blacks, and they made no exception for Ali.

Ali grew another inch, combining size with his remarkable speed. He became a professional boxer, employing a manager, trainer, and financial advisors. Over the next two years, he defeated several opponents. With some of his earnings he bought a new car and a house for his parents in suburban Louisville. Ali's behavior brought him as much attention as his fighting. He was cocky and articulate during his frequent TV appearances. Some newswriters called him "Mighty Mouth" when he said things like "I'm not just the greatest, I'm the double greatest" and "They say that the greatest was Sugar Ray; but they have yet to see Cassius Clay."

In 1964, he had the chance to fight heavyweight Sonny Liston, who had not lost a fight in nine years. At age 22, Ali proved his ability by defeating Liston. Ali was the new world champion. Soon after this he decided to change his religion and join the Nation of Islam. He took the Muslim name Muhammad Ali. Some people criticized his actions and hoped he would lose in the ring. But Ali successfully defended his title against Liston, then beat former champion Floyd Patterson.

During the mid-1960s, the United States was becoming more involved in the Vietnam War in Southeast Asia. Young men were being drafted to fight there, and Ali was inducted in 1967. He refused to enter the army, saying his religious beliefs forbade him to fight. Some Americans praised Ali for risking prison to stand up for his beliefs. Others called him a draft dodger and traitor. His titles were taken from him and he was not allowed to box. Ali toured the country giving speeches, often on college campuses.

After a long court battle, Ali was convicted of draft evasion and sentenced to five years in jail and a $10,000 fine. His lawyers appealed his case, asking a higher court to rule on it.

In another lawsuit, a judge ruled that Ali could still box professionally. The new heavyweight champion was Joe Frazier, and a match was set for 1971. Newspapers called it "The Fight of the Century." Each man earned $2.5 million just for taking part. They fought fiercely for fourteen rounds, during which Joe Frazier kept the edge. In the fifteenth round, Frazier knocked Ali down.

He got up, but all the judges named Frazier the winner. Ali was upset not to regain his title, but he talked calmly after the fight.

That same year, he won his legal battle when the Supreme Court said he was not guilty of draft evasion. The Court declared that Ali should not have been drafted at all. Ali spent the next three years fighting other champions and earning about $5 million. He won all but one fight, to Ken Norton, whom he later beat. He also won a rematch with Joe Frazier. But Frazier had lost the heavyweight title to George Foreman, so Ali did not become the champion after he won. For that, he would have to fight Foreman.

Millions of people sat before their televisions to watch the fight between Ali and Foreman. Sixty thousand fans gathered at the stadium in Kinshasa in the African nation of Zaire. People favored Foreman, who was seven years younger than the 32-year-old Ali. But Ali fought brilliantly, tiring his opponent. In round eight, he knocked Foreman out. He could still "float like a butterfly and sting like a bee," as he liked to say.

Ali fought Frazier a third time in 1975, and beat him again. Although he was wealthy enough to retire, Ali kept boxing. In 1978 he lost his heavyweight title to 24-year-old Leon Spinks. Unwilling to quit, Ali fought him again that year and regained his title. In 1979 he announced that he was quitting. But only a year later, Ali agreed to fight Larry Holmes. After being badly beaten, Ali quit for good.

As Ali entered his forties, he looked ill. His movements were slow and awkward; his walk was shaky. He seemed to have trouble speaking. People guessed that boxing had damaged the fighter's brain. But Ali had Parkinson's disease, an illness of the nervous system for which he was taking medication. "I feel fine," he insisted. "I'm older and fatter, but we all change."

Even so, fans felt sad to see the former champ looking old and sick. He urged them not to worry, saying, "I have a beautiful wife and . . . eight kids in all. . . . All are healthy. I have more fans and loved ones than any one person in the world. I've been invited to the countries of the world. . . . I'm happy and doing real good."

Arbus, Diane

(1923–1971)

AMERICAN PHOTOGRAPHER

> Taking pictures is like tiptoeing into the kitchen late at night and stealing Oreo cookies.
>
> —Diane Arbus, in a lecture on her art

Diane Nemerov was born on March 14, 1923, in New York. Her father was a businessman who specialized in high fashion clothing. Her brother, Howard, was one of America's finest poets.

In the spring of 1937 Diane's father arranged for her to take sketching lessons from the store's illustrator. There she met Allan Arbus, who was working part-time. She was fourteen and he was nineteen, but she fell in love with him immediately.

In 1938 her parents enrolled her in the Cummington School of the Arts near Northampton, Massachusetts. She studied painting and met Alexander Eliot, who became a lifelong friend; later he was the art editor for *Time* magazine. Less than a month after her eighteenth birthday, Diane Nemerov married Allan Arbus. They rented an apartment across the hall from Alexander Eliot and his wife, Anne.

Allan Arbus joined the Army in 1943 and was sent to train in New Jersey. He took photography courses and each evening he taught his wife everything he had learned during the day. Diane Arbus also studied for a short while with the documentary photographer Berenice Abbott.

At the end of World War II the Arbuses went into business as fashion photographers. Diane's father hired them to photograph newspaper advertisements for his store. They were soon working for numerous fashion magazines, including *Vogue* and *Glamour*. They also provided ads for Greyhound Bus Company and Maxwell House Coffee. In 1957 they decided to break their business partnership, and a year later they separated.

Diane Arbus, wearing her camera at all times, began frequenting sideshows and circuses. She was fascinated by the performers and became friends with many of them, who let her photograph them. In 1959 she was hired by *Esquire* magazine to photograph New York. She worked for five months, taking pictures of eccentric citizens of the city, the homeless, and other ignored aspects of city life.

She also traveled around the city with newspaper photographer Weegee. He drove around New York in a beat-up Chevrolet, listening to the police radio and taking photographs of crimes and fires and other catastrophes. Arbus admired his factual and detached approach to his photos.

In 1965, Arbus began teaching photography courses. Three of her photographs were exhibited at the Museum of Modern Art, and she was worried how people might react to her bold pictures. Most people did not like them; some even spit on them as they hung on the museum walls. Her work did receive some good critical reviews, however, and she received the first of her two Guggenheim fellowships.

It was not until the 1980s that Arbus's style and content were considered significant and a major influence in photography. Along with Robert Frank, she helped changed the attitude of documentary photography from the benevolent style of the 1930s and 1940s to a more glaring and unsettling honesty in pictures.

Arbus also continued shooting fashion photographs as well. She had many assignments from the *New York Times* to photograph children's fashions, and in 1971 the London *Sunday Times* hired her to take wedding photographs of Tricia Nixon, daughter of President Nixon. For much of her work she was paid half of what a man would be paid. She constantly argued that she was "a photographer, not a woman photographer," and wanted to make women photographers considered the equals of their male colleagues.

Although Arbus was divorced from Allan Arbus in 1969, he continued to support her financially throughout her life. She had fought depression much of her life, and in the late summer of 1971 she complained that her photography no longer satisfied her. She was worried that she would only be remembered as "the photographer of freaks." She was convinced that her pictures had no value, and in late July she committed suicide.

Arendt, Hannah

(1906–1975)

GERMAN-BORN AMERICAN
PHILOSOPHER AND
POLITICAL SCIENTIST

The sad truth is that most evil is done by
people who never made up their minds to
be either good or evil.

—Hannah Arendt

Although she rejected the label of philosopher, preferring to call herself a political scientist, at the heart of Hannah Arendt's political writing was always an
acute ethical consciousness; Arendt's best work is about good and evil as the
byproducts of political systems. And in a century that produced some of the
most appalling evils known to history, her analysis is essential reading. In her
last book, Arendt came to the conclusion that only the "activity of thinking"
could enable humanity to turn its back on evil.

Born Johanna Arendt in Hannover, Germany, on October 14, 1906, she was
the pampered only child of Paul Arendt, an engineer, and his wife, Martha. Her
family were well-to-do assimilated Jews, and she went to the best schools,
where she was an outstanding student. Hannah's father died when she was only
seven, and she was raised by her mother. She would later recall that her father's
death had "scarred" her, but that on the whole she was a happy child, growing
up in Königsburg, in Prussia.

As a teenager, Hannah was willful, stubborn, perhaps a little spoiled, but
immensely intelligent. She read voraciously—poetry, philosophy, fiction. She
also wrote poetry, most of it reflecting a typically teenage obsession with death.
After reading the work of Sören Kierkegaard, she decided she would study theology.

However, at the University of Marburg, she met and studied with Martin
Heidegger, the first of three great German philosophers whom she would encounter during her student days. She would have an affair with Heidegger, who
was seventeen years her senior and married; it would last on and off until his involvement with the Nazis in the mid-thirties. He steered her into philosophy as
a discipline and instilled in her a reverence for the process of thinking.

After her year at Marburg, Arendt matriculated at Freiburg, where she studied with Heidegger's teacher, Edmund Husserl. Under his tutelage, she was in-

troduced to phenomenology, the philosophical school of which he was the foremost exponent. Finally, Arendt moved on to Heidelberg, where she studied with one of the great thinkers of German existentialism, Karl Jaspers, with whom she would remain friends for the rest of his life. With Jaspers as her advisor, she wrote (and later published) her dissertation on St. Augustine's concept of love.

In 1929, Arendt married another philosophy student, Gunther Stern. While he was studying for his advanced degree, she began work on her first book, a study of Rachel Varnhagen, a prominent Jewish salon hostess in eighteenth-century Germany. In Varnhagen, she had found someone with whom she had definite affinities, a woman of intellect who was also a pariah because of her gender and ethnicity, but who was an almost totally assimilated Jew.

The book was nearing completion in 1933 when history intervened. Arendt was arrested by the Gestapo. She was held for eight days and then released. After a brief stay in Prague, she went to Paris, France. She had left without travel papers of any kind, and for the next eighteen years, until she took United States citizenship, she would be a stateless person.

Stern joined her in Paris, but their marriage was at best fragile. In 1936, she would meet Heinrich Blucher, a communist activist; in 1940, she would divorce Stern and marry Blucher.

In Paris she was joined by her mother (who had smuggled out what little money the Nazis hadn't confiscated by disguising gold coins as coat buttons). Arendt took a job with Youth Aliya, a group that aided Jewish orphans by relocating them in Palestine. With the outbreak of World War II and the quick German march across Europe, the trio were no longer safe in Paris. They managed to obtain emergency visas and went to New York.

In New York the three refugees lived in a small, cramped apartment. Arendt began writing a newspaper column for the German-language daily *Aufbau*. Finally, in 1942, she secured her first teaching position in the United States, a class on modern European history at Brooklyn College. Through the 1940s, she would take a number of different jobs and write on a freelance basis for a variety of periodicals.

The revelation that the Nazis had embarked on a program of the systematic extermination of Europe's Jews shook Arendt to the very core of her being. "The abyss had opened," she would recall later. Out of the fires of the Auschwitz concentration camp came her most important work, *The Origins of Totalitarianism* (1951), a three-volume study of the new, modern phenomena of the totalitarian state, which she called the "embodiment of radical evil." Such an evil is so great and all-encompassing, so mindless that, she says, "anger could not revenge, love could not endure, and friendship could not forgive." She argued that anti-Semitism was merely the first part of a larger movement of political repression and the dehumanizing alienation that had become an integral part of post-Renaissance European politics, with its emphasis on mass society. In the work as a whole, Arendt argued that participation in the political process was the only guarantor of freedom; without the mass participation of the people, the State is run by private interest groups or cults of personality such as arose around Hitler and Stalin. In her later book, *On Revolution* (1963), she contrasted the American Revolution and the French Revolution as examples of the successful way to share power and responsibility and a disastrous perversion of the stated ideals of "liberty, equality, and fraternity."

The Origins of Totalitarianism was essentially the first systematic examination of this new political phenomenon. Coming not too long after the conclusion of the war and the beginning of the Cold War, it was a big seller, giving Arendt and Blucher some measure of financial security. A Guggenheim Foundation grant followed, designed to fund a study by Arendt of the Marxist elements of Russian totalitarianism. She was then teaching philosophy at the University of Chicago and later at the New School for Social Research. She was also writing magazine and journal articles at a furious pace.

In 1963, Arendt stepped into the most damaging and violent controversy of her career. The Israeli government had seized Nazi leader Adolf Eichmann from his hiding place in Argentina and transported him to Jerusalem, where he was placed on trial for his role in the design and execution of the "Final Solution," the extermination of six million Jews and countless millions of others in the death camps. Arendt was asked to cover the trial by *The New Yorker*. The resulting articles and the book that came from them, *Eichmann in Jerusalem: A Report on the Banality of Evil*, stirred tremendous anger in Jewish communities around the world. As the subtitle suggests, Arendt believed that the evil that Eichmann represented was neither demonic nor mysterious, and that to demonize it in that way was to dignify it. Eichmann was a bureaucrat, thoughtless, calculating, and bland, not a satanic figure. Although she had misgivings about the legality of the trial itself, Arendt had no problem with the verdict. On the other hand, she was disturbed by the glossing over of what she felt was Jewish collaboration, by the Nazi-appointed community councils, with the murderers. She was the first writer to raise this issue, which has been a source of considerable argument ever since.

Arendt found herself under concerted attack in the United States, Israel, and Europe. Gershom Scholem denounced her book as "heartless . . . sneering and malicious," and speakers attacked her at meetings of campus Jewish student groups all over America. She was also defended by many in the Jewish community. Eventually, the rift would heal. Arendt remained an active member of the board of directors of the Conference on Jewish Social Studies and a supporter, although a critical one, of the State of Israel.

In the 1960s and 1970s, Arendt continued teaching, lecturing, and writing. Her essays on the student rebellion of the 1960s, the Vietnam War, and Watergate were collected in *Crises of the Republic*. In 1969, Jaspers died, and the following year Blucher. For the first time in many years, Arendt felt alone and lonely.

Her response was to return one last time to philosophy, her first love. She began work on a projected three-part study, *The Life of the Mind*. In the course of its three sections, "Thinking," "Willing," and "Judging," she would examine the preconditions necessary to a life of contemplation and the mechanisms by which these actions were performed. In the first volume, *Thinking*, she also returned once more to the question of Eichmann and the nature of evil, reasserting that his actions lacked motive, interest, or will, hence any capacity to distinguish right from wrong. Regrettably, Arendt died before she could finish the final volume of the trilogy; she suffered a fatal heart attack in December 1975. In her typewriter was a sheet of paper with the single work *judging* written on it. The first two volumes were published posthumously in 1979.

In the preface to *The Origins of Totalitarianism*, Arendt wrote that what she was striving for was "comprehension." She defined it as "the unpremeditated, attentive facing up to, and resisting of, reality—whatever it may be." She had faced the worst realities of a bloody century and resisted them with integrity and intellectual strength.

Armstrong, Louis

(1900–1971)

AMERICAN MUSICIAN AND COMPOSER

> People love me and my music, and you know I love them. The minute I walk on the bandstand, they know they're going to get something good. I see to that.
>
> —Louis Armstrong, during a radio interview in England, January (1959)

More than any other American musician, the life and career of the trumpeter and vocalist Louis Armstrong tells the history of jazz music from its start in the Dixieland clubs in the black quarter of New Orleans to its worldwide popularity as a uniquely American art form.

Daniel Louis Armstrong was born on July 4, 1900, in a two room shack in the poor black ghetto of New Orleans. His father, Willie, was a turpentine worker who left his mother, Maryann, when Louis was five years old. Louis and his sister Beatrice lived with his mother and grandmother while his mother worked as a housemaid in the early 1900s.

As a boy Louis would sing for pennies on the street, and he later formed a quartet in which he played a guitar that was built out of an old cigar box. At night he would hang around the seedy bars in the Storyville district of New Orleans. As legend has it, on New Year's Eve in 1913 Louis borrowed his stepfather's gun and fired it into the air six times. As a punishment he spent the night in jail.

Louis, always getting into trouble with the law over petty crimes, was frequently put into the Colored Waif's Home for Boys. There the home's drill instructor and bandmaster, Peter Davis, gave the boy a bugle and taught him how to play it and read music. In a year Louis graduated to the cornet and was leading the home's brass band. When Louis was released from the home in 1915, he delivered coal, did errands for people, and searched in garbage cans for food.

Armstrong began to take cornet lessons from Joe (King) Oliver, a Dixieland musician who played the popular music of the day—ragtime, blues, and sentimental songs. In 1917 when King Oliver left to play in Chicago, Armstrong replaced him in Kid Ory's band. Soon people took note of the young man's talent on the cornet and his ability to improvise as he played. In 1920 Armstrong joined Fate Marable's band, which played on the riverboat *Dixie Belle* as it traveled up and down the Mississippi. A year later Armstrong wrote his first song, "I Wish I Could Shimmy Like My Sister Kate."

In 1922 King Oliver invited Armstrong to Chicago to join his Original Creole Jazz Band. There, the two men played cornet together. Armstrong quickly matured as a musician, and he soon made the first of his hundreds of recordings. In 1924, he married the pianist of the Creole band, Lillian Hardin, who encouraged her husband to join Fletcher Henderson's orchestra in New York, where Armstrong made recordings with the great blues singer Bessie Smith. By then Louis was playing the trumpet and also singing with his raspy voice. He was the first musician to use scat singing. Many other jazz singers would adopt this practice, such as Ella Fitzgerald.

Back in Chicago in 1925, Armstrong formed his own small band of five musicians known as the "Hot Five," who began recording a series of more than sixty performances that featured Armstrong's most creative trumpet playing. These records set the style of the improvised jazz solo that almost every musician of the day tried to copy. Songs like "Potato Head Blues" became the trademark style of "Satchmo," a nickname shortened from "Satchelmouth" because of the largeness of Armstrong's lips and cheeks when he played the trumpet.

A turning-point came in Armstrong's career after he returned from his first concert tour in Europe in 1932. Satchmo began to perform with big bands, which paved the way for the swing band era in music around 1935. Armstrong also started performing more popular songs and moved away from the free-form jazz improvisations that made him famous during the 1920s. He took on a broader appeal as a popular entertainer. Armstrong was the first black performer to have a sponsored radio show and to appear regularly in Hollywood feature films. The first was *Pennies from Heaven* (1936) with Bing Crosby, and there would be twenty-eight other films in the next thirty-two years.

In 1945 after World War II, the big-band era came to an end, and Satchmo changed with the times. He performed with a smaller band in a New Orleans–style format, Louis Armstrong and the All Stars. During this period Satchmo sometimes made a return to his previous years as an innovative jazz player, but often he used his band as a showcase for singing pop songs like "Hello, Dolly." During the late 1940s and 1950s, the U.S. State Department hired Armstrong to give a series of goodwill concerts in many countries around the world. Perhaps the highlight was his trip to Africa in 1956, when Armstrong was greeted by more than one hundred thousand people in Accra, West Africa. His response was: "After all, my ancestors came from here and I still have African blood in me."

After the race riots in the late 1950s in Arkansas and other parts of the South, Armstrong was critical of the policies of President Eisenhower, and he canceled a tour of Russia because of the poor treatment of black Americans by the U.S. government.

Armstrong suffered a heart attack in 1959 and, because of other health complications, greatly reduced his activities as an entertainer. Wherever he played, he continued to be admired for his contributions to American music. In the late 1950s the American conductor Leonard Bernstein lauded Armstrong's career both as a performer and composer of jazz music, influencing classical music as well as new generations of jazz trumpet players like Dizzy Gillespie and Miles Davis.

In early 1971, despite his deteriorating health, Satchmo insisted on playing an engagement at the Waldorf-Astoria Hotel in New York, followed by a few television appearances. He made his last recording at the end of February 1971. Louis Armstrong died on July 6, 1971, at his home in Corona, New York.

Armstrong, Neil Alden

(1930–   )

AMERICAN ASTRONAUT AND FIRST
PERSON TO WALK ON THE MOON

One small step for man, one giant leap for mankind.

> —Neil Armstrong, setting foot
> on the Moon, July 20, 1969

Neil Alden Armstrong was born in his grandparents' farmhouse near Wapakoneta, Ohio, on August 5, 1930. He was an exceptionally intelligent boy who learned to read before he started school. In the first grade he read ninety books. He skipped the second grade; tests showed that he was already reading as well as most fifth-graders.

Neil was interested in music—an interest he probably got from his mother. During his free time, he played the horn and the piano, took part in Boy Scout activities, and looked at the starry sky through a neighbor's telescope. He had no way of knowing, as he studied the pitted surface of the Moon through the small telescope, that one day he would be the first human being to walk there.

When Neil was six, his father took him on an airplane ride, and the boy discovered a new and lasting love: flight. He became obsessed with the idea of flight. He filled his room with model airplanes, and he loved to hang around airports doing odd jobs for the pilots. Sometimes he even dreamed that if he held his breath, he would rise into the air and fly.

Armstrong learned to fly before he learned to drive a car. By the age of sixteen he had obtained his pilot's license. He started college at Purdue University in Indiana, studying aeronautical engineering—the science of designing aircraft. When war broke out in Korea (1950–53), he left college to serve as a pilot in the U.S. Navy. Although he was the youngest pilot in his squadron, Armstrong flew seventy-eight combat missions over Korea from the aircraft carrier *Essex*. His most dangerous moment came when one of the wings of his jet was damaged on a bombing run. He managed to keep the plane in the air long enough to get out of enemy territory before parachuting to safety. Later, as an astronaut, he would show the same blend of skill and coolness in an equally dangerous crisis.

Armstrong could have made a career in the Navy, but after the war was over he chose to return to civilian life. He left the Navy and returned to Purdue for a degree in aeronautical engineering, which he received in 1955. He married and had three children: two sons and a daughter (the daughter died at an early age). By this time Armstrong had moved his family to California and gone to work at Edwards Air Force Base in California for the National Aeronautics and Space Administration (NASA), which was developing high-speed rocket planes.

As a test pilot, Armstrong was one of a select few pilots who pushed at the very frontiers of flight by flying experimental planes, such as the X-15, always trying to go faster, higher, and farther. In 1962 Armstrong won an award for his work as an X-15 test pilot, and that same year he joined NASA's astronaut training program.

His first mission into space came in 1966 when he piloted the *Gemini 8*, a spacecraft that orbited the Earth. The *Gemini 8* flight included both a triumph and a near-disaster. It was the first mission in which a spacecraft docked, or joined, another spacecraft while in orbit. Under Armstrong's control, the *Gemini 8* capsule docked smoothly with an unoccupied vehicle that had been launched earlier. This successful docking proved that spacecraft could meet and refuel in orbit. It paved the way for later missions that would involve more than one spacecraft and would require astronauts to move from one vessel to another.

But soon after the docking procedure, *Gemini 8* ran into trouble. The two-person spacecraft went out of control and began spinning wildly in space, revolving once a second. Armstrong and his partner, astronaut David Scott, were becoming dizzy and disoriented. Armstrong radioed mission control on Earth: "We've got serious problems here. . . . We're tumbling end over end!" Faced with a crisis, growing dizzier by the second, Armstrong managed to bring the wildly tumbling craft under control. Then, seeing that he had used up much of the vessel's fuel in the emergency maneuvers, he made a quick decision to leave orbit earlier than planned. The capsule made a safe splashdown in the Pacific Ocean.

Gemini 8 could have been lost, but Armstrong saved the mission—and his life. Impressed with his calm nerves and clear thinking, NASA chose him three years later for the most historic space flight of all: *Apollo 11*, which made the first landing on the Moon. In preparation for the mission, he spent more than four hundred hours in flight simulators, training machines that were identical to the spacecraft's cabin.

Armstrong was named commander of the three-person *Apollo 11* crew. Armstrong was chosen for his leadership abilities. As commander, Armstrong would have a unique honor: He would be the first human being to step onto the surface of the Moon.

The *Apollo 11* mission was the climax of a long race between the United States and what was then called the Soviet Union to see who would be first on the Moon. The Soviets actually launched their own spacecraft, the *Luna 15*, just three days before *Apollo 11* blasted off on July 16, 1969. But *Luna 15* was unoccupied, and aboard *Apollo 11* three astronauts were riding into history.

They blasted off from the Kennedy Space Center in Florida. More than a million people came from all over the country to camp patiently in fields and along roads outside the space center, waiting to see *Apollo 11* take off. They were not disappointed. The launch took place at 9:32 P.M., blazing a fiery trail into the night sky. Even ten miles away the powerful rocket engines shook the Earth and roared in the sky; inside the space capsule, the astronauts were shaken in their spacesuits as the rocket lifted them away from Earth.

Once the spacecraft was safely in orbit around the Moon, Armstrong and Aldrin prepared to descend to the surface in the lunar module, or LM, which was called the *Eagle*. Collins remained behind in the orbiting capsule, the *Columbia*. The LM was going to land on an area of the Moon's surface called the Sea of Tranquility.

Searching for a clear landing spot, Armstrong saw that the LM's precious fuel was being gobbled up fast. He had just minutes left to land the *Eagle,* or they would have to cut short the mission and return to the *Columbia* without touching down on the Moon. Seeing a suitable landing site, Armstrong took over the piloting of the LM and brought it down manually, carrying out this tricky maneuver with skill. A moment later he radioed to mission control in Houston: "Tranquility Base here. The *Eagle* has landed."

Those words, carried to millions of listeners around the world, signaled that a new era in human history had begun. For the first time, people had ventured not just into space but onto another world. Then, when Armstrong—clad in his spacesuit—stepped out of the LM onto the surface of the Moon, he uttered the often-quoted statement that it was a "giant leap for mankind." One billion people watched that step on television. President Richard Nixon radioed his congratulations. "Because of what you have done," he told the astronauts, "the heavens have become a part of man's world."

In honor of the pioneers of flight, Armstrong and Aldrin carried with them a tiny scrap of the *Kitty Hawk,* the Wright brothers' first plane. They also carried an American flag, which they set up on the Moon's surface, and a plaque that read: "We came in peace for all mankind."

Earlier, some scientists had thought that anyone who stepped onto the Moon's surface might sink helplessly into deep, fine dust. Armstrong's first step proved that these fears were unfounded. "The surface is fine and powdery," he reported. "I can pick it up loosely with my toe. . . . I only go in a small fraction of an inch, maybe an eighth of an inch. But I can see the footprints of my boots and the treads in the fine, sandy particles." These were the first footprints in the Moon's eons-long history.

A mishap nearly marred the astronauts' return. One of their spacesuits accidentally broke off part of a switch that controlled the rocket that the LM would use to take off from the Moon. Mission control in Houston suggested that they take apart a ballpoint pen and use it to replace the broken switch. Fortunately, the pen did the job. The *Eagle* left the Moon, rejoined the *Columbia*, and made a safe journey back to Earth, where the three astronauts received a hero's welcome.

Perhaps Armstrong felt that having made the first landing on the Moon was enough fame and adventure for anyone. He made no further spaceflights. He took an administrative job in NASA's Washington, D.C., offices. In 1971, Armstrong left the space program to teach aerospace engineering at the University of Cincinnati.

Ashe, Arthur

(1943–1993)

AMERICAN TENNIS CHAMPION

When Arthur Ashe was growing up in Richmond, Virginia, there were few black players in major tournaments. Tennis was dominated by wealthy people, mostly white men. As a child, Arthur admired tennis pro Pancho Gonzales, whose skin color, he said, was "closest to mine." When he first played at age 7, he borrowed a racket and used a court that was for "Negroes only."

Arthur Ashe's father was a park police officer. His mother died when he was 6. (Arthur later said that she had taught him to read when he was 4, as well as having taught him "about manners.") To help him cope with his grief, Arthur ran, swam, and played baseball with his brother John. Eager to learn tennis, he asked a playground coach for lessons. He worked so hard that he beat much older boys in a tournament when he was 9.

Arthur's coach asked Dr. R. Walter Johnson to watch his small, thin student play. Dr. Johnson had helped Althea Gibson and other black athletes. He agreed that Arthur was promising, and asked him to join the young people who came to his home in the summer to practice on his tennis court. Studying with Dr. Johnson and playing with his group improved Arthur's game greatly.

Arthur continued to win matches, but was not allowed to play against whites in segregated Virginia. Efforts to enter him in tournaments sponsored by the U.S. Lawn Tennis Association (USLTA) met with resistance. Meanwhile, Arthur moved to St. Louis to work with a new coach in 1960. He was enrolled in the USLTA's Junior Singles Indoor Tournament. There he won first place, impressing people with his form, hitting power, and agile movements on the court.

Arthur finished high school in St. Louis. He had the highest grades in his class and earned a scholarship to UCLA, (University of California at Los Angeles). Ashe was happy to attend a school known for both its strong academic program and fine tennis team.

In 1963, Ashe won the National Clay Court Championship and played in his first Wimbledon (All-England) Tournament. That year he became the first black on the U.S. Davis Cup team, coached by his idol, Pancho Gonzales. He helped the team to win the cup for the United States. Ashe said Gonzales gave him expert help: "He could look at you hitting the ball and diagnose all your mistakes."

In 1964 Ashe got his chance to play in the USLTA championships at Forest Hills, New York. He reached the quarterfinals. That year he received a special honor: the annual Johnston Award, given to the player who stands for the best character and sportsmanship in tennis. When he accepted it, Ashe said, "I hope I can prove to be the exception to the rule that good guys always finish last!"

Ashe was ranked third in 1965, and he seemed to become tense on the court. People said he had lost his concentration. He regained his edge during that year's Davis Cup matches, helping the U.S. team win again. By college graduation in 1966, Ashe was ranked second among men players. Then, in 1968, he made it to the final round at the U.S. Open tournament, which he won in five difficult sets. He earned another major title at the Australian Open in 1970.

For several years, Ashe had wanted to play in the South African Open tournament. The government there enforced strict race segregation laws and would not let him compete. In 1971 he made a goodwill trip to Africa, playing in exhibitions and speaking to young people. He was finally allowed to play in the 1973 Open.

As a professional, Ashe won many titles, including the men's doubles at Wimbledon. In 1975 he reached the men's singles final. He played 22-year-old Jimmy Connors, ten years younger than Ashe and ranked first in the world. When Ashe won the first set, the crowd began to get excited. He had planned his strategy carefully and was returning Connors's powerful serve well. He played a strong net game, hitting accurate volleys. Arthur Ashe beat Connors in four sets, and became the first black man to win Wimbledon.

By 1977 Ashe needed surgery for a long-standing heel injury. He married Jeanne Moutoussamy, a photographer who worked for NBC-TV. He was busy endorsing products, doing TV commentary, and developing a program to teach tennis to inner city children. Then, at age 36, he suffered from a heart-attack, but he recovered. He and his wife adopted a baby girl, whom they named Camera.

Ashe's many fans were saddened in 1992 when he announced that he had AIDS, which impairs the body's ability to fight disease. A blood transfusion during heart-bypass surgery in 1983 appeared to have caused it. Ashe was praised for his dignity and courage. He told people he had learned to live with AIDS and was taking medications to control its effects. Ashe had spent much of his life on causes that would benefit others; now he became an important and articulate spokesperson for AIDS education and treatment.

Early in life, his father had told him, "Treat everybody with the same respect and don't sweat the little stuff—or, for that matter, the big stuff. You'll never know the difference a hundred years from today." Arthur Ashe said these words had inspired him to deal with the challenges of his life, including racism. He called AIDS "one more challenge." Ashe died in 1993. His courage and contributions continue to inspire people all over the world.

Ashrawi, Hanan

(1946–   )

SPOKESWOMAN FOR THE PALESTINE LIBERATION
ORGANIZATION AND PALESTINIAN RIGHTS

> We have seen you look back in deepest sorrow at the tragedy of your past and look on in horror at the disfigurement of the victim turned oppressor.
>
> —Hanan Ashrawi, to the Israeli people, 1991

Palestine Liberation Organization (PLO) activist Hanan Ashrawi was born Hanan Mikhail in 1946 in Ramallah, in what is now called the West Bank, a disputed area of Israeli-occupied land inhabited mostly by Arabs and Palestinians. The youngest of five girls, she was taught by her father, a local politician, to treasure the concept of an independent Arab Palestine.

Palestine had been controlled by the Ottoman Empire (what is today Turkey and Syria) for centuries before it came under British control at the time of Ashrawi's childhood. In the struggle for the creation of Israel in 1947–48, the territory that Palestinian Arabs had hoped would become their independent country was divided among the newly created state of Israel and other neighboring countries, including Egypt and Jordan. This left the Palestinian Arabs with no land to call their own. Since that time, particularly since the Six-Day War of 1967, when Israel claimed additional Arab lands, they have been under the control of Israel.

In the 1960s, Ashrawi studied at the American University in Beirut, Lebanon, where she earned a master's degree in literature, and joined the General Union of Palestinian Students, a political group. During this time she first met Yasir Arafat, the leader of the PLO. In 1973, she began teaching literature at Bir Zeit University in the West Bank. Later she traveled to the United States to earn a doctorate in literature from the University of Virginia in 1981. Throughout her academic career, she was noted for having a sharp intellect, strong determination, and an ability to persuade others. Returning to the West Bank, Hanan Mikhail married a filmmaker named Ashrawi and had two daughters. She also resumed her teaching career at Bir Zeit University.

In the 1970s, Ashrawi became increasingly active in the movement for Palestinian human rights, which she believed were becoming more and more abused under Israeli occupation of the West Bank. The standard of living was declining; there were increasing restrictions on where Palestinians could travel in the region; protest demonstrations were crushed, often violently, by the Israeli army; and, at the same time, large numbers of immigrant Jews were being encouraged by the Israeli government to settle in the West Bank territory. A military invasion of Lebanon by Israel in 1982, in which Palestinian refugees were killed, spurred Ashrawi to take more direct action to help her people.

Initially Ashrawi organized protests against Israeli military actions. Then, in 1987, the *intifada* (mass riots and demonstrations by Arab citizens against Israelis) erupted in the West Bank and she suddenly gained international exposure when she was interviewed on ABC television's *Nightline* to represent the Palestinian position. In the following months she would appear on U.S. television several times. She became known as an impressive, passionate, yet thoughtful and articulate voice for Palestinian Arabs and the cause of independence. "They are holding a whole people captive against their will. They are stealing these people's land and resources and freedoms and rights and the possibility of a future" is how she summed up her position sometime later.

Despite a setback caused by the PLO's support for Iraq's Saddam Hussein against the United States and its allies in the 1990 Persian Gulf war, Ashrawi and Palestinian leaders, particularly Yasir Arafat, pursued a settlement of the Middle East crisis. By 1991, she was having unpublicized talks with U.S. Secretary of State James Baker. She persuaded him to support the PLO's right to be represented at peace talks scheduled to take place in Madrid that fall. These talks were a continuation of the peace process begun by the Camp David Accords in the late 1970s. However, for the first time, the negotiations included representatives of the PLO, which, to much of the world, was characterized as a terrorist organization bent on armed conflict rather than peaceful negotiation.

As the voice of the PLO, Hanan Ashrawi surprised the world. Not only did Palestinian leaders in Madrid express a willingness to accept a path to independence that included intermediate stages, but Ashrawi also provided a new tone of optimism and hope to a process that had been mired in bitterness and suspicion. Without yielding her principles, she offered a new face of the PLO.

"Let us end the Palestinian-Israeli fatal proximity in this unnatural condition of occupation, which has already claimed too many lives. . . . Set us free to re-engage as neighbors and equals in our holy land," she said.

After the Madrid conference in 1991, the Israeli government attempted to arrest Hanan Ashrawi on the grounds that she had violated the country's laws by speaking to a meeting of the PLO in Algiers (the PLO agreed to accept the peace terms at that meeting). International outrage, including support from U.S. President George Bush, caused the government to back down, and Ashrawi remained defiant. "I refuse to be intimidated, and I refuse to be silenced," she told *The New York Times*.

After 1991, the Middle East peace process continued to move forward in small steps. A conference in Washington at the end of that year represented another triumph for Ashrawi and the Palestinians when she smoothly turned Israel's refusal to accept a schedule arrived at by U.S. government officials into a public relations success for the PLO. Suggesting that Israel was suddenly trying to change the rules, Ashrawi gained additional support for the Palestinian position. Since that time, despite the historic Oslo Peace accords in 1993, violence, continued terrorism, and massive protests have continued to mark the slow march to peace and independence for Arab Palestinians in the Middle East. In 1996, Ashrawi was elected to the newly-formed Palestinian government.

Astaire, Fred

(1899–1987)

AMERICAN DANCER AND
CHOREOGRAPHER

To catch the public, dances must have a personality and a pattern. The times my dances have clicked are the times they had a reason, when they told a part of the story, and when they belonged in the plot. It is extremely important for a dance cue to flow naturally into and out of the story.

—Fred Astaire

One of the most popular dancers of his time, Fred Astaire could perform the most difficult dance steps with such grace and ease that he was admired by both ballet-trained and modern dancers alike. During his career Astaire appeared in over a dozen stage musicals and thirty Hollywood films, often as a leading actor, dancer, and choreographer.

Frederick Austerlitz, Jr., was born in 1899 in Omaha, Nebraska, the second child of Frederick Austerlitz, Sr., a brewer from Austria, and Ann Gelius Austerlitz, a housewife. His sister, Adele, was one-and-a-half years older than he was. His mother changed their name to Astaire when the children were young because it would look better on a theater marquee if either of them ever decided to get into show business. Ann wanted to escape the confines of Omaha, and she believed it was possible if her children became famous entertainers.

Young Adele and Frederick were taking lessons in singing and dancing before they were five years old. When Frederick, Sr., was laid off from his brewery job, the family decided that Ann would take the children to New York, where vaudeville acts were booked for tours across the country. In 1905, the children enrolled at Claude Alvienne's Dancing School; they also studied singing and dramatic reading. Two years later Fred and Adele Astaire made their debut as a brother-and-sister dancing act. They were paid fifty dollars a week for their first engagement.

Frederick, Sr., joined his family in New York and acted as the duo's business manager, booking his children in theaters across the country on the vaudeville circuit. Fred was responsible for singing most of the songs in the act. Ann tutored the children when they were traveling between jobs. While they soon became successful, the two children, ages ten and twelve, were forced to grow up with adult comics, animal trainers, and acrobats, not with other children in a grammar-school setting. In 1908, the child-labor laws took effect, stating that only children over fourteen (sixteen in some states) could work. As a result, Fred and Adele stopped performing for a few years and went to a public school in Highwood Park, New Jersey.

Before the Astaire duo act started to perform again in 1912, Ann took the youngsters to Ned Wayburn, the best dance instructor in New York, so they could learn the new craze that was sweeping the country—tap dancing. Soon the Astaires mastered ballroom dancing, the tango, and the waltz. Every time Fred learned a new dance step, he tried to incorporate it into their act. Their salary had risen to $150, and then to $200, per week. By 1917 they were making almost twice that amount, and they performed in the musical *Over the Top* on Broadway. After playing in several hit musicals, the Astaires starred in the 1924 musical comedy *Lady, Be Good!* written by George and Ira Gershwin.

In 1932, Adele married an English lord in London, and she retired from show business. Fred was now a solo act. He was asked to go to Hollywood for a screen test to see how he would look on film, but studio executives were not pleased with the results. So he went back to New York and starred in another Gershwin musical, *Girl Crazy*, in which he was paired with singer/dancer Ginger Rogers. It turned out to be a good match of their individual styles. Fred again went to Hollywood for a screen test, and both he and Rogers got movie contracts. They performed together in eight musical comedies from 1933 to 1939—including *The Gay Divorcee* (1934), *Top Hat* (1935), and *Shall We Dance* (1937).

Throughout the 1940s and 1950s, Astaire was teamed up with several well-known performers and actors, such as Rita Hayworth, Judy Garland, Cyd Charisse, and Audrey Hepburn, but none of the pairings quite matched the excitement that was generated when he performed with Ginger Rogers. From 1959 to 1981 Astaire played dramatic roles in eight films, most of which received critical praise. In 1981, Astaire became the ninth recipient of the American Film Institute's Life Achievement Award. He died of pneumonia at the age of eighty-eight in 1987.

Auden, W(ystan). H(ugh).

(1907–1973)

ENGLISH POET, PLAYWRIGHT, ESSAYIST, CRITIC, AND
OPERA LIBRETTIST

> I always have two things in my head—I always have a theme and the form. The form looks for the theme, theme looks for the form, and when they come together you're able to write.
>
> —W. H. Auden

Certainly, few poets in the English language managed to produce more verse of such high quality as Auden. He was versatile, equally at home writing highly structured rhymed verse in a variety of forms and free verse; he was as comfortable turning out opera librettos for some of the foremost composers of this century as he was translating Bertolt Brecht or Dag Hammarskjöld.

Wystan Hugh Auden was born on February 26, 1907, in York, England. His father was a doctor, the chief medical officer of the city of Birmingham; his mother was a nurse. As a boy, Auden shared his father's fascination with the sciences. Science would figure prominently in his poetic output as an adult, and until he was in college, he had thought he would pursue a career in the sciences.

Auden was shipped off to boarding school as a boy. He was an excellent student. At Gresham's, the secondary school he attended, Auden first began writing verse. He also realized that he was gay, and that middle-class values no longer held him. By the time he left Gresham's, he had also left the Church.

After a year of science at Christ Church College, Oxford, he also left the field of science, switching his major to English.

Oxford was a stunning experience for Auden. He became the center of a circle of friends—other writers, like Stephen Spender, C. Day Lewis, Louis MacNeice—to whom he would remain close all his life. They shared his literary interests and his left-wing politics. Auden's first book of poetry, *Poems* (1928), was a slender volume of which Spender hand-printed thirty copies while the young men were still undergraduates.

The 1930s proved to be a golden decade for Auden and his circle. After a brief sojourn in Berlin, Auden returned to England and published his first two commercially produced books of verse: *Poems* (1930), and *The Orators* (1932). He also wrote a dramatic piece, *Paid on Both Sides: A Charade* (1930), a T.S. Eliot tale of a feud between two families.

Auden had quickly established himself as the spokesman for a new generation of poetic talent. Between 1932, when the twenty-six-year-old Auden produced *The Orators*, and 1940, the year of *Another Time*, he wrote and published a travel book with Louis MacNeice; another on his own; three plays with Christopher Isherwood; and another book of poems, *On This Island* (1936).

Auden was visibly identified with progressive politics in this decade, even volunteering to serve as an ambulance driver on the side of the Spanish Republic as the civil war in Spain raged. (His stay was somewhat mysteriously brief; apparently he was a dreadful driver.) He also went to China later to report on the invasion by the Japanese.

In 1935, Auden married Erika Mann, daughter of the great German novelist Thomas Mann. They had never met; Auden married her to give her the protection of British citizenship so that she could leave Nazi Germany. Her father was considered a traitor to the Fatherland; the Nazis had threatened to cancel her German citizenship, rendering her stateless and unable to cross borders without a passport.

It was in this period, too, that Auden turned to the theater with an old friend, Christopher Isherwood. Isherwood knew Auden from their days together at prep school. Both writers had come a long way since then, and their three collaborations—*The Dog Beneath the Skin*, *The Ascent of F6*, and *On the Frontier*—represented a serious attempt to create a new verse drama.

Auden's Spanish trip took place in 1937. Immediately after his return home, he wrote one of his best-known poems, "Spain," perhaps the best-known political poem ever written. Auden would later exclude the poem from his 1950 *Collected Poems*, angrily rejecting the closing lines, "History to the defeated/May say Alas but cannot help nor pardon." Auden felt that those lines, suggesting that the victors were always morally right, expressed "a wicked doctrine." It was characteristic of Auden to submit his poems to rigorous rewriting, even omitting some from later collections, if he found their moral ideas objectionable in retrospect. Another of his poems to suffer that fate, "September 1, 1939," closes with the line, "We must love one another or die." Years later, Auden would grimace at that line, saying, "That is a lie. Perhaps if it said, 'We must love one another *and* die'. . . . " The poem does not appear in the final edition of his *Collected Poems* (but it does appear in his *Selected Poems*, along with "Spain").

Auden continued to be politically active until the coming of World War II. He produced another travel book, this time with Isherwood, called *Journey to a War*. He also wrote the soundtrack for an acclaimed documentary film about the British postal service, *Night Mail*. His finest work in response to the threat of war hanging over Europe, though, was a sequence of twenty-seven sonnets that appeared in *Another Time* under the title "In Time of War."

Another Time is significant for a different reason. It includes the first poems Auden wrote in America; Isherwood and Auden had emigrated there at the end of the decade. It was a decision that would prove controversial in an England being battered by Nazi bombings day and night. For Auden, it was a deliberate decision to become an exile. He had used the theme of exile throughout his poetic output of the 1930s; now he was experiencing it firsthand. Isherwood opted for the West Coast, settling in Los Angeles. Auden stayed in New York.

Auden was undergoing other, more complex changes than just a move from London to New York City. He had grown disaffected with the left, and he was undergoing a gradual conversion back to the Christianity of his youth. He had also met and fallen in love with a young American man, Chester Kallman, who became his lifelong partner.

Auden divided his time between New York and teaching assignments in the Philadelphia area, at the highly respected colleges Swarthmore and Bryn Mawr. He also was turning out major poetry in great quantity, including one of his most overtly religious works, "For the Time Being," which was dedicated to his mother, who had died in August 1941. In addition, he wrote an opera libretto, *Paul Bunyan*, for Benjamin Britten in 1941.

By 1943, Auden had finished another major collection of poetry, but it would be two years before it could be published, due to wartime paper shortages. He had wanted the book to be titled *Poems: 1928–1945*, but Random House insisted on *The Collected Poetry*, a title whose finality dismayed the author.

Although the end of the war allowed him to return to Europe, and he would do so periodically throughout the rest of his life, Auden was by that time a confirmed New York City resident. He had given up teaching, although he traveled widely, lecturing and reading from his poetry. He and Kallman collaborated on a libretto and lyrics for Igor Stravinsky's *The Rake's Progress* (1947). His next volume of poetry, *The Age of Anxiety*, a dialogue among four people in a Third Avenue bar, won the Pulitzer Prize in 1948.

In the 1950s and 1960s, Auden continued to produce verse, criticism, and essays at a tremendous rate. He spent five years between 1956 and 1961 at Oxford as professor of poetry. He delighted in sprinkling his lectures and his verse with obscure words gleaned from the *Oxford English Dictionary*; nothing gave him greater pleasure, he said, than an unusual word used precisely.

Auden and Kallman bought a large home near Vienna, Austria, in the 1960s, and began to divide their time between New York and the Austrian house.

He continued to spend summers in Austria. He was preparing to give a lecture in Vienna at the Austrian Poetry Society on September 29, 1973, when he collapsed and died in his hotel room. His body was flown back to England, where it was buried. Thirteen months later, a memorial stone in his honor was added to Poet's Corner at Westminster Abbey, placing Auden where he rightly belonged, among the greatest poets in the English language.

Balanchine, George

(1904–1983)

RUSSIAN-BORN AMERICAN DANCER AND CHOREOGRAPHER

Georgi Melitonovitch Balanchivadze was born in St. Petersburg, Russia, in 1904. His father was a respected composer and his mother had hoped that Georgi would one day enter the military profession. When Georgi was ten years old, he visited the Imperial Ballet School with his mother. The governor of the school suggested that he try out as a student, and in 1914 he was accepted. Like other students, Georgi lived at the school and studied other subjects while receiving intensive training in ballet.

In 1921 Georgi graduated from the Academy of Opera and Ballet, and in 1924 he became a member of the Soviet State Dancers. Performing artists in the Soviet Union at that time were restricted as to where they could perform. In addition, they could only perform works created by musicians, choreographers, or directors who were recognized and approved by the government. In 1924, the government allowed the Soviet State Dancers to go to Europe to perform. When the government told the dancers to return to the Soviet Union, Georgi decided to defect and move to Paris, where he would be free to dance wherever he wanted to. He then changed his name to George Balanchine.

Balanchine joined the Ballet Russe as a choreographer, or dance director. The leader of the company was a former Soviet citizen, Sergei Diaghilev. In 1933, a wealthy American ballet enthusiast, Lincoln Kirstein, invited Balanchine to come to New York to found a company. He agreed, and created the

American Ballet Company in 1934. From 1935 to 1938, Balanchine was associated with the Metropolitan Opera, and he composed the ballet "Slaughter on Tenth Avenue" for the musical *On Your Toes* in 1936. In 1940 he staged the dances for the all-black musical *Cabin in the Sky*. From 1940 to 1946 Balanchine composed a dozen ballet works, largely for his ballet company in New York, but also for companies in the Paris Opera House.

In 1946 Balanchine became the artistic director of the Ballet Society in New York, for which he composed five original ballets. With Lincoln Kirstein as general manager and Balanchine as artistic director, they created the New York City Ballet Company in 1948. George Balanchine has been called the finest choreographer of our time by many dance critics, and throughout his career he created hundreds of ballets and original dance pieces for operas, musical comedies, and motion pictures.

Baldwin, James

(1924–1987)

AMERICAN ESSAYIST, NOVELIST, SHORT-STORY WRITER, PLAYWRIGHT, AND POET

James Baldwin was born in Harlem (a neighborhood in New York City) in 1924. In 1927 his mother Berdis, a domestic servant, married David Baldwin, a religious fanatic who was a factory worker during the week and a preacher in a storefront church on weekends. Baldwin's childhood was marked by poverty and the strictness and hostility of his stepfather. While his parents worked, Baldwin cleaned their home and cared for his eight siblings. He became very withdrawn as a child, and his only escape was through books, movies, and his natural talent and love of writing.

Baldwin had read Harriet Beecher Stowe's *Uncle Tom's Cabin* by the time he was eight years old. After this, he read works of Charles Dickens, Robert Louis Stevenson, and Fyodor Dostoevsky, as well as the entire Schomburg collection of black literature and history. At Frederick Douglass Junior High School, Baldwin met the famous black poet Countee Cullen, to whom he showed his writing. He, like many others, recognized Baldwin's talent and encouraged him to continue reading and writing.

In 1938, at the age of fourteen, Baldwin was feeling overwhelmed not only by the dangers of the Harlem streets, but also by the tensions within his own family. Because of this desperation, and with the hope of placating his stepfather, Baldwin turned to the church for help. He quickly became a young minister himself, and became fairly well known as he preached in various Harlem churches. Since Baldwin was still in high school, he felt he had to play down his religious activities while at school or when associating with school friends. They often went to Greenwich Village, and it was there that Baldwin met the black artist Beauford Delaney, who introduced him to the gay culture in the Village. The contradictions between Baldwin's religious activities and his secular life grew deeper when he had his first homosexual relationship.

In 1942 Baldwin graduated from DeWitt Clinton High School in the Bronx, gave up preaching, and decided to leave Harlem. Traveling to New Jersey, he found a job as a defense worker. He encountered even more racism in New Jersey than in New York, and he relates his experience there in *Notes of a Native Son:* "I learned in New Jersey that to be a Negro meant, precisely, that one was never looked at but was simply at the mercy of the reflexes the color of one's skin caused in other people."

Baldwin returned to New York. He settled in Greenwich Village in New York, a community where many artists lived, and decided to work on a novel. In 1944, he met black novelist Richard Wright, who was his literary idol. Wright helped him get a fellowship in 1945, but Baldwin's novel, which was loosely based on his family experiences, was rejected by two publishers.

While revising his novel, Baldwin began receiving public attention in 1947 for the essays and reviews he wrote. He was awarded another fellowship based on text he created to accompany a series of photos of storefront churches. Baldwin still didn't have a book contract, though he had outlined another novel and continued to publish articles and short fiction in periodicals. When one of his friends committed suicide, Baldwin felt so exhausted and frustrated by the events in his life that the only recourse seemed to be a self-imposed exile. Using the rest of his grant money, he traveled to France, where he would spend most of the remainder of his life.

For Baldwin, life in France was even harder financially than it had been in New York. He also discovered that although there seemed to be less prejudice against blacks, there was greater prejudice against the Arab population living in France. Baldwin found a niche with a group of writers that included Jean-Paul Sartre, Simone de Beauvoir, and Jean Genet, as well as the American expatriates Saul Bellow, Truman Capote, and Richard Wright. Baldwin wrote two essays that secured him a place as a controversial critic of black culture. The first, "Everyman's Protest Novel" (1949), examined the limits of Stowe's *Uncle Tom's Cabin.* The second, "Many Thousand Gone" (1951), was a critique of Wright's novel, *Native Son.* Baldwin asserts in both of these essays that an individual sense of identity and self-worth is necessary for social reform to occur. This is a theme that carries through in most of his work.

Baldwin finally finished his first novel, *Go Tell It On the Mountain*, in 1952, although it wasn't published until 1953. The novel explores a young man's coming-of-age as well as racial and sexual tensions within black society. While his later works focus on the social origins of black oppression, *Go Tell It On the Mountain* examines tensions within the family unit.

Baldwin next published a collection of essays in 1955, titled *Notes of a Native Son*. In 1956, he published his second novel, *Giovanni's Room*. This was one of the first contemporary novels to deal with the subject of homosexuality.

Although Baldwin never returned to America to live, he did visit. He began to identify himself more as an American than a Frenchman once the Supreme Court ruled against segregation in 1954. In 1957 Baldwin traveled to the American South and met Martin Luther King, Jr., who was just becoming a popular figure of the civil rights movement. Baldwin became a speaker for King and a spokesperson for the Congress on Racial Equality (CORE) and the Student Nonviolent Coordinating Committee (SNCC). Although his exact role in the civil rights movement is unclear, the movement did have an obvious impact on his writing. Baldwin still believed in the importance of individual self-realization, but he increasingly recognized the ways in which society prevented this from happening freely.

Baldwin's third novel, *Another Country* (1962), took six years to write. Although it was published to negative reviews, the book sold millions of copies. In this novel, Baldwin shifts from holding the individual responsible for his condition to recognizing the harmful effects of society. Identity becomes a social issue because of the effects of racism and homophobia.

While he was writing *Another Country*, Baldwin published another collection of essays entitled, *Nobody Knows My Name* (1961). Using his own experiences with the civil rights movement, he explored black people's role in white society.

Baldwin's later novels, which include *Tell Me How Long the Train's Been Gone* (1968), *If Beale Street Could Talk* (1974), and *Just Above My Head* (1979), continue to examine issues of race, sexual identity, and family relationships and tensions. His later nonfiction titles include *No Name in the Street* (1972), which describes race relations in the 1950s and 1960s; *The Devil Finds Work* (1976), which looks at American racial stereotypes and issues in the movies; and *The Evidence of Things Seen* (1985), Baldwin's last book, about a string of child murders in Atlanta, Georgia.

In the 1980s, Baldwin continued to teach at American colleges, though his health was beginning to decline. In 1987 he died of cancer in France.

Ball, Lucille

(1911–1989)

AMERICAN ACTOR
AND COMEDIAN

We were no Hollywood couple. People told
us that we were crazy, that we were committing career suicide. I didn't listen.

—Lucille Ball

Lucille Desiree Ball was born in Celoron, New York. After her father died
when she was four, she became very close to her grandfather, and together they
would go to vaudeville shows and movies. Lucille's mother would give her costumes and makeup, and she would pretend to be an actor. In high school, she
played the lead in *Charlie's Aunt*, and helped with everything else for the show.
At fifteen, Lucille enrolled in the John Murray Anderson—Robert Milton Theater School in Manhattan, but returned home after six weeks because she could
not make the adjustment. She then tried to be a model at Hattie Carnegie's
salon, but had little success.

At the age of seventeen, Ball was stricken with rheumatoid arthritis, and it
was three years before she recovered and could walk again. When she was well,
her next job in New York was as the Chesterfield Cigarette Girl, which led to
her last-minute replacement as one of the twelve Goldwyn Girls in the 1933
Eddie Cantor movie *Roman Scandals*. Once in Hollywood, small parts in over
a dozen movies followed. Unlike many other female actors of the time, she was
willing to do physical stunts, like wearing mud packs and falling into swimming
pools.

Ball got her first screen credit and a small speaking part in 1935, and a second role in *That Girl from Paris* (1936). That job led to a leading role in the musical *Hey Diddle Diddle*, which never made it to Broadway. Ball decided that
comedy was the right direction for her. During the late 1930s, she turned to
radio, landing a role as a featured comedian on Jack Haley's *Wonder Bread
Show*. However, she was still dependent on acting for her livelihood. She made
over twenty-two films during the next six years, working with comedians like
Buster Keaton, the Marx Brothers, and Laurel and Hardy.

It was during the filming of *Too Many Girls* in 1940 that Lucy met the

Cuban musician Desi Arnaz, who had a small part in the movie. They started dating; she married him six months later. For the next ten years, the couple spent a lot of time apart because of their separate careers. Desi was drafted into the army during World War II, creating even more distance between the couple.

Playing a crippled nightclub singer in *The Big Street* in 1942, Ball received good reviews and the attention of the MGM studio bosses, who suggested she dye her hair red. They signed her for several starring roles. She played the dizzy wife of a bank executive in the radio show *My Favorite Husband* (1948–51). Lucy's reputation as a comedian prompted Bob Hope to ask her to costar with him in *Sorrowful Jones* and *Fancy Pants*.

Ball thought that television offered a promising future, so she and Desi did a guest appearance on Ed Wynn's comedy show. When CBS wanted to use the plot of *My Favorite Husband* for a television show and offered Lucy the part, she insisted that Desi play her husband. The studio did not like the idea at first, because the couple was not "average" enough for a television show. But Lucy was stubborn. To prove that a comical redhead and a Cuban bandleader could be accepted by American audiences, Lucy and Desi took their act on an extensive vaudeville tour, then made their own pilot on film. Six months after the debut of *I Love Lucy* on October 15, 1951, the show was rated the top program on television.

The half-hour sitcom influenced television programming for many years. Each episode was filmed with three cameras before a live audience. With the hit show, Lucy and Desi were able to sell rerun rights to CBS, which enabled them to form their own production company, called Desilu. The show *I Love Lucy* won five Emmy Awards and over two hundred other awards. The Ricardo family made such a hit that when Lucy and Ricky's fictional son, "Little Ricky," was born, forty-four million viewers watched the show. The television birth coincided with the actual birth of Lucy's real-life son, Desi, Jr. The original show ran until 1957 when it became the *Lucille Ball–Desi Arnaz Show*, which aired monthly until the couple's divorce in 1960.

Ball's dream of Broadway success came true in December 1960 when she acted in the musical comedy *Wildcat*. In 1961, the former comedian Gary Morton became Lucy's husband and executive producer. Lucy bought out Desi's shares in Desilu Productions and started on another project. Ball portrayed widowed "Lucy Carmichael" on "The Lucy Show" from 1962 to 1968. Then she sold Desilu Productions to Gulf and Western Industries for seventeen million dollars. She formed Lucille Ball Productions and presented "Here's Lucy," in which she played widowed mother Lucy Carter. Her own son and daughter played the two children on the show, and the series ran from 1968 to 1974.

Ball returned to Hollywood to make several movies after her last series finished its run: *The Facts of Life, Critic's Choice, Yours, Mine, and Ours*, and Lucy's last film, *Mame*. In 1972 Lucy passed up another contract for another television series in favor of retirement. She said she was starting to feel "a little alone out there, at my age, acting silly."

On March 4, 1984, Ball was inducted into the Television Academy Hall of Fame for her contributions to the television industry.

In 1989 Lucille Ball died at her home in Beverly Hills, California.

Barnard, Christiaan Neethling

(1922–   )

SOUTH AFRICAN HEART SURGEON

> It is the duty of the doctor to serve the public and also to let the public know what is going on.
>
> —Christiaan Barnard, in a 1968 interview

Dr. Christiaan Barnard was a groundbreaking surgeon whose sense of duty to the public pushed him beyond what most of the rest of his profession thought possible. By performing the first human heart transplant, Barnard became an international celebrity. Far more important, he launched a whole new field of medicine, one that remains in the forefront of research, and controversy, today.

Christiaan Neethling Barnard was born on November 8, 1922, in Beaufort West, South Africa. His father was a Dutch Reformed minister in the Afrikaner community, and the family was extremely poor. Christiaan was one of four sons. He went to local secondary schools. Then he attended the University of Cape Town, where he earned a medical degree in 1953. Early in his career, as he worked as a general practitioner physician, he became fascinated with heart surgery, using dogs in his research.

In 1955, Barnard went to the United States, where he studied under the noted surgeon Owen Wangensteen, M.D., at the University of Minnesota. In 1957 he earned a Ph.D. degree. While at the University of Minnesota he also performed his first heart operation.

Barnard returned to South Africa the following year and became director of medical research at the University of Cape Town. It was then that he began experimenting in earnest with organ transplantation. In 1960, he gained his first international attention when he created a two-headed dog, giving one animal a second head through the use of medical transplantation. In the field of heart research he was experimenting with the use of artificial valves to replace damaged ones.

By 1967, Barnard had spent ten years studying every aspect of heart surgery, as well as researching the possibilities of transplantation. He decided to attempt to transplant a human heart. The first step was to find a suitable patient: Louis Washkansky, a fifty-four-year-old grocer with life-threatening heart disease. Assembling a team of thirty doctors, nurses, and technicians, Barnard then had to wait for the appropriate donor. On December 2, 1967, Denise Duvall, a young woman whose blood type was compatible with that of Washkansky, was fatally injured in an automobile accident in Cape Town. Obtaining permission from her father to use Duvall's heart upon her death, Barnard and his team began to do what had never been attempted before.

Duvall's heart was removed, chilled and kept alive with a heart-lung machine while Washkansky's diseased heart was removed. Then transplantation took place as the woman's heart was connected to the grocer's blood vessels and arteries. By the time the new heart had been warmed to thirty-five degrees, it showed signs of functioning on its own. The use of electric shock succeeded in starting it to beat again. The heart-lung machine was disconnected, and Washkansky's chest was closed.

During the very first heart transplant there was little experimental knowledge about what drugs and how much of them should be used. Eighteen days after his operation, Louis Washkansky died of double pneumonia because the drugs used to prevent rejection of his new heart had destroyed too much of his natural defense system to fight against infection.

Despite the death of his patient, Dr. Barnard became famous around the world, appearing on television and even meeting with President Lyndon B. Johnson of the United States. The attention, and the criticism from some of his colleagues who believed that the South African was deliberately trying to gain publicity, did not prevent Barnard from continuing his pioneering work. On January 2, 1968, he performed another heart transplant, this time placing the heart of Clive Haupt, a mixed-race stroke victim, into Philip Blaiberg, a fifty-eight-year-old white dentist. Given South Africa's system of apartheid, this decision caused further controversy, and Barnard was once more accused by some doctors of continuing to seek undue personal attention.

Barnard and his team had learned much from their first transplant attempt about the correct use of drugs to prevent rejection of a new heart without weakening the body's natural immune system. The Blaiberg operation was considerably more successful; after seventy-four days in Groote Schuur Hospital, the patient with the new heart was released to go home.

As surgeons around the world also began to perform heart transplants, those of Dr. Barnard continued to be more and more successful. Several of his early patients were still alive when he retired in 1983. During his career, he not only performed the world's first heart transplant, but contributed valuable information about the development of certain types of heart disease. The first to perform open-heart surgery in South Africa, he also developed a new type of artificial heart valve.

Basie, Count

(1904–1984)

AMERICAN BANDLEADER AND PIANIST

The singer Lena Horne once said: "Count Basie isn't just a man, or even just a band. He's a way of life." His way of life was playing the piano, leading his band, and creating an environment in which many young soloists developed into highly talented musicians from the roaring 1920s into the 1980s.

William Basie was born in Red Bank, New Jersey, on August 21, 1904. His parents gave him his first piano lessons. But it was in New York that he became inspired. Of all the ragtime pianists that were popular at the time, Basie's keyboard idol was Fats Waller. Young Basie used to go to the old Lincoln Theater in Harlem to listen to Waller playing the pipe organ. When Waller got used to seeing Basie around the theater, Fats started giving the young boy lessons.

Soon Basie was playing almost as well as his famous teacher. One time when Waller was booked to play a tour on the vaudeville circuit, Basie was asked to fill in for him, which the young musician was happy to do, playing everywhere from big houses in Chicago to tiny tent theaters in the most rural areas of the South. Most of the shows were booked by TOBA (Theater Owners Booking Association), which handled black entertainers. Basie traveled hundreds of miles with shows working with blues singers such as Clara Smith and Maggie Jones.

Around 1925, Basie joined a road show presided over by Gonzelle White and played with him for almost two years until the band ran out of money in Kansas City. Basie took a job as a piano player in a silent movie house for a year. In 1928 he joined Walter Page's Blue Devils, which included Hot Lips Page, Buster Smith, Eddie Durham, and Jimmy Rushing. The band broke up in 1929 and Basie joined Bennie Moten's Orchestra. When Bennie Moten died in 1930, Basie started his own band for a radio show that was broadcast live from the Reno Club in Kansas City every Sunday night. Decca was the first record label to sign up the Count Basie band: the contract was for twenty-four 78 rpm records a year for three years; $750 was paid to Basie for each of the three years.

During the 1930s Count Basie and his Orchestra toured around the country from the Grand Terrace Hotel in Chicago to the newly opened Apollo Theater in Harlem and New York's Roseland Ballroom. In 1937, singer Billie Holiday joined Count Basie's band for about one year. The arrival of singer Helen Humes in 1938 was the last important addition to a band that had become nationally famous.

By 1948, the popular style of music was changing, and audiences wanted to hear the new jazz music of smaller bands like Dizzy Gillespie, Stan Kenton, and Woody Herman, and less of the big band jazz that Basie was famous for playing. Keeping up with the new trends in music, Basie broke up his big band in 1950 and formed a smaller sextet group made up of younger musicians. In 1954 Count Basie made his first trip to Europe, touring Scandinavia, France, and Switzerland.

However, the one element still missing from his new group was a singer. But on Christmas Day 1954 the singer arrived in the person of Joseph Goreed Williams. In 1955, Count Basie and his band recorded the hit single "April in Paris." In April 1957, Count Basie made his first visit to Britain. The demand for the band was so great that they made arrangements to bring the band back in October of the same year. In between the bookings in Britain, Basie played for an audience of eight thousand at the Newport Jazz Festival, an annual gathering of great jazz musicians.

The period when Basie was making records for Roulette found the band at its best. Just before *The Atomic Mr. Basie* album was made, Basie completed thirteen weeks at the Waldorf-Astoria Hotel in New York. This was the first time that a black band played the Waldorf. And in November 1957, Basie was chosen to play a Royal Command performance in London.

During the 1960s and 1970s, Count Basie continued to make recordings with several singers of note: Frank Sinatra, Sarah Vaughan, Tony Bennett, Ella Fitzgerald, and Sammy Davis. But in 1976 he suffered a heart attack, and had to leave the band for a while to recuperate. In 1982, when he played in Britain for the last time, he came riding onstage in a motorized wheelchair. Basie was the last of the great piano-playing band leaders, outliving Duke Ellington, Earl Hines, and Claude Hopkins. Basie showed that a big band could keep dancers happy and still captivate dedicated jazz lovers.

Count Basie died of cancer on April 26, 1984, at his home in Hollywood, Florida.

The Beatles

The Beatles, one of the best-selling bands of all time, hailed from Liverpool, England. Of the four members of the band, John Lennon (1940-1980), Paul McCartney (1942-), George Harrison (1943-), and Ringo Starr (1940-), Lennon and McCartney remain the best known for their ground breaking songwriting and technical achievements in the recording studio.

John Winston Lennon grew up in Liverpool, raised by an aunt. He attended Liverpool Art College, where he met artist Stuart Sutcliffe (who later died of a brain hemorrhage) but his attention was already focused on music. In 1955, influenced by the popularity of skiffle, a speeded-up jug-band blues sound, Lennon persuaded his aunt to buy him a banjo. Lennon ultimately purchased a guitar, and inspired by rock and roll artists such as Elvis Presley and Chuck Berry, formed a band called the Quarry Men with Stu Sutcliffe on bass. In 1956, he met Paul McCartney.

Paul McCartney, born in 1942, was also from Liverpool. He learned to play the piano by ear as a child, but the influence of American rock-and-roll inspired him to switch to guitar as a teenager. After accepting Lennon's invitation to join the Quarry Men, the two quickly became friends and spent long hours writing songs and playing guitar. When Sutcliffe left the group, McCartney took up the role of bassist. It was McCartney who introduced his guitarist friend George Harrison to Lennon and asked that Harrison be admitted into the group. Harrison proved his prowess on guitar with the tune "Raunchy," and Lennon welcomed him in. Harrison, another Liverpool native, was born into a working class family in 1943. He was the youngest of the Beatles and practiced playing guitar until his hands bled. In the years that followed, Harrison would become the group's lead guitarist, despite his outwardly reserved nature.

The Quarry Men's style evolved from skiffle into rock and roll as they played more and more shows. Their name also went through change, and by the time they settled on the Beatles in 1960, they had been known as Johnny and the Moondogs, the Nurk Twins, Long John and the Silver Beetles, and the Silver Beetles. Their first big break came in 1960 when they were hired to play an extended run at the Kaiserkeller Club in Hamburg, Germany, where they further continued to develop into experienced musicians. With a shortage of drummers in Liverpool, the group went through a succession of percussionists until they brought in Pete Best. They played a second run in Hamburg in 1962 with Best on drums, during which time they met drummer Ringo Starr.

Ringo Starr was born Richard Starkey in 1940 in the Liverpool suburb called the Dingle. Starr was not a healthy child, and was in and out of hospitals for most of his youth. Nicknamed Ringo by his mother because of his penchant for wearing rings, he began to pursue his lifelong interest in drums in 1959, when he bought his first set. By 1961 he was playing with Rory Storm and the Hurricanes, and his drum solos and vocal performances became known as "Starrtime." In 1962, just as the Beatles signed their first recording contract, Pete Best was fired and replaced by Ringo.

Managed by Brian Epstein and produced by George Martin, the Beatles became England's most beloved foursome, with hits such as "Love Me Do," "Please Please Me," and "She Loves You." In 1964, the band made its first triumphant trip to America, where they appeared on *The Ed Sullivan Show* and drew the largest audience in television history until that time. Beatlemania became an international phenomenon: their haircuts and clothes were emulated; their records sold millions of copies; and their concerts drew thousands of screaming fans. The "Fab Four," as they were known, displayed their wit and charm in the films *A Hard Day's Night* and *Help!*

The Beatles were the first English rock band to write their own songs, most of which were composed by McCartney and Lennon. The two sometimes wrote together, but most of the time they acted as each other's editors, helping to fix or finish a song that the other was working on. Together, they revolutionized popular music with timeless classics such as "All My Loving," "Can't Buy Me Love," "Eight Days a Week," "Ticket to Ride," "Eleanor Rigby," "Yesterday," "With a Little Help from My Friends," and "Hey Jude" (their most successful single). The group's albums—*Rubber Soul, Revolver, Sergeant Pepper's Lonely Hearts Club Band, The Beatles* (also known as *The White Album*) and *Abbey Road*—are among the finest ever recorded.

As Lennon became increasingly involved with Japanese avant-garde artist Yoko Ono, McCartney took over the direction of the band. The Beatles played their famous rooftop concert in 1969, which was included in the film *Let It Be* and produced on record by Phil Spector. Replacing Brian Epstein (who had died in 1967 from a sleeping pill overdose), businessman Allen Klein tried to sort through the Beatles' confused financial affairs, notably their floundering record company, Apple. Relations among the four Beatles heated up, until McCartney publicly announced his resignation from the band in 1970.

The individual Beatles continued to work as soloists. Lennon, who had released *Two Virgins* in 1968, founded the Plastic Ono Band and recorded three hit singles, "Give Peace a Chance," "Cold Turkey," and "Instant Karma." His album *The Plastic Ono Band* remains one of the most brilliant and disturbing introspective works from a rock star. In the 1970s, as Lennon protested the Vietnam War and became active in various social and political causes, he wrote songs about peace and a progressive vision of humanity such as "Imagine." In 1975, he retired from rock and roll, resisting attempts by concert promoters to get the Beatles back together. In 1980, he and Ono recorded *Double Fantasy*, which became a number-one seller, with a number-one single, "Starting Over." After a recording session on December 8, 1980, Lennon was shot to death by a deranged fan, Mark Chapman, outside his apartment in New York City. Mourners worldwide paid tribute to Lennon, who was the voice of his generation.

McCartney's first two solo albums were not well received, but he formed a new band, Wings, featuring his photographer wife Linda Eastman as keyboardist and backup singer. By the mid-1970s he was back at the top of the record charts with the best-selling album, *Band on the Run* and two hit singles, "My Love" and the title track. The theme song he wrote for the James Bond movie *Live and Let Die* was nominated for an Academy Award. Although Wings eventually disbanded, McCartney continues to write, record, and perform and recently composed the well-received *Liverpool Oratorio*.

George Harrison's solo career began in 1968 with *Wonderwall*. His second solo album, the three-record *All Things Must Pass*, was an artistic and commercial success that included the number-one single, "My Sweet Lord." In 1971, Harrison sponsored and hosted two benefit concerts at New York's Madison Square Garden for the starving people of Bangladesh. The Concert for Bangladesh, as it came to be known, featured such rock stars as Ringo Starr, Eric Clapton, Leon Russell, and Bob Dylan. The event is noted as one of the most successful benefit concerts ever, raising more than $10 million, and was filmed as a documentary and released as a Grammy Award winning three-record set. Harrison's record sales declined by the mid-1970s and he began to focus on other projects. He produced albums for other musicians and produced films (several with the Monty Python comedy troupe). In 1987 he made a musical comeback with *Cloud Nine*, which spawned two hit singles, "Got My Mind Set on You" and "When We Was Fab." Harrison also had two hit albums with the Traveling Wilburys, an all-star band featuring Bob Dylan, Roy Orbison, Tom Petty, and Jeff Lynne.

Ringo Starr, who occasionally sang lead vocals on Beatles songs such as "Yellow Submarine" and Octopus' Garden," had several hit singles during the 1970's ("It Don't Come Easy," "Back off Boogaloo," and "You're Sixteen") and continues to tour periodically with Ringo Starr and the All Starr Band. Starr was the only Beatle to establish an acting career beyond their mid-1960's movies, starring in *The Magic Christian* (1969), *Born to Boogie* (1974), *The Last Waltz* (1978), and *Caveman* (1981), which co-starred his wife, actress Barbara Bach. He has also had a recurring role as the conductor on the children's show *Shining Time Station*.

The impact of the Beatles on modern music cannot be overestimated; they remain, perhaps, the most influential rock-and-roll band of all time, having blended all types of music and influence into their repertoire. They were elected into the Rock and Roll Hall of Fame in 1987. In 1995, after years of lawsuits over royalties, the surviving members of the Beatles reunited to record a few songs written by John Lennon and recorded by him on rough demo. Using digital technology, they were able to combine Lennon's original vocals with their own, and 1996 saw the release of the first Beatles single in more than twenty-five years. The song, "Free as a Bird," was included as part of the Beatles' *Anthology*, a collection of never-before released versions of some of their most popular songs as well as some that had never been heard outside of the studio. *Anthology 2* and *Anthology 3* followed. Not surprisingly, *Anthology* became their sixteenth number one, proving that the Beatles popularity is indeed enduring.

Beauvoir, Simone de

(1908–1986)

FRENCH NOVELIST AND EXISTENTIALIST PHILOSOPHER

His death separates us. My death will not reunite us. It is so. It is already beautiful that
our lives could intertwine for so long a time.

—Simone de Beauvoir, from
Adieux to Sartre

If, as one commentator put it, the primary theme of existentialism is the "dilemma of human freedom in a world in which God does not exist," then Simone de Beauvoir's simple, dignified farewell to her lifelong lover, companion, and friend Jean-Paul Sartre suggests that Beauvoir had made her peace with that world before she left it.

Simone de Beauvoir was born on January 9, 1908, in Paris, France, the oldest child of a comfortably upper-middle-class family. Her father, Georges de Beauvoir, was a lawyer by profession, but he was also an avid devotee of the theater and literature. Her mother, Françoise Brasseur de Beauvoir, came from a very religious Catholic background, and she tried to pass her religious beliefs on to her two daughters, Simone and Helen, who was born two year later.

When she was six, she started her education at a private girls' school. She grew up sharing her father's enthusiasm for literature, reading everything she could. By the time she was eight, she knew she would be a writer.

Around the age of fourteen, Simone began to question the tenets of her faith, coming to the decision that there was no God. That decision carried with it the realization of anguish, solitude, and the inevitability of death. As an adult, Beauvoir and Jean-Paul Sartre, her lifelong lover and companion, would spend their entire lives developing a philosophy that would answer those anxieties. As a teenager, Simone could only begin to face them by understanding that they were the price of a radical kind of freedom that came from recognizing oneself at one's own cause and end.

It was at approximately that time that the Beauvoirs' financial situation began to deteriorate. Both of Simone's parents came from money, and they reacted in different, but equally inappropriate, ways to their financial losses. Georges became indifferent, careless, almost irrationally critical of Simone's schoolwork, and would disappear for days; Françoise immersed herself increasingly in religion. By the age of seventeen, Simone would come to despise the bourgeois pieties of her parents and the values that they had tried to instill in her. Her commitment to a career as a writer became stronger than ever.

Beauvoir was still an outstanding student. She obtained a degree in literature and philosophy, and was accepted for postgraduate work at the École Normale Supérieure, the top postgraduate progam in France, a training ground for future university professors. There she would take the *agrégation*, the competitive exam for teaching posts. Her fellows students were a dazzling lot: Maurice Merleau-Ponty, Paul Nizan, Raymond Aron and a gangly bespectacled philosophy student who had failed the *agrégation* on his first try, Jean-Paul Sartre.

Sartre impressed Beauvoir with the wide sweep of his mind—he seemed to be interested in everything—and by his firm conviction that he would be a successful writer. For the first time in her life, Simone had met someone who was her intellectual equal, perhaps someone who could even dominate her. It was the beginning of a relationship that, despite some rocky periods, would last the rest of their lives. When the results of the *agrégation* were posted, Sartre had finished first in the nation, Beauvoir second. At twenty-one, she was the youngest person ever to have passed the exam on the first try, and one of the examining professors remarked, "Of the two, it is she who is the philosopher."

Although Sartre spent time in Berlin, Germany, in 1933, neither of them saw the storm clouds of war approaching; they would tour Austria and Germany together the following year, still convinced that Nazism was a passing trend. Although they would become the leading socialist activists of their generation in the years after World War II, in the 1930s neither Beauvoir nor Sartre was particularly political, so events in Europe caught them as much by surprise as they did many others.

They were more preoccupied in the middle of that turbulent decade by a small tempest of their own, when Sartre began a relationship with a former student of Beauvoir's, Olga Kosakiewicz. It would be the only time that a "contingent" relationship would threaten their household, and Beauvoir would retell the story in her first published novel, *She Came to Stay* (1938), much to Olga's dismay.

When war was declared in September 1939, Sartre was called up for military service. His military career was a brief one; in June 1940 the French army surrendered and he was declared a prisoner of war. By 1941 he was back in Paris.

Although they managed to avoid the worst privations of the war, Beauvoir and Sartre were forever changed by it. They pledged to be more involved in the world and society around them. They collected and distributed information for the resistance, and after the Nazis dismissed Beauvoir from her teaching position, she began a novel about the resistance that would eventually become *The Blood of Others* (1945).

As the war ended, Beauvoir and Sartre became part of a group of French intellectuals that included Albert Camus and André Malraux, who were concerned with the direction that postwar French society would take. In 1945, the two of them founded a magazine, *Les Temps Modernes* (Modern Times), which would provide them with a pulpit from which to address the ramifications of day-to-day political life, a useful complement to the larger concerns of their books.

In the late 1940s, Sartre suggested to Beauvoir that she undertake a book on the status of women. In 1949, Beauvoir finished what became her best-known book, *The Second Sex*. It became a contemporary bible of feminism, particularly in the United States, where many feminist thinkers—Betty Friedan and Gloria Steinem chief among them—would attest to its importance and influence.

During a lecture tour of the United States, Beauvoir met and became involved with the American novelist Nelson Algren. The relationship continued for several years. She would re-create the relationship in her 1954 novel, *The Mandarins*, a study of the disillusionments of postwar intellectual life. In the early 1950s, she also began a six-year-long relationship with Claude Lanzmann, then a young journalist, and today a famous filmmaker and editor of *Les Temps Modernes*. He was seventeen years her junior, and, as she would later admit, the affair was as much a way of fighting off her sense of growing older as anything else.

When the Soviets suppressed the workers' uprising in Hungary in 1956, Beauvoir and Sartre immediately denounced the repression and broke off relations with the Communist Party. At the same time, they were spearheading a small, but growing minority that supported the Algerian revolution and called for France to give independence to that African colony. Beauvoir was among the first to hear of torture of Algerian prisoners by French military forces; she organized opposition to the use of torture and even served as editor of a first-person account by an Algerian woman. Right-wing French terrorists bombed Sartre's apartment afterward. Undaunted, Beauvoir and Sartre were among the first to sign the "Manifesto of the 121," a petition of prominent intellectuals urging young Frenchmen to resist the draft.

Françoise de Beauvoir was then dying of cancer. Simone went to her side and was with her through the last months of her struggle. After her mother's death, she wrote a moving account of those last days, *A Very Easy Death* (1964).

In 1968, with French students taking to the streets, Beauvoir and Sartre were vocal and highly visible in their support. When the government successfully regained control of the situation, it added to their sense that the structure of French society was intractable. Beauvoir was coming to a similar conclusion about the status of women; her travels in the so-called socialist countries had made it clear that even they had done little to improve the lives of their female population. She stepped up her own activism in feminist causes, marching with the 1970 Women's Liberation Movement demonstration in Paris, starting a feminist section in *Les Temps Modernes,* and assuming the presidency of the French League of Women's Rights. The last years of her life were spent writing and nursing Sartre, who by then was blind and quite ill.

Beauvoir died of pneumonia in a Paris hospital, almost exactly six years to the day after Sartre. She was buried in the Montparnasse cemetery in the same grave with his ashes.

Beckett, Samuel

(1906–1989)

IRISH PLAYWRIGHT,
NOVELIST, AND POET

"I'll never know, in the silence you don't know, you must go on, I can't go on, I'll go on," is how Samuel Beckett closes his monumental trilogy of novels, consisting of *Molloy* (1951), *Malone Dies* (1951), and *The Unnameable* (1953). Those words could be said to represent everything in Beckett's universe, one of the most original and striking in literature.

Samuel Beckett was born on Good Friday, April 13, 1906, in Foxrock, Ireland, near Dublin. He was the second son of a well-to-do Protestant family. Beckett's father was a highly successful surveyor, his mother was a former nurse with a domineering personality.

In school, Beckett was a standout athlete, a good cricketeer, swimmer, and boxer. In fact, Beckett would eventually hold the rather unusual distinction of being the first Nobel Prize winner who also was listed in *Wisden,* the cricketeer's annual.

He entered Trinity in 1923, to study law and accounting so that he could join his father's firm. However, he proved a terrible student. It was only in his third year of college that Beckett, discovering a talent for languages, suddenly blossomed. By the end of his junior year, he had won the Foundation Scholarship in Modern Languages, summered in France, and returned to receive his degree in 1927, finishing at the head of his class in his major. Moreover, he won the gold medal for outstanding scholarship and a cash award. He was named as a *lecteur* (reader) at the prestigious École Normale Supérieure in Paris, an appointment that was scheduled to last for three years.

In Paris, Beckett met the two men who would alter his life forever. The first was a fellow graduate of Trinity, Thomas McGreevy, an extroverted Irish Catholic who was part of an extensive network of Irishmen in Paris. He, in turn, introduced Beckett to another Paris-based Irishman: James Joyce.

By 1931, Joyce was one of the most famous authors in the world, one whose work Beckett admired greatly. Joyce was losing his eyesight, and numerous young men volunteered to read to him and run various small errands for him. Beckett became one of the most trusted of this group, a surrogate son to Joyce.

Joyce was hard at work on the book, then titled *Work in Progress*, that would eventually become the famous *Finnegans Wake*, and he asked young Beckett to contribute an essay to a collection being assembled to explain that most difficult work. Beckett's article, entitled "Dante . . . Bruno. Vico. Joyce," was his first published piece of writing. It was an astute analysis of the influence of fellow exiles Dante, Giordano Bruno, and Giambattista Vico on the *Wake*.

Beckett's next piece of writing was a book-length poem, *Whoroscope*, written in 1931 for a competition. The Joyce-influenced poem won.

As a direct result of that victory, editor Charles Prentice (a friend of McGreevy's and Aldington's) was convinced that the young Irishman would be a good choice for a brief study of Marcel Proust that his firm, Chatto and Windus, was planning. This long essay, published in 1931, displays a seldom-seen side of Beckett: he was an exceptionally keen literary critic.

He returned to Dublin, where he found life in his mother's home intolerable. He tried moving in with cousins in Germany, but that only brought a slight improvement.

He returned to Paris, where, in hopes of earning enough money to live on, he started writing short stories. He also began a novel (which would eventually see the light of day in 1934 as a collection of short stories, *More Pricks Than Kicks*). Eventually, he was forced by circumstances to return once again to the family home in Dublin.

More Pricks was published but didn't sell; he was forced to resort to writing criticism and journalism to supplement the allowance that his mother grudgingly gave him.

His next novel, *Murphy*, was refused by almost every publisher in London. Beckett spent his time in libraries, reading voraciously but aimlessly. Finally, in 1937, a desperate Beckett returned to Paris. Shortly after, the publishing firm of Routledge accepted *Murphy* for publication, and the book came out in 1938.

On January 7, 1938, Beckett and friends were walking on a Paris street when a pimp named Prudent came up to him and asked for money. Beckett refused, and Prudent stabbed him, puncturing a lung and just missing his heart. Beckett had a successful convalescence in a nearby hospital. After his release, he visited Prudent in jail. "Why did you stab me?" he asked the pimp.

"I don't know," was the reply.

That bizarre incident helped crystallize the writer's growing belief of the absurdity of existence and unknowable nature of even one's own life.

Despite that incident, 1938 was turning into a good year for Beckett. In addition to the publication of *Murphy*, he met and became involved with a young French pianist, Suzanne Deschevaux-Dumesnil; the couple would remain together for the rest of Beckett's life, finally marrying on March 25, 1961.

The coming of war shattered whatever domestic tranquility Beckett may have achieved for himself. Although as an Irish citizen he was officially neutral, he could not stand by while his friends were disappearing. In 1940, he joined one of the first resistance groups. When the war ended, Beckett was awarded the Medal of the Resistance and the Croix de Guerre. During the nearly three years that he was in Rousillon, Beckett wrote another novel, *Watt*, which was not published until 1953.

With the end of the war, Beckett seemed to be slipping back into the round of depression and Dublin trips that had characterized his anguished 1930s years. Once more, he tried his hand at theater as a way of jump-starting his creative juices.

As an exercise, he decided to try once again to write a play, this time in French. Between October 9, 1948, and January 19, 1949, he wrote easily. The result was a new play that heralded a new kind of theater: *Waiting for Godot*.

On January 5, 1953, *Waiting for Godot* had its Paris premiere. The play was a hit, with audiences coming to see it largely out of curiosity—a play in which nothing happens? Beckett was, at last, receiving recognition. However, the play was not staged in English until the 1955 London production, and the American production, in 1956, was an unqualified disaster. Eventually, though, *Godot* would be recognized as a masterpiece and a landmark work in the history of modern theater.

Like *Godot*, *Endgame* (1957) was originally written in French. Beckett's decision to abandon his native language to write in a foreign tongue was a carefully considered one. Writing in French gave him several advantages. First, he was somewhat more restricted in his vocabulary simply by virtue of unfamiliarity. So, he had to write simply, eschewing "fancy" writing and easy tricks. It also allowed him to sidestep any literary influences that he might have had to deal with in English.

Now firmly established as both novelist and playwright, Beckett entered a period of great productivity. *Krapp's Last Tape* (1960), his first postwar play written in English, a series of short mime (the art of acting merely by using bodily movements, and no spoken dialogue) pieces, and *Happy Days* (1963) followed in rapid succession.

In 1969, Beckett received the Nobel Prize for Literature in recognition of his body of work. Characteristically low-key, Beckett sent his publisher to accept the award, and he donated most of the money to needy artists.

Beckett remained unchanged by his fame. He began to shift his writing style toward an even more strict minimalism, making no concessions to readers or viewers. Later works like "Breath" (1970), *Not I* (1970), and *That Time* (1976) are less than a half-hour in length; "Breath" has only 120 words and last about thirty-five seconds. Likewise, his novels were getting shorter and more compressed.

In 1988, Beckett suffered a fall in his apartment. To avoid further danger, he moved to a nursing home. There he watched tennis and soccer on television and read. On July 17, 1989, Suzanne died. He attended the funeral, then returned to the nursing home. As his own health began to fail, he was moved to a hospital, where he died on December 16, 1989.

Begin, Menachem

(1913–1992)

ISRAELI INDEPENDENCE LEADER
AND PRIME MINISTER

We must foster friendship and understanding between us and every nation, great or small, strong or weak, near or far, which recognizes our independence . . . and which is interested, even as we are, in international justice and peace among nations.

—Menachem Begin, speaking at
the White House, 1979, after
winning the Nobel Peace Prize

From freedom fighter in the battle to create the state of Israel to Nobel Prize winner for his efforts to bring peace between Jews and Arabs, Menachem Begin led one of the most fascinating lives of any of the prominent leaders in the twentieth-century Middle East.

Menachem Begin was born in what is now Poland, in Brest-Litovsk, on August 16, 1913. He was educated first in Jewish religious schools and later attended the University of Warsaw, where he earned a law degree. As a young man he joined Betar, the youth wing of the Revisionist Zionist Movement, a political group committed to creating an independent Jewish state in the Middle

East. For much of the twentieth century, until the formation of Israel as a state in 1948, Palestine, the ancestral birthplace of Judaism, was under the political control of England and predominantly settled by Arabs.

Begin's political life began during Palestinian riots between 1936 and 1938, when he organized demonstrations against the British representative in Poland. He also tried to encourage Jews to immigrate illegally to Palestine and was arrested by the Polish police. After working for Betar in Czechoslovakia for a short time, he returned to Poland in 1939 to become the organization's leader. At the beginning of World War II, he escaped the Nazi invasion of Poland but was later arrested in the Soviet Union because of his Zionist views and sent to prison in Siberia until 1942.

Freed because he was Polish and the Soviets were opposed to Germany's occupation of Poland, Begin reached Palestine in 1942. By 1943 he had become the leader of an underground group called Irgun Tzevai Leumi, which was also dedicated to a free Jewish state in Palestine. In the years that followed, Begin's guerrilla warfare against the British made him not only a criminal wanted by the English, but a controversial figure among other Jewish groups pledged to an independent Jewish state. He earned a reputation in other parts of the world as a terrorist who, it was believed, participated in such acts as the bombing of the King David Hotel in Jerusalem and a massacre of hundreds of Arab men, women, and children at Deir Yassin. Even after the formation of Israel in 1948, he and his men were attacked on the orders of the country's first prime minister, David Ben-Gurion, who feared that Begin was less interested in peace between the Arab Palestinians and Jews than in total victory for Israel.

With the creation of Israel, Begin turned from warfare to politics, creating the right-wing Herut Party and serving in the new country's legislature, the Knesset (parliament). Until 1967, he was a strong nationalist voice in Israel, opposed to any kind of conciliation or compromise on issues affecting the country's relations with its Arab neighbors.

At the time of Israel's victory in the Six-Day War of 1967, in which the country claimed large amounts of land from Egypt and other neighbors, Begin served in the government as minister without portfolio. In 1970, he and other members of the Gahal Party (formed by Begin in 1965 as a merger between his party, Herut, and the Liberal Party) resigned when they considered the United States to be too favorable toward Arabs. Shortly after, Gahal merged with another right-wing party, Likud, and Begin became Israel's opposition leader.

Likud won the national elections in 1977, and Menachem Begin became Israel's first non-socialist prime minister. Only months later, he welcomed the president of Egypt, Anwar el-Sadat, to Jerusalem. It was the first time an Arab leader had made an official visit to Israel. This historic meeting led to the signing of the Camp David Accords, a series of agreements negotiated between Egypt and Israel with the help of U.S. President Jimmy Carter, in 1978. In recognition of their efforts to defuse the tensions in the Middle East, the Israeli and Egyptian leaders were awarded the Nobel Peace Prize. In March 1979, Begin and Sadat met at the White House in Washington to sign an Egypt-Israel peace treaty.

Begin's success in coming to terms with his country's most powerful neighbor was of major benefit to Israel. But it also meant giving up land in the Sinai peninsula (the expanse of desert that had acted as a buffer zone between Egypt and Israel) taken during the Six-Day War. There was also considerable opposition in Israel to the treaty's terms. Begin's Likud Party, nevertheless, won the elections of 1981 and he remained prime minister.

Throughout Begin's political career he was noted for his excellent speaking skills, which rallied supporters and swayed public opinion. He also presided during a period of strength for Israel; the economy was strong and, despite some disagreements with the United States, foreign relations with non-Arab countries were favorable to Israel. Even the United States, which objected to many of Begin's positions regarding a Middle East peace, provided record amounts of military and economic aid to the tiny nation.

To the surprise of many, Menachem Begin announced his resignation from government in 1983 at the peak of his success. One factor behind the decision was the 1982 war with Lebanon, in which Israel suffered serious casualties while trying to destroy the Palestine Liberation Organization's armies that were based there. The fighting provoked considerable debate in Israel, and Begin was said to have been dismayed by the high number of Israeli deaths. Another factor may have been the death of his wife the previous year. Begin himself had always maintained that he would retire from public life upon turning seventy. He died in Jerusalem nine years later, on March 9, 1992.

Bell, Alexander Graham

(1847–1922)

SCOTTISH-BORN AMERICAN
INVENTOR OF THE TELEPHONE

As I placed my mouth to the instrument, it seemed as if an electric thrill went through the audience, and that they recognized for the first time what was meant by the telephone.

—Alexander Graham Bell,
  describing one of his first
  demonstrations of his
  invention in 1877

Alexander Bell was born in Edinburgh, Scotland. His father, Alexander Melville Bell, was a well-known teacher of the deaf. To distinguish himself from his father, eleven-year-old Alec took the middle name "Graham," naming himself after a friendly Canadian traveler who had been a guest of the Bells.

Alec enjoyed reading about science. His favorite subject was phonetics, the study of speech. Melville Bell taught this subject at Edinburgh University. But Alec's father did little to encourage him. Alec was shy and his grades at Edinburgh Royal High School were poor. Melville Bell clearly felt that Alec's charming older brother, nicknamed Melly, was the most promising of his children.

Alec's grandfather saw that this quiet boy was neglected at home. Also a speech teacher, he lived and taught in London, England. When Alec was fifteen, he invited the boy to visit him, hoping that an adventure might help open Alec up.

Alec's year with his grandfather proved to be a turning point in his life. Away from his demanding father, he felt freer. Instead of constantly having to prove himself, he at last could act however he wished. At home, his parents discouraged him from reading books for fun. But his grandfather loved to read novels and plays. Together, he and Alec read through the plays of Shakespeare, many of which Alec learned to recite word for word. When Melville Bell came to take his son home, he could barely recognize him. Alec had an air of confidence that made him seem like a different person.

Alec did not stay at home for long. Soon after he returned, he took a summer job at Weston House, a boarding school in Elgin, Scotland. There he taught music and public speaking.

Soon after Alec returned home, his grandfather died. In a few months, the Bell family moved to his London house. Alec taught speech for several years until, after the deaths of Melly and his youngest brother Ted from tuberculosis, the family moved to Canada.

Alec traveled south to Boston, Massachusetts, where, like his father, he taught the deaf to speak. In 1873, he was named a professor at the School of Oratory at Boston University. While there, he met a young deaf woman named Mabel Hubbard. They soon fell in love, but her parents refused to let them marry.

At about the same time, Bell started experimenting with machines that transmitted sound. "If I can make a deaf-mute talk," he said, "I can make metal talk." Bell wanted to find a way to make a metal disc vibrate in response to sound. He then hoped to send the vibration along an electrified wire so that it could re-create the sound on the wire's other end. Bell knew a great deal about acoustics, the science of sound. But he knew nothing of electrical engineering. To help him he hired a young engineer, Thomas Watson.

For several years, Bell and his assistant worked on how to send sound over a distance. Finally, in March 1876, they staged an experiment to test their latest attempt to make a telephone. The men strung a wire from Bell's laboratory to his bedroom in his house. While Watson waited in the bedroom, Bell went to his lab and said into their phone's mouthpiece, "Mr. Watson, come here. I want to see you." As fast as could, Watson ran the lab. He had heard every word clearly.

With the help of Mabel Hubbard's father, Bell founded the Bell Telephone Company to market his invention on July 9, 1877. Confident that Alec Bell would become a success, Hubbard's parents finally gave Mabel and Alec their blessing. The couple was married two days later.

However, Bell's troubles were not over. In 1878, he was forced to go to court to defend his rights to the telephone. Another inventor, Elisha Gray, claimed he had developed it first. The case went to the Supreme Court. After hearing months of testimony, the court finally ruled that Alexander Graham Bell was the one and only inventor of the telephone.

The case made Bell famous, but more important to him, it ensured that he would become wealthy from his invention. Bell used his money to help the deaf. For several years, he funded a school for the hearing-impaired. He also founded the American Association to Promote the Teaching of Speech to the Deaf. Through this charity, he helped pay Annie Sullivan to teach a deaf-mute child named Helen Keller to communicate. Keller was so grateful that years later when she wrote her autobiography she dedicated it to Bell.

Bell used his wealth to fund still other projects. He provided the money needed to start *Science* magazine. With his father-in-law, he also founded the National Geographic Society, which would come to publish its own periodical, *National Geographic.*

About the only extravagance Bell allowed himself was Beinn Bhreagh, a fifty-six-acre estate on Cape Breton Island in Canada. He and his wife spent almost forty summers in this lush setting. It was there, after a long bout with diabetes, that Bell died in 1922.

Many years later, his name is still familiar to many Americans. But Bell would probably be alarmed by the reasons why. While most people now think of him as the inventor of the telephone, he had hoped he would be remembered for the service he valued most—being a teacher and helper to those who could not hear.

Ben-Gurion, David

(1886–1973)

FIRST PRIME MINISTER OF ISRAEL

> In Israel, in order to be a realist you must believe in miracles.
> —David Ben-Gurion, in a 1956 newspaper interview

In the struggle to create an independent Jewish state in the Middle East, there were those who used guerrilla warfare and armed conflict to rise to positions of leadership. On the other hand, a person who stands as the finest example of one who used political pressure, negotiation, firm resolve, and public opinion to achieve success was David Ben-Gurion.

Ben-Gurion was born David Green on October 16, 1886, in Plonsk, Poland. He was one of eleven children. His father practiced law unofficially and was an early follower of Theodor Herzl, the founder of Zionism. David was educated in religious Jewish schools (yeshivas), and even as a teenager he was active in organizing Zionist political groups. In 1906 he moved to Palestine, where he worked as a guard of Jewish settlements and as a farmer. He also founded the Palestine Labor Party and edited its newspaper (at this time he adopted the pen name Ben-Gurion). In 1913 he traveled to Constantinople (now Istanbul) to attend college. (The Ottoman Empire, now roughly equivalent to Turkey, but encompassing much more Middle Eastern territory, controlled Palestine at that time.)

During World War I, in which the Ottoman Empire supported Germany, Ben-Gurion returned to Palestine. However, he was deported because of his political views. He moved to the United States with Isaac Ben-Zvi, a friend and colleague who would later become one of Israel's first presidents. In addition to creating an organization to encourage American Jews to emigrate to Palestine, Ben-Gurion joined the Jewish Volunteers, a group that supported Great Britain's forces in the war. In 1917, the British issued the Balfour Declaration, which called for a Jewish state in Palestine. Initially, many Zionists were supportive of English interests.

Palestine was taken from the Ottoman Empire during the war. In 1923, the British took control of the territory at the request of the League of Nations, the international organization that preceded the United Nations. Ben-Gurion, who had returned to Palestine to continue his work with the Labor Party (he also founded the General Federation of Jewish Labor in 1921), became active in the Jewish Agency. This organization was established to encourage and manage Jewish immigration to Palestine. He became its chairman in 1935.

In 1939, however, the British government reversed its course on the immigration issue and declared that Jewish arrivals would be limited, and then stopped altogether by 1944. Relations between the British and Jewish leaders in Palestine began to fall apart. During World War II, Ben-Gurion had the challenge of supporting the Allied war effort against Nazi Germany and continuing his efforts to encourage Jewish immigration. In 1942, he called for the establishment of an independent Jewish state in Palestine that would recognize the rights of all non-Jewish residents.

After World War II, the situation in Palestine turned violent, with many Jewish leaders turning to guerrilla warfare against Arabs opposed to a Jewish state and toward the British occupying forces. In 1947, England turned the problem over to the newly created United Nations. A plan was created that called for a U.N.–controlled area around Jerusalem and two independent countries—one Arab and one Jewish. This solution did little to please either the Arabs or the Jewish settlers. In May 1948, David Ben-Gurion declared the creation of a new nation of Israel "based on the precepts of liberty, justice, and peace taught by the Hebrew prophets." There was no provision made for an independent Arab state.

The new country was quickly attacked by its Arab neighbors, and although an armistice was agreed to, no peace treaty was signed. In the meantime, the leaders of the newly created state of Israel were busy drawing up a constitution and electing David Ben-Gurion as the first prime minister to govern the country. Israel was formally recognized by the United Nations in May 1949, one year after it was created.

Ben-Gurion served until 1951, when religious conservatives in Israel's Knesset (the equivalent of the U.S. Congress) who were unhappy with his socialist programs forced a no-confidence vote. After traveling to the United States to raise money for the new country, new elections put him back in office. He resigned again in 1953, this time because of poor health, and for two years he worked as a laborer on a kibbutz. Then, in 1955, he returned to government service as prime minister to try to resolve the problem of Arab terrorist attacks on Israel's borders. He decided on a policy of immediate armed response, a practice that Israel often maintained from that point on.

In 1956, Egypt attempted to nationalize the vitally important Suez Canal, prompting immediate response from several European powers. Israel also declared that its security was threatened by the Egyptian move and quickly conquered the Sinai peninsula and took control of Gaza. Israel withdrew from these areas in 1957.

Ben-Gurion served as prime minister until 1963 but remained in politics until 1970, serving in the Knesset. In the 1967 Six-Day War, during which his country quickly conquered the Sinai, Gaza, and other areas, he was opposed to Israel's keeping much of the same land it had given back to its neighbors in 1957. In addition to his key leadership positions during the founding of Israel, David Ben-Gurion established the continuing close connection between Israeli nationalism and the Jewish religion through his lifelong work to encourage Jewish people of all countries to move to the Middle East and become citizens of Israel. He died on December 1, 1973.

Bergman, Ingmar

(1918–   )

SWEDISH FILM DIRECTOR

When you read, words have to pass through your conscious mind to reach your emotions and your soul. In film and theater, things go directly to the emotions. What I need is to come in contact with others.

—Ingmar Bergman, in a 1972 interview

Ingmar Bergman is one of the legendary filmmakers of the twentieth century. He was born on July 14, 1918, in Uppsala, Sweden, about fifty miles north of Stockholm, the capital. His family was very poor while Bergman was a child. His father, a chaplain, did not make much money. Bergman himself did not care for his father's religion; he found his preaching a bore. Moreover, tensions developed between Bergman and his father.

Bergman's lifelong addiction to film took hold at age ten, when he began going with his older brother to see films at school. The movies they saw were primarily documentaries, nature films, and feature films designed specifically for children. He had been fascinated by films ever since he had seen the classic *Black Beauty* when he was six years old. Indeed, his ambition was to be a projectionist, a person who operates a motion picture projector.

At about that same time, in 1928, an aunt sent his brother Dag a movie projector as a Christmas present. Bergman swapped half of his toy army soldiers for the projector. Soon afterward, he began buying films from a photography store; he would cut and splice (connect together) different parts of different films to create his own films.

As a teenager, Bergman's love for films continued to increase. He went to the movies at every opportunity. He particularly liked horror films such as *The Mummy* and *Frankenstein*.

When he was sixteen years old, Bergman participated in a student exchange program, which enabled him to visit Germany. At that time, Adolf Hitler and the Nazis were solidifying their power throughout Germany, and Bergman received a heavy dose of Nazi propaganda, or political publicity. He has said that when he returned to Sweden he was a pro-Nazi teenager. However, after World War II ended and Bergman saw newsreels of the Nazi death camps and other atrocities, he realized the evil he had been associated with. The effect was traumatic. As a result, Bergman would forever turn his back on politics.

While at college, Bergman studied literature and art history. However, he soon decided that he wanted a career in the theater. He knew that his parents would not favor such a decision. He felt his parents were old-fashioned, stuck in the conservative Sweden of the nineteenth century. They were devoted to duty and opposed to new ideas. Bergman was rebelling against what they valued in life. He broke free from his parents' control after a fight over his career plans turned violent. He left home and did not see his parents again for four years.

The 1940s proved to be important years for Bergman. They were the years in which Bergman began his theater career, which laid the foundation for his subsequent career as a film director. He directed his first play in 1938; by 1940, he was directing plays at the Student Theater in Stockholm. He also began writing his own plays in the early 1940s.

In 1943, Bergman married Else Fisher, and the two of them lived as bohemians. At that time, he was also hired by Sweden's largest film company to be a scriptwriter. By 1945, Bergman was directing his first film, *Crisis*. With this film, he began his practice of letting members of his theater productions have roles in the film. Unfortunately, *Crisis* was not successful.

Despite his initial failure, Bergman met with critical success in 1951 with *Summer Interlude,* and then again in 1953 with *Sawdust and Tinsel.* By the late 1950s, Bergman had hit his stride as a film director with *Wild Strawberries* and *The Face.*

In two of his classics from this period—*The Seventh Seal* (1957) and *The Virgin Spring* (1959)—Bergman drew on his childhood environment. Growing up in Uppsala gave him a deep appreciation for Nordic history, which Bergman incorporates in these two films as the backdrop for his exploration of the themes of death, betrayal, and disillusionment. In *The Seventh Seal,* for example, a disillusioned knight tries to solve life's mysteries while playing a game of chess with Death. The brooding film captures Bergman's own sense of despair that resulted, in large part, from the effects of World War II. Bergman has said that films reveal much more about their creators than one might think.

In the mid-1960s, Bergman's films changed their focus. Rather than examining one's place in the universe, Bergman explored themes such as the artist's place in society. While maintaining his high critical standards, Bergman was also becoming more commercially accessible in style, and by 1972 he directed his most popular film, *Cries and Whispers.* Other well-known and highly praised works include *Fanny and Alexander, The Magic Flute,* and *Scenes from a Marriage.*

Despite the success of *Cries and Whispers,* Bergman ran into serious troubles by the mid-1970s. Tax problems he was experiencing in Sweden led Bergman to suffer a nervous breakdown. After he recovered his health, he left Sweden to protest his mistreatment by tax authorities. By 1979, the tax issues were cleared up, and Bergman returned to Sweden. He retired from filmmaking in 1982.

Bergman's work reflected his own growth and development as a person. As he changed over time, he made changes in his directorial methods. He also adjusted his style to work with commercial and technological changes. In so doing, Bergman's creative versatility enabled him to further an already distinguished career.

Bernstein, Leonard

(1918–1990)

AMERICAN CONDUCTOR, PIANIST, AND COMPOSER

The conductor must not only make his orchestra play; he must make them want to play. He must exalt them, lift them, start their adrenaline pouring, either through cajoling or demanding or raging. But however he does it, he must make the orchestra love the music as he loves it.

—Leonard Bernstein

Leonard Bernstein's career of nearly fifty years as a musician, composer, conductor, and teacher got off to a dramatic start in 1943. That year, at the age of twenty-five, he made his conducting debut with the New York Philharmonic Orchestra at Carnegie Hall by stepping in for Bruno Walter at the last moment—and electrified the audience. During the 1950s, with his popular series of televised Young People's Concerts and lectures, and the major role he played in elevating the Broadway musical theater to the level of opera, Bernstein introduced classical music to a wide audience.

Leonard Bernstein was born in 1918 in Boston, Massachusetts. His father was a businessman who started the Samuel Bernstein Hair Company, which provided barber shops with cosmetics. Leonard's mother, Jennie, worked in a factory before becoming a full-time mother to him and his sister Shirley and brother Burton. Leonard was a sickly child who suffered from asthma and hay fever. His family moved around the Boston area frequently as he grew up, and he often had to make new friends whenever he lived in a new neighborhood.

Leonard did well in school, and after returning home one day when he was ten, he saw a piano that his aunt had lent to the family. He soon started to improvise at the piano and play whenever he could, and it was not long before he was taking lessons. When he was fourteen, his father took him to hear the Boston Pops Orchestra, an experience that young Leonard never forgot.

When Bernstein was fourteen years old, he auditioned for the best piano teacher in Boston, Heinrich Gebhard. It was arranged for Leonard to take lessons with one of the master's assistants, Helen Coates, for $6 a lesson. After four years with Ms. Coates, Leonard studied with Gebhard and dreamed of becoming a professional musician. In 1935 Bernstein graduated from Boston Latin School, and at seventeen he was admitted to Harvard University.

At Harvard, Bernstein's teacher in music composition was the American composer Walter Piston. Apart from taking his studies very seriously, Bernstein wrote music reviews for the university journal. His first published article in the journal was about a concert by the Boston Symphony Orchestra conducted by Sergei Koussevitsky, who would later become Leonard's greatest mentor, friend, and adviser. In 1939, Bernstein graduated from Harvard *cum laude* (with honors), and made his debut as a conductor. Bernstein went to New York for the summer and began writing songs in collaboration with Betty Comden and Adolph Green for a nightclub cabaret. He met many people in the music world (such as the American composer Aaron Copland, who also became one of Bernstein's lifelong friends).

In 1939, Bernstein attended the Curtis Institute of Music in Philadelphia, where he studied piano and conducting with Fritz Reiner, the chief conductor of the Pittsburgh Symphony Orchestra. In the summer of 1940, Bernstein was invited to further his studies in conducting at the Berkshire Music Center with Sergei Koussevitsky, who appointed Bernstein as his assistant conductor in 1942. (When Koussevitsky died in 1951, Bernstein became the head of the summer Tanglewood Festival until 1955.)

In the winter of 1942, Bernstein worked in New York as a piano teacher while writing some popular and classical music. After Bernstein's dramatic conducting debut with the New York Philharmonic in 1943, a concert that was broadcast live around the country, he became famous and began to receive invitations to write music for and perform with several orchestras.

The mid-1940s through the 1950s were very productive years for Leonard Bernstein. His first Broadway musical, *On the Town*, opened in New York in 1944. Other Bernstein musicals that were to follow included: *Trouble in Tahiti* (1952), *Wonderful Town* (1953), *Candide* (1956), and his most famous and popular musical work, *West Side Story* (1957), conceived and choreographed by Jerome Robbins. Shakespeare's tragic love story *Romeo and Juliet* provides the basic plot outline of *West Side Story*. The show tells the story of a contemporary love affair that develops between two people whose friends and family members belong to two rival gangs in a tough New York City neighborhood.

From 1951 to 1956, Bernstein was a professor of music at Brandeis University in Waltham, Massachusetts. He taught music theory and composition to both beginners and advanced students. He inspired musicians to expand their repertory and talents. Any student who studied conducting under Bernstein was rewarded with the professor's enthusiastic encouragement. The success of Bernstein's television series *Omnibus* and Young People's Concerts in the mid-1950s was the result of his contagious enthusiasm for his subject matter and the non-threatening manner that he used to introduce young people to classical music. Bernstein won an Emmy Award for the show in 1956–57.

In 1958, at the age of forty, Bernstein became the first American-born music director of the New York Philharmonic. During the 1950s and 1960s he appeared as a guest conductor with many symphony orchestras in places around the world, including Israel, Austria, Italy, and Russia. His style of conducting was highly theatrical. Bernstein used a little nod of his head or moved his hand slightly for a quiet note. Then he would swing his arms dramatically for a loud crescendo.

In 1969, Bernstein resigned as musical director of the New York Philharmonic in order to spend more time composing and on other projects. He was, however, named laureate conductor and allowed special performances with the Philharmonic. He took the orchestra on a Bicentennial tour of eleven European cities in the summer of 1976, giving thirteen concerts in just seventeen days.

In addition to being an excellent pianist, composer, and conductor, Bernstein liked to write poetry and he published several of his sonnets. He also enjoyed teaching, and in 1973 he lectured at the Massachusetts Institute of Technology; he was also the Charles Eliot Norton Professor in Poetry at Harvard University. In 1976, he published *The Unanswered Question: Six Talks at Harvard.*

Bernstein's seventieth birthday in 1988 was the cause of many tributes to him around the world, including a major celebration at Tanglewood. One year later, to celebrate the fall of the Berlin Wall, Bernstein conducted performances of Beethoven's Ninth Symphony on both sides of the wall.

In recognition of his outstanding contributions to music around the world, Bernstein received honors from Finland, France, Italy, Austria, and Sweden. In 1981 he became a member of the American Academy of Arts and Letters, and two years later he was made a member of the Vienna Philharmonic. He won the Gold Medal of the Philharmonic Society of London in 1987, and became President of the London Symphony Orchestra. In 1988, two years before his death, Bernstein was made laureate conductor of the Israeli Philharmonic.

Bethune, Mary McLeod

(1875–1955)

AMERICAN EDUCATOR, REFORMER,
AND GOVERNMENT OFFICIAL

Mary McLeod Bethune was born on July 10, 1875, one of seventeen children born to former slaves in rural South Carolina. Educated in Christian schools and colleges, Mary studied to be a missionary teacher in Africa, only to discover that as a black woman, she would not be given the post she sought in Africa. She taught instead at a number of black colleges before moving to Florida in 1899 to open her own mission school. She founded the Daytona Normal and Industrial Institute in 1904, a school that became a model for its quality education, its able administration, and its progressive relationship with Daytona's mixed-race community.

She built the institute into a large, prosperous school, which eventually became Bethune-Cookman College in 1929. She headed the school until 1942, when her career took a sharp turn toward public service in Washington, D.C.

All through the 1920s and 1930s, Mary Bethune worked tirelessly to organize and inspire black women to become involved in social and political issues such as segregation, discrimination, and international relations, through the National Association of Colored Women (NACW) and the National Council of Negro Women (NCNW). Her work with the NCNW brought her in contact with Eleanor Roosevelt, who saw Bethune's value as a voice for black concerns in her husband's administration. In 1935, Bethune was appointed an adviser to the National Youth Organization (NYA), an agency charged with helping young people find work during the Depression and World War II.

Mary Bethune used her role in the NYA as a springboard to ever-increasing influence within the Roosevelt government with respect to black interests and founded the Federal Council on Negro Affairs. This group became informally known as the "black cabinet," and was made up of black people in government who sought to generate support for the New Deal among the black population while working to generate support within the government for anti-discrimination policies. Bethune was fiercely loyal to Roosevelt and she took seriously what she considered to be her responsibility to represent the administration to the black community. She traveled throughout the country promoting the New Deal and encouraged blacks to unite with their fellow Americans to win the war. She also campaigned for civil rights through grass-roots organizations, marching, demonstrating, and picketing businesses that did not admit or hire blacks.

Mary McLeod Bethune left government in 1944, and retired in 1949 to her home in Daytona Beach, Florida, where she died on May 18, 1955. During her lifetime, she uniquely mastered the political arts of cooperating, negotiating, lobbying, and persuading, and used these skills to advance the rights and interests of black people. She was keenly aware of the racial climate of the times, and worked carefully around it to achieve her goals and improve race relations. Bethune was by far the most influential black woman of her day.

Bettelheim, Bruno

(1903–1990)

AUSTRIAN PSYCHOLOGIST

> Our hearts must know the world of reason, and reason must be guided by an informed heart.
> —Bruno Bettelheim, from *The Informed Heart*

As an educator, writer, and psychologist, Bruno Bettelheim's unique vision and strong commitment to social issues made him one of the most influential thinkers in his field. In a lifetime spanning virtually the entire twentieth century, his own life, including time spent in Nazi concentration camps, helped shape the ideas that would provide valuable insights for future generations of psychologists and social scientists.

Bruno Bettelheim was born in Vienna, Austria, on August 28, 1903. He was educated in Germany as well as in his home country, where he graduated from Vienna's Reform Realgymnasium in 1921. Very early in life he came to believe that the arts—music, literature, painting—provided the keys to creating a peaceful and stable society. World War I occurred just as he was going through adolescence, and he gave this fact much significance in shaping his future thoughts and beliefs.

Bettelheim continued his education at the University of Vienna where he was strongly influenced by Sigmund Freud, the most famous psychoanalyst of the twentieth century. Then, as he was Jewish, Bettelheim was arrested in 1938 when Adolf Hitler's Nazi regime came to power in Austria. He was deported to Germany and imprisoned in the Dachau and Buchenwald concentration camps, where he managed to apply his studies to psychological research on his fellow prisoners. He was particularly interested in how the totalitarian life in such a forced environment affects the human spirit and in how human beings adapt to these conditions in order to survive. When the results of his work were finally published in 1943, they attracted worldwide attention.

Bettelheim was released from prison in 1939. He immediately immigrated to the United States, where he worked at the University of Chicago as a researcher for the Progressive Education Association until 1942. He then became a professor of psychology at Rockford College in Illinois, from 1942 to 1944, when he returned to the University of Chicago. There he was made director of a program to study children of normal and high intelligence who had serious emotional problems. It was in the field of psychological research with children that he made his greatest contributions to science.

Among Bettelheim's beliefs was a conviction that, in order to live "socially useful and emotionally satisfying" lives, children needed more than love from their parents. They needed an environment that was stable and nurturing, which would make it possible for them to realize and meet their everyday needs. He drew lessons from the study of seriously disturbed children to apply to normal society. And he believed that the goal of psychotherapy for disturbed individuals was to "restore meaning to their lives."

Bettelheim also turned his attention, and his writing, to social issues such as racial prejudice. In fighting this problem he insisted that it was important to deal with the realities of the racial groups involved rather than the stereotypes and myths that tended to put the discussion in the context of "melodrama." In particular, he called for the use of reason instead of emotion in attempting to solve this, and other, social concerns.

Bettelheim became a naturalized U.S. citizen in 1944 and was on the faculty of the University of Chicago until 1973. Throughout his life he believed that correcting society's injustices and inequities was a matter of moral necessity, even if there could be no scientific method used to accomplish those goals. In writing about tolerance, for example, he said, "We must recognize from the start that the issue is a moral one, to be decided on moral grounds regardless of whether present methods of investigation can provide the supporting arguments or not."

He continued his writing after retirement from the University of Chicago, publishing a number of books, including a study of fairy tales, and in 1987, *A Good Enough Parent: A Book on Child-Rearing*. Bruno Bettelheim died in Silver Spring, Maryland, on March 13, 1990.

Bonhoeffer, Dietrich

(1905–1945)

GERMAN THEOLOGIAN

Dietrich Bonhoeffer was a German Lutheran pastor and theologian. Arrested and sent to Buchenwald concentration camp in 1943 by the Nazi government for plotting to kill Adolf Hitler, Germany's leader, he was hanged by the Nazis in 1945.

Bonhoeffer was born in the German town of Breslau in 1905. He studied religion in Berlin and New York, and was influenced by his German teacher Karl Barth. Religion, to Bonhoeffer, had to be something *lived*, not just written, preached, and thought about. He began his ministry in the 1930s, at the same time that Hitler began ruling Germany. Bonhoeffer joined the "confessing Church," a group of Lutherans opposed to the evils of Hitler and his regime. He taught theology in Berlin, but he fled to the United States in 1939 so that he would not have to serve in the German army. A month later, however, he returned to Germany. According to Bonhoeffer, being a true Christian meant fighting Hitler, not escaping him. He joined a group of people who were plotting to overthrow Hitler, and he continued writing about the duties of a Christian. In 1943, he was arrested for taking part in a plot to kill Hitler. While in prison, he wrote letters and diaries, which were eventually published after his death. He condemned the organized churches of his day, because they had not taken a stand against Hitler. He felt that human beings had to create a religion that did not rely on a supernatural God to make them behave. He was hanged by the Nazis in 1945, shortly before Hitler took his own life. Bonhoeffer's life, even more than his writings and preaching, had a huge impact on Christianity in the second half of the twentieth century.

Bonner, Yelena

(1923–   )

RUSSIAN HUMAN RIGHTS ACTIVIST

Yelena Bonner, the wife of 1975 Nobel Peace Prize winner Andrei D. Sakharov, fought for human rights within the Soviet Union from the 1960s until the collapse of the Soviet Union in the late 1980s. Despite constant harassment by the KGB and ill health, Bonner was able to serve as Sakharov's contact with the outside world, and she received the Nobel Peace Prize in his name in 1975.

Bonner was born in Moscow in 1923. Both of her parents were active in the Communist Party of the Soviet Union. When Bonner was fourteen, both of her parents were arrested during the dictator Joseph Stalin's purges. Her father was killed, and her mother was imprisoned until 1954. Bonner and her brother moved in with their aunt and uncle, but they, too, were soon purged. The children were raised by their grandmother, and Bonner worked as a maid and a file clerk while in high school. In 1940, she became involved with Communist Party youth groups, and she volunteered for the army after Germany's leader, Adolf Hitler, invaded the Soviet Union with his army in 1941. She was injured in the war, and nearly lost her vision. She finished World War II as a lieutenant. After spending two years struggling to regain her sight, Bonner enrolled in medical school in Leningrad (now St. Petersburg). There she met her first husband and had two children. Following her graduation, she worked as a pediatrician (children's doctor), and then in Iraq as a foreign-aid health worker. She also edited a book of poems of Vsevolod Bagritsky, her first love, who had died in World War II.

In 1965, Bonner joined the Communist Party only after it denounced Stalin. She wrote that she never believed that her parents had done anything wrong, and never forgave Stalin for what he had done. Also in 1965, she separated from her husband and began pursuing political interests. When the Soviet Union invaded Czechoslovakia in 1968, she began to oppose the Communist Party. She started publishing underground (secret) newspapers, and she met fellow dissident Andrei Sakharov at the trial of another dissident in 1970. They were married in 1971, and Bonner resigned from the Communist Party.

For the next fifteen years, Bonner and Sakharov were harassed by the KGB for their work to end human rights abuses in the Soviet Union. They were spied on by secret police, questioned endlessly about their work, prohibited from attending dissident trials, forbidden from owning a telephone, and not allowed to travel within or outside the country. They formed a watchdog group in Moscow, along with other dissidents, to monitor the human rights abuses in the Soviet Union. They often used the hunger strike as a means of political protest, for the couple was well known in the West and it would have been a great embarrassment to the Soviet government had they been allowed to die of hunger. Several times, Bonner and Sakharov were taken to a hospital and force-fed to end their strikes. Alone among the dissidents, Bonner was not arrested. She reported that she was spending her political prisoner's day all by herself, because all the people who had protested against the holding of political prisoners had become political prisoners themselves.

Bonner had to fight to receive the exit visas she needed to travel to Europe and the United States for medical treatment. On one of her trips, in 1975, she was in Italy when the Nobel Committee announced that her husband had won the Peace Prize. She traveled to Norway to accept it in his name, and she put the $143,000 prize money in a Western bank, so the KGB would not confiscate it.

Sakharov was exiled to Gorky in 1980, and he was not allowed to leave that city. Bonner visited him frequently and carried his messages to the world. On one trip to the United States, she managed to write her memoirs in a hospital bed while recovering from heart surgery. In 1984, Bonner was arrested by the KGB as an evil influence on her husband, and she was sentenced to internal exile in Gorky, along with her husband. She received a travel visa in 1985, after another hunger strike, and while in the United States she met with government officials and received a pledge from President Ronald Reagan that he would do everything he could to free Sakharov. On the same trip she met with British Prime Minister Margaret Thatcher and French President François Mitterand.

In 1986, one day after their first telephone was installed, Bonner and Sakharov received a phone call from Soviet Premier Mikhail Gorbachev, doing away with their exile and inviting them back to Moscow, to live as free citizens. The couple returned to Moscow and threw themselves once again into human rights work. Their efforts paid off. Many dissidents were released from Soviet jails, and those Soviet citizens who wished to emigrate were being allowed to do so. In 1989, shortly before his death, Sakharov was elected to the Congress of People's deputies. Yelena Bonner has continued to represent courage and strength in the face of great opposition. In January 1995, Bonner asked U.S. President Bill Clinton to pressure Russian President Boris Yeltsin to stop his military attacks on Chechnya, a breakaway Russian republic.

Borges, Jorge Luis

(1899–1986)

ARGENTINIAN SHORT-STORY WRITER, POET, NOVELIST, AND ESSAYIST

Jorge Luis Borges's writings are at once playful and funny, and yet unnervingly true to life, a literary hall of mirrors in which art imitates life imitating art imitating life.

Nowhere else but in the world of Borges could mapmakers create a map so accurate that it is the exact size of the country it depicts and, eventually, blankets. The Borges fictional world is a funny, eerie mixture of mazes and labyrinths, a world in which the wall dividing fiction from reality is more like a sieve.

Borges was born in Buenos Aires, Argentina, on August 24, 1899. He was the son of Jorge Guillermo Borges, a lawyer; and Leonor Acevedo de Borges, a prominent translator of English and American fiction. His mother's family was quite distinguished, including famous Argentine patriots like Francisco Narciso de Laprida and Col. Isidro Suárez, who fought in the nation's war of independence. As he grew up, Jorge learned English and Spanish virtually simultaneously.

Jorge was a frail, bespectacled child who found refuge from a threatening world in his father's enormous library. There he read everything from Percy Shelley and John Keats to Greek mythology. He developed a taste for literature of the fantastic that would remain with him his entire life. By age nine, the young boy had translated Oscar Wilde's *The Happy Prince* into Spanish. His father's literary career had been cut short by hereditary blindness (which would eventually strike Jorge, too), so the family was delighted by the precocious boy's writing endeavors.

From 1914 to 1921, the Borges family lived in Europe. Borges and his sister, Norah, were educated at the College Calvin in Geneva, Switzerland. The instruction there was conducted in French, so Jorge acquired a third language and, since he concentrated on the study of Latin, a fourth. He also began reading extensively in French and German literature. At the end of their European sojourn, the family spent a year in Madrid, Spain, during which time Borges met and became involved with some of the literary avant-garde of the Spanish capital. He also published his first poems.

The Borges family returned to Buenos Aires in 1921. Jorge threw himself into the life of the city, which would be a major subject of poetry for him. He wrote and published widely, two volumes of poetry and two books of essays in five years. His early work is filled with a romantic view of Argentina that faded as time went on. Borges became a contributing editor of *Sur* (*South*), a magazine of the literary avant-garde founded by Victoria Ocampo; he reviewed films and books for the magazine, as well as contributing poetry.

However, it was not until 1935 that Borges established his real literary trademark. That year he published his first narrative fiction in a collection entitled *A Universal History of Infamy*. These stories, and the ones that followed in *Ficciones* (*Fictions*, 1944), represented a significant transition for Borges. A series of essays on nonexistent books and authors, these "stories" veer between clever literary play and disorienting labyrinths of truth and illusion.

It was a difficult time for Borges personally. He was forced to seek regular work, taking a position as a librarian in 1937, the beginning of what he called "nine years of solid unhappiness." In 1946, after he publicly attacked the Argentine dictator Juan Perón for his support of Hitler and the Nazis, Borges was fired from his job at the library.

Although he was painfully shy, Borges was finally forced to take a teaching position in order to survive. He moved into an apartment in Buenos Aires with his mother; he would occupy the apartment for most of the rest of his life. In 1955, when Perón fell from power, Borges was offered the position of director of the National Library, which he accepted and held until he retired in 1975. He also was made a professor of German, English and American literature at the Faculty of Philosophy and Letters.

By that time, about 1953, Borges was beginning to feel trapped by his reputation as a writer of fantastic tales. The encroaching hereditary blindness that had afflicted his father was finally affecting him as well. For the next twenty years, he would write no stories. Instead, he collected previous essays (which would be published in 1964 as *Other Inquisitions*) and dictated a series of short fables and prose poems, which were published in 1960 in Argentina, and in 1964 in the United States as *Dreamtigers*. Borges also began writing poetry again.

More important, he began a fruitful collaboration with his lifelong friend Adolfo Bioy Casares. Their first book, *Chronicles of Bustos Domecq* (1967) was a witty satire on the literary world, a series of essays and stories by the nonexistent Bustos Domecq.

Beginning in the 1960s, Borges started traveling widely. He lectured and spoke on campuses around the world. He made a lengthy visit to the United States, during which he spoke at universities in Massachusetts, Oklahoma, Texas, and New Hampshire. His reputation outside Argentina was secured by new translations of his best works into English. In 1961, he was awarded the prestigious Fomentor Prize with Samuel Beckett.

Borges married Elsa Astete Millán in 1967, and she accompanied him to the U.S., but they divorced in 1968 and he moved back in with his mother. He married Maria Kodama two months before his death in 1986. A regular traveling companion of his during the last six years of his life, she had collaborated with him on a collection of travel writing, *Atlas* (1985), combining his text with her photographs. He died in Geneva, a place from his youth.

Bradley, Omar

(1893–1981)

GENERAL IN COMMAND OF AMERICAN FORCES IN EUROPE
DURING WORLD WAR II

Omar Bradley was born on February 12, 1893, in Clark, Missouri. He graduated from the United States Military Academy at West Point in 1915. He served at various military posts over the next few years, including four years as an instructor in mathematics at West Point. In 1925, he graduated from the army's Infantry School at Fort Benning, Georgia, and in 1929 he finished his studies at the General Staff College at Fort Leavenworth, Kansas. He returned to West Point as an instructor in tactics in 1934 and in 1938 joined the General Staff of the War Department in Washington, D.C.

In 1943, at the height of World War II, Bradley was assigned to the headquarters of General Dwight Eisenhower in North Africa. He took over the Second Army Corps from General George Patton and led it in the capture of Bizerte and Tunis, eventually forcing the surrender of General Erwin Rommel's famed Afrika Korps, capturing twenty-five thousand German troops. He was made field commander of American land forces under Eisenhower, with more than one million men under his command. He planned overall battle strategy during the drive into Germany and had to mediate disputes between aggressive, temperamental commanders like Patton and British General Bernard Law Montgomery. Polite and well-mannered toward reporters and politicians, Bradley was a popular general, but he tolerated no failure from his subordinates. He eventually achieved the rank of five-star general and from 1947 to 1953 he served as chairman of the Joint Chiefs of Staff. He died in New York City on April 8, 1981.

Brancusi, Constantin

(1876–1957)

ROMANIAN SCULPTOR

> I could have had money if I had done other things. But I chose sculp-
> ture. If I got as far as Paris and lived as I did, it was because that was
> what I wanted. My game is my own.
>
> —Constantin Brancusi, in 1938, on the darker days of his career

Constantin Brancusi was one of the twentieth century's greatest sculptors. He
was born in Pestisani Gorj, Romania, in 1876, in the village of Hobitza. Brancusi experienced an unhappy childhood: He did not get along with his strict father, and he got along even less with his stepbrothers, who used to beat him.
When he was eleven years old, he finally ran away from home. In nearby Tirgu
Jiu, Brancusi worked at a variety of odd jobs to survive. He then moved on to
Craiova, where he worked as a waiter.

Because of his small stature, he used to climb inside wine casks to clean
them. Later, he constructed a violin from the wood of a discarded cask. Such
talent caught people's attention, and eventually Brancusi was accepted into a
local arts-and-crafts school. His entry into the school was even more remarkable, since Brancusi lacked any type of formal education. Indeed, throughout
his life, he wrote French phonetically rather than using standard grammatical
spelling.

Despite his lack of a formal education, Brancusi was an outstanding student.
He completed the five-year arts-and-crafts program in only four years. Then he
went to an art school in Bucharest, Romania's capital, where he once more distinguished himself by winning honors.

In 1904, Brancusi went to Paris, France, where he initially earned a living as
a dishwasher before obtaining a Romanian scholarship to study at an art
school. In Paris, the massive and powerful sculpture works of Auguste Rodin
had the greatest influence on Brancusi. Rodin's sculptures represented the pin-
nacle of artistic achievement to Brancusi, who sought to produce works that
were equally as great.

In 1913, five of Brancusi's sculptures were exhibited at the armory show in
New York City. One year later, he had his first one-person exhibition in New
York. From 1914 onward, Brancusi was assured of financial stability because of
intense interest in his work by American collectors.

Brancusi's sculptures reflect the primitivism in vogue with the Paris avant-
garde. However, because he grew up in a culture imbued with peasant and folk
art traditions, Brancusi was not drawn, as so many of his Paris contemporaries

were, to the exotic and the magical elements in primitivism. Rather, he respected primitive or tribal art's formal craft, its ability to make the very simplest of forms express complex meaning. In his own sculpture, Brancusi likewise sought such simplicity—the ability to reduce and to concentrate the complex. His method greatly influenced subsequent practitioners of modern art.

Brancusi sought to reveal the essential quality of whatever he was sculpting. He wanted to get below the surface of appearances; his sculptures were abstract, rather than realistic representations of people or things. For these very reasons, he refused the offer by Rodin, Europe's most renowned sculptor at the time, to work in his studio as an apprentice carver. Brancusi went on in his work to simplify forms; he intentionally eliminated all recognizable detail from his sculptures. He emphasized the general rather than the specific in his art.

As his reputation grew, he remained a very private person. And, in the 1920s, when he was internationally recognized, Brancusi became even more solitary and isolated.

When he died in 1957, Brancusi left the French government his art studio and all of its contents, which included versions of the majority of his most renowned works. Brancusi's art has inspired countless sculptors. He has remained the central figure of twentieth-century abstract sculpture.

Brandeis, Louis D.

(1856–1941)

LAWYER AND ASSOCIATE
JUSTICE OF THE U.S.
SUPREME COURT

Those who won our independence believed . . . liberty to be the secret of happiness and courage to be the secret of liberty.

—Louis Brandeis, in *Whitney v. California* (1927)

Louis Dembitz Brandeis was born in Louisville, Kentucky. He was the youngest of four children. Both of his parents were members of distinguished Jewish families in the European city of Prague. They had emigrated to the United States in 1848. Louis's father established a successful grain and farm produce business in Louisville.

Louis attended public school in Louisville and graduated with honors from high school at the age of fifteen. His family encouraged Louis's interest in learning and culture. In 1872, when his father's business failed, the Brandeis family returned to Europe for a long visit. Brandeis attended school in Dresden for three years during this period. Later he wrote how valuable the experience had been.

Brandeis returned to America in the summer of 1875 and entered Harvard Law School that September. Brandeis quickly became known throughout the university for his brilliance. He finished his legal studies in two years, graduating at the top of his class in 1877. Brandeis's academic record at the law school was so outstanding that it has never been surpassed by any other student.

Brandeis stayed another year at Harvard University to do graduate study in law. Then, in 1878, he moved to St. Louis, and practiced law in a firm there. However, he missed the stimulating atmosphere in Cambridge and Boston, and the humid climate in St. Louis made him ill. After only nine months there, he returned east and opened a law office in Boston with a law school classmate, Samuel D. Warren, Jr. Warren's family were prominent Bostonians, and Brandeis met many important residents of the city, including Oliver Wendell Holmes, Jr. During his first two years of practice, Brandeis also served as a parttime clerk to the chief justice of the Massachusetts Supreme Court, Horace Gray. Shortly afterward, Gray was appointed to the U.S. Supreme Court as an associate justice. Later Holmes, and eventually Brandeis, would also serve on the U.S. Supreme Court.

Brandeis's law practice was successful, and he became a wealthy man. In the 1890s, however, Brandeis began devoting more and more time to social welfare. He believed that privileged people had a responsibility to help those who were less fortunate. "Responsibility," he often said, "is the great developer of men." Brandeis donated his time and legal services to several civic organizations, including the Public Franchise League, which he helped found in Boston in 1900.

As the unpaid legal adviser to the State Board of Trade, Brandeis worked for the adoption of fair rates in the gas industry. (At that time, before the widespread use of electricity, gas was the major source of lighting in Boston and other cities.) He also worked on behalf of consumers in the fields of life insurance, railway transportation, and banking. His reputation as an outstanding lawyer grew, and he now argued cases regularly before the U.S. Supreme Court.

An important part of his presentation was what came to be known as the "Brandeis brief." Most briefs are short. Brandeis's briefs were lengthy and detailed. He would quickly sum up the principles of law involved in a case, then write as many as a hundred pages offering additional information—facts and figures that supported his argument. Brandeis's unique approach worked: he usually won the cases he defended, and he earned the praise and admiration of the justices of the Supreme Court. Later, as a member of the Court, he wrote his opinions in a similar lengthy, careful manner.

Brandeis became an authority on labor relations, and he often worked with employers and employees who were Jewish immigrants. Brandeis's family had not followed any religious practices, and Brandeis had always moved in non-Jewish circles. By 1912, however, his increasingly frequent contact with Jews reawakened an interest in his Jewish origins. He became a student of Zionism. In 1914, when headquarters of the World Zionist Organization were established in the United States, Brandeis became the chairman of its operating committee.

In 1912 Brandeis was an active supporter of Woodrow Wilson in his campaign for the presidency of the United States. After Wilson's election, Brandeis became one of his most important advisers. Brandeis played a leading role in the establishment of the Federal Reserve banking system in 1913 and the Federal Trade Commission in 1914. When a vacancy arose on the Supreme Court, Wilson nominated Brandeis for the seat in January 1916. There was great opposition to Brandeis's appointment. Critics said that Brandeis was not qualified because he had no previous experience as a judge. Many of his supporters, however, agreed with Brandeis that anti-Semitism caused the opposition. Finally, in June 1916, Brandeis's appointment was approved by the Senate, and Brandeis took his seat as the first Jewish member of the U.S. Supreme Court.

On the Court, Brandeis joined his friend Oliver Wendell Holmes, Jr., who had been appointed in 1902. During nearly forty years of service, Brandeis was a firm supporter of liberties guaranteed by the Bill of Rights—freedom of speech, assembly, and the press. Although Brandeis often dissented from the majority decision, he lived to see many of his dissents later written into law.

During his years on the Supreme Court, Brandeis devoted all of his time and energy to his duties as an Associate Justice. He and his wife, whom he had married in 1891, lived quietly in Washington, D.C. They avoided most of the social life in the capital, but saw friends and associates regularly at a tea that they hosted each week at their home.

In February 1939, in his eighty-third year, Brandeis retired from the Court. He continued to live in Washington during the winter, but spent his summers on Cape Cod. Brandeis suffered a heart attack in the fall of 1941 and died several days later in a Washington hospital. His ashes were buried beneath the University of Louisville Law School.

Brecht, Bertolt

(1898–1956)

GERMAN PLAYWRIGHT, POET,
NOVELIST, SHORT-STORY WRITER,
AND ESSAYIST

Playwright Eugen Berthold Brecht was born on February 10, 1898, in Augsburg, Germany, to a well-to-do middle-class family. (He later abandoned his first name and changed the spelling of his second to the harder-sounding Bertolt.) His father, Friedrich, was business director of a paper company, working his way up from his beginnings as a clerk for the firm. Although he was a Catholic, he allowed his wife, Sofie, to raise the boy in her Protestant faith. Young Eugen went through the usual schooling—four years of elementary school, followed by the *Realgymnasium* (secondary school).

From an early age, Brecht was both a writer and a rebel. He began writing poems while still a teenager, and he had a short play published in his school journal in 1914. But, by 1916, he came close to being expelled from school for his opposition to the war effort. In 1917, he had enrolled in medical studies, hoping to avoid the draft. Despite his ostensible medical studies, he was called upon to do military service. He served as a medical orderly in the venereal disease ward of the local military hospital; it was an experience that he would recount with gruesome relish in years to come.

All through that period, Brecht was writing poetry and working on his first play, *Baal*. With the war over, he was to witness the ferocious power struggles out of which the Weimar Republic was born. Inspired by the turmoil around him, Brecht took time out from writing *Baal* to write *Drums in the Night*, a stark drama of postwar malaise; using the 1918–1919 revolt as a background, he presented a strong anti-war message. It is believed that this play was sufficient to get Brecht on the Nazis' blacklist as early as 1925, eight years before they would actually come to power.

Baal, the first of Brecht's plays to be staged, follows the exploits of a carousing, singing poet, not unlike the playwright himself. In 1919, Brecht had a son by Paula Banholzer, whose parents prevented her from marrying him. Three years later, Brecht married actress Marianne Zoff. They had a daughter, Hanne, who would also become an actress.

Brecht had been to Berlin a few times in the postwar period, and he quickly realized that the capital was where the real action was in the arts. He had dropped out of the university in 1921. Even though he wrote and staged two more plays in Munich—*In the Jungle of Cities* (1923) and *Edward II* (1925), which was a free adaptation of Christopher Marlowe's play of the same title—it was clear to Brecht that his career wouldn't advance much further without a move to Berlin, the center of German theater. He left Marianne and Hanne in Muenster and moved to Berlin in September 1924. He soon moved in with actress Helene Weigel, who would eventually become the second Mrs. Brecht.

In Berlin, Brecht experienced quick success. He finished *A Man's a Man*; staged several of his earlier plays; found a publisher; and began assembling a creative team, some of whose members would be with him for several years, including his "secretary," Elisabeth Hauptmann. By September 1927, *A Man's a Man*, heavily reworked from its first draft, had premiered in Berlin.

The following year, Brecht met and teamed up with a young composer of great promise, Kurt Weill, and his wife, the actress and singer Lotte Lenya. The result of this collaboration would be one of the great successes of German theater history. The team created a musical play that today is in the standard repertoire around the world—*The Threepenny Opera*. With its jagged musical rhythms and cynical worldview, *The Threepenny Opera* was an unprecedented piece of theater, even in the Berlin of the Weimar Republic. The play was a huge hit, the music was played everywhere in Berlin, and Brecht and Weill were the toasts of the city. More than one critic accused Brecht of stealing from seventeenth-century writer John Gay's *The Beggar's Opera* and the poems of François Villon, and Brecht never exactly denied it, but as one of his defenders said, "He stole, but he stole with genius."

Brecht, who was a prolific poet, was one of the great lyric poets of the German language. Moreover, it is in his poetry that Brecht unburdened himself of many of his political doubts and personal insecurities, ranging from the poignant verses about his exile in the 1930s and 1940s, to his sardonic and witty skewering of Hollywood and darker ponderings of the failures of Stalinism.

Brecht and Weill's next collaboration, *Happy End*, was a transparent attempt to cash in on the success of *The Threepenny Opera*. The story was supposedly written by a nonexistent Dorothy Lane (with the translation credited to Hauptmann). The score was one of Weill's richest, but the show was a disappointment.

By that time, Brecht had fully enveloped himself in Marxism, and his next several plays reflected his newfound political fervor. With Weill, he wrote *The Rise and Fall of the City of Mahagonny*, a cynical play about a mythical gold-rush town in America in which the only crime is to be broke; it is punishable by death. Nazi sympathizers found this less than amusing, and that disrupted the opening-night performance, which they denounced as the work of "a communist and a Jew."

Brecht and Marianne Zoff divorced in 1927. In 1929, he married Weigel. Their son, Stefan, had been born in 1924, their daughter, Barbara, in 1930. When the Nazis came to power in 1933, Brecht knew that he had to leave the country, taking his family with him. He was, according to some sources, the number-five man on the Nazis' blacklist, and when they held their massive book-burnings, his were among the first books cast into the flames. The day after the Reichstag burned down (a fire that the Nazis set and blamed on the communists), Brecht was gone.

Over the next fourteen years, Brecht and his family were on the move constantly, with stops in Denmark, Finland, Sweden, Switzerland, Czechoslovakia, Austria, France and, finally, the United States. In one of his poems, he commented, only half-jokingly, that he kept a full suitcase under his bed at all times.

The six years in which the Brechts lived in Denmark were, ironically enough, tremendously productive ones for the playwright. He wrote a great deal of poetry, plus four plays, including the two dramas that are, arguably, his finest achievements: *Galileo* (1938–1939) and *Mother Courage and Her Children* (1939). In these two masterpieces, Brecht shoves aside ideology and theory repeatedly to create magnificent moments of theater, while still allowing himself to rage against greed, war, political repression, and betrayals.

Brecht, over the years, developed a theory of what he called "epic" theater. He distinguished epic theater from Aristotle's vision of drama, in which the purpose of the play is to allow the audience to reach an emotional catharsis, usually through identification with the characters. In epic theater, the appeal is to the intellect. Brecht's theoretical writings on drama are fascinating reading and were highly influential.

Brecht's stay in America was less than satisfying, although it provoked some of his best poetry. He went almost immediately to Hollywood, where he hoped to find work writing for film.

Brecht would only manage to complete one film assignment during his seven years in California, an interesting Fritz Lang anti-Nazi film, *Hangmen Also Die* (1943). However, while in Hollywood, he met and became friends with the actor Charles Laughton, who had been one of the principal inspirations for *Galileo*. Laughton was thrilled at the chance to play the role, and the two worked extensively on an English-language version of this play about scientific responsibility and intellectual freedom. The final result, which premiered shortly after the atomic bombs were dropped on Hiroshima and Nagasaki, was both a critical and commercial failure.

Two of his best late plays were written in the United States with an eye toward Broadway, *The Caucasian Chalk Circle* and *The Good Woman of Sechuan*. Neither would make it to the mainstream American stage for a generation.

With the war over, Brecht was ambivalent about returning to a war-ravaged

Germany. Unfortunately, he was had his mind made up for him. The House Un-American Activities Committee, determined to sweep "communist influence" out of the film industry, subpoenaed many Hollywood writers to be questioned about their political activities and their friends. The original group of nineteen was whittled down to eleven, with Brecht one of them. Brecht, as a legal alien, was on shakier ground than the other ten; his testimony makes for fascinating reading as he nimbly waltzes around the committee's questions, suddenly not understanding English or misinterpreting queries. When he was asked if he had ever belonged to the Communist Party, he emphatically answered, "No, no, no, no." It probably was true; Brecht was a Marxist, but he wasn't a joiner.

The next day, he was on a plane to Zurich, Switzerland. After extended negotiations with the communist government in East Germany, Brecht and Weigel settled in East Berlin. He became an honored citizen of the German Democratic Republic, with his own theater and company, the Berliner Ensemble. He trained the company in his theories of drama, and the troupe quickly became legendary throughout the world. Brecht was not about to bend his principles as a playwright into line with the prevailing Stalinist aesthetic of "socialist realism." He worked more as a director than as a playwright during the remainder of his life, and kept writing poetry as well, although much of it, critical of the East German government, could not be published in his lifetime.

On August 14, 1956, during rehearsals for *Galileo*, Brecht died. He was buried in the Dorotheen Cemetery in Berlin. In one of his poems, he offered the best possible epitaph for himself: "I need no gravestone, but/If you need one for me,/I would like it to say/He made proposals. We/accepted them./By such an inscription, we/Would all be honored."

Breuer, Marcel

(1902–1981)

HUNGARIAN ARCHITECT AND FURNITURE DESIGNER

> Mass production and standardization had already made me interested in polished metal, in shiny and impeccable lines in space, as new components of our interiors. I considered such polished and curved lines not only symbolic of our modern technology, but actually to be technology.
>
> —Marcel Breuer's comments on his tubular steel furniture

Marcel Lajos Breuer was one of the twentieth century's premier modern architects and furniture designers. He was born in Pecs, Hungary, on May 22, 1902. Growing up, he wanted to be an artist, but in 1920 he became disillusioned with his goal while studying at a Vienna art academy. Fortunately, his dream did not die. He became excited once more about the prospects of an art career when he heard of the newly opened Bauhaus, a school of architecture and the applied arts in Weimar, Germany. Breuer quickly moved from Vienna to the Bauhaus and enrolled as a student.

At the Bauhaus, Breuer was a success both as a student and then as a teacher. After four years of performing outstanding schoolwork, Breuer was hired as a member of the Bauhaus faculty in 1924. He served dual roles as both a teacher and as the head of the carpentry and furniture department.

Breuer's research in design and his interest in industrial mass production and standardization led to his invention of tubular-steel furniture, a hallmark of modern design. Breuer was the first modern architect who designed furniture that was both a machine-made product and aesthetically attractive. Breuer believed that furniture design was a type of architecture—he felt that the two design approaches were not that different from each other.

While working as a designer and teacher, he did not forsake the desire that brought him to the Bauhaus in the first place. Indeed, Breuer devoted much time to painting and to the study of architecture. He also worked diligently in his efforts to make the Bauhaus specialize in building and industry and to downplay its arts-and-crafts orientation.

In 1928, Breuer left the Bauhaus and moved to Berlin to open his own architecture office. The following year, the great worldwide economic depression hit Germany, and all construction came to a standstill. As a result, Breuer refocused his energies back to tubular-steel furniture.

Like so many others from the Bauhaus, Breuer left Germany in 1933 when the Nazis first ascended to power. Breuer immigrated to England, where he entered an architectural partnership with F.R.S. Yorke. In 1937, however, he emigrated from England to the United States in order to teach for architect Walter Gropius at Harvard University. He taught design at Harvard's School of Architecture, and from 1938 to 1941 Breuer teamed up with Gropius to build a number of houses.

Breuer left Harvard in 1946 and opened his own architecture and design office in New York. He spent the rest of his career working on larger projects such as major public buildings and complete residential neighborhoods in the United States, Europe, and South America.

Breuer belongs to the second wave of great twentieth-century architects. His designs reflect his commitment to Bauhaus principles of functionality. He also developed his ideas of design by making use of American building methods such as wood-frame houses, which particularly fascinated him.

Buck, Pearl S.

(1892–1973)

AMERICAN NOVELIST AND
HUMANITARIAN

Pearl S. Buck was born in Hillsboro, West Virginia. Her parents were missionaries who worked in China, where Buck was taken when she was an infant. Instead of staying in the missionary compound, the family lived in the community. Buck was a bright and curious child and an excellent student. She read the Bible, Chinese sagas, and the literature of Charles Dickens, Theodore Dreiser, and Sinclair Lewis. Buck's mother often gave her writing "assignments" which she would correct, and she encouraged Buck to submit her work for publication.

Buck attended Randolph-Macon Women's College in the United States when she was seventeen. In her senior year she won two literary prizes. She graduated in 1914 and stayed in the United States to teach. Buck married in

1917, and she and her husband, an agricultural specialist, settled in northern China. They both taught at the university in Nanking, and Buck began to publish articles in journals in 1923.

Buck's first child was born mentally retarded, and she brought her to the United States for treatment in 1925. While in the United States, she got her Master's degree from Cornell University, and then she returned to China.

Buck's first novel, *East Wind: West Wind*, was published in 1930. It depicted a Chinese couple caught between the old ways and the influence of modern western culture. The novel offered insights into Chinese culture. The setting was authentic and an element of suspense kept readers turning the pages.

The Good Earth, published in 1931, reflected Buck's complete knowledge of Chinese life. The book reaches a universal level, however, as it explores birth, marriage, illness, family relationships, and death. It conveys Buck's deep belief that human nature can rise above any hardship. Buck published a sequel to *The Good Earth* in 1932 entitled *Sons*, and a third volume, *A House Divided*, in 1935.

Buck's book *The Mother* (1934) depicts the joys, sorrows, despair, and hope experienced during motherhood. In 1936, Buck published a biography of her mother, *The Exile*, and one of her father, *Fighting Angel*. Both books told about the sacrifices her parents made for the missionary cause, and the hardships and dangers they faced living in China.

In 1934 Buck returned to the United States. She had divorced and remarried, and she began to write about American topics and settings. In *The Proud Heart* (1938), Buck eliminated the use of the Chinese saga that so influenced her earlier works, and tried to create a new American style.

Buck's writing philosophy included the use of the Chinese saga. This style reflected an omniscient (all-knowing) point of view, and action and suspense were employed to keep the reader interested. Buck was cautious of being didactic or "preachy" in her novels, although she did want them to convey her values and beliefs such as the importance of eliminating racism, poverty, and war.

Buck won a Nobel Prize in 1938. She began to write for larger audiences, including magazine articles on contemporary issues. She produced a lot in order to maintain a steady readership and convey her messages to as many people as possible. Through her writing, Buck seemed to continue her parents' humanitarian work.

In 1941, Buck established the East and West Association to promote understanding between these two regions of the world. She founded Welcome House, an adoption agency for children fathered by American servicemen. The Pearl S. Buck Foundation has set up agencies in several countries to help Amerasian children with basic necessities, medical care, and education. Buck was always outspoken on human rights issues, and the royalties earned on her books continue to work for these causes.

Byrd, Richard Evelyn

(1888–1957)

AMERICAN AVIATOR AND POLAR
EXPLORER; FIRST PERSON TO FLY
OVER BOTH THE NORTH POLE AND
THE SOUTH POLE

Whoever should elect to inhabit such a spot
must reconcile themselves to enduring the
bitterest temperatures in nature, a long
night as black as that on the dark side of the
moon, and an isolation which no power on
Earth could lift for at least six months.

—Richard Evelyn Byrd,
from *Alone*, 1938

Richard Evelyn Byrd was born in Winchester, Virginia. Quite early in life he
proved himself to be a confident and resourceful traveler, able to do things on
his own. He made a trip around the world—alone—at the age of twelve.

After attending military school and the U.S. Naval Academy, Byrd joined
the navy. Sports injuries to his legs made him unfit for active service, but he was
trained as a naval aviator, or pilot. He became extremely enthusiastic about the
benefits and possible uses of airplanes, which were still fairly new, and
throughout the rest of his career he worked on many projects related to flight,
such as planning air service across the Atlantic Ocean and carrying the first
load of airmail from the United States to Europe.

Byrd's greatest fame, however, came as a polar explorer. He combined his
knowledge of aviation with a desire to know more about the Arctic and Antarctica, two of the world's last remaining unexplored frontiers. He was a pioneer
in the use of aircraft for polar exploration.

In 1924, Byrd made his first polar venture, commanding a naval flight group
in Greenland and Ellesmere Island, two large Arctic islands that have served as
the starting points for many polar expeditions. Two years later he organized a
private expedition and, with fellow pilot Floyd Bennett, flew his own plane
across the North Pole. An Italian explorer named Umberto Nobile had flown
a dirigible over the pole, but Byrd's was the first airplane to make the flight.

The Arctic flight made Byrd an international hero, and he was easily able to
get support for an expedition to Antarctica. The Antarctic expedition included
three planes, ninety-eight sled dogs, and fifty men. Byrd established a base
called Little America at a place called the Bay of Whales, on the Ross Ice Shelf,

one of the major features of the Antarctic coast. Little America remained the focus of American exploration in Antarctica for years afterward.

Byrd succeeded in flying over the South Pole on November 29. The flight took just under sixteen hours. A few years earlier, Norwegian explorer Roald Amundsen, the first person to reach the South Pole, had needed three months to cover the same distance. With the airplane, Byrd had launched a new era of polar exploration.

He returned to Antarctica in 1934, this time to spend the winter season there making meteorological studies. The expedition set up headquarters at Little America, but Byrd had something special in mind for himself. He chose to spend the entire winter in an isolated camp called Bolling Advance Base, 123 miles inland from Little America. It was the first time such a feat of endurance had been attempted, and Byrd tried it because he wanted to see how the solitude and the six-month-long winter night would affect him. Bolling was the first inland camp in Antarctica, and the only one for the next twenty-one years. During his lonely experiment, Byrd ran into trouble when carbon monoxide fumes from his stove made him ill. Fortunately, a team from Little America reached him after five months, in time to save his life. He wrote about his time at Bolling in *Alone*, published in 1938.

Byrd followed the 1934 expedition with a series of Antarctic trips. In each trip he continued to play a personal role in the exploration, photographing, and mapping of the southern continent, often from the air. In 1946 he headed Operation Highjump, the largest expedition ever sent to Antarctica. With an aircraft carrier, six airplanes, several ships called ice-breakers that could push through pack ice, and four thousand men, Operation Highjump was designed to photograph the Antarctic coast so that new, more accurate maps could be made.

Both before and after World War II (1939–45), Byrd served as the U.S. government's head of Antarctic programs. He made a final flight over the South Pole in 1956, one year before his death in Boston. During his lifetime and later, Byrd was honored as a pioneer of both aviation and Antarctic studies. In books such as *Skyward* (1930) and *Discovery* (1935), as well as in the many articles he wrote for *National Geographic* and other publications, he alerted people in the United States and around the world to the wonders of flight and to the harsh beauty of Antarctica.

Cagney, James

(1899-1986)

AMERICAN ACTOR,
SINGER, AND DANCER

James Cagney grew up in a tough neighborhood on New York City's Lower East Side. He attended the city's public schools where individual attention from teachers was rare. Cagney studied hard and was accepted into Columbia University. Unfortunately, he had to drop out after a year because of a lack of money. He took whatever work he could find, including jobs in billiard halls and as a delivery boy. Cagney turned to show business in the hopes of making a better living.

Cagney's first acting job was in a vaudeville show in which he played the part of a female in the chorus line of *Every Sailor* (1919). He went on to appear as an actor and a dancer on the vaudeville circuit throughout the 1920s until he finally got one of the leading roles in *Penny Arcade* on Broadway. When the play was later made into a film, Cagney went to Hollywood and re-created the role in *Sinner's Holiday* (1930). He stayed in Hollywood and made a few other movies until he appeared as a gangster in the movie *Public Enemy* (1931), which brought Cagney into the limelight. Other memorable gangster movies that he acted in were *Angels with Dirty Faces* (1938), *The Roaring Twenties* (1939), and *White Heat* (1949).

Cagney costarred with the actor Pat O'Brien in eight films. Although Cagney was best known for his gangster roles, he made some musicals in which he sang and danced. His first musical was *Footlight Parade* (1933), and his best effort came in 1942 in *Yankee Doodle Dandy* (in which he played the role of George M. Cohan, the patriotic American actor, singer, and producer). For this performance Cagney won the Academy Award for best actor.

Cagney's movie career slowed down in the mid-1940s, but he started his own production company and starred in *Blood on the Sun* (1945). In the 1950s, Cagney's popularity faded, and it was not until he played an aging gangster in a movie with Doris Day, *Love Me or Leave Me* (1955), that his career picked up again. He planned on retiring from acting after appearing in Billy Wilder's *One, Two, Three* (1962). He moved to his farm in upstate New York and lived there quietly for twenty years. After he suffered a stroke his doctor suggested that it would be good for his health to return to acting. Cagney returned to the screen in a featured role as the police commissioner in *Ragtime* (1981). He had aged greatly but could still deliver his lines in his familiar forceful manner.

Cagney's style of acting was simple and straightforward. He said in his autobiography, *Cagney on Cagney*, "Never settle back on your heels. Never relax. If you relax, the audience relaxes. And always mean everything you say."

James Cagney died after having a massive heart attack on his upstate New York farm in 1986.

Campbell, Kim

(1947–   )

PRIME MINISTER OF CANADA

Avril Phaedra "Kim" Campbell was born on March 10, 1947, in Vancouver, British Columbia. She grew up with her father, a Vancouver attorney, and stepmother and attended Vancouver's Prince of Wales High School. Campbell studied political science at the University of British Columbia, where she met and married math professor Nathan Divinsky.

In 1980, while still in law school, Campbell won a seat on the Vancouver school board. Her sharp, intelligent manner got her noticed, and she became increasingly involved in political matters. In 1988, she won a seat in Parliament, and in 1990 Prime Minister Brian Mulroney appointed her as Canada's first female attorney general and justice minister. As attorney general, she managed to push through a tough gun-control law, as well as legislation to protect the rights of those who have been raped. Eventually she was appointed Canada's defense minister. In June 1993 Canada's ruling Progressive Conservative party chose her to succeed Mulroney, who resigned the previous February. Campbell is the first woman to become prime minister of Canada. She is a strong and memorable person who is likely to leave an indelible mark on Canadian politics, as well as on the international political landscape.

Camus, Albert

(1913–1960)

FRENCH NOVELIST, PLAYWRIGHT,
PHILOSOPHER, AND JOURNALIST

We must realize that we cannot escape the
common lot of pain, and that our only justi-
fication, if one there be, is to speak insofar as
we can on behalf of those who cannot.
—Albert Camus

Albert Camus was a giant among French postwar writers, a man of high moral integrity who would not be tied to anyone's party line. Although it is fashionable to lump him together with the existentialists because of his concept of life as "absurd," he was an independent thinker whose relationship with them is tenuous, at best. Rather, Camus was one of the great voices of humanism in a world shattered by war, mass murder, and torture.

Albert Camus was born on November 7, 1913, in Mondovi, Algeria. His father, who was French, was killed in battle early in World War I, before Albert was even one year old. His mother, who was Spanish, was forced to take menial jobs to support her two sons. Albert grew up in extreme poverty, but through his intellectual achievements he was able to lift himself up. His teachers recognized in the young boy an exceptional mind and encouraged him to try for scholarships. As a result, he was able to go through school to the University of Algiers. He was a brilliant student, particularly in philosophy, and an ardent fan of sports and the theater. However, his schooling was frequently interrupted, first by a bout with tuberculosis at seventeen, then later by the need to take part-time work in order to survive.

As a university student, he experimented with many things: He played goalie for a local sports club; married; joined the Communist Party briefly; and worked for the university's meteorological service. After completing his thesis, on the relationship between Hellenism and Christianity, he edited a newspaper and tried his hand at directing a theater group. For almost his entire life, he would remain a wanderer who would change jobs and travel almost on a whim. He would not buy a house until the year before his death.

Tuberculosis was part of the reason for his rootlessness. He was often confined to sanitaria with the illness, was unable to get teaching work because of it, and would be declared unfit for military service when World War II came.

In a way, his sickness left him with no choice but to become a writer, and he published his first two books shortly before the war.

With the outbreak of war, Camus moved to Paris and began work on his first novel, the book that would secure his reputation, *L'Étranger* (*The Stranger;* 1942). This story of a man completely alienated from the people and places around him, who almost inadvertently commits a murder and is sentenced to death, is undoubtedly Camus's best-known book.

Camus was unable to find work in German-occupied Paris, so he returned to Algiers in 1941 and began writing *The Myth of Sisyphus* (1942), a philosophical essay in which he elaborated on the thinking behind the earlier novel. Death, Camus says, is the arbitrary and hence absurd ending to man's achievements in life. As a result of death, life itself is meaningless, unable to provide a basis for human values. And yet, he argues, suicide is not an appropriate response to the absurdity of life. "There is nothing to equal the spectacle of human pride," he says, and suicide is a renunciation of that pride. Rather, it is meaningful to struggle against the absurdity as a manifestation and display of that pride. Struggle transforms absurdity from passive despair to revolt against the world's indifference to mankind.

In 1942, Camus returned once more to France, this time to join the resistance. He worked as an underground journalist until France was liberated in 1944. For the next three years, he would edit *Combat*, the former resistance newspaper that had became a prominent voice of liberal thought. He also wrote his first two plays, *The Misunderstanding* (1944) and *Caligula* (1945), both of which deal with moral questions as seen through the lens of "absurdity."

Finally, in 1947, he wrote and published his second novel, *The Plague*, an attempt to portray a positive figure in struggle. Dr. Rieux, the hero of *The Plague*, organizes to help fight an outbreak of bubonic plague in the Algerian city of Oran; his work is seen as heroic in the face of arbitrary and dreadful suffering.

The Plague marks a major turning point in Camus's thought. Where his work had focused on the absurd before, his attention had shifted to the revolt that he deemed an essential part of life's meaning.

In his next book, the philosophical essay entitled *The Rebel* (1951), Camus argues that man should not tolerate the absurdity of the world; at the same time, he says that revolt and revolution are significantly different things. Revolt, an individual protest, is an act on behalf of humane values, tolerance, and moderation. By contrast, he argues, revolution inevitably leads to tyranny, no matter how well intentioned the revolutionaries may be. He denounced Marxism as a philosophy that would use any means to achieve its ends. The book provoked a storm of controversy, and Camus came under attack from French philosopher and novelist Jean-Paul Sartre.

Camus followed *The Rebel* by returning to the theater, and would not produce a major book until 1956's *The Fall*.

In 1957, Camus received the Nobel Prize for Literature and published a collection of short stories, *Exile and the Kingdom*. He then began work on a new novel, *The First Man*, (published posthumously in 1994), and a play on the Don Juan theme. But on January 4, 1960, while returning to Paris from a vacation, he was killed in a car crash. He was forty-six.

Capra, Frank

(1897–1991)

AMERICAN FILMMAKER AND ACADEMY AWARD WINNER

> I would sing the songs of the working stiffs, of the short-changed Joes, the born poor, the afflicted. Above all, I would fight for their causes on the screens of the world.
>
> —from Frank Capra's autobiography, *Name Above the Title*

Francesco Capra was born on May 18, 1897. His family moved to California in 1903, during a time of hard economic times in Italy. More than two million Italians came to America during the early 1900s. In trying to support the family, his father worked at a variety of jobs, and Capra's mother worked as a fruit picker.

At Throop College of Technology (which became the California Institute of Technology) Capra studied engineering and earned the best grades in his freshman class. He was awarded a travel scholarship and visited New York, where he toured the Eastman plant and saw film being made.

During World War I, Capra tried to enlist in the military, but the Army sent him back to school to study. In 1919, he had a tiny acting part in a John Ford Western, *The Outcasts of Poker Flat*, and he began to consider making his career in the movies. Francesco Capra legally changed his name to Frank Capra when he became an American citizen in 1920.

Capra quickly began working in San Francisco—building sets, carrying props, and assisting the director of slapstick comedies. In 1924, Capra moved to Hollywood, where he wrote jokes for Hal Roach's *Our Gang* comedies.

Columbia Pictures, a small studio in 1927, hired Capra to direct films and he quickly earned money for the studio and gained some critical attention. In 1928, he directed *Submarine*, Columbia's first movie with sound.

In 1934 Capra directed *It Happened One Night*, starring Clark Gable and Claudette Colbert. The film is now considered a classic, and it made 1934 one of the most profitable years for Columbia Pictures. The film made Capra famous and earned him an Academy Award as well as winning five Oscars in all.

Capra then directed *Mr. Deeds Goes to Town* (1936), for which he was awarded another Oscar for Best Director. His next film, *You Can't Take It with You* (1938), gave him his third Academy Award in five years and made him one of the premier directors in Hollywood.

During this time Capra served as president of the Academy of Motion Pictures and helped negotiate contracts between the Screen Directors Guild and the studios. Capra's actions on behalf of the guild helped promote the film industry to the public and avoided a possible labor strike.

Mr. Smith Goes to Washington (1939), about an idealistic man who fights corruption in government, made Jimmy Stewart a star and was nominated for eleven Academy Awards. The film also caused controversy: Joseph Kennedy (President John Kennedy's father) offered Columbia Pictures two million dollars not to release the film, as he believed the film would help Adolf Hitler's cause in Germany.

Capra ended his productive twelve years with Columbia Pictures in 1939, since he sought more creative freedom. Every major studio in Hollywood wanted to hire the popular director, but he chose instead to start his own company, Frank Capra Productions, Inc. His first film as an independent filmmaker was *Meet John Doe* (1941). The film was a commercial and critical disappointment that ruined the company. Capra quickly signed with Warner Brothers Studio and directed *Arsenic and Old Lace* in order to pay his debts.

On December 12, 1941, five days after the Japanese bombed Pearl Harbor, Frank Capra once again enlisted in the army. One of the few directors in Hollywood to suspend his career and serve in the military during World War II, Capra continued to make films for the U.S. Army to gain public support for the war effort. One of the films he made for the army was awarded an Academy Award for the Best Documentary of 1942. Capra was discharged with the rank of colonel at the end of the war and returned to Hollywood.

Capra formed another independent company, Liberty Films, Inc., and made *It's a Wonderful Life*. While the film has since become a popular Christmas season favorite, it was a box office failure. The critics admired the film, however, and it was nominated for five Academy Awards. The financial failure of the film once again ruined Capra's plans for complete creative control and he returned to the studio system.

Frank Capra only directed seven more films in his career and left Hollywood after two bitter failures. He also left during a time when the House Un-American Activities Committee (HUAC) was trying to expose "communists" in Hollywood and the rest of America. Capra's films had been criticized by many people for his attacks on big business and government, and Capra had worked with many writers and friends who supported the communist cause. Capra had even supported the war relief effort in the Soviet Union at the end of World War II when the Soviets were U.S. allies.

The powerful director Cecil B. DeMille demanded that all directors sign loyalty oaths, pledges of one's allegiance to the United States and cooperation with HUAC. Capra did not believe that he should have to sign anything, but he also feared that he would be asked to testify before HUAC in a public hearing or be blacklisted in Hollywood, as many filmmakers were in the 1950s, so he went into retirement.

Capra returned to Hollywood when the blacklisting stopped, but he and movies had changed. He was not the great director he had been before World War II; in 1961 he made *Pocketful of Miracles*, which has been called by many critics one of the worst movies of all time.

Cardozo, Benjamin N.

(1870–1938)

ASSOCIATE JUSTICE OF THE U.S.
SUPREME COURT WHO INFLUENCED
THE JUDICIAL PROCESS

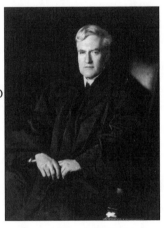

Benjamin Cardozo was born in New York City. As a child he was privately tutored by Horatio Alger, the writer of popular stories for boys. Cardozo graduated from Columbia University at the age of nineteen. A year later, in 1890, he received a master's degree from Columbia. Cardozo attended classes at Columbia Law School but never received a degree in law. He was admitted to the New York bar in 1891.

Cardozo practiced law for more than two decades in New York. He acquired a reputation for being thorough and well prepared, and he won most of his cases. Cardozo's quiet private life ended in 1914, when he became a justice of the New York State Supreme Court. Not long after assuming that office, Cardozo was appointed by the governor to become associate judge of the Court of Appeals. This was the state's highest court. In 1926 Cardozo was elected chief judge of the Court of Appeals.

Six years later, President Herbert Hoover appointed Cardozo an associate justice of the U.S. Supreme Court. Cardozo became the second Jewish

Supreme Court justice, after Louis Brandeis. Cardozo replaced Oliver Wendell Holmes, Jr., who had just retired, serving on the U.S. Supreme Court for six years, until his death in 1938.

Benjamin Cardozo is considered one of the great judges in the history of the United States. Throughout his career he had a major influence on judicial policy. Cardozo believed that courts did not just "find" the appropriate laws and apply them to each case. He thought that courts also had a responsibility to recreate laws. On the U.S. Supreme Court, Cardozo was a pathfinder. He often joined Justices Brandeis and Harlan Stone in writing dissenting opinions. These dissents were later accepted in other cases by a majority of the justices and became the law of the land.

Cardozo was noted for his clear and elegant writing style. In addition to his many legal opinions, he also wrote a number of books. Among them are *The Nature of the Judicial Process* (1921) and *Law and Literature and Other Essays* (1931).

Carter, Jimmy

(1924–   )

GOVERNOR OF GEORGIA AND THIRTY-NINTH PRESIDENT
OF THE UNITED STATES

James Earl Carter, Jr. was born on October 1, 1924, in Plains, Georgia, to a family of farmers. He studied briefly at Georgia Southwestern College and at the Georgia Institute of Technology before entering the United States Naval Academy in Annapolis, Maryland in 1942. He graduated in 1946 and in the same year married Rosalynn Smith. He served briefly on several battleships and then transferred to the navy's submarine school in New London, Connecticut. He served on submarines until 1952, when he began to work with Admiral Hyman Rickover on the development of the first nuclear-powered submarines. He resigned his commission upon the death of his father and took over the family's prosperous peanut farm.

In 1962, Carter was elected to the Georgia State Senate. He was generally against segregation but did not speak against it forcefully. After two terms in the State Senate, he ran for governor in 1966, but was defeated by the segregationist Lester Maddox. In 1970, he successfully ran for governor. He worked to reform the state government, cut the budget, and ended segregation in Georgia.

In 1976, Carter decided to run for President. He was not well known outside Georgia, but other factors were in his favor. In the aftermath of the Watergate scandal, Republican President Nixon resigned the presidency in disgrace, and his replacement, Gerald Ford, seemed beatable. Carter ran as an "outsider" attacking government corruption and won the election.

One of Carter's main initiatives as President was a new energy program. He created the Department of Energy to set policy for conserving resources and searching for new sources of energy. He took government controls off prices of oil and natural gas, hoping to create an incentive to conserve through higher prices, but the program was not popular with American car owners. In 1977, Carter negotiated a new treaty with Panama, returning the Panama Canal to the Central American nation in exchange for rights to use the canal forever. Following efforts begun by Richard Nixon, Carter established full diplomatic relations with China. He also tried to negotiate SALT II, an agreement with the Soviet Union to limit the production of nuclear weapons. The treaty was signed, but the Soviets then invaded Afghanistan and the Senate did not ratify the treaty.

In 1978, Carter was successful in bringing together Israel's prime minister, Menachim Begin, and Egypt's President, Anwar Sadat, at the Camp David presidential retreat in Maryland. Here a peace agreement was reached in which Israel returned territory captured from Egypt in previous wars and Egypt agreed to live in peace with Israel. But other Arab states rejected the agreement, isolating Egypt, and Sadat was assassinated by Muslim extremists in October 1978.

In 1979, a revolution in Iran overthrew the government of the pro-American Shah Mohammad Reza Pahlavi and installed a government led by the Islamic fundamentalist clergyman Ayatollah Ruholla Khomeini. When Carter allowed the ailing Shah to come to the United States for medical treatment, angry students in Tehran seized the American embassy and held fifty-two Americans hostage. Carter spent the last year of his term trying to negotiate the release of the hostages.

Americans became frustrated with the President's inability to quickly resolve the situation, and Carter's popularity declined. He also failed to deal decisively with "stagflation," a combination of high inflation and high unemployment driven in part by the rising cost of energy. In the 1980 presidential election, Carter was defeated by Ronald Reagan. Carter retired to Plains, Georgia and makes public appearances and international diplomatic journeys on human rights issues. He is frequently involved in efforts to build affordable housing through the organization Habitat for Humanity.

Cartier-Bresson, Henri

(1908–)

FRENCH PHOTOGRAPHER

> For photographers, there are two kinds of selection to be made, and either of them can lead to eventual regrets. There is the selection we make when we look through the viewfinder at the subject; and there is the one we make after the films have been developed and printed.
>
> —Henri Cartier-Bresson, in a 1952 essay

Henri Cartier-Bresson, a founder of photojournalism (the art of telling a story visually through pictures), has been one of the twentieth century's most acclaimed and influential photographers. He was born in 1908 in France. The son of a wealthy thread manufacturer, Cartier-Bresson grew up in a life of privilege. When he was young, he liked to sketch and to paint. His parents encouraged him to pursue his artistic interests.

Although he did not graduate from high school, his artistic and intellectual talents were impressive. Indeed, Cartier-Bresson studied at an art school from 1927 to 1928, and then he studied literature for eight months at England's prestigious Cambridge University.

After completing his studies, he led an adventurous life. In 1931, Cartier-Bresson traveled in Africa, where he worked as a wild-game hunter. However, he eventually contracted malaria and had to return to France to recuperate. During his recovery, he became interested in photography and bought a camera.

His early photographs suggest his interest in surrealism—his use of light and shadow as well as motion and space suggest surrealism's dream quality and its dynamic energy. His photographs also reveal the strong influence of Eugène Atget, André Kertész, and Man Ray. In time, Cartier-Bresson became the most influential photojournalist of his day, surpassing his early European influences, Atget and Kertész. Indeed, through his innovative, artistic techniques, Cartier-Bresson represented the high-water mark of the Paris school of photography that included Atget and Kertész; nevertheless, he humbly considers himself as a photojournalist.

In 1935, Cartier-Bresson traveled in the United States, where he studied filmmaking with an American cinematographer. Back in France, in 1936, Cartier-Bresson worked as an assistant for the renowned French film director Jean Renoir. The next year, Cartier-Bresson directed a documentary, *Return to Life*. Despite his progress in filmmaking, Cartier-Bresson ended his budding cinematic career to concentrate on photography.

During World War II, Cartier-Bresson served in France's film and photography army unit. He was captured by the Germans, however, and spent three years in a prisoner-of-war camp before escaping to freedom and returning to Paris. After the war, Cartier-Bresson photographed France's postwar desolation. In 1946, he helped to found Magnum Photos, an agency for photographers. This was an endeavor that enabled him to travel and to work independently. He made photographs of people and places in China and the Soviet Union for magazines in Europe and in the United States. For thirty years, Cartier-Bresson worked in conjunction with Magnum Photos—during that time he produced the photographs for which he is most renowned. Photography critics applauded his ability to capture, in his black-and-white images, emotion and expression in people and in the everyday and the commonplace event or setting. By the early 1970s, however, Cartier-Bresson stopped making photographs to concentrate on his first love, painting and sketching.

Cartier-Bresson will be remembered and studied for his mastery at catching on film what he himself called "the decisive moment": the instant when the photographic subject—whether a person, an event, or a scene—is at the highest intensity level in terms of action and emotion. In learning to capture on film "the decisive moment," Cartier-Bresson revealed an internal perspective and not simply what is externally noticeable in a snapshot. As a result, he greatly enhanced modern photography's development.

Caruso, Enrico

(1873–1921)

ITALIAN OPERA SINGER

Considered by the man in the street, whether or not he knows anything about opera, to be the most famous opera singer of our time, Enrico Caruso was born in Naples, Italy, in 1873. Displaying an amazing tenor voice, which is the highest male voice, at a young age, Caruso studied voice with Guglielmo Vergine from 1891 to 1894. He made his professional debut when he was just twenty-two, in a new opera by Domenico Morelli, *L'Amico Francesco*. During the engagements that followed, Caruso learned sixteen major roles in two years. With each successful opera, Caruso's name became more famous in local circles. In 1897, he sang in the world premiere of the opera *L'Arlesiana*. In 1898, upon the sudden death of tenor Roberto Stagno, Caruso was chosen to star in the new opera *Fedora*. He scored a huge success, and, as he later put it, "contracts descend on me like a big rainstorm."

After touring Russia and Argentina, (1899–1901), Caruso's domination of the field began to pick up steam. He made operatic debuts in all the important opera houses of Europe, including Teatro alla Scala of Milan (1900), Teatro San Carlo of Naples (1901), Covent Garden in London (1902), Paris Opera House (1904), and Vienna Opera House (1906). Caruso's most important debut came in 1903, when he sang at the Metropolitan Opera House in New York as the duke in *Rigoletto.* The Met became his artistic home for the rest of his career. He sang 628 performances in that house; and 234 at the Brooklyn Academy of Music, in Philadelphia, and on tour. During his eighteen seasons at the Met, he was featured in seventeen opening nights and performed thirty-nine of his greatest roles, including Canio in *Pagliacci*, Radames in *Aïda*, Samson in *Samson and Delilah*, the title role in *Faust*, Don José in *Carmen,* and many others.

By the time Caruso had reached his mid-thirties, he had become the most popular and highest-paid singer in the world. His fees at the Metropolitan Opera House eventually rose to $2,500 a performance (a huge sum at the time). He charged more in other places, receiving $10,000 a performance in Cuba in 1920, and $15,000 in Mexico City the year before that.

Caruso began to make recordings in 1902. His first records, recorded in Milan, were so successful that Caruso has been credited with popularizing the phonograph and turning it from the toy it was then regarded as into a musical instrument. He signed an exclusive contract with the Victor Talking Machine Company in 1904, and all his later recordings were made in New York or in Camden, New Jersey. Despite their primitive sound quality, most of Caruso's recordings are still in circulation and sell well to this day.

Caruso's voice was said to have an appeal that went right to the senses. His vocal production was flawless, producing a sound of rare beauty. The quality of his voice has been described in many languages as "golden" and "velvet." Crossing the depth of a baritone with the smooth high sound of a tenor, Caruso was unique among tenors. He worked on his acting interpretations throughout his career, and his style, which was ahead of its time, has had a lasting influence on operatic singing in this century. His acting, which was criticized at first, improved with the years. His last role, as Eleazar in *La Juive* (The Jew), was regarded as a great acting as well as vocal performance.

Dying in 1921, at the relatively young age of forty-eight, Caruso's career spanned only twenty-six years. But his name is still the first name that comes to mind when one thinks of opera.

Casals, Pablo

(1876-1973)

SPANISH CELLIST

If, today, the cello is considered a major concert instrument, it is due to the amazing career of Pablo Casals. Casals was born in 1876 in Vendrell, Catalonia, Spain, to a musical family. His father was an organist and piano teacher who gave the boy his first instruction in music. Seeing great musical potential in the youngster, Casals's father encouraged him to take violin lessons, which he did until he was twelve years old. When the family moved to Barcelona, Casals found the instrument that interested him most, and he began to study the cello with José Garcia. He also studied harmony with José Rodoreda. Casals's progress was so fast that he soon was able to assist his teachers in class. In 1891, he graduated from the Municipal School of Music and began his concert career.

In 1894, Casals went to Madrid, Spain's capital, where his masterful playing attracted the attention of Count Morphy, secretary to the queen of Spain. As a result of Morphy's recommendation, Casals was paid by the government to study and to play the cello at the court of the queen. With the money he made, Casals continued his musical education with Tomas Breton. By 1895, Casals was playing the cello at the famed Paris Opéra and organizing his own string quartet.

It was in 1899, when he performed Lalo's *Cello Concerto*, that Casals's career really took off. His playing of the famous piece so stunned and delighted audiences and critics that Casals began giving concerts all over Western Europe. He also appeared to great acclaim in the United States from 1901 to 1904, and then again from 1914 to 1917. It was during that period that Casals married his student, the Portuguese cellist Guilhermina Suggia, divorced her, and then married American singer Susan Metcalfe.

In 1919, Casals established himself in Barcelona as the leader of Orquestra Pau Casals. The orchestra's first concert took place on October 13, 1920. At the same time, Casals was part of the celebrated Cortot-Thibaud-Casals Trio.

During the Spanish Civil War (1936–1939), Casals remained in Spain, but when the Loyalist government was defeated, he chose to leave Spain and move to Prades, France, which is on the Spanish border. There, in 1950, he set up a summer series devoted to chamber music concerts, which attracted international attention. By that time, Casals's fame as a musician had become legendary. It was well acknowledged that as a cellist, there was no one better and very few, if any, equals.

Casals composed several cello pieces, including *La Sardana*, a piece for an ensemble of cellos. His Christmas oratorio, *El Pesbre (The Manger)* was performed for the first time in Acapulco, Mexico, in December 1960. Casals also wrote a choral work entitled *La Vision de Fray Martin (The Vision of Fray Martin)*.

Casals died in Puerto Rico, in 1973, just three years short of the age of one hundred. In 1976 the Spanish government issued a postage stamp in honor of the one hundredth anniversary of his birth.

Chagall, Marc

(1887–1985)

RUSSIAN-FRENCH PAINTER

But my art, I thought, is perhaps a wild art, a blazing quicksilver, a blue soul flashing on my canvas.

> —Marc Chagall, in his
> autobiography, *My Life*

Marc Chagall was one of the best-known artists of the twentieth century. His spectacular paintings combined fantastic imagery with scenes of Jewish life and folklore. His work had a major influence on the painters who came after him. Chagall was born in 1887 into a Hasidic (ultra-Orthodox) Jewish family, living in the provincial capital of Vitebsk in western Russia.

From an early age, Chagall displayed his artistic talents. He spent only three months in a local art school before being sent to an art academy in St. Petersburg. There, he saw paintings by the young French artists, the Fauves, whose luminous use of color influenced his subsequent work.

In 1914, a patron provided Chagall with enough money to go to Paris to study painting. He studied at several academies and also met many avant-garde artists and writers. That same year, three of his paintings were exhibited in Berlin, Germany, and he was given the opportunity to have a one-person exhibition at a larger Berlin gallery. His paintings attracted attention because of Chagall's skillful experimentation with dreamlike images that reflected rural Russian scenes from his youth. At this time, Chagall was quickly ascending the artistic ladder of fame. However, his rising career took a detour when he visited his home in Vitebsk and World War I began. The war put a halt to art exhibitions, and to make matters worse, Germany and Russia were on opposing sides of the conflict.

Chagall's life became even more complicated after the Russian Revolution in 1917. Chagall had supported the revolution, and the local Soviet leaders appointed him commissar of fine art in Vitebsk. He was hired to reorganize the local art school, but his job did not last long. By that time, his own artwork consisted of a mixture of fantasy and modern French techniques that seemed unintelligible to the local political leaders, who fired him. Chagall left Vitebsk for Moscow in 1919. He spent the next three years in the Russian capital painting murals, designing stages and sets for a newly created state Jewish theater, and writing his autobiography.

By 1922, Chagall found the artistic atmosphere in Russia stifling, so he returned to Berlin, where he worked on illustrations for the German edition of his autobiography. In 1923, he returned to the congenial artistic atmosphere of Paris, where he became the leader of a group of immigrant Jewish artists that met regularly. While he continued painting, Chagall also kept himself busy by doing etchings and illustrations for books.

During the 1920s, his reputation was steadily on the rise as his paintings were attracting more and more attention. Using rich, sensuous colors, Chagall created a unique style that combined fantastic imagery with Russian folk scenes. His success was such that, in 1924, his first retrospective exhibition was held in Paris. Two years later Chagall had his first one-person showing in New York. By the 1930s, Chagall was quite famous; things were going very well for him. In 1931, he published his autobiography. And in 1937, he became a French citizen and lived in Paris until World War II, when Adolf Hitler's Nazi-based campaign to murder Jews forced him to flee. Chagall left France and came to the United States in 1941.

Chagall kept busy during the war years, designing stage sets and costumes for ballets in Mexico and in the United States. In 1946, after the war ended, he was honored with a large retrospective exhibition of his works at the Museum of Modern Art in New York, which solidified his status as a premier international artist.

In 1947, Chagall returned home to France for the opening of an exhibition of his work at the modern art museum in Paris, and in 1948 he moved back to France for good. He continued to paint, while also doing work with ceramics and sculpture in the 1950s. In the late 1950s and early 1960s, he designed stained-glass windows as well. In 1975, he returned to Moscow for a visit at the invitation of the Soviet government. He died in France ten years later.

Chanel, Gabrielle Bonheur

(1883–1971)

FRENCH FASHION DESIGNER

Gabrielle Chanel, or "Coco," as she was called for most of her adult life, was a leader of the women's fashion industry in the 1920s and again in the 1950s. She was also a manufacturer of perfume, whose trademark brand, Chanel No. 5, is among the best known in the world.

Gabrielle Chanel was born in the province of Auvergne, France, in 1883. Little is known about her childhood because in later life she found it amusing to tell her friends conflicting stories about how she grew up. In one story, she was raised in a stable; in another, she lived with a wealthy family and was taught by a governess. One widely believed tale is that as a child she cut up the living room curtains to make clothes for her dolls.

It is known that she was orphaned early in her life and went to work with her sister in a Deauville hat shop at age seventeen. Shortly afterward, the two young women moved to Paris, where Gabrielle opened a millinery shop of her own.

One of her pleasures was to go horseback riding alone in the Paris parks, early in the morning, when the cocks were crowing. From this habit she acquired the nickname "Miss Cocorico," which she later shortened to "Coco."

Chanel herself told to a newspaper reporter, in 1954, a story about her first venture into designing clothing. She was employed as a groom, at a stable where wealthy Parisians kept their horses, when one chilly morning she put on a polo player's sweater to keep warm. That gave her the idea of making jersey pullovers for women. Charles Ritz, an American fashion importer who used the stables, gave her some bolts of beige wool jersey that he could not sell because buyers thought they looked too much like "winter underwear." Chanel fashioned the fabric into turbans and matching pullovers, sold them to horsewomen, and launched a fashion trend that later was to be called the "beige decade."

During the 1920s, Chanel became famous for designing naturally fitting, comfortable, dresses and simple hats that were popular among younger women rebelling against the highly formal and structured clothing of earlier designers. Her clothing exhibited a flair for "simple elegance," the fashion press decreed. At the height of her career, she employed 2,400 people in her clothing business; she also manufactured perfumes, textiles, and costume jewelry.

She considered five to be her lucky number, and when she introduced a perfume—packaged in a simple bottle, contrasting with the elaborate containers of the day—she named it No. 5. It became the most famous perfume in the world.

Chanel retired from creating clothing in 1938 when Italian designers captured women's imagination and the business of French designers declined. Her perfume business continued to prosper through World War II. When American soldiers brought Chanel No. 5 home to their wives and girlfriends, it became so popular in the United States that she opened a showroom in New York.

In 1954, she announced a comeback, claiming she was distressed that the fashion industry of France had been taken over by men. Her show that year was declared a failure by fashion journalists, who saw it as a disappointing repetition of the designs that had made her famous twenty years earlier. But it became clear that women liked them, and soon the industry was again busy producing clothing by Chanel.

During her "second career," Chanel concentrated on designing clothing that could be mass-produced. Again she became known for creating dresses that were both attractive and comfortable.

Personally, Chanel was a small, energetic woman who spoke in a low, quiet voice and loved confrontation ("I prefer vitriol to honey," she once declared). She lived in a Paris apartment so filled with art objects, rare books, and collections of bronzes, crystal, and figurines that she found it more comfortable to sleep at the elegant Ritz Hotel, across the street.

Chaplin, Charlie

(1889–1977)

BRITISH-BORN AMERICAN FILMMAKER AND ACTOR

Charles Spencer Chaplin was born in a poor district of London, England on April 16, 1889. His mother spent most of her life in and out of mental hospitals. His father was a successful vaudeville performer until he began to drink heavily. After his parents separated, Chaplin and his brother spent most of their childhood in a workhouse. Barely able to read or write, Chaplin left school to become a performer. By the age of nineteen he had become one of the most popular music-hall performers in England.

In 1910, Chaplin traveled to the United States. While performing in a small acting company, Chaplin was noticed by the director Mack Sennett, who hired the young actor to direct films at Keystone studios. In his first year at Keystone, Chaplin made thirty-five films, including his first feature, *Tillie's Punctured Romance*.

After leaving Keystone to direct and write his own pictures, Chaplin experimented with different characters before creating the little tramp in 1915 that made him famous. The tramp, with his derby hat, baggy pants, mustache, and cane, became so popular that he is almost the symbol of silent films.

In 1919 Chaplin formed United Artists (UA) studio with the director D. W. Griffith, and the actors Mary Pickford and Douglas Fairbanks. Chaplin made all of his major films for UA, including *The Gold Rush* (1925) and *The Circus* (1928). Three of his most respected movies, *City Lights* (1931), *Modern Times* (1936), and *The Great Dictator* (1941), were made after sound had been introduced into the movies, but Chaplin used many of the techniques of silent film. When he did use sound, however, he displayed a clever and humorous understanding of its effects.

After World War II, Chaplin abandoned his tramp character and his popularity lessened. During the 1940s and 1950s, Chaplin outraged many Americans with his political views. He was a socialist and an atheist, which made him politically suspect during the early days of the Cold War.

While on vacation in Europe in 1952, Chaplin was notified that he would not be allowed to return to the United States. He had never been an American citizen and so required permission to live and work in America. Chaplin sold all of his American possessions and settled in Switzerland with his fourth wife, Oona O'Neill, the daughter of playwright Eugene O'Neill.

Chaplin turned to more autobiographical subjects in his next films. *Limelight* (1952) told the story of a performer's fading popularity, and *A King in New York* (1957) was based upon the harassing investigations of Senator McCarthy and the House Un-American Activities Committee.

At age eighty-three, Charlie Chaplin returned to the United States to receive an honorary Academy Award. His tearful acceptance speech opened with a remark that perfectly fit his career as a great silent filmmaker: "Words are so futile, so feeble."

Charles, Ray

(1930–   )

AMERICAN MUSICIAN, COMPOSER, AND SINGER

> I look at music the same as I look at my bloodstream, my respiratory
> system, my lungs. It's something I have to have. I was born with
> music inside me.
>
> —Ray Charles

One of the greatest pop singers of his generation, Ray Charles is a multitalented
musician—a composer, pianist, saxophonist, and band leader. His unique style
combines the power of gospel music with the soulfulness of rhythm and blues
and a cool measure of jazz. The music of Ray Charles is a passionate celebration
of the joy and pain of the black American experience.

Ray Charles Robinson was born in 1930 in Albany, Georgia. His father was
a railroad repairman who was frequently away from home, so his mother,
Aretha, had to care for Ray and his older brother by herself. When Ray was just
a few years old, his brother drowned. By age five, Ray's vision began to deteriorate rapidly; he became totally blind from glaucoma, a disease of the eye, two
years later. His mother sent him to the St. Augustine School for Deaf and Blind
Children in St. Augustine, Florida, where he discovered his talent for music
and the piano. His mother died from food poisoning when he was fifteen, and
he immersed himself in music for consolation. Ray spent many hours playing
the piano and singing the blues, learning from every musician who would play
for him.

At the age of sixteen, Ray Charles joined an all-white country and western
band called the Florida Playboys. For a year he played in many beer halls and
honky-tonks. After saving just $600, he decided to get as far away from Florida
as he could, and he wound up in Seattle, Washington. Charles sang in a local
talent show there and found steady work with other musicians. When he was
seventeen, he formed the McSon Trio, which was fashioned after the popular
Nat King Cole Jazz Trio. In 1948 the McSon Trio recorded its first record,
"Confession Blues." Charles's first big rhythm-and-blues hit was "Baby Let Me
Hold Your Hand," which sold 100,000 records in 1950. Then he moved to Los
Angeles to get into the music scene.

Charles was barely twenty years old when he began living on the road, touring with a number of different bands, developing his musical style for ten years.
He was encouraged by a record executive who heard him and gave him a
recording contract with Atlantic Records. The smash hit "I Got a Woman"
showed off Charles's style of inspirational gospel and rhythm and blues, which

would influence the work of two generations of musicians, from Loretta Lynn to the Beatles to Stevie Wonder. Ray Charles became a worldwide star by 1959 with the rousing record "What'd I Say." People of all races and ages appreciated the Ray Charles big-band sound created by eighteen musicians (including the Raelettes, his female backup singers). "The Genius of Ray Charles" tour, marking his last album for Atlantic Records, culminated in sold-out appearances at Carnegie Hall in New York.

In 1960, Charles produced the soulful song "Georgia on My Mind," which won two Grammy awards. Over the next ten years, he recorded twenty-four albums and fifty-three singles, including the albums *Genius + Soul = Jazz* and *Modern Sounds in Country and Western Music*. He also made several television appearances under the ABC-Paramount label. Ray Charles was the first black musician to "cross over" and achieve fame in country and western, pop, and rhythm-and-blues music styles. In 1963, Ray Charles Enterprises was formed, along with his own label—Crossover. During the late 1960s Charles hosted several more television specials and became a benefactor of the United Negro College Fund and other charities.

In the 1970s and 1980s, his band toured the globe for nine months each year. His style encompassed everything from country ballads to smooth, improvised jazz instrumentals to funky blues. He wrote the music for several highly successful advertising campaigns, including the "You've got the right one, baby—*uh-huh*!" for Diet Pepsi.

Ray Charles says he will never retire from performing and songwriting. As long as he can breathe, he believes he will be making music for millions of fans around the world.

Chavez, Cesar

(1927–1993)

AMERICAN LABOR UNION
ACTIVIST

Cesar Chavez was born on March 31, 1927, on a farm near the town of Yuma, Arizona. Cesar's grandfather, for whom he was named, had been a poor farm worker in Mexico. He brought his family to America, settling on a 160-acre section of what is now Arizona where he grew corn, lettuce, beans and a little cotton.

But with the coming of the Great Depression the family could no longer make a living from working the land. In 1937, they sold the farm and house for whatever the bank would offer and headed for California. The members of the Chavez family became migrant workers, who moved from farm to farm as the seasons changed. Cesar went to more than thirty elementary schools in California and Arizona. Finally, when he reached the seventh grade, he dropped out of school entirely. Although he was just a boy, Cesar had to work: ten to twelve hours a day, six and sometimes seven days a week, he toiled in the fields with his family.

During World War II, Chavez served in the United States Navy. After the war, he continued working as a migrant laborer. He married and started a family, the work paid very poorly, and it was always a struggle to make ends meet.

One day in 1952, an organizer named Fred Ross approached Chavez and asked him to help convince other Mexican-American farm workers to start helping themselves. Chavez agreed, and spent the next ten years working with Ross and his boss, Saul Alinsky. Alinsky's group was called the Community Service Organization (CSO). As part of the CSO, Chavez helped Mexican-Americans register to vote, so they could participate in elections. He helped farm workers who were in trouble with the police or who needed money. He showed workers how to petition farm owners for toilets, clean housing and safe drinking water. While helping others, Chavez was also helping himself: he was improving his English, studying the law, and learning to become an effective public speaker.

In 1962, Chavez left the CSO to take a non-paying job with the newly formed National Farm Workers Association. Going from farm to farm, he urged workers to join the union. Many were afraid because they thought the big growers would take away their jobs. But slowly, Chavez was able to convince them to organize and the union grew. They started a credit union, a gas station, and a grocery store. The union was able to offer burial arrangements so workers would not have to go into debt to pay for the funeral of a family member, and also hired lawyers to help workers who had been cheated by their bosses.

Chavez helped organize strikes, which meant that unless conditions improved for the workers, they would refuse to work. The growers did become angry when they saw the crops rotting in the fields with no one to pick them. There were fights and beatings. Some union members were sent to jail. But Chavez believed the changes he sought could come about without violence, and he continued to work peacefully towards achieving his goals.

In 1965, Chavez and the union called for a boycott against the grape growers. The boycott gained national attention. In front of supermarkets all over America people carried signs that said "Don't Buy Grapes!" Donations of money poured in from all over the country. Important political leaders, like Robert F. Kennedy, Eugene McCarthy, and Hubert Humphrey gave their support to the migrant workers.

Through it all, Chavez worked to keep up the spirits of the workers. He spoke at churches, colleges and union meetings. He organized a march from Delano, California to the state capital at Sacramento—a distance of three hundred miles. Some of Chavez's followers grew impatient, and wanted the union to use violence to get their demands met. But Chavez refused. Like Martin Luther King Jr., he believed that resistance and negotiation were the best weapons of all.

Slowly, the boycott began to work. Some of the growers agreed to let Chavez and his union bargain for the migrant workers. That meant more money and better working conditions. In 1970, the grape boycott ended and Chavez called for a national boycott of lettuce that lasted until 1978.

Chavez was an active union member until his death in 1993. Along with his children and grandchildren, he continued to march, demonstrate and organize to improve working conditions for migrant farm workers throughout the United States.

Chichester, Francis

(1901–1972)

ENGLISH ROUND-THE-WORLD
SAILOR AND AVIATOR

If anything terrifies me I must try to conquer
it.

> —Sir Francis Chichester, from an
> interview in *Life*
> magazine, June 9, 1967

Sir Francis Charles Chichester ranks among the twentieth century's greatest
adventurers and daredevils. He not only became a pioneer of aviation while
barely knowing how to fly, but he also became legendary as a sailor, taking up
the sport at the age of fifty-two after being diagnosed with a serious illness.
Ever seeking new challenges with boundless enthusiasm, Chichester even
sailed alone across the Atlantic on a thirty-five-cent bet.

Francis was born on September 17, 1901, in North Devon, England. Even
as a young schoolboy, he was rebellious and often in trouble, much to the con-
sternation of his father, who was a preacher in the small town where the family
lived. Hoping their son would attend one of England's best universities, Francis's parents were further disturbed when he decided to quit school altogether
at seventeen.

After trying his hand at farming near home, Chichester gave in to his urges
to escape what he considered a life of strict routines. With the equivalent of
about fifteen dollars in his pocket, he hired on to a ship sailing to New Zealand
in 1919, working in the engine room shoveling coal. Once on the other side of
the world, he tried everything he could think of to make a living, including
being a professional boxer, lingerie salesman, lumberjack, and coal miner.
Nothing worked until he teamed up with a partner, eventually going into the
lumber business. Chichester and Geoffrey Goodwin also started an airline,
though Chichester did not know how to fly.

With financial success, Chichester decided to return to England in 1929.
There, hardly more than a few days after receiving his pilot's license and buying a small plane called a Gipsy Moth, he set out for Australia, determined to
beat the solo flying record for that route—which, at that time, was fifteen days.
He did not set a record, but his success at what amounted to teaching himself

to fly while he flew halfway around the world encouraged Chichester to take other flights.

In 1930, he attempted the longest seaplane flight of his day by flying from New Zealand to Australia. Halfway through his flight he had to stop for repairs at Lord Howe Island, but the feat was notable, especially because of the information about flight navigation that Chichester collected en route. The navigation system he devised was later adapted by the British Royal Air Force for use in World War II. A year later, in 1931, he set off from England on a round-the-world seaplane journey but got only as far as Japan, where he was seriously injured in a crash.

It took Chichester until 1936 to recover from the many broken bones and other injuries he had sustained. When the bones had all healed, he promptly flew another plane from Sydney, Australia, back to London, stopping in Beijing, China, along the way.

With the outbreak of World War II, Francis Chichester offered his services to the Royal Air Force in England. Rejected as a pilot because he was too old—he was almost forty at the time—he was put to work with the air ministry, where he developed navigation manuals and taught navigation to pilot trainees. After the war he put his fascination with navigation to use by creating a company that produced jigsaw puzzles made from maps. This venture expanded into a full-scale publishing company specializing in navigation publications and provided Chichester with another solid income.

He was not content to stay at home in England, however. At the age of fifty-two, he decided to take up sailing. He rebuilt a small sloop and called her *Gipsy Moth II*, after his first airplane, and proceeded to enter ocean races. Then, in 1957, Chichester was told by his doctors that he had serious lung cancer. Undaunted, he quit smoking, became a vegetarian, and moved to France, a country that has much better weather than England. By 1959, he was racing again, with a new sailboat, the *Gipsy Moth III*. The next year, he challenged a member of the British Royal Ocean Racing Club to a solo transatlantic (from England to New York) race. The winner would collect the equivalent of thirty-five cents. Chichester arrived in New York days ahead of his competition and was hailed by the international media as a hero. After a second, record-setting solo sail across the Atlantic, his accomplishments were recognized by Queen Elizabeth II of England when she made him a Commander of the Order of the British Empire (C.B.E.).

Despite his age (he was in his sixties by then), Chichester's quest for new adventures continued. Buying a larger boat, called *Gipsy Moth IV*, and financed by several corporations and a newspaper, he set sail for an around-the-world solo voyage. He left England in August 1966, headed for the Cape of Good Hope, at the southern tip of the African continent, off South Africa. After almost three months at sea, his automatic steering mechanism gave out. Then after 107 days at sea, he reached landfall in Sydney, Australia. Almost two months later, he was off again, heading back to England via Cape Horn, at the southern tip of South America.

Nine months after leaving home he was back on British soil, and again, navigation was the key to his success. Chichester was not the first to sail around the world alone, but his trip was distinctive because he relied more heavily on navigation at sea than anyone else ever had. As he told *Life* magazine shortly after arriving home, "I went around the world seeing land at only four places."

Francis Chichester was dubbed Sir Francis by Queen Elizabeth II in 1967. After a remarkable life of adventure around the world, he died at home in England on August 26, 1972.

Chisholm, Shirley

(1924–)

UNITED STATES REPRESENTATIVE

Shirley Chisholm was born on November 30, 1924, in the Bedford-Stuyvesant section of Brooklyn, New York. She graduated from Brooklyn College with a degree in sociology and studied elementary education at Columbia University. Early in her career, she worked for various child care agencies, and in 1959 she worked for New York City's Bureau of Child Welfare. She was also active in the Brooklyn branch of the National Association for the Advancement of Colored People.

In 1964, Chisholm was elected to the New York State Assembly. In 1968, she was elected to the United States Congress, defeating the widely respected civil rights leader James Farmer. Small and frail-looking, but passionately outspoken, Chisholm fought hard to be assigned to important House committees. She supported the creation of a Department of Consumer Affairs and sponsored a bill to extend the powers of the Department of Housing and Urban Development. She also worked to create equal employment opportunities for minorities and supported antipoverty legislation. She favored school decentralization to promote community control, and she opposed the war in Vietnam. After retiring from Congress in 1983, Chisholm became a popular lecturer at colleges and universities. She gave an inspiring speech at the Democratic National Convention in 1992, which reminded a nation of viewers that she was an important trailblazer and was still a vital voice for liberal causes.

Churchill, Sir Winston

(1874–1965)

WARTIME PRIME MINISTER OF
THE UNITED KINGDOM

You ask what is our policy? I say it is to wage war by land, sea, and air. War with all our might and with all the strength God has given us, and to wage war against a monstrous tyranny never surpassed in the dark and lamentable catalogue of human crime.

—Winston Churchill, speaking to
the British people during World War II

One of the legendary figures of the twentieth century, Sir Winston Churchill is remembered and honored as much for what he said and symbolized as for what he actually accomplished. With an eloquent gift for using the English language, he rallied the British people to survive against terrible odds in World War II, only to be voted out of office as soon as the fighting stopped. One of history's most inspiring speakers, he also found time to write many books, among them the *History of the English-Speaking Peoples*, for which he was awarded the Nobel Prize for Literature (1953).

Winston Leonard Spencer Churchill was born on November 30, 1874, to Lord Randolph Churchill and Jenny Jerome, an American daughter of a wealthy businessman. Descended from the Duke of Marlborough, Winston was born in England's Blenheim Palace. He enjoyed a close relationship to his mother, but held a distance from his father for most of his life.

As a boy, Winston was a discontented, mediocre student. He attended Harrow, a prestigious preparatory school, and then went to Sandhurst, England's premier military academy. He took a liking to journalism while in the army. In 1895, he traveled to Cuba with his regiment and wrote stories for the *Daily Graphic*, a newspaper. A year later he was in India, where he wrote a novel as well as reports on the military campaigns of that period. "Nothing in life is so exhilarating as to be shot at without result," he wrote during this period. Then, during the Boer War in southern Africa (1899–1902), a conflict between England and the Dutch settlers there, he worked as a correspondent for the *Morning Post*.

Churchill entered politics in 1899 largely because that was what young men of his elevated social class and family traditions in England were expected to do. He failed to win a seat in the House of Commons until the next year. Thus was launched a political career of more than sixty years. Ironically, although he gained legendary status as a political leader, he lost a surprising number of elections during his years of service. He joined the Liberal Party in 1904 in an effort to further social reforms in England. As a young politician he stressed the need to address the issue of poverty and called on private business to work for the good of society. "There is no finer investment for any community than putting milk into babies," he once said. He worked particularly hard at resolving problems of unemployment.

In the first decades of the twentieth century, Winston Churchill held many government positions. He was Lord of the Admiralty, but his unsuccessful strategy for the navy during World War I led to his dismissal. For part of the war he rejoined the army and fought on the front lines in France. He also served in the Colonial Office, administering England's far-flung colonial empire, but another controversy provoked by his headstrong opinions led to another dismissal, and he was defeated in his campaign for the House of Commons in 1922.

Having left the Liberals to join the Conservatives, Churchill was made Chancellor of the Exchequer in 1924, but disagreements on economic policy and defense led to his resignation from the Conservative "shadow" cabinet (the Conservatives were not in power at this time) in 1931. He continued to disagree with the Conservatives about the role of the British empire, remaining a staunch supporter of England's control over other parts of the world.

Winston Churchill will always be remembered primarily for his role during World War II. Summoned in 1940 to be prime minister and minister of defense just as Nazi Germany was unleashing enormous force against England, he was tireless in providing inspiration for the people to survive the terrible ordeal. Throughout the Battle of Britain, in which England was bombed several times a day by German airplanes, Churchill rallied his citizens, urging them on.

"Let us therefore brace ourselves to our duties, and so bear ourselves that, if the British empire and its Commonwealth last for a thousand years, men will still say, 'This was their finest hour,'" he said in 1940, upon taking office.

Despite his supportive leadership during the war, Churchill and his party were turned out of office in 1945. Controversy about some decisions made during the fighting and about his role in carving up Europe at the Yalta Conference of that year were factors in his defeat. In any case, Churchill was back in office by 1951, to serve another four years as prime minister in more peaceful times.

In 1955, Sir Winston Churchill retired from a highly distinguished career in public life. He settled in at his family estate to paint landscapes, write books, and continue to express his strong opinions about British life and international politics. He died on January 24, 1965.

Cocteau, Jean

(1889–1963)

FRENCH FILMMAKER

From the 1920s until his death, Jean Cocteau was a true Renaissance man of the avant-garde arts. Not only was he an innovative filmmaker, but he was also an actor, a playwright, a poet, a novelist, a painter, and a graphic artist. Cocteau was born on July 5, 1889, near Paris. Educated in local schools, Cocteau directed his first film in 1930.

Cocteau was an eccentric personality. He moved back and forth between different artistic mediums in an attempt to present his dominant theme: the predicament of the creative person, whom Cocteau termed the poet, in a hostile world. For Cocteau, the poet is anyone—a painter, a sculptor, a designer, an architect, or a writer—who has the imagination and creativity necessary to transform aspects of the everyday world into artistic works.

As a filmmaker, Cocteau wrote and directed his own scripts. Critics usually focus on his film trilogy—*The Poet's Song, Orpheus*, and *The Testament of Or-*

pheus—about the poet as Orpheus, a character from Greek mythology who almost rescues his wife, Eurydice, from Hades by charming Pluto, the god of the underworld, with his music and song.

Cocteau was renowned for describing his use of film as "cinematic poetry." He said that film allowed him a poetic freedom to say things visually rather than with ink and paper. Cocteau continued to think of himself, however, primarily as a writer, a literary person. He declared that his profession was not that of a filmmaker. Indeed, he often posed as merely an amateur filmmaker, despite the fact that many critics considered the works in his trilogy as cinematic masterpieces.

Many critics have seen the influence of surrealism in Cocteau's films: in his cinematic juxtaposition of images that do not flow together and, thereby, challenge the audience's sense of what they are watching. Cocteau, however, rejected such characterizations. He is, perhaps, best considered as a leader of the French avant-garde arts.

Conrad, Joseph

(1857–1924)

POLISH-BORN ENGLISH NOVELIST,
SHORT-STORY WRITER, AND
MEMOIRIST

I have been called a writer of the sea, of the tropics, a descriptive writer, a romantic writer—and also a realist. But as a matter of fact, all my concern has been with the "ideal" value of things, events, and people. That and nothing else.

—Joseph Conrad

Novelist Joseph Conrad was born on December 3, 1857, in Berdichev, Poland, in the heart of what was then the Polish Ukraine; his name was Józef Teodor Konrad Korzeniowski. The boy's father, Apollo, a member of the landed gentry and an intellectual, was also a fervent Polish nationalist struggling against Russian annexation of his native land, and a writer and translator. His mother, Eva, was an activist like her husband. When Józef was only four, his parents were arrested by czarist police and deported to northern Russia with their young son. There, he watched as his mother died of tuberculosis in 1865.

In 1869, Apollo Korzeniowski was released from penal exile. He and his son, now eleven, returned to the Austrian-ruled part of Poland. Józef always remembered his father's death that year, his health shattered by the fierce Russian winters.

Józef went to live with Tadeusz Bobrowski, his mother's brother, a prosperous lawyer who urged the boy to reject his father's idealistic virtues for a more practical vision of the world. For the rest of his life—and throughout his writing—Conrad would feel pulled by these two, Tadeusz and Apollo, the conservative and the impulsive, the realist and the idealist.

Józef wanted to go to sea, an unusual desire for someone who had grown up in landlocked Poland. When he was seventeen, he left Poland for Marseilles, France, with the reluctant consent of Bobrowski, and joined the French maritime service. Józef would now acquire his second language, French, over the course of several years as an ordinary seaman. He also acquired knowledge of sailing and of the world, traveling to the West Indies and other exotic locales.

Involved in an unsuccessful gun-smuggling operation, in 1878 Conrad gambled and lost badly in Monte Carlo and attempted suicide, shooting himself in the chest. Once again, Bobrowski rescued him, paying off his gambling debts and overseeing his convalescence. Upon his recovery, Józef took a berth on a British freighter and traveled to England, which became his permanent home.

As a British seaman, Józef made voyages to the Far East, Australia, and the Congo. Conrad taught himself English by reading the works of Charles Dickens, William Shakespeare, Anthony Trollope, Lord Byron, and John Stuart Mill. He worked himself up from regular seaman to a master's certificate in the British Merchant Marine, and in 1886 he became a naturalized British citizen named Joseph Conrad.

He began writing when he was thirty-one, writing in a language he hadn't learned until he was in his twenties, a remarkable enough feat under any circumstances. But more than that, he was writing well.

By 1895, he had published his first book, *Almayer's Folly*. The following year, he published *An Outcast of the Islands*. Now a professional writer, in 1896 he married Jessie George; she bore him two sons, and the family enjoyed a comfortable and quiet domestic life.

Conrad found the process of writing a terrible strain. He was a slow writer, yet in a career that would last only thirty years, he turned out some thirty-five volumes of work: novels, short stories, two plays, essays, criticism, and memoirs.

Conrad drew heavily on his own experiences for his fiction. His first two books were inspired by a trader he had met on the Southeast Asian Malay Peninsula, where the novels are set, and his recollection of that environment is detailed and colorful. His third published novel, *The Nigger of the "Narcissus"* (1897), was based on his experiences as second mate of a ship bearing that name. This was the book that launched his reputation as a chronicler of seagoing life and the first of his work to receive serious and favorable reviews.

Conrad returned repeatedly to the image of the ship's captain as bungler. In his story, "Youth" (1898), the novella *Typhoon* (1902), and even, to some extent, in his first great novel, *Lord Jim* (1900), the authorities in charge of the vessels on which the action takes place are incompetent.

In 1899 Conrad authored a novella that is among his most famous, *Heart of Darkness*. This tale of dissolution and obsession in the depths of the Congo (which served as the basis for the film *Apocalypse Now*) is a brilliant miniature in which all the Conrad themes appear, crystallized. The story is told in flashback, narrated by Marlow, a captain who turns up in several Conrad books, usually as a narrator within the text.

Marlow turns up again, although in a less central role, in *Lord Jim*. Once more, Conrad returns to the Far East and offers what seems to be an adventure tale; but it is, in reality, a complex fable of moral failure and redemption through a quasi-suicide.

In his short story "The Secret Sharer" (1910), a young captain takes on board a fugitive with whom he finds a deep affinity. For Conrad, these doubles are not "two sides of a coin" but, rather, an indication of how complex a moral equation good and evil really are.

Conrad's early work received considerable critical approval, but sold only modestly. Still, he continued to write novels, moving away from the world of the sea and his exotic ports of call and increasingly into the netherworld of political extremism. In *Nostromo* (1904), *The Secret Agent* (1907), and *Under Western Eyes* (1911), Conrad explores exile in its literal sense, centering his narratives on men who are as swept up in history as the sailors in *Typhoon* are by the sea. Conrad takes this theme to its final fruition in his last great novel, *Victory* (1915), returning once again to the most isolated parts of South Asia for the story of a self-imposed exile, Heyst.

In 1913, Conrad published *Chance*, a lesser novel utilizing Marlow as a narrator once more; it became his biggest seller to date, the book that allowed him finally to stave off some of his economic terrors. He was able to give up a lot of his journalistic hack work and turn his attention to novels and short stories fulltime.

The years of constant work were taking their toll on Conrad's health, and he traveled little. He did return to Poland once, in 1914, and had the bad luck to be stranded there when World War I broke out. He was able to return home, thanks to the intervention of the American ambassador. In 1923, he made his only visit to America, for a highly successful reading tour. In 1924, he was offered a knighthood by England's royal family, but he turned it down; perhaps he was expressing some loyalty to his original Polish identity. At the time of his death, he was at work on a romantic adventure set in the Napoleonic period, which was published posthumously as *Suspense*.

Cousteau, Jacques

(1910–   )

FRENCH UNDERSEA EXPLORER,
INVENTOR, FILMMAKER, AND
AUTHOR

We want to explore the themes of the
ocean's existence —how it moves and
breathes, harmonizes the physical and biological rhythms of the whole earth, what
hurts it and what feeds it—not least of all,
what are its stories.

>—Jacques Cousteau, from *The
Ocean World of Jacques Cousteau*

Inventor of the aqualung, three-time Oscar-winning filmmaker, and pioneer of
a global environmental movement, Jacques-Yves Cousteau has spent a lifetime
exploring the earth's oceans and bringing his discoveries to the people of the
world through books, films, and television. Helping to create the first cameras
to be used for underwater filming, as well as the machines that enable people
to dive to, and even live at, the bottom of the sea, he has been instrumental in
unveiling the mysteries of how animals and plants live in our planet's waters
which make up 70 percent of the earth's surface.

Cousteau was born on June 11, 1910, in Saint André-de-Cubzac, a small
market town in Bordeaux, France. Jacques's early life was marked by his parents' frequent travels—his father was a financial advisor and assistant to
wealthy American businessmen. With his parents often away, Jacques and his
older brother, Pierre Antoine, were left in France at boarding school. His parents' trips gave Cousteau an early interest in discovering the rest of the world.

At the age of ten, Cousteau and his family moved to New York. Jacques and
his brother learned English in school in Manhattan and spent the summer at
camp in Vermont. It was at camp that Jacques began to develop his love of underwater exploration, trying to devise ways of staying below the surface as long
as possible. By the age of eleven, he also showed a talent for designing mechanical things by building a model of a crane used to load ships and improving on its design.

Cousteau was not a particularly good student, however. His great love was
the movies, a passion that has lasted his entire life. When the family moved
back to Paris in 1922, he bought one of the first movie cameras to be sold there
and proceeded to spend most of his time and money making his own melodra-

mas. It was not until after the age of sixteen, when he was sent away from home to boarding school in Alsace, a region of eastern France near Germany, that he took his studies seriously; he then became an excellent student.

Upon graduation in 1929, Cousteau attended the naval academy at Brest, in Brittany, on France's northwest coast, where he studied aviation, never failing to take his camera along on flights. An automobile accident, which left his left arm broken and his right arm paralyzed, prevented him from furthering his career as a flyer. However, with the navy, he traveled the world in the early 1930s.

As a young officer, Cousteau was assigned to Toulon, a large French port on the Mediterranean Sea. It was there, in the late 1930s and early 1940s, that, while swimming to regain strength in his arms, he discovered the real joy of exploring under the sea. With two friends, Cousteau experimented with ways of seeing and breathing underwater. They created new types of masks, goggles, and snorkels and even built a watertight case for Cousteau's camera.

It was at that time that Cousteau also developed his own approach to scientific investigation, one that would shape his entire life to come. Cousteau and his friends discovered the joy of studying marine life in its natural environment: instead of bringing sea animals to land, they would go study them where they lived naturally. This idea inspired more than forty years of exploration in every part of the world, every ocean, even the Amazon River in South America. It also led to Cousteau's strong interest in protecting the world's environment.

In 1937 Cousteau married Simone Melchior, who became a member of virtually every expedition her husband ever mounted. (Their two sons, Jean Michel and Philippe, shared in their father's work as well.)

With the outbreak of World War II in 1939, Cousteau was assigned to the cruiser *Dupleix*, in the Mediterranean, to fight the Italians and German submarines. By 1941, when Germany occupied his homeland, Cousteau joined the French resistance (he was later given the country's highest military honor for his work in the wartime underground).

During the war he continued to work with friends to develop ways to breathe underwater. In 1943, with another colleague named Émile Gagnan, Cousteau created a working model of the aqualung, the breathing device that the entire world now associates with scuba diving. His invention also made possible one of today's most exciting sports, scuba diving for pleasure (Cousteau's father made his first dive when he was in his seventies).

By 1949, Cousteau was able to raise enough money to buy and transform a military minesweeper into a state-of-the-art scientific research ship. The *Calypso*, as she was called, was to become the most famous ship of its kind, taking part in dozens of worldwide expeditions beginning in 1951 and going through the 1980s.

With his first underwater exploration, in 1951, of the huge coral reefs in the Red Sea, which divides Africa from the Arabian peninsula, Jacques Cousteau began a lifetime of ocean exploration that continues today. In 1952, he discovered a one-thousand-year-old Roman freighter in the Mediterranean Sea that yielded valuable archeological treasures. A few years later the *Calypso* provided the first photographs of one of the world's deepest ocean trenches, more than four miles below the surface. In 1957, Cousteau was named director of the prestigious Oceanographic Institute in Monaco. Soon this museum and scientific laboratory became the most famous in the world for oceanographic research.

In the 1960s, Cousteau mounted a series of expeditions designed to see if man could live underwater. Successful attempts were made to place groups of men in underwater "houses" as much as three hundred feet below the surface, where they lived for up to twenty-eight days. At this time Cousteau believed strongly that the future of mankind would include happy colonies of humans living in the ocean, harvesting marine life, mining the sea floor.

Later, Cousteau changed his mind. During the 1970s, his became an outspoken voice for protecting the oceans. In the 1980s, his concern for conservation and protecting the environment led to the development of a new kind of computer-operated "windship" could save energy and money by eliminating the need to burn oil for fuel.

Jacques Cousteau's work has been honored with the highest awards from France, Britain, and the United States, where he received the U.S. Presidential Medal of Freedom in 1985. His success as an underwater explorer, however, is not just due to his intelligence and commitment to learning. His greatest strength has been as a communicator. The reason the world knows so much about him and his work is because of the popularity of his movies, books, and television specials. They also helped pay for his expeditions.

Cousteau's boyhood passion for making movies has never left him. With André Laban, he developed the first underwater cameras for television use and produced films of his expeditions that were seen around the world. Three— *The Silent World* (1957), *The Golden Fish* (1959), and *World Without Sun* (1966)—won Academy Awards (Oscars) in Hollywood. CBS television's Omnibus did three specials about him. ABC television helped produce a series of one-hour specials about every aspect of the oceans and their marine life, and the National Geographic Society, in Washington, D.C., not only financed several expeditions but produced twelve television specials about them.

By bringing the amazing world of the oceans vividly alive to millions through his enormously popular films and books, he has helped generations of people understand and care about one of the earth's most valuable resources; its precious oceans.

Croce, Benedetto

(1866–1952)

ITALIAN PHILOSOPHER

Historical judgment is not a variety of knowledge, it is knowledge itself; it is the form which completely fills and exhausts the field of knowing, leaving no room for anything else.

—Benedetto Croce

Benedetto Croce is easily the best-known Italian philosopher of this century, a protean figure whose works range through almost all the issues that philosophy touches upon. He wrote compellingly on the subject of history and its writing, politics and political theory, and literature and literary criticism. However, it is in the area of aesthetics that he made his most profound impact. It may be fairly said that Croce is almost alone among twentieth-century philosophers in writing a major work on aesthetics.

Benedetto Croce was born on February 25, 1866, at Pescasseroli, in the Abruzzi region of Italy, the son of wealthy Neapolitan landowners. Croce never had to earn a living, which made it possible for him to devote himself from early youth to his studies and to writing. His parents were killed in an 1883 earthquake that also left him injured; for the next three years, he would live with his uncle, in Rome.

In Rome, Benedetto attended the university. There he encountered Antonio Labriola, one of the first great Italian Marxist thinkers. Labriola, a professor of ethics, introduced Croce to Marx, who had a lasting effect on Croce's thought. At first, Croce would embrace Marxism and establish ties to other European socialists. By 1900, as he pursued his philosophical investigations into the roots of Marxist thought, he drifted away from doctrinaire Marxism.

In 1898, at the height of Croce's work on Marxism, he began a correspondence with another young Italian, Giovanni Gentile, who was doing work in similar areas. It was the beginning of a friendship and collaboration that would last twenty-five years, but would end in a serious rupture.

In 1886, having completed his studies at Rome, Croce moved back to Naples, where he would live for the rest of his life. In 1893, he published his first philosophical essay, "History Brought Under the General Concept of

Art." By 1900, in addition to his work in Marxism, he had begun sketching his great book on aesthetics. In 1903, he founded the journal *La Critica*. The following year, he became an editorial advisor to a major publishing house, Laterzi. Between his own writing and these two crucial positions, Croce would dominate Italian literary and philosophical life for the rest of his career.

In 1902 Croce published his first major work on aesthetics, *Aesthetics as a Science of Expression and General Linguistics*. At the heart of this work was Croce's actual project—to complete a total reassessment of every aspect of nineteenth century idealism. He began a systematic study of Hegel's philosophy of spirit. Over the next several years, Croce would produce volumes on ethics, logic, and history.

At the heart of Croce's thought are his ideas about aesthetics. Like so much of his other work, they are the product of a deep commitment to the idealism of Hegel and Giambattista Vico. As is usually the case in idealist aesthetics, Croce regarded art as a form of cognition—that is, knowledge. Reason may give us knowledge of the universal, he said, but our intuition—of which art is an expression—gives us knowledge of the particular. Works of art are "pure" intuitions because they are "immaterial." In other words, they are constructed completely by the mind, rather than adapted by the mind from matter, from the "phenomenal" world.

In 1910, Croce was made a life member of the Italian Senate, but he had avoided partisan politics. He remained neutral upon Italy's entry into World War I. Although he had been associated with the Italian Socialist Party (PSI) earlier, he had broken with it, believing that what Italy needed was a spiritual rebirth. He began drifting to the right politically, finding the rabid nationalists more to his taste. Serving as minister of education in 1920–1921, he drafted an extensive reform program for the Italian educational system, but it was rejected until the fascists came to power in 1923 and implemented it.

When Mussolini and the fascists seized power and, among other things, implemented his educational reforms, Croce looked on them with a mixture of skepticism and quiet generosity. However, when Mussolini established an actual dictatorship in January 1925, Croce was unequivocal in his denunciation of the fascist leader. Gentile had written a "Manifesto of Fascist Intellectuals," to which Croce replied with a "Protest." As a result of this bitter exchange, their friendship was ended, and Croce became a celebrated and visible symbol of resistance to the dictatorship. For the next fifteen years, he would maintain that role, although it would cost him a period of political isolation.

Finding himself suddenly removed—forcibly—from political life, Croce had the time to return to his books. With his 1936 *Poetics*, he reached the final development of his ideas about aesthetics. He wrote extensively as a literary critic, a forum from which he offered constant opposition to fascism. When the Mussolini government fell, Croce became a leader of the Liberal Party, and in 1944 he served once again, briefly, as a cabinet member. For his eightieth birthday, he founded the Institute for Historical Studies, which is still located in his former home. In 1950, he suffered a serious stroke, but he kept working right up to his death.

Dali, Salvador

(1904–1989)

SPANISH SURREALIST PAINTER

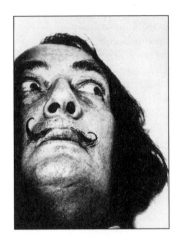

The new images which paranoiac thought may suddenly release will not merely spring from the unconscious; the force of their paranoiac power will itself be at the service of the unconscious.

> —Salvador Dali, in an essay from 1930

Salvador Dali, the twentieth century's most well-known surrealist painter, was born on May 11, 1904, in Figueras, Spain. In his autobiography, Dali claimed that his childhood was an unhappy one. He said he was a vain and mean child and that he suffered from fits of hysteria.

Dali studied art in Madrid, Spain's capital, where he was deeply influenced by the supernatural paintings of Giorgio de Chirico and Carlo Carrà. At the same time that he was attracted to the fantastic and the supernatural, Dali was also interested in realistic representation. In his own artistic career, Dali made great use of both realistic and supernatural imagery, often combining them in his distinctive paintings.

While in school in Madrid, Dali's closest friend was Luis Buñuel, who would become Spain's first great film director. Buñuel's first two films were made in collaboration with Dali.

Throughout his life, Dali was an iconoclast. He sought to attack established rules and expectations. While a student at a Madrid art school, Dali was suspended for encouraging students to riot. A little later, he was imprisoned briefly for being a subversive. Then he was expelled from his art school in 1926 for his excessive behavior. Later in life, he channeled his eccentricity toward attracting as much attention as possible to himself. He believed that public attention served to fuel his creativity.

After being expelled from art school, Dali began exhibiting his paintings in Madrid and in Barcelona in 1927. One year later, Dali made two trips to Paris, where he visited with artist Pablo Picasso. The next year, some of his paintings were included in a Paris exhibition. His works reflected the style for which he is best known, surrealism. Surrealist art emphasized the irrational, the bizarre, and the accidental; it sought to reach the unconscious, hidden processes of the mind. Dali became the most recognizable member of the surrealist movement.

In his paintings, Dali skillfully used meticulous detailing to create a dream-like picture of reality. He carefully constructed hallucinatory imagery with strikingly realistic detail, thereby calling the viewer's attention to his or her understanding of reality. His most renowned work, the 1931 painting *The Persistence of Memory*, featured gold watches bent and dripping from the sun's rays as if they were made of wax. This and other paintings such as *The Origin of the Fleeting Wish* attracted attention from art lovers and the general public as well.

In his theory of surrealism, Dali developed what he called "critical paranoia." He believed that the artist should acquire a state of genuine delusion while maintaining an awareness that he or she had deliberately suspended his or her control of reason and will. Such a method, Dali argued, would enable one to tap rich artistic and poetic talents hidden within one's unconscious. Moreover, he argued that "critical paranoia" could be a useful way of life.

Over time, Dali developed his own extravagant public behavior as an art form. For example, in 1936, he appeared at the opening of the London surrealist exhibition wearing a scuba-diving suit. Through a variety of extravagant antics, Dali made himself one of the most celebrated and influential avant-garde artists.

In 1937, Dali visited Italy, and his style underwent a change, for a while, in the direction of a more academic style. Around that time, he was also expelled from the surrealist group of artists for refusing to support the cause of worldwide Marxist revolution. The surrealists charged Dali with supporting fascism by glorying in public attention.

In 1940, he moved to the United States, where he lived for fifteen years. In the U.S., Dali directed his efforts toward attracting publicity. He had his first retrospective exhibition at the Museum of Modern Art in New York in 1941. He attracted more attention between 1942 and 1944 by publishing his autobiography.

In the early 1950s, Dali finally abandoned surrealist imagery in favor of realistic modes of past masters. He returned to Spain in 1955. Ten years later, he published *Diary of a Genius*. Throughout the remainder of his life he continued to be a very visible, flamboyant celebrity. His critical reputation remains strong; he is still viewed as one of the most versatile twentieth-century artists. He died on January 23, 1989.

Davis, Miles

(1926–1990)

AMERICAN JAZZ TRUMPETER

Miles Davis was born in St. Louis, Missouri, in 1926, and by the age of thirteen was already playing the trumpet in his high school band. Two years later he was playing professionally in local bands. In 1944, he moved to New York to study at the Juilliard School. The jazz saxophonist Charlie Parker was Miles Davis's idol ever since the young trumpeter heard his recordings. The two musicians met and started playing together in live performances and recordings from 1945 to 1948. In 1948, Miles Davis began to lead his own groups playing bop music.

In 1955, Davis played at the Newport Jazz Festival, and then formed a quintet with pianist Red Garland, double bass player Paul Chambers, drummer Philly Joe Jones, and tenor saxophonist John Coltrane. It was not unusual for Davis to play with a variety of musicians, such as pianists Chick Corea and Keith Jarrett and guitarist John McLaughlin.

In the mid-1970s a serious illness combined with injuries suffered in an auto accident forced him to retire. With the help of a physical therapist and a driving passion to return to music, he made a number of recordings in 1980 and toured with numerous musicians, including saxophonist Branford Marsalis, beginning in 1984.

Later in his life, Davis began painting abstract art works, and he held several one-man shows in galleries around the world. Miles Davis died at his home in Los Angeles, California in 1990, leaving behind a long legacy of musical innovation.

Dayan, Moshe

(1915–1981)

ISRAELI MILITARY COMMANDER AND POLITICIAN

Moshe Dayan, Israeli military leader and minister of foreign affairs, was born on May 20, 1915, on a kibbutz in what was then Palestine, in the Middle East. His father was a farmer and a leader in the cooperative settlement movement.

At the age of twenty-one, Dayan joined the British-controlled Supplementary Police Force in Palestine. By 1940, however, he had become a member of the underground Jewish guerrilla fighters who were battling the British in an attempt to establish an independent Jewish state in the Middle East. The British eventually relinquished control to the United Nations and Israel came into being in 1948.

In the struggle for Israel's existence, Dayan moved from fighting the British in 1947 to fighting the Egyptians in 1948 when that country resisted the creation of a Jewish state. He had become a military leader of the Jewish forces by 1949 and represented his new country at peace talks that year. He again earned national recognition as a war hero in 1956, when he commanded the Israeli attack on Egypt when the latter tried to nationalize the Suez Canal.

Dayan retired from the Israeli army in 1958 and entered politics, serving as the minister of agriculture and later joining the opposition party, Rafi, in 1965. In 1967, Dayan became minister of defense and masterminded, along with military Chief of Staff Yitzhak Rabin (who later became Israel's prime minister), the Six-Day War, in which Israel conquered the combined forces of Egypt, Saudi Arabia, Iraq, Jordan, and Syria and claimed large amounts of Arab lands (most of which have since been returned). After the brief war Dayan made further efforts to strengthen Israel's military, anticipating years of continued warfare in the Middle East.

Though primarily a military figure, Dayan objected to accusations that he viewed armed response as the only successful strategy in protecting Israel's security. He also cared deeply about the men and women who had to do the fighting, even those on the side of the enemy. Making a strong distinction between soldiers and terrorists, he insisted on the proper, humane care of prisoners of war and Arab settlers living on Israeli soil. As minister of agriculture, he believed that Arabs deserved equal treatment and the same opportunities as Jewish inhabitants.

In 1977, Moshe Dayan was named minister of foreign affairs for Israel, a position he held during the successful peace negotiations between his country and Egypt, which were moderated by U.S. President Jimmy Carter. Dayan resigned from government in 1979 due to conflicts with Prime Minister Menachem Begin, another former freedom fighter for Israel. With a keen interest in archaeology, he retired to a farm in the countryside. Dayan died on October 16, 1981.

de Gaulle, Charles

(1890–1970)

FRENCH STATESMAN AND
WARTIME LEADER

Je suis la France.
—Charles de Gaulle, 1940

"I am France." Few people in history would dare make such a monumental claim. But few people other than Charles de Gaulle (whose name literally means Charles of France) have had the supreme self-confidence not only to make the claim, but to make good on it. At a turning point in history, when many of his fellow citizens were caving in to the forces of Nazi Germany, de Gaulle did indeed take personal responsibility for saving France. From that day on he devoted his life to celebrating the glories of his country's culture, history, and people, and turning France into a power equal (some believed he meant superior) to any nation on earth. Along the way, this towering (physically, as well as politically) figure of world affairs managed to be a thorn in the side of most of his allies, especially the United States, and even to his countrymen.

Charles André Joseph Marie de Gaulle was born in Lille, a city in northern France, on November 22, 1890. His father was a teacher who never recovered emotionally from France's crushing defeat in the Franco-Prussian War of 1870. He raised his son Charles to seek revenge on Germany. Charles also was taught at an early age to revere his family's long history in fighting for France, a history that dated to the fourteenth century. A great-great grandfather had been a counselor to the king of France, and de Gaulle's grandfather had written a history of Paris.

In 1909, de Gaulle began courses at Saint-Cyr, France's most prestigious military academy. Despite being called "the Big Asparagus" because of his height, he did well and graduated in 1912 with an assignment to join Henri Pétain, one of France's top military leaders at the time. De Gaulle served in the army as a captain during World War I. At one point he was so badly wounded that his body was about to be buried by the Germans. Suddenly, he regained consciousness, and they imprisoned him. He escaped several times, only to be recaptured. At the end of the war he received three awards for bravery.

Never one to be hesitant about offering his opinions, de Gaulle was repeatedly at odds with his superior officers after the war. Much of his theory about military strategy at this time was ignored by the French, only to be read and used by the Germans, with great success, during World War II. Sadly, it was through the use of much of de Gaulle's strategy that the Nazi armies quickly conquered France in 1940, at the beginning of the war. While many of the French military leaders surrendered (including de Gaulle's former mentor and hero, Pétain, who later became head of the German-controlled Vichy government in France), Charles de Gaulle refused. He escaped to England, where, on a radio broadcast from London, he uttered his famous declaration: *"Je suis la France,"* he proclaimed, and promised that the French people would fight back and win.

Despite his relatively low rank—brigadier general—he managed to convince Winston Churchill, the British prime minister, that he could rightfully claim leadership of French forces. De Gaulle, who had been tried, convicted, and condemned to death by a French court in German-occupied France, created the Free French Army and for the rest of the war worked, and squabbled intensely with, the other Allied leaders, including Winston Churchill, Franklin D. Roosevelt, and most of the military commanders (including his fellow Free French officers). He also directed the French resistance to German control of France.

In 1944, after the massive invasion at Normandy, de Gaulle triumphantly returned to France and was immediately elected premier.

By 1946, the majority of politicians had sided against de Gaulle, despite his wartime role. Always somewhat contemptuous of politics and what he considered petty issues, de Gaulle resigned. In 1947, however, he created "The Rally of the French People," a populist movement that became an enormously powerful force in French politics without actually being a formal party or winning an election. During this time, de Gaulle also was urged to take over the government by armed force, which he refused to do. He retired once again in 1955.

De Gaulle was back in politics in 1958 after a rebellion by French army officers in Algeria and their threat to invade Paris. The French government collapsed, and de Gaulle was made president of the Fifth Republic of France.

As president from 1958 to 1969, de Gaulle presided over a stormy period in French history. As Europe became increasingly drawn to the American side of the Cold War between the Soviet Union and the United States, de Gaulle adamantly insisted on France's independence. He opposed all efforts to unify Europe, demanded that NATO move from French soil, condemned the Soviet Union for its totalitarian actions in Eastern Europe, supported the Vietnamese liberation movement against the United States, and declared China a threat to world peace.

Under de Gaulle, the French economy prospered, an ambitious nuclear program was begun, and France regained its premier position as leader in Western arts and culture. But de Gaulle's sometimes belligerent individualism and almost total refusal to play politics also made enemies around the world and at home. In 1968, as student riots swept many world capitals and major cities, the students and workers of France almost toppled de Gaulle's government. A year later, finally having had enough of his style of autocratic rule, the people of France drove de Gaulle from office by voting against his plans to reorganize government. He had promised to resign if the country rejected his programs, and, once again, he kept his word. Charles de Gaulle resigned and retired quietly to his home at Colombey-les-Deux-Églises in April 1969. He died there on November 9, 1970, days before his eightieth birthday.

de Klerk, Frederik Willem

(1936–)

SOUTH AFRICAN LEADER WHO
ENDED APARTHEID

> My hands are not dripping with blood. I am using my hands and my mind and my energy and I am giving everything I have to work for peace.
> —Frederik de Klerk, upon receiving Nobel Peace Prize, 1993

Inheriting a racially divided and violence-prone country, Frederik de Klerk, with remarkable courage and determination, presided over one of the most profound transformations any society could make. When he became the leader of South Africa, a minority of white men and women controlled the lives, freedom, and welfare of millions of black Africans who had settled in southern Africa. When he left office in 1994, apartheid had been dismantled and a black man had taken his place.

Frederik Willem de Klerk was born in Johannesburg, one of South Africa's largest cities, on March 18, 1936. Politics ran in his family, with his uncle J.G. Strijdom serving as prime minister and the initiator of many laws of apartheid. His family was also religiously conservative and belonged to the Afrikaner ethnic group, the descendants of Dutch settlers who had arrived at the southern tip of the African continent at about the same time that black African tribes were moving south from central and eastern Africa.

When the English claimed the Cape Colony (at the southern tip of South Africa) in the early 1800s, the Dutch, or Boers, were forced north, where they established colonies and fought not only the British but the black Zulu tribes. By the mid-1900s, the Afrikaners had come to control the politics of South Africa and had created a society based on the complete separation of races—apartheid. Strict laws against criticizing the government or objecting to apartheid were enforced by a powerful national police force and military. Whatever the claims by the white apartheid supporters, black South Africans were kept not only separate but unequal. They were provided with the least education, the poorest-paying jobs (often requiring travel of hundreds of miles), and were not allowed to participate in the election process.

De Klerk entered politics after studying law at Potschefstroom University. In 1972 he was elected to represent Vereeniging, a town in the Transvaal province. This was an area where much of South Africa's enormous mineral resources were mined, and it was also a center of Afrikaner political activity.

Frederik de Klerk, who came up through the ranks of the National Party, which had created and supported apartheid, stepped into a prominent political life just as resistance to apartheid was intensifying—at home from black South Africans, and abroad from most governments of the world. Initially, he showed no signs of questioning the party policies. He served in South Africa's governments in the 1970s as minister in a variety of areas, including post and telegraph, sports and recreation, and mineral and energy affairs. He also climbed the ladder of success in the National Party in the Transvaal. In 1989, de Klerk became party chairman when Pieter W. Botha, who was also president, became ill.

In August of that year, de Klerk gave the first sign that his political philosophy was not geared strictly along the lines of apartheid rules. He publicly met with neighboring Zambia's president, Kenneth Kaunda, a black man, to discuss the racial situation in South Africa. When Botha suddenly resigned only weeks later, de Klerk became acting president. Elections in September confirmed the National Party's majority and he was officially the new leader.

On February 11, 1990, de Klerk announced that Nelson Mandela, the most powerful black leader of South Africa, who had been imprisoned for his democratic beliefs for more than twenty-seven years, would be freed. Mandela's party, the African National Congress (ANC), which had been banned, would be allowed to function. De Klerk also allowed other opposition parties, including the communists, to take part freely in politics.

De Klerk and Mandela met for the first time in May 1990, putting into operation a process that would totally transform South Africa within four years. All laws of apartheid would be abolished and free elections for all South African citizens, regardless of color, would be held. The process was not a peaceful one. Extreme violence plagued the black townships (perhaps the most well known of these downtrodden communities was Soweto, on the outskirts of Johannesburg) as both white and black instigators attempted to terrorize the country. De Klerk's own security forces were repeatedly implicated in much of the violence, and Mandela's ANC was locked in a fierce battle for power with the Inkatha Zulu parties. The black leader of the Communist Party was murdered.

Despite the horrific violence that made newspaper and television headlines around the world, and despite frequent disagreements with each other, de Klerk and Mandela maintained their course, equally determined to make a changed South Africa work. Finally, in April 1994, in an election that saw blacks voting for the first time (some walking hundreds of miles and waiting days on line at polling places to do so), the ANC won 62 percent of the popular vote. Nelson Mandela was elected president of a country that had held him behind bars as a political prisoner for a third of his life. Frederik Willem de Klerk, the man who had the courage to stand up to his traditions, friends, and colleagues and put the process of black equality in motion, accepted the position of deputy president. In may of 1996, deKlerk resigned from the Mandela government, saying that South Africa was now ready for a strong opposition party, which he is determined to lead.

De Valera, Eamon

(1882–1975)

LEADER OF IRISH INDEPENDENCE

You have but one life to live and but one death to die. See that you do both like men.

> —Eamon De Valera, to his men
> fighting the British

Eamon De Valera, who worked to achieve Irish independence from Britain, was born in New York City on October 14, 1882, the son of a Spanish musician and an Irish mother. When he was only two, his father died and Eamon was sent to Ireland to be raised by his grandmother. He was an outstanding athlete at Blackrock College in Dublin and later went to the National University of Ireland, where he received a degree in mathematics in 1904.

Having learned Gaelic, the native language of Ireland, from his grandmother, De Valera continued to study it after university. This led to an involvement in the Gaelic League, which promoted traditional Irish culture and the arts, and very quickly to membership in the Irish Volunteers, a guerrilla warfare group determined to achieve Irish independence. In 1916, De Valera was captured by the British and sentenced to death; only his American birth saved him from dying. He was released in 1917 and was recognized among Irish supporters as the leader for independence. In 1918, his followers won the elections in Ireland and declared a separatist republic, with De Valera as president. The move was not recognized by the British, but it generated a great deal of sympathy and financial support from Irish-Americans in the United States.

In 1921, De Valera agreed to a truce in the fighting with British forces in Ireland. England initially refused to accept his terms for peace, offering instead a dominion status for the country and continued British control of Northern Ireland. When his delegates at the London conference accepted these terms, De Valera was outraged and refused the agreement. Despite his protests, however, the Irish legislature approved the terms, and civil war broke out in 1922.

De Valera continued to fight those who favored partial independence from Britain although they had won the civil war. In 1926, however, he left the increasingly extreme Republicans and started Fianna Fail, an opposition political party. In 1932, with a majority in the Dail, or legislature, De Valera's party elected him prime minister. For the next sixteen years he worked to achieve total Irish independence from Britain. His continued battle against British-controlled economic policy led to Ireland's increasing economic independence. In 1937, his party adopted a constitution that gave Ireland complete independence without calling it a republic. By 1938, De Valera had accomplished all his goals except uniting Northern Ireland with the rest of the country.

During World War II, De Valera insisted on Ireland's neutrality, which proved to be popular. Fianna Fail continued to win elections until 1949, when it lost power. Then, in 1957, De Valera and his party again won a majority and he served again as prime minister. Almost blind, having suffered from failing eyesight for decades, he was elected president of the Irish Republic (a largely ceremonial position) in 1959 and again in 1966, fifty years after he first entered politics and helped define twentieth-century Irish history. Eamon De Valera died in Dublin on August 29, 1975.

Diaghilev, Sergei

(1872–1929)

RUSSIAN IMPRESSARIO

Sergei Diaghilev was neither a dancer, choreographer, designer, nor composer, but his gift for putting talented artists together in the right combinations made him one of the most notable impresarios in the world and secured his place in the history of ballet. Without his influence, the dance careers of choreographers and dancers such as Anton Dolin, Alicia Markova, and George Balanchine would have been quite different.

Diaghilev was born near Novgorod, Russia, in 1872. His lonely and isolated early life gave no indication of his later flamboyant success. At eighteen, his parents sent Diaghilev to St. Petersburg to study law. He had wanted to become a composer, but showed no real talent in that direction.

In St. Petersburg, while staying with relatives, he got involved with a group of young writers and artists whose radical views would influence his later career. They provided his basic education in the arts. Diaghilev became the editor of the group's periodical, *The World of Art*, from 1898 to 1904, and organized exhibitions of modern Russian paintings. He took one of those exhibitions to Paris in 1906, and followed it up the next year with a series of concerts of Russian music.

In 1908, he introduced Modest Mussorgsky's *Boris Godunov* to the West. The opera was such a success that a second major French season was planned. This time ballet was to be included, along with several operas. But when financial support for the opera season was decreased, the less-expensive ballets of choreographer Mikhail (or Michel) Fokine replaced most of the costly opera productions. The exotic visual impact of the presentation, coupled with the quality of Russian male dancing (particularly by the great dancer Vaslav Nijinsky, who was later to be one of Diaghilev's most popular attractions), drew a great response. This experience defined Diaghilev's mission in life. In 1911, *Les Ballets Russes de Sergei Diaghilev* (The Russian Ballets of Sergei Diaghilev) became a permanent organization.

Of all the major personalities in dance history, Sergei Diaghilev is genuinely unique. By creating a glamorous public image that contrasted sharply with the reality of his near poverty, he turned his *Ballets Russes* into what many believe to be the most popular dance company of all time, encouraging dozens of dance careers and influencing the art form.

An important factor in Diaghilev's continued involvement in ballet was his nurturing of Nijinsky's talent. He urged the younger man to try his hand at choreography. World War I and the Russian Revolution cut the company off from its homeland forever. Always drawn to young talent, Diaghilev began to work with other choreographers. He took the young dancer Léonide Massine under his creative wing and helped him to develop into a great choreographer. Diaghilev also began to work with writers and artists such as Jean Cocteau, Pablo Picasso, and even the fashion designer Coco Chanel.

In 1921, after Massine left the company, Diaghilev introduced the nineteenth-century classic ballet *The Sleeping Beauty* to the West. He hoped that it would run for thousands of performances and bring him the fortune he so badly needed. The production, which opened in London, was extremely lavish, but it was not the success that Diaghilev expected. The London public had been

carefully conditioned by Diaghilev's more contemporary ballets to expect
something different, and they were confused by the nineteenth-century piece
that was put before them.

The company, financially devastated and on the verge of ruin, was miraculously invited to take up residency in Monte Carlo, and it was the small principality in the south of France that became the company's permanent base.
There, Nijinsky's sister and George Balanchine became his last choreographers. Suffering from diabetes, Diaghilev died during his 1929 summer holiday
in Venice.

DiMaggio, Joseph Paul

(1914–   )

AMERICAN BASEBALL PLAYER

To many people, the name Joe DiMaggio is synonymous with the game of baseball. From the late 1930s and through the 1940s, this legendary player made
headlines. In 1969 some sports experts named DiMaggio the greatest living
baseball player. Other outstanding players, such as Willie Mays and Mickey
Mantle, looked up to him. Mantle once said, "I think he was the greatest player
ever."

Joe was born in Martinez, California, one of nine children. His Italian immigrant father operated a fishing boat off the coast of San Francisco. At one
time, Joe and his two brothers expected to follow him and become crab fishermen. Young Joe was a bit shy, because he grew up speaking only Italian and his
English was awkward. He enjoyed playing baseball. When one of his older
brothers joined a team in the Pacific Coast League, Joe began to think of baseball as a career.

In 1932 he joined his brother Vince on the San Francisco Seals. The team
needed a shortstop, so Vince had said, "My kid brother can play short." Joe

spent a number of games sitting on the bench, though, until he improved his fielding ability. DiMaggio's throws were not accurate in the beginning. As a batter, he was more successful right from the start.

By 1934 some major league teams had noticed him, but DiMaggio suffered from leg injuries that season and did not play much. Still, the New York Yankees decided to take a chance on the promising young player. DiMaggio showed them what he could do by hitting 29 home runs for the Yankees in 1936 and achieving a batting average of .323. (A batting average over .300 is considered very good.) Three years later, DiMaggio hit .381, which was to be the highest batting mark of his major league career.

The year 1941 was his best ever. "Joltin' Joe" managed to get at least one hit in 56 games in a row. Some people hailed this as a record that might never be broken. DiMaggio modestly said luck had played a big part in his hitting streak, adding, "Manager Joe McCarthy and my teammates gave me plenty of help that year."

Like other men his age, Joe DiMaggio served in the armed forces during World War II. He returned in 1946 to play once again with the Yankees. He enjoyed two fine seasons until a recurring problem with his heel required surgery in 1948. A second operation was needed in 1949. DiMaggio came back to help his team win the American League pennant that year and the next.

DiMaggio was 37 years old when he felt forced to retire in 1951; old injuries were keeping him from playing as well as he wanted to. The veteran of eight All-Star Games and ten World Series said, "I feel that I have reached the stage where I can no longer produce for my ball club, my manager, my teammates, and my fans the sort of baseball their loyalty to me deserves."

DiMaggio kept busy after retiring from the game. He served as a sports commentator and worked with his brother Tom to build up a restaurant business in San Francisco. He was married to movie actress Marilyn Monroe in 1954, but they later divorced. People wrote songs and movies that featured the beloved "Yankee Clipper," and DiMaggio wrote his autobiography. He endorsed commercial products and kept active in baseball as a batting coach for the Yankees.

Praising DiMaggio's ability, sportswriter Grantland Rice once wrote, "Joe DiMaggio possesses that magic gift of perfection in his swing at the plate. If ever an athlete was meant for a sport, Joe DiMaggio was meant for baseball."

Disney, Walt

(1901–1966)

AMERICAN FILM PRODUCER AND
AMUSEMENT PARK OWNER

What we're selling here is the name Walt
Disney.
> —Walt Disney, to a young artist
> on his staff in 1939

Born in Chicago, Illinois, Walter Elias Disney had a difficult childhood. His father, Elias, had trouble keeping a job, so the Disney family moved frequently. Perhaps frustrated by his own lack of success, Elias Disney was stern with Walt and his three brothers and one sister. They were not allowed to have toys or play games and were beaten whenever they misbehaved.

Walt decided to quit school in the ninth grade. After working a few odd jobs, he tried to enlist in the army to help fight in World War I (1914–18), but was rejected because he was too young. He instead joined the Red Cross, and drove an ambulance through battlefields in France.

After the war, Disney moved to Kansas City, ready to strike out on his own. As a teenager, he had had enough art training to land several jobs as a commercial artist. Interested in cartooning and animation, Disney soon moved to California and began making short animated movies. His most successful ones featured Oswald the Rabbit.

Deciding audiences liked his animal characters best, Disney started drawing another, Mortimer Mouse. As he later explained, he thought of the character as "a nice fellow who never does anybody any harm." When he showed his wife, Lillian, his new creation, she offered one suggestion. She said its name sounded too stuffy. She suggested that Disney call the character "Mickey" instead. In 1928, Disney released the first Mickey Mouse cartoon, *Steamboat Willie*. It was also the first animated cartoon with a soundtrack. Disney himself provided Mickey's voice.

Mickey Mouse was an instant sensation. Within a few years, he was an international star, and his creator was acclaimed as the most innovative person working in movies. The pressure of fame was difficult for Disney. He had a mental breakdown in 1931, but when he recovered he launched into work with more energy than ever.

In the 1930s, Disney became even more famous and successful. He created still more characters, including Donald Duck and Pluto, and his studio of animators produced a huge number of cartoons. Among them was *Snow White and the Seven Dwarfs*, the first feature-length cartoon ever made. It won an Academy Award, as did many of the studio's other films.

Disney and his business ran into trouble in 1941. Many of his animators went out on strike, complaining that, despite his studio's success, Disney paid them little. He was also a demanding boss, often unreasonably so. He would often yell at employees, behavior he was known to explain away by saying, "I was just excited. When I am excited, I get loud." The strike was quickly settled, but it so upset Disney that he nearly had a second breakdown.

In the 1940s, Disney also had his first financial failures. Eager to do anything to get his audience back, he ventured into different types of films. He tried combining live actors with animation in films such as *Song of the South*. He then experimented with producing nature films and live-action movies for children.

Successful again, in the 1950s Disney moved into yet another area—television. Featuring the highly popular *Davy Crockett* serial, the weekly series *Disneyland* (later called *The Wonderful World of Disney*) premiered in 1954. The next year, Disney created the *Mickey Mouse Club*. This daily show starred a group of teenagers known as the "Mouseketeers."

Now at the height of his success, Disney conceived an idea that most people in the entertainment industry called insane. While at an amusement park with his daughters, Disney decided to make "Disneyland" real. Like other amusement parks, it would have rides, food, and other entertainments for families. But instead of being just a place to while away an afternoon, Disney saw his amusement park as a vacation destination.

The park Disney had in mind was going to cost a fortune to build. All his employees tried to discourage him, but Disney would not listen. Using most of the profits his company had made over the years, he bought land in Anaheim, California, and on it built Magic Kingdom, Tomorrowland, and other attractions based on his movies.

His fantasy complete, Disneyland opened its doors in 1955. It proved to be Disney's greatest success. Just as he had predicted, families were happy to travel hundreds, even thousands of miles to spend a week in Disneyland. Within years, it had become one of the greatest American tourist attractions, luring nearly as many visitors as the Grand Canyon.

The Disney Studios continued to produce television shows and movies. But in the 1960s many critics complained that they lacked the quality of the Disney features made decades before. Disney's answer to these criticisms was *Mary Poppins*. This musical about two children and their babysitter won five Academy Awards and was the studio's biggest hit yet. Two years after the film's release, Walt Disney died of lung cancer. The huge entertainment empire Disney had created grew even larger after his death. In 1971, the company opened its second amusement park, Walt Disney World in Florida. Nearby is EPCOT (Experimental Prototype Community of Tomorrow), a vast complex of exhibits celebrating the inventions of the future.

Although the company expanded, it seemed to many to have lost its heart once Disney died. Disney's drive had set his business in motion, but his vision had kept it alive. Always willing to experiment with an idea, Disney constantly gave his fans new forms of entertainment before they could get bored with the old ones.

In the 1980s, a new president, Michael Eisner, helped to revive some of the old Disney spirit. He has helped to form the Disney Channel, a cable television network, and build a new amusement park in France. And under his command the movie division has flourished. In addition to producing films for adults, it has had great success with new animated features, including *The Little Mermaid*, *Beauty and the Beast*, and *Aladdin*.

Domingo, Placido

(1941 –   )

SPANISH OPERA SINGER
AND CONDUCTOR

Hailed as the most gifted all-around operatic artist of his generation, Placido Domingo's tenor voice has been compared to that of famed Italian opera singer Enrico Caruso. Born in Madrid, Spain, in 1941, Domingo's parents were both singers. After touring Mexico, they settled there and gave performances with their company. When Domingo was seven, his parents sent for him and he performed with them when he was still a child. It was clear that young Domingo was gifted. Encouraged by his parents, he soon began studying with voice teachers in Mexico City. While still a teenager, Domingo made his operatic debut in Mexico City in a production of *Rigoletto*. With his powerful voice and tall, dark good looks, he managed to support himself for several years in Mexican productions of Broadway musicals.

In 1961, Domingo sang his first major role in the United States (Alfredo in *La Traviata*), but it was not until 1968, when he sang the role of Maurizio in the opera *Adriana Lecouvreur*, that he made his New York Metropolitan Opera debut. As he learned more and more operatic roles, Domingo's reputation grew. In the 1970s, Domingo's growing celebrity was matched only by that of the Italian tenor Luciano Pavarotti.

The role with which Domingo has come to be most associated is the title role in *Otello*, which is based on Shakespeare's famous play *Othello*. An actor as well as a singer, Domingo brings a well-thought-out, internal characterization to a role frequently overplayed by other opera singers. His Otello has dignity and a rare quality of yearning. Domingo has also been praised for his acting and singing in the standard romantic tenor parts: Don José in *Carmen*, Gustavo in *Un Ballo in Maschera*, and Roldolfo in *La Bohème*, to name a few.

Domingo has made a number of operatic films (*La Traviata* in 1983, *Carmen* in 1984, and *Otello* in 1986), and is also one of the most-recorded classical artists in the world. He has recorded all his operatic roles, many of them two or three times. In addition, Domingo has recorded a number of operas that are only rarely performed (*Louise* and *Iris*, for example), and a great many light and popular songs in English, French, German, Italian, and Spanish. Having been brought up in an atmosphere of popular song, it comes naturally for Domingo to sing everything from American composer John Denver's country songs to the theater music of English composer Andrew Lloyd Webber. He has said that by reaching out to a wider audience, he feels that he could help bring millions of people to opera.

Domingo is also the first major operatic singer to become a conductor. He has conducted more than a dozen different operatic works in the world's major opera houses, and he has begun to conduct symphony orchestras.

In 1986, Domingo commissioned composer Gian Carlo Menotti to write the opera *Goya* (based on the life of Spanish artist Francisco Goya) for him, and he triumphantly sang it in its Washington, D.C., premiere.

Today, Domingo shows little signs of reducing his commitments, adding a hectic schedule of concerts to his already crowded professional life. He has become the artistic consultant to the Los Angeles Opera, and has become increasingly identified over the years with the Hispanic world, devoting time to Mexican earthquake relief, singing Spanish and Latin-American music, and helping to direct the musical program for the 1992 Seville (Spain) International Festival.

Dos Passos, John

(1896–1970)

AMERICAN NOVELIST, POET,
PLAYWRIGHT, AND ESSAYIST

John Dos Passos was greatly influenced as a child by his parents. His father, who had fought in the Civil War, was a criminal and business lawyer and author. He lovingly exposed him to a broad range of interests: food, fox hunting, finances, politics, and music.

Dos Passos attended private schools and went to Harvard University in Boston in 1912. Here he began to publish in literary journals and became interested in the imagist movement. Dos Passos graduated from Harvard in 1916. He joined the Norton-Harjes volunteer ambulance service, not because he wanted to contribute to the First World War, but out of a love of adventure. He served with the ambulance corps in Italy and France.

Dos Passos published his first novel, *One Man's Initiation*, in 1917. It was based on his experiences during the war, such as his encounters with death, fear, foreign places, corruption, and anarchy. His next novel, *Three Soldiers*, was published the following year. He wrote the book while working as a freelance journalist in Spain. The novel gave a vivid account of army life, as it depicted soldiers being broken down by the army.

Dos Passos wrote many poems set in Spain and Portugal, and they were collected in a volume entitled *A Pushcart at the Curb*. He wrote a play, *The Garbage Man*, which was produced at Harvard in 1925, and a collection of essays on Spain, *Rosinante to the Road Again*, published in 1922.

The *U.S.A. Trilogy* is perhaps Dos Passos's most famous works. It consists of *The 42nd Parallel* (1930), *1919* (1932), and *The Big Money* (1936). Dos Passos wanted the trilogy to offer a history of social changes throughout twenty-five years, as experienced by twelve Americans. He experimented with narrative form in these books by using three techniques: "newsreel," "camera eye," and biographical sketches. The "newsreel" technique incorporated newspaper quotations, political speeches, and even songs into the narrative. The "camera eye" referred to brief prose poems depicting poignant or decisive moments in the narrator's life. Dos Passos wrote about the lives of prominent Americans and public figures, such as labor leaders, politicians, and artists.

Dos Passos also wrote historical nonfiction books later in his life. Dos Passos' work chronicles America's changing moods and provides an interesting commentary on the American experience.

Dubcek, Alexander

(1921–1992)

REFORM LEADER OF COMMUNIST CZECHOSLOVAKIA

> I realized in this crazy-house setting nothing made any sense—not the ideals I cherished and thought we shared, not the treaties we had concluded . . . Did it make any sense, under these circumstances, to sign another worthless "agreement" with them?
>
> —Alexander Dubcek, from *Hope Dies Last*

Alexander Dubcek, whose attempts to democratize communism met with both great success and terrible failure, was born in the Slovakia part of Czechoslovakia on November 27, 1921. He was one of two sons of parents who had met in the United States, where they were living as immigrants. Alexander's father was a cabinetmaker and pacifist living in Chicago. When World War I broke out and he refused to be drafted into the army, the Dubceks were forced to return to Europe.

As a boy, Alexander lived in several parts of the Soviet Union, after his father joined the Communist Party and worked in factories in several cities. The family returned to Slovakia in 1938, the year the Germans began their takeover of Czechoslovakia, which led to the outbreak of World War II. In 1939, Dubcek joined the Czechoslovakian Communist Party, which had been banned by the Nazi occupiers. He spent the war as a guerrilla fighting the Germans. His brother, also a member of the underground, was killed.

Working in a factory after the war, Dubcek was given his first political position in 1949, as secretary of a local committee. By 1951, he was a member of the central committee of the Slovak Communist Party in Bratislava, where he also studied law. By 1955, he was a professional politician. He also traveled to Moscow to continue his political studies. He continued to earn more and more responsible positions in the Slovak Communist Party, becoming its chairman in 1964.

After 1964, Dubcek began to shift his political thinking to become more liberal. He spoke out in favor of economic reforms that focused more on a private economy and affiliated himself with leading intellectuals and artists. He also took a strong position in insisting that Slovak communists, as a minority in Czechoslovakia, had been slighted by Russian-controlled leaders. In 1967 many of the same elements of society for which Dubcek had expressed support, including the intellectuals and writers, forced a change in government. While Antonin Novotny, the leader of Czechoslovakia and Dubcek's former mentor, was in Moscow, Dubcek and his followers engineered an overthrow of party leadership. In January 1968, Dubcek was made the leader of the Czechoslovakian Communist Party, the first Slovak ever to hold that position.

Among Dubcek's first decisions was a relaxation of the communist control over the media. Other democratizations followed, including increased freedom for labor unions, economic enterprises, and governmental institutions such as the courts. As he was liberalizing the governing cabinet, Dubcek consistently insisted that his reforms would not weaken Czechoslovakia's adherence to the Soviet-led philosophy of government. Meanwhile, his government continued to broaden individual freedoms, expand opportunities for private enterprise in business, and stimulate trade with Western Europe. During this time, the arts in the capital city of Prague and other cities flourished, providing some of the world's most innovative cultural experiments.

By July 1968, much of the rest of the Soviet bloc had become alarmed by the reforms taking place in Czechoslovakia. Dubcek was invited to meet with his colleagues in other communist countries, but he refused. They responded by condemning his actions at home. Then the Soviet Union agreed to meet with him and a compromise was agreed upon, one which, on paper, seemed to guarantee the Czech leader's ability to continue his programs. Only days later, on August 21, 1968, the Soviet army invaded Czechoslovakia. Despite overwhelming popular support, what became known as the "Prague Spring" was crushed. Dubcek, under the weight of the Soviet armed forces, was compelled to give in. "We hope you will trust us even though we might be forced to take some temporary measures that limit democracy and freedom of opinion," he told his people.

Within days, many of the traditional Soviet limitations on individual freedoms were reimposed, with the support of the Czechoslovakian Communist Party, which had decided to put itself in the hands of those with the most military power. Dubcek was forced out of office, only to be returned by huge popular acclaim in 1989, when the Soviet Union was collapsing. He was made leader of the Social Democratic Party and was elected speaker of the Parliament, but his tenure was to be short. Alexander Dubcek, the man who had valiantly tried to bring about democratic reforms within the confines of the communist system, died on November 7, 1992.

Du Bois, W.E.B.

(1868–1963)

AMERICAN HISTORIAN,
SOCIOLOGIST, AND SOCIAL
ACTIVIST

The cost of liberty is less than the cost of repression.

—W.E.B. Du Bois, from *John Brown* (1909)

William Edward Burghardt Du Bois was born in Great Barrington, Massachusetts. His mother, Mary Burghardt, was the descendant of a slave who had been brought to Massachusetts from West Africa in 1730 and freed later in the century when the state banned slavery. William's father, Alfred Du Bois, was the son of a mulatto father who had been born in the West Indies and came to America in the early 1800s. Alfred Du Bois married Mary Burghardt in 1867 and a year later their only child, William, was born.

Shortly after William's birth, Alfred Du Bois left his family, and Mary and her son never heard from him again. The two lived with Mary Du Bois's father for five years. Then they moved to their own house in the center of Great Barrington. William entered grade school, where he quickly became an excellent and hardworking student. From this time he also had a series of odd jobs to help support himself and his mother.

As a teenager Du Bois edited the high school newspaper, and became local correspondent for a black newspaper based in New York. He started a club, the Sons of Freedom, to encourage African-Americans to be active in town affairs.

After graduating from high school at the age of sixteen, Du Bois worked for a year to save money to go to college. Leading citizens of Great Barrington also raised money to pay for his education. Du Bois had dreamed of going to Harvard, but he was rejected there. Instead he attended Fisk University, a school for African-Americans in Nashville, Tennessee.

At Fisk, Du Bois was an outstanding student. He edited the university newspaper and became a good public speaker. During summer vacations he taught in a small rural school for blacks in Tennessee. Here he saw for the first time the terrible poverty of blacks in the South. Du Bois became interested in improving the lives of all black people. He decided that he would try to live "a life that shall be an honor to the race."

Du Bois graduated from Fisk in three years and applied again to Harvard for graduate work. Harvard accepted him but did not accept his Fisk degree. In September 1888 he enrolled at Harvard as a third-year student. Majoring in philosophy, Du Bois became one of the top students in his class and was befriended by one of his professors, the famous philosopher William James. After graduating in 1890 he continued his studies at Harvard for two years on a fellowship. In 1892-94, Du Bois traveled abroad and studied for two years at a university in Berlin.

Du Bois returned to the United States to teach at Wilberforce University, a black institution in Ohio. Du Bois received his doctor of philosophy degree in 1895. A year later his dissertation, on the slave trade, was published by Harvard University. Also in 1895, Du Bois married Nina Gomer, a student at Wilberforce. In 1897 the couple had a son who died in infancy; in 1900 they had a daughter.

In 1897 Du Bois began teaching at the University of Pennsylvania, in Philadelphia. His research on a black neighborhood in the city was published as *The Philadelphia Negro* in 1899. In the book, Du Bois criticized upper-class blacks as well as whites for denying opportunities to poor blacks, and said that upper-class blacks had a responsibility to help less fortunate members of their race.

In the fall of 1899 Du Bois was hired to teach history at Atlanta University, another black institution. Here he formed a lifelong friendship with another teacher, John Hope, who later became president of the university. During his eleven years at Atlanta, Du Bois became increasingly well known as both a scholar and an activist. Soon after arriving, he launched a series of annual conferences on the problems of black Americans. In 1900 he traveled abroad to set up an award-winning exhibition on black American life at the Paris Exposition. He also met in London with other black leaders and founded the Pan-African Association. Its purpose was to work for the rights of Africans and their descendants throughout the world. Du Bois was elected chairman of the association.

Back in America, Du Bois wrote articles on Pan-Africanism and other political and social issues for many well-known national periodicals. Some of these were collected and published in 1902 as *The Souls of Black Folk*. The book attracted wide attention and is one of Du Bois's most famous works.

One of the essays in *The Souls of Black Folk* criticized Booker T. Washington, the American black educator who had founded the Tuskegee Institute in Alabama. Washington believed that, instead of concentrating on gaining more rights, black people should learn practical skills and use these skills to work for the economic improvement of the entire South. Du Bois thought that Washington was wrong. Black people were being increasingly attacked by whites throughout the country, and Du Bois thought that action was needed to stop these attacks. Du Bois also believed that blacks should be given as much education as possible, especially those blacks who were obviously smart and talented. He called for leadership by the group of blacks that he named the "talented tenth"—the most educated in America. In 1904 Du Bois and other African-Americans who shared his ideas founded the Niagara Movement to work for black rights.

Du Bois left Atlanta University in 1910 and moved to New York. That year a new organization called the National Association for the Advancement of Colored People (NAACP) had been founded. Du Bois became the group's director of publicity and research. He founded and edited the NAACP's monthly journal, *The Crisis*, which had a nationwide circulation. After the death of Booker T. Washington in 1915, Du Bois was hailed as the country's outstanding black leader. That same year he published another widely read book, *The Negro*, a cultural and political history of the black race.

In *The Crisis*, Du Bois publicized the problems of black Americans during his twenty-four years as editor. Du Bois also continued to be a leader of the Pan-African movement. He organized several international conferences that called for African independence. During these years he published more scholarly articles and books, as well as poems and short stories. He became a leader of the *"Harlem Renaissance,"* a flowering of culture in New York's black community during the 1920s.

Du Bois resigned as editor of *The Crisis* in 1934 and returned to Atlanta University. Chairman of the sociology department, he did more research on African-American life. In 1939 Du Bois published *Black Folk Then and Now: An Essay in the History and Sociology of the Negro Race*. His autobiography, *Dusk of Dawn* was published in 1940.

Du Bois retired from Atlanta University in 1944, at the age of seventy-six. He worked as a speechwriter for the NAACP, and also continued as an active member of the Pan-African Association. During the early 1950s, Du Bois was accused by the U.S. government of being a member of the Communist party and an agent of the Soviet Union. Although he was acquitted after a brief trial, the charges ruined his reputation. He was no longer considered an important leader of the black community. To make matters worse, the State Department took away his passport, and he was unable to travel abroad.

Finally, in 1959, when his passport was returned, Du Bois visited the Soviet Union for five months, then spent ten weeks in Communist China. In 1960 Du Bois traveled to Africa for the inauguration of Kwame Nkrumah as the first president of Ghana. Because of Du Bois's long association with the Pan-African movement, he was still admired throughout Africa. At the invitation of Nkrumah, Du Bois moved to Ghana in 1961 with his second wife. (His first wife had died in 1950.) He spent the final years of his life writing an encyclopedia of African life and culture.

Du Bois died in August 1963, at the age of ninety-five, in Accra. He received a state funeral and was buried in the city, just outside government headquarters.

Durant, Will

(1885–1981) and

Durant, Ariel

(1898–1981)

AMERICAN WRITERS OF POPULAR
PHILOSOPHY AND HISTORY

Will Durant was born in North Adams, Massachusetts. He received a bachelor's degree in 1907 from St. Peter's College in Jersey City, New Jersey, and a master's degree the following year. For several years Durant studied at a Catholic seminary in New Jersey to become a priest. In 1911 he left the seminary and moved to New York City. He taught at an experimental school there for two years. In 1913 he married one of his pupils, Ada Kaufman.

Ada Kaufman was born in Prosurov, Russia. She emigrated to the United States with her family as a small child. When she met Will Durant, he began calling her Ariel. Later she changed her first name legally to Ariel. Ariel and Will Durant had a daughter and an adopted son.

From 1914 to 1927 Will Durant became director of the Labor Temple School, an adult education center in New York. He gave lectures in history and philosophy to working men and women. He also attended Columbia University as a graduate student in philosophy and received his doctoral degree in 1917.

Durant published his lectures in pamphlet form during the early 1920s. They were later collected in one volume and published as *The Story of Philosophy: The Lives and Opinions of the Great Philosophers* (1926). The book was a survey of Western philosophy from Plato to John Dewey. It was written for the average reader. *The Story of Philosophy* became a best seller in twelve languages. It has sold more than two and one-half million copies since it was first published.

Will Durant left the Labor Temple School to become a full-time writer. During the late 1920s and early 1930s he published seven books on philosophy, history, and current affairs. He began collaborating his wife, Ariel, on a long series of books called *The Story of Civilization*. In 1935 the Durants moved to Los Angeles. That same year the first volume of *The Story of Civilization* was published. It was called *Our Oriental Heritage*.

Between 1935 and 1975, Durant and his wife wrote and published eleven volumes in the series. However, Ariel Durant was not listed as the coauthor for the first six volumes. In 1968 Will and Ariel Durant were awarded the Pulitzer Prize for general nonfiction for the tenth volume, *Rousseau and Revolution* (1967).

Will and Ariel Durant described their life and work together in *A Dual Autobiography*, published in 1977. Ariel Durant died in Los Angeles in the fall of 1981. Will Durant died less than two weeks later.

Earhart, Amelia Mary

(1898–1937?)

AMERICAN PIONEERING AVIATOR

We must earn true respect and equal rights from men by accepting responsibility.

> —Amelia Earhart, to women
> students at Purdue
> University, Indiana, 1935

Amelia Mary Earhart was born in Atchison, Kansas, on July 24, 1898. Her father, Edwin Earhart, worked for several railroad companies, first as a lawyer and then, after suffering from alcoholism, as a clerk. Her mother, Amy Otis Earhart, was free-spirited, and active, the first woman to have climbed to the summit of Pikes Peak, Colorado, the highest mountain in the United States outside of Alaska.

Both parents filled Amelia and her younger sister, Muriel, with the spirit of independence and adventure. Amelia grew up with a sense of confidence in herself and the belief that she could do anything she set her mind to do.

Earhart saw her first airplane in 1908 at the Iowa State Fair. Even before that, however, Earhart had enjoyed the sensation of flight. She had built a rickety wooden roller coaster in her backyard and practiced riding it on a board until she could do so without falling off. "It's just like flying!" she had exclaimed to Muriel.

High school was a difficult time for her. Her father's alcoholism caused him to lose a string of jobs, and the family moved repeatedly while he looked for work. Earhart attended six different high schools before graduating from Hyde Park High School in Chicago in 1916.

Her family then sent Earhart to a fashionable girls' academy called the Ogontz School in Rydal, Pennsylvania. She did not complete her studies there, however. In 1917 she visited her sister, who was going to school in Toronto, Canada. There Earhart saw Canadian soldiers who had been wounded fighting in Europe, which was in the throes of World War I (1914–18). Deciding that she must do something to help, Earhart left school and became a nurse's aide in a Toronto hospital. In her spare time, she studied automobile engine mechanics, because she was curious about how engines worked. This experience would be useful to her later on, when she would take care of her own airplane engines.

In 1919, Earhart began studying medicine at Columbia University in New York City. The following year she moved to Los Angeles, California, where she gave in to her longstanding curiosity about flight. She took flying lessons and received her pilot's license in 1922. At that time, there were only about a dozen licensed women pilots in the whole world. She even owned a small plane for a while, but it proved too expensive to maintain, and she had to sell it. She set a women's altitude record in October of 1922, reaching a height of nearly three miles above the earth.

Earhart's parents were divorced, and the young pilot moved to Boston with her mother. She worked at several jobs and tried to return to school, but she was restless. She wanted to be flying, but there were no jobs in aviation for women.

Earhart celebrated with the rest of the world in 1927, when Charles Lindbergh became the first person to fly alone across the Atlantic Ocean. A publisher, George Palmer Putnam, decided that it would make an interesting story if Earhart flew across the ocean. No woman had yet crossed the Atlantic by air. Earhart would simply be a passenger. Yet the chance to be part of a record-setting flight was too good to miss, and she agreed.

The *Friendship*, a small red-and-gold plane, left Newfoundland, Canada, on June 17, 1928. Finally, after nearly twenty-one hours in the air, they sighted land in the distance. They had reached Great Britain, and Earhart had become famous, even though she had not piloted the plane. Keeping her promise to George Putnam, she wrote a book about the trip called *20 Hours, 40 Minutes: Our Flight in the Friendship*.

Putnam became Earhart's business manager as well as her friend, and with his help she was soon earning enough money to buy her own plane. The two were married in 1931.

Earhart had been preparing for a bigger challenge: a solo flight across the Atlantic. This time she would not be a passenger. She would fly her own plane across the ocean alone, just as Lindbergh had done. She took off from Newfoundland on May 20, 1932. Before long, Earhart encountered serious mechanical problems.

A raging storm buffeted the plane for hours. One of the plane's exhaust pipes burst into flame. Still Earhart kept on. At last she saw a patch of ground below and managed to land on it. It turned out to be a farm in Ireland. She had succeeded in crossing the Atlantic, the first woman to do so on her own. The flight had also set a women's distance record of 2,027 miles.

Earhart was now a figure of world renown.

In 1932, Earhart set a new women's speed record for a nonstop flight from California to New Jersey. In January of 1935 she flew alone from Honolulu, Hawaii, to Oakland, California, in eighteen hours. Later that spring she made the first solo flights from Los Angeles to Mexico City and from Mexico City to New Jersey. It seemed that there was nothing she could not accomplish in the air.

In 1937, Earhart told a reporter, "I have a feeling there is just one more good flight left in my system." It would be a long flight: 27,000 miles. Earhart planned to fly around the world. An American pilot named Wiley Post had made a round-the-world flight in 1931 and again in 1933; he had died in 1935 while trying to do it for a third time. No woman had yet attempted it.

She would fly east from California rather than west. She took off on May 20, 1937, with navigator Fred Noonan.

Earhart flew the plane—which she had named the *Flying Laboratory*—to Puerto Rico and then to the easternmost point of Brazil. From there she crossed the Atlantic to Dakar in West Africa. She flew across the widest part of Africa, above the Sahara Desert, and then across the Arabian Peninsula to Karachi, in present-day Pakistan. She and Noonan spent two days there while the *Flying Laboratory* was overhauled.

Leaving Karachi, the two aviators flew to Calcutta, India. They managed to take off from Calcutta safely, and they made stops in Burma, Indonesia, Australia, and Papua New Guinea. By the time she reached New Guinea, Earhart had flown 22,000 miles.

The next leg of the flight was the most dangerous. Earhart and Noonan were scheduled to fly to Howland Island, a tiny speck in the vast Pacific Ocean, 2,556 miles from New Guinea. It was vitally important that their navigation be accurate. There was possibly another danger. Japan had begun setting up outposts among the Pacific islands, and many people in the United States feared that the Japanese would be hostile toward any Americans who happened to enter their territory.

Earhart and Noonan left New Guinea on July 2. Seven hours later she radioed her position. *The Flying Laboratory* was on course and had covered eight hundred miles of the distance to Howland Island. About nine hours later, Earhart radioed another message, which was picked up by a U.S. Coast Guard vessel that had been stationed in the area to help in case of trouble. Static blocked most of her words, but she was heard to say "cloudy and overcast." An hour later she radioed the words, "We are circling." It seemed that she believed she was near Howland Island. Five hours later she reported that she was flying back and forth, looking for the island. She was not heard from again.

The *Flying Laboratory* would have run out of fuel by mid-morning on July 3. But she had not landed on Howland Island by that time. Therefore the plane must have gone down, either at sea or on another island. A massive search began. The U.S. Navy used ships and planes to cover a 265,000-square-mile area. Ham radio operators in the United States and around the world listened to the airwaves in the hope of hearing a report that Earhart's plane had been spotted. Putnam, waiting anxiously in San Francisco, asked the Japanese government to help in the search but received no reply.

By late July, the searchers were forced to give up. No trace of Earhart, Noonan, or the *Flying Laboratory* had been found. The most famous woman pilot in the world was presumed to be dead.

Rumors about Earhart's fate surfaced over the years. Some said she had been taken prisoner by the Japanese, although there has never been any evidence to support this sensational theory. In the 1960s, several pilots tried to recreate Earhart's last flight, hoping to pick up clues about what happened to her, but they found nothing. In the late 1980s, one investigator claimed to have uncovered wreckage from her plane on a remote island north of Howland Island. An expedition was sent to recover the wreckage, but it has not yet been thoroughly proved to be that of the *Flying Laboratory*. Perhaps Amelia Earhart's fate will remain a mystery forever.

Eastman, George

(1854–1932)

AMERICAN INVENTOR OF THE
KODAK CAMERA AND FLEXIBLE
FILM

George Eastman was born in Waterville, New York, but at six moved to the nearby city of Rochester. There his father founded the Rochester Mercantile College, the first business school in the country.

When George was fourteen, his father died. To support his widowed mother, the boy went to work, first in a real estate office, later in an insurance company and in a bank. In ten years, he saved enough money for him and his mother to live comfortably without fear of ever going hungry.

Only then did Eastman feel confident enough to pursue his life's goal—to go into business for himself. While on vacation, he had stumbled on an idea. To better share his trip with his mother when he returned, Eastman had taken photographs of the sites he saw. As he learned, the science of photography was so new that taking pictures could be a frustrating hobby. It required heavy, expensive equipment, including a huge camera, a tripod, glass plates, chemicals, and a tent. It also demanded a great deal of time. Early photographs had to be developed immediately, so creating one image could take as much as an hour of a photographer's time.

Eastman set out to discover a simpler way to make photographs. Even though he had almost no formal education, he started reading every science book he could find. He taught himself French and German so he could read articles in European scientific journals.

In an English journal, he finally found the information he was looking for. It described a type of gelatin that could replace a photographic solution called collodion. Photographs were then printed on collodion-coated glass plates, which had to be covered by another chemical, silver nitrate, before the plate was exposed to light. Using gelatin instead of collodion eliminated this step, simplifying the photographic process.

In 1879, Eastman started manufacturing his gelatin-covered (also called "dry") plates. The venture was a success, but Eastman continued his experiments. He spent so much time at work that his mother often showed up at his factory and asked him to come home.

Eastman's long hours paid off when, in 1884, he made his greatest invention. He had been looking for a way to take photographs without using glass plates, which were bulky and broke easily. His solution was film made from a paper base covered with gelatin. Before he could sell his film, Eastman had to invent a camera that could use it. In 1888, he succeeded and started marketing a lightweight box camera, the first that did not need a tripod. It was not only convenient, but also fairly cheap. Eastman's camera, the Kodak, cost only twenty-five dollars.

The Kodak camera changed the world of photography. Previously only professional photographers or devoted hobbyists were willing to spend the time and money needed to take pictures. Now almost everyone could afford to photograph their friends and family for fun.

Eastman proved to be a clever businessman as well as a skilled inventor. The demand for his Kodaks was so huge that his factory had to grow quickly. Fast growth can sometimes overwhelm a business owner. But Eastman ran his company well. By 1900, he was managing the work of more than three thousand employees and had supervised the building of Kodak Park, a large complex of factories and offices in Rochester.

Eastman's success was amazing. However, it brought him little pleasure or satisfaction. Always a gloomy man, his outlook became even more bleak after his mother died in 1907. His depression grew until 1932, when at the age of seventy-eight George Eastman killed himself: Behind he left a sad, simple suicide note, reading only, "My work is done, why wait?"

Edison, Thomas Alva

(1847–1931)

AMERICAN INVENTOR OF THE ELECTRIC LIGHT BULB, PHONOGRAPH, AND FIRST MOVIE CAMERA

> Genius is one percent inspiration, ninety-nine percent perspiration.
> —credited to Thomas Alva Edison in *Harper's Monthly* (1932)

Thomas Alva Edison was born in Milan, Ohio, but soon his family moved to Port Huron, Michigan. His father, Samuel, was unsuccessful at business, but had a fun-loving nature. Thomas had more in common with his mother. Saddened by the death of two sons and one daughter, Nancy Edison was stern, sober, and always dressed in black.

At a young age, Thomas seemed so serious that Samuel Edison worried about the boy, especially after he started school. Thomas's classmates teased him mercilessly, making fun of the weak, somber boy. His teacher, who thought Thomas was retarded, provided little comfort. After only three months, he ran away from the school one day and refused to return.

His mother then began teaching Thomas at home, but his real education came from his own reading. His favorite book was titled *The School of Natural Philosophy*. It described science experiments that he could perform at home in a laboratory he set up in his basement.

To pay for laboratory supplies, Thomas started selling newspapers and sandwiches on a train that ran from Port Huron to Detroit. For twelve hours each day, he rode the train, reading books or napping when he was not working. He later remembered the three years he had this job as the happiest time of his life.

When he was fifteen, Edison found work as a telegraph operator. It was a perfect position for a young man interested in science. The telegraph had recently been invented by Samuel Morse. By using Morse Code, an operator could send messages along an electrically charged wire. Before telephones, the telegraph was the only way to communicate information quickly over a long distance.

For the next three years, Edison moved around the country, from telegraph office to telegraph office. Even though he was a skilled operator, he had trouble keeping any job for long. He often got fired for fiddling with his latest experiment when he was supposed to be attending his telegraph station.

In 1868, his years of experimenting finally began to pay off. That year he invented the duplex telegraph. It sent two messages along the same wire at the same time. News of the invention impressed several investors. They offered Edison money to help him develop other ideas he had. With their financing, Edison could afford to become a full-time inventor.

By 1871, he and a partner had set up a business in Newark, New Jersey. There he met and married a fifteen-year-old worker, Mary Stilwell. The couple had two boys and one girl, whom Mary Edison reared on her own. Her husband spent little time at home, preferring to be in his workshop all day and often all night.

Edison decided to expand his business in 1876. He had a huge factory built in nearby Menlo Park. It was to become the first private research laboratory in the United States.

Edison told a newspaper reporter that he and his employees planned to create "a minor invention every ten days and a big thing every six months or so." The goal seemed impossible, but he made good on his boast. When news spread of the hundreds of inventions coming from his factory, Edison became known as the "Wizard of Menlo Park."

Probably the most important invention credited to Edison was the electric light bulb. There had been earlier electric lamps, but none worked as well as those with Edison's bulbs. And unlike the previous inventions, they could be safely used in people's homes.

The phonograph was another of Edison's inventions. His machine was crude, but it was the first device that could record and play back sounds.

Reporters began flocking to Menlo Park. They knew their readers were eager to hear about what was coming next from Edison's invention factory. Many tried to find out what Edison was working on behind a closed door in a dark room. In 1889, the secret was revealed. He had invented the Kinetograph, the first movie camera.

In all, Edison, with the help of his staff, received 1,093 patents in his name from the U.S. government. Each patent declared him the owner of a new invention. Because of this achievement, the press called him a genius. Many of his fellow inventors, however, had less generous names for Edison. They accused him of stealing their ideas and challenged a number of Edison's patents in court. With a team of highly paid lawyers, Edison usually won these cases.

Edison's many patents earned him huge sums of money as well as many enemies. But being rich meant little to the inventor. Edison did not seem to have much use for his money. Some reporters concluded that all he cared about was helping others with his life-enhancing inventions. Edison, however, had another explanation for why he worked so hard: "I don't care so much about making my fortune as I do for getting ahead of the other fellow."

Spurred on by a love of competition, Edison continued to invent despite a series of illnesses that plagued his last years. In 1931, he died from several ailments at the age of eighty-four. On the day of his funeral, President Herbert Hoover proposed a fitting tribute. At the president's request, people all over America dimmed the lights in their homes to honor the man many considered the greatest inventor in history.

Einstein, Albert

(1879–1955)

PHYSICIST

Science without religion is lame, religion without science is blind.

—Albert Einstein, in a paper for a conference in 1940

Born in Ulm, Germany, Albert Einstein moved to the city of Munich when he was a baby. His father and uncle operated a small factory there.

Albert liked studying nature and taking music lessons from his mother. He had little interest in school, however. His teachers branded him as a poor student because he would never do what he was told.

When he was twelve, Albert read a book about a type of mathematics called geometry. For the first time, he found a school subject that excited him. On his own, Albert started reading more and more about math and science.

In 1894, the family business failed, and the Einsteins moved to Italy. Albert liked the warm Italian climate, but feared that without the business his family would not be able to send him to college. By that time, he was determined to become a science teacher. A few of his cousins offered to pay his way as long as he learned to live very cheaply. Albert was delighted. He did not mind being poor as long as he had a chance to learn.

Albert Einstein applied to the Federal Institute of Technology in Switzerland, an excellent school for the study of physics. The school turned him down when he failed a basic science test. He knew a great deal about physics and math, but almost nothing of biology or languages. Only after spending a year catching up on these subjects was Einstein admitted into the institute.

Einstein graduated in 1900 and spent the next year looking for a teaching position without success. Finally, he gave up his plans to teach. Instead, Einstein became a clerk in the Swiss patent office. The job paid fairly well and left him with plenty of free time to read and study physics.

At the time, physics was a changing field. Many European scientists were questioning old theories about energy and matter. Einstein was particularly interested in light. Recent experiments had shown that if a beam of light is turned on a metal plate, a shower of tiny particles called electrons are released. Einstein theorized that the light itself was made up of particles. (These were later called photons.) When the photon hit the plate, it bumped into the electrons in the metal. When the particles met, some of the photons' energy was transferred to the electrons, thus setting them in motion. Einstein called this process the photoelectric effect. In 1905, he wrote a paper about his theory, which was published in a scientific journal. The same year, Einstein published another article. It dealt with the relationship between time, motion, and space. Einstein claimed that time is relative, meaning that it changes depending on other factors. For instance, according to Einstein, a person in a very fast-moving spaceship would experience time differently from a person on earth. A few days in the spaceship would be like a few years spent on the planet.

In the same paper, Einstein set forth a simple equation, $e = mc^2$. The e meant energy. The m meant matter. The c meant the speed of light. Simply put, the equation said that if matter moves very quickly, it becomes energy. The idea that matter and energy are really the same thing was completely new. It suggested not just a new way of thinking about physics, but also a new way of looking at the world.

At first, few scientists noticed the clerk's papers. But as years passed, some began to perform experiments to test Einstein's ideas. All the experiments proved that he was right. Soon Einstein was hailed as a great scientist. He was offered a job as a professor at the University of Zurich in 1909. A few years later, he was asked to head the Kaiser Wilhelm Institute in Germany. When he arrived there, he was pleased to discover that he was now a celebrity in his native country.

At the institute, Einstein made new discoveries about the force of gravity. While there, he also won the Nobel Prize in 1921 for his work years before on the photoelectric effect.

In the 1930s, Einstein's fortunes changed. Adolph Hitler came to power, and his followers, the Nazis, hated Jews. Although he was not religious, Einstein was born to Jewish parents. The Nazis began threatening to kill him. Einstein decided to leave Germany forever. In 1933, he moved to the United States. He went to work at the Institute for Advanced Study at Princeton University in New Jersey.

In 1939, war broke out in Europe. Rumors began to spread among American scientists that Hitler's Nazis were building a new type of weapon—the atomic bomb—based on Einstein's idea that matter can be turned into energy.

Several of these scientists visited Einstein in August 1939 to discuss the Nazi weapon. It was clear that the United States might enter World War II (1939–45) to battle Germany. Einstein's visitors felt that the United States needed to start work on its own atomic bomb. Without the weapon, they felt that the American army would have no chance of defeating the Germans. Einstein agreed to write a letter to President Franklin D. Roosevelt, asking that the United States begin atomic bomb research as soon as possible.

Largely because of Einstein's note, the U.S. government launched the Manhattan Project to build an atomic bomb. Years later, the American army dropped two of the weapons on cities in Japan, which had joined forces with Germany. The bombings ended the war, but the destruction they caused angered and depressed Einstein. He spent the rest of his life promoting peaceful uses for atomic power.

Einstein also devoted himself to developing a new idea called the unified field theory. With it, he sought to show a special relationship between the laws of gravity and the laws of electromagnetism. Before he finished his work, he died in 1955 at the age of seventy-six. Since then, other scientists have studied the unified field theory, but it is yet to be proved.

During his career, Einstein completely changed the world of science. Because of his contributions, he is regarded by many as the greatest scientist who ever lived.

Eisenhower, Dwight D.

(1890–1969)

SUPREME COMMANDER OF THE ALLIED FORCES
DURING WORLD WAR II AND THIRTY-FOURTH
PRESIDENT OF THE UNITED STATES

Dwight David Eisenhower was born in Denison, Texas on October 14, 1890. When Eisenhower was a year old, his family moved to Abilene, Texas where his father worked as a farmer, mechanic, and railroad worker. At school, Eisenhower was bored with his studies, but he liked to read military history. Unable to afford college after high school, he hoped to have the government pay for his education by applying for admission to the United States Military Academy at West Point, New York. He was accepted in June 1911.

After graduation from West Point, Eisenhower was sent to Fort Sam Houston near San Antonio, Texas. Here he met Mary Geneva Doud, known as "Mamie," whom he married in 1916. When the United States declared war on Germany in 1917, Eisenhower hoped for a combat assignment, but was instead assigned to various army posts in the South and Midwest. He graduated first in his class from the army's Command and General Staff School and rose to the rank of brigadier general.

When the Japanese attacked the American naval base at Pearl Harbor in December 1941, General George C. Marshall, army chief of staff, called Eisenhower to Washington and made him head of the Far Eastern Section of the War Plans Division. Eisenhower had the unenviable task of supervising the flow of supplies to General Douglas MacArthur's troops in the Philippines. It was widely expected that MacArthur's army would be beaten. MacArthur and his troops left the Philippines in April 1942. Though Eisenhower felt he had done what he could for MacArthur, the defeat left a lasting bitterness between the two men. General Marshall, however, was impressed with Eisenhower's work, and in June 1942 he appointed Eisenhower commander of the European theater of war operations and sent him to England.

In England, Eisenhower set to work developing plans for an invasion of Europe. Our ally the Soviet Union was besieged by several huge German armies, and Joseph Stalin was demanding that the Allies launch such an invasion to relieve the pressure on Russia. But Winston Churchill, the British prime minister, remembered the losses suffered by England in World War I, and argued against a European landing. Over his own objections, Eisenhower was instead put in charge of a more modest invasion of North Africa, where German armies under General Erwin Rommel were pushing toward Egypt and the Suez Canal. Rommel was eventually driven out of North Africa, but both Eisenhower and his troops lacked combat experience and suffered heavily during the campaign.

From North Africa, the Allies struck north into Sicily and Italy, where Eisenhower showed great skill and diplomacy in moderating disputes between his temperamental commanders. When the Germans were finally driven out of Italy, it became obvious that the rugged Italian Alps would prevent a large army from continuing an offensive into Germany from the south. Attention now turned back to planning the invasion of Europe from England.

On June 5, 1944, making the most momentous decision of his career, Eisenhower ordered the commencement of "Operation Overlord." Early the next morning, on what was called D-day, thousands of ships and landing craft appeared off the coast of France in the province of Normandy. After a fierce naval bombardment, more than one hundred fifty thousand Allied troops assaulted the German beach defenses and slowly pushed their way into France. In less than a year, Allied forces liberated Paris, contained a massive German counterattack in the Ardennes forest of Belgium, crossed the Rhine River into Germany itself, and linked up with Soviet armies at the Elbe River. On April 30, 1945, Adolf Hitler committed suicide and on May 7 Germany surrendered. Chief of Staff General Marshall told Eisenhower, "You have completed your mission with the greatest victory in the history of warfare." In August 1945, Japan surrendered and the war ended.

When he returned to the United States, Eisenhower was arguably the most popular man in America. Both the Republicans and Democrats wanted him as their presidential candidate for the 1948 election, but Eisenhower declined. In 1952, however, Eisenhower ran on the Republican ticket. With Richard M.

Nixon as his running mate, Eisenhower defeated his Democratic opponent, Adlai Stevenson, and entered the White House in January 1953.

Eisenhower's approach to problems was sometimes cautious, sometimes tough, but best described as practical. For example, he quickly recognized that the Korean War, which had plagued the last two years of the Truman administration, had deteriorated into a bloody, unwinnable stalemate, and he negotiated a peace with the North Koreans in July 1953.

Many of Eisenhower's efforts as President had long-lasting repercussions. He greatly expanded the espionage activities of the Central Intelligence Agency and secretly supported the overthrow of the nationalist government and returned the pro-Western Shah to power. As the first step toward the controversial involvement of the United States in Vietnam, he refused the French aid in their effort to retain control of their Indochinese colonies. After a crushing defeat at Dien Bien Phu by Ho Chi Minh's Communist and nationalist rebels, the French abandoned their interests in Indochina. But the United States refused to recognize the peace agreement. Eisenhower then formed SEATO, the Southeast Asia Treaty Organization, which extended military protection to the non-Communist governments of the region.

In the summer of 1956, President Gamal Abdel Nasser of Egypt nationalized the Suez Canal, and Britain and France invaded Egypt to reclaim the canal. Eisenhower refused to support the invasion, and England and France had to withdraw under strong international criticism. Eisenhower believed that the European powers should give up their dreams of empire and withdraw from their overseas colonies. He then intended for the United States to step in and protect these areas from the advance of communism.

Eisenhower was reelected to a second term as President in 1956 and faced difficulties on the domestic front as well as internationally. During his first term, he had given orders to desegregate the armed forces, and in 1954, in the wake of the Supreme Court's order to desegregate southern schools, Eisenhower faced riots in Little Rock, Arkansas by angry white people who were resisting integration of local high schools. Reluctantly, and after much delay, he ordered federal troops into Arkansas to quell the riots.

In 1960, Eisenhower hoped to resolve the escalating nuclear arms race between the United States and the Soviet Union, and arranged to meet Premier Nikita Khrushchev in Paris to discuss the issue. But shortly before the meeting, Khrushchev announced that the Soviets had shot down an American U-2 reconnaissance aircraft for violating Soviet airspace. The expansion of CIA espionage activities that Eisenhower had authorized now came back to haunt him; due to the U-2 spy plane incident, the Paris peace summit collapsed.

The Twenty-second Amendment to the Constitution, ratified in 1951, had limited Presidents to two terms, and in 1960 Eisenhower stepped down and retired to a farm in Gettysburg, Pennsylvania. In March 1969, at the age of 78, he died at Walter Reed Army Hospital in Washington, D.C.

Eisenstaedt, Alfred

(1898–1995)

POLISH-BORN AMERICAN PHOTOGRAPHER

Alfred Eisenstaedt was born in Poland on December 6, 1898. As a soldier in the German army during World War I, Eisenstaedt injured his legs and during his long recovery, he visited museums and was interested in the photographs and art he saw. His uncle gave him a camera and he taught himself how to use it, using the family bathroom as a crude darkroom to develop his photographs.

In the mid-1920s, he encountered the work of Erich Salomon, a German photographer who had taken pictures of European diplomats. Salomon's pictures of powerful people made Eisenstaedt determined to become a professional photographer. He soon began to work as a freelance photographer for German magazines.

Sensing that Adolf Hitler was leading Germany into another war, Eisenstaedt came to the United States in 1935 and became a naturalized citizen in 1943. He worked as a freelance photographer in New York, selling his pictures to *Vogue*, *Harper's Bazaar*, and other magazines. He then met the publisher Henry Luce, who was starting a picture magazine called *Life*. He became the staff photographer for *Life* magazine in 1936 and his picture of a West Point cadet was used for the cover of the magazine s first issue.

During World War II Eisenstaedt remained in the United States, but his photograph of a sailor kissing a nurse during the Victory over Japan (V-J Day) celebration in Times Square became one of the most famous images from the war.

When Eisenstaedt learned his craft, cameras were slow and unresponsive; he helped pioneer the use of the small camera that has become the hallmark of the photojournalist. He made his photos with the available light on the scene.

Eisenstein, Sergei Mikhailovich

(1898–1948)

RUSSIAN FILMMAKER

Sergei Eisenstein was a film pioneer whose influence has been far-reaching. He was born on January 3, 1898, in Riga, a seaport in Latvia. Eisenstein was an only child; his parents separated when he was eleven years old. His overbearing father was an architect, engineer, and the head of construction for a local railroad company. Eisenstein's mother was the daughter of a self-made merchant. She and her husband did not get along; she regarded him as vulgar and raised Sergei to be a man of culture.

Eisenstein was shy and lonely as a child. He was not athletic, but he was intellectually gifted. He had learned French and German before he entered school. He also distinguished himself as an artist. His real loves, however, were theater and opera.

Eisenstein's father was a tyrant; his despotic behavior motivated Eisenstein's support of social protest to overthrow unfair authority. In order to please his father, Eisenstein enrolled, when he was seventeen, at the Institute of Civil Engineering in Petrograd. He was firmly committed to following in his father's footsteps as an engineer. However, the beginning of the Russian Revolution, in 1917, made Eisenstein change his plans.

The revolution motivated him to stage his own personal revolution and break away from his father's authority. With his newfound independence, Eisenstein volunteered to fight with the Red Army. During his military service, Eisenstein found the opportunity to direct public performances. He was pleased with the work, and when the revolution ended, he became an artist. He joined the "workers'" theater and became a set designer for a Moscow theater.

After designing sets and costumes for a few years, he began making films. He made silent films and was influenced by the work of the German director Fritz Lang, and the American filmmaker D.W. Griffith. Eisenstein's first movie, *Strike*, premiered in Moscow in 1925. Eisenstein made only seven films in twenty-two years. However, his movies have had a lasting impact on filmmaking. Indeed, at the 1958 World's Fair in Brussels, Belgium, an international jury of more than one hundred film critics and historians voted Eisenstein's *The Battleship Potemkin* the best film ever made.

The Battleship Potemkin was his second film; he made it when he was twenty-seven years old; it took only four months to complete. Critics regard the film as a masterpiece of cinematic art. Particularly, Eisenstein has been hailed for his use of photomontage, the rapid succession of film images shown in order to reveal an association of ideas. The montage technique allowed Eisenstein to control the viewer's emotions in a much more sophisticated way than earlier filmmakers had been able to do. The competing imagery of photomontage also illustrated Eisenstein's belief that "art is conflict."

A trip to the United States in 1929 was disastrous. He was unable to find a Hollywood studio to support him for a film version of Theodore Dreiser's great novel, *An American Tragedy*. He then went to Mexico at the invitation of Mexican painter Diego Rivera, hoping to make a movie about life in Rivera's country. However, trouble started when Eisenstein arrived. He was arrested without cause; then, after he was released and his film project was under way, the movie's financial backer canceled the film. Eisenstein was stranded in Mexico;

to compound his problems, the U.S. government denied him permission to reenter the country. Eisenstein finally made it back to Moscow, but he never received the film he shot in Mexico.

Although he was home, Eisenstein was, in reality, no better off. He was attacked in the Soviet press for his long absence and for trying to make films that were not in accord with the official Soviet artistic policy of realism.

He did regain Soviet government favor in the late 1930s, but he was again censured in the 1940s for a film he was making about Ivan the Terrible. On February 11, 1948, Eisenstein died of a heart attack. He was still in the prime of his life—forty-nine years old.

Eliot, T. S.

(1888–1965)

AMERICAN POET, EDITOR, AND CRITIC

Thomas Stearns Eliot was born in St. Louis, Missouri, where he attended private schools. He entered Harvard University in 1906, and studied under the literary critic Irving Babbitt, who led a movement in literature called New Humanism. This trend advocated classical standards and conservative moral values in modern literature. Eliot's studies under Babbitt would become a big influence on his later work.

Eliot published verse and prose at Harvard. Moving to London, he met poet Ezra Pound, who helped Eliot publish his first poem, "The Love Song of J. Alfred Prufrock," in 1915. Pound praised Eliot in American and British journals, and Eliot's first critical piece was on Pound. It was entitled, *Ezra Pound, His Metric and Poetry*, and it was published in 1917.

Eliot's poetry publications include *Poems* (1920), "The Waste Land" (1922), "The Hollow Men" (1925), *Poems (1905–1925)* (1925), "Ash Wednesday" (1930), *Sweeny Agonistes* (1932), *The Rock* (1934), *Collected Poems* (1936), *Old Possum's Book of Practical Cats* (1939), *East Coker* (1940), *Burnt Norton* (1941), and *The Dry Salvages* (1941). Eliot repeatedly used certain symbols and themes in his poems, such as childhood, sexuality, symbols of Christianity, and images of nature. His style, which used symbolism as well as controlled and precise language and irony, was later imitated by other writers. His work as a poet helped to shape the development of twentieth-century Anglo-American literature.

Eliot's critical work explored the techniques of Elizabethan playwrights and seventeenth-century poets. He wrote essays on classical literature, French symbolist poetry and twentieth-century literature. Eliot was also interested in the theater, especially in reviving drama written in verse. He believed that in order to succeed and become popular, verse drama had to realistically portray ordinary life just as modern drama did. His plays included *Murder in the Cathedral* (1935), *The Family Reunion* (1939), *The Cocktail Party* (1950), and *The Confidential Clerk* (1954).

Eliot was a powerful force in both English and American literature. His reviews and introductions to books helped to promote new authors. His own work earned him a Nobel Prize for literature in 1948.

Ellison, Ralph Waldo

(1914–1994)

AMERICAN NOVELIST
AND ESSAYIST

Ralph Ellison was born in Oklahoma. His father, who died in 1917, was an avid reader who named his son after the transcendental writer Ralph Waldo Emerson. Both of Ellison's parents believed that African-Americans could achieve the wealth and position of white society through education and work.

As a teenager, Ellison read everything he could, from fairy tales to the realist adventures of James Fenimore Cooper. He worked at various odd jobs and, wherever he was, liked to listen to peoples' stories and tell his own. Ellison wanted to be a musician, and studied the saxophone and trumpet in high school. He especially admired jazz musicians and would often listen to them rehearse.

Ellison attended the Tuskegee Institute in 1933. He studied music, drama, painting, and photography, and he became more interested in poetry, especially that of T.S. Eliot. Ellison spent the summer of 1936 in New York. Although he had planned to return to Tuskegee, he was immediately attracted to Harlem, a mostly black community in Manhattan, where he would live the rest of his life.

Ellison tried to find a job playing the trumpet, but the competition was just too tough. During the Great Depression, Ellison lived and worked at the Harlem YMCA. He worked a variety of jobs during the mid-1930s, but when he met poet Langston Hughes and author Richard Wright, they encouraged him to write a short story. Ellison did, and although "Hymie's Bull" was not published, he determined to become an author. Ellison studied the work of writers such as Fyodor Dostoevsky, James Joyce, Gertrude Stein, and Ernest Hemingway. In 1938, he was hired by the Federal Writers' Project, a government program, to study the use of folklore, history, and language in fiction.

Realism in literature was popular during the 1930s, and Ellison believed that this was an appropriate style for radical writers. He believed that African-American literature should raise the consciousness of its readers. Ellison published eight stories between 1938 and 1944, and he also wrote critical essays. He wrote much more than he actually published, and considered the unpublished work as exercises.

In 1945, Ellison decided to write a novel about black identity, history, and heroism. He started with the line, "I am an invisible man," and began writing the manuscript for *Invisible Man* full-time. The story is about an ambitious black man who moved from the South to New York to advance himself. The text is influenced by blues, spirituals, sermons, and folklore. Ellison worked on the book for five years, and it was published in 1952.

Following *Invisible Man*, Ellison published a collection of essays, *Shadow and Act* (1964). This book contained reviews, interviews, and autobiographical essays. Before *Invisible Man* was published, Ellison had outlined a novel which he wanted to be even better than his first. Although several sections of the new novel have been published and read publicly, the book remains unfinished. His writing seemed to stop with the assassinations of John F. Kennedy, Martin Luther King, Jr., Malcolm X, and Robert F. Kennedy, as the novel's plot involved the assassination of an important politician. Ellison's fiction seemed to be becoming all too real.

Ellison continued to write stories in the 1960s and 1970s. In 1987, he published *Going to the Territory*, a collection of personal and cultural essays, speeches, and interviews written from 1957 to 1986. In this book Ellison explored the complex cultural experience and identity of America. He died on April 16, 1994.

Ralph Ellison's work contained accurate and intense descriptions of African-American life. He wrote with humor as well as an almost tragic sense of awareness about America's confusion over its identity. Ellison believed that writers should help shape and renew national identity and pride, and for his devotion to that objective we can be grateful.

Faulkner, William

(1897–1962)

AMERICAN NOVELIST AND
SHORT-STORY WRITER

William Faulkner was born in Mississippi, the setting for much of his work. His father ran a livery stable and hardware store, and later became business manager at the University of Mississippi. Faulkner had three brothers.

Being a below-average student, Faulkner left high school in the tenth grade to take a job in his grandfather's bank. In his spare time, he read a lot, wrote poetry, and painted. Faulkner wanted to join the U.S. Army, but he was rejected because he was short (only 5′5″) and underweight. Instead, he joined the Royal Flying Corps in Canada, and the events during World War I influenced his writing.

Faulkner attended the University of Mississippi and studied English literature, Spanish and French, though he dropped out after one year. He went to New York for a brief time and worked in a bookstore. He returned to Mississippi and did a variety of odd jobs, such as housepainting, store clerk, dishwashing, and even rumrunning. Rumrunners smuggled liquor during the Prohibition era, a time when alcoholic beverages were illegal.

During this time, Faulkner became friends with a man named Phil Stone. Stone recommended authors for Faulkner to read, and they often talked about books together. When Faulkner wrote *The Marble Faun*, a book of poems, Stone helped finance its publication in 1924. An interesting anecdote about the publication of this book is that it gave Faulkner his current name. That is, the family name was really spelled Falkner, but the printer mistakenly added a "u" to make it "Faulkner." Faulkner decided to keep the new spelling.

After the publication of *The Marble Faun*, Faulkner traveled to New Orleans where he wrote articles for newspapers and magazines. He also composed his first novel, *Soldier's Pay*. It was published in 1926 to good reviews, and it brought him a contract for a second novel. Faulkner returned to Mississippi to write.

Mosquitoes, published in 1927, had a New Orleans setting. *Sartoris*, published two years later, was a fictional account of Faulkner's own family history. While he was writing this book, he was also beginning to write *The Sound and the Fury*, which was published in the same year. Faulkner married in 1929 and became a very prolific author. He wrote all of his major works in just ten years. Although he worked on movie scripts in Hollywood and made trips to New York, he generally stayed in Mississippi.

Faulkner combined reality and myth in his fiction. He viewed the novel as an art form, which is apparent in the complex structure and style of his books. The numerous revisions and drafts of his manuscripts suggests that he was dedicated to the craft of fiction-writing. Faulkner's work is rooted in the South and in southern history. He explored not only the problems and issues of the twentieth century, as the realistic writers of his time (such as Theodore Dreiser, Sinclair Lewis, and John Dos Passos) were doing; but he dealt with universal themes—anguish, endurance, and love.

Many of Faulkner's novels are set in a southern place known as Yoknapatawpha County, an imaginary region which has hunting country and swamps, dusty roads and a railroad, and a river running through it. It was home to many generations of Indians, slaves, plantation owners, aristocrats, and war veterans. There were doctors, preachers, lawyers, peddlers, and farmers. Faulkner used his vivid imagination to create this mythic place—its landscape and its people.

Faulkner's novels include *As I Lay Dying* (1930), *Sanctuary* (1931), *Light in August* (1932), *Absalom, Absalom!* (1936), *The Unvanquished* (1938), *The Hamlet* (1940), *Intruder in the Dust* (1948), *Requiem for a Nun* (1951—a sequel to *Sanctuary*), *A Fable* (1954), *The Town* (1957), and *The Mansion* (1959). His short-story collections include *These Thirteen* (1931), *Doctor Martino and Other Stories* (1934), and *Go Down Moses and Other Stories* (1942).

Fellini, Federico

(1920–1993)

ITALIAN FILMMAKER

When I decide to make a film, my initial stimulus is the signing of the contract.

For people who live in the imagination, there is no lack of subjects. To seek for the exact moment at which inspiration comes is false. Imagination floods us with suggestions all the time, from all directions.

What we need, in order to give an exact shape to this imagination, is to find a reason—any reason—to begin; we need to connect it with physical reality. I need brutal reason. Without this I would never give a concrete form to my ideas, I would do nothing.

—Federico Fellini, in his 1974 autobiography

Federico Fellini, one of the great international film directors of the twentieth century, was born on January 20, 1920, in Rimini, Italy, a town about one hundred miles south of Venice. As a child, Fellini enjoyed a reasonably comfortable middle-class life. His father, a traveling salesman for a candy and jelly company, was often away on business while Fellini was growing up. As a result, Fellini's mother was in charge of raising Federico, his brother, and sister.

As a child, Fellini already exhibited artistic talent. Like his mother, Fellini loved to draw. He did not enjoy school and took every opportunity to draw rather than to study. Despite Fellini's poor school performance, his father was planning on Federico's becoming a lawyer. The particulars of Fellini's early life are unclear; he often revised information about his life that he had given previously. The fact that his films are so autobiographical makes the jumbled details of his early life all the more frustrating.

Film historians are fairly certain that Fellini did, as a child, run away from school to join a traveling circus. After a few days, he was reunited with his parents, but the experience had a profound impact on Fellini. Throughout his film career, the circus continually served as an inspiration to Fellini.

In Fellini's senior year of high school, he and his friends spent their free time wandering the streets. They had no plans for the future; their goals seemed no higher than to attempt delinquent mischief. Fellini's street experiences parallel what he presented in his 1953 film, *The Loafers*.

After graduating from school, Fellini left home and moved to Florence to go to college. There, he earned a living working as a proofreader and as a cartoonist for a comic-strip magazine. He lived in Florence for only half a year, however. He moved on to Rome, where he had promised his father that he would enter law school. He did enroll at the University of Rome, but it is not clear whether he ever went to a single class. He was, however, able to avoid being drafted into the Italian army to serve in World War II because he was enrolled as a student.

Fellini's real desire was to become a famous journalist. He worked for a while as a police and court reporter for a Rome newspaper. Then he began drawing cartoons and writing short stories for the magazine *Marc' Aurelio*. However, his friendship with an actor, Aldo Fabrizi, ended up directing Fellini away from journalism and toward theater. Fellini toured with Fabrizi's troupe, working as scenery painter, a secretary, and, occasionally, as an actor. Fellini drew on these experiences for the first film he directed, *Variety Lights*, which he co-directed in 1950 with Alberto Lattuada.

A formative stage of Fellini's career began shortly after World War II, when the Italian movie director Roberto Rossellini met Fellini and asked him to help write the script for a documentary film Rossellini was going to make. The documentary turned into a feature film, and Fellini ended up working as Rossellini's assistant director for three other films—*Paisan; Rome, Open City*; and *L'Amore*.

After working for Rossellini, Fellini codirected *Variety Lights* in 1951. The film was not a success, and neither was his next one, *The White Sheik*, in 1952. Nevertheless, Fellini went forward and directed *The Loafers* in 1953—the movie was a great success. It catapulted Fellini into international renown as a director. His next film, *La Strada*, was an even greater success; many critics have hailed the film as presenting a strong feminist message for equality. *La Strada* won the Oscar as the Best Foreign Film of 1954.

In 1960, Fellini released *La Dolce Vita*, an international hit. The film, a satire of Rome's high society, is told from the point of view of Moraldo, a journalist, who tries but is unable to remove himself from the decadence he despises. As critics have pointed out, *La Dolce Vita* is a highly autobiographical film. The film won the grand prize at the 1961 Cannes Film Festival and it went on to be a huge box-office success.

He released his next great film, *8½*, in 1963. The film got its unusual title because it was, apparently, Fellini's eight-and-one-half work (he had made seven films by himself, and three as collaborations). The film *8½* mixed fact and fantasy and was easily Fellini's most unconventional film. With *8½*, Fellini won his third Oscar for Best Foreign Film. He won a fourth Oscar for Best Foreign Film in 1973 with *Amarcord*. And, in 1992, Fellini received a Lifetime Achievement Award at the Academy Awards ceremony.

Fellini continued to make films through the 1970s and 1980s. While none of his later films was a cinematic masterpiece, they all reflected the masterful Fellini style that his fans loved. His 1990 film, *Voices of the Moon*, brought together the major themes of his films of the 1970s and 1980s.

Fermi, Enrico

(1901–1954)

ITALIAN-BORN AMERICAN
PHYSICIST

Born in Rome, Italy, Enrico Fermi was an excellent student from his earliest years in school. He particularly liked learning about mathematics and science. As a teenager, every week he walked two miles to a market where he could buy cheap used books on these subjects.

In 1918, Fermi received a scholarship to the University of Pisa. When he was only twenty, he was awarded a Ph.D. in physics, graduating with high honors. After briefly studying in Germany, Fermi joined the faculty of the University of Rome.

In 1932, the neutron was discovered. This tiny particle is found in the nucleus (center) of the atom—the basic unit of all matter. Using homemade equipment, Fermi began a series of experiments involving neutrons. In one, he shot neutrons into uranium at a high speed. The experiment produced uranium atoms with extra neutrons. For this research, Fermi was awarded the Nobel Prize in physics in 1938.

The same year, Fermi and his family left Italy. The Italian government had passed laws that discriminated against Jews, such as Fermi's wife. To escape persecution, the Fermis decided to start a new life in the United States.

While teaching at Columbia University in New York City, Fermi learned of a new theory developed by Lise Meitner, a young physicist in Germany. Drawing from Fermi's work and her own experiments, she came to believe that a neutron could split uranium atoms, releasing energy and more neutrons in the process. Fermi saw that these released neutrons could split still more uranium atoms and unleash still more energy. If this chain reaction continued, it would create an incredible explosion.

Fermi worried that he was not the only scientist with this idea. He heard rumors that Italy's German allies were working on making a bomb from atomic energy. At the time, the United States was preparing to fight Germany and Italy in World War II (1939–45), which had already broken out in Europe.

With funds from the U.S. government, Fermi went to work testing his theories. It took years to stockpile enough uranium, but finally in December 1942 Fermi was ready. At the University of Chicago, he oversaw the world's first controlled nuclear chain reaction. Fermi's experiment proved that it was possible to build an atomic bomb.

The United States then assembled hundreds of scientists to work toward this goal. Their efforts, known as the Manhattan Project, produced the first atomic bombs, which helped the United States and its allies win the war. Having become a U.S. citizen, Fermi was pleased by this outcome, but was upset that his discoveries had made such a devastating weapon possible.

After the war, Fermi continued to teach and perform research at the University of Chicago until his death in 1954. The U.S. Atomic Energy Commission now honors this great scientist by awarding the annual Enrico Fermi Award. It is given to people who contribute to the development of atomic energy—one of the most important peacetime uses of Fermi's work.

Feynman, Richard P.

(1918–1988)

AMERICAN PHYSICIST

Scientific knowledge is an enabling power to do either good or bad—but it does not carry instructions on how to use it.

—Richard P. Feynman, in a 1957 address to the National Academy of Sciences

Richard Phillips Feynman was born in New York. When his mother was pregnant, she predicted he would become a scientist. His father helped make her prophesy come true by teaching Richard about mathematics when he was still a toddler. He went on to learn calculus on his own before he entered junior high school. Richard also built a laboratory in his house. There he satisfied his "puzzle drive," as he named his desire to learn how everything from radio to typewriters worked.

In high school, Feynman was a brilliant student, but took to being unruly and playing pranks to prove that even though he was the smartest student in school, he still had a sense of fun.

After graduating, Feynman earned a bachelors degree in physics at the Massachusetts Institute of Technology. He then continued his studies at Princeton University in New Jersey. By the time he received his Ph.D. in 1942, the United States had entered World War II (1939–45) to battle German troops in Europe. As a promising physicist, Feynman was asked to work on the Manhattan Project in Los Alamos, New Mexico.

At Los Alamos, Feynman became friends with many of the greatest scientists of the day, such as Hans Bethe and Enrico Fermi. They were as impressed with Feynman as he was with them. J. Robert Oppenheimer, the chief scientist of the Manhattan Project called him "by all odds the most brilliant young physicist here." He added that Feynman was "a man of thoroughly engaging character and personality."

In July 1945, Feynman watched the Trinity test, at which the first atomic bomb was exploded in the New Mexico desert. Initially, he was thrilled that he and the rest of the Los Alamos team had succeeded. But soon, he became depressed as he thought about his part in creating this devastating new weapon. Adding to his despair was the sudden death of his wife from tuberculosis, a disease of the lungs.

After the war, Feynman became a professor at Cornell University in New York State. There he grew anxious about his growing reputation. He worried about not being able to live up to the expectations other scientists had for him. Feynman emerged from his funk only after he resolved to ignore their wishes and just study physics "for the fun of it."

One day, while sitting in a cafeteria at Cornell, Feynman saw a student toss a plate up into the air. To amuse himself, he began making some calculations about how the plate had wobbled and spun as it fell crashing to the ground. The game led him to think about the movements of electrons. These particles are found in all atoms—the basic building blocks of all matter.

As Feynman recalled, he "continued playing with [the idea] in a relaxed fashion." Soon he developed a new theory about quantum mechanics. At the same time, he invented a type of graph that helped him understand and compute related mathematical problems. These drawings became known as Feynman diagrams. They are now a standard tool physicists use to study atomic particles. For their invention and his new theories, Feynman won the Nobel Prize in physics in 1965.

In 1950, Feynman left Cornell to join the faculty at the California Institute of Technology (Caltech), where he continued his research in particle physics. He made important discoveries about the force that holds together the nucleus (center) of the atom. He also developed a theory that led physicists to find the parton, a particle found in the nucleus.

At Caltech, Feynman was as well-regarded for his teaching as for his research. Many of his lessons were collected in *The Feynman Lectures on Physics* (1963), a three-volume text that is still considered a classic.

In addition to several other works on physics, Feynman also wrote two books about his life, *Surely You're Joking, Mr Feynman!* (1985) and *What Do You Care What Other People Think?*. Intended for a popular audience, they recount amusing stories about adventures he had. Feynman wrote of playing the bongos in a Brazilian band, taking wild gambling trips to Las Vegas, and chasing after women.

In February 1986, Feynman was asked by President Ronald Reagan to serve on a team investigating the cause of the *Challenger* disaster. This space shuttle had exploded, killing its seven-member crew, a month earlier. Always distrustful of authority, Feynman grew weary of the formal proceedings and started his own investigation. He made news with his harsh criticism of the National Aeronautics and Space Administration (NASA) for mismanaging the shuttle's launch.

One incident during the investigation was reported all over the world. The investigators thought that the shuttle had exploded because its flexible, rubbery O-rings, which acted to seal some explosive substances, had been allowed to become cold and brittle. When they questioned a NASA official about the matter, he said that there was no way to test the theory. Feynman then stopped the hearing and asked for a glass of ice water. When he had the glass in hand, he clamped a piece of O-ring material to it. Several minutes later, he pulled the O-ring back and showed everyone in the room that it had become stiff. With his simple experiment, Feynman had proven that the official was either a liar or a fool.

Two years later, Feynman died of cancer at the age of sixty-nine. His obituaries hailed him a genius. Some even called him one of the greatest intellects of all time. His students and fellow scientists honored and mourned him equally as a great scientist and as a lively and entertaining friend. Feynman's life had shown to them and to the public how much joy and excitement could be found in the study of science.

Fields, W. C.

(1879–1946)

AMERICAN ACTOR, COMEDIAN, AND SCREENWRITER

Born to a poor family in Philadelphia, Pennsylvania, William Claude Fields ran away from home when he was eleven years old. At the age of fourteen, he got a job as a juggler in an amusement park, and began his climb as an entertainer on the vaudeville circuit. Fields's reputation grew as he toured the world with his comic juggling and billiards acts, eventually joining the Ziegfeld Follies on Broadway in New York. The only movie that Fields appeared in during that period was a silent short film made of his vaudeville act called *Pool Sharks* (1915).

Fields was the star of the Broadway comedy *Poppy* in 1923, in which he played the part of a con man who gets tripped up in a series of comic mishaps. This part established the character that the actor portrayed in show business for the rest of his career. Like all great comedians, Fields knew that audiences laughed at the misfortunes that happen to everyday people. Using this wisdom, he made many hilarious silent films during the 1920s and 1930s. When sound came to the movies, Fields's success continued. Four of his most famous comedies, which he wrote, acted in, and directed, are *You Can't Cheat an Honest Man* (1939), *My Little Chickadee* (1940) (which also starred Mae West), *The Bank Dick* (1940), and *Never Give a Sucker an Even Break* (1941).

Fields's brand of comedy influenced the actors Charles Chaplin and Buster Keaton, two other great clowns of film. He also left a permanent impression on future comedians in American films, and his trademark style was imitated by countless impersonators. Fields appeared in several more films in the early and mid-1940s, but his alcoholism and various medical problems led to his death in 1946.

Fitzgerald, F. Scott

(1896–1940)

AMERICAN NOVELIST AND SHORT-STORY WRITER

Francis Scott Fitzgerald, born in Minnesota, grew up during World War I. He attended Princeton University, where he began writing. He left before graduating and entered the army, during which time he began "The Romantic Egotist." While stationed in Alabama in 1918, he met Zelda Sayre, whom he married in 1920. In that same year, "The Romantic Egotist" was published as *This Side of Paradise*. The novel caused him almost instant success, and Fitzgerald was considered a major American author.

The 1920s were a time of indulgence and excess, and Fitzgerald's life reflected this. He spent a lot of money, drank alcohol in public despite the Prohibition laws, and he traveled across the country and in Europe. Fitzgerald published several stories and a second novel, *The Beautiful and the Damned* (1922).

Fitzgerald published two collections of stories: *Flappers and Philosophers* (1920) and *Tales of the Jazz Age* (1922). The latter received bad reviews, and this prompted Fitzgerald to turn to more serious fiction about historical and social issues. In 1925 he published *The Great Gatsby*, a story about a self-made American businessman who cannot find true happiness. The novel was such a success that Scribners published another story collection, *All the Sad Young Men*, in 1926.

With the stock market crash of 1929, the decadent 1920s ended, as did much of Fitzgerald's career. His wife had begun to suffer from mental illness, and Fitzgerald paid for her medical treatment by writing short stories for magazines such as the *Saturday Evening Post* and *Esquire*. He sacrificed quality for quantity, needing more and more money during the Depression. Many of these stories were based on his own life experiences.

In 1934, Fitzgerald published his fourth novel, *Tender Is the Night*. It is a semi-autobiographical story about a successful doctor whose career is destroyed by his wife's mental illness. Fitzgerald even used his own wife's medical records and letters in the novel. It was published to good reviews but poor sales.

Fitzgerald's story collection, *Taps at Reveille* (1935), did not sell well either. Again in need of money, he went to Hollywood in the mid-1930s to work on screenplays, such as *A Yank at Oxford*, *The Women*, *Three Comrades*, and *Gone with the Wind*. He began another novel about a Hollywood movie mogul. *The Last Tycoon* was unfinished when Fitzgerald died, but was published in 1941 as a series of unrevised chapters and notes.

Fitzgerald's work is invaluable for its depiction of American life between the two world wars. His short stories are often included in anthologies, and *The Great Gatsby* is popular with both literature students and general readers. Two collections of Fitzgerald's stories are: *The Stories of F. Scott Fitzgerald* (edited by Malcolm Cowley), and *The Short Stories of F. Scott Fitzgerald* (edited by Matthew Bruccoli).

Fleming, Peggy Gale

(1948–)

AMERICAN FIGURE SKATER

The 1968 Winter Olympic Games were turning out to be a disappointment for the United States. No American had yet won a gold medal. Then figure skater Peggy Fleming glided gracefully onto the ice. She began her long freestyle program, the last of three events that would determine the outcome of the women's figure skating contest. With masterful control, she performed a complex program of artistic dance movements and athletic spins and jumps. For her performance, Fleming captured a first-place gold medal, the only one won by an American that year.

Peggy Fleming was born in San Jose, California. The family moved to Cleveland, Ohio, where Peggy first tried skating at age 9. Like many future champions, she showed a natural ability on the ice. Her movements were coordinated and graceful right from the start. Seeing his daughter's talent, Mr. Fleming encouraged her. The family, which included three other daughters, made financial sacrifices so that Peggy could take lessons, rent practice time on the rink, and travel to competitive events.

After the Flemings moved back to California, Peggy entered and won the Pacific Coast junior championship. In 1961, she won the novice championship. That year, American figure skating suffered a tragic setback. Eighteen members of the Olympic team had been killed in an airplane crash in Belgium. One of those killed was Peggy's coach, Billy Kipp. Peggy later said, "It all seemed so awful that I could hardly believe it." She vowed to do her best, both to honor Kipp and to strengthen America's chances in international contests.

Peggy won the national women's title in 1964—the youngest winner in its history. Chosen for the Olympic team, she competed in the Games, held in Innsbruck, Austria, and placed sixth. Just 15 years old, she was only three places away from a medal. Getting steadily better, she placed third in 1965 at the world championship in Colorado.

Peggy had trouble at the Colorado competition because of the high altitude. Because skating contests were held at other places high above sea level, including the upcoming world championship in Switzerland, Peggy would need to move to one. That meant heavy expenses and more sacrifices on the part of her family.

The Flemings united to help Peggy's skating. Her father found a job in Colorado Springs so that she could train there. Her mother, an able seamstress, sewed her costumes.

The renowned coach Carlo Fassi began working with Peggy. She attended a special school with a flexible schedule so she could skate for several hours a day. Fassi also brought along choreographers to plan Peggy's routines on the ice. Heavy training and physical conditioning helped her to win her first world crown in 1966. She fought off the icy-cold weather at the outdoor rink to skate brilliantly.

Sadly, her father died of a heart attack shortly after Peggy became world champion. She continued her heavy training schedule, combining it with classes at Colorado College. Along with her goal of winning the next Olympics, she wanted to become a professional skater in order to help her family.

Fleming overcame a bad moment at the next world contest. She fell while doing a difficult jump. Rising quickly, she went on to master the rest of the program and kept her title.

At 20 years old, Fleming was more physically and mentally mature, and it showed in her skating. She was slender, at 105 pounds and 5 feet 3 inches tall. Gliding across the rink, she looked delicate and graceful and was often called a "ballerina on ice."

During the Olympics in Grenoble, France, Fleming got off to a shaky start. But she quickly regained her concentration and took charge of the ice with great style. Skating to the music of Tchaikovsky and Saint-Saëns, she danced and spun. She completed a double-axel spread eagle, something no woman had ever done before in a world contest, an extremely tricky jump. Her performance was called "exquisite" and "the best ever."

After winning her gold medal, Fleming won one last world championship, then began skating professionally with the Ice Follies. She was also in demand to promote commercial products and to appear on television as a skating commentator. She was featured in two TV specials: "Here's Peggy Fleming" and an ice show filmed in Russia.

In 1970 Peggy Fleming married medical doctor Greg Jenkins and six years later gave birth to son Andrew. She appeared in ice shows and professional skating contests during the 1980s. There audiences and TV viewers got to see the airy grace and smooth footwork that were the trademarks of this world champion skater.

Fokine, Michel

(1880–1942)

RUSSIAN CHOREOGRAPHER, DANCER, AND TEACHER

Michel Fokine, regarded in his time as an excellent dancer, earned his place in the history of ballet not as a dancer, but as a choreographer and teacher. Born Mikhail (he later changed it to Michel) Mikhailovich Fokin in St. Petersburg, Russia, Fokine entered the Imperial Ballet School at the age of nine, against his father's wishes. Nine years later, he graduated and joined the Maryinsky (now the Kirov Ballet) company.

His debut took place on his eighteenth birthday, when he danced in *Paquita*, which was staged by choreographer Marius Petipa. By 1902, he was teaching and choreographing his first dances for student recitals. His first piece was a short ballet, *Acis et Galatée* (1905). That same year, he created *The Dying Swan*, a short solo for dancer Anna Pavlova. He dashed off the choreography in one afternoon, and Pavlova used the piece as her signature dance for the next twenty-five years.

From the beginning, Fokine wanted to introduce fresh ideas into what he saw as the stale, outdated formulas of the nineteenth-century ballet. To put his new ideas into action, Fokine had to teach the dancers to express mood, emotion, and action. For the first time, dancers were expected to listen to the music and respond to the feeling in it. When he staged his Greek-themed *Eunice* in 1907, he asked that the dancers perform barefoot. The shocked management of the Maryinsky theater finally compromised and allowed the dancers to appear without shoes, but they had to wear tights with painted-on kneecaps and toenails. In his other major ballets, such as *Petrouchka* (1911) and *The Firebird* (1910), only the leading ballerinas would wear shoes and traditional tutus; other characters were dressing in more realistic costumes.

In 1909, Fokine was hired by producer Sergei Diaghilev as the principal choreographer for his *Ballets Russes* company. Until he left the company in 1914, he created most of the ballets for the troupe, including the classic *Les Sylphides*. Fokine loved to work with composers, and Igor Stravinsky was one of his best collaborators during that time. Together they created the classic ballets *The Firebird* and *Petrouchka*.

After leaving Diaghilev, Fokine returned to Russia. Then, with the coming of the Russian Revolution, he went to Scandinavia. Eventually, he settled in the United States. He continued to teach and choreograph, but his later ballets didn't live up to his best work of earlier years. His final years were spent mostly restaging his ground-breaking triumphs of earlier seasons.

Fonteyn, Margot

(1919–1991)

ENGLISH DANCER

Margot Fonteyn, one of this century's most famous ballerinas, was born Peggy Hookham in Reigate, Surrey, England, in 1919. She began studying in England and continued her lessons in Shanghai, China, where her family moved. In 1934, at the end of a six-month visit to London with her mother, Peggy auditioned at Sadler's Wells and received a postcard telling her to report for rehearsals as one of the snowflakes in *The Nutcracker*.

Modeling her early dancing on her idol Alicia Markova, Fonteyn's potential was quickly recognized by both artistic director Ninette de Valois and choreographer Frederick Ashton. They soon cast her in leading classical roles in *Swan Lake*, *Giselle*, and *The Sleeping Beauty*.

From 1935 to 1963, Fonteyn served as Ashton's favorite dancer and inspiration. He created many of his most impressive roles for her, ranging from plotless dances—such as *Symphonic Variations*, *Scènes de Ballet*, and *Birthday Offering*—to dramatic ballets like *Apparitions*, *Cinderella*, and *Ondine*. *Ondine* was about a water sprite who falls in love with a mortal. Ashton meant it as a tribute to Fonteyn's unique style.

When she reached forty, Fonteyn stepped down from her place as a regular member of the Royal and took on guest-star status. Such a formality was a required step for ballerinas at the Paris Opéra. Retirement seemed to be on the horizon, until the Russian dancer Rudolf Nureyev appeared on the scene. His fiery passion, mixed with Fonteyn's cool reserve, led to the most legendary of ballet's partnerships. As a team, they became huge box-office draws and appeared all over the world in such pieces as *Marguerite and Armand* and Kenneth MacMillan's *Romeo and Juliet*. The pair created headlines wherever they went.

Outside her associations with Ashton and Nureyev, Fonteyn created Ophelia in Robert Helpmann's *Hamlet*; performed in a modern version of *Paradise Lost*, by Roland Petit, in 1967; appeared in John Cranko's *Poème de l'Extase*, in 1970; and danced in the title role of *The Merry Widow*, by Ronald Hynd, for the Australian Ballet, in 1975. Earlier in that same year, without her toe shoes, she backed up Nureyev in American choreographer Martha Graham's *Lucifer*.

Fonteyn's magic was captured by the camera on several occasions, including the filming of *Ondine* in 1958; *Romeo and Juliet* in 1966; and *Marguerite and Armand* in 1973. In 1979, she devised and narrated a six-part British Broadcasting Company (BBC) television series entitled *The Magic of Dance*. This was a personal look at the art form she loved so much, and it was later published in book form. This joined her previous book, *Margot Fonteyn: An Autobiography*, which was published in 1975, and a pair of lavish photo books on her career, produced by Keith Money.

Fonteyn became Dame Margot in 1956. In 1979, she was canonized by the Royal Ballet with that rarest of all honorary titles—prima ballerina assoluta (absolute first ballerina).

Ford, Henry

(1863–1947)

AMERICAN AUTOMOBILE MANUFACTURER

> The man who has the largest capacity for work and thought is the man who is bound to succeed.
>
> —from Henry Ford's *My Life and Work* (1922)

Henry Ford was born on a farm near Dearborn, Michigan. Throughout his youth, Henry helped his father tend the family fields, but he found farm work boring. School, likewise seemed like a waste of time to him. Henry much preferred playing with machines. He liked taking them apart just to see whether he could put them back together.

When Henry was thirteen, he saw something that would change the course of his life. Riding along a dirt road on a horse-driven wagon, he and his father noticed a man driving a strange machine alongside them. The machine consisted of a steam engine on a platform mounted on wheels. Standing on the platform, the rider had to pour coal constantly into the engine to keep the machine moving. The vehicle was impractical and dangerous, but it captured Henry's imagination. From that day, Henry started working toward a goal—to build a low-priced, self-powered automobile that could replace the horse and wagon.

To make a living, Ford moved to Detroit, Michigan, when he was sixteen. Soon the Edison Illuminating Company offered him a job as its chief engineer. Now married and the father of a baby boy, he welcomed the extra money this well-paying position brought in.

While working for Edison, Ford attended a banquet for the company's founder. Thomas Alva Edison was world famous, considered by many to be the greatest inventor in history. After the dinner, Ford approached Edison and asked him what he thought of his idea for an automobile. The inventor told him, "Keep on with your engine. If you can get what you are after, I can see a great future."

Excited by Edison's faith in his vision, Ford started working on his vehicle in earnest. Late one night in the spring of 1896, he finished the project. His automobile was so large that Ford had to break down a wall of his workshop to get it on the road. Then, at four in the morning, he, his wife, Clara, and his son Edsel took a ride in the first Ford motor car.

For the next few years, Ford improved his design and tried to find partners to help him start an automobile company. After several false starts, he founded the Ford Motor Company in 1903. That year, the company's first car (the Model A—also called the Fordmobile) went on sale for $800.

Ford was not satisfied. He worked on improving the car's design, first creating the Model B, then the Model C, then the Model D. For five years, he worked through the alphabet until the Model T was born. The Model T was everything Ford wanted in his car: It was simple, practical, and could be sold at such a low price that most Americans could buy one.

To make the Model T, Ford created a large factory in Highland Park, Michigan. There he tried to find ways to make his car even cheaper to build. One innovation was the *assembly line*—a line of workers, each of whom did just one task. At the beginning of the line, a worker would put together the first pieces. As the mechanism traveled from one worker to another, more and more pieces were added to it. Finally, when it reached the end of the line, the car was completely assembled.

Other factories had used assembly lines. But no manufacturer had ever before used one to make a product as complicated as a car. The Model T included more than five thousand separate parts. Each had to be fitted perfectly if the finished car was to work properly.

Ford drove his assembly line workers to do their jobs faster and faster. Eventually, they were so well trained that they could complete a car in only ninety-three minutes. The work was dull, but Ford's employees were well paid. Ford offered most of his factory workers five dollars a day when the average wage was eleven dollars a week.

Because his factory was so efficient, each year Ford's Model T cost less to build. He passed this savings on to his customers. In 1908, a Motel T was priced at about $1000; in 1925, it cost only $250. The price was so low that, by the mid-1920s, just about every American family owned an automobile. Ford had fulfilled the promise he made to the public when he formed his company: "I will build a motor car for the great multitude."

By the 1920s, Ford had plenty of competitors. The largest was General Motors (GM). Each year this company introduced new features on its cars. For instance, GM cars had heaters and came in colors other than black. Ford thought these frills were unnecessary. He refused to change the basic design of the Model T for twenty years.

But automobile customers liked the luxuries GM offered. Because basic prices had become so low, they did not mind spending just a little more for a comfortable, attractive car. Model T sales dropped as buyers came to prefer fancier automobiles.

In desperation, Ford brought out a new design—the Model A. For a time, the Model A satisfied customers' desire for something new. But other companies kept improving their own models. Soon the Model A seemed just as old-fashioned as the Model T.

Almost single-handedly, Ford had created the car industry. By doing so, he changed the way Americans lived. In cars, they could travel more easily than ever before. Easy transportation allowed them to see new places, meet new people, and develop new ideas about the world.

But at his death in 1947, Ford's company was on the verge of bankruptcy. He had been able to build an inexpensive car, but he could not read public tastes. His grandson, Henry Ford II, who took over the company in 1945, was more skilled at pleasing customers. In just ten years, he made the company profitable again. Building on the car empire his grandfather had created, he once again made the Ford Motor Company one of America's greatest success stories.

Ford, John

(1895–1973)

AMERICAN FILMMAKER

Sean Aloysius O'Feeney was born in Cape Elizabeth, Maine, on February 1, 1895. He was the thirteenth child of Irish immigrant parents. Shortly after he was born, the family moved to Portland, Maine, where his father owned a saloon. As a child, Sean painted and sketched and wanted to be an artist. His older brother, Francis O'Feeney, went to Hollywood and worked as a movie director for Universal Studios, changing his last name to Ford.

After he graduated from high school, Sean O'Feeney joined his brother in Hollywood and changed his name as well. Francis Ford helped his younger brother get work as a stunt person and actor, in the movies, including a small role as a Ku Klux Klan member in D.W. Griffith's landmark film *Birth of a Nation* (1915).

By 1917, Ford began directing short Westerns, calling himself Jack Ford until 1923, when he changed his name to John Ford. His first important film was *The Iron Horse* (1924), about the building of a railroad, which revealed Ford's mastery of film technique.

In the 1930s, Ford made movies of every kind, from comedies to action films, and worked with a number of popular actors, including Boris Karloff and Shirley Temple. His reputation grew in 1935 when he earned a Best Director Oscar for *The Informer*, a drama set in Ireland.

Ford was soon hired to direct the film version of John Steinbeck's novel, *The Grapes of Wrath* (1940), which earned him another Academy Award. A Hollywood film had never addressed so frankly a social issue as Ford did in his retelling of Steinbeck's story of a family's struggle to escape the Dust Bowl during the Great Depression.

After serving as a filmmaker for the government during World War II and making the classic documentary *The Battle of Midway* (1942), John Ford returned to Hollywood and began a series of Westerns that became his best-known films and popularized the Western genre.

Ford had not made a Western since *Stagecoach* (1939), but *My Darling Clementine* (1946), the intelligent and stylish story of Wyatt Earp and the gunfight at the OK Corral quickly set the standard for all Westerns and has become an American film classic. Two other Westerns, *Fort Apache* (1949) and *She Wore a Yellow Ribbon* (1949), helped establish John Wayne as one of the biggest stars in Hollywood.

The Searchers (1956) also starred John Wayne and told the story of a ruthless and frustrated man's search for his niece who had been kidnapped by Comanche Indians. The film is regarded as John Ford's masterpiece, and considered to be one of the finest films ever made in color.

John Ford was often seen on the set of his films dressed in worn khaki trousers, tennis shoes with holes in the toes, an old jacket, and a battered hat. He liked to work with a glass of brandy in one hand and a cigar in the other. He made nearly 120 films in his career and received four Academy Awards, as well as a Lifetime Achievement Award in 1973. When the director Orson Welles was asked what American directors he respected, he replied, "The old masters, by which I mean John Ford, John Ford, and John Ford."

Forster, E(dward). M(organ).

(1879–1970)

ENGLISH NOVELIST, SHORT-STORY WRITER, AND ESSAYIST

> Human beings have their great chance in the novel.
>
> —E.M. Forster

Edward Morgan Forster, one of the key figures in English literature in this century, was born on January 1, 1879, in London, England. His father, an architect, died when he was only a year and a half old. Consequently, he was raised by his mother and other female relatives. His relationship with his mother, perhaps the central one in his life, was alternately warm and difficult. He grew up with her in their home, Rooksnest, in the Hertfordshire countryside. Rooksnest became the model for the house in *Howards End* (1910), perhaps his best novel. When his great-aunt, Marianne Thornton, died in 1887, she left him a sizable inheritance, which allowed him to go through college and his writing career with few money worries. His typically gracious thank-you to her was to write her biography in 1956.

Edward's school years were unhappy ones, and he re-created that misery in the Sawston School sequences of *The Longest Journey* (1907). However, he found the University of Cambridge to be an endlessly exciting intellectual challenge, with faculty members and classmates who broadened his horizons. It was at Cambridge that he first met Goldsworthy Lowes Dickinson, a teacher who helped shape his thinking so much that he later wrote a biography of him (1934); and the club called The Apostles, whose members were the core of the Bloomsbury Group. His college friends included biographer Lytton Strachey, economist John Maynard Keynes, and Leonard Woolf, Virginia Woolf's husband, an important political activist, publisher, and memoirist in his own right.

Forster had done some writing for campus magazines toward the end of his Cambridge years, but his first real publications came later, primarily essays and profiles written for *Independent Review*, which numbered among its editors several of his former teachers, including Dickinson.

After graduation, Forster had traveled to the Mediterranean with his mother. There he fell in love with the "pagan" cultures of Greece and Italy, a passion that would be reflected in his novels. Upon his return to England, he moved back in with his mother and began to write.

This was the beginning of a phenomenally productive time for Forster; between 1903 (when the magazine was founded) and 1910, he wrote four of his six novels and several of his best short stories. He was at his best when writing about the lives of the upper middle class, from which he himself had emerged.

The four novels of that period—*Where Angels Fear to Tread* (1905), *The Longest Journey* (1907), *A Room with a View* (1908), and *Howards End* (1910)—are among the finest produced during the Edwardian period.

Ironically, Forster had begun writing *A Room with a View* as the first of all his novels. Although commenced in 1902, it was not finished for six years, but the result was one of his most endearing works, a charming social comedy which remains one of his most popular books.

However, it was *Howards End* that won Forster recognition as a major novelist; it was a work of genius that won unanimous raves and also delighted the reading public. It is the widest ranging in social scope of any of Forster's first four novels. In it, he attempts nothing less than a novel that will serve as a snapshot of English society in its entirety.

While he was writing *Howards End*, Forster had made the acquaintance of a young Indian student, Syed Ross Masood. Masood introduced Forster to the culture and arts of India. That interest was fed further by a former classmate, Malcolm Darling, who had been a tutor to the rajah of Dewas State Senior. In 1912, Forster, accompanied by Dickinson and another friend, set out for India.

India was a thrilling experience for Forster, "the greatest opportunity of my life." The exposure to an entirely alien culture forced him outside himself in a way that enriched his thinking and writing. He began work on *A Passage to India* (1924), the last of his novels published during his lifetime, shortly afterward.

Upon his return home to England in 1913, Forster began work on a new novel, *Maurice*, about a young man at Cambridge and his growing realization that he is attracted to men. He finished a first draft of the book within a year, but he would not allow it to be published during his lifetime because of its subject matter. It was published in 1971, shortly after his death, with the dedication, "To a Happier Time."

With the coming of World War I, Forster was determined to do something concrete for his country. He joined the Red Cross in 1915, working for the next four years as a "searcher," someone who looks for missing soldiers. In that capacity, he was sent to Alexandria, Egypt.

The spectacle of English colonialists mistreating Egyptians helped to clarify some of Forster's thinking about India as well as Egypt. After writing two travel books set in Egypt, he began work on *A Passage to India*, a book that many critics believe is his masterpiece. This tale of cross-cultural misunderstanding leading to scandal and a false accusation of rape was the culmination of Forster's work as a fiction writer. He gave up writing novels and only authored a few more stories, those having homosexuality as a subject, which were not published until after his death.

His two best collections of essays, *Abinger Harvest* (1936) and *Two Cheers for Democracy* (1951), display him at his best—a warm, witty, and thoughtful man with deep commitment to other people. During World War II, he became famous throughout Great Britain for his radio lectures and opposition to the Nazis.

After the war, Cambridge offered him a fellowship as writer-in-residence at King's College, a position that came with the use of a small cottage on the grounds. This became a fruitful time for Forster; he wrote short stories, a book of Indian reminiscences, *The Hill of Devi* (1953), the libretto for Benjamin Britten's opera *Billy Budd* (1951), and a commemorative biography of his great-aunt. (The cottage would come in handy after his death; Cambridge extended the same fellowship to W.H. Auden, another alumnus.)

Forster continued to write through the mid-1960s. He was concerned about the threat of nuclear war, testified for the defense in the obscenity trial of the publishers of *Lady Chatterley's Lover*, and traveled abroad extensively, including a third trip to his beloved India. He had a major stroke in 1964 and another the following year. After that, his health deteriorated gradually. A massive stroke on May 22, 1970, finally led to his death, on June 7. In the 1980s and 1990s, most of his novels were filmed, quite successfully, by the team of Ismail Merchant and James Ivory, and by the noted director David Lean, who did *Passage to India*. They led to a renewal of interest in Forster's work.

Fossey, Dian

(1932–1985)

AMERICAN ZOOLOGIST

If mountain gorillas are to survive . . . far more active conservation measures urgently need to be undertaken. The question remains, is it already too late?

—from Dian Fossey's *Gorillas in the Mist* (1983)

Dian Fossey was born in San Francisco, California. As a little girl, Dian loved animals, but her parents would not allow her to keep any pet except a goldfish. She later said that the death of her fish Goldie was the most painful event of her childhood.

After high school, Fossey went to the University of California at Davis to study to be a veterinarian (a doctor for animals). Rethinking her career, she soon transferred to San Jose State College. She graduated from there in 1954 with a degree in occupational therapy.

Fossey loved riding horses. To better enjoy her hobby, she moved to Kentucky, a state known for its fine thoroughbreds. There she took a job at the Kosair Crippled Children's Hospital at Louisville. She directed the hospital's therapy for disabled children.

Fossey enjoyed her work, but always felt there was something missing in her life. She longed to go to Africa and see the wildlife there. As she explained in 1983, "I had this great urge . . . I had it the day I was born. Some may call it destiny. My parents and friends called it dismaying."

Knowing that "dreams seldom materialize on their own," Fossey decided to take some action to make her wish come true. She left her job and took out a loan from a bank to pay for a seven-week trip to Africa in 1963. Her first stop was Tanzania, where she met Louis Leakey. Leakey was a well-known scientist who was searching for fossils of ancient humans. Fossey then went on to Zaire. There she saw mountain gorillas for the first time. She later described the experience with great passion: "Immediately I was struck by the physical magnificence of the huge jet-black bodies blended against the green palette wash of the thick forest foliage."

Several years after Fossey returned home, Louis Leakey paid her a visit in Louisville. He told her she should return to Africa for a long-term study of gorillas. Needing little persuasion, Fossey packed up and arrived in the village of Kabara in Zaire in late 1966.

Fossey knew that mountain gorillas were very shy. For many months, she just watched them, looking for a way of communicating without scaring them. Mimicking the sound of their chestbeats, she first tried slapping her thighs to attract their attention. The gorillas responded, but not quite the way she had hoped. Whenever Fossey made the noise, they looked at her with nervousness. She later discovered that gorillas only beat their chests when they were upset and alarmed.

Other techniques proved more successful. Fossey found the gorillas liked seeing her pretend to eat their favorite foods or imitate the ways they groomed themselves. Gradually, she earned the animals' trust.

Just as Fossey's work began to pay off, she was captured by armed guards. Different political groups were fighting for power in Zaire. The army was leery of outsiders in their country and wanted Fossey to leave. Escaping from the guards, she went to the tiny country of Rwanda. There, with Leakey's help, she established the Karisoke Research Centre.

At Karisoke, Fossey began studying fifty-one gorillas who lived nearby. Through her careful observations, she was able to identify fifteen sounds they made to communicate with one another. She learned that they chuckled when they played, grunted when they were scolding their children, and growled when they sensed danger.

Even more fascinating to Fossey was the closeness of gorilla families. When family members were ill, others would pitch in to nurse them back to health. If a baby gorilla was threatened, its relatives would risk their own lives to save it.

To Fossey's horror, the animals she called "gentle giants" often had to fight to stay alive. Rwanda was full of hunters known as poachers. They shot gorillas because they could sell their skins as trophies to wealthy Europeans. Other hunters captured the animals so they could be sent to live in zoos. So many mountain gorillas were being killed or confined that the animals were in danger of becoming extinct.

Fossey constantly chased away poachers from the gorilla families she studied. But despite her efforts, a favorite young gorilla, whom she named Digit, was murdered in 1978. Fossey decided to use Digit's death to tell the world what was happening. She saw that the event was covered on news broadcasts. She also asked for donations to the Digit Fund to finance patrols to watch for poachers.

During the fund drive, some people claimed that Fossey's many years in the wild had made her insane. She maintained that she "cried a lot" after Digit's killing, but assured the public she "didn't go bonkers." Still, she knew she needed a break. It was difficult to get food rich in calcium at Karisoke. As a result, her bones were so brittle that she, in her own words, "was a walking skeleton." In 1980, she returned to the United States to restore her health and to teach at Cornell University. Fossey also took the time to write a book, *Gorillas in the Mist* (1983). Later made into a movie, it recounts her many years of living among mountain gorillas.

After a few years, Fossey was eager to go to Africa. As she said herself, she was "more comfortable with gorillas than with people."

Within months of her return, Dian Fossey's body was discovered in her home. She had been murdered, but by whom remains a mystery. Although the theory is unproven, most who knew her believe that she was killed by angry poachers.

Famous in her lifetime, Fossey remains well-known after death. Her fierce dedication to her work has inspired many students to travel to Africa and perform their own research. But many more people have been moved by her familiar stories of the "gentle giants." Through her careful research, Fossey proved that her gorilla friends were not so different from humans. Her efforts have rallied thousands to fight their slaughter and that of other endangered species.

Frank, Anne

(1929–1945)

DUTCH DIARIST

> It's an odd idea for someone like me to keep a diary, because it seems to me that neither I—nor for that matter anyone else—will be interested in the unbosomings of a thirteen-year-old schoolgirl.
>
> —Anne Frank

That was what Anne Frank wrote in the third entry in the diary she had received six days earlier as a birthday present. Had she been a thirteen-year-old schoolgirl under any other circumstances, that assessment might have been right. But Anne Frank was a German-born Dutch Jew, living during the Nazi occupation of The Netherlands, and her diary was to become one of the most-read books of the second half of the twentieth century.

Anneliese Frank was born on June 12, 1929, in Frankfurt-am-Main, Germany, the second daughter of Otto and Edith Frank, a well-to-do couple. When the Nazis came to power in 1933, the Franks left Germany for The Netherlands, settling in Amsterdam. When the Nazis invaded The Netherlands in 1940, it brought Anne's childhood to a premature end. Under Nazi rule, Jews were to forbidden go to school with non-Jews, so she had to change schools, going to a Jewish Montessori school. Jews were forced to observe a curfew—they were forbidden to be out after eight P.M. They were required to wear a yellow fabric Jewish star on their outer garments. They were no longer permitted to own businesses.

On June 5, 1942, Anne's older sister, Margot, received a summons to report for forced labor. Wasting no time, the Franks went into hiding. Along with four others, they moved into a hidden apartment atop the offices of Otto's business (the "Secret Annex"). Gentile friends brought them food and other necessities, but they couldn't leave the apartment. They hid there for twenty-five months.

Anne, who aspired to be a writer, recounted the daily life of the eight inhabitants of the small apartment in a style that is surprisingly mature, given her youth, but sprinkled with enough teenage silliness that, given what would happen, makes it almost unbearably poignant to read. At the outset, Anne explains to Kitty, her name for the diary, that she is writing in the hopes that it will be a substitute for the really good friend that she feels she lacks. At that point in the book, before the immediate threat of arrest and transportation to a concentration camp, she has no idea that she will never get the chance to make a "true" friend under ordinary circumstances ever again.

On August 4, 1944, an anonymous tipster informed the Occupation Forces of the existence of the Secret Annex. During the chaos that ensued when the Gestapo (Hitler's special police) arrested the Franks, the diary was knocked to the floor in the attic. There it was recovered by Miep Gies, a Dutch friend who had been helping the Franks survive their ordeal. The Franks were taken to Westerbork transport camp and then sent to the Auschwitz death camp on September 3, part of the last transport to leave Westerbork. Anne and Margot would, in turn, be sent on death marches to Bergen-Belsen, where they died of typhus in March, only two months before the end of the war in Europe. Of the eight people hidden in the apartment, only Otto Frank survived.

When he returned to Amsterdam, Miep gave him Anne's diary. At first he was reluctant to make it public. After he had read it to friends, however, they urged him to try to get the book published. In 1947, under the title *The House Behind*, the diary was published in The Netherlands. Shortly thereafter, it was translated into other languages and became an international sensation. The English-language edition, *Anne Frank: The Diary of a Young Girl*, was published in 1953. Since then, the book has been adapted for the stage and filmed with enormous commercial success.

The version of the diary that was published after the war had been edited by Otto Frank; among other edits, he chose to omit passages in which his daughter mused about sex. In 1984, after his death, a second volume, *Tales from the Secret Annex*, was published. This collection includes several short stories, an unfinished novel, and some passages deleted from the diary. In 1995, a definitive English-language edition was published, restoring virtually all the material that Otto Frank had deleted.

Today, as Michael Berenbaum, executive director of the United States Holocaust Memorial Museum, has observed, Anne Frank is the most famous child to die in the Holocaust. The Amsterdam house in which the Franks were hidden has been turned into a museum, and is run by a youth organization that bears her name, dedicated to fighting racism and anti-Semitism throughout the world. The museum is one of the most popular tourist stops in the country; in 1988 alone, 564,000 people came to see the Secret Annex.

And Anne's diary, which has never gone out of print since that initial publication in 1947, has once again reached *The New York Times* best-seller list in the new edition.

Foyt, Anthony Joseph

(1935–   )

AMERICAN RACE CAR DRIVER

It was 1967. A.J. Foyt was rounding a turn at the Indianapolis 500 race. As he came through a chute and looked ahead, he saw a startling and grim sight: Five cars had crashed on the straightaway. Twisted pieces of metal lay strewn over the track. Smoke rose above the wreckage. Seconds earlier, Foyt had been enjoying the prospect of surging to the lead for his third Indy 500 victory. Now he feared he was about to crash.

With amazing skill, Foyt managed to guide his speeding car around the debris and shattered cars. The 33-year-old driver won the race in what was certainly one of the most challenging final laps of his career.

Anthony Joseph Foyt was born in Houston, Texas. As a child, he spent plenty of time around cars. His father owned a garage and had once been a race driver himself. Foyt enjoyed driving motorcycles, old stock cars, midget racers, and sprint cars. When he quit school at age 17, he devoted his time to learning everything he could about racing.

Later, Foyt would tell people how he had built and tested all his own cars in those days. "I . . . learned all the pitfalls of racing," he said. "It meant that nobody could put anything over on me, because I knew what I could do."

Foyt was winning national midget racing contests by the time he was 20. In 1958, at age 23, he qualified to drive in the Indianapolis 500, considered one of the top races in the world. But when his car spun on an oily spot on the track, he had to withdraw. The next year he returned to Indy to place 10th. In 1960 he won several championship races and a USAC (United States Auto Club) title.

In 1961, Foyt had a bad moment during the Indy 500, which he managed to win for the first time. He ran out of gas with ten laps left in the race. Hastily, he stopped to refuel, but in the meantime another car took the lead. Then problems overtook driver Eddie Sachs, who was in front of Foyt. When a worn tire on his car began to vibrate, he stopped to replace it. That gave Foyt just enough time to win the race, by a mere eight seconds.

In 1963 Foyt took part in some international races. He won a 252-mile race in the Bahamas. His 1964 record was outstanding as Foyt won ten races, seven of them in a row. That year, he reclaimed the Indy 500 title he had lost two years earlier, and was considered the top driver in the United States.

Although Foyt had had several close calls, he was not seriously injured in a crash until 1965. At a speed of 140 miles per hour, he had to slow down when two cars ahead of him cut their speed to enter a turn. His brakes did not work.

Foyt's car slid off the track and fell over an embankment. He suffered several broken bones and spent a few months in casts, resting in bed.

By 1967 he was back to win the Indy 500 and the national driving championship again. He won his fourth Indy championship in 1977. Foyt had said he might retire after achieving this historic fourth win, but he kept on racing, sometimes better than ever. He had won more than 150 USAC races during his long career.

Foyt was sometimes criticized for impatience and a quick temper. Some people thought he was arrogant, but others found the tough-talking Texan to be friendly. Other racers respected A.J. Foyt's skills and cool head on the track. Mario Andretti, who had raced against him many times, once said, "A.J. is a great race driver. If you are leading a race and he is in the field, you know that sooner or later he'll be nipping at you."

Frankfurter, Felix

(1882–1965)

ASSOCIATE JUSTICE OF THE U.S. SUPREME COURT

> As judges we are neither Jew nor Gentile, neither Catholic nor agnostic.
>
> —Felix Frankfurter, in *West Virginia State Board of Education v. Barnette* (1943)

Felix Frankfurter was born in 1882 in Vienna, Austria. He emigrated to America and settled in New York with his family in 1894. Frankfurter spoke no English when he arrived in the United States. However, eight years later he graduated third in his class from City College of New York. After working for a year, Frankfurter entered Harvard Law School. He graduated at the top of his class in 1906 with highest honors.

For several years Frankfurter served as an assistant to Henry Stimson, U.S. Attorney for the Southern District of New York. In 1911 Stimson became secretary of war in the cabinet of President William Howard Taft. Frankfurter moved to Washington, D.C. and continued as Stimson's assistant.

In 1914 Frankfurter became a professor of law at Harvard Law School. He taught at the law school for twenty-five years. However, he was also active in other areas during this time. After the United States entered World War I in 1917, Frankfurter served as a legal adviser to Secretary of War Newton D.

Baker. During the Paris Peace Conference in 1919, Frankfurter was a legal adviser to President Woodrow Wilson.

In the 1920s Frankfurter was a supporter of Zionism. One of his friends and fellow Zionists was Associate Justice Louis Brandeis of the U.S. Supreme Court. Frankfurter also helped to found the American Civil Liberties Union and the *New Republic*, a weekly magazine.

In 1930 Frankfurter became an adviser to Franklin D. Roosevelt, then the governor of New York. When Roosevelt became President of the United States in 1933, Frankfurter continued as one of Roosevelt's advisers. In 1939 Frankfurter resigned from the faculty of Harvard Law School when Roosevelt appointed him an associate justice of the U.S. Supreme Court.

As a Supreme Court justice, Frankfurter participated in many important decisions. One of them was the famous 1954 case *Brown v. Board of Education of Topeka*. The Supreme Court's decision in this case outlawed segregation in all U.S. public schools. The decision was unanimous. Before the Court voted, Frankfurter and Chief Justice Earl Warren worked hard for a unanimous decision. They had to do lots of research about other segregation cases and decisions. Then they tried to show their fellow justices that segregation was not legal under the terms of the U.S. Constitution.

Frankfurter was a strong supporter of basic rights guaranteed by the Constitution. However, he did not believe that Supreme Court justices should let their personal opinions decide court cases. Every decision had to be based on precedent. This policy is known as judicial self-restraint. The judges had to restrain or keep themselves from trying to remake the law.

During his long career Frankfurter corresponded with many well-known people who were his friends. These included Alfred North Whitehead and John Dewey, as well as fellow jurists Louis Brandeis, Benjamin Cardozo, Learned Hand, and Oliver Wendell Holmes, Jr.

Frankfurter was the author of several books, including *The Business of the Supreme Court* (1927), *Mr. Justice Holmes and the Supreme Court* (1938), and *Felix Frankfurter Reminisces* (1960). He suffered a stroke in the spring of 1962 and retired from the Supreme Court later that year. In 1963 President John F. Kennedy awarded Frankfurter the Presidential Medal of Freedom. Frankfurter died in Washington, D.C. two years later.

Freud, Sigmund

(1856–1939)

AUSTRIAN PSYCHOANALYST

> Have not the unconscious impulses brought out by dreams the importance of real forces in mental life? Is the ethical significance of repressed wishes to be made light of—wishes which, just as they lead to dreams, may some day lead to other things?
>
> —from Sigmund Freud's *The Interpretation of Dreams*

The name Freud is, without a doubt, one of the twentieth century's best known. A towering figure in the development of human psychology, Sigmund Freud and his ideas have permeated virtually every aspect of modern culture, from advertising and art to medicine.

Sigmund Freud was born in Freiberg, in what is now the Czech Republic, on May 6, 1856. His father was a merchant and married to his second wife, who was twenty years younger than he. Sigmund, the oldest child in the second family, later claimed to have been confused as a child about his family relationships.

In 1860, the family moved to Vienna, Austria, after Jakob Freud's business collapsed. For much of the rest of his childhood, Sigmund lived in miserable economic conditions. Though he was Jewish, he did not practice his religion past his teen years. Upon graduating from secondary school in 1873, he enrolled at the University of Vienna, where he studied medicine. He received his medical degree in 1881.

In 1882, Freud became a resident at the Vienna General Hospital. There, for three years, he was particularly interested in research on the anatomy of the human brain. He also experimented with the use of cocaine in the treatment of mental disorders and was reputed to have become addicted to it for a time (he openly admitted using the drug). About 1886, Freud married and opened his own office as a neuropathologist. He also worked at the Kassowitz Children's Clinic, where he specialized in neurology (the study of the nervous system).

In his early career, Freud did valuable research in neurophysiology. But by 1893 he was involved in his own self-analysis, and it was during this period, leading up to the turn of the century, that he began to formulate many of the ideas that would later provide the basis for modern psychoanalysis.

Freud was one of the first to believe that mental disorders could be caused purely by psychological factors rather than by physical disease or damage. At first working with Josef Breuer, he began to formulate concepts of psychology that evolved into a distinct system of psychoanalysis. One of his most important contributions was the idea of free association, in which a therapy patient is encouraged to express whatever comes to mind, rather than being asked specific questions to answer. The therapist would then analyze the meaning of the associations. He also developed the concept of transference, which describes the patient's transference of emotions and sexual feelings from his unconscious to the therapist.

Freud developed profoundly new concepts of the unconscious mind—the ego, id, and superego—and proposed that the basis for neuroses, or mental disorders, were sexual in origin. He believed that during the developmental stages of life, infantile sexuality plays a crucial role in helping shape the personality. He outlined a complex system of psychosexual development in human beings, the most controversial of which was an Oedipal stage, which described the child's sexual feelings for its mother.

Another area of interest to Freud was dreams. He suggested that these were essentially the mind's way of fulfilling wishes. These concepts were all applied to other areas of human culture, including religion and mythology.

The early part of the twentieth century was a period of time when there was an enormous public interest in psychology. Freud quickly established himself within the scientific community. But he was not the only leader in psychology; two others, Carl Jung and Alfred Adler, who initially studied with Freud and others, established themselves almost as equals, offering variations of psychoanalysis that sometimes differed greatly from those of the master. By 1914, the three had split into sharply divided camps, each gathering his own school of supporters.

During World War I, Sigmund Freud had two sons in the army and was living in war-torn Vienna under difficult economic conditions. He complained only about the scarcity of cigars. In 1923, he was diagnosed with cancer of the jaw, and for much of the rest of his life he lived in excruciating pain.

Much of Sigmund Freud's status in the field of psychology can be attributed to his popularity not in Europe, but in the United States. Though he had little interest in the country and, in fact, was severely critical of American society, predicting its collapse, the American medical profession adopted Freud's theories wholeheartedly. This was due, in part, to the large number of scientists, doctors, and psychologists from Germany and Austria who had fled to America during the Nazis' rise to power in Europe. To Adolf Hitler's way of thinking, psychoanalysis was a Jewish conspiracy, and most psychologists, many of whom were Jewish, were forced to flee Germany in the early 1930s.

Freud remained in Austria until 1938, when Nazi Germany occupied his country. Arrangements were made and bribes paid to allow him and his daughter, Anna Freud, herself a prominent psychoanalyst, to immigrate to England. Freud died shortly afterward of cancer, on September 23, 1939.

Friedan, Betty

(1921–   )

AMERICAN FEMINIST, WRITER,
AND COFOUNDER OF NOW

First, she must unequivocally say 'no' to the
housewife image. This does not mean, of
course, that she must divorce her husband,
abandon her children, give up her home.
She does not have to choose between marriage and career; that was the mistaken
choice of the feminine mystique.

—from Betty Friedan's *The*
Feminine Mystique (1963)

Writer Betty Friedan helped launch the women's movement with her 1963
book, *The Feminine Mystique*. She exploded the myth that all women could
find fulfillment solely through their husbands and children. Yet while expanding the opportunities available to women, she warned her readers not to reject
the family. Though not the sole source of fulfillment for women, the family
could and should remain one source, she insisted.

Betty Naomi Goldstein Friedan was born in Peoria, Illinois. Her father, an
immigrant Jew, began his life in the United States by selling buttons on street
corners, but through hard work became owner of a jewelry store. Her mother
edited the women's page of a Peoria newspaper, but was forced to quit her job
when she married. Her discontent with life solely as a housewife and mother
made a lasting impression on Betty.

Betty Goldstein began writing in high school, where she started a literary
magazine. After graduating in 1938, she edited the college newspaper at Smith
College in Northampton, Massachusetts. She received an undergraduate degree in psychology in 1942, then worked for a year as a researcher in psychology at the University of California at Berkeley.

She moved to New York in 1943, taking a job with a news service. When
men returning from World War II re-entered the economy in 1945, Goldstein
was forced to leave her job. Except when on maternity leave in 1949, Betty
Friedan, who got married in 1947, worked as a reporter from 1945 to 1954.
When she requested a second maternity leave in 1954, Friedan was fired and
her job was given to a man. The injustice of both firings fueled Friedan's dawn-
ing feminism. Yet from 1954 to 1957, Friedan unwittingly supported the myth

that women were happy confining themselves to domestic affairs through the articles she contributed to women's magazines.

Frustrated, she set out to prove that education did not destroy a woman's femininity or create conflict and frustration in their lives. Friedan published her findings in *The Feminine Mystique* in 1963. The book attacked the myth, which she called "the feminine mystique," that women should define themselves solely as wives, mothers, and consumers. This myth, Friedan argued, made women feel guilty and inhibited their growth, preventing them from forming their own identities, fully using their talents, and realizing their goals. The bestseller helped spark the nationwide women's movement. Friedan became a prominent spokesperson, appearing in television interviews and going on national speaking tours.

While teaching courses on non-fiction writing at New York University and the New School for Social Research from 1965 to 1970, Friedan increased her political activism. In 1966, she co-founded the National Organization of Women (NOW) and served as its first president. Under Friedan, NOW called for greater enforcement of existing laws—especially a section of the Civil Rights Act of 1964 that outlawed discrimination (unequal treatment) in hiring and promotions based on sex. NOW also urged the passage of new laws to protect the rights of women. It supported the proposed Equal Rights Amendment to the Constitution as well as the legalization of abortion. To help achieve this latter goal, Friedan co-founded the National Conference for Repeal of Abortion Laws in 1968. The group later changed its name to the National Abortion Rights Action League after the 1973 Supreme Court decision in the case of *Roe v. Wade* established a woman's right to a safe, legal abortion. Rejected by younger, more radical feminists, Friedan declined to seek reelection to the NOW presidency in 1970. That same year, however, she called for a one-day national women's strike for equality to mark the fiftieth anniversary of women gaining the vote. The event became the largest U.S. demonstration for women's rights in fifty years.

After Congress passed the Equal Rights Amendment in 1972, Friedan spent the next ten years campaigning for state approval of the amendment. Despite the efforts of Friedan and other feminists, the amendment fell three votes short of approval. In 1973, she helped found the First Women's Bank and Trust Company in New York. Three years later, she published *It Changed My Life*, an account of her campaigns for women's rights since the publication of *The Feminine Mystique*.

Friedan had always insisted that men should be regarded as allies. Although she believed women should not have to limit their interests to family and home life, she also recognized their importance to most women. Her 1981 book, *The Second Stage*, reflected this emphasis on the family. Feminists in the 1980s and 1990s, she suggested, should attempt to win changes in job policies and home life. To allow men and women to share household and family duties, she advocated more flexible work schedules and allowing either parent to take a leave of absence from work for pregnancy and childbirth. She also called for improvements in child care. Friedan's emphasis on home and family drew a heated response. Many feminists accused her of turning her back on the movement she had helped initiate. Others criticized her for ignoring issues of rape and violence against women. Friedan insisted that she was merely dealing with the reality of changing family life. The family, she contended, was too important an issue to leave to conservative activists like Phyllis Schlafly.

The differences between Friedan and many other feminists became clear in 1986. A California bank had challenged a law guaranteeing women that they would not lose their jobs during maternity leaves. In the interests of equality, NOW wanted the law extended to men who took "paternity leaves," too. Friedan—and in 1987, the Supreme Court—disagreed. Friedan favored equal treatment of men and women. But she also believed that because women carry and deliver babies, they needed the added protection of the law. This, she insisted, would insure that equal rights would not be held hostage to biology.

In 1988, Friedan began teaching such courses as "Women, Men and the Media" at the University of Southern California. She has continued to write articles and to promote issues of concern to women and families. In 1989, Friedan turned her attention to what she calls the "age mystique": the myths Americans have about aging. Friedan objects to American culture's tendency to portray the natural process of aging solely in negative terms, using such words as "decay" and "decline." To counter this, Friedan has begun offering her view of aging as a source of freedom and as an opportunity for older Americans to discover hidden strengths.

Frost, Robert

(1874–1963)

AMERICAN POET

Robert Frost was born in San Francisco. After his father's death in 1885, Frost's mother moved the family back to New England, where they lived in New Hampshire and Massachusetts. Being a teacher, Frost's mother introduced her son to poets such as William Wordsworth and Ralph Waldo Emerson, who wrote about peoples' connection to nature.

Frost did not like to study or read until he was twelve. He then found that he enjoyed high school, and he graduated in 1892 as co-valedictorian. The woman who was also valedictorian would become his wife three years later. Frost entered Dartmouth College in 1892, but dropped out after one semester. He worked at a textile mill and taught. His first poem, "My Butterfly," was published in *The Independent* in 1894. In the same year, he published four more poems in a book, *Twilight*. He printed just two copies of the book, one for himself and one for his fiancée.

Frost studied at Harvard University from 1897 to 1899. In 1900, he moved to a poultry farm in New Hampshire where he would live for twelve years. He almost died of pneumonia in 1906. Frost wrote poems which he occasionally sold for publication, but the money was not enough to live on. From 1905 to 1911 he taught English to support the family. In 1912, he sold the farm and sailed to England, wanting to establish himself as a poet.

Frost settled near London, and published two books, *A Boy's Will* (1913) and *North of Boston* (1914). They did establish him as a poet, and in 1915, Frost returned to the United States. A shy man who found success hard to handle, Frost settled on a farm in New Hampshire. He published *Mountain Interval* in 1916, and the following year began teaching at Amherst College in Massachusetts. He moved to a farm in Vermont, and founded the Bread Loaf School of English at Middlebury College. Frost also taught at Wesleyan College, the University of Michigan, Dartmouth College, Yale University, and Harvard University.

Despite the success of Frost's career, his personal life was a bit darker. His first child had died of cholera in 1900. Both his younger sister and a daughter suffered from mental illness, and he lost yet another daughter in childbirth. In 1938 his wife died and his son committed suicide shortly afterward. Because of these tragedies, Frost often suffered from severe bouts of depression.

Although he did not receive public recognition as a poet until he was forty years old, Frost became a very popular author. He won four Pulitzer Prizes for poetry, served as poetry consultant to the Library of Congress in 1958, won several honorary degrees, and he was invited to read his poem, "The Gift Outright," at the presidential inauguration of John F. Kennedy.

Fulbright, J. William

(1905–1995)

UNITED STATES REPRESENTATIVE AND SENATOR

James William Fulbright was born on April 9, 1905, in Sumner, Missouri. The family moved to Fayetteville, Arkansas a year after his birth. Fulbright graduated from the University of Arkansas at Fayetteville in 1925. He earned a Rhodes scholarship and spent several years at Oxford University in England. In 1934, he graduated from George Washington University Law School and went to work as an attorney for the Department of Justice. From 1939 to 1941 he served as president of the University of Arkansas.

In 1942, Fulbright was elected to the United States Congress. In 1943, two years before the end of World War II, he introduced a resolution calling for the creation of an organization of states to preserve the peace. He believed that "only by the collective action of a dominant group can security be attained." This resolution became the foundation of American support for the United Nations at the end of the war.

In 1944, Fulbright was elected to the United States Senate. He eventually became chairman of both the Senate Banking and Currency Committee and the Foreign Relations Committee. He voted to approve the United Nations Charter and America's participation in the organization. In 1945, the Senate passed the Fulbright Act, authorizing funds for American scholars to study abroad and for foreign students to study in the United States. In 1954, Fulbright cast the only vote in the Senate to cut off funds for the Permanent Subcommittee on Investigations, chaired by Senator Joseph McCarthy.

During the late 1960s, Fulbright, by then one of the most powerful senior members of the Senate, began to criticize America's increasing involvement in Vietnam, and eventually, along with Senators Wayne Morse and Eugene McCarthy, he came to lead congressional opposition to the war. His position on the war cost him his longtime friendship with President Lyndon Johnson. He also advocated less belligerent policies toward Communist China and Cuba.

In 1974, swept along by the anti-incumbent tide caused by the Watergate scandal, Fulbright was challenged and defeated by Dale Bumpers. Though he made his reputation as a maverick and a critic, he came to be known as one of the nation's elder statesmen on foreign affairs. He died on February 9, 1995.

Fuller, Buckminster

(1895–1983)

AMERICAN ENGINEER

Now there is one outstandingly important fact regarding Spaceship Earth, and that is that no instruction book came with it.

> —from Buckminister Fuller's *Operating Manual for Spaceship Earth* (1969)

Richard Buckminster Fuller, Jr., was born into a rich family in Milton, Massachusetts. As a small child, he had very poor vision. His life changed completely when at age four he was fitted with his first pair of glasses. Fuller later recalled, "I was filled with wonder at the beauty of the world and I have never lost my delight in it."

At Milton Academy, an expensive private high school, Fuller showed a talent for science and mathematics. But he had little patience for the school's regulations and his teachers' discipline.

Like his father, grandfather, and great-grandfather, Fuller went to Harvard University after graduation. Even though he was an intelligent student, he was soon expelled for "irresponsible conduct." During a weekend in New York, Fuller spent all of his tuition on a wild party for the performers in a Broadway show. A few months later, Harvard agreed to readmit Fuller. But in less than a year, he was again asked to leave because he would not respect the university's rules. With this experience, Fuller's formal schooling came to an end.

For the next ten years, Fuller worked at several jobs that he found uninteresting. After spending some time in the U.S. Navy, he was a manager for a canned meat factory, a salesman for a trucking company, and a machinist for a brick manufacturer. When he was dismissed from the brick company in 1927, Fuller became depressed and started drinking heavily. In desperation, he moved to a cheap apartment in Chicago, Illinois, and spent the next two years trying to sort out his life. He finally decided that he had no interest in making money. Instead, he wanted to devote himself to learning about the world and helping humankind. Specifically, he hoped to find "ways of doing more with less to the end that all people—everywhere—can have more and more of everything."

Toward this goal, Fuller started designing houses and cars that were comfortable but required few materials to make. He started a company, Dymaxion Corporation, to sell his inventions. Because of his natural skills as an engineer, Fuller was also hired as a consultant for *Fortune* magazine and for the U.S. government during World War II (1939–45).

After the war, Fuller made his greatest invention—the geodesic dome. This structure looks like half of a sphere. Its framework is made from building material arranged in a grid of triangles. The design is extremely economical. Geodesic domes require little material to build but are very sturdy.

In 1949, Fuller founded a company, Geodesics, Inc., to manufacture his domes. At first, he had few buyers. Buildings made with geodesic domes looked too strange to most contractors. Gradually, however, people warmed to Fuller's design. In 1953, the Ford Motor Company hired Geodesics to create a ninety-foot domed cover for one of its factories. The next year the Marine Corps and the U.S. Air Force asked for Fuller's help in constructing portable domes for temporary military installations.

Soon Fuller was traveling to countries such as Afghanistan, Japan, and India, to build structures for their governments. By the end of the 1950s, the geodesic dome was hailed worldwide as one of America's greatest contributions to architecture. During official talks with the U.S. government in 1959, Nikita Khrushchev, the premier of the Soviet Union, made a point of announcing, "I would like to have . . . Fuller come to Russia to teach our engineers."

That year, Southern Illinois University offered Fuller a job as a research professor. With the guarantee of a regular income, he was free to give up business and spend his time lecturing, teaching, and inventing. He excited hundreds of students with his innovative ideas. One of the most unique was the World Game. This computerized game had a serious purpose. Fuller invented it to show students that if the world's resources were distributed properly, every person would have enough food and possessions to live well. In 1972, Fuller moved to Philadelphia, Pennsylvania, where he continued his work at the University City Science Center.

Throughout the 1970s and 1980s, Fuller's reputation grew, especially among America's youth. He continued to design practical buildings, such as theaters and auditoriums. But he also came up with detailed plans for many strange and fantastic structures. For example, he designed a huge dome to cover New York City. He claimed it could conserve much of the energy used by the city.

Fuller communicated many of his ideas in his books, which have sold more than one million copies around the world. The most popular is *Synergetics: Explorations in the Geometry of Thinking* (1975). Called a "major intellectual achievement" by *Newsweek* magazine, it sets forth some of Fuller's notions about human thought and the universe.

In 1983, Buckminster Fuller died in Los Angeles at the age of eighty-seven. As in his lifetime, he continues to be regarded as one of the most inventive thinkers of the twentieth century.

Gagarin, Yuri

(1934–1968)

SOVIET COSMONAUT

> Here we go!
> —Yuri Gagarin, on liftoff for the first space flight

Yuri Alexeyevich Gagarin, the very first man to fly in space, was born on March 9, 1934, in Klushino, a small Soviet Union town west of Moscow, near Smolensk. The son of a carpenter on a collective farm, Yuri had little intention of becoming a national hero known around the world when he went to agricultural school and then to the Saratov Industrial Technical School, where he studied to become a factory worker. It was only because of his interest in flying that his future career was set.

After being encouraged by his flying-club colleagues, Yuri joined the Soviet air force in 1955. He finished training in 1957, then, for two years was stationed in the Arctic region as a pilot. In 1959, he decided to try to join the Soviet space program.

As one of the first class of cosmonaut recruits, Gagarin was stationed in Moscow. For two years the group trained, always aware that the United States also was attempting to put the first man in space.

Gagarin had little warning that he was to be the cosmonaut chosen to make history. In early April 1961, the State Commission for Space Flight made its selection. Less than two weeks later Gagarin was in the remote central Asian region of Kazakhstan, where Baikonur, the Soviet launch site, had been built. On April 12, 1961, perched in a tiny, four-and-a-half-ton capsule on top of the giant R-7 rocket with its twenty-four engines, Yuri Gagarin was hurtled into space, the first human being to leave the earth's atmosphere and make an orbit (a full circling) around the globe.

Gagarin's space capsule circled the earth at a top altitude of 187 miles from the Russian steppes (dry, treeless land with harsh temperature extremes), out across the Pacific Ocean and North America, above the Atlantic Ocean and Africa. Approaching the Soviet Union again, the craft reentered earth's atmosphere and Gagarin landed by parachute after escaping the space capsule, near Vostok. In only a few years, Gagarin's relatively unsophisticated spacecraft would be replaced by lunar landing modules, space shuttles, and enormously complex space stations. But in 1961, the entire world was astounded by his brief, record-setting circling of the world.

Gagarin's flight did not last very long—it was less than two hours. But it marked one of the greatest milestones in human history, and ignited a space race between the United States—which had hoped that Alan Shepard would be the first man to orbit the earth—and the Soviet Union. This rivalry ended only with the collapse of the Soviet Union in 1990.

Following the historic 1961 flight, Gagarin spent months traveling the world as a celebrity. He visited continental Europe, England, and North America, though not the United States. Upon returning home, he was honored with several awards, including the Order of Lenin. He was made Hero of the Soviet Union and Pilot Cosmonaut of the Soviet Union. Gagarin was then put in charge of the Soviet Union's cosmonauts in training. In 1964, he was named deputy director of the Star Town Training Center, where his country's space program was headquartered.

From 1964 to 1968, Gagarin participated in the Soviet space program in several capacities. He helped train the first Soviet women cosmonauts and was on the command control team for several space flights. In 1967, he was chosen to be backup command for the *Soyuz 3* mission, scheduled for the following year. Then, on March 27, 1968, Gagarin was killed in an airplane crash along with his instructor. It was a training flight of a two-man jet airplane, a routine procedure Gagarin had performed many times before, and an ironic fate for the man who took such tremendous risks in being rocketed into space.

A life cut short by sudden tragedy has not prevented Yuri Gagarin from leaving his mark on the world. In addition to receiving several honors in the Soviet Union—his hometown of Gzhatsk, a cosmonaut training school, and the Red Banner Air Force Academy have all been named for him—there is even a crater on the moon that bears his name. His feat launched the twentieth century's most exciting field of exploration, the conquest of space.

Gandhi, Indira

(1918–1984)

PRIME MINISTER OF INDIA

My father was a statesman, I'm a political
woman. My father was a saint, I'm not.
—Indira Gandhi, from *New York
Review of Books*, 1975

No relation to the famous Mohandas Gandhi, Indira Gandhi nevertheless was
part of one of the twentieth century's most remarkable, and violence-touched,
political families. Daughter of independent India's first leader, she led her
country through one of its most important eras, only to be murdered in the end
by her own bodyguards.

Indira Priyadarshini Nehru was born on November 19, 1917, in Allahabad,
India. At that time India was a British colony, and her father, Jawaharlal Nehru,
was, along with Mohandas "Mahatma" Gandhi and others, deeply involved in
the independence movement. In 1947 Nehru would become India's first prime
minister.

Indira received two educations: one from the everyday, frequently tumul-
tuous life as the daughter of an independence leader during a time when his actions were often deemed illegal; the other in some of India's and England's
finest schools. Prior to India's independence, Indira attended Santiniketan
University in her own country, and then Oxford University in England. In
1942, she married a lawyer and newspaper publisher named Feroze Gandhi.
Both were jailed by the British that same year for their involvement in the
struggle for India's freedom from England.

In 1947, when her father became prime minister of the newly independent
nation of India, Indira served as official hostess, becoming active in many issues relating to children, women, and welfare. During the early years of independence, she also gave birth to two sons, Rajiv and Sanjay. By 1955, she had
become prominent in her father's political organization, the National Congress
Party, which had been the primary force for independence. In 1959 she was
elected as president of the party.

Jawaharlal Nehru died in 1964, and Gandhi was asked to be minister of information and broadcasting in the succeeding government of Lal Bahadur

Shastri. Then, following his death in 1966, she was elected to lead the Congress Party, which won the national elections. Indira Gandhi filled the position of prime minister at a time when her country was in turmoil. A war with neighboring Pakistan had just ended, there were severe food shortages due to a two-year period of little rain, and unemployment plus higher prices were causing significant discontent among India's millions of poor people. By 1967, the Congress Party was losing power quickly.

Gandhi favored using strong government action to improve social and economic conditions. In 1969 she nationalized the largest banks in order to make more money and credit available to small businesses and farmers. But this and other actions alienated many leaders in her own party who favored a more free-market approach to the economy. The conservatives and older party members forced her to form a separate, liberal wing of the party. In 1970, Gandhi was compelled to govern with a coalition of liberal parties and was nearly voted out of office.

In 1971 she called for national elections a year ahead of schedule in order to consolidate her support. With a campaign message of increased, rapid change to improve the quality of life for all Indians, Gandhi and her supporters won a huge victory, taking two-thirds of the legislature seats. Her challenges, however, were not easy ones. Another war with Pakistan broke out, and it resulted in the creation of an independent state of Bangladesh (formerly East Pakistan), which received India's support. While this gained popularity for Gandhi, it also drained the national treasury, and at the same time the economy was stagnant. These factors resulted in India's worst economic crisis since independence, and civil unrest increased.

Gandhi also faced strong opposition in the legislature. When a court accused her of election abuses during the 1971 campaign and ordered her to leave office for six years, she took her son Sanjay's advice and declared a state of emergency, imposing strong measures against demonstrations and political opposition. When elections were held in 1977, Gandhi was voted out of office and arrested for corruption, though she was jailed only briefly. A year later, however, she was forced to give up her seat in Parliament (she had lost as prime minister, not as a legislator) and again was briefly jailed. But, as often happens in politics, her arrests and battles with the courts served only to increase her popularity again. In 1980, Gandhi was back in office.

Again, her term of office was difficult. Persistently unfavorable economic conditions continued to stir civil dissatisfaction and violence that the government could not control. Additionally, her refusal to condemn the Soviet Union's invasion of nearby Afghanistan brought criticism at home and from foreign leaders. In 1980, her son Sanjay was killed in an airplane crash. In June 1984, Gandhi ordered troops to put down a separatist movement by the Sikhs in Punjab, a large province in the northeast of India. Attacking the Sikhs' most revered shrine, the Golden Temple in Amritsar, the government troops killed several separatists and the Sikh people were outraged. Four months later, on October 31, 1984, Indira Gandhi was murdered by two of her own Sikh bodyguards. Rajiv Gandhi succeeded his mother as prime minister during a period of increased rioting and violence. On May 21, 1991, he, too, was assassinated while campaigning for reelection.

Gandhi, Mohandas

(1869–1948)

LEADER OF NONVIOLENT INDIAN INDEPENDENCE MOVEMENT

My personal faith is absolutely clear. I cannot intentionally hurt anything that lives, much less fellow human beings, even though they may do the greatest wrong to me and mine. Whilst, therefore, I hold the British rule to be a curse, I do not intend harm to a single Englishman or to any legitimate interest he may have in India. . . . I know that in embarking on nonviolence I shall be running what might be termed a mad risk. But the victories of truth have never been won without risks, often of the gravest character. Conversion of a nation that has consciously or unconsciously preyed upon another, far more numerous, far more ancient and no less cultured than itself, is worth any amount of risk.

—Mohandas Gandhi, on achieving goals through nonviolent means

Mohandas Karamchand Gandhi, known to the people of India as Mahatma ("great soul"), led the Indian people in a nonviolent struggle to gain independence from Great Britain. Much of what is known about his early life comes from his autobiography, *My Experiments with Truth*. He was born on October 2, 1869, in Porbandar, India, into a Vaisya (merchant) caste family of grocers and moneylenders. He was influenced deeply by his mother, a follower of a religion called Jainism, which preached nonviolence to all living things, as well as strict vegetarianism. Gandhi, a shy and serious boy, was married at the age of thirteen (a common occurrence at the time in India; less so in the twentieth century) to a girl named Kasturba, according to their parents' plans. In time they had four children of their own.

During Gandhi's childhood, the British ruled over a vast foreign empire, including India and South Africa. As a subject of the British crown, Gandhi was allowed to study law in London, and then he later returned to India to practice law in 1891. He was not very successful, however, and in 1893, he began to work for an Indian law firm in South Africa. He immediately felt the prejudice of that society toward Indians (for more than a century, South Africa, especially the east coast city of Durban, has been home to a large Indian population), and he remained there for twenty-one years, editing a newspaper called *Indian Opinion*, and leading the campaign for Indian rights in South Africa.

It was during this time that Gandhi developed his method of nonviolent struggle, which he called *satyagraha* ("steadfastness in truth"). The truth that he proclaimed was that all people, even violent oppressors, could become just and loving if their violence was met by love, rather than by more violence. He organized campaigns of civil disobedience, in which many people broke laws they considered unfair and peacefully accepted the consequences. He organized strikes by Indian mine workers, and was himself arrested by the British many times. The effectiveness of his efforts convinced many people that nonviolent struggle could be an effective tool in winning India's independence from Great Britain.

In 1915, Gandhi returned to India and organized workers who were angry at the unfair treatment they received at the hands of the British rulers of India. He used *satyagraha* to successfully oppose British laws that made it illegal to organize opposition to the government. At one point, his followers became so frustrated that they began to riot. Gandhi immediately called off the protests, and he began a fast to impress upon his followers that their behavior was more important than the immediate results of their movement. On April 13, 1919, in the northeast Indian city of Amritsar, British troops opened fire on a crowd of unarmed Indians demonstrating for independence, killing hundreds of them. Gandhi turned to direct political protest, leading the Indian National Congress in a three-year policy of noncooperation with the government. In 1930, he led hundreds of people on a two-hundred-mile march to the sea, where they made salt from sea water to protest the Salt Acts, which forced people to buy salt only from the British government. He led boycotts of British goods, and encouraged Indians to learn how to weave, to foster economic self-sufficiency, the dignity of labor, and independence from the British textile industry.

Gandhi led a life of total simplicity. He gave up the Western suits that he had worn as a young lawyer, and instead wore *dhotis*, traditional Indian garments of white cloth that were wrapped around the body, rather than tailored. Many Indians had been ashamed of wearing their traditional clothes, and Gandhi restored their pride. He wove all his own clothes, often spending several hours a day at the loom.

In his life he spent a total of seven years in jail. In addition to fighting the policies of the British government, he also worked for changes in Indian society. He tried to raise the status of the Untouchables, the lowest caste in India, whom he called Harijans ("children of God"). He worked to bring about peace between the Hindus and Muslims who shared the vast Indian subcontinent. When India finally achieved independence in 1947, Gandhi fought against its partition into a Hindu state (India) and a Muslim state (Pakistan). He began a hunger strike on January 13, 1948, at the age of seventy-eight, to protest the terrible violence that was occurring among Hindus, Muslims, and others. So great was his moral influence that five days later the leaders of the warring groups agreed to stop the fighting. On January 30, 1948, on his way to a prayer meeting in Delhi, Gandhi was assassinated by a Hindu fanatic who opposed his tolerance of Muslims.

People from all over the world mourned Gandhi's death. He showed that great love, great courage, and great strength could combine to change the world. He spoke of his whole life as an experiment with truth, and never claimed to have discovered all of it. His methods and philosophy have formed the basis of many other social justice movements around the world, including the civil rights campaign of Dr. Martin Luther King, Jr., in the United States in the 1950s and 1960s. Many of the activists whose biographies appear in this volume were inspired by Gandhi's example.

García Lorca, Federico

(1898–1936)

SPANISH POET AND PLAYWRIGHT

Returning to Granada in July 1936, Federico García Lorca looked over the vast expanses of his native Spain and told his companion, "Rafael, those fields are going to be filled with the dead." Could he have suspected that within a month, he would be one of those dead? The greatest Spanish poet of the twentieth century was murdered by fascists sometime on August 18 or 19, 1936. He was one of the first prominent victims of the Spanish Civil War.

Federico García Lorca was born on June 5, 1898, at his family's home on the fertile plains outside Granada, Spain. His father, Federico García Rodriguez, was a successful landowner and farmer; his mother, Vicenta Lorca Romero (his second wife), was a schoolteacher. He was the eldest of four children, part of a close-knit extended family that included uncles, aunts, and cousins, all of them in the area around Granada. The family's fortunes were secured and, consequently, García Lorca would have the luxury of being able to be a writer without financial worries for the entirety of his life.

In 1909, the family moved to nearby Granada so that the children could receive a better education. Federico distinguished himself in school mainly as a daydreamer and joker. But at his first love, music, he excelled. Studying with Antonio Segura Mesa, a well-known piano teacher, García Lorca aspired to attend the Paris Conservatory and have a career on the concert stage. Unfortunately, his parents were less enthusiastic about that idea. When Segura Mesa died in 1916, Federico's dream died with him.

García Lorca's father intended his eldest son to become a lawyer and a man of stature. But Federico was already dabbling in literature when he entered college. He was bored by most of his classes at the University of Granada, with the notable exception of his literature class. His professor, Martín Dominguez Berrueta, firmly believed in the broadening effects of travel, and he encouraged Federico in that pursuit. Following his professor's advice, he traveled extensively in Spain, and his first published book, *Impressions and Landscapes* (1918), is a record of those trips.

During the summer of 1919, Granada was visited by Gregorio Martínez Sierra, an important theatrical producer who was on the lookout for an innovative talent. After hearing García Lorca read, he asked the young poet to try his hand at writing a play based on one of his poems. The play that resulted, *The Butterfly's Evil Spell* (1920), was a disastrous failure, and it would be seven years before García Lorca tried to have another play of his produced.

By 1920, García Lorca had accumulated a large body of poems. In early 1921, his *Poems 1921* received a few respectful reviews then dropped out of sight.

Poems of the Deep Song (1931) grew out of a competition that García Lorca entered, half in jest, to compose an example of the Andalusian genre, *canto jonde* (deep song), a Gypsy-influenced song style of which he was quite fond. This interest, which not only produced one of his best collections of poetry, also brought him into contact with the Gypsy community, leading to another "song" book, *Romancero Gitano* (1928), a series of poems in the style of the Gypsy *romance* songs, mostly ballads.

One reason why it took so long for García Lorca to publish his poetry in book form was that he was much more comfortable reading it aloud. Read aloud, the poem retained not only the sound values that he worked so hard to put into it, but also had more *duende*, one of those untranslatable local terms that can best be described as a combination of "magic" and "soul." For García Lorca, *duende* was the key element not only in his poetry and in Spanish culture, but in all great art.

The late 1920s were a complicated time for him. He was embarking on new projects—drawing and publishing a literary magazine—and experimenting with new poetic forms. He was also coming to terms with his homosexuality.

Contact with Salvador Dalí and filmmaker Luis Buñuel helped draw García Lorca definitively into the Spanish surrealist orbit. That change in direction can be clearly seen in his poetry written in the late 1920s and early 1930s, with their juxtaposition of unusual images and metaphors, and their fascination with the bizarre and unpleasant.

In 1929, García Lorca took his first trip outside Spain, going to Columbia University in New York, by way of France and England. He spent much of his time with the Spanish-speaking faculty members or with the Spanish or Latin American writers circles scattered around the city. At night he would go back the dorm and write poetry. He went to the theater, movies, up to Harlem, and was on hand when the stock market crashed, in 1929.

The literary product of this period, generally not a happy one for García Lorca, was *A Poet in New York* (which was not published until after his death). One of his most famous books, it is full of dark and brooding poems in which the city is seen as a dreary world of machines and oppressed people of color.

By the spring of 1930, he accepted an invitation to lecture in Havana, Cuba. He spent two months there, delighted to be in a warm atmosphere with a Spanish-influenced culture.

On his return to Spain, García Lorca stayed at his father's country house near Granada, and he embarked on what became the most productive period of his writing life. He helped found a theater company, La Barraca, in response to the founding of the first Spanish Republic, with its democratic ideals and artistic openness, and he wrote his best plays for them, *Blood Wedding*, *Yerma*, and *The House of Bernarda Alba*. These are stark poetic tragedies about violence tearing apart families and communities, and they are among the most successfully realized verse plays written in this century.

The death in the bull ring of an old friend, the bull fighter Ignacio Sánchez Mejías, in 1934 was a terrible blow to García Lorca, who began work shortly after on a long poem, *A Flood of Tears for Ignacio Sánchez Mejías* (1935). The poem was yet another success for García Lorca, coming on the heels of *Blood Wedding* and *Yerma*.

García Lorca was now a public figure. Over the last months of his life, he was hard at work on additional plays and a book of sonnets. But in 1936, fascist forces led by Francisco Franco attempted a coup (an overthrow of an existing government) that led to a civil war that raged for three years.

García Lorca returned to Granada in July to see his family and to celebrate his father's saint's day. He arrived on July 14; Franco's troops began their rebellion in the North African colonies three days later. On the twentieth, fascist sympathizers in the Granada garrison rose up in concert with them and took control of most of the city. Gangs of thugs roamed the streets, picking up anyone whose politics (or faces) they didn't like and killing them. García Lorca knew they would be looking for him; he was an artist of known liberal sympathies, and a gay man. Sometime on the day of August 16, García Lorca was arrested by a former member of Parliament, Ramón Ruiz Alonso. He was taken to the government headquarters and held there for about thirty-six hours, tortured, shot with other prisoners, and buried in an unmarked grave. He was thirty-eight.

He left behind a large number of unfinished books of poetry, but his legacy was firmly established. He was the best of the many great poets of the so-called Generation of 1927, one of the most important poets of the first half of this century.

García Márquez, Gabriel

(1927–   )

COLOMBIAN NOVELIST, SHORT-STORY WRITER, SCREENWRITER, AND JOURNALIST

Faced with [the possibility of the destruction of humanity on Earth] that must have seemed a mere utopia through all human time, we, the inventors of tales, who will believe anything, feel entitled to believe that it is not yet too late to engage in the creation of the opposite utopia. A new and sweeping utopia of life, where no one will be able to decide for others how they die, where love will prove true and happiness be possible, and where races condemned to one hundred years of solitude will have, at last and forever, a second opportunity on earth.

—Gabriel García Márquez, in his Nobel Prize lecture

Gabriel García Márquez was born on March 6, 1927, in Macondo, a small town near the Atlantic coast of Colombia, Arataca. Gabriel was the oldest son of Gabriel Eligio García, the town's telegraph operator. His mother's family had opposed her marriage to García, who had been on the other side in bloody political fighting, but when Gabriel was born, they gladly accepted their new grandson, and for the first eight years of his life, he was raised by them.

García Márquez has said that his childhood was a wondrous time. He came under the spell of his grandmother, a fantastic weaver of tales; and his military hero grandfather, also a splendid storyteller. From his grandmother, the young boy heard yarns of the supernatural that would eventually find their way into his novels in the form of "magical realism"; from her husband, he heard stirring stories of the military exploits of men of valor and power who would serve as the models for many of his protagonists. When his grandfather died in 1936, that idyllic time ended, and Gabriel went to the port city of Sucre to live with his parents.

Reunited with his parents, Gabriel was sent to school in nearby Baranquilla, then was awarded a scholarship to the national high school in Zipaquirá, near the capital, Bogotá. He graduated from the school in 1946 and began law studies while living in Bogotá.

In 1947, the young law student published his first short story, an eerie tale of the supernatural, "The Third Resignation." Over the next five years, he would publish fourteen more tales in the city's newspapers. Already he was being drawn away from the legal profession toward literature. Events would shortly propel him in that direction even more quickly.

On April 9, 1948, a popular progressive politician was assassinated. It was the beginning of a period of near civil war that Colombians refer to as *la violencia;* it lasted into the 1960s and claimed the lives of several hundred thousand people. For the duration of the street fighting, the university was closed down, and García Márquez transferred to the university at Cartagena.

In Cartagena, he found himself a position as a reporter on the city's daily newspaper. That was the end of law school. He would move from one newspaper to another, and by 1955 he had become a nationally known journalist, working in the capital. In the meantime, he was also still writing fiction, introducing the fictional town of Macondo in a 1955 story, "Monologue of Isabel Watching It Rain in Macondo." He published his first novel, *Leaf Storm*, the same year. While he was on assignment in Europe for *The Spectator*, his Bogotá paper, Rojas Pinilla, the dictator of Colombia, closed down the paper for embarrassing his government with its reporting. García Márquez found himself alone and penniless in Paris, France.

He began writing two new books simultaneously, *In Evil Hour* (1957) and *Nobody Writes to the Colonel* (1961). When he completed the first of these, he traveled through Eastern Europe, then to London, England, where he stayed for two months before returning home.

Back in Colombia, he married his childhood sweetheart, Mercedes Barcha, and he resumed his newspaper work. When Fidel Castro took power in Cuba in 1959, García Márquez agreed to serve with the Cuban news agency Prensa Latina, opening a Bogotá office, working in Havana and finally in New York. After a year, he resigned and moved with his now growing family (Mercedes had had a boy) to Mexico City. In quick succession, he had three books published there—the two that he had written in Paris; and a collection of short stories, *Big Mama's Funeral* (1962).

In the 1960s, García Márquez was active in the busy Mexican film industry, but he was not satisfied. One day in January 1965, García Márquez was driving from Mexico City to Acapulco when he had a vision of the magical history of

Macondo. For the next eighteen months, he wrote in a veritable frenzy. The result was *One Hundred Years of Solitude*, a masterpiece that propelled him to the front ranks not only of Latin American novelists, but of world literature.

One Hundred Years is the multigenerational saga of Macondo, from its founding by the Buendía family to its destruction by a hurricane a century later. Like his other books, it is at once poetic, dreamlike, and yet fast-moving, a tragicomic family chronicle that takes in both the real and the fantastic.

With this global success, García Márquez could afford to live comfortably for a while. He moved with his family to Barcelona, Spain, where they lived for the next four years. Then he established a home in Cuernavaca, Mexico, shuttling between there and Colombia, after being invited to return home by the president of the country.

García Márquez published two more successful books: a collection of short stories set in Macondo, *Innocent Erendira* (1971); and a novel about an aging dictator, *Autumn of the Patriarch* (1975). He also resumed his journalistic activities because there were issues he felt the need to address. He founded a progressive political magazine in Bogotá, and has written newspaper columns on and off since, as well. One product of his journalistic writing was *Clandestine in Chile* (1986), a short book about the filmmaker Miguel Littin, a Chilean who secretly returned home from exile to make an underground film about the brutal dictatorship of General Augusto Pinochet.

In 1982, García Márquez was awarded the Nobel Prize for Literature. He has continued to turn out novels of considerable stature. His novella, *Chronicle of a Death Foretold* (1981), was filmed by the Italian director Francesco Rosi, and served as the basis for a musical play in 1995. A series of films based on several of his stories was made and released in 1989. His three most recent novels have varied widely in subject matter and tone. *Love in the Time of Cholera* (1984), is a gentle comic fable of the growing relationship between two elderly people. By contrast, *The General in His Labyrinth* is a somber portrait of the great liberator Simón Bolívar at the end of his life. García Márquez's latest novel, *Of Love and Other Demons* (1994), is a dark and brooding tale of the supernatural, eros, and death.

García Márquez has been a figure of some controversy because of his frank and open championing of socialism and his friendship with prominent political figures ranging from Cuba's Fidel Castro to France's François Mitterrand. However, he has eschewed the opportunity to write directly political fiction (although his general political sentiments are unmistakable), preferring to explore the inner resources of the heart and possibilities of the fabulous.

Gates, Bill

(1955–   )

AMERICAN FOUNDER OF
MICROSOFT

[I want] to have a computer on every desk
and in every home, all running Microsoft
software.

—Bill Gates, on his personal goal.

William H. Gates was born in Seattle, Washington. The only son of a lawyer
and a teacher, he grew up in a close family. Recognizing his exceptional intelligence at an early age, his parents sent him to Lakeside School, a challenging
and expensive private school near their home.

When Bill was thirteen, Lakeside bought some time for its students on a
computer at a local company. A math whiz, he liked computing instantly.

Gates soon found a practical use for his new obsession. At fourteen, he
founded and became the president of Traf-O-Data. Towns outside Seattle
hired the company to use computers to monitor traffic. In its first year, Gates
and his friends earned $20,000. But they had trouble keeping clients once it
was discovered that the company was operated by a group of high school students.

While he was still in high school, Gates's talent became known to TRW, a
nearby computer company. It offered him a position as a computer programmer. Lakeside gave him permission to put his studies aside in his senior year to
take the $20,000-a-year job.

In 1973, Gates left home to attend Harvard University. There, he began
studying to become a lawyer. For a while, his interest in computers waned. But
in late 1974, his old friend Paul Allen came to Gates with an idea that would
change his life. Allen had seen an article in a magazine about the Altair 8800,
the first home computer. The computers Gates and Allen had worked on as
boys were huge and difficult to operate. The Altair was different. It was small,
and its inventor hoped someday to make it so easy to run that anyone could
learn to use it.

According to the article, no one had developed software for the Altair yet.
Without software the invention was worthless. Knowing that the Altair's manufacturer, MITS, was eager to start selling the computer, Gates and Allen im-

mediately called the company's president. When the young men told him they had created the software the Altair needed, the president asked them to meet with him at MITS headquarters in Albuquerque, New Mexico.

The invitation was both thrilling and terrifying to Gates and Allen. They were eager to work with the president. But they had lied to him on the telephone. They had not even begun work on creating the software they said they had already developed.

Frantic but confident, Gates and Allen started work. For days and nights at a time, they barely left Gates's dorm room as they puzzled over the problem. Even though they knew nothing more about the Altair than what they had read, they soon had the software other programmers had been unable to make. Gates later said, "That's the coolest program I ever did. We just had this book that described the machine. If we had read the book wrong, or the book was wrong, we were hosed." Luckily for him and his friend, their software worked perfectly.

Deciding to waste no time, Gates dropped out of college, moved to Albuquerque, and, with Allen, founded a company named Microsoft. They started making software for MITS until the computer firm went out of business. Microsoft then moved to the Seattle area and started working with other, bigger companies, such as Apple Computers, Commodore Computers, and the Tandy Corporation.

Microsoft's big break came in 1980. In that year, Gates made a deal with IBM, the largest computer company in the United States. For IBM, he created MS-DOS—Microsoft disc operating system. This program would be used to operate all of the home computers made by IBM. For the rights to MS-DOS, IBM agreed to pay Microsoft royalties. These royalties now amount to more than $200 million a year.

In 1983, Allen became ill with cancer and left the company. Suddenly, Gates had to run the fast-growing Microsoft alone. Working long hours, he quickly rose to the occasion. Unlike many programmers, he proved to be as brilliant at running a business as he was at running a computer.

Gates's business skill has made him one of the richest people in America. He owns almost half of Microsoft's stock. The price of the stock rose so high in 1987 that Gates's share was valued at more than a billion dollars. At the time, he was only thirty-one, making him the youngest American billionaire ever.

Gates continues to head Microsoft, but has publicly said he hopes soon to stop working so hard and take some time off to raise a family. To his competitors, this comes as good news. As one rival, Willard Peterson of the WordPerfect Corporation, has said, "We'd love to see Bill get married and have a few kids. We'd love to see him mellow out."

Gehrig, Henry Louis

(1903-1941)

AMERICAN BASEBALL PLAYER

The new player waited in the batter's box. It was June 1, 1925, and 21-year-old Lou Gehrig had been sent to bat as a pinch hitter for one of his teammates. His single was the first of many hits he would pile up. For the next fifteen seasons and for 2,130 games in a row, Lou Gehrig would be playing ball for the New York Yankees. The "Iron Man of Baseball" would have played even longer, but a tragic disease ended Gehrig's career at age 36.

Henry Louis Gehrig was born on June 19, 1903, in New York City. His parents were German immigrants and Lou was the only one of their four children to survive to adulthood. His father worked at different jobs, mostly as a janitor and ironworker, and Lou's mother worked as a cleaning woman. When he was old enough, Lou got jobs after school and during the summers to help his family. Bright and athletic, he worked hard at both school and sports, including soccer, football, and baseball. His parents had high hopes for their son and expected him to go to college.

In high school Lou stood out among all his peers in the New York area. When he started college at Columbia University, he played both football and baseball. Lou had a scholarship to Columbia but had to work as a waiter in a restaurant after classes to supplement it. His mother worked extra hours as a cook to help her son.

Lou was a sophomore in college when a Yankee scout made him a timely offer, including a $1,500 bonus, to join the team. Both his parents had been ill, and Lou knew his earnings were needed. In 1923 and 1924, Gehrig was a pinch hitter. He spent games on the bench waiting until someone on the regular roster was unable to play. Then came his turn, in June 1925. From then on, he was one of the Yankees' most reliable batters and their everyday first baseman.

At that time, Babe Ruth was the big star of the Yankees. Gehrig followed him in the batting order, and some thought he hit the ball harder, although not always farther. Babe's home runs and flamboyant personality brought him most of the attention. Gehrig was a quiet man who spent his time off the field with his family and wife Eleanor. Called a "gentle giant," Gehrig was loved by his teammates and considered to be the second-best player in the group. "I'm not a headline kind of guy," he would say when people commented on how his teammate, Ruth, dominated the news.

Gehrig was known for the steady confidence he inspired in his teammates and his ability to hit when the stakes were high. In each of his thirteen full seasons he drove in more than 100 runs; he led the league five times, once driving in 184 runs. He hit a total of 493 home runs (plus 10 in several World Series) and was voted Most Valuable Player in the American League four times—an all-time record.

In 1938 Gehrig felt unusual weakness and pain in his arms and legs. He had been playing baseball for a long time, so it seemed possible that his problems stemmed from years of exertion. But when the symptoms got worse, Gehrig could no longer hide or overcome them. He could not control the bat properly or throw the ball in from the infield. People wondered what was wrong. Manager Joe McCarthy had such a high regard for Lou that despite the sagging performance, he said, "Gehrig plays as long as he wants to play."

On May 2, 1939, Lou Gehrig asked that he be removed from his team's lineup. He said it "would be best for the club." Gehrig was diagnosed with a disease called amyotrophic lateral sclerosis. The disease causes hardening of the brain and the spinal cord, which contains the motor nerves that move parts of the body. Victims of the disease become paralyzed, then die.

Gehrig faced the news that he had an incurable disease with the same courage and lack of self-pity he had shown throughout his life. On July 4, 1939, more than sixty thousand fans and teammates jammed Yankee Stadium for "Lou Gehrig Appreciation Day." Moved to tears, Lou Gehrig stood at home plate and spoke through a microphone, thanking his friends and expressing his feelings. "Today I consider myself to be the luckiest man on the face of the earth," he said. He called his illness "a bad break" and went on to praise the people he had loved and worked with during his life—his parents, his wife, his fellow Yankees. At times, he needed help to stand up. People wept openly, including Babe Ruth, as Gehrig spoke. A special election brought him into the Baseball Hall of Fame that same year.

Lou Gehrig died on June 2, 1941, just before his 38th birthday. His courageous story was reenacted in a movie called *The Pride of the Yankees*, in which Gehrig was portrayed by popular film star Gary Cooper. In 1969, sportswriters chose him as the best first baseman of all time. His friend and manager Joe McCarthy once said of Gehrig, "He's been a great ball player. Fellows like him come along once in a hundred years. . . . More than that, he's been a vital part of the Yankee club . . . He's always been a perfect gentleman, a credit to baseball. We'll miss him."

Geisel, Theodor Seuss

(1904–1991)

AMERICAN AUTHOR AND ILLUSTRATOR

Best known as the beloved "Dr. Seuss," Theodor Seuss Geisel was born in Springfield, Massachusetts. His father was a superintendent of Springfield's public parks, and his mother was an author and vice-president of Beginner Books, which Geisel founded. Geisel received his B.A. from Dartmouth College in 1925, and did graduate study at Oxford University in England and the Sorbonne in Paris.

Geisel thought that he would become a college English professor. However, after graduate school in 1926, he worked as a freelance cartoonist for magazines. When Geisel wrote a cartoon about a pesticide that was produced by the Standard Oil Company, the company hired him in 1928 to draw their advertisements. For fifteen years, Geisel produced unusual insects and monsters for their motor oil division.

On a boat trip from Europe to the United States in 1936, Geisel began to compose a nonsense poem set to the beat of the ship's engine. He then drew pictures to go with it, and in 1937 he published *And to Think That I Saw It on Mulberry Street*. His first children's book, set in Springfield, portrays the vivid imagination of a young boy. In the story, a horse-drawn wagon becomes a parade of odd vehicles and creatures.

During World War II, Geisel stopped writing in order to work for the war effort. He made documentary films for the Information and Education Division of the U.S. Army. Geisel won two Academy Awards for his documentaries, "Hitler Lives" and "Design for Death," about the Japanese war effort.

Geisel's early books were all successful, but his book *The Cat in the Hat* made him an icon of children's literature. The story, which used a small number of simple rhyming words, changed the way young children could learn to read. With the success of *The Cat in the Hat*, Geisel founded Beginner Books. The publishing company was later bought by Random House, and Geisel became its president.

All of Geisel's books are written in a rhyming, swiftly paced style. They are whimsical, fantastical, and convey a sense of morality. Some of his classics include *Green Eggs and Ham* (about trying new experiences), *The Lorax* (about the environment), and *Fox in Socks* (a book of tongue-twisters). A few of his later books seemed to address an adult audience as well. *The Butter Battle Book* is about the nuclear arms race, and *You're Only Old Once* is about growing old.

Theodor Seuss Geisel is an important figure in American literature because he revolutionized the teaching of reading as well as children's book publishing.

Gershwin, George

(1898–1937)

AMERICAN PIANIST
AND COMPOSER

Jacob Gershwin was born in Brooklyn, New York, to poor parents. Before he changed his name to George, he taught himself to play the piano by age twelve; two years later he was a pupil of Charles Hasibitzer. Gershwin dropped out of New York's High School for Commerce to work for Jerome H. Remick and Company, a music publisher on Tin Pan Alley. Gershwin made $15 a week as a song plugger (someone who promoted a company's songs by playing them for interested performers).

In 1917, Gershwin became the rehearsal pianist for *Miss 1917*, a musical by Jerome Kern and Victor Herbert. During that time he was studying music harmony and orchestration with private teachers and writing his own songs. By 1918 a music company offered him $35 a week for the rights to publish whatever he wrote. His first hit song was "Swanee," sung by Al Jolson in 1920. He wrote the score for the Broadway musicals *A Dangerous Maid* (1921) and *Our Nell* (1922). In 1924, he wrote the music, and his older brother Ira the lyrics, for *Lady, Be Good!* which starred Fred Astaire on Broadway.

Gershwin was not just a popular composer; he was also the first musician to bring jazz music into concert halls, and he became famous for composing and performing *Rhapsody in Blue* and *An American in Paris*. Then in 1929 he made his debut as a conductor of the New York Philharmonic Orchestra in Lewisohn Stadium. In addition to writing the stream of pop songs like "S'wonderful" (1927), "Embraceable You" (1930), and "I Got Rhythm" (1934), he went to Hollywood and wrote scores for films in the late 1930s such as *Shall We Dance?*, *Damsel in Distress*, and *Goldwyn Follies*.

As prolific as Gershwin was, he still made time to tour in American cities and perform with major orchestras. By far the most ambitious work that he was to compose in his short life was the full-length opera *Porgy and Bess* (1935), which was based on Dubose Heyward's novel about the lives of rural blacks living in South Carolina. The drama of the story was as moving as the music was lively and powerful.

George Gershwin died of a brain tumor at the age of thirty-eight when he was at the height of his creativity. Over fifty years after his death, his work is as popular and relevant as ever.

Giacometti, Alberto

(1901–1966)

SWISS SCULPTOR

> The explanation as to why my figures had become so thin did not occur to me until later, on a day when I was carrying a sculpture to an exhibition. I picked it up with one hand and put it on the seat of the taxi. At that moment I realized that it was very light and that life-size figures irritate me, after all, because a person passing by on the street has no weight; in any case, he's much lighter than the same person when he's dead or has fainted. He keeps his balance with his legs. You don't feel your weight. I wanted—without having thought about it—to reproduce this lightness . . .
>
> —Alberto Giacometti, in a conversation published in 1963

Alberto Giacometti was born in Bogonava, near Stampa, Grisons, in the alpine region of southern Switzerland on October 10, 1901. He was surrounded by art almost from birth. Giacometti's father, Giovanni Giacometti, was a landscape painter; and his godfather, Cuno Amiet, was also a painter, a Fauve, and one of Switzerland's principal advocates of Art Nouveau. From a young age Giacometti exhibited talents for drawing, painting, and modeling. In fact, he could not decide initially whether to become a painter or a sculptor. Eventually, however, he chose the latter career.

Giacometti went to the public schools at Grisons. He studied painting with his father in 1919, and in 1920 he and his father went to the Venice Biennale, an important international art fair. Giacometti remained in Italy until 1921 to continue his studies. In 1922, he moved to Paris, France, and for the next two years he studied drawing and sculpture with Antoine Bourdelle at the Académie de la Grande Chaumière. Bourdelle had been one of the sculptor Auguste Rodin's assistants, and his influence on sculpture was significant. Giacometti left the Grande Chaumière after three years, believing that Bourdelle could no longer teach him anything.

From 1925 onward, he shared a studio with his brother, Diego, who was also a sculptor and designer. Together, they designed furniture, lighting fixtures, vases, and other furnishings. The family affair continued in 1927 when Giacometti's first exhibition in Switzerland was held at the Gallery Aktuaryus in Zurich; the show included paintings by his father.

Three distinct phases marked Giacometti's career. The influence of cubism is evident in his early work. As he moved beyond cubism in the late 1920s into his second phase, he first began to attract attention as an avant-garde sculptor. In 1926 he abandoned the academic style of sculpture. From that point, through the first half of the 1930s, Giacometti associated with the surrealists. In 1932, during his surrealist phase, his first one-man exhibition in Paris took place at the Gallery Pierre Colle.

Giacometti struggled with an artistic conflict between abstract forms and the literal representation of the human body. By the middle of the 1930s, he decided that his surreal constructions carried him too far beyond actuality's bounds; as a result, Giacometti rejected the surrealists and returned to a much more representational aesthetic. For the next decade, he worked on a theory of perception. Seeking to represent reality, Giacometti searched for new ways of seeing; one practical result was his sculptures with small heads and figures to emphasize objects seen.

During World War II, Giacometti lived in Geneva, but he returned to Paris in 1945. In the late 1940s and early 1950s, he developed his elongated (stretched) and skeletal style of human figuration for which he is renowned. The early 1950s marked his third phase. Giacometti underwent another artistic crisis that led to his development of another mystical conception of art. He now viewed his work not as the representation of explicit reality *per se*, but what lay behind appearances, an intangible reality. By the late 1950s, Giacometti garnered international fame.

One of the many highlights in his artistic career was his set design for Samuel Beckett's influential play, *Waiting for Godot*, which was first performed in Paris in 1953. The 1955 retrospective of his works at the Guggenheim Museum in New York and at the Arts Council in London also ranked as career highlights, as did, a decade later, the retrospectives held at the Tate Gallery in London and the Museum of Modern Art in New York. In 1964, Giacometti received the Guggenheim International Award; one year later, he received the Grand Prize in Art of the City of Paris.

Gide, André

(1869–1951)

FRENCH NOVELIST, DIARIST,
TRAVEL WRITER, PLAYWRIGHT,
AND ESSAYIST

My writings can be compared to Achilles's
spear, with which a second contact cured
those it had first wounded. If one of my
books disconcerts you, reread it; under the
obvious poison, I took care to hide the anti-
dote; each one of them aims less to disturb
than to warn.

—André Gide

French writer André Gide was born on November 22, 1869, in Paris, France,
to conservative, wealthy parents. His father was a professor of law at the University of Paris; his mother was from a wealthy family with extensive estates in
Normandy. André was sent to the exclusive École Alsacienne when he was
nine, but was expelled after only a few months. His father died when he was
only eleven, and his mother, convinced that he was too delicate for school, kept
him home.

Madame Gide was a severe, austere Protestant who controlled every aspect
of André's life, from what he wore to what he read, and who continued to give
him advice until her death, when Gide was twenty-five.

Although Gide showed great promise as a pianist, after he finished his bachelor's degree (B.A.), he decided to pursue a career as a writer. To that end, he
sequestered himself in a Swiss mountain resort town and wrote his first novel,
The Notebooks of André Walter (1891). Although the novel suffers from the im-
maturity of its author, it already shows signs of the key themes and structures
of Gide's fictional world—the renunciation of love in the name of a desire for
purity, the use of a structuring device that draws attention to the process of
writing. The book was printed at Gide's own expense, and nobody outside his
immediate circle of friends and family bought it. That summer, he and his
cousin Madeleine announced their engagement.

André Walter was a novel about the failure of renunciation, while *The
Lovers' Attempt* (1893) was a novel about the failure of physical love, focusing
on a young couple who soon grow bored with their happy relationship. Gide
was attending the regular Tuesday-evening gatherings at the home of the great

symbolist poet Stephane Mallarmé. The influence of the symbolists—with their hazy imagery and abstract metaphors—can be seen in the second book.

In the fall of 1893, Gide left for a trip to North Africa with a friend, Paul Albert Laurens, a young painter. Freed from the claustrophobic atmosphere of the Paris salons, and far away from the prying eyes of his mother, Gide basked in the North Africa sun and breezes, opening himself up to his senses, and admitting to himself that he was sexually attracted to men. When he encountered writer Oscar Wilde on a second North African jaunt the following year, Wilde and his lover, Lord Alfred Douglas, recognized Gide's reticence and talked him out of it. Fully aware now of his gayness, Gide would carry the opening of that door into his writing, which became more open and disciplined, as well.

The two books that grew out of his African trips, *Marshlands* (1895) and *Fruits of the Earth* (1897) were, respectively, a satirical jibe aimed at the Parisian claustrophobia, and a celebration of the liberation he had finally embraced. A philosophy of complete detachment, accompanied by personal liberation, was a radical position to adopt at the turn of the century, and Gide's mother was horrified. She had objected at first to his proposed marriage to Madeleine, but now she saw her niece as a potentially stabilizing influence, to replace her own when the time came for her to depart. That time came in 1895, and the wedding took place five months after her death. Gide reflected on the difficulties of the marriage in both *Strait Is the Gate* and *The Immoralist* (1902).

With the latter novel, Gide entered into the peak of his fiction writing, a period of intense productivity that lasted through the publication of *The Counterfeiters*, in 1926.

The Immoralist was by far Gide's most infamous novel, a first-person story told by a man who, after a brush with death, resolves to live for himself, a decision that ultimately leads to the death of his wife. Gide felt that this was a book that only a small handful of people would understand, so he restricted the first edition to a tiny press run of only three hundred copies.

In 1909, Gide and a group of friends founded *La Nouvelle Revue Française* (*The New French Review*, NRF), which quickly came to be one of the most influential journals and publishing houses in French literature, a position its publishing arm still holds today. Gide entrusted his next major novel, *Strait Is the Gate* (1909), to the journal. The success of NRF helped contribute to Gide's reputation as a man of letters. *Strait* is a mirror image of *The Immoralist*, with a female protagonist who lives only for others and is destroyed by her self-sacrificing nature.

Lafacadio's Adventure (1914) outraged many readers with its scathing satire of Catholicism, unquestioning acceptance of homosexuality as normal, and a hero who cheerfully commits a murder just to prove a point.

World War I presented a series of turning points for Gide. He worked for the Red Cross aiding Belgian refugees. In his journals (which were published in four volumes after his death), he admitted that the terrible destructiveness of the war was leading him to a crisis of conscience and the abandonment of conventional religion. But his growing love affair with Marc Allegret (who would one day become a noted French filmmaker) became a source of comfort. It was the first time he had ever been in a relationship that combined romantic and physical love. When he and Allegret took a trip to England in 1918, Madeleine, enraged, burned all his letters. He was appalled, for he thought the letters contained his best work.

With the end of the war and the coming of the 1920s, Gide was beginning to achieve some fame beyond literary circles. His preaching of an ethic of complete sincerity struck a responsive chord in the surrealists, among others. But in 1924, perhaps in keeping with that philosophy, he risked everything by publishing a Socratic dialogue under the title *Corydon*, in which he offered a systematic defense of homosexuality. *If It Die . . .* , his autobiography, published two years later, took that logic to the next level.

As a result of these two books, many of Gide's friends abandoned him. To escape their negative feelings toward him, he sold off his estates and traveled to French Equatorial Africa with Allegret. The trip that produced his first travel book, *Travels in the Congo* (1925), a work that turned out to be a bitter attack on the brutality of French colonial rule and racism.

He returned to France, where his latest novel, *The Counterfeiters*, had been published in his absence. This intricate novel-within-a-novel is one of the key works of the high-modernist period.

In the 1930s, Gide became involved with the political left, opposing the fascists in Spain and the rising tide of Nazism. In 1936, he visited the Soviet Union, where he was acclaimed as the world's greatest living novelist. He was appalled by what he saw there, however. On his return home, he wrote two books in which he turned away from his previous support for the Soviet system. He never again allowed himself to become politically active.

During World War II, Gide lived in Provence, France, and in North Africa in Algeria. After the conflict's conclusion, he wrote and published his last major work, *Theseus* (1946), in which he reworked the Greek myth of the slayer of the Minotaur as a philosophical parable.

In 1947, Gide received the Nobel Prize for Literature. His career, though, was essentially over. He died on February 19, 1951, in Paris, at the age of eighty-two.

Gorbachev, Mikhail

(1931–   )

ARCHITECT OF SOVIET PERESTROIKA

The guilt of Stalin and his immediate entourage before the party and the people for the mass repressions and lawlessness they committed is enormous and unforgivable.

—Mikhail Gorbachev, 1987

Soviet leader Mikhail Gorbachev was born in Stavropol in the Soviet Union on March 2, 1931. From a peasant family, he spent his youth driving farm equipment and experiencing the difficulties that most of the Soviet workers felt during the rule of Joseph Stalin, when the agricultural and industrial systems were seriously deficient. In 1952, Gorbachev joined the Communist Party, and in 1955 he received a law degree from the University of Moscow.

When Stalin died in 1953, the Soviet Union went through a period of confusion, with its leaders competing for power. Nikita Khrushchev, who eventually took over as Soviet leader, launched a new era in Soviet politics when he was the first to publicly condemn Stalin and his brutal policies. It was this fresh approach that attracted Gorbachev. After finishing law school he returned to Stavropol to work for the Young Communist League, or the Komsomol, with the encouragement of Yuri V. Andropov, a rising star in the Communist Party. Andropov made Gorbachev secretary of the regional Central Committee in 1966.

When Khrushchev was deposed in 1964, Gorbachev and others hoped for a more rapid program of political, social, and economic reforms. Instead, Leonid Brezhnev took control of the country. With his conservative approach, he reversed many of the gains that had begun under Khrushchev. Gorbachev bided his time, working within the party system under the protection of Andropov. In 1978, Brezhnev made him a party secretary for agricultural administration. Gorbachev vigorously set about dealing with the problems and shortages related to agricultural production and transportation. In 1980, he and Andropov, who succeeded Brezhnev upon the latter's death, became members of the Soviet Politburo, the ruling body, and quickly put the Soviet Union on a fast-paced modernization program. Both men understood that significant change to a system more closely resembling Western economies was necessary if the Soviet Union were to survive.

Andropov died soon after taking office, and again Gorbachev had to wait while the successor, Konstantin U. Chernenko, a conservative, slowed down the reforms again. Then, in 1985, after Chernenko died, Gorbachev finally controlled the power of the Soviet Union. His goals were to improve relations with the Western powers, improve the economy by adopting Western concepts of trade and production, and reinvigorate the Soviet political process by attracting the country's most creative and imaginative minds to plan policy. This process, called *perestroika*, succeeded in opening up all aspects of Soviet life to question and discussion for the first time. Restrictions on freedom expression of opinion by individuals and by the media were loosened, and the Soviet Union hurtled into a period of breakneck change.

Gorbachev's reforms and transformations also unleashed other forces. Ancient ethnic resentments among the many groups of people that made up the vast Soviet Union came violently to the surface, and a new wave of anti-Semitism washed over much of the country. Changes in the economy did more to raise hopes than improve the lives of most people, and bitterness turned into blame of the Soviet leader's increasing reliance on Western ideas. Meanwhile, Gorbachev was becoming the darling of the international media. To improve international relations, and cut spending at home, he pulled Soviet troops out of their disastrous and expensive war in Afghanistan. He traveled to Europe and the United States to negotiate major disarmament agreements. When the Eastern European countries of the Soviet bloc began crumbling in 1989, Gorbachev made it clear that he supported democratic reforms there; he said also that the Soviets would not invade those countries, as they had always done before.

While Gorbachev was becoming more and more popular in other countries, at home Soviet politicians and a significant portion of the general population were rising up against him. In 1990, Soviet nationalists blamed him for corrupting Russia's cultural heritage by introducing so many Western ideas. And Soviet liberals like Boris Yeltsin complained that more changes still had to be made in order to transform the Soviet Union into a democracy. Gorbachev continued to be blamed for making changes that did not have immediate positive results for the economy. That same year he won the Nobel Peace Prize for his efforts to defuse the Cold War between the USSR and the U.S. But increasing resentment at home finally brought him down.

In August 1991, a group of conservative leaders attempted to seize control of the government. The Soviet people demonstrated in the streets, with Yeltsin as their leader. After three days the coup d'état attempt collapsed, and Gorbachev, who had vanished during the turmoil, emerged to take office again, but only briefly. In September, he ordered the Communist Party to be abolished.

Then the Council of People's Deputies voted to eliminate the Soviet Union itself, creating a series of confederated republics instead. On December 21, 1991, Russia and ten other Soviet republics joined in a Commonwealth of Independent States. On December 26, 1991, Mikhail Gorbachev resigned. He continues to be an active, if marginalized, figure in Russian politics.

Gordy, Berry, Jr.

(1929–)

AMERICAN FOUNDER OF MOTOWN RECORDS

Berry Gordy, Jr., one of America's most successful African-American businessmen, was born and reared in Detroit, Michigan. His parents, Berry, Sr., and Bertha, owned a carpentry business and a general store. All of their eight children—Berry was their seventh—displayed musical talent at an early age.

Berry dropped out of high school and was drafted at twenty-two. While in the army, he studied for and passed a high school equivalency exam.

Once he was out of the service, he returned to Detroit and married Thelma Coleman in 1953. As they started a family, Gordy held several jobs. He first tried prizefighting. He then found a job at a car factory. While working there he began running a record store, the 3-D Record Mart. Gordy soon closed the shop because it was bringing in little money.

In his spare time, Gordy wrote songs. For years he submitted his tunes to contests, but he never won a prize. Finally, in 1957, a singer named Jackie Wilson decided to record a song Gordy wrote with his sister Gwen and a friend, Tyran Carlo. The song ("Reet Petite") was a hit. It made both Wilson and Gordy stars of the music industry.

Wilson and other singers recorded many more of Gordy's songs. Every time someone bought one of these records, Gordy received a royalty.

Even though he was making more money than he had at his other jobs, Gordy was not satisfied. The company that owned his songs—a music publisher—also received a royalty. Gordy did not like the arrangement. He felt that because he had actually written the song, he deserved the music publisher's royalty, too.

In 1958, Gordy decided to start his own music publishing company. He named it Jobete. Gordy made up the word using parts of the names of his first three children—Hazel *Jo*y, *Be*rry and *Te*rry.

The same year Gordy became a record producer. As a producer, he hired singers and musicians and chose the songs they recorded. At first, he sold the recorded songs to record companies. The record companies then sold the records to stores. But Gordy soon realized that he could make more money if he sold the records himself.

In 1959, Gordy borrowed $800 from his family and used it to found the Motown Recording Company. Motown began operating out of a small apartment with only six employees. One of them was Raynoma Liles, who became Gordy's second wife after he and Thelma Gordy divorced. Gordy's relatives, especially his sisters, also helped him run the small company.

From the beginning, Motown was a success. Gordy had a gift for finding talented performers and guiding their careers. Among his discoveries were Smokey Robinson and the Miracles, Stevie Wonder, Diana Ross and the Supremes, and the Jackson 5.

Gordy also had a keen sense of the type of songs the public wanted to hear. He once told Robinson, "Songs are more than rhymes. Songs need a beginning, middle, and end. Like a story."

Many of his singers and other employees have said that Gordy acted as though Motown was a family rather than a company. Some appreciated Gordy's fatherlike manner. Michael Jackson, who was the lead singer of the Jackson 5, has said, "Berry was my teacher and a great one. He told me exactly what he wanted and how he wanted me to help him get it." Other Motown artists felt that Gordy was too controlling. They often complained that he forced singers and songwriters to compete against each other rather than letting them work together as a team.

In 1972 Gordy moved the Motown offices to Los Angeles, California. By this time, Motown's record sales had begun to drop. Gordy decided to devote much of his time to producing movies and television shows starring Motown singers. The most successful was *Lady Sings the Blues*. This 1972 movie told the story of a famous blues singer, Billie Holiday. Diana Ross earned an Academy Award nomination for her performance as Holiday.

Gordy had another success with a 1983 television special called "Motown 25—Yesterday, Today, and Forever." The two-hour program brought together Motown's greatest talents. It was the most-watched variety special in the history of television.

In 1988, Gordy sold Motown Records to MCA, Inc. for $61 million. He continues to head the Gordy Company, which includes Jobete and Motown's movie and television divisions.

Graham, Martha

(1894–1991)

AMERICAN DANCER AND CHOREOGRAPHER

> Communication, whether it be in the dance, or whether it be in the spoken word, is now the great need of the world.
>
> —Martha Graham, speaking about the role of dance as an art form, *The Notebooks of Martha Graham*, 1973

Martha Graham was born in Pittsburgh, Pennsylvania, to Dr. and Mrs. George Graham. Martha and her two sisters were tutored in private school, and when Martha was ten years old, the family moved to Santa Barbara, California. Her mother nurtured her early interest and talent for music and dance, and she attended the Denishawn School in Los Angeles. When Martha's father, a strict Presbyterian, heard of her wish to be a ballet dancer, he strongly objected and withdrew her from Denishawn. She did not return to the school until 1916 after her father died.

In 1920, at the age of twenty-six, Martha Graham made her professional debut in Los Angeles. She was slender and, at just five feet three inches tall, rather short for a ballet dancer, but she made a dramatic entrance. A critic at the dance concert wrote that Martha Graham created "a new system of leverage balance and dynamics . . . she has found an original way of communication."

Martha Graham continued to perform at dance concerts around the country. She began teaching dance at the Eastman School of Music in New York, where she experimented with group choreography in 1924. Because of the relative novelty of modern dance at that time, some audiences who were more accustomed to traditional ballet ridiculed rather than encouraged Martha Graham's attempt to discover new styles of dance. But critics were generally unanimous in their support of her efforts.

By 1930, Martha Graham had founded the Dance Repertory Theatre and her school of contemporary dance in New York. Each year she gave at least one recital. Also in 1930, she danced the female lead in Igor Stravinsky's *Rite of Spring*, and introduced several Indian dances at the Bennington Dance Festival. Martha Graham drew on all human experience as the subjects of her dances—from Greek drama to Biblical and historical legends.

In 1940, in New York, Graham premiered *Letter to the World*, based on the work of Emily Dickinson, with several of the dancers enacting aspects of the poet's life while speaking lines from her poems.

For four months in 1954, Martha Graham made a successful tour of Europe with her dance company. For sixteen weeks in 1955–56, they performed in countries of the Far East and Near East under the Department of State's International Exchange Program. During 1956, she also lectured in Athens, Rome, and Paris. The friendliness of audiences in Asia deeply impressed Graham, who after her return home received a tribute from Paul G. Hoffman, director of the United Nations Special Fund: "I would like to salute Miss Graham as not only a very wonderful dancer who has danced her way into the hearts of millions, but as the greatest single ambassador we have ever sent to Asia."

In 1957, she filmed an educational documentary picture titled *A Dancer's World*. *Appalachian Spring*, with music by Aaron Copland, was filmed in 1958. One of her most ambitious works in 1958 was *Clytemnestra*, which was based on the Greek tragedy.

Graham collaborated with choreographer George Balanchine in 1959 to produce *Episodes,* a ballet in two sections set to music by Anton Webern. In her part of the ballet, Graham, with her company, danced a dramatic characterization of Mary Stuart in her struggle for power with Queen Elizabeth.

She created a rare humorous piece in 1960 titled *Acrobats of God*, which depicts the trials and glories of the dancer with wry wit. Another dance of the 1960 season, *Alcestis*, is an addition to her cycle of dances inspired by Greek drama and legend.

Dancers and would-be dancers come from all over the world to the Martha Graham School of Contemporary Dance in New York, which has eight or more teachers and some 250 to 300 students. Graham also taught at the Neighborhood School of the Theatre and the Juilliard School of Music, and she was an accomplished lecturer.

Some critics feel that Graham's works contained too much symbolism. Possibly because of obscurity, and possibly because of the difficulty of the psychological experiences that she tried to communicate, a Graham piece is never merely diverting or entertaining. "I want to make people feel intensely alive," Graham said in an interview in 1960. "I'd rather have them against me than indifferent."

Greer, Germaine

(1939–   )

AUSTRALIAN FEMINIST WRITER AND THEORIST

In the early days of the contemporary feminist movement, one writer could almost always be counted on to stir up a fuss, to nettle the male chauvinists and to out-debate, out-think, and out-write their literary spokesmen. Germaine

Greer has a doctorate in English literature, but her fame has nothing to do with Shakespeare, the subject of her dissertation. She is famous for speaking out against the oppression of women in the most outrageous way imaginable.

Germaine Greer was born on January 29, 1939, in the Melbourne beach suburb of Elwood, the eldest child of a conservative, well-to-do family. Her father, Eric, was a successful newspaper advertising executive who was away fighting in World War II for most of Germaine's childhood. When he returned, he was so visibly aged from his ordeal in the siege of Malta that his wife didn't recognize him. Greer would later write a prize-winning book about her search for her father's real identity, *Daddy We Hardly Knew You* (1989). The changes in him could not have helped a marriage that was suffering from communication problems. Indeed, Germaine's mother and father broke up about the same time that Germaine began to fight with her mother.

Germaine, a product of Star of the Sea Convent in Melbourne, was an outstanding student who won a junior scholarship in her twelfth year, and followed it with a scholarship to the University of Melbourne in 1957. She continued to be a brilliant student, graduating with first-class honors as an English and French literature double-major. She then went on to Sydney University for a master's degree in English, and first-class honors again.

For the next three years, Greer worked as a schoolteacher. Then in 1964 she won another scholarship, that time to Newnham College, Cambridge University, England, where she received her doctorate in 1967 with a dissertation entitled "The Ethics of Love and Marriage in Shakespeare's Early Comedies."

Although she had become a lecturer at Warwick University, she was making more of a name for herself as a journalist, contributing not only to academic journals, but also to *Rolling Stone*; *Oz*, a famous British counterculture magazine of the 1960s; and even a pornographic magazine, much to the dismay of her colleagues at the university. She also experimented very briefly with marriage, to a Cambridge graduate student named Paul de Feu, who was working as a roof tiler in London. They were divorced in 1973, although the marriage really didn't last that long.

In 1970 Greer published the book that launched her reputation as a serious feminist, a book that would influence women on both sides of the Atlantic—*The Female Eunuch*.

The book was a huge success, a runaway best seller that catapulted Greer on to the television talk shows. After a triumphant tour of the United States, she returned home to Australia for a book tour; one of her first actions was to apply for membership in the Sydney Journalists' Club, which at the time did not admit women. She was turned down for membership but was invited to speak, an invitation she understandably refused. While in Australia, she also gave testimony in several obscenity trials, continuing her championing of free speech. She was ruthlessly frank with her fellow Australians, and it cost her; she left the country vowing not to return as long as the conservative Liberal Country Party held power.

The royalties from *The Female Eunuch* enabled her to buy a beautiful house in the Tuscan hills of Italy, and she split her time between that home and a town house in London. Her next book, *The Obstacle Race* (1978), expanded on the thesis of *Eunuch*, by demonstrating with specific examples of the way that women artists are inhibited in the male-dominated art world.

In her next book, though, *Sex and Destiny: The Politics of Human Fertility* (1984), Greer shocked her fans and supporters by attacking the West's enforcement of family planning in the Third World and her sudden new emphasis on the importance of motherhood to women. This seemed a betrayal of the ideas expressed in *The Female Eunuch*, and many feminists were infuriated.

Her most recent works suggest, however, that her position, while not necessarily compatible with conventional feminism, is still staunchly pro-feminist. She helped edit a collection of seventeenth-century women's verse, and another of the uncollected poetry of Aphra Behn. Her 1991 book, *The Change*, discusses menopause in terms no less aggressive and combative than those that distinguished her greatest success years earlier.

Gretzky, Wayne

(1961–   )

CANADIAN HOCKEY PLAYER

Wayne Gretzky is fast on the hockey rink, but he's not the fastest player of all. Yet his ability to shoot accurately and his ability to anticipate where the puck is going, his weaving ability, and his excellent control of the stick have enabled Gretzky to play record-breaking hockey. Former hockey great Maurice Richard said of him, "He's moving all the time, and it seems like the players who are trying to check him just can't catch him." While playing this rugged game, Gretzky has even managed to win awards for gentlemanly conduct on the ice.

Wayne started to skate at age 3 in his hometown of Brantford, Ontario. In a backyard rink, he hit pucks with his father, zigzagging through tin cans set up on the ice. His father later said that he had tried to teach his son concentration, something that would later show up in his game. "He puts so much thought in what he's doing," Wayne's father remarked. "He doesn't just chase the puck around."

Wayne was so good he always played with boys older than himself as he grew up. By 17 he was a pro. He started out with the Indianapolis Racers in what was then the American Hockey Association. Then he was traded to the Edmonton Oilers. By 1982, his contract called for a salary of more than $1 million a year.

When people called him "the Great One" and "the best player ever," Gretzky responded modestly, saying, "Nobody will ever duplicate Howe, Esposito, Richard, Jean Beliveau . . . The really great players play at the same level year after year. . . . The important thing now to me is the consistency." Having won the Hart Trophy (given to the league's most valuable player) eight years in a row, Gretzky is well on his way.

Griffith, D. W.

(1875–1948)

AMERICAN FILMMAKER

David Wark Griffith was born on January 22, 1875, in the family farmhouse in Floydsfork, Kentucky. Griffith's father, Jacob, was a plantation owner who kept slaves and served as a colonel under General Thomas "Stonewall" Jackson during the Civil War. As a result of a complication of one of his old war wounds, Griffith's father died in 1882.

The Griffiths then moved to Louisville, where David's mother ran a boardinghouse and Griffith worked in a bookstore to support the family. The bookstore was a gathering place for many local writers, and Griffith was intent on becoming a playwright. By his early twenties, Griffith began working as an actor, even though his mother did not approve.

Acting was an insecure profession, and Griffith had to take many other jobs in order to earn money. He worked in a steel mill and also worked aboard ships. Sometimes he could not find any work and was forced to beg for food. In 1906, while performing in Boston, Massachusetts, Griffith married Linda Arvidson Johnson, another actor in the company.

By 1907 he had sold only one play and he realized that he had failed as a playwright and an actor. With the help of a friend, Griffith found work with the Lasky Company as an assistant to a cinematographer, or cameraperson. Griffith later took a job at American Biograph studios, and within a few weeks he was given his first chance to direct a film. During his years at Biograph, Griffith made more than four-hundred films. He also worked with some of the best actors of the time, including Mary Pickford, Lionel Barrymore, and Dorothy and Lillian Gish.

In 1913, Griffith became dissatisfied with Biograph; he wanted more money and more creative control. Within less than a year he started to work on the first and best remembered of his films, *The Birth of a Nation*. The film, which was the longest and most expensive film of that time, takes place during the Civil War and the Reconstruction period of the South after the war. The film's hero triumphs with the help of the Ku Klux Klan and the film was criticized severely for this reason. Nevertheless, the technical aspects of the film make it one of the most influential films in history.

President Woodrow Wilson described *Birth of a Nation* as "history written by lightning," and the film was a huge success, despite its shortcomings. The success led Griffith to begin immediately on another film, *Intolerance* (1916), which many film historians regard as the greatest film ever made. The film, however, was a commercial failure.

After the failure of *Intolerance*, Griffith started his own studio, United Artists, with the help of Douglas Fairbanks, Mary Pickford, and Charlie Chaplin. From 1921, Griffith felt stifled by the studio he helped create. The independence he had worked best under was gone, now that he had to report to accountants. He made his last film in 1931.

Griffith was the first filmmaker to master the art of editing, enabling him to switch from character to character, or story to story, without confusing the audience. Griffith also helped pioneer a new style of acting in film. Instead of having his actors portray emotion with large gestures, as was the standard method, Griffith moved the camera closer to the actors in order to catch small movements and subtle, more natural expressions. Griffith established the importance of the director in making a film, where as before the cameraman had always been the most important person. Griffith died of a brain hemorrhage in a small hotel room where he lived in Hollywood, in 1948.

Guevara, Ernesto "Che"

(1928–1967)

LATIN AMERICAN REVOLUTIONARY

> Guerrilla war is a people's war, a mass struggle. To try to carry out this type of war without the support of the population is to court inevitable disaster.
>
> —Che Guevara, on revolution

Ernesto "Che" Guevara was a revolutionary who worked to overthrow dictatorships in Cuba, the Congo, and Bolivia. His guerrilla tactics helped Fidel Castro overthrow the dictatorship of Fulgencio Batista in Cuba in the 1950s, and he became a world ambassador for the Cuban revolution and the Cuban minister of industries. He left Cuba after a bitter disagreement with Castro, and was killed in Bolivia in 1967. He remains a symbol of armed struggle against dictatorship to this day.

Guevara was born on June 14, 1928, in Rosario, Argentina. His family was middle class, and both of his parents were politically active when he was growing up. His father fought against Nazi propaganda in Argentina, and opposed the dictatorship of Juan Perón. His mother was arrested for her political activity. The two of them supported their son's revolutionary activities all their lives.

Guevara attended medical school in Argentina. He took time out to travel the length of South and Central America by motorcycle, and he eventually reached Miami, in the United States. He was struck by the poverty of the people everywhere. In 1953 he traveled to Bolivia, where he met radical revolutionaries who were trying to overthrow the right-wing governments of Latin America. He trained as a guerrilla fighter, traveling through Costa Rica, Guatemala, and Mexico. He met Fidel Castro in Mexico in 1955, and joined a group of exiled Cubans who were plotting to return to Cuba and set up a socialist state. They trained outside of Mexico City, led by Alberto Bayo. Guevara, Castro, and the others were arrested in Mexico in 1956, but were released after a month in prison.

From 1956 to 1959, Castro and Guevara carried out a guerrilla war against the Batista regime. On January 1, 1959, Batista fled Cuba for the Dominican Republic, taking with him more than $300 million that he had stolen from the Cuban people while he was their leader. Guevara helped set up a socialist economy in Cuba, and also established good relations with the Soviet Union, China, and many Third World countries. Partly due to a boycott of Cuba and a failed invasion by the United States, the Cuban economy never regained its health. Guevara began criticizing the Soviet Union, Cuba's biggest financial supporter, for abandoning its mission to help the poor of the world. He felt that the Third World needed to develop its own brand of revolution, and not depend on the Soviet Union. Castro needed the Soviet Union too much to risk offending its leaders, so he sent Guevara out of the country on other missions. Guevara disappeared in 1965, and reappeared in the Congo, in Africa, where he joined leftist forces in the civil war there. In 1966, he traveled to Bolivia, where he engaged in jungle warfare against the right-wing government. His idea for freeing the Third World countries from Western capitalism was to create many small revolutions all over the world. In Bolivia, he tried to repeat the success of Cuba, in which a small group of fighters won the sympathy of the peasants and overthrew the government. In October 1967, he was captured by the Bolivian government. Deciding that a trial would create too much public sympathy, Bolivian president Barrientos ordered that Guevara be executed on October 9, 1967. Two days later, the Bolivian government released a photo of an air force colonel pointing to a bullet hole in Guevara's chest, to prove to the world that he was really dead. Millions of people around the world honored the life and ideals of the man who had opposed both the capitalism of the West and the orthodox communism of the east. Guevara had truly fought for the oppressed peasants of the Third World.

Hale, Clara

(1905–1992)

AMERICAN SOCIAL REFORMER

> I love children. I think all children are born with something special. And you can bring it out and make them good people. But they need love. We give out love and they give love in return.
>
> —Clara Hale, interview with Tom Seligson, "How Mother Hale Saves Young Lives," in *Parade*, November 18, (1984)

Social activist Clara McBride Hale offered love and care to babies that others ignored. For more than twenty years, "Mother Hale" rocked, nurtured, and nursed back to health babies born to drug-addicted mothers. Since pregnant addicts pass on their addictions to their babies through the bloodstream they share, the babies Hale tended were born addicted, too. Hale offered comfort and love to hundreds of babies while helping them through the pain of withdrawal.

Clara McBride was born and reared in Philadelphia, Pennsylvania. Her father died during her infancy. Clara's mother supported the family by cooking and renting out rooms in their home. Clara later credited her mother with teaching her to take pride in herself and to love others. After graduating from high school, she married and moved to Harlem in New York. Clara Hale worked nights for several years, cleaning theaters to add to the income from her husband's floor waxing business. When Thomas Hale died in 1932, Clara Hale was left a widow with three children. While continuing to clean theaters at night, Hale cleaned homes during the day. In order to stay home with her children, Hale started a day-care center in her home. She also began taking foster children into her home. The city paid Hale $2 a week to take care of each child. In addition to those receiving day care, Hale usually housed seven or eight foster children. Over twenty-seven years, she cared for forty foster children.

In 1968, Hale decided to retire. After just one year, however, she began caring for drug-addicted children. Hale's new career began in 1969, when her daughter, who holds a doctoral degree in child development, noticed a young heroin addict falling asleep one day in a Harlem park. A two-month-old baby was falling out of the young woman's arms. Lorraine Hale talked to the addict, gave her her mother's address, and told her she could get help there. The next day, the addict agreed to turn the baby over to Clara Hale while she underwent drug treatment. Word of Hale's action spread quickly, and two months later, Mother Hale had crammed cribs in every room of her apartment to care for twenty-two addicted babies.

For eighteen months, Hale's work was financed solely by her three children, who worked overtime to raise the money needed to care for the babies. In the early 1970s, the New York City Department of Social Services for Children began to provide funding. With money provided by the federal government, the Hales renovated a five-story home in Harlem. In 1975, Hale House—the only institution in the country that treated victims of their mothers' drug abuse—officially opened in its new location. Hale House could care for as many as fifteen children, ranging in age from ten days to four years, at a time. Hale began to hire and train child-care workers and sleep-in aides to help her care for the addicted babies. In time, Hale House also employed a social worker, a teacher, and a part-time staff of doctors and nurses.

Hale House usually began its program of care within ten days of a baby's birth. The babies would receive comfort in Hale's room until the withdrawal symptoms ended weeks or even months after their arrival. The addicted babies would often suffer from diarrhea and vomiting; they would scratch themselves until they bled and cry endlessly until withdrawal was completed. She would walk with the babies, talk to them, sing to them, or rock them—whatever worked to stop their crying. After withdrawal had ended and the babies slept through the night, they would be moved to the nursery where the child-care staff would take care of them.

Mother Hale always stressed that Hale House was not an orphanage. Her goal was to reunite healthy parents and children. Ninety-seven percent of the babies were returned to their mothers after completed drug treatment. An average of less than one child a year was ultimately put up for adoption.

In 1985, President Ronald Reagan saluted Mother Hale as "a true American hero" in his State of the Union address before Congress. The recognition brought national attention to Hale House. Although the government cut funding to Hale House in 1989, private donations increased rapidly following Reagan's address. Hale House expanded its program in the 1990s to offer housing and education to mothers who have completed their drug-treatment programs. Hale also opened a home for infants and mothers with the deadly disease AIDS (Acquired Immune Deficiency Syndrome). Although Clara Hale died in 1992, Hale House, today run by Lorraine Hale, has continued to provide love and care to the babies of addicts and of mothers with AIDS.

Hamilton, Edith

(1867–1963)

AMERICAN CLASSICAL SCHOLAR AND EDUCATOR

> The spirit of the West, the modern spirit, is a Greek discovery and the place of the Greeks is in the modern world.
> —from Edith Hamilton's *The Greek Way* (1930)

Edith Hamilton was born in Dresden, Germany, while her parents were on a trip to Europe. The Hamilton family home was an estate in the center of Fort Wayne, Indiana. Edith was the eldest of five children. She had three sisters who were close to her in age and a much younger brother. One of Edith's sisters was Alice Hamilton, who grew up to be a world-renowned physician and social activist.

Edith's father, a businessman, was wealthy and well-educated. Her mother, whose favorite hobby was reading, was active in community affairs. She was a leader of the temperance movement and strongly supported women's suffrage.

Edith and her sisters were educated at home by both of her parents and by private tutors. Her father began teaching Edith Latin when she was seven.

Later all of the sisters also learned Greek, French, and German. In addition, the parents stressed religious education. The entire family attended the local Presbyterian church, and the children were required to study the Bible.

At the age of seventeen Edith Hamilton was sent to Miss Porter's School in Farmington, Connecticut. While she was there (1884–86), her father's business failed. All the Hamilton sisters realized that they needed to prepare themselves to earn their own livings. Edith Hamilton decided to become a teacher and to earn a degree at Bryn Mawr, a prominent women's college in Pennsylvania. Hamilton studied science and mathematics on her own to pass Bryn Mawr's difficult entrance examinations. She was admitted to the college in 1891.

Hamilton majored in Greek and Latin at Bryn Mawr. She received both a bachelor's and a master's degree in 1894, and then did further graduate work in Latin during 1894–95. In 1895 Hamilton was awarded the college's highest honor, the Mary E. Garrett European Fellowship. This award paid for her to study abroad for a year. During 1895–96 Edith Hamilton and her sister Alice studied in Germany, first in Leipzig and later in Munich. Edith Hamilton later recalled that she was not allowed to sit with male students at German university lectures. Instead she had to sit by herself on the lecture platform.

In 1896 Bryn Mawr College President M. Carey Thomas asked Hamilton to become head of the recently founded Bryn Mawr School in Baltimore. This was the only girls' school in the country that offered nothing but college preparatory courses. During the next twenty-six years Hamilton made the school into one of the leading institutions of its kind in the country. The school's curriculum included rigorous training in Greek and Latin language and literature. Hamilton believed strongly in Greek philosophy and ideals, and she made these the basis of school policy. Each year, in addition to her administrative duties, Hamilton taught a course for seniors on the Roman poet Vergil.

Following a disagreement with Thomas, Hamilton suffered a decline in health and resigned from Bryn Mawr School in 1922. Later she admitted that she had never been happy at the school. In 1923 Hamilton bought a house on Mount Desert Island, Maine, and moved there with her friend Doris Fielding Reid. The two women shared a home for the rest of Hamilton's life. In 1924 they moved to an apartment in New York City but kept their Maine house for summer vacations. One of Reid's nephews came to live with them when he was five, and Edith Hamilton later adopted him.

In New York Hamilton began a new life. Doris Reid went to work for an investment firm while Hamilton kept house and entertained. She became a member of the city's literary and theatrical community. One of her friends was Rosamond Gilder, who edited *Theatre Arts Monthly*. In the late 1920s Gilder persuaded Hamilton to write articles for the magazine on ancient drama and culture. Hamilton also published a translation in verse of *Prometheus*, a play by the Greek writer Aeschylus.

Hamilton's writing attracted wide attention. A New York editor asked her to write a book about ancient Greek thought and culture. The resulting book was *The Greek Way*, first published in 1930. It became a best-selling popular account of the ancient civilization. From then on, Hamilton was an established professional writer. She published articles and book reviews on the Greeks, the Romans, and the Bible in the nation's leading magazines.

In 1943 Hamilton moved to Washington, D.C. with Reid, who had become head of her company's office there. By this time Hamilton had published four more books, including *Prophets of Israel* (1936), an account of biblical figures. In the nation's capital she continued to write articles, reviews, and two more books. She also lectured and gave radio talks, and many well-known people in all fields came to visit her at her home.

In 1955 Hamilton was elected to the American Institute of Arts and Letters. Two years later she was elected to an even more prestigious group, the American Academy of Arts and Letters. Also in 1957 Hamilton was made an honorary citizen of Athens. She traveled to Greece for the award, and the public ceremony was written about in newspapers across the United States. Hamilton was also interviewed about the event on American television.

In her nineties Hamilton co-edited *The Collected Dialogues of Plato*, which was published in 1961. At the time of her death in Washington, D.C., in 1963, Hamilton was planning to write another book about the Greek philosopher, Plato.

Hammarskjöld, Dag

(1905–1961)

SWEDISH STATESMAN
AND DIPLOMAT

A mature man is his own judge. In the end, his only form of support is being faithful to his own convictions. The advice of others may be welcome and valuable, but it does not free him from responsibility.

—Dag Hammarskjöld, on
human responsibility

Dag Hammarskjöld was a Swedish government minister who became the second secretary-general of the United Nations. He helped resolve many international crises, and he was revered as a man of peace around the world. He died in a plane crash in 1961.

Hammarskjöld was born on July 29, 1905, in Uppsala, Sweden. His father was the prime minister of Sweden, and had also served as a representative to the League of Nations. In 1914, his father, then Sweden's prime minister, declared that Sweden would not take part in World War I because international disputes should be settled by law, not war. Hammarskjöld attended Uppsala University, where he received a degree in literature and philosophy by age nineteen. He later studied law and economics. In 1936, he was named Swedish undersecretary of finance. Although Sweden was officially neutral in World War II as well, Hammarskjöld arranged for financial help for the Norwegian government-in-exile in London. Norway had been conquered by Nazi Germany in 1940.

After World War II ended, Hammarskjöld worked to rebuild the countries of Europe. He worked as an economic advisor in Paris, and got his first taste of international diplomacy. In 1952, he worked out a peaceful settlement when the Soviet Union shot down a Swedish plane. Hammarskjöld's efforts may have prevented war.

In 1953, Hammarskjöld was appointed secretary-general of the United Nations. He took an organization that was not taken seriously by the governments of the world and turned it into a powerful force for peace. He helped avert an international crisis between China and the United States at the end of the Korean War. China had captured some American pilots and refused to release them. Hammarskjöld negotiated with the Chinese for their release. He also tried to bring peace to the Middle East. He secured a ceasefire in the first Arab-Israeli war, in 1948, and another one in the second war in 1956.

Hammarskjöld was killed in a plane crash on September 18, 1961, while he was on his way to the Congo, in Africa, to negotiate a ceasefire in a civil war. After his death, he was awarded the Nobel Peace Prize in 1961 for his life's work to bring international conflicts to peaceful conclusions. He made the United Nations an important international organization, and won the respect and trust of world leaders who did not trust one another. In the speech he gave upon becoming secretary-general of the U.N., he quoted a Swedish poet: "The greatest prayer of man is not for victory, but for peace."

Hand, Learned

(1872–1961)

AMERICAN JURIST AND
POLITICAL ACTIVIST

Learned Hand was born Billings Learned Hand in Albany, New York. His father, a leading judge and lawyer in the state, died when his son was fourteen. Hand attended Harvard University, where his teachers included Josiah Royce, William James, and George Santayana.

After graduating in 1893, Hand went on to Harvard Law School, where he studied under the school's famous dean, Christopher C . Langdell. After graduation in 1896, Hand dropped his first name, Billings. However, throughout his life close friends called him "B.," a short version of his nicknames "Bunny" and "Buck."

Hand practiced law in Albany until 1902, when he married and moved to New York City. Here he became a partner in a law practice, but most of his work bored him. He preferred to discuss legal and political issues with groups of friends. Hand also became active in civic reform groups. During this time he began writing articles for legal journals, including the *Harvard Law Review*.

In 1909 President William Howard Taft, a Republican, appointed Hand as a district judge in New York City. During Hand's years in this post he became a good friend and adviser to former U.S. President Theodore Roosevelt. In 1912 Hand left the Republican party to support Roosevelt's campaign for re-election to the presidency as a Progressive party candidate. Hand helped found the *New Republic* in 1914 and wrote articles for the magazine for several years.

In 1924 Hand was appointed to the Court of Appeals for the Second Circuit, which covered New York, Connecticut, and Vermont. At that time this was the leading appeals court in the country. Hand became chief judge of the court in 1939 and served in that post until 1951. Hand continued as a judge of the court until his death ten years later.

Hand is considered one of the leading American judges of the twentieth century. No other federal judge served longer than Hand in this century. During his career as a judge he wrote about three thousand opinions that covered every area of the law. According to legal scholars, Hand's written opinions played a major role in the development of American law. Many of these opinions have been referred to by other lawyers and judges in their own writings.

As both a judge and a private citizen, Hand was a strong defender of freedom of speech and other rights under the U.S. Constitution. For many years he was considered a likely member of the U.S. Supreme Court. One of his closest friends, Justice Oliver Wendell Holmes, Jr., supported Hand's appointment. However, William Howard Taft, who had become chief justice of the Supreme Court in 1921, used his influence to keep Hand from a Court seat. (Taft had become angry with Hand in 1912, when Hand left the Republican party and supported the Progressive party.)

In 1952 a collection of Hand's speeches, court opinions, and articles was published as *The Spirit of Liberty*. The title comes from a famous statement by Hand in one of his written opinions: "The spirit of liberty is the spirit which is not too sure that it is right." Hand worked right up to the time of his death in 1961 in New York.

Havel, Vaclav

(1936–   )

PRESIDENT OF CZECH REPUBLIC

> I assume you did not propose me for this office so that I, too, should lie to you.
>
> —Vaclav Havel, inaugural address, 1990

A man of great courage and integrity, Vaclav Havel went from prison to lead the Velvet Revolution in Czechoslovakia. As president of the Czech Republic, the playwright and philosopher provided world leadership in addressing issues of international importance.

Vaclav Havel was born on October 5, 1936, in Prague, capital of what was then Czechoslovakia. He grew up in a world of intellectual pursuits, with a father who ran a restaurant and entertained many of the country's artists and thinkers.

Havel's life was significantly changed in 1948 when Czechoslovakia became communist and the family's wealth was confiscated. His parents were forced to take low-paying jobs, and the children were forbidden by the government to attend regular schools. Vaclav worked in a scientific laboratory and went to school at night. As a teenager he began writing, and discussing philosophy with friends. In 1956 he took his first step toward dissent by attending a government conference for writers and asking that poets who had been banned from publication be reinstated.

In 1957, Havel joined the army and organized a theater company in his regiment. This experience prompted him to seek work in the theater after his military service was completed two years later. By 1968, he was the playwright for a progressive theater company. The 1960s were a productive period for Havel, who published several plays that became successful not just in Czechoslovakia, but also in Europe and elsewhere. In 1964 he married Olga Splichalova, who would become his confidante and advisor, as well.

The "Prague Spring" of 1968, as the remarkable outburst of creativity among the artists and writers of Czechoslovakia was called, died suddenly when the Soviet Union invaded Czechoslovakia in order to put an end to the reforms of Alexander Dubcek, the country's liberal communist leader. Havel called on the West to protest the abuses to civil and human rights being imposed, and the new Czech government responded by banning his works. Working in a brewery, he continued to write and smuggled his work out of the country. Rather than flee to another country where he could write in freedom, Havel chose to stay and work for change.

In 1975, Havel published a letter to his government describing the miserable conditions and the lack of values in Czech society. Two years later he joined hundreds of other intellectuals in protesting Czechoslovakia's failure to abide by the Helsinki Agreement on human rights and became the group's spokesman. He was arrested and given a suspended sentence. In 1978, he helped establish the Committee for the Defense of the Unjustly Persecuted and he was again arrested, this time sentenced to four years at hard labor. His letters to Olga about the experience were later published in a book.

Through the 1980s Havel continued to be the eloquent voice of freedom in Czechoslovakia. Havel's message was all the more powerful because he addressed these issues in relation to the very essence of what it meant to be human and to have a conscience, a soul. The government responded by continually harassing him. In January 1989, he was arrested again.

Upon his release in the fall of 1989, Havel established the Civic Forum, a coalition of groups who jointly advocated a nonviolent approach to change. As profound changes were beginning to sweep through the communist bloc, the well-thought-out, principled activities of the Civic Forum led the way into what was called the Velvet Revolution, the bloodless collapse of communist Czechoslovakia and the establishment of democracy. On December 19, 1989, the country's parliament elected Vaclav Havel president.

Havel's popularity served him well. The Soviet Union withdrew its troops from Czech land, the U.S. Congress celebrated the new Czech leader, and Havel began what he warned would be a slow and painful process toward democracy and a free-market economy. Keeping his promise, free elections were held in 1990, and Havel was reelected president.

After 1990, Havel presided over the personally painful partition of Czechoslovakia into two new countries based on the two major ethnic groups—the Czechs (the Czech Republic) and the Slovaks (Republic of Slovakia). Havel was unable to prevent the Slovaks, who believed that they were not equally treated within a unified Czechoslovakia, from establishing their own country. Havel was elected president of the Czech Republic and continued to work for peaceful relations and economic cooperation between the two countries.

Havel, whose courage and eloquence were honored with awards from many countries, continued to speak out on international issues, including the need for ethnic groups to find ways to live together and the necessity to arrive at global solutions to environmental and human rights challenges. In all his actions and pronouncements, he seemed to raise the discussion above the level of politics and special interests.

In accepting the Philadelphia Liberty Medal in 1994, Vaclav Havel said, " . . . in today's multicultural world, the truly reliable path to coexistence, to peaceful coexistence and creative cooperation, must start from what is at the root of all cultures and what lies infinitely deeper in human hearts and minds than political opinion . . . It must be rooted in self-transcendence. Transcendence as a hand that reaches out to those close to us, to foreigners, to the human community, to all living creatures, to nature, to the universe; transcendence as a deeply and joyously experienced need to be in harmony even with what we ourselves are not . . . Transcendence as the only real alternative to extinction."

Hawking, Stephen William

(1942–   )

ENGLISH THEORETICAL PHYSICIST

> In the front row a young man in a wheelchair was, very slowly, signing his name in a book that bore on its earliest pages the signature of Sir Isaac Newton. When at last he finished, there was a stirring ovation. Stephen Hawking was a legend even then.
>
> —Carl Sagan, on Stephen Hawking, in 1974

The history of twentieth-century science is full of courageous men and women who triumphed over adversity to make a brilliant contribution to our knowledge of the universe. There is no better example than Stephen Hawking, the

British theoretical physicist who captivated the world with his daring theories and remarkable ability to explain the universe.

Stephen William Hawking was born in Oxford, England, on January 8, 1942. After graduating from St. Alban's School, he enrolled at Oxford University, earning a bachelor's degree (B.A.) in 1962, and then a Ph.D. at the University of Cambridge, in 1966. His fields were mathematics and physics. Upon receiving his doctorate, he was made a fellow at Gonville and Caius College at Oxford.

Hawking took up where Albert Einstein and other earlier theoretical physicists had left off, investigating the theory of relativity. His particular interest was black holes. In 1971, he proposed that when the Big Bang, the explosion that created the universe, occurred, objects were created that were no bigger than a proton (a subatomic particle within the nucleus of an atom), but having millions of tons of mass. What made these objects, called mini–black holes, particularly interesting was that they, theoretically, must behave according to the laws of gravity (because of their mass) and according to the laws of quantum mechanics.

In 1974, Hawking further predicted that black holes must give off subatomic particles, despite their huge mass, until their energy is used up, at which point they explode. His brilliance, in part, stemmed from his ability to develop theories that explained how the universe could operate according to both classic laws of physics and quantum theory, one of which would seem to contradict the other.

Hawking was honored for his theories by being made the youngest fellow of the Royal Society, at the age of thirty. Also, in 1979, he received the Lucasian professorship of mathematics at Cambridge, a position once held by Sir Isaac Newton, the man who discovered gravity and who is considered one of the greatest scientists of all time.

Another major accomplishment of Hawking has been his ability to capture the imagination of the public and focus their attention on ideas that are, for virtually all of mankind, extraordinarily hard to comprehend, even if they remain fascinating. Hawking's *A Brief History of Time: From the Big Bang to Black Holes*, written in 1988, became an international best-seller. In less than two hundred entertaining pages, the physicist explained the history of the universe, black holes and all. A film based on the book also won critical and popular acclaim.

Making these accomplishments all the more remarkable was the fact that, in the 1960s, Stephen Hawking was diagnosed with amyotrophic lateral sclerosis, a disease that attacks the nervous and muscular systems and cannot be cured. Despite suffering greater and greater symptoms of the disease, which affected his speech, as well as the use of his muscles, Hawking continued to work, displaying an inspiring attitude toward life.

"Apart from being unlucky enough to get ALS, or motor neuron disease, I have been fortunate in almost every other respect. The help and support I received from my wife, Jane, and my children, Robert, Lucy, and Timmy, have made it possible for me to lead a fairly normal life and to have a successful career," Hawking wrote in *A Brief History of Time.*

Heifetz, Jascha

(1901–1987)

RUSSIAN VIOLINIST

Considered by critics to have been the world's greatest violinist, Jascha Heifetz was born in Russia in 1901 to a musical family. His father was a music teacher who gave the boy a specially made one-quarter-size violin when he was three years old. Heifetz learned to play music before he could talk, and it was clear that his talent was very special. At seven, he was playing concerts in Russia; at twelve, he made his debut with the Berlin Philharmonic. Famed violinist Fritz Kreisler was present when the boy played in Berlin, and he was quoted as saying, "I felt like breaking my violin."

In 1917, the Heifetz family, who were Jewish, left Russia because of anti-Semitism and moved to America. It was there that sixteen-year-old Heifetz made his triumphant New York Carnegie Hall debut. Concerts in many other countries followed. In 1940, Heifetz estimated that he had spent 66,000 hours—or two-fifths of his life—playing the violin, and that he had traveled enough to equal two roundtrips to the moon. For all this, Heifetz became the highest-paid violinist in history. He was paid $2,250 per concert, a phenomenal amount of money at that time.

Heifetz's fame in the music world led Hollywood filmmakers to seek him out. He made four films, including *They Shall Have Music* (1939) and *Carnegie Hall* (1947).

Through the years of doing concerts and recording (1917 to 1965), Heifetz also taught violin at the University of California at Los Angeles. He gave his last concert in 1972 at the Los Angeles Music Center.

Hellman, Lillian

(1905–1984)

AMERICAN PLAYWRIGHT

Lillian Hellman, an only child, was born in New Orleans. Her father was a shoemaker. Her father's trade led them to spend half of the year in New York, and half in New Orleans. As a teenager, Hellman kept a diary, and she knew from a young age that she wanted to be a writer.

Hellman left New York University after her junior year. She was married from 1925 to 1932, and then lived with the author Dashiell Hammett, a loyal literary adviser, for many years. In 1934, Hellman wrote her first play, *The Children's Hour.* The plot involves a girl who tells a lie about two of her teachers—that they are lesbians—and ruins their lives, due to the homophobic climate at the time. The play was banned in Chicago and Boston because the story was so controversial.

In 1937, Hellman was invited to the Moscow theater festival. She then traveled to Spain where there was a civil war going on. Her observances on both of these trips led her to hate fascism (governments of dictatorship), and helped to form her political views.

Hellman's play, *The Little Foxes* (1939), opened on the eve of World War II. *Watch on the Rhine* (1941) was based on her own experiences in Europe. The play won the New York Drama Critics Circle Award in 1941, and a film version was made in 1943. Hellman drew on her own family experiences for *The Autumn Garden* (1951), about a reunion of friends.

In 1952, Hellman was called to appear before the House Un-American Activities Committee. She was living with Hammett, a communist, and she was suspected of communist leanings herself. Hellman agreed to answer questions about herself, but not about others. During her hearing, she pleaded the Fifth Amendment, which states that no one can be forced to testify as a witness against herself.

Hellman was let off the hook by the committee, but during the 1950s, she had only two theatrical successes. *The Children's Hour* was revived on Broadway, and she adapted Jean Anouilh's play, *L'Alouette* (the story of Joan of Arc) into *The Lark*.

Hellman wrote *Toys in the Attic*, one of her most popular plays, in 1960. The play won the New York Drama Critics Circle Award, and its success allowed Hellman to care for Hammett, who was then dying of lung cancer.

By the 1960s, after the success of *Toys in the Attic*, Hellman began to feel negatively about theater. The public seemed to prefer television and movies to plays, and nonfiction also gained popularity. Hellman's last play, *My Mother, My Father and Me* (1963), ran for only two weeks.

Hellman wrote three autobiographies: *An Unfinished Woman* (1969), which won the National Book Award, *Pentimento* (1973), and *Scoundrel Time* (1976). She is best known for her plays, which depict her concern for other people as well as her insight into social issues.

Hitchcock, Alfred

(1899–1980)

ENGLISH FILM DIRECTOR

Alfred Hitchcock was a master director of suspenseful movies. His use of soundtrack music, camera angles and movements, and complex editing techniques revolutionized the motion picture industry, and helped him create some of the most exciting and scary films of all time.

Hitchcock was born in London, England, in 1899, to Emma Hitchcock and her husband, Joseph, a poultry dealer and fruit importer. Many of his early experiences influenced his later movie themes. When he was five, his father punished him for some minor offense by sending him to the local police station with a note. The policeman in charge of the station read the note and locked Hitchcock up for five minutes, saying, "This is what we do to naughty boys."

As part of his stern Catholic upbringing, Hitchcock attended a convent school run by the Faithful Companions of Jesus. Hitchcock next attended an equally strict Jesuit school, St. Ignatius College, in Stamford Hill. There students received frequent corporal (physical) punishment, usually beatings with a hard rubber cane. Hitchcock recalled the dread of those beatings, likening it to "going to the gallows." He learned to keep a low profile and keep out of people's way as a means of avoiding attention and punishment.

Hitchcock then matriculated at the University of London, where he studied engineering. He also learned some art, navigation, and political science. Upon graduation, he took a job making calculations for a cable company's technical installations. He tired of this, and took an art job in the advertising department of a London store. In 1920, he tried to get into the British motion picture industry. At first he wrote title cards for the silent movies of the Famous Players-Lasky Company, which became Paramount Pictures. On these cards was written the dialogue that was spoken by the silent actors. Hitchcock innovated by drawing designs and pictures on the cards. Soon he had become a scenario writer, and by 1923 he had received his first credit on a film, as art director of *Woman to Woman* for the Gainsborough Pictures company in Islington, London. The first movie that he directed was a low-budget picture shot in Munich, Germany, *The Pleasure Garden*. In 1926 he married Alma Reville, his assistant director for this film. He directed many other films during the late 1920s, and was chosen to direct the first talking British film, *Blackmail*, in 1930.

It was not until 1935, however, that he developed the style for which he is famous. He made six movies for Gaumont-British that became known as the Hitchcock Cycle: *The Lady Vanishes*; *The Man Who Knew Too Much*; *Secret Agent*; *Sabotage*; *The Girl Was Young*; and *The Thirty-Nine Steps*. This last movie was named best-directed motion picture by the New York Film Critics Circle. Hitchcock visited the United States, and was impressed with the advanced technology of the Hollywood studios. He signed a contract to direct five films for Selznick-International. The first of these, *Rebecca*, won the Oscar for Best Picture in 1940. Hitchcock remained in America and became a permanent resident. For the next twenty-plus years, he directed at least one film per year for various Hollywood studios. Among them were *Spellbound* (1945), *Dial M for Murder* (1954), *Rear Window* (1954), *To Catch a Thief* (1955), a remake of *The Man Who Knew Too Much* (1956), *Vertigo* (1958), *North by Northwest* (1959), *Psycho* (1960), and *The Birds* (1963).

From the 1940s on, Hitchcock made a cameo appearance in each of his films. It became a game among his fans to try to spot him. In *Lifeboat* (1944), his picture appears on a newspaper that one of the characters is reading, in a before-and-after advertisement for a weight-reduction system (Hitchcock at one point weighed 290 pounds, and "slimmed" down to 220). Many of his films included such subtle touches of humor.

Hitchcock was a master of human psychology. Even in tense and surreal situations, his characters act believably. He also had a wonderful grasp of the psychology of his audience, and knew exactly how to maintain and build suspense almost to unbearable levels. His popularity with audiences allowed him to work with the biggest stars of the day, including Cary Grant, James Stewart, Laurence Olivier, Joan Fontaine, Ingrid Bergman, Kim Novak, and Grace Kelly. Despite having once caused a commotion by quipping that "all actors are children" and "should be treated like cattle," he never argued with a performer on the set, and never raised his voice while directing. He used a very persuasive and energetic style to get what he wanted out of his actors.

In the 1950s Hitchcock saw opportunities in the emerging field of television. He produced a weekly television series, *Alfred Hitchcock Presents*, starting in 1955. He himself directed most of the episodes. He also lent his name to many anthologies of mystery stories written by writers less famous than himself. To ensure quality, he supervised the production of these volumes.

Unlike the chaotic world portrayed in his films, Hitchcock's private life was a model of routine and order. He and his wife had one child—a daughter, Patricia—and when he was not shooting a film, he was almost always home with his family. He loved food and wine, hated exercise, and remarked when asked if he were overweight because of his love of food, "I am not really a heavy eater, unless you mean that I am heavy, and I eat."

In 1979, Hitchcock received a Lifetime Achievement Award from the American Film Institute, and the following year was knighted by Queen Elizabeth II of England, despite the fact that he had taken U.S. citizenship. He was working on a new film, *The Short Night*, when he was taken ill. He died on April 29, 1980, in Bel Air, California.

Holmes, Jr., Oliver Wendell,

(1841–1935)

JUSTICE OF THE U.S. SUPREME COURT

> Life is an end in itself, and the only question as to whether it is worth living is whether you have enough of it.
> —Oliver Wendell, Holmes, Jr., from a speech
> to the Massachusetts Bar Association, 1900.

Oliver Wendell Holmes, Jr. was born in Boston, Massachusetts. He was the son of the famous poet and physician Oliver Wendell Holmes, Sr.. The most well-known scholars and writers of the time were friends of the Holmes family. They included Ralph Waldo Emerson, Louis Agassiz, James Russell Lowell, Henry Wadsworth Longfellow, William Prescott, John Greenleaf Whittier, and Nathaniel Hawthorne. Many of Oliver Jr.'s childhood friends grew up to be famous too. They included the future historian Henry Adams, the novelist Henry James and his brother, the philosopher William James.

Holmes was educated at local private schools. He was also taught informally by Emerson. From this philosopher and poet Holmes developed a lifelong interest in philosophy. He entered Harvard University in 1858. The Civil War broke out during his senior year and Holmes immediately joined the army. However, his battalion was not called up to fight, and he returned to Harvard to finish his degree. After graduation in the spring of 1861 Holmes joined a company of volunteers from Massachusetts. He fought in some of the bloodiest battles of the war and was wounded three times.

Holmes returned to Boston in 1864 and entered Harvard Law School. He graduated in 1866 and began to practice law in Boston. About this time he made his first visit to England. Here he met some of the country's leading citizens, including the economist and philosopher John Stuart Mill.

As Holmes's law practice grew, he also began to write about legal matters. In 1870 he became a regular contributor to the *American Law Review* as well as its coeditor. A year earlier he had begun to revise James Kent's *Commentaries on American Law*. The twelfth edition of this work, edited by Holmes, was published in 1873.

Holmes's first and most important book, *The Common Law*, was published in 1881. This was a collection of lectures that he delivered at the Lowell Institute in Boston. It is considered a classic work on American common law. It has been reprinted many times and translated into several foreign languages. Shortly after the publication of *The Common Law*, Holmes was appointed a professor at the Harvard Law School.

Holmes held the position for only one year. In 1883 he was appointed to the Massachusetts State Supreme Court. He served on the court for nineteen years. During the last three years he was the court's chief justice. In his years on the Massachusetts State Supreme Court Holmes wrote some 1,300 opinions. Most of them concerned disputes between individuals.

In 1902 President Theodore Roosevelt appointed Holmes to the U.S. Supreme Court. Holmes became known as one of the most brilliant justices in the history of the Court. Many legal scholars believe that he was the equal of Chief Justice John Marshall. He wrote many dissents that later became the majority view of the Court.

Holmes was a leader of the liberal wing of the Supreme Court. He was known as a strong supporter of civil liberties. However, he believed that citizens had to use common sense in exercising their rights. One of his most famous opinions was written in the case known as *Schenck v. United States* (1919). In that opinion Holmes said that the right to free speech did not mean that anyone could, for example, falsely shout "Fire!" in a crowded theater and cause a panic. If speech caused a "clear and present danger," it could be punished by law. The so-called "clear and present danger" doctrine became a standard for later decisions by the Supreme Court.

Holmes served for thirty years on the Court. He retired in 1932, several months before his ninety-first birthday. He died in Washington three years later. During his lifetime he published several books in addition to *The Com-*

mon Law. Speeches first appeared in 1891; revised editions were published in 1913 and again in 1938. Holmes's *Collected Legal Papers* came out in 1920. Many of his letters have also been collected and published.

Hopper, Edward

(1882–1967)

AMERICAN PAINTER

Edward Hopper was born in the small Hudson River town of Nyack, New York, on July 22, 1882. His father owned a dry goods store where the young Hopper worked after school. By 1899, Hopper had already decided to become an artist, but his parents persuaded him to study commercial illustration because it seemed to offer a more secure living. Hopper commuted to New York to attend the Correspondence School of Illustrating for a year, before moving to New York and studying at the New York School of Art. The painters Rockwell Kent and George Bellows attended the prestigious New York School of Art at the same time.

Like the majority of the young artists of the time, Hopper wanted to study in France and with his parents' help, he left for Paris in October 1906. It was a great time in the history of art in Paris; with Picasso and Matisse gaining attention, but Hopper was ignorant of it all. "Whom did I meet? Nobody. I'd heard of Gertrude Stein, but I don't remember having heard of Picasso at all," Hopper recalled of his time in Paris.

In August 1907, Hopper returned to New York, where he illustrated for a number of magazines. He hated the work and later in life he refused to discuss this period of time.

Hopper began exhibiting his paintings in 1908 and sold his first painting at the landmark Armory Show of 1913, where Americans saw modern painting from around the world for the first time. As the public's interest in modernism increased, Hopper's realistic paintings went ignored for a time, and he did not sell another painting for ten years. Hopper earned a living by illustrating posters for the American Red Cross and many Hollywood movies.

In 1923, Hopper met Josephine Verstille Nivison, a former student at the New York School of Art, and she encouraged Hopper to paint with watercolors. Soon his work was being widely praised and the Brooklyn Museum purchased *Mansard Roof*. A year later, Hopper and Nivison were married.

Hopper quit his job as an illustrator and began painting with new energy and determination. His wife encouraged his work and was the model for almost all of the female figures in his paintings. In 1930 the Museum of Modern Art in New York purchased *House by the Railroad*, the first painting in the museum's permanent collection. The painting of a nineteenth century house standing alone near railroad tracks has become a famous image in American art, praised for its stark imagery and realism.

Beginning in 1930, the Hoppers began to spend time on Cape Cod, where Edward Hopper painted numerous watercolors and oils. Hopper was soon categorized as a regionalist. Hopper disliked the label and began exhibiting paintings that revealed the more international influences in his work.

Hopper was elected to the National Academy of Design in 1932, but he refused the honor due to the Academy's rejection of his work in the past. A year later, the Museum of Modern Art exhibited a retrospective of his painting, the highest honor given by the museum.

In 1942 Hopper produced his masterpiece, *Nighthawks*, which depicted a lonely couple in an all-night diner. His fame once again subsided as the emergence of the abstract expressionists overshadowed the realists, who were now seen as obsolete. Hopper was hurt by the criticism, and in 1953 he helped start the magazine *Reality*, which argued in favor of realistic art.

In 1956 Hopper appeared on the cover of *Time* magazine, which argued that Hopper should be considered as one of America's great artists, alongside other realists like John Singleton Copley and Thomas Eakins. His work has increasingly come to be accepted as among the finest of this century, and his reputation continues to grow.

Hopper, Grace

(1906–1992)

AMERICAN NAVAL OFFICER, MATHEMATICIAN, AND COMPUTER SCIENTIST

Grace Murray Hopper was born on December 9, 1906, in New York. She graduated from Vassar College and received her doctorate in mathematics from Yale. She worked as a mathematician and computer programmer in private industry before joining the navy in 1943, where she worked on sophisticated computer and language research. She left the regular navy in 1946, but remained in the reserves until 1966, when she returned to active duty to oversee the standardization of the navy's computer and language programs.

Hopper's pioneering work in the field led to the first practical computer program that could translate human programming instructions into codes that could be read by a computer. She is credited with coining the term "bug," which refers to all kinds of computer snags or failures, and which she claimed came from an incident involving an actual bug (a moth, she said) and the circuit panel of a large computer she was programming.

After four decades of service in the navy, in 1983 Hopper received a special presidential appointment to the rank of rear admiral. She was the oldest officer on active duty in the armed service at the time of her retirement in 1986. Hopper died on New Year's Day, 1992, at her home in Arlington, Virginia.

Horowitz, Vladimir

(1904–1989)

RUSSIAN PIANIST AND COMPOSER

Vladimir Horowitz was, for most of the twentieth century, the most talked-of pianist in the world. His playing made listeners wonder how any human being could combine such limitless technique with such serious musical understanding. Horowitz was born in Kiev, Russia, in 1904. His mother, an excellent pianist, was a conservatory graduate; it was from her that Horowitz got his early interest in music. His mother gave him his first piano lessons when Horowitz was six. It was clear that he had great promise and needed more instruction than his mother was able to give.

When Horowitz was ten, his parents sent him to the Kiev Conservatory to study with Felix Lumenfeld. At seventeen, Horowitz graduated with honors. During those years, Horowitz's father decided not to let the boy perform until he had finished his education, but when the Russian Revolution came in 1917, the family lost their home and money, and all thoughts of Horowitz's further schooling ended.

In 1922, an uncle of Horowitz's, who was a music critic, arranged for his nephew's first public appearance. He became an immediate sensation in Russia and gave seventy concerts the next year, twenty-three of them in Leningrad (now St. Petersburg). By 1924, Horowitz was ready to begin his first European tour. He played triumphantly in Germany, Holland, Italy, France, Spain, Belgium, and England. Everywhere he went he created a sensation. The noted French critic Henri Prunières wrote: "He has all the technical gifts in addition to exquisite musical sensitiveness."

After several very successful European tours, Horowitz decided to go to the United States. He made his American debut at New York's Carnegie Hall in 1928, playing Tchaikovsky's *B-Flat Minor Concerto* with the New York Philharmonic. The Russian pianist electrified the audience with his superb technique. He smashed out chords and played so rapidly that the eye could not follow the movements of his fingers. Within a short time, Horowitz was famous all over the world. Most astonishing was the fact that at that time Horowitz practiced for only three or four hours a day, while other pianists practiced three times that amount without nearly the same results. At the time, Horowitz said, "When I practice I get worse."

In 1933, Horowitz married Wanda Toscanini, the daughter of the great Italian conductor Arturo Toscanini. In 1936, they moved to Switzerland, then to Paris, and retired from public life for two years. It was reported that Horowitz did not touch a piano during this time, but when he made his encore appearance at the keyboard in Paris in 1939, he seemed to be a greater pianist than he had been before.

With World War II escalating in Europe, Horowitz returned to New York in 1940 to live; in 1944, he became an American citizen. His reception when he played at Carnegie Hall that year was loud and joyous and almost as long as the concert itself. The critics agreed that his playing was as dazzling as ever, and perhaps even more expressive.

During that time, Horowitz was composing as well as playing. Later on, he would play his variation on themes from the opera *Carmen*, or his piano version of John Philip Sousa's *Stars and Stripes Forever*.

Horowitz interrupted his public appearances once again in 1953, due to ill health. It was not until 1965 that he made his triumphant comeback at Carnegie Hall. Once again he was hailed as a genius. He resumed his career in concert recitals, although not as a soloist with orchestras. Twenty-five years later, to mark the fiftieth anniversary of his American debut, Horowitz, conducted by Eugene Ormandy, played Rachmaninoff's *Piano Concerto Number Three* with the New York Philharmonic. Horowitz also had the distinct honor of being invited back to his native Russia by the government in power at the time. He played a series of concerts that had audiences swooning.

Hughes, Langston

(1902–1967)

AMERICAN POET, SHORT-STORY
WRITER, AND PLAYWRIGHT

We younger Negro artists . . . intend to express our individual dark-skinned selves
without fear or shame. If white people are
pleased we are glad. If they are not it doesn't
matter. We know we are beautiful. And ugly
too . . . We build our temples for tomorrow,
strong as we know how, and we stand on top
of the mountain, free within ourselves.

—Langston Hughes, from "The Negro Artist and
the Racial Mountain," *The Nation*, June 23, 1926

Born in Missouri, Langston Hughes grew up with his mother and maternal
grandmother. His father had failed as a lawyer in Oklahoma because of the
racist climate there, and he left the family to emigrate to Mexico. Hughes's
childhood was marked by financial and emotional poverty. His mother had to
work quite often, and he became a lonesome child. Hughes' grandmother
taught Hughes the importance of civil rights, and encouraged him to read and
write.

Hughes went to high school in Ohio, and published twenty short stories and
poems in the school literary magazine. His poetry was influenced by the works
of Walt Whitman, Carl Sandburg, Paul Laurence Dunbar, and W.E.B. DuBois.
Through his grandmother's tales of slavery, as well as his awareness of the ongoing segregation of blacks, Hughes responded to racism through his poems.

Hughes spent a year at Columbia University. He left to take a string of odd
jobs, such as delivery boy, vegetable farming, and working on ships in the Hudson River. Hughes took steamer ships to Africa and then Europe, where he settled in Paris.

In 1924, Hughes returned to the United States. He had published some
poems in magazines, and in 1926, he published his first collection, *The Weary
Blues*. The poems in this volume combined traditional verse with the rhythms
of blues and jazz. The publication of this book established Hughes's prominence, along with other African-American writers such as Countee Cullen, in
the Harlem Renaissance.

Hughes enrolled at the mostly black Lincoln University in Pennsylvania in
1926. While he was in college, Hughes published his second volume of poetry.

The poems in *Fine Clothes to the Jew* (1927) explored the themes of the blues—sexuality, violence, sadness, poverty, tragedy—but they did not adhere to traditional poetic forms. Hughes graduated from Lincoln in 1929, and began writing with the support of a patron, Charlotte Mason, a white woman who supported black artists. She advised Hughes and edited his work.

Hughes published his first novel, *Not without Laughter*, in 1930. The story was about a black boy growing up in the Midwest trying to survive racism and poverty. In the same year, Mason stopped supporting Hughes, though the reasons why are unclear. It may have had to do with the play he was writing with fellow author, Zora Neale Hurston. In 1930, Hurston claimed that *Mule Bone* was hers alone. Given the stressful events during that year, Hughes traveled to Cuba and Haiti to recover.

When he returned to the United States, just as the country was entering the Great Depression, Hughes began a year-long tour of the South to read his poetry and sell books. From the South he went west, and his writing shifted from blues poetry to radical political work. When he reached the west coast, Hughes joined a group of African-Americans who were going to make a film on race relations in the Soviet Union. Although the film project fell through, Hughes toured that country in 1932 with other writers, and wrote some of his most radical verse.

Hughes returned to the United States in 1933, and found another patron, Noel Sullivan. With Sullivan's support, Hughes wrote a series of protest stories which were collected in *The Ways of White Folks* (1934). When his father died in 1934, Hughes went to Mexico where he worked on translating Mexican writers. He hoped to find publishers for them in the United States, but his efforts proved unsuccessful.

Hughes returned to the United States in 1935 and lived with his mother in Ohio. He learned that a play he had written in 1930, *Mulatto: A Play of the Deep South*, was about to be produced on Broadway. Hughes' play ran longer than any other drama by a black author until Lorraine Hansberry's *A Raisin in the Sun*. In 1939, Hughes accepted a job as a writer in Hollywood to work on script for *Way Down South*. The following year, he published his autobiography, *The Big Sea*, and began to shift away from radical leftist politics.

Hughes published several poetry collections in the 1940s, including *Shakespeare in Harlem, Jim Crow's Last Stand, Fields of Wonder*, and *One-Way Ticket*. By the end of the decade, he was under investigation for his earlier radical poems. In 1953, he was subpoenaed by the House Committee on Un-American Activities, and he cooperated with the questioning.

Hughes had always enjoyed music and he collaborated as lyricist on several musicals, including *Street Scene* (1947), *Trouble Island* (1949), *The Barrier* (1950), *Simply Heavenly* (1957), *Black Nativity* (1961), *Jericho-Jim Crow* (1964), and *The Prodigal Son* (1965). In the latter three, he succeeded in bringing gospel music to the stage.

Wanting to help young writers get published, Hughes published anthologies of African-American literature. He collaborated with Arna Bontemps on *The Poetry of the Negro 1746–1949* (1949), and published *New Negro Poets* (1964) and *The Best Short Stories by Negro Writers* (1967). This volume contained the first story every published by Alice Walker, author of *The Color Purple*.

In addition to poetry, short stories, and songs, Hughes published numerous nonfiction books, including *A Pictorial History of the Negro in America* (1956) and *Black Magic: A Pictorial History of the Negro in American Entertainment* (1967). Hughes also published two books of work by Africans: *An African Treasury: Articles, Essays, Stories, Poems* and *Poems from Black Africa, Ethiopia, and Other Countries.*

Hughes' last volume of poetry was published after his death in 1967. *The Panther and the Lash* contained poems about civil rights and the black power movement of the 1960s. African-American society was Hughes' tireless source of inspiration—he celebrated this culture and its members were his main audience.

Ionesco, Eugène

(1912–1994)

FRENCH-ROMANIAN PLAYWRIGHT

Eugène Ionesco was a famous post–World War II dramatist. He was a major figure in the Theater of the Absurd, a style of drama that emphasized the uselessness of traditional values and the alienated condition of humanity.

Ionesco was born November 24, 1912, in Slatina, Romania. His father was Romanian, and his mother was French. Within a year of Ionesco's birth, his family moved to Paris, France, where Ionesco lived for the next twelve years. French was Ionesco's first language, and he only learned Romanian when he and his family moved back to Romania in 1925.

As a young child, Ionesco loved the Punch and Judy puppet theater shows, and when he was older, he and his friends pretended to be actors. At age thirteen, Ionesco even wrote a patriotic play.

However, Ionesco's early love of drama soured as he matured. He preferred writing poetry and literary criticism; and, after graduating from the University of Bucharest, he earned his living as a French teacher. He did not intend to become a playwright.

Ionesco rekindled his early love of drama by accident. While trying to learn English, he turned his language lessons into a parody of a play: He used the wooden dialogue of his English exercises to mock the conventions and pretenses of theater. The result turned out to be his first absurdist play, *The Bald Soprano*, which premiered in 1950. *The Bald Soprano*, like most of Ionesco's other plays, made fun of conventional behavior and middle-class values. Although critics initially dismissed the play, Ionesco realized that he was destined to be a playwright.

In 1951, Ionesco staged his second absurdist play, *The Lesson*; and his next play, *The Chairs*, followed one year later. Throughout the 1950s, Ionesco continued his writing, and by the end of the decade, in 1959, he staged his most famous play, *Rhinoceros*, which attacks the horrors of conformity.

Ionesco's plays helped to redefine postwar drama; he influenced countless playwrights and theatergoers. His artistic treatment of twentieth-century alienation has made his works appealing to audiences throughout the last half of the century.

Jackson, Jesse

(1941–   )

AMERICAN CIVIL RIGHTS ACTIVIST
AND CANDIDATE FOR THE
DEMOCRATIC NOMINATION FOR
PRESIDENT

Jesse Louis Burns was born to Helen Burns of Greenville, South Carolina on October 8, 1941. When he was two years old, his mother married Charles Jackson, a postal worker, and the boy was given Jackson's name. Taunted by other children because of his illegitimacy, the young Jackson sought out his natural father, Noah Robinson, a textile worker with his own family. As a teenager, Jackson was welcome in both the homes of his adoptive father and his biological father, but he never lost the feeling that he had been deprived of a normal family upbringing. It didn't help to be growing up in segregated Greenville, where blacks had to sit at the back of buses and Whites Only signs confronted them at restaurants, movie theaters, and public bathrooms.

In high school, Jackson studied hard and was chosen for the National Honor Society. He was also a star player on the all-black football and basketball teams. He turned down a contract with the San Francisco Giants when he learned that another player, a white player who was not as good as Jackson, had been offered better terms. In 1959, he chose to attend the University of Illinois at Champaign on a football scholarship. Faced with discrimination against black students and athletes, Jackson left Illinois after a year. He enrolled at the mostly black Agricultural and Technical State University at Greensboro, North Carolina, where earlier that year four black students who had been refused service at an all-white Greensboro lunch counter started the sit-in protest movement that rapidly spread across the South.

After enrolling at Texas A&T University, Jackson excelled as an honor student and athlete. In 1962, he married Jacqueline Lavinia Davis, the daughter of migrant farm workers. By 1963, Jackson was a leading student activist who had been arrested for organizing protest marches and sit-ins. He became the local field director for CORE, the Congress of Racial Equality. Upon graduation, he decided to become a preacher, and in 1964 he secured a scholarship to the Chicago Theological Seminary.

On March 5, 1965, the Reverend Martin Luther King, Jr. and his Southern Christian Leadership Conference (SCLC) staged a march from Selma, Alabama to the state capital of Montgomery to demand voting rights for blacks. At the Edmund Pettus Bridge on the outskirts of Selma, the police attacked the marchers with tear gas and clubs. King issued a call for all clergymen to come to Selma and help, so Jackson left Chicago to join the protest. In Selma, he got to know King's associate, the Reverend Ralph Abernathy, and he joined the SCLC. After passage of the Voting Rights Act of 1965, the SCLC turned its attention to discrimination in northern cities, and Jackson found himself back in Chicago in 1966, organizing protests with King against segregated housing. In Chicago, Jackson also started Operation Breadbasket, a program to force businesses to hire more blacks. Jackson's relationship with King was often strained, however. Many in the civil rights movement regarded Jackson as too independent and ambitious.

On April 4, 1968, Martin Luther King, Jr. was assassinated in Memphis, Tennessee. Abernathy took over the leadership of the SCLC, but Jackson, a more passionate speaker, began to gain followers among urban black youth who were losing patience with the SCLC's nonviolent tactics and emphasis on integration Jackson's approach focused on black economic power, on getting more jobs for blacks, and on patronizing black-owned businesses. In 1971, Jackson and Abernathy had a falling-out over Operation Breadbasket's finances, and Jackson resigned from the SCLC.

Jackson immediately formed Operation PUSH (People United to Serve Humanity) with the help of money from prominent members of the black community. Operation PUSH continued Operation Breadbasket's stress on black economic improvement, but it did something else that the SCLC had never done: it took an interest in electoral politics and endorsed candidates who supported black causes. It engaged in an unsuccessful effort to unseat the powerful Chicago mayor, Richard J. Daley. In the 1972 presidential election, Jackson endorsed Senator George S. McGovern of South Dakota. McGovern represented the left wing of the Democratic party and was opposed to the Vietnam War. Though McGovern lost the election to Richard M. Nixon, at the Democratic National Convention Jackson succeeded in opening the party to many new black delegates, and he became a political force the Democrats began to pay attention to as they sought black votes.

In the late 1970s, Jackson organized PUSH-Excel, an extension of Operation PUSH that focused on black education and the problems of drug and alcohol abuse. Jackson promoted black pride and self-esteem, and the federal government provided $5 million for his school programs. In 1983, he helped Harold Washington to become the first black mayor of Chicago, finally taking the city away from the political machine of his old enemy, Mayor Daley, who was now dead. In 1984, he decided to challenge Walter F. Mondale for the Democratic nomination for President. Jackson appeared to be doing well after he traveled to Syria and secured the release of an American airman being held captive there. But his popularity later declined, in part because of his association with the militant Black Muslim leader Louis Farrakhan. Mondale won the Democratic nomination, but was defeated in the general election by Republican Ronald Reagan.

In 1986, Jackson formed the National Rainbow Coalition, which he meant to become a progressive force within the Democratic party. The Rainbow Coalition was well organized, well financed, and broadbased, and became Jackson's political base of support for his 1988 presidential campaign. Jackson sought to appeal not only to blacks, but to labor, liberals, women, and gay rights activists. Jackson took positions popular with the Democratic left—for instance, he supported restricting the right of large corporations to move jobs overseas, creating new government-financed health and housing programs, and increasing assistance to the poor. In some early 1988 Democratic primary elections, Jackson beat his main opponent, Governor Michael Dukakis of Massachusetts, in several states, becoming for a time the Democratic front-runner. Dukakis eventually won the nomination, but lost the election to George Bush.

In 1989, Jackson moved from Chicago to Washington, D.C., and in 1990 was elected its "shadow senator," a nonvoting, nonsalaried position created by the city to lobby for statehood and representation in Congress. When in August 1990 Iraqi President Saddam Hussein invaded Kuwait, Jackson flew to Iraq and negotiated the release of three hundred captured Americans and foreign nationals. Later in the year, he began to host a weekly television talk show on civil rights and other issues.

Jackson remains a controversial figure. Many black leaders have criticized his outspokenness and feel that his positions are too liberal for today's more conservative Democratic party. But he remains a powerful voice for millions in the black community and others who have felt left out of the political process.

John XXIII

(1881–1963)

ITALIAN RELIGIOUS LEADER (POPE) AND REFORMER

> Our duty is to dedicate ourselves willingly, eagerly, and fearlessly to
> the work required by our own era, thus proceeding on the way the
> Church has followed for twenty centuries.
>
> —Pope John XXIII, on the obligations of the Catholic Church

Angelo Roncalli, who took the name John XXIII when he was elected pope in
1958, presided over the most far-reaching reforms in the Roman Catholic
Church in four centuries. He made the Church more accessible to common
people, worked for world peace, and brought about a mending of relations between Christians and Jews. He became one of the most beloved religious leaders the world had ever known.

Roncalli was born in Sotto il Monte, the village in northern Italy where his
family had farmed for five hundred years. The third of thirteen children, he
helped his father work the fields and gather wood for fuel. Later in life, he
would maintain close contact with his native village. At the age of eleven, he enrolled in a seminary to become a priest. He studied from 1882 to 1890 in Bergamo, and later at the Pontifical Seminary in Rome. He was ordained as a priest
in 1904. From 1905 to 1914, he worked as the secretary to the bishop of Bergamo, Giacomo Radini-Tedeschi, who became a second father to Roncalli. He
taught at the seminary where he had studied and began the practice of publishing a newsletter to tell people what the parish was doing. He also started
writing a history of the saints.

In 1914, Radini-Tedeschi died, and World War I began. Roncalli was
drafted into the Italian army, and served for over two years. After the war he
briefly became spiritual director of the Bergamo seminary, but in 1921 Pope
Benedict XV appointed him to reorganize the Society for the Propagation of
the Faith, an organization that supported Catholic missionary activity outside
Italy. In 1925 he was assigned to the Vatican diplomatic corps and was made an
archbishop. He succeeded in improving the Vatican's relations with Bulgaria
and Turkey. During World War II, when the rest of the world did not want to
believe that the Nazis were murdering six million Jews, Roncalli passed this information on to the Vatican. Shocked when the pope ordered him to do and
say nothing because the Vatican had to remain neutral in the war, Roncalli defied the pope's orders. He used the contacts that he had made in Turkey to help
Eastern European Jews escape from the Nazis.

Late in 1944, he received an appointment to become papal ambassador to

France, a country that had been terribly divided by the German invasion. The Vatican had recognized the German puppet government in France, and many French bishops, including the archbishop of Paris, were being accused of collaborating with the Nazis. Roncalli protested that he could not handle such a difficult assignment. He was told that he was the pope's personal choice.

Once in France, Roncalli performed brilliantly. He persuaded many of the collaborating bishops to resign, promoted bishops who had fought in the resistance, and became one of the most popular men in France. In 1953, at the age of seventy-one, Roncalli was reassigned to be patriarch of Venice. In 1958, he traveled to Rome to vote for the man who would replace Pope Pius XII, who had just died. On October 28, 1958, he was elected pope, at the age of seventy-seven. He took the name John, to honor his father's name and the name of the church in which he was baptized.

People expected John XXIII to be a quiet pope who would not do anything remarkable. He soon proved them wrong. Uncomfortable with the formalities that separated the pope from other people, he began inviting guests to join him for dinner, and traveling through Rome. He visited churches, hospitals, orphanages, prisons, and slums, often unannounced.

John had spent many years in the Vatican's diplomatic service. He knew firsthand how much work needed to be done to bring people of different religions and backgrounds together, to end war and promote love and peace. He created a special department in the Vatican to improve relations with non-Catholics.

He took stands on important political issues of the day. On Easter Sunday, 1963, he released a papal document that was for the first time addressed to all people of the world. Called *Pacem in Terris* (Peace on Earth), it proclaimed that every person had the right "to worship God in accordance with the right of his own conscience and to profess his religion in public." It pushed for increased participation of women in the modern world, and opposed the building and testing of nuclear weapons. It acknowledged that communist countries had an important role in creating a peaceful and just world. It spoke of conciliation between Catholics and non-Catholics, East and West, and rich and poor.

John's most important act was the convening of a council to change some fundamental Catholic traditions. Opened in October 1962, Vatican II, as it was called, brought about revolutionary changes in the Catholic Church. John died in June 1963, as the council was just getting under way, and so he did not live to see the great changes it brought about. When it ended, the Catholic Church no longer considered Protestants to be heretics, and had apologized to Jews for centuries of Catholic anti-Semitism. Jews were no longer to be thought of as "Christ killers," and the Catholic Church would stop trying to convert them. Within the Church itself, big changes were put into place. Priests could celebrate mass in languages other than Latin, so all people could understand the service. Religious freedom of Catholics was expanded, and nonclergy were allowed a greater role in the Church. In a few short years as pope, the humble farmer's son had given to millions of people around the world hope that peace and justice were possible. When he died, he was mourned by Catholics and non-Catholics alike.

Johns, Jasper

(1930–   )

AMERICAN PAINTER
AND SCULPTOR

Jasper Johns was born in Augusta, Georgia, on May 15, 1930. He never had any formal art training and he attended the University of South Carolina for two years before moving to New York.

Johns was drafted into the army during the Korean War, and when he returned to New York, he became close friends with the artist Robert Rauschenberg, who lived in the same apartment building. Johns and Rauschenberg discussed art and discovered that they were both interested in moving away from the abstract expressionist style popular at the time. The abstract expressionists were concerned with painting as a process, and not necessarily the final product.

One of Johns's first paintings to attract attention was *Flag* (1955), in which a boldly painted U.S. flag covers the entire canvas. At first, people did not know how to approach the painting, since it seemed to lack any emotion or setting; it was just a flag. Johns, however, was cleverly questioning the process of painting itself, the act of representing real objects through paint.

Johns soon began painting targets, numerals, and letters of the alphabet—all two-dimensional objects. He deliberately selected popular and simple objects in order to focus attention on the differences and similarities between the real object and its painted image. He also created a series of sculptures of beer cans, flashlights, and cans with brushes in them, that were so carefully constructed, that it was difficult to recognize them as art and not mistake them for the actual objects.

The later work of Johns is characterized by camouflaged images embedded in his paintings. He often has taken other paintings and copied a single image from the work and placed it in his own canvas, sometimes using different colors and distorting the image. "Not mine but taken," Johns has often said about his method of creating his art.

Johnson, Lyndon B.

(1908–1973)

UNITED STATES SENATOR, VICE PRESIDENT, AND THIRTY-SIXTH PRESIDENT

Lyndon Baines Johnson was born in Stonewall, Texas on August 27, 1908. His father, Sam Ealy Johnson, Jr., was a member of the Texas House of Representatives from a district of poor farmers and ranchers. His mother, Rebekah Baines, was a college student and a part-time reporter for an Austin newspaper when she met her husband. Raised in Johnson City, Texas, Johnson developed an early interest in politics because of all the local politicians who came to visit his father. In 1924, Sam Johnson became ill and retired from the Texas legislature. The family was deeply in debt and fell into poverty. In 1927, Lyndon enrolled at Southwest Texas State Teachers College in San Marcos. He graduated in 1930 in the midst of the Depression and taught at Sam Houston High School for a year.

Johnson began his move into politics when he went to Washington. D.C. as an assistant to freshman Representative Richard M. Kleberg and became a diligent student of the inner workings of the Washington political scene. When Franklin Roosevelt was elected in 1932, Johnson worked hard to get Texas farmers to cooperate with Roosevelt's farm program to grow less food and raise the prices of their crops. In 1934, he married a reporter for the *Daily Texan*.

Johnson befriended a powerful member of Congress, Sam Rayburn, who in 1935 secured him a job as the Texas state director of Roosevelt's National Youth Administration. In 1937, he was elected to the U.S. House of Representatives. In one of his first efforts in Congress, he helped to build a dam at the junction of the Colorado and Pedernales rivers, bringing electricity to rural Texas. The effort earned him the recognition and friendship of Roosevelt and the bright, young New Deal activists working with the President. Johnson was easily reelected to Congress in 1940.

Johnson ran for the Senate in 1941, but was narrowly defeated. When the Japanese attacked Pearl Harbor on December 7, 1941, Johnson became the first member of Congress to volunteer for military service. He became a lieutenant commander in the navy and was sent to Australia to report on the military preparations of General Douglas MacArthur. He managed to hitch a ride on an American aircraft sent to bomb New Guinea. The aircraft was attacked and badly damaged by Japanese Zeros and had to make an emergency landing. For his coolness under fire, MacArthur awarded Johnson the Silver Star. Johnson returned to Washington and in 1942 was elected to a third term in Congress.

Johnson made a second bid for the Senate in 1948 and won the election. He became an expert on national defense. He befriended many politicians, and by 1955 he became the Senate majority leader, the most powerful Democrat in the Senate. His ability to influence senators became legendary. The work exhausted Johnson, however, and in the summer of 1955 he suffered a heart attack.

He was back in the Senate in January 1956, facing a difficult debate over civil rights. In 1954, in *Brown v. Board of Education*, the Supreme Court had decided on the basis of a case in Topeka, Kansas that segregation in public schools was unconstitutional, but several southern states had refused to abide by the decision. President Dwight Eisenhower wanted Congress to pass a law creating a Civil Rights Division in the Justice Department that could sue southern states that refused to desegregate or give blacks the right to vote. Johnson broke with his fellow southern Democrats and worked to secure passage of the Civil Rights Act of 1957. In the wake of the Soviet launching of *Sputnik*, Johnson also sponsored the Space Act of 1958, which created the National Aeronautics and Space Administration (NASA).

Johnson had earned the reputation of a pragmatic senator who could get things done, and he began to consider a run for the presidency. In the election of 1960, he lost the Democratic nomination to John F. Kennedy, the young senator from Massachusetts. But Kennedy chose Johnson as his running mate, and in November they defeated their Republican opponent, Richard M. Nixon. But as an energetic and ambitious politician, he was bored with his duties, which were often largely ceremonial. Then suddenly, on November 22, 1963, Kennedy was assassinated in Dallas, Texas, and Johnson became President.

Johnson swore to "devote every hour of every day during the remainder of John Kennedy's unfulfilled term to achieving the goals he had set." Motivated by his New Deal liberalism, and relying on the friendships he had made in Congress, Johnson secured passage of a great many reform bills.

The first of the reform measures was the Tax Reduction Act of 1964. Next came the Civil Rights Act of 1964, which forbid discrimination against blacks in public accommodations. Two other civil rights laws extended the federal guarantee of black voting rights and prohibited discrimination in housing. The

Medicare program offered funds to help pay the medical costs of the elderly, and the Medicaid program offered similar benefits to the poor. Federal money was given to the nation's schools through the Elementary and Secondary Education Act and the Higher Education Act. Johnson also created the Department of Housing and Urban Development, the Department of Transportation, the National Endowment for the Humanities and the Arts, and the Corporation for Public Broadcasting. Through the Economic Opportunity Act of 1964, Johnson spent $3 billion on antipoverty programs, including the Job Corps, Volunteers in Service to America (VISTA), the Model Cities program, Project Head Start, and the Food Stamps program. The popularity of these liberal programs gave Johnson an easy victory against Republican Barry Goldwater in the 1964 presidential election.

After 1964, however, Johnson's attention and energy were absorbed by the war in Vietnam. In South Vietnam, a corrupt and undemocratic government, supported by the United States, was under increasing attack from guerrillas supported by North Vietnam. Despite the government's weakness, Kennedy had decided to support South Vietnam to prevent the entire country from falling to the Communists. At the time of Kennedy's death, there were seventeen thousand American troops fighting in South Vietnam. Continuing Kennedy's policy, Johnson began a rapid buildup of military forces in Vietnam. By 1968, there were more than five hundred thousand American soldiers serving in South Vietnam, and American aircraft were bombing the cities of North Vietnam.

The war did not go well. The stubborn resistance of Ho Chi Minh and his armies could not be broken. The hardships of jungle warfare demoralized American troops. At home, the costs of the war were taking funds away from Johnson's antipoverty programs. A broad antiwar protest movement developed, bringing riots and huge demonstrations across the country. Some of Johnson's closest advisers turned against him, as television brought the death and destruction of the war into American living rooms every night. In June 1968, after continual assurances from Johnson that the war was being won, Communist troops launched the Tet Offensive, penetrating South Vietnamese cities and exposing the inability of the Americans to defend the country.

Johnson grew increasingly isolated as his popularity fell. As the 1968 presidential elections grew close, Johnson was challenged for the Democratic nomination by two antiwar candidates: Senator Eugene McCarthy and Robert Kennedy, the former President's younger brother. Fearing defeat at the polls and exhausted by the war, on March 31, 1968 Johnson surprised the nation by announcing that he would not run for reelection. The Democratic nomination went to Vice President Hubert Humphrey, who was later defeated by Republican Richard M. Nixon, who claimed to have a secret plan to end the war.

Johnson retired to the LBJ ranch in Texas. He wrote his memoirs and supervised the building of the Lyndon B. Johnson Presidential Library at the University of Texas in Austin. On January 22, 1973, the day after Nixon announced a cease fire in Vietnam, Johnson suffered another heart attack and died.

Lyndon Johnson had a genuine vision of America as a "Great Society" in which a nationwide war against poverty could be waged through a vast program of economic and social welfare legislation. But his administration created much controversy, and he is generally regarded as a tragic figure whose progressive programs would have earned him the reputation of a great President had he not been insistent on fighting an unpopular war against a determined enemy.

Johnson, Philip

(1906–   )

AMERICAN ARCHITECT

Philip Cortelyou Johnson was born in Cleveland, Ohio, on July 8, 1906. He was educated at Harvard University and graduated in 1930. He immediately accepted the job as director of the department of architecture at the newly established Museum of Modern Art (MOMA) in New York, and remained there until 1936, when Johnson returned to Harvard to get a professional degree in architecture.

In 1932, in collaboration with Henry Russell Hitchcock, Johnson organized the now famous exhibition, *The International Style: Architecture Since 1922*, with a catalogue that became the most important text on modern architecture. The exhibit was important because it illustrated the great works of early modern architects, mostly European, including Mies Van der Rohe.

Johnson organized Mies van der Rohe's first visit to the United States. Johnson hired the famous architect to design his New York apartment, and then found Mies van der Rohe other clients. Mies van der Rohe eventually became an American citizen and one of the most influential architects in the United States. Johnson wrote a book on Mies Van der Rohe, which is still regarded as one of the best books on the architect.

After working as an author, critic, and museum director, Philip Johnson built his first important building at the age of forty-six. The Glass House in New Caanan, Connecticut, was based upon several designs of Mies Van der Rohe's, who had wanted to build a completely transparent structure. Johnson used other architect's ideas in order to create his own unique work. While the Glass House was both admired and ridiculed, it remains a landmark in post–World War II American architecture for its entirely modern design.

Johnson never again matched the excellence of his first effort, but in the years following the Glass House, he designed and built a series of middle class family houses that rate as some of the best houses ever designed. He also helped Mies Van der Rohe design the Seagram Building in New York, which is regarded as the finest skyscraper ever built.

The 1960s were a period of creative uncertainty, as Johnson began to question the ideas of modern architecture he had championed for so long. His designs began to borrow more from early American architects, especially Henry H. Richardson and Charles McKim. Johnson's design for a new section of the Boston Public Library (1973) shows the influence of the nineteenth-century buildings; while the American Telephone and Telegraph (A. T. & T.) skyscraper in New York (1980) is a modern building, it still manages to include McKim's ideas of detail and design in the steel-and-glass construction.

Philip Johnson's experimentation in his architecture and his combining of modern and old techniques has irritated and surprised other architects and critics, but has also given the architect an important and unique place in the history of American architecture.

Johnson, Rafer Lewis

(1936–   )

AMERICAN DECATHLON COMPETITOR

When Rafer Johnson was 16, he was already a fine runner and baseball player. One day he attended a track and field meet at Tulare, California, a town not far from where he lived. At the meet, Johnson saw Olympic gold medal winner Bob Mathias win a decathlon event. Watching the various events, Johnson decided to train for the decathlon, a decision that led him to an Olympic gold medal in 1960.

Rafer Johnson was born in Texas but grew up in Kingsburg, California, where his parents moved with their six children. Rafer was a good student as well as baseball player during his early teens. He enjoyed track and field and could jump a distance of 21 feet when he was 15. In high school, he played football and basketball and continued to add more decathlon events to his training, including the broad jump, high hurdles, and discus throw. At 6'3"½ and 190 pounds, he was strong and had the agility needed for these different kinds of events.

In 1954 Johnson entered a national decathlon championship sponsored by the Amateur Athletic Union. Despite his inexperience, he finished third. While practicing long hours for several sports, he had managed to maintain an A average in school and to serve as class president his senior year. After graduation, he entered UCLA (University of California at Los Angeles), where he trained in track and field with a well-known coach.

Johnson won the decathlon at the 1955 Pan American games. Not only did he defeat other decathletes from North and South America, he broke the previous world record held by American Bob Mathias and came close to the points earned by the Russian man who had won the world decathlon title that year. Shortly thereafter, the Russian, named Vasily Kuznetsov, topped his previous world record.

Now 20 years old, Rafer Johnson competed in his first Olympics, in Melbourne, Australia. Unfortunately, he was having problems with his knees and had to drop out of the long jump. Although injured, he won a silver medal, finishing second in the decathlon. The next year at a world championship, he finished second to Kuznetsov, then beat him later the same year during another competition. The world title went back to the Russian in 1959.

As the Olympics drew near, Johnson suffered another setback: His back was seriously hurt in an auto accident. He could not train all year, although he did some coaching at UCLA. Courageously, he worked to regain his edge before the Summer Games in Italy.

When they began, Rafer Johnson walked at the head of the U.S. team as it arrived for the opening ceremonies. He had been chosen by his teammates to carry the flag, always a great honor.

During the two days of competition, Johnson was part of a three-way race for the gold medal. He did especially well in the discus and javelin throw. When the time came for the 1,500-meter race that would determine the decathlon winner, Johnson ran hard, knowing he must be either first or a close second to win. He managed to stay right behind the leading runner to win the decathlon. Johnson said he was relieved to have finished and now felt like going for a long, relaxing walk.

Retiring from competition, Rafer Johnson was a popular public speaker and received many awards for his contributions to American sports. He was active in the civil rights movement and political events, and has pursued new careers in business and acting.

Jordan, Michael Jeffery

(1963–   )

AMERICAN BASKETBALL PLAYER

Michael Jordan's former college coach once said, "Jordan was a hero so many times at the end of games it was uncanny." One such moment came during the 1982 NCAA (National College Athletic Association) championship game while Jordan was a freshman on the University of North Carolina team. Its Georgetown opponents led by one point, 62–61. From seventeen feet away, Jordan received the pass. In the last second, he hurled the ball toward the basketball hoop and scored.

Michael Jordan was born in Wilmington, North Carolina, in 1963, the third of five children. His father worked as a supervisor at a General Electric plant, and his mother was a customer service representative at a local bank. The family was close. Michael later said, "My parents warned me about the traps—the drugs and drink, the streets that could catch you if you got careless. They gave me guidance and taught me to work hard."

Michael played several sports as a child, and his parents always watched him compete. In high school, he competed in track and field, baseball, football, and basketball. Worried about injuries in football, his mother steered him toward basketball. Michael was not an instant success. He was short and underweight at 14.

By his senior year, Michael had shot up to 6'6"1/2". All the hours of practicing and running began to pay off as a taller, stronger player took shape. As he neared graduation, colleges began to offer him athletic scholarships. Michael chose the University of North Carolina (UNC) for its sports and educational programs. He especially liked coach Dean Smith. Michael enrolled as a geography major, planning to teach in college after he finished playing basketball.

By the end of his freshman year, Jordan was regarded as one of best defensive guards in the country. He got praise for his ability to follow the ball and to sense where it was going. People marveled at his high leaps and knack for making baskets from many places on the floor. He helped the United States to win the Pan-American Games in Caracas in 1983, scoring 12 points in the second half of the game against the Brazilian team.

Jordan continued to amaze other players and fans, who thought he was superhuman on the court. He was voted top college player for the 1983–84 season. Jordan spent summers working with young people at basketball camps.

Just before his senior year, Jordan decided to turn pro, knowing his earnings would help his family. The Chicago Bulls chose him with their first pick that spring. As a rookie, Jordan played well and seemed at ease. With Jordan at guard, the Bulls rose to the top of the National Basketball Association's Central Division. Ticket sales rose. He was named Rookie of the Year, and ranked third in scoring, with an average of 28.2 points a game. He made 2.39 steals per game and led his team in assists and rebounds.

During the 1985–86 season, Jordan fell during a game and broke some bones in his left foot. He missed most of the season and was depressed about not getting to play.

When he tried exercising and playing basketball at a local gym, his foot felt strong. But was it as good as before? Jordan asked to play in the last fifteen games of the season, and the Bulls finally agreed. He scored about 22 points a game and looked as good as ever during the playoffs. Opponents still complained that trying to guard Jordan was an impossible task.

In 1986–87, Michael Jordan collected an astonishing 159 points in one three-game period, racking up 59 of them during thirty-seven minutes of playing time in one game. His average of 37.1 points per game that year topped the NBA. He also became the first player since Wilt Chamberlain to score over 3,000 points in a single season.

As the 1990s began, Jordan seemed better than ever. One of his great thrills was playing with other basketball superstars like Larry Bird and Magic Johnson in the 1992 Olympics at Barcelona, Spain. The Dream Team brought the United States a gold medal.

His good manners and talent led people to call Michael Jordan the "Gentleman Superstar." He said, "I'm very grateful that a lot of people respect me for my ability. But it's equally important that people respect me as a man." Besides setting an example for young people, Jordan has given his time and money. He was involved in Special Olympics and Head Start programs for preschoolers and has frequently spoken out about drugs, saying, "I'm strictly against drugs and alcohol and I want people to know that I'm not afraid to say no. If they're put in the same situation and if they saw that I said no, then they can say the same thing."

Already a legendary sports hero, Jordan has used his influence in public service messages and commercials on behalf of important causes. A basketball and a pair of shoes—Air Jordan—were named for him. When Smith Sports Center was established in Chapel Hill at UNC, the school retired Jordan's number 23 jersey. Only ten other UNC players have been so honored. Basketball player Clyde Drexler once said of Jordan, "He's a pro's pro. We even like to see him play—when we're not playing against him."

Joyce, James

(1882–1941)

IRISH NOVELIST, SHORT-STORY WRITER, POET,
AND PLAYWRIGHT

James Joyce is *the* central figure in the modernist period of Western literature, perhaps the central figure in Western literature in this century. His completed output was slender—three novels, one collection of short stories, two books of poetry, and a play—but his influence on other writers has been incalculable.

James Joyce was born on February 2, 1882, in Dublin, Ireland. His father, John, had secured a job through his connection to the leader of the Irish Parliamentary Party, Charles Stewart Parnell. When a divorce scandal (in intensely Catholic Ireland) wrecked Parnell's career, the older Joyce lost his job as well. His mother dreamed of the priesthood for James, who was the oldest of ten children who survived to adulthood.

Dublin was the second-largest city in the British Empire, but a provincial backwater culturally, despite the rising tide embodied by William Butler Yeats and the Celtic Twilight movement. These writers, harkening back to a misty, lost tradition of Gaelic fairy stories, were of no interest to Joyce. He wanted to connect to modern literature, to his beloved Henrik Ibsen (Joyce taught himself Norwegian in order to read the playwright in the original), and to the history of English literature that the Gaelic revivalists rejected.

Young James was sent to Clongowes Wood College, a well-regarded Jesuit-run school outside Dublin, from the age of six. The school was strict, but instilled in the boys a love of language and a sense of intellectual commitment. James was an excellent student, but was homesick at the school. Eventually, his father's financial problems forced him to withdraw, continuing his schooling at another Jesuit institution in Dublin proper. After 1894, he won prizes for academic achievement virtually every year.

In 1898, Joyce enrolled in University College, Dublin, a Catholic school. It was there that he displayed great talent as a writer and first expressed his enthusiasm for Ibsen, a controversial choice at the turn of the century. In the summer of 1900, Joyce wrote his first serious imaginative work, a drama called *A Brilliant Career*, the story of a doctor who marries a woman he doesn't love in order to advance his career. The play was never produced, never published, and, as far as is known, no manuscript exists.

Given his superb record as a secondary-school student, Joyce was a bit of a disappointment to his family during his college years. Although he graduated in 1902, he was an undistinguished student, bored by the college curriculum.

Joyce enrolled in medical school, but he spent most of his time in the summer of 1902 pursuing a literary career. His father's fortunes continued to decline, and it was unclear how Joyce could possibly pay for medical school. Joyce took this opportunity to depart for Paris, France, supposedly to look for a medical school there. In reality, it was the first step in his eventual disengagement from an Ireland he was coming to hate.

In Paris, Joyce took a few classes and then came home for Christmas at his mother's urging. He quickly returned to France, only to be summoned once again by a telegram that arrived on Good Friday, April 10, 1903: MOTHER DYING COME HOME. FATHER. Joyce returned home immediately. His mother died of cancer in mid-August. The following summer, Joyce, still in Dublin, met and began wooing an uneducated hotel maid, Nora Barnacle. Their first encounter took place on June 16, 1904, at Finn's Hotel, where she was employed. In honor of that occasion, he set the action of his novel *Ulysses* (1922) on that day, now known as Bloomsday for the book's protagonist, Leopold Bloom. By October, the couple was ready to run off together to the Continent. Except for two brief visits, Joyce never returned to Ireland.

The couple settled in Trieste, in northeastern Italy, where Joyce supported himself by teaching English in the Berlitz school. Their son, Giorgio, was born in 1905. He was followed by a much-troubled daughter, Lucia, in 1907.

That was also the year in which Joyce published his first book, a collection of poems, *Chamber Music*, and the year in which he finished *The Dead*, the moving novella that ends *Dubliners*; and the year in which he scrapped an autobiographical fragment, *Stephen Hero*, and began rewriting it completely as *Portrait of the Artist as a Young Man*.

Joyce returned to Ireland briefly in 1909, trying to find a publisher for *Dubliners*. Perhaps the worst setback came on September 11, 1912, when the printer, outraged by what he called "unpatriotic" material in the book, burned the proofs. That was the last straw for Joyce; he left Ireland that same night, never to return.

In 1914, *Dubliners* was finally published by Grant Richards. The years in between had taken a hard toll on the Joyce family in Trieste. In fact, the Joyce-Barnacle relationship was under tremendous strain (they were not married, and would not be until 1931). Joyce had conceived a passion for one of his students, while a friend of theirs had propositioned Nora. That strain was reflected in his next piece of writing. In 1913, just before this crisis period passed with the publication of *Dubliners*, Joyce began writing his only published play, the aptly titled *Exiles*. Not surprisingly, it is about a writer facing a marital crisis after returning to Dublin.

With the outbreak of World War I, Joyce had to leave Italy, so the family moved to Zurich, in neutral Switzerland. By then, *Dubliners* had finally been published, *Portrait* and *Exiles* were finished, and Joyce had completed a rough draft of the first three chapters of *Ulysses*.

Ulysses was published in 1922 in Paris. As the title suggests, the book parallels *The Odyssey*, with the role of Odysseus assumed by a warm, decent Dublin Jew, Leopold Bloom, and Stephen Dedalus, back in Dublin once more after a period in Paris, as his surrogate son for a day. But the book also draws on a vast array of other literary works in its mind-bogglingly complex structure. There are references to *Hamlet*, to Sinbad the Sailor, the Wandering Jew, Moses, Christ, Icarus, Lucifer, and the Prodigal Son. The book is a dazzling kaleidoscope of writing styles, as well, with Joyce parodying numerous other writers.

Ulysses, published at the high point of the modernist period, can be read as a response to the recently concluded Great War, reflecting the collapsing values of Western civilization.

The book had a notorious and difficult publication history. *Ulysses* was originally serialized in *The Little Review*, a distinguished literary magazine, but the serialization was halted in America by court order when the U.S. Post Office complained that certain episodes were obscene. In England, copies were burned on the boat docks. For several years, Americans had to go to Paris to buy *Ulysses*, then had to smuggle the blue-covered book past customs inspectors eager to protect America from this "dirty" book. Finally, in 1933, the U.S. District Court declared that the book was not obscene. Of course, all this controversy boosted sales, and Joyce approached much of it with good humor: He finally had a best-seller.

Joyce, in the meantime, had begun work on his next book, tentatively titled *Work in Progress*. Beginning in 1925, pieces of the book appeared in serial form in the magazine *transition*. Joyce would continue working on this final book for seventeen years; it was finally published as *Finnegans Wake* in 1939.

Finnegans Wake is probably the most difficult great book ever written, the key text of the high-modernist era. It is dense with literary allusions, and full of puns in every sentence in a dozen different languages; it requires us to learn how to read all over again.

The Paris years were good ones for Joyce. He found himself famous at last, surrounded by admirers and colleagues. And, for the first time, he was financially comfortable. The family could afford to take vacations, and the new-found leisure probably contributed to the lengthy writing period for *Wake*. But even the good times were rocky. Joyce's eyesight, never good, was failing. His daughter Lucia was gradually sinking into schizophrenia, although Joyce denied this for a long time before she was to be institutionalized.

It is not known what Joyce planned to do after he finished and published *Finnegans Wake*. He supposedly told one friend that his next book would be a simple one, that since *Wake* was about a river, this one would be about the sea. He really never had the chance to think about it. World War II broke out almost immediately after the book was published, and the Joyces were once more forced to seek refuge. They stayed briefly in the south of France, then were finally admitted to Switzerland (after dispelling a rumor that Joyce was Jewish). Three weeks after they settled in Zurich once more, Joyce was admitted to the hospital with a perforated duodenal ulcer. He died on the operating table of peritonitis.

In evaluating Joyce's legacy, many people focus on his innovations in novelistic technique, such as his use of stream-of-consciousness, and his wildly inventive and unconditional play with language. These are true and important, but we should not overlook his largeness of spirit; Joyce's vision embraces all of humanity, and does so with zest and humor.

Jung, Carl

(1875-1961)

SWISS PSYCHOANALYST

Man, as we realize if we reflect for a moment, never perceives anything fully or comprehends anything completely.

> —Carl Jung, from *Man and His Symbols*

Three names dominate the early days of psychoanalysis—Sigmund Freud, Alfred Adler, and Carl Jung. Jung, the most creative thinker of the three and the one whose intellectual curiosity led him to search for and assimilate ideas from virtually every culture in the history of mankind, made enormous contributions not only to the study of, and therapy for, the human mind, but to art, religion, history, economics, and scientific philosophy.

Carl Gustav Jung was born in Kesswil, Switzerland, on July 26, 1875. His family was strongly religious; his father and eight uncles were all ministers, and their influences played a major role in shaping the young man's ideas later. When, late in Jung's life, his father began to doubt his religion and turned to science to find answers, the relationship between father and son soured. Carl's mother was sickly and superstitious and confided in her son, thus providing a very different influence from that of her husband. The boy was an only child until he was almost ten years old, and he spent his early childhood with the poor farming people of his area, from whom he absorbed a fascination with folklore and an appreciation of nature.

The family moved to Basel, Switzerland, in 1879, and Carl enrolled in the

Universitat Basel in 1895. He received a degree in medicine in 1900 and moved to Zurich, where he began a lifelong career in psychiatry. At that time Sigmund Freud, the father of pyschoanalysis, was considered to be the towering figure of the field; he headed the branch of psychoanalytic thinking that was referred to as the Vienna School. Jung belonged to the less traditional Zurich School, and he soon became its preeminent figure.

One of Jung's first contributions was what came to be called the "association method." In essence, it relied on helping the patient in analysis come in touch with nonconscious factors in his or her psyche. He spoke on this subject when he and Freud were invited to the United States to attend the twentieth anniversary of Clark University, in Massachusetts.

In 1911, Jung founded the International Psychoanalytic Society. Continuing his work with patients and his research, he made a number of other innovative contributions to his field. These included a new perspective on the psychological interpretation of myth, fantasy, and dreams. He created the term "collective unconscious," which described a level of awareness deeper than the personal unconscious and one that people of similar traditions and cultures share, without realizing it consciously. His work in this area led him to study traditional cultures around the world. One of his trips was made to investigate the Pueblo Indians of Arizona and New Mexico.

Jung also was the first to explore the importance of symbolic language, dreams, and the arts in getting in touch with the unconscious. On this issue he parted with the thinking of Freud, who was unwilling to pursue such a daring approach. Jung resigned from the Psychoanalytic Society in 1913 over this disagreement. The concept of extrovert and introvert types of personalities was also a contribution made by Jung.

In 1937, Jung spoke at Yale University, in New Haven, Connecticut, about the connection between religion and psychology, claiming that the "religious function" was in each individual and that, for reasons of mental health, it was important to be in touch with that need. Then, in 1944, the University of Basel created a special position for him in medical psychology. At the time he also pursued an interest in alchemy in response to his observation that many of his patients had dreams about the subject. He was particularly interested in the symbolic and artistic elements of the concept.

Jung resigned his teaching position at Basel in 1945. In 1948, he created the C.G. Jung Institute Zurich. He was given honorary doctorate degrees by Oxford University, Harvard University, the University of Calcutta (India), and several other schools. He also was inducted into the Royal Society of England in honor of his ground-breaking ideas.

Carl Jung died in Switzerland on June 6, 1961.

Kafka, Franz

(1883–1924)

CZECH NOVELIST, SHORT-STORY WRITER, AND DIARIST

> I think we ought to read only the kind of books that wound and stab us.
>
> —Franz Kafka

Kafka was born in Prague, Czechoslovakia (then part of the Austro-Hungarian empire), on July 3, 1883. His father, Hermann, was a wealthy Jewish wholesaler in fancy goods, a self-made man who dominated his son, who alternately idolized and detested his father over the course of his life. Franz's mother, Julie, was a capable and intelligent woman, a virtual partner in the family business. Franz was the oldest surviving child, two older brothers having died in early childhood. He had three sisters, the oldest of whom was six years younger than he, so he occasionally found himself in the role of protective big brother.

Kafka was brought up with little sense of Jewish identity; in his famous letter to his father, dated November 1919, he reproached the older Kafka for not instilling in him that sense of identity, of historical belonging. Hermann was a domineering presence in the household, pushing Franz repeatedly into situations in which he would excel but be miserable. His father insisted on German schools and a German university, where Kafka was unhappy much of the time, yet was an excellent student.

At university, Kafka studied law, but he was becoming attracted to the idea of being a writer, and began to move in Prague literary circles.

Most important for his future, Kafka met and became friends with eighteen-year-old Max Brod at a meeting of the "Section for Literature." Brod, a year younger than Kafka, was much further along in his literary ambitions, lecturing on Arthur Schopenhauer and Friedrich Nietzsche. Like Kafka, Brod was studying law. They remained intimate friends for the rest of Kafka's life, and Brod later played a pivotal role in preserving Kafka's literary output.

In June 1906, Kafka completed a doctor-of-laws degree and took a job with a small Italian insurance company. Two years later, he was employed by the government-run Workers' Accident Insurance Bureau; a job he held for the next sixteen years. In the meantime, he was writing, slowly and painstakingly. In 1906, he had entered a short-story contest sponsored by a Viennese magazine. He published eight short sketches in the journal *Hyperion* in 1908; after much prodding from Brod, Kafka allowed them to be collected into a small book.

Outside the office, Kafka was studying Czech and becoming mildly active in

Czech nationalist politics. He considered himself a socialist, a position he had embraced as early as secondary school. He was a sickly young man, suffering from migraine headaches and nervous upsets. He experimented with vegetarianism, hoping that his problems would decrease.

Kafka also began to explore his Jewish heritage, studying the ancient mystical texts of the Cabala. From his diaries, one can see that he was becoming deeply involved in Jewish traditions. In his writings, one can see his affinity for the ideas of the mystics who believed in a hidden world that was integrally connected to the visible one.

On August 12, 1912, he met with Max Brod to give him the manuscript of a collection of short pieces to be published under the title *Meditations*. The next night, visiting Max once again, Kafka was introduced to a charming and attractive Jewish woman from Berlin, Felice Bauer. Thoroughly smitten, Kafka wrote to her on September 20, beginning a stormy relationship that continued in one form or another for five years. Over that time, he proposed marriage twice, each time breaking off the engagement.

Felice inspired him as a writer. Six weeks after their first meeting, he wrote "The Judgment," one of his best short stories, in a single exhausting night. *Meditations* was published, and he sent a copy to Felice. He began the novel that would eventually be published posthumously as *Amerika*; the first chapter was published in 1913. And he started work on his most famous story, *The Metamorphosis* (which was published in 1915).

A novella, *The Metamorphosis* begins with a matter-of-fact statement: "As Gregor Samsa awoke one morning from uneasy dreams he found himself transformed in his bed into a gigantic insect." From this stunning beginning, Kafka constructs a startling parable of family relations. Gregor's passivity and the constant struggle for dominion within the family unit are unnervingly portrayed.

The outbreak of war in 1914 barely registered in Kafka's world. Kafka's government position made him exempt from the draft. He was much more preoccupied with his writing and his formal engagement to Felice. Kafka's health was beginning to decline as the tuberculosis that would eventually kill him began to attack his lungs. In 1915, he won the Theodor Fontane Prize for "The Stoker," the excerpt from *Amerika*. In 1916, he wrote and published another major story, "In the Penal Colony," and began work on *The Trial*.

The Trial, which was published posthumously, opens with a brutally blunt and simple statement: "Someone must have traduced Joseph K., for without having done anything wrong he was arrested one fine morning." The book has the free-flowing logic of a dream, with places and incidents tumbling over one another. The result is both nightmarish and funny.

By the end of 1917, Kafka was diagnosed with tuberculosis of the lungs. He broke off his relationship with Felice Bauer once and for all. His doctors recommended a rest cure in a sanitarium.

As the war dragged on, food shortages, coal shortages, and the like were crushing the inhabitants of the city. Kafka tried to keep writing, keep working, and stay healthy. After retiring from his job in 1922, he moved from sanitarium to sanitarium. He was writing some of his best stories at the time, and working on "The Castle" (which was published in 1926).

In summer 1923, he met a young Polish Jew, Dora Dymant, the daughter of an Orthodox rabbi, many years younger than the forty-year-old Kafka. He had finally found a woman with whom he could settle down happily. The couple moved back to Prague, and Kafka wrote one of his rare optimistic stories, "A Little Woman." But his health was failing; between Christmas and New Year's Day, he lay in bed with a high fever. On March 17, 1924, Max Brod, who had been sending the couple food parcels regularly, took Franz to his home. The nearly six-foot-tall Kafka was down to 108 pounds, almost unable to speak or eat as the disease spread to his larynx. But he kept writing, finishing one last story, "Josephine the Singer, or The Mouse People."

On June 2, Kafka, who was by then in a sanitarium once more, was feeling a little better, and he ate some strawberries and cherries. He was apparently working on the proofs of a collection of his stories, *A Hunger Artist*. He fell asleep at midnight, with Dora by his bedside. He died on June 3 at the age of forty, weighing a mere ninety pounds.

Kafka had told Max Brod that he wanted his diaries, his letters, and all his manuscripts destroyed upon his death. He had published only a handful of stories in his lifetime and, had Brod followed those instructions, he probably would have been forgotten not long after his untimely death. Instead, Brod shepherded the unfinished material into print.

Kafka's influence on subsequent literature has been enormous. No one better embodies the feelings of alienation and displacement experienced by man in the face of the mass society and mass destruction of the last hundred years. As Frederick Karl, one of his biographers, observed, no other writer in this century has had his name used as an adjective (Kafkaesque) to describe a worldview. "No other contemporary or near contemporary literary figure has given his name to such a state of being, to such a majestic sense of demonic forces," Karl wrote. "*Proustian* or *Joycean* suggests a literary style, a manner, even a tone, but not a way of life."

Kasparov, Gary

(1963–   )

RUSSIAN CHESS PLAYER

Many experts consider Gary Kasparov the greatest chess player of all time. In 1985, he became the youngest world champion ever by defeating Anatoly Karpov in a long, tense match. Always outspoken, Kasparov was not afraid to use his lofty position to challenge the world chess authorities, even at the cost of his title.

Gary Kasparov was born Harry Weinstein on April 13, 1963, in Baku, the capital of what is now the country of Azerbaijan. His father died in a traffic accident when Kasparov was a child, and the government authorities who took care of him changed his name to Gary Kasparov. Kasparov is a Russian variation of his Armenian mother's maiden name, Kasparyan.

Like Anatoly Karpov, Kasparov learned chess through a correspondence course, under the guidance of Mikhail Botvinnik. His chess hero as a child was Alexander Alekhine, the two-time French champion. Kasparov began forging his own path to the championship at the age of twelve, when he won both the Azerbaijan and Soviet junior championships. On his seventeenth birthday, he was awarded the title of grand master, establishing himself as one of the world's top players.

Kasparov's game reminded chess experts of previous grand masters like Russians Mikhail Tal and Anatoly Karpov. Kasparov could be fiery and aggressive on the board, but he maintained a solid defensive game as well. He developed a reputation for arrogance that both intimidated and irritated his opponents.

In 1984, Kasparov first challenged Karpov for the world championship. The tense match was stopped by an international chess official before its conclusion, in a controversial and unpopular decision. In the 1985 rematch, Kasparov defeated his opponent and claimed the world title. He defeated Karpov in a 1986 match as well, leaving no confusion as to who was the world's greatest living player.

The outspoken Kasparov was not content simply to defend his title, however. In 1994, dissatisfied with chess's governing body, the International Chess Federation, he formed his own group, the Professional Chess Association, and set up a match with Britain's Nigel Short. The federation refused to recognize this match and stripped Kasparov of his champion's title. Only thirty-one years old, Gary Kasparov was still widely considered the best player on the planet, with or without official recognition.

Keaton, Buster

(1895–1966)

AMERICAN ACTOR
AND FILMMAKER

Born Joseph Francis Keaton to a vaudeville family, Keaton received his nickname from an old family friend, the famous escape artist Harry Houdini. At the age of six months Keaton fell down a flight of stairs without a scratch; "Buster" was a vaudeville term for a comic fall. By the age of three, Keaton had joined his family in vaudeville as the "Three Keatons." Buster was soon the star attraction, but after his father began drinking heavily (making their acrobatic act very dangerous), the trio disbanded. Buster went to New York to appear as a solo act on Broadway for $250 per week in *The Passing Show of 1917.*

Keaton met up with an old friend of his from vaudeville, Rosco "Fatty" Arbuckle, who invited him to watch the filming of a comedy short at Arbuckle's studio. Keaton became fascinated with the camera and decided to leave Broadway to work for $40 per week for Arbuckle. He learned all he could from Fatty. His first film was *The Butcher Boy* (1917), in which he established his role of an ordinary man who constantly endures the comic disasters of fate with an unsmiling face. Keaton took over Arbuckle's film studio in 1921, when he began writing, directing, and acting in his feature comedies, such as *The Playhouse, The Boat* (1921), and *Cops* (1922). In the early 1920s, Keaton and Charlie Chaplin were the kings of comedy.

Keaton was ahead of his time with *Sherlock Junior* (1924), a film in which Keaton, as a film projectionist, jumps in and out of the movie that he is projecting in the film. *The Navigator* (1926) was his biggest box-office success, and *The General* (1926) had one of the greatest chase scenes in all of film comedy. In fact, the Marx Brothers used the same idea for the climax of their film *Go West* (1940).

Keaton was his own boss, making movies the way he wanted. But he made the mistake of letting someone talk him into giving up his own studio to make movies for MGM in Hollywood. From the start, MGM tried to change the way Keaton made his films. His first movie, *The Cameraman* (1928), was a hit, but he had to fight MGM for every gag he wanted to put into the film. The next two comedies were moderately successful, including his first "talkie," *Free and Easy* (1930). But every film thereafter was a flop. Keaton was screen-tested to become a dramatic actor, but nothing came of it. By 1933 Keaton was drinking heavily, had gotten divorced from his wife, and was broke. Then MGM fired him from the studio.

During the next two decades, Keaton occasionally appeared in films, in minor roles. It was not until Chaplin made *Limelight* (1952) that the public started to notice the comic artistry of Buster Keaton. In 1957 Donald O'Connor starred in the *The Buster Keaton Story*, a movie that introduced his work to a new generation to the once famous silent film star. Keaton spent the rest of his life making guest appearances in movies such as *It's a Mad, Mad, Mad, Mad World* (1962) and *How to Stuff a Wild Bikini* (1965). Keaton died in 1966.

Keller, Helen

(1880–1968)

AMERICAN SOCIAL REFORMER, FEMINIST, PACIFIST, AND ADVOCATE FOR THE BLIND AND DEAF

I look upon the world as my fatherland, and every war has to me a horror of a family feud. I look upon true patriotism as the brotherhood of man and the service of all to all.

> —Helen Keller, "Menace of the Militarist Program", *New York Call*, Dec. 20, (1915)

Helen Keller overcame deafness, muteness, and blindness to achieve her ideal of serving others. Having overcome so much herself, she took on a mission to help the disadvantaged—especially as an advocate for the blind and deaf—through lectures, fund-raising and personal appeals to lawmakers. Although she became a symbol of the triumph of courage, will, and intelligence over adversity, Keller was a writer and educator, a social reformer, and a feminist.

Helen Keller was born in Tuscumbia, Alabama. She could see, hear, and by the time she was one, speak. In 1882, Helen suffered from a severe illness that left her deaf, blind, and mute at nineteen months. A wild, willful child, Keller invented sixty signs on her own as a way of making her desires known. In 1886, Keller's mother sought help from the Perkins Institution for the Blind in Boston. The institution recommended Anne Sullivan, a recent Perkins graduate, as Keller's teacher and governess. Sullivan, partially cured of her own blindness, would exercise the greatest influence on Keller as a child—and throughout her life.

Using a combination of love and discipline, Sullivan in 1887 tamed Helen's wildness within two weeks. Sullivan taught Helen the "manual alphabet": an alphabet for the deaf that uses the positioning of fingers to form letters. Within a month, Helen realized that everything had a name, and that the manual alphabet was her path to knowledge. This moment of realization was later portrayed in the famous water-pump scene in William Gibson's play and movie, *The Miracle Worker*. By spelling out the names of objects in Helen's hand, Sullivan taught her more than three-hundred words in a few months. After four months of teaching, Helen wrote her first letter—to her mother.

In 1888, Sullivan brought Helen to Boston to live at the Perkins Institution. By this time, the press had already begun to praise Helen's accomplishments. While at Perkins from 1888 to 1894, Helen learned to read and write in Braille. Helen begged Sullivan to teach her how to speak, eventually convincing her teacher to cooperate. Helen learned to speak by placing her fingers on Sullivan's throat to "hear" (through her fingers) the vibrations when she spoke. From 1890 to 1894, she took speech classes at the Horace Mann School for the Deaf in Boston. During this period, she demonstrated her first charitable impulses. She helped raise money for a deaf, blind, and mute boy to receive schooling at Perkins. In 1894, Sullivan brought Helen to New York to attend the Wright-Humason School, which taught deaf children how to speak.

After Helen's father died in 1896, Sullivan raised funds to allow her student to enroll in the Cambridge School for Young Ladies. Through this school, and two years of work with a private tutor, Helen Keller gained admission to Radcliffe College—with advanced credit in Latin—in 1900. Keller took on a full course load at Radcliffe. Sullivan attended all classes with her, spelling lectures into Keller's hands. With the help of Sullivan and Harvard University literature instructor John Macy, Keller wrote an autobiography, *The Story of My Life*, published in 1902. Keller used the money earned from the book to buy a farm in Wrentham, Massachusetts. The following year, she published a second book, *Optimism*, an essay that conveys her faith in life's essential goodness. In 1904, she received honors and applause upon her graduation from Radcliffe.

In 1905, Sullivan married Macy, who joined her in working with Keller. The following year, the governor of Massachusetts appointed Keller to the nation's first State Commission for the Blind. Keller soon raised eyebrows by campaigning against sexually transmitted disease, a previously unmentionable subject. Keller, however, insisted on addressing it, because it caused blindness in newborn infants. *The World I Live In*, a collection of essays about the way Keller perceived the world was published in 1908.

At this time, Keller became active in other social reforms as well. She joined the Socialist Party in 1909 and was also committed to the cause of women's suffrage. She supported striking textile workers in Lawrence, Massachusetts in 1912. The following year, Keller published a collection of socialist essays, *Out of the Dark*.

Anne and John Macy separated in 1913, though they never divorced. That year, Keller and Anne Sullivan Macy began a series of cross-country lecture tours. They were joined by Polly Thomson, a young woman who served as Keller's secretary, housekeeper, and hairdresser. Thomson would remained with Keller for almost fifty years.

Keller continued to work toward social reforms. In 1915, she called for a general strike against war when the U.S. began to abandon its neutrality in World War I. Keller joined Industrial Workers of the World, and she appealed to the governor of Utah to spare the life of IWW organizer and songwriter Joe Hill. As a feminist, she endorsed the birth-control movement promoted by Margaret Sanger. She also supported the National Association for the Advancement of Colored People, founded in 1909 to work toward the goal of equal rights for African Americans. She also urged the passage of laws that would prohibit child labor and outlaw the death penalty.

In 1924, Keller began serving as a spokesperson for the American Foundation for the Blind (AFB). In addition to helping the foundation raise funds, Keller in the 1930s sought out lawmakers to win new laws to benefit the blind. Her lobbying helped secure federal money to fund reading services for the blind, as well as other laws benefiting the blind. Keller helped insure the inclusion of a section of the Social Security Act of 1935 that allows the blind to receive federal grant money.

When Anne Macy died in 1936, Keller and Thomson went abroad. She lectured throughout Japan, the first of a series of international tours. *Helen Keller's Journal*, published in 1938, expressed her feelings since Macy's death and explored who she was without Macy. During World War II (1941–45), Keller toured military hospitals to build morale. After the war ended, Keller spent ten years lecturing on blindness throughout the world: in Europe, Australia, New Zealand, South Africa, the Middle East, Latin America, and India. In 1961, the year after Thomson died, Keller suffered the first of a series of small strokes. Three years later, President Lyndon Johnson awarded her the Medal of Freedom.

Kennedy, John F.

(1917–1963)

UNITED STATES REPRESENTATIVE, SENATOR,
AND THIRTY-FIFTH PRESIDENT

John Fitzgerald Kennedy was born in Brookline, Massachusetts, a suburb of Boston, on May 29, 1917. His father, Joseph Kennedy went to Harvard, where he experienced discrimination because of his Irish Catholic background. He was a millionaire by the time he graduated. In 1913, at the age of twenty-six, he became the youngest bank president in the country. He became chairman of the Securities and Exchange Commission, and served President Franklin Roosevelt as United States ambassador to Britain. Kennedy's mother, Rose Fitzgerald, was the daughter of a former mayor of Boston.

John Kennedy attended Choate, an exclusive private school in Wallingford, Connecticut. He enrolled at Princeton University, but became ill and had to leave. In 1936, he entered Harvard University. During a summer break, he traveled in Europe and then wrote his senior thesis on the growing threat of Nazi Germany. After his graduation in 1940, the thesis was published under the title *Why England Slept*, and it became a best-seller.

In September 1941 he joined the United States Navy—following the example of his older brother Joseph, who was a naval air cadet. On December 7, 1941, the Japanese attacked Pearl Harbor and the United States was at war. Kennedy was assigned to the Office of Naval Intelligence, but became bored with his duties and wanted a combat assignment. In July 1942, he transferred to Midshipmen's School at Northwestern University in Evanston, Illinois and volunteered for service aboard a patrol torpedo (PT) boat.

Kennedy was sent to the South Pacific island of Tulagi, where he took command of PT 109. On the evening of August 1, 1943, PT 109 was rammed and cut in half by the Japanese destroyer *Amigari*. Two of Kennedy's crew were killed, and of the eleven survivors three were badly injured. Over the next six days, the crew swam to and hid on three different islands until they found natives who could carry Kennedy's plea for help, carved on a coconut, back to an American base. The crew was rescued, and Kennedy's heroism in keeping his men together was front-page news in New York and Boston.

Kennedy tried to stay in the navy, but he contracted malaria and his back problems grew worse. He took medical leave and returned to Boston, only to learn that on August 12, 1944, his brother Joseph, stationed in England, was killed while on a secret bombing mission. All of the hopes and ambitions the family had for Joe now fell on John Kennedy's shoulders.

In 1946, Kennedy was elected to the United States House of Representatives. He was a best-selling author and a war hero, and his youth, charm, and Irish Catholic background appealed to the working-class voters of Massachusetts. He moved to the Georgetown area of Washington, D.C. Though he was reelected to Congress in 1948 and 1950, Kennedy was depressed by personal tragedy (on May 12, 1948, his sister Kathleen was killed in a plane crash) and bored by his limited role in the government. In 1952, Kennedy decided to run for the United States Senate, where there was more debate about his real area of interest, foreign policy. With his younger brother Robert running his campaign, he defeated Republican Henry Cabot Lodge by a narrow margin.

On September 12, 1953, Kennedy married Jacqueline Bouvier. "Jackie" was from a wealthy, prominent Washington family, and the wedding was an important social event. The couple's sophistication and polished good looks helped promote Kennedy's career.

In 1954, Kennedy underwent serious back surgery and had to remain less active during the long and painful recovery, but by 1956 his career was back on the rise. In 1957 he won the Pulitzer Prize for his new book of essays, *Profiles in Courage*. He easily won reelection to the Senate in 1958, and in January 1960, he decided to run for the presidency. He won the Democratic nomination that summer and chose Senator Lyndon B. Johnson of Texas as his running mate. His opponent was Republican Vice President Richard M. Nixon.

The election was a hard-fought one, and the first in which the candidates debated on live television. In November 1960, Kennedy narrowly defeated Nixon and became President.

His energetic and informal working style, his appointment of many bright, young cabinet advisers, his lavish entertaining, and his association with people in the arts earned for his administration the nickname of "Camelot," taken from the idyllic court of the mythical English King Arthur. Among Kennedy's first initiatives were the Food for Peace program, in which surplus American food was sent to poor countries, and the Peace Corps, in which skilled young Americans were sent to underdeveloped nations to build schools and health clinics, to improve agriculture, and to share American technology and values. Then came the Alliance for Progress, which provided economic aid to Latin American countries as a way to check the spread of communism. Kennedy was fearful of this possibility, especially since Fidel Castro had established a Communist state in Cuba in 1959.

The problem of Cuba would plague Kennedy throughout his term as President. When he entered the White House, he was told of a secret plan by his predecessor, President Eisenhower, to have the Central Intelligence Agency organize a group of Cuban exiles to invade Cuba and overthrow Castro. Kennedy allowed the plan to go forward, and in April 1961, fifteen hundred Cuban exiles landed at the Bay of Pigs on Cuba's southern shore. But Kennedy had miscalculated. There was no popular uprising against Castro in Cuba, and within days the battered invasion force had surrendered. The Bay of Pigs operation was a complete disaster, and Kennedy was widely criticized at home and abroad. He had to bargain with Castro and trade agricultural machinery for the release of the captured Cuban exiles.

Castro, fearing another American invasion, invited the Soviet Union to install medium range missiles on Cuban soil. The missiles could reach some areas of the United States and were capable of carrying nuclear warheads. When American intelligence aircraft discovered the missile sites, Kennedy reacted swiftly. On October 22, 1962, he revealed the presence of the missiles to the American people in a televised public address, demanded that Cuba remove them, and sent American naval forces to blockade Cuba and to challenge arriving Soviet ships. For several tense days, Americans wondered if the United States and the Soviet Union would go to war over Cuba. Finally, on October 27, Soviet Premier Nikita Khrushchev backed down, agreeing to remove the missiles if Kennedy promised not to support another invasion of Cuba. Kennedy's handling of the Cuban missile crisis restored his reputation after the Bay of Pigs disaster, but many Americans were growing wary of Kennedy's tendency to provoke military confrontations.

In August 1961, Soviet-controlled East German troops blocked the border between East and West Berlin to stop East German refugees from escaping to the western-controlled zone of the city. Kennedy ordered American troops to protect the roads leading into Berlin, which was deep within Soviet-controlled territory. For several days American and Soviet tanks faced each other in a tense standoff, until Khrushchev backed down and Soviet forces withdrew. But the East Germans built a high wall across the border between East and West Berlin, and tensions between the superpowers over Germany remained high.

In Southeast Asia, Kennedy involved the United States in a military conflict that was to last fifteen years. After the French were driven out of Indochina by Communist and nationalist rebels, civil war broke out in the three new nations of Laos, Cambodia, and Vietnam, where Communist and nationalist forces led by the North Vietnamese leader Ho Chi Minh sought to overthrow corrupt local governments. Kennedy saw these local conflicts as another confrontation between the superpowers and sent military supplies and a small force of American troops to defend the governments of Laos and South Vietnam.

Kennedy's most serious domestic problem was in the area of civil rights. He had campaigned for the presidency with a pledge to fight segregation, and throughout the southern states black Americans under the leadership of the Reverend Martin Luther King, Jr. were organizing to fight discrimination and extend black voting rights. "Freedom Riders," busloads of blacks and whites supporting equal rights, traveled to southern cities and were harassed and beaten by angry southerners. Kennedy sent six hundred federal marshals to Montgomery, Alabama to protect the Freedom Riders. He used the Justice Department to take legal action against southern states that prevented blacks from voting. He also appointed the first black jurist, Thurgood Marshall, to the

United States Supreme Court. In September 1962, when a black student, James Meredith, was refused admission to the University of Mississippi, Kennedy sent the National Guard to Oxford, Mississippi to protect Meredith from angry white mobs. Kennedy sent more troops to Alabama in June 1963 when Governor George Wallace refused to desegregate the state university and riots broke out. In August 1963, Martin Luther King, Jr. led a huge march on Washington to support a comprehensive civil rights bill Kennedy was trying to push through Congress. But Kennedy moved cautiously in supporting the legislation. His mind was focused on America's international problems and he did not want to divide the country on the issue of civil rights. The civil rights bill did not become law during his term as President.

On November 22, 1963, while traveling in a motorcade through the streets of downtown Dallas, Texas, President Kennedy was assassinated, supposedly by a gunman, Lee Harvey Oswald. Vice President Lyndon Johnson was left to deal with the difficult problems of civil rights and American intervention in Vietnam. Historians still argue over how Kennedy would have handled these problems had he lived. The assassination itself has provoked an endless debate over what actually happened and who was responsible.

Kennedy, Robert F.

(1925–1968)

UNITED STATES ATTORNEY GENERAL AND SENATOR

Robert Francis Kennedy was born on November 20, 1925, in Brookline, Massachusetts, the son of Joseph Kennedy, a wealthy investment banker and ambassador to England, and the younger brother of John Kennedy, the future President of the United States. Kennedy enlisted in the navy and in 1946 served as a seaman aboard a destroyer named after his father. In 1948, he graduated from Harvard University. Two years later he married Ethel Skakel, and in 1951 he graduated from the University of Virginia Law School.

Kennedy went to work for the Justice Department in Washington, but returned to Massachusetts in 1952 to manage his brother John's campaign for the Senate. He then worked as legal counsel to the Senate committee led by Joseph McCarthy of Wisconsin, which was investigating alleged Communist subversion. In 1956, he worked for the presidential campaign of Democrat Adlai Stevenson, but Stevenson lost to Dwight Eisenhower. After the campaign, he took the position of chief counsel for the Senate Rackets Committee, which investigated corruption in labor unions. He tried unsuccessfully to depose Jimmy

Hoffa, president of the International Brotherhood of Teamsters, whom he believed to be linked to organized crime. His questioning of Hoffa in Senate chambers before television cameras made Robert Kennedy a national figure.

In 1959, Kennedy left the Rackets Committee to manage John's campaign for the presidency. After winning the election in 1960, President Kennedy appointed his younger brother attorney general. As head of the Justice Department, Kennedy's most serious problem during this period was protecting civil rights demonstrators who were demanding voting rights and desegregation in the South. Constrained by the need not to offend southern white Democrats, he could not always act decisively, and he received much criticism for not being able to control violent attacks on black protestors.

Kennedy was more than attorney general; he was the President's brother and closest adviser. He played a key role in approving the disastrous invasion of Cuba by Cuban exiles in 1961 and in the President's handling of the Cuban missile crisis of 1962. When the President was assassinated in 1963 and Lyndon Johnson took his place, Robert Kennedy, who had never gotten along well with Johnson, left the Justice Department and successfully ran for the United States Senate in 1964.

In 1968, President Johnson's popularity was at an all-time low as a result of his escalation of the war in Vietnam. When Senator Eugene McCarthy of Minnesota almost defeated Johnson in the New Hampshire Democratic primary election, Kennedy sensed that Johnson could be beaten and announced his own candidacy for the presidency. Kennedy campaigned as an antiwar and pro-civil rights candidate. Johnson declined to run for reelection, and the contest for the Democratic nomination became a three-way race between Kennedy, McCarthy, and Vice President Hubert Humphrey. On June 5, 1968, celebrating his victory in the California Democratic primary election at the Ambassador Hotel in Los Angeles, Kennedy was shot and killed by an assassin. Vice President Humphrey went on to win the Democratic nomination, but Republican Richard Nixon won the White House.

Keynes, John Maynard

(1883–1946)

ENGLISH ECONOMIST

But I wish to extend the English language.
—John Maynard Keynes

John Maynard Keynes, the English economist, not only extended the English language—by introducing what became known as "Keynesian" economics—but he revolutionized his field and the way the twentieth century has approached it. Sometimes called the godfather of the New Deal, his theories were crucial to the basic concept of governmental regulation of economic activity, a philosophy that has dominated national policies in Europe and the United States since World War II.

Keynes was born on June 5, 1883, in Cambridge, England. After attending the prestigious Eton school, he entered the University of Cambridge, where he earned a master's degree in economics in 1905. For two years he worked for the British colonial service in India, then returned to teach at Cambridge. He remained at Cambridge for the rest of his career, although he also took other assignments from time to time. In 1915, for example, he began a four-year service with the British Treasury.

It was in that position that he represented the British Treasury Department at the peace conference that ended World War I. In 1919, he quit, strongly opposing the agreement reached at Versailles, France, and predicting that it would only pave the way to future war. By 1939, with the outbreak of World War II, Keynes had been proven right.

Keynes's position, published in a book in 1919, earned him instant criticism and fame throughout Continental Europe, England, and the United States. In the ensuing years, through books and lectures, he began to develop economic theories that would eventually dominate the field of international economics. He announced the end of laissez-faire economics; he claimed that the relationship between saving and investment was crucial to preventing depressions; and he called for getting rid of the gold standard, in which the value of nations' currencies were tied to the price of gold. During the Great Depression, which began in 1929, he was the first economist to call for huge government spending to regain economic strength. President Franklin Rooosevelt listened, and the New Deal was successful in reversing the depression in America.

With the approach of World War II, Keynes argued that government should reverse its course and attempt to slow down the economy. He also called for the rearmament of England, but he hoped the country would still follow a path of positive pacifism rather than fighting in the war. But, by 1938, he was critical of British government efforts to avoid fighting Adolf Hitler; during the war itself, Keynes was a strong supporter of the war effort.

Keynes's major contribution to economics was the principle of regulation of economic activities highlighted by a strong, active role of government. He died shortly after World War II, on April 21, 1946, at the age of sixty-three.

Killy, Jean-Claude

(1943–   )

FRENCH SKIER

> When he has a sore throat, France gargles.
> —a writer's joke about Jean-Claude Killy, demonstrating
>   how beloved he was by all French people

In 1964, members of the French national ski team began to notice a change in Jean-Claude Killy. The grim, brooding young man they had always known was suddenly a carefree prankster, playing practical jokes, squirting water at them from a seltzer bottle, and putting a picture of a skull on his ski helmet. Even more surprising, he began to dominate on the slopes as he never had before.

The change in Killy's attitude came from his observations of American skiers, who were always lighthearted and fun-loving no matter how they fared in competition. The dour Killy thought he could take a lesson from their approach, and he did.

His first life as a slaloming sourpuss began on August 30, 1943. Raised by his divorced father at a ski resort in the French Alps, Killy seemed destined for the slopes from the beginning. He was on skis at the age of three, taking instruction from his father. Five years later, he was up to twelve ski runs a day, and was soon competing in junior regional meets. He won those easily, often against older, more experienced competition. A shy boy with low self-esteem, he loved the attention that came with winning. Skiing quickly became his passion. At age fourteen, he was suspended from school for cutting classes to head out to the slopes. At sixteen, he left school for good, determined to pursue skiing as a career.

During his childhood, and for the rest of his life as an active skier, Jean-Claude Killy was hindered by illness and injury. Depression over his parents' divorce kept him off the slopes for more than a year at one point. When he was fifteen, he broke his leg and developed tuberculosis. Another three months was lost sitting out that time. Nevertheless, Killy persisted, and he finally earned a place with the French national ski team.

Just when it looked as if he was about to break through at the 1962 World Championships, he broke his ankle. After being drafted into the French army for a brief period, he developed the liver disease called jaundice. Hoping to rally his health for a shot in the 1964 Olympics, Killy found himself beset yet again, this time by an intestinal disease. He competed in the games, but finished poorly. As his development as a skier suffered because of the time lost to illness, Killy became increasingly despondent. It was then that he made the decision to overhaul his attitude.

The new, lighthearted Killy began to make dramatic progress as a skier. In an important victory, he won the prestigious Hahnenkamm combined, defeating Austrian legend Karl Schranz. In 1965, he put together an impressive string of wins, capping it off with a world record time in the downhill at the World Championships in Portillo, Chile. Pouring all his free time into training, Killy continued to dominate the tour in 1967, winning the first-ever World Cup competition with 225 total points, the maximum score. Having upgraded his outlook and shaken the injury bug, Killy looked to shine at the upcoming Olympic Games in Grenoble, France.

On advice from former gold medal skier Toni Sailer, Killy took a few days off before those games began. The recharged Frenchman then greeted the "hometown" crowd with a history-making performance. He became the first skier since Sailer to win all three alpine events—downhill, slalom, and giant slalom—proving both his ability and his versatility on the slopes.

After capping off his Olympic year with another World Cup trophy, Killy retired from amateur skiing. He devoted himself to becoming an international celebrity, endorsing products and appearing in movies. He became a matinee idol in his native country. The glamorous life proved boring for him after a while, however, and he briefly returned to skiing as a professional. After winning a number of pro titles, he retired for good to the ski lodge where he had lived as a child. Financially independent, he devoted his free time to dangerous hobbies like motorbike racing, skydiving, and bullfighting. A fierce competitor who never lost his edge, Killy remains to this day a revered figure in his native France.

King, Billie Jean

(1944–   )

AMERICAN TENNIS PLAYER

"There's nothing else quite like it," Billie Jean King once said about the experience of being an athlete. "It's music, it's dancing, it's the greatest thing in the whole wide world."

Billie Jean Moffett discovered the joy of sports at an early age while growing up in California. She was the best athlete, boy or girl, at her elementary school. She liked many sports, including football, baseball, softball, and track and field. Her whole family was athletic. Her father enjoyed baseball and basketball, while her mother was a good swimmer. Her brother Randy, a baseball player, later became a pitcher for the San Francisco Giants.

Billie Jean later said, "The first time I saw a professional baseball game with my father, what struck me like a thunderbolt was that there were no women on that baseball diamond. . . . Throughout my adolescence, I found a subtle pressure against being an athlete." People called her a tomboy—an unflattering label in those days. Her mother said she should find a sport more suitable for girls, like golf, swimming, or tennis.

The first time Billie Jean played a formal tennis match, she lost twelve games in a row and was frustrated. But a city recreation department pro named Clyde Walker was giving free lessons every week at a nearby park. He taught her the proper grip and how to swing at the ball. Billie Jean worked hard on these skills, hitting a ball against a backyard fence. She even went to other parks where Clyde was teaching in order to get more instruction. Billie Jean told her parents that one day she would be "the Number One tennis player in the whole world."

She meant it. She kept practicing and walked four miles to school to build up her strength. But she was having some problems with her game. Aggressive and fast, she enjoyed rushing the net to hit the ball before it bounced (called a volley shot). Her coach wanted her to be more patient, urging her to wait in the backcourt more often and to hit ground strokes after the ball bounced.

She experienced some awkward moments. At a tournament at the Los Angeles Tennis Club, 11-year-old Billie Jean felt out of place among more affluent players. She had brought a sack lunch, while they bought hamburgers at the clubhouse. Then she was left out of a group picture because she was wearing shorts and a shirt, not a tennis dress. Billie Jean said, "It turned me upside down." Later she would work to make tennis less stuffy and more available to less wealthy people.

Billie Jean kept playing in regional tournaments, and began to win. By her mid-teens, she had perfected a strong serve-and-volley game and was making fewer errors. When she was 15, her town raised money to send her to the national girls championships in Ohio, where she reached the quarterfinals.

By age 16, Billie Jean ranked No. 19 in the nation; the next year, she was No. 4. She missed her high school graduation because she was playing at Wimbledon, the English championship. When she took the doubles title with Karen Hantze, they were the youngest winners ever. The crowds liked Billie Jean and cheered her on.

Despite a busy tournament schedule, Billie Jean entered Los Angeles State College as a history major. While there, she met Larry King, who was studying law. As a sophomore, she made it to the Wimbledon finals in 1963, but lost to Margaret Smith Court. The older champion told Billie Jean that she was good enough to win but that she didn't practice enough year-round.

Billie Jean left college to focus on tennis. She worked with Merlyn Rose in Australia to improve her shots and her game strategy. Her serves and strokes became more deadly once she learned make them bounce in unexpected directions. She went on a diet to get in shape. In 1965 Billie Jean married Larry King. She also defeated all the American women she played. Two years later she reached her goal of winning the Wimbledon singles title as well as the U.S Open at Forest Hills. She won Wimbledon again in 1968 and added her first Australian Open title. She also won many doubles championships.

Billie Jean was happy to be earning a good living at tennis. But she resented the fact that men made much more prize money than women. She led a battle for equal prize money and helped to organize important new women's tournaments, including the Virginia Slims circuit. As the first woman athlete to earn $100,000 a year, in 1971, she said she hoped "to show the world that women can earn a good living in sports. It'll open up more avenues for women in other sports." She won nineteen of the thirty matches she played that year. With others, she formed the Women's Tennis Association, and served as its first president.

Billie Jean was nearly 30 when she beat teenager Chris Evert to win her fifth Wimbledon singles title in 1973. Then she played the famous Battle of the Sexes match against male player Bobby Riggs at the Houston Astrodome. More than thirty thousand people attended, while thousands more watched on TV. Bobby Riggs, age 55, had beaten Margaret Court and then challenged Billie Jean to a $100,000 "winner-take-all" showdown.

Riggs was favored, but Billie Jean vowed to beat him. She ran down each ball, and used a variety of skillful shots, and rushed the net to defeat Riggs. At the end, Billie Jean gave a clenched-fist salute and yelled, "Right on!" She said, "Maybe it means people will start to respect women athletes. Not just me; there are plenty to take my place."

By 1975 King had been No. 1 for seven years. She was 31 and people began calling her "the Old Lady." Because of chronic knee problems and several operations, she knew she might have to give up playing in big tournaments. But she missed tennis and worked hard to get back in top shape. "I'm stubborn enough to continue the pain and the drudgery and the therapy," she said.

In the meantime, she and Larry had developed World Team Tennis matches and Billie Jean was part of the New York Sets, the team based in New York City. With Larry, she published a magazine called *WomanSports*. She was also a popular sportscaster.

People were impressed but not completely surprised when Billie Jean won her record-breaking twentieth Wimbledon title during the women's doubles final in 1979. She kept on playing tennis into the 1980s, often in matches for over-35s.

By the 1990s, tennis was widely popular and women were earning big prizes in a variety of tournaments. Nobody had done more for tennis or for women athletes than Billie Jean King.

King, Martin Luther, Jr.

(1929–1968)

AMERICAN CIVIL RIGHTS LEADER

Martin Luther King, Jr. was born on January 15, 1929, in Atlanta, Georgia. His father was pastor of Atlanta's Ebenezer Baptist Church, one of the more prominent black churches in the city. Though the King family lived in middle-class comfort, the burden of segregation was heavily felt. Since 1896, when the Supreme Court in *Plessy v. Ferguson* ruled that "separate but equal" facilities for blacks were constitutional, the southern states had passed a series of Jim Crow laws to segregate whites and blacks. Growing up in Atlanta, King discovered that he could not eat at certain restaurants, that no hotels or motels would admit his family, and that most parks and swimming pools were for whites only. Blacks attended separate schools, sat at the back of buses, and used separate bathrooms at public facilities. And though the right of blacks to vote was guaranteed by the Fifteenth Amendment, local laws disqualified many of them. If a black person resisted the system, he might be arrested by police or killed by members of the Ku Klux Klan.

In 1944, King entered all-black Morehouse College, intending to become a lawyer. But he became interested in religion as a force for social change, and in 1951 he obtained his divinity degree from Crozer Theological Seminary in Chester, Pennsylvania. He received a scholarship to Boston University's School of Theology, where he met and married Coretta Scott in 1953. In 1954, he accepted the position of pastor of the Dexter Avenue Church in Montgomery, Alabama. King envisioned a new role for the black church—not simply to offer comfort to the oppressed, but to actively organize and lead the black community to change its conditions. He was deeply influenced by the philosophy of Mohandas K. Gandhi, who had led India to independence from Britain in 1947. Gandhi believed in nonviolent civil disobedience, and had frustrated the British with marches, strikes, boycotts, and his refusal to obey British laws. King thought these tactics could be applied to the civil rights struggle. In the same year he went to Montgomery, the Supreme Court in *Brown v. Board of Education* ruled that "separate but equal" facilities were not constitutional, reversing its decision of fifty years before and setting the stage for an era of civil rights activism.

At the Dexter Avenue Church, King began to develop a powerful, rhythmic speaking style that stirred his congregation. He befriended Ralph Abernathy, pastor of the First Baptist Church, who had similar ideas of making the churches agents of social change. On December 1, 1955, Rosa Parks, a seamstress's assistant in a Montgomery department store, was arrested for refusing to give up her seat on the bus to a white man. Lawyers for the local branch of the National Association for the Advancement of Colored People (NAACP) felt the Parks case could be taken to the Supreme Court and used to destroy the Jim Crow laws. They called on black ministers for support. King and Abernathy organized a black boycott of the Montgomery bus system, which began on December 5. King was harassed by the police, and on January 30, 1956 his home was bombed. On November 13, the Supreme Court struck down Alabama's segregation laws as unconstitutional, and on December 13, 1956, more than a year after the boycott had begun, city officials relented and integrated Montgomery's buses. King's speeches and organizing activities had been widely covered in the press. He emerged from the successful boycott as a national spokesperson for black causes, having proved his theories of nonviolent protest could work.

Similar boycotts were organized in other southern cities, and black ministers formed the Southern Christian Leadership Conference (SCLC), with King as its president. In 1960, King moved from Montgomery to Atlanta, Georgia to manage the SCLC's new campaign to register black voters. In February 1960, black college students in Greensboro, North Carolina sat down at an all-white lunch counter and refused to move until they were served. With King's support, they formed the Student Nonviolent Coordinating Committee (SNCC) to teach other students the tactics of nonviolent resistance. Sit-ins spread throughout the South. In September 1960, King was arrested for sitting in at an Atlanta lunch counter, and was sentenced to four months' hard labor at Reidsville Penitentiary. The harshness of the sentence shocked the nation. Senator John F. Kennedy of Massachusetts used his political connections to get King released, and in November 1960 black voters gave Kennedy the margin he needed to win the presidential election.

In 1961, King joined with James Farmer of the Congress of Racial Equality (CORE) to end segregation on interstate buses and trains. Integrated groups of blacks and whites, called Freedom Riders, boarded buses and trains together and traveled south. They were viciously attacked by police and Klansmen. For two years, the Freedom Riders struggled to integrate transportation facilities. King was arrested several times and threatened by white mobs. In 1961, he went to Birmingham, Alabama, one of the most segregated cities in America, to lead mass demonstrations for civil rights. Many black children participated in the marches, and when Sheriff Eugene "Bull" Connor attacked the demonstrators with fire hoses and police dogs, television coverage of the police attacking children enraged people all over the country. King was arrested again, and on a piece of prison toilet paper he wrote his famous "Letter From a Birmingham Jail," laying out his philosophy of nonviolent protest.

In 1963, A. Philip Randolph, a prominent black labor leader, brought other activists together to organize a massive demonstration in the nation's capital to push for more civil rights legislation. More than two hundred thousand people attended the March on Washington on August 28, 1963, and millions more watched on television. King was the last speaker of the day, and gave his famous "I Have A Dream" speech, in which he envisioned an America free of race prejudice. In 1964, Congress passed a new Civil Rights Act forbidding discrimination in public accommodations, and in the same year King was awarded the Nobel Peace Prize.

King now turned his attention to extending black voting rights. SNCC and SCLC began a series of marches and demonstrations in the town of Selma, fifty miles west of Montgomery, Alabama, as part of a voter registration drive. King, Abernathy, and thousands of demonstrators were arrested. Others were chased with electric cattle prods. Once out of jail, King called for a march from Selma to the capital of Montgomery. In their first attempt on March 7, 1965, the marchers were attacked by state police and more than 140 people were injured. King sent out a call for all clergymen across the country to join him in Selma for another attempt. Governor George Wallace tried to forbid the march, but on March 24 several thousand marchers reached Montgomery for a large rally. Thanks to King's relentless determination, Congress passed a new Voting Rights Act that year.

In 1966, King traveled to Chicago to work with Jesse Jackson's Operation Breadbasket, an effort to improve black economic conditions. King was appalled by the poverty, substandard housing, and social disintegration he discovered in the black ghettos. He began to develop a broader interest in economic reform and in President Lyndon Johnson's antipoverty efforts. But he saw the war in Vietnam as an obstacle to those reforms. In 1967, at Riverside Church in New York City, he made a major speech against the war.

In April 1968, King went to Memphis, Tennessee to support a strike by black sanitation workers, who wanted the city to recognize their union. On March 4, while standing on the balcony of the Lorraine Hotel, King was shot and killed by an assassin. Over the next few days, riots broke out in the black communities of Chicago, Detroit, Boston, Memphis, New York, and Washington.

King was buried in Atlanta. His wife Coretta survives him and has become a leading spokesperson in the struggle for black equality and the continuation of her husband's efforts. Without ever having held political office, Martin Luther King, Jr. had moved millions to march, demonstrate, risk imprisonment and beatings, and even face death. He achieved a stature equal to his hero, Gandhi, and led a movement that destroyed many of the more blatant and humiliating practices of segregation in America.

Kissinger, Henry

(1923–)

UNITED STATES NATIONAL SECURITY ADVISER AND
SECRETARY OF STATE

Henry Kissinger was born on May 27, 1923, in the city of Furth, Germany, a few miles from Nuremberg. His parents were Jewish, and his father, Louis Kissinger, lost his job as a teacher in 1935 when the Nazi party took control of the city. In 1938, the family left Germany for England and then made their way to the United States, where they settled in New York.

Kissinger attended the City College of New York, and in 1943, at the age of nineteen, he was drafted into the army. By 1944, he found himself back in Germany, this time working as an interpreter for the Eighty-Fourth Infantry Division. When the Germans surrendered, he was given the job of rebuilding local government in the cities of Krefeld and Hesse. By 1946, he was training American intelligence agents at the European Command Intelligence School at Oberammergau.

From 1947 to 1950, Kissinger attended Harvard University, and graduated with high honors. In 1950, he married Anneliese Fleischer, the daughter of German refugees, and continued with his postgraduate work at Harvard. His graduate thesis, *A World Restored: Metternich, Castlereagh, and the Restoration of Peace, 1812*, revealed Kissinger's basic conservatism and fear of revolution, as well as his fascination with the great diplomats and power politics of the nineteenth century. In 1951, he became director of the Harvard International Seminar program, where he met many future foreign leaders. In 1957, as head of Harvard's influential Council on Foreign Relations, Kissinger authored *Nuclear Weapons and Foreign Policy*, a report that challenged government leaders to find an alternative to full-scale nuclear war as a military option and argued that "limited exchanges" of nuclear weapons were possible without leading to world war.

The book became a best-seller, and intrigued many international relations experts who felt the country was trapped in its policy of nuclear deterrence, under which the United States could not pursue its foreign policy aims without triggering a nuclear war with the Soviet Union. But others feared Kissinger's argument, which seemed to treat the atomic bomb as just another conventional weapon.

By the early 1960s, Kissinger was a full professor at Harvard, a recognized authority on foreign policy, an adviser to the Kennedy administration, and a close friend of Governor Nelson Rockefeller of New York, who had presidential ambitions. In 1962 he stopped advising Kennedy and went on to support the efforts of Rockefeller to obtain the Republican nomination in three presidential campaigns. In 1968 Richard Nixon defeated Rockefeller and won the general election against Democrat Hubert Humphrey.

Kissinger had spoken out strongly against Nixon, and was surprised when the new President asked him to become his chief adviser on the National Security Council. The first order of business was to find a solution to the Vietnam War, which had begun under President Kennedy and had, under President Lyndon Johnson, become an unwinnable stalemate involving half a million American troops. Nixon and Kissinger approached the government of Ho Chi Minh in North Vietnam in the hope of negotiating a settlement, but the North Vietnamese stubbornly insisted on the complete withdrawal of American troops. In 1969, to force the Vietnamese to negotiate, Nixon began a secret bombing campaign in Cambodia, and in 1970 American forces invaded that country, seeking out the Cambodian outposts that served as bases for the North Vietnamese soldiers. But the invasion toppled the legitimate government of Cambodia and widened the scope of the war. Nixon then began to slowly withdraw American troops, at the same time increasing the bombing of North Vietnamese cities.

At home, Americans demonstrated against the invasion of neutral Cambodia and the increased scale of bombing. Many of Kissinger's former friends and academic colleagues called for his resignation. Finally, on January 23, 1973, meeting in Paris with the North Vietnamese negotiator Le Duc Tho, Kissinger obtained an agreement for a cease-fire and disengagement of American troops. Both Kissinger and Le Duc Tho received the Nobel Peace Prize for their efforts, but Le Duc Tho refused to accept the prize and Kissinger later returned his award when the North Vietnamese overran South Vietnam in 1975.

One area in which Nixon and Kissinger achieved a more clear-cut foreign policy victory was in normalizing relations with China. Relations with China had been nonexistent since the Korean War of the early 1950s. Taking advantage of growing tensions between China and the Soviet Union, Kissinger met secretly with Chinese Premier Zhou Enlai in Beijing in July 1971, and arranged for Nixon to visit China in February 1972. The visit was a great success, and in the following years normal diplomatic and commercial ties were established. Kissinger had planned to leave the Nixon administration at this point, but in August 1973, he found he could not refuse Nixon's offer to become secretary of state. As Nixon became absorbed in defending himself during the Watergate scandal, in which agents working for his reelection committee had burglarized Democratic party headquarters in Washington, Kissinger found himself virtually in charge of American foreign policy.

He faced a crisis in the Middle East on October 6, 1973, when the armies of Egypt and Syria attacked Israel in what came to be known as the Yom Kippur War. When the United States resupplied Israel by military airlift, Arab nations cut off the sale of oil to the United States and other Western nations. Shortages were felt immediately within the United States and the price of gasoline rose drastically, Kissinger negotiated a cease-fire on October 22, 1973, then traveled to the Middle East to bring about a permanent disengagement. Since none of the leaders of the warring countries would meet with their enemies, Kissinger spent months flying back and forth between Cairo, Tel Aviv, and Damascus, delivering proposals and counterproposals, adding a new term to the language of foreign affairs: "shuttle diplomacy." Kissinger succeeded in getting all parties to disengage on May 31, 1974. It was a diplomatic triumph, and Kissinger was widely acclaimed.

Meanwhile, back home, things had gone downhill for his boss. In August 1974, President Nixon was forced to resign his office as a result of investigations into the Watergate scandal.

Kissinger continued to work as secretary of state under President Gerald Ford. He retired from the government in 1977, and in 1982 founded Kissinger Associates, a consulting firm that advises private companies on how to do business in foreign countries. He continues to be in great demand as an adviser, lecturer, and writer.

Korbut, Olga

(1955–   )

RUSSIAN GYMNAST

Tears streamed down Olga Korbut's face as the scores were announced for the performance on the uneven bars. The tiny Soviet gymnast had dazzled everyone the previous day with an array of breathtaking moves, but a tiny slipup on the bars had cost her a chance at the all-around gold medal. An international audience of millions watched as their Olympic heroine was denied the honor everyone knew she deserved. It was to be one of the few disappointments in Olga Korbut's career.

Olga Valentinovna Korbut was born on May 16, 1955, in Grodno, a city in what was then part of the USSR (now the Republic of Byelorus). She was the youngest of four girls. Her oldest sister, Ludmila, was also a gymnast, and the family believed firmly in the importance of athletics.

Olga was a happy-go-lucky child who was always running and jumping. She was bothered by the fact that she was always the smallest girl in her class at school, but in her career as a gymnast her size would be an asset. She excelled in physical education class, though her grades in other subjects suffered. When she was nine, she was chosen by government officials to attend a special sports school so she could train full-time in gymnastics.

At sports school, she trained under Renald Knysh, who drove his students hard. He believed in instilling fearlessness in his pupils, and he accomplished this by installing felt matting on every surface of the gymnasium so that young gymnasts would not be afraid to try the riskiest possible moves. Always a daredevil, Olga took to his system immediately. Under Knysh's guidance, she perfected the tricky backward somersault that would become one of her trademark moves on the balance beam. She also worked with him on the creative elements of the gymnastics program, using choreography, or artistically arranged moves, to create an individual style that greatly added to her charm.

The work was grueling, requiring her to perform some moves as many as four hundred times a day. Olga was willing to put up with the training program if it meant she had a chance to join the 1972 Soviet Olympics team. While she was still considered too young for such intense competition, she was allowed on the team as an alternate, ascending to the regular squad only when another gymnast took ill.

Before Olga Korbut made her debut, few people paid attention to Olympic gymnastics. The sport was considered too technical and lacked the personality of the more popular track and field events. When Olga took center stage, that changed. She impressed the international audience with her smile, her enthusiasm, and her obvious delight in every move she made on the floor. Next to Korbut's prancing and leaping, the motions of the other competitors looked stiff and mechanical. The old style of gymnastics finally met its new face.

Korbut was more than just a dancer on a wooden beam, however. She also showed her technical mastery by choosing the most difficult program possible. Only the trickiest elements—somersaults, pirouettes, complicated backflips—found their way onto Korbut's menu. No gymnast before her had dared to challenge herself in this way. The program later came to be known as "the Korbut elements" in her honor.

Apart from her slip on the uneven bars, Korbut's all-around program was all but perfect. She completed a backward somersault on the unevens, and that sent a hush through the crowd. Her astonishing backward somersault on the balance beam earned her a gold medal in that event, and she took top honors in the floor exercise as well. When she returned to the floor the day after her slip, the packed crowd in Sportshalle Stadium greeted her with a thundering ovation. The weeping, bitterly disappointed figure of the previous day had given way to the fierce competitor who refused to quit. Though she came in seventh in all-around scoring, Korbut went home with two gold medals and was the real winner of the Munich Olympics.

Named Associated Press Woman Athlete of the Year for 1972, Olga Korbut became an international celebrity. Olga Korbut Fan Clubs sprang up all over the world, as her performance ignited interest in gymnastics across Europe and North America. When she toured America with a team of gymnasts in 1973, she was greeted with a fervor usually reserved for rock stars. Engaging and warm, with an ever-present smile, she defied American stereotypes of cold, calculating communists and became a symbol of warming U.S.–Soviet relations.

Like Sonja Henie before her, Olga Korbut revolutionized her chosen sport while building international goodwill and bringing attention to a long-overlooked Olympic event.

Krishnamurti, Jiddu

(1895–1989)

INDIAN RELIGIOUS FIGURE

A charismatic figure whose lectures thrilled thousands (and, with the advent of videotape and cable television, millions), Jiddu Krishnamurti offered an idiosyncratic version of Indian religious philosophy and mysticism. Krishnamurti was born in Madanapalle, a small town north of Madras, India. Narianiah Krishnamurti, his father, was a Brahman (a member of India's highest social class), a rent collector and, later, a district magistrate under the British. His mother died when he was only ten, leaving his father to care for Jiddu and his brothers until he retired from government service and moved to the grounds of the International Theosophical Society.

Narianiah was an adherent of theosophy, the philosophy espoused by the International Theosophical Society, founded by Madame H.P. Blavatsky and H.S. Olcott. Theosophy—drawn in equal parts from Buddhism, Brahmanism, and salesmanship—held that the spiritual destiny of mankind was in the hands of the "masters," highly developed human beings who had moved beyond material existence to live on a higher plane.

In 1909, the year that the Kirshnamurtis moved to the society's headquarters outside Madras, the organization was headed by its president, Annie Besant, and her collaborator, Charles W. Leadbeater. Leadbeater claimed that his clairvoyant powers had identified Jiddu as a possessor of rare spiritual potential after he saw the little boy's aura while he was playing on the beach at the estate. Leadbeater and Besant believed that Jiddu was destined to become the Lord Maitreya, the World Teacher, who would be a logical successor to Lord Krishna and Jesus Christ as a spiritual leader.

First, however, Jiddu had to be trained and prepared for this great duty. He and his brother Nitya were placed on "probation" and entered into a period of rigorous training. A group of wealthy English and American patrons funded his upbringing, through the Order of the Star in the East, an organization founded to promote Krishnamurti's new role.

In 1911, the boys were taken to England for a visit by Besant and Leadbeater. After their return, Narianiah signed a paper giving them permission to educate the two boys in England. But by the end of 1912, he had filed suit to regain custody, charging that Leadbeater and the teenage Jiddu were having an intimate relationship. The case dragged through the courts, while the boys remained in England. In 1914, the Indian courts found for the father, but Besant won an appeal, before the Privy Council in London, in which both she and Leadbeater were found not guilty of any of the charges brought against them. Jiddu took his entrance exams for Oxford University, but failed them. He would never receive a university education, although he would study privately for many years.

From 1920 to 1929, Krishnamurti's brilliance as a public speaker and his unusual message made him a great drawing card for the theosophists. Nitya died in California in 1925 during one of their lecture tours, leaving Jiddu in a depression that he would later refer to indirectly in a remark about the "bondages of the mind."

Krishnamurti was beginning to strike out on his own course, to the increasing dismay of Besant, Leadbeater, and other heads of the society. In 1929, he announced that he was dissolving the Order of the Star, and he resigned from the society. He spent the rest of his life traveling, writing, and lecturing.

Krishnamurti's teachings revolved around a form of spiritual purgation that he called "the Process." During a three-day period in 1922, he experienced a spiritual transformation; the Process that resulted would occur for about an hour every evening, causing him great head pains. At that time, witnesses said, his "higher self" would depart his body and enter into a transcendent state of consciousness. Krishnamurti said that the Process allowed him to know oneness with all life and unconditional freedom. He taught that the source of man's sorrow is that his mind is conditioned; for anything new to arise and for sorrow to end, the mind must be deconditioned. In some way, the Process allowed him to achieve that state, but even he couldn't explain how.

Kroc, Ray

(1902–1984)

AMERICAN FOUNDER OF THE MCDONALD'S RESTAURANT CHAIN

Raymond Albert Kroc was born to middle-class parents in Chicago, Illinois. He attended public school until the United States became involved in World War I (1914–18). He joined the army and served overseas as an ambulance driver.

When Kroc returned home, he decided to pursue a career as a jazz pianist, but had little success. After a stint working at a Chicago radio station, Kroc took a job in business. For seventeen years, he was employed by the Lily Cup Corporation. He then struck out on his own. Kroc first tried selling real estate in Florida. After going, in his own words, "stone broke," he went into business marketing a milkshake machine to small restaurants.

Two of his customers were Mac and Dick McDonald. The brothers owned a hamburger stand in San Bernardino, California. One day in 1954, Kroc went out of his way to visit the restaurant. He wanted to find out how such a little operation kept eight of his machines in constant use.

Kroc quickly understood the secret of the McDonalds' success. Their menu was small, and they spent little time with each customer. But what they lacked in variety and service, they made for with speed, quality, and price. Kroc learned what the McDonalds' many customers already knew. If you wanted a tasty, cheap meal in a hurry, there was no place better to go than to the Mc-Donalds' stand.

Kroc made a deal with the brothers. He wanted to build other restaurants using the McDonalds' menu and system for preparing food. In exchange for using their name and ideas, he offered to give them a penny for every two dollars his restaurants earned. To the McDonalds, Kroc seemed to be offering them money for nothing. They were happy to accept his terms.

In 1955, Kroc opened his first McDonald's restaurant in Des Plaines, Illinois. There he refined the McDonald brothers' system of using an assembly line. Assembly lines were then common only in factories. Kroc adapted the idea to food preparation. At McDonald's, one worker might be responsible just for putting the pickles on the hamburgers, while another might do nothing but squirt ketchup on the buns. Although working this way was surely boring to the employees, it allowed the restaurant to make the largest number of hamburgers in the smallest amount of time possible.

Kroc paid almost as much attention to his restaurant's atmosphere as to its food. He declared that above all a McDonald's always had to be clean. Nothing made him angrier than to see trash in its parking lot. His employees were also expected to be well-groomed. Among his rules were that no order-taker could have bad skin, bad teeth, or a tattoo.

Kroc's McDonald's was an immediate success. Convinced his idea was a good one, he proceeded with his plan for a chain of similar restaurants. Kroc tried to build them close to highways. As Kroc predicted, families on a trip were always looking for a clean restaurant where they could grab a quick meal. Outside each McDonald's, Kroc erected two giant golden arches that hungry travelers could easily spot far down the road.

By recognizing that many Americans would want a simple, dependable meal at a low price, Kroc built a restaurant empire of more than ten thousand outlets around the world. At his death, his fortune totaled $600 million, which made him one of the five wealthiest people in the United States.

Kurosawa, Akira

(1 9 1 0 –   )

JAPANESE FILMMAKER

> . . . if I were to write anything at all, it would turn out to be nothing but talk about movies. In other words, take "myself," subtract "movies," and the result is zero.
>
> —Akira Kurosawa, from his 1982 autobiography

Akira Kurosawa has been one of the twentieth century's greatest film directors. He was born on March 23, 1910, in Tokyo, Japan. Before Kurosawa was born, his father had been in the military, but he then moved on to become a teacher. Kurosawa's mother was the daughter of a merchant. His parents provided him with a strict but secure middle-class environment.

Kurosawa's love of movies started when he was a child. He credits his father's enlightened attitude toward the cinema as strengthening his own attachment to film. When Kurosawa was young, the cinema was still in its infancy, and most educated, middle-class people looked upon movies as a lower-class form of entertainment. Kurosawa's father, a teacher, did not share this prejudice against films and regularly took his family to the movies (mostly American and European films).

While Kurosawa found pleasure in movies, he found nothing but pain in school. He was very shy and felt isolated from his classmates and his teachers. To make matters worse, he did poorly in all subjects except writing and painting. His alienation at school paralleled his detachment from current events. In his autobiography, Kurosawa said he was simply unaware of such dynamic international events as World War I and the 1917 Russian Revolution. He did not begin to recognize that he was living in a dangerous world until he was in middle school.

As a teenager, Kurosawa wanted to become a painter, and his father encouraged him to go to art school. Kurosawa was influenced by the works of Paul Cézanne and Vincent Van Gogh. Kurosawa failed the art school entrance examination and was not admitted as a student. Nevertheless, he continued his pursuit on his own to be a painter.

However, when he was nineteen, the Great Depression, which had worldwide effects, made art supplies too expensive to buy. Looking for other artistic avenues, Kurosawa turned to literature, theater, music, and film. He particularly loved to read, but he was also becoming even more fascinated by film. Moreover, his older brother was working on silent films. On his brother's advice, Kurosawa saw Fritz Lang's 1932 movie *The Testament of Dr. Mabuse*, and he was impressed by Lang's directing. Over the next four years, Kurosawa would finally give up painting and, on a whim, would begin his film career.

In 1935, Kurosawa happened to see a "want ad" from a film company seeking to hire new assistant directors. On the spur of the moment, Kurosawa decided to give film a try. He was hired and began as an assistant director. He slowly moved up the industry ladder as he learned all aspects of the cinema. After working as an assistant director, he began writing film scripts. Then he learned the art of film editing. And, by 1942, he had already directed his first feature film, *Judo Saga*, which was a hit.

Kurosawa's success continued with the release of his next film, *The Most Beautiful*, in 1944. He married the actress Yaguchi Yoko one year later. However, despite these milestones, Kurosawa has not been pleased by everything that happened during this important period in his life. While he was directing his first films, Japan was engaged in World War II. In his autobiography, Kurosawa said he was ashamed that he did not offer any political protest against his country's militarism.

After the war ended, Kurosawa's career continued to run smoothly. In 1948, he met the actor Toshiro Mifune, who went on to star in most of Kurosawa's films. Three years later, in 1951, Kurosawa directed his first cinematic masterpiece, *Rashomon*, which won the top prize at the Venice Film Festival. It later won the Oscar for Best Foreign Film. The movie reflects the theme that dominates all of Kurosawa's films: People are fundamentally incapable of existing in peace and harmony with their neighbors. *Rashomon* was also a landmark in film history because it introduced the Western, industrialized world to the Japanese film industry.

Following *Rashomon*, Kurosawa enjoyed fifteen consecutive years of cinematic success. His 1954 classic, *Seven Samurai*, became a classic American western when John Sturges remade it for American audiences under the title *The Magnificent Seven*. And Kurosawa's 1963 hit film, *High and Low*, revealed the influence of Fritz Lang's movies on him.

Kurosawa's success ended in the mid-1960s. He had developed the reputation of being difficult, if not impossible, to work with. As a result, he had trouble finding people willing to finance his films. In 1971, one year after his first cinematic failure, *Dodes' Kaden*, Kurosawa tried to commit suicide. However, after overcoming depression and ill health, he rebounded in 1976 with the film *Dersu Uzala*, which won the Academy Award for Best Foreign Film. For the next two decades, Kurosawa was, once more, directing great films. His 1980 movie, *Kagemusha*, won the grand prize at the Cannes Film Festival. Five years later, he directed *Ran,* an award-winning adaptation of Shakespeare's tragic masterpiece, *King Lear*.

Kurosawa is recognized as a true cinematic master. He has been intimately involved in the entire process of filmmaking. He edited or personally supervised the editing of his movies. He has also written screenplays for other film directors. He continues to live with his wife in Tokyo.

La Guardia, Fiorello H.

(1882–1947)

AMERICAN POLITICIAN AND MAYOR OF NEW YORK CITY

Fiorello H. La Guardia was born in New York on December 11, 1882, the son of Italian immigrants. His father was an army bandmaster, a job that took him to remote military posts in the United States, and La Guardia was raised in Prescott, Arizona. He returned to New York in 1906 and in 1910 earned his law degree from New York University. He set up a law practice and specialized in representing unions and striking workers. In 1915 he was appointed deputy attorney general for the state, and the next year he ran for Congress, becoming the first Republican ever elected from his district.

La Guardia interrupted his political career in 1917 and became an army aviator in France during World War I. He was known as the "flying congressman." When he returned to Congress in 1919, however, La Guardia was far from a model Republican. He opposed Attorney General A. Mitchell Palmer's deportation of immigrants. He took up the cause of women's suffrage, and fought hard to save New York's five-cent subway fare. By 1921, the Republican party tried to abandon La Guardia for being too radical, but he threatened to run against it on an independent ticket. Knowing that his popularity in New York was very high, the Republican party relented and supported him for reelection to Congress for five terms over the next ten years. He continued to fight for a shorter workday, old-age pensions, unemployment insurance, and other reform measures that were of vital interest to the Italian and Jewish working-class immigrants of his district. Opposed to Prohibition, he set up a homemade brewery in a Washington drugstore and defied the government to arrest him.

In 1934, he ran for mayor of New York City, supported by a coalition of progressive Republicans, liberals, Socialists, and labor groups, and was elected. He took the city by storm, balancing the budget, cutting his own salary, and appointing city officials on the basis of merit rather than party affiliation. He began a host of new projects to improve parks, hospitals, roads, schools, housing, and mass transit. He was passionate, outspoken, and flamboyant, and had a memorable sense of humor. During a newspaper strike, he went on the radio every day to read the comics to those accustomed to reading them in their papers.

La Guardia died in 1947. He was without doubt the most popular mayor in the city's history, serving from 1934 to 1945. Though some criticized him for his tough methods, La Guardia managed to be both a man of the people and a clever politician, one who measured individuals by their skills and achievements rather than by their political party affiliation.

Lang, Fritz

(1890–1976)

GERMAN FILMMAKER

Fritz Lang was one of the master filmmakers before World War II. He was born on December 5, 1890, in Vienna, Austria. His father, an architect, wanted Lang to follow in his footsteps. Lang, however, wanted no part of the lifestyle his father led. Nevertheless, to make his father happy, Lang agreed to begin pre-architectural studies. He lasted only one semester, however. He wanted to be a painter.

In his autobiography, Lang described himself as a "visual person." Through his special cinematic vision, Lang created one of the great film careers of the twentieth century.

He ran away from home and went to Brussels, Belgium, to study art. He then traveled throughout North Africa and Turkey before finally winding up back in Europe, first in Paris, and then in Germany, to study painting in Munich.

When World War I began, Lang returned to Vienna and was drafted into the army. During the war, he was wounded several times while serving on the Italian front. While recuperating in the hospital, Lang kept busy by writing film plots.

His actual entry into the film industry occurred quite by chance. While at a Vienna café in 1918, a stranger asked him if he wanted to act in a play; the acting role led to a job as a scriptwriter for a film production company. After writing film scripts for a while, Lang then became a director in 1919. One of his films that year, *The Spiders*, was a commercial success. Two years later, in 1921, Lang directed his first great film, *Destiny*.

Throughout the 1920s, Lang directed a series of hit films; perhaps his most notable film of the period was his 1926 futuristic fantasy, *Metropolis*. However, in the early 1930s, the Nazis censored Lang's *The Testament of Dr. Mabuse*. Lang turned down the Nazis' offer to head the German film industry, and he left Germany.

Lang went to the United States to work in Hollywood in the 1930s. After directing nineteen films, Lang eventually got fed up with the Hollywood studio system and returned to Germany. However, his newer German films were not as well received as his earlier ones had been. When he retired, Lang moved back to Beverly Hills, California, where he died in 1976.

Lawrence, D(avid). H(erbert).

(1885–1930)

ENGLISH NOVELIST, SHORT-STORY WRITER, POET, ESSAYIST, TRAVEL WRITER, AND PLAYWRIGHT

In what is perhaps the most famous statement of his worldview, D.H. Lawrence wrote to a friend: "My great religion is a belief in the blood, the flesh, as being wiser than the intellect. We can go wrong in our minds. But what our blood feels and believes and says is always true." The notion was cribbed from political philosopher Friedrich Nietzsche, but Lawrence really tried to live it. The characters in his best novels surrender to it completely.

David Herbert Lawrence was born on September 11, 1885, in Eastwood, a small town near Nottingham, England. His father, Arthur, was a coal miner (although one who rose to the position of subcontractor, thanks to his considerable managerial skills); his mother, Lydia, was a former schoolteacher and an intellectual.

As was clear from his highly autobiographical novel *Sons and Lovers* (1912), Lawrence's parents had a turbulent marriage that alternated between blistering fights and sulky, uneasy truces. The frail, sensitive Lawrence took after his mother, to his father's dismay. It is surprising, then, that Lawrence believed in instinct over intellect, a view that favored his hated father's kind of behavior over that of his mother.

Lawrence raised himself out of the working class by sheer effort; he attended local schools, finishing with a teaching certificate from Nottingham University College. Then he worked briefly as a clerk at a surgical instruments company and in local elementary schools, before finally getting a teaching position in the London suburb of Croyden in 1908, following in his mother's career path.

Lydia Lawrence was stricken with cancer and died in 1910. Lawrence was at once traumatized and liberated by her death. He had already begun writing his first novel, *The White Peacock* (1911), a tale of an unhappy marriage and its breakdown. Lydia's death released him to write the story of his own childhood and adolescence.

At Croyden, Lawrence met and became friends with Ford Madox Hueffer (who changed his last name to Ford during the anti-German hysteria that accompanied the outbreak of World War I). Hueffer was already the influential editor of *The Little Review*, and was well connected in London literary circles. In Lawrence, he saw a young man of unusual talent, and he gladly introduced him around. By 1912, Lawrence had published two novels: *The White Peacock*, which received some favorable notices; and *The Trespasser* (1912), which was much less satisfactory.

Lawrence had never liked teaching, but it provided a steady income. Now a published novelist, he wondered whether the time had come to make the great leap and try to write full-time. He decided to see an old friend, Professor Ernest Weekley, to ask for advice. Weekley was at the university lecturing, so Lawrence sat down with Frieda, Weekley's wife, to wait.

Two months later, Frieda left her husband and three children to join Lawrence on the Continent. They were married on July 13, 1914, and stayed together until his death.

They made a strange, contradictory couple, the embodiment of the Lawrentian ideal of love between polar opposites. The Baroness Frieda von

Richthofen Weekley was one of three celebrated and beautiful von Richthofen sisters, German aristocracy from the most elevated circles of the German social world, nieces of the German foreign minister.

Matters became complicated when Lawrence was mistaken for an English spy and threatened with arrest and deportation. The subsequent contretemps broke the story of his affair with Frieda into the newspapers and, although Frieda's father got the mess straightened out, nobody saw the humor in it at the time.

Now that the relationship was public knowledge, Lawrence's choices had been made for him. He had married not only up in class, but out of his country as well. For the rest of his literary life, he would return repeatedly to such alliances of opposites. For the rest of his personal life, he would be an exile, buffeted by political events, personal tragedies, and ill health.

Lawrence became a prodigious writer, turning out short stories, novels, travel books, and poetry in great quantities. He had to; he needed the money. The couple traveled through Europe before returning to London on the eve of World War I. It proved to be a bad decision; when the war broke out and Frieda's cousin, Baron Manfred von Richthofen, began shooting down English pilots at an impressive rate, the English government began eyeing her suspiciously, and the couple's neighbors were less than cordial.

With a mixture of reluctance and relief, the Lawrences took a cottage in remote Cornwall. The accommodations were cheap, and the countryside was quiet and isolated, allowing Lawrence to write. They were soon joined by their friends Katherine Mansfield and John Middleton Murry, with whom Frieda had an affair. Lawrence began working on a two-novel series, tentatively titled *The Sisters*, that would explore the erotic and emotional lives of a pair of middle-class English girls. Eventually, these became *The Rainbow* (1915) and *Women in Love* (1920).

Lawrence was appalled by the war, believing it to mark the self-destruction of Western civilization. Having married a von Richthofen and being opposed to the war made him and Frieda targets of much suspicion in provincial Cornwall. Worse, *The Rainbow* ran into censorship troubles with its frank depiction of sexual love, and the book was suppressed. No publisher would touch *Women in Love* as a result, and the book was not published until 1920.

Disgusted with England, Lawrence decided to embark on a wide-ranging odyssey after the war ended. Australia, Ceylon, San Francisco, New Mexico, Mexico, Italy, southern France, the island of Capri—Lawrence and Frieda tried them all. Indeed, some of his finest writing can be found in his travel books, particularly *Twilight in Italy* (1916), *Sea and Sardinia* (1921), *Mornings in Mexico* (1927), and *Etruscan Places* (1932).

Many of Lawrence's heroes are wanderers. Lawrence also returned constantly to the theme of erotic love between opposites. His frank depiction of sexual behavior landed him in trouble again and again, most famously leading to the suppression of one of his last and greatest books, *Lady Chatterley's Lover* (privately printed in 1928, then in 1932 as an expurgated, or edited, edition). This novel combines many of Lawrence's key concerns in a tale of the affair between a titled woman, trapped in a marriage to a crippled, impotent war hero, and her gamekeeper: misogyny (the disliking of women), sexual awakening, love out of one's class, an almost cultlike devotion to earth as the source of the lifeforce, and World War I as the destroyer of young promise.

Chatterley occupied Lawrence for the last several years of his life. He actually produced three complete versions of the novel in the two years before it was privately printed. The unexpurgated version was not available in the United States until 1959.

In 1925, Lawrence's health was broken, as tuberculosis took a heavy toll on him. He and Frieda returned to Italy, where he worked on *Chatterley*. To compound his troubles, police closed an exhibition of Lawrence's erotic paintings in London in 1929. In less than a year, he was dead.

Leakey, Richard

(1944–   )

KENYAN PALEONTOLOGIST

Richard Erskine Leakey, son of the famous paleontologists Louis Leakey and Mary Leakey, was born in Nairobi, Kenya, on December 19, 1944. With little formal higher education (he studied for two years in a secondary education program in London, England), he embarked on a career in his parents' footsteps only after pursuing several other interests first, notably working as a safari guide in East Africa. His extensive knowledge and understanding of physical anthropology and human evolution came from his experience growing up in Kenya with his scientist parents.

Flying a small plane over the Lake Natron region of northeastern Tanzania in 1963, he observed an area of exposed cliffs and sediment that promised to offer good fossil hunting. Shortly thereafter a jawbone of *Zinjanthropus*, a manlike creature that lived almost two million years ago, was found at Lake Natron, and Leakey decided to devote his full energies to the search for man's origins. In 1967, he took part in an expedition to Ethiopia, to the north of Kenya. On that trip, he located a prime research site on the shores of Lake Rudolph (now called Lake Turkana) in northern Kenya. This site, Koobi Fora, would eventually yield almost five hundred fossils of man's ancestors.

These finds led Leakey to propose a theory that three distinct hominids lived side by side in Africa at a very early period in man's evolution. Only one, *Homo habilis* (meaning "skillful man"), survived to evolve into *Homo erectus* and then *Homo sapiens*, the species that mankind belongs to today. In 1972, Leakey, along with fellow paleontologist Glynn Isaac, found an almost complete skull of *Homo habilis* (broken into more than three hundred pieces, which were then carefully reassembled), which proved to be two and a half million years old. His team later discovered other proof that man's direct ancestors lived in eastern Africa as early as three and a half million years ago. In 1984, they found an almost complete skeleton of *Homo erectus* that dated to more than one and a half million years old.

In 1968, Richard Leakey was made the director of Kenya's national museum, a post his father also had held. Traveling the world to raise funds for research, he also founded the Louis Leakey Memorial Institute for African Prehistory. In the late 1980s he was asked by the Kenyan government to head the country's wildlife conservation efforts. Leakey gained wide respect among wildlife and environmental groups around the world for his attempts to preserve Kenya's natural treasure of endangered animal species. In the early 1990s, however, Leakey was involved in a small-plane crash in which he lost both legs, and Kenya's national politics were becoming an impediment to his work. Both factors led to his resignation from the Kenya Wildlife Service, and he returned to private research.

Le Corbusier

(1887–1965)

SWISS ARCHITECT AND ARTIST

> The house is a question of materials. Its walls, floors and roof are questions of suitability: which part supports, which is supported, which does neither one nor the other. The various compartments of the house raise the question of utility: what function is served by one or the other: what is its appropriate form, its size and its capacity for providing light.
>
> —Le Corbusier, in a 1930 essay

Le Corbusier was not only one of the twentieth century's most influential and outstanding architects, he was also an innovative painter. He was born in 1887, in La Chaux-de-Fonds, in the Jura mountains of Switzerland, near the French border. Le Corbusier's real name was Charles Edouard Jeanneret; he began using the pseudonym Le Corbusier in 1920, although he continued to sign his paintings "Jeanneret." His pseudonym was derived from one of his grandparent's names.

His father, a watch enameler, wanted Le Corbusier to take over his trade. As a result, Le Corbusier began taking classes in 1900 at a local art school. By 1902, he enrolled in the school's engraving program. However, his poor eyesight forced him to leave in 1905. He began to study decorative arts, and a professor who recognized Le Corbusier's design talents encouraged him to become an architect.

In 1907, Le Corbusier traveled throughout Europe, studying a variety of building designs. In 1908, he moved to Paris and began working for Auguste Perret, a well-respected architect. Le Corbusier worked for Perret for fourteen months, during which time he learned the basics of using reinforced concrete. Le Corbusier became convinced that reinforced concrete would be the material to revolutionize architecture's future.

In 1913, Le Corbusier established his own architecture office in his hometown. He had decided to specialize in building with reinforced concrete. After only one year back in La Chaux-de-Fonds, he moved to Paris in 1916. There, he met the painter Amédée Ozenfant; together, they collaborated to create purism, an approach to modern design that extended the premises of cubism. The aim of purism was, on the one hand, to create an impersonal machinelike precision, and, on the other hand, to exclude emotion and expressiveness. As a movement in painting, purism thrived from about 1918 to 1925; subsequently, Le Corbusier incorporated its impersonal precision into his theories of architecture.

In 1922, he and a cousin opened an architectural firm in Paris that soon attracted young architects from around the world. Le Corbusier's 1923 influential book, *Towards a New Architecture*, functioned as a blueprint for rationalist innovation in modern architecture. That same year, Le Corbusier became a founding member of C.I.A.M., the International Congress of Modern Architecture, an international organization created to exchange design ideas.

Le Corbusier's architectural theory sought to eliminate resemblances to past stylistic forms. Through the use of new materials for construction, especially reinforced concrete and metal-framed window series, Le Corbusier revolutionized the possibilities of architectural design. He sought to bring the precision of the machine into daily life.

When the international economic depression hit in the 1930s, Le Corbusier found less work as an architect, so he began devoting his energies to theories of town planning. He sought to restructure cities in order to take full advantage of technological and transportational progress. Although his ideas were put to little use in France, his design theories exerted tremendous influence in other countries, particularly in Brazil, India, and the United States.

The international scope of his influence was increased further in 1946 when he founded ASCORAL, a broad-based research group of architects, engineers, and scientists. That same year, he was also appointed to a team of international architects commissioned to design the United Nations building in New York. In 1957, he designed the National Museum of Western Art in Tokyo, Japan. And from 1961 to 1964, he designed the Carpenter Center for the Visual Arts at Harvard University in Cambridge, Massachusetts.

Many of Le Corbusier's designs were completed after his death, in 1965. His functionalist approach had a tremendous impact on the modern movement in architecture. His influence was unparalleled in his day.

Lenin, Vladimir

(1870–1924)

FOUNDER AND FIRST PREMIER
OF SOVIET UNION

History teaches that no oppressed class has ever come into power, and cannot come into power, without passing through a period of dictatorship.

—Vladimir Lenin, 1919

Evil revolutionary or savior of a nation—however one views the life of Vladimir Ilyich Lenin, it is an indisputable fact that the man who led the Russian Revolution, launched the Soviet Union, and left a legacy of political philosophy that helped create governments around the world was one of the major figures of the twentieth century.

Lenin was born on May 4, 1870, in what was then called Simbirsk, Russia. His actual family name was Ulyanov. His father was a school inspector who had been honored by the government for his service. His mother was of German descent and taught him to play the piano, read, and sing. Lenin received awards in school for being top student and applied to Kazan University in 1887, the same year his older brother was executed for trying to kill Czar Alexander III.

Expelled almost immediately from the university, Lenin organized a group of followers of Karl Marx and began to form student protests against the ruling czar. Later, he opened a law practice, having passed the exams without ever taking the courses. In 1893, he moved to St. Petersburg and continued to advocate Marxist philosophy. He was arrested in 1895 and sent to Siberia, where he met his wife-to-be, Nadezhda Konstantinovna Krupskaya. During his exile, Lenin wrote a book, *The Development of Capitalism in Russia*, which suggested that a revolution by the middle class was necessary in order for Russia to become a socialist state governed by the workers.

In the first decade of the twentieth century, most of the revolutionaries from Russia were forced to live in other parts of Europe to avoid being arrested at home. In 1903, the Social Democrats' Second Congress was held in Brussels and London. The result of the meeting was the party's split into two groups, the Bolsheviks, led by Lenin, and the Mensheviks. From that time until 1917, when the Russian Revolution actually began, these two groups, and many others, would continue to struggle for supremacy as the leaders of the revolution. In 1912, Lenin declared the Bolsheviks a separate party. When World War I began, he called for the defeat of Russia so that the czar and his government would be weakened. In 1916, he wrote that the war would mean the economic weakening of the capitalist governments fighting one another and thus pave the way for socialist revolution.

On November 7, 1917, Lenin and Leon Trotsky launched the Russian Revolution, which resulted in the overthrow of czarist Russia and the creation of the All-Russian Congress of Workers' and Soldiers' Deputies. The new government was called the Russian Soviet Republic and Lenin became its leader, though he had no experience of any kind holding a public office. His philosophy taught that a dictatorship of the proletariat was a necessary step leading to the "withering away of the state [or government]."

Lenin's first task was to resolve the civil war that erupted between the Bolsheviks and the Mensheviks, now called the White Russians, which was not accomplished until the end of 1921. Lenin also renamed the Bolsheviks, calling them the Communist Party. He solidified his control by dissolving the Constituent Assembly, which had few Bolsheviks in it.

In 1922, Lenin suffered a stroke and remained ill for two years. He died on January 21, 1924, in Gorky. While he is most often thought of as the father of the Soviet Union, it is important to point out that the country that evolved until the leadership of later rulers—notably Joseph Stalin, who was one of Lenin's lieutenants—bore little resemblance in reality to the state that Lenin himself envisioned. Few political leaders in history have been such masters as Lenin was at applying pure theory to practical implementation of policy. He believed strongly that the path of communism, which admittedly included a stage of dictatorship, would lead to the freeing of all people from political, economic, and every other kind of oppression. What he did not count on was that, by putting that process in motion, his successors would settle for totalitarianism instead of proceeding to Lenin's Marxist-inspired communism.

Lévesque, René

(1922–1987)

CANADIAN JOURNALIST, LEGISLATOR,
AND GOVERNMENT OFFICIAL

Born on August 24, 1922, at Campbellton, New Brunswick, René Lévesque was a liaison officer and European war correspondent for the American armed forces during World War II. In 1946, he joined Radio-Canada International, becoming head of the radio-television news service in 1952. Beginning in 1956, Lévesque hosted the television series "Point de Mire" and became known as one of Quebec's most influential television commentators. Following the 1959 television producers' strike, Lévesque joined the Quebec Liberal Party and was elected to provincial office in 1960.

From 1960 to 1961, Lévesque was minister of water resources and public works, and from 1962 through 1966, he was minister of natural resources and of family and social welfare. He was responsible for the government's decision to nationalize the previously private electric utilities, and he called for reform of general political procedure. Disillusioned with the Liberals' positions on constitutional issues and the federal government, Lévesque became an independent in 1967 and founded a group that a year later became the Parti Quebecois (PQ).

In 1970, the PQ won nearly a quarter of the vote in the general elections, and by 1973 it was the primary opposition party to the Liberals. In 1976, Lévesque and the PQ defeated the Liberal government, promising a public referendum on the issue of provincial sovereignty. Lévesque, now the Premier of Quebec, and the PQ quickly reformed the automobile insurance industry, re-zoned agricultural lands, abolished secret electoral funding, and established French as the official language of Quebec. The sovereignty referendum took place in 1980 and only received 40 percent of the vote, an intensely personal defeat for Lévesque that is said to have broken his heart and initiated his decline. In the early 1980s Parti Quebecois began to lose popularity, and in 1984 Lévesque announced he would no longer push for Quebec's independence, an announcement that prompted several of his ministers to resign in protest. Lévesque himself resigned as head of the party in 1985 in order to resume his work in broadcasting and journalism. He died on November 1, 1987 in Montreal, Quebec.

Rene Lévesque was first recognized as one of French Canada's most influential television journalists. He is remembered as the founder of the Parti Quebecois and leader of the movement for Quebec independence, an effort which continues to press for French-Canadian separatism and is a constant source of conflict within Canadian government and politics.

Lindbergh, Charles Augustus

(1902–1974)

AMERICAN AVIATOR

Charles Augustus Lindbergh was born on February 4, 1902, in Detroit, Michigan. His father was a politician and writer; his mother was a science teacher. He was their only child.

Lindbergh's parents had a somewhat troubled marriage, and they were often separated for long periods of time. Lindbergh was mostly raised by his mother. He was not a notable student. He went to eleven different schools, and his grades were not particularly good. In 1918, he graduated from high school in Little Falls, Minnesota. He spent the next two years running his father's farm in that community, but he was busy figuring out how he could become a flier. He began studying engineering at the University of Wisconsin, but in his second year of college he dropped out and entered a flying school in Lincoln, Nebraska.

Since childhood, Lindbergh had loved the sight of airplanes whirling in the sky. On his first airplane ride, at the age of nineteen, he decided to become a pilot. The nation's skies were filled with pilots and airplanes returning from World War I (1914–18). Public enthusiasm for flying was high, and flight shows were popular attractions in big cities and small towns alike. To make a living, many pilots gave flying lessons or became barnstormers—stunt fliers who went from town to town, giving people rides for a small fee or performing daring feats such as loops and spins.

In Nebraska, Lindbergh happily made a place for himself in the community of barnstormers and mechanics. Tall and slender, he was called "Slim" by the other pilots. Later, his boyish good looks would help endear him to the public. While he was learning to fly, Lindbergh worked as an assistant to a barnstorming pilot. He was a wing-walker—a stunt performer who left the cockpit of a plane and walked along its wings while it was in flight, to the delight of crowds below. He also parachuted from airplanes, a sight that was still new to audiences. In addition, he was responsible for cleaning the plane and doing mechanical repairs. All of his barnstorming experiences were valuable to him, since they taught him a lot not just about airplanes but also about his own courage and nerve.

By 1923, Lindbergh had saved enough money to buy a plane of his own, a war-surplus training plane. He barnstormed for a year and then entered the U.S. Army flight school in San Antonio, Texas, graduating first in his class in 1925. This made Lindbergh a second lieutenant in the Army Reserve.

St. Louis, Missouri, had several airfields and had become a center of aviation in the Midwest, so Lindbergh looked for work there. A brand-new service called airmail had just been introduced. Lindbergh was made the chief pilot for the St. Louis-to-Chicago run, carrying canvas bags of mail through the night sky from one city to the next. As he flew, he began thinking about bigger challenges.

Two English pilots had flown a plane across the Atlantic Ocean by the shortest possible route, from Newfoundland, Canada, to Ireland. Then a businessman had offered a prize of $25,000 to any pilot who could fly *without stopping* from New York City to Paris, France—a distance of 3,600 miles, much farther than the Newfoundland-to-Ireland trip. A number of pilots had their eyes on that prize. Lindbergh decided to win it.

Lindbergh wanted to make the trip alone, something that no one thought was possible. But he knew that he could stay awake for forty hours, if necessary. He felt that a small plane, carrying as much fuel as possible and nothing else, had the best chance of making good time across the ocean.

Lindbergh won support from some St. Louis businessmen, and a small company called Ryan Airlines offered to build his plane. Lindbergh helped design the airplane, which he named the *Spirit of St. Louis*. It carried large fuel tanks but had a tiny cockpit, with barely enough room for the pilot's wicker seat.

Lindbergh tested the *Spirit of St. Louis* by flying it from San Diego, California, to Roosevelt Field in New York City. The plane handled well, and Lindbergh set a new transcontinental speed record. Reporters greeted him at the end of this flight and peppered him with questions about the coming transatlantic trip. They were amazed to learn that "Lucky Lindy," as Lindbergh was called in the press, did not plan to carry a radio or even a parachute. Every possible ounce of weight was to be devoted to fuel.

After days of frustrating delays caused by waiting for good weather, Lindbergh was finally ready. He took off on the morning of May 20, 1927, from

Roosevelt Field, with five ham sandwiches and a quart of water to get him to Paris. Lindbergh was alone.

After seven hours, he was crossing Nova Scotia, northeast of Maine. After twelve hours, he was leaving the coast of Newfoundland behind. Night fell as he headed out across two thousand miles of ocean. He ate a couple of his sandwiches and prepared for a long, tiring night.

The *Spirit of St. Louis* crossed the French coastline as the thirty-third hour of Lindbergh's flight approached. He celebrated by eating a sandwich. As night fell for the second time, he saw the lights of Paris ahead. The Eiffel Tower, Paris's unmistakable landmark, beckoned him on. He flew around it once and then came in for a smooth landing at Bourget Airfield. The flight had lasted thirty-three and a half hours.

Instantly, Lindbergh became a hero to the world. Thousands of people greeted him at Le Bourget Airfield when he landed, and he was welcomed by cheering crowds when he returned to the United States. For many years after his historic flight, Lindbergh was perhaps the best-known private citizen in the world. He also became a spokesperson for aviation, working to promote flight services and passenger travel. He called attention to the benefits of aviation by making spectacular demonstration flights and setting new records.

In 1927, Lindbergh flew nonstop from Washington, D.C., to Mexico City. It was the first time such a flight had been made. While in Mexico, Lindbergh met and fell in love with Anne Morrow, daughter of the U.S. ambassador to Mexico. They were married in 1929.

The next phase of Lindbergh's public life was a sad and painful episode. The Lindberghs' first child, a boy, was born in 1930. In 1932, he was kidnapped and killed. The case shocked the nation and resulted in a huge search by law-enforcement officials. An immigrant carpenter named Bruno Hauptmann was convicted of the crime. He was electrocuted, although some people claimed that he was not really guilty. To escape the grief of their loss and the unwelcome publicity, the Lindberghs moved to England.

Lindbergh was in the news again in the late 1930s, as the nations of Europe moved toward World War II (1939–45). Returning to the United States in 1939, he became an antiwar activist and urged the United States to stay out of the war; he felt that Germany's military might was too great for the United States to overcome. This position made him unpopular with many Americans, including President Franklin Roosevelt, who considered Lindbergh unpatriotic. Yet when the United States entered the war, Lindbergh helped industrialist Henry Ford manufacture bombers, and he flew fifty combat missions in the Pacific. In 1954, President Dwight Eisenhower rewarded Lindbergh with the rank of brigadier general in the Air Force Reserve.

Lindbergh devoted the rest of his life to working as an advisor for Pan American Airways and to supporting the conservation movement. Long before environmentalism became fashionable, he spoke about the need to preserve endangered species and indigenous peoples whose way of life was threatened by Western civilization. His autobiography, *The Spirit of St. Louis,* was published in 1953 and won a Pulitzer Prize. Lindbergh died of cancer on the island of Maui, Hawaii, in August of 1974.

Louis, Joe (Joe Louis Barrow)

(1914–1981)

AMERICAN BOXER

Joe Louis, nicknamed the "Brown Bomber," held the heavyweight boxing title longer than any boxer before him—nearly twelve years. But before winning the title in 1937, he had been beaten by a German fighter named Max Schmeling. It bothered Louis. He often remarked, "I won't be champion until I get that Schmeling." In 1938 the two men fought in a rematch at Yankee Stadium that was to become legendary.

Among other things, there were political aspects to this match. Schmeling was a German, from a country ruled by dictator Adolf Hitler and his militaristic Nazi party. Many Americans feared that Nazi aggression would engulf Europe and even spread to the United States. Joe Louis was an American and a special hero to black Americans. He belonged to a race the Nazis had labeled "inferior."

From the time Joe Louis entered the ring that night, he struck Schmeling relentlessly. The fight lasted only 2 minutes and four seconds into the first round when the referee called an end to it. A sportswriter for the *New York Times* wrote about Joe's "lightning attack. Lefts and rights—Bang! Bang! Bang!" Americans celebrated. Louis had beaten Schmeling, and now he felt the world title was truly his.

Joe Louis Barrow was born into stark poverty to a share-cropping family in Alabama. He had almost no schooling until the family moved to Detroit when he was 12. Joe could not read or write, and he had tremendous difficulty trying to catch up. He was placed in Bronson Vocational School to learn cabinetmaking, then auto body work. His mother wanted him to play the violin. But Joe started using his music-lesson money for boxing lessons at the community center where some of his friends boxed.

Joe persisted with boxing even after he was soundly beaten in his first amateur fight. Fighting as Joe Louis, he went on to won 50 of his 54 amateur bouts. He worked to get his 6'1½", 200-pound frame in shape and to throw quick punches, one after another. After he won the Golden Gloves light heavyweight award, he came to the attention of a lawyer manager who hired a famous trainer for him.

For more than eleven years, the methodical, fast-punching Louis defeated all challengers. He inspired young fighters like Rocky Marciano and impressed fans with his skill and modest ways. When World War II began, Louis enlisted in the army. He went to bases around the world meeting service people and fighting exhibitions. His patriotism promoted unity among all Americans in fighting against a common enemy during a grim period in history.

After the war, Joe Louis defended his title in a 1947 fight against Jersey Joe Walcott. But it was a split decision, and he realized that his reflexes and ability were weakening. After defeating Walcott again in 1948, Louis left pro boxing. Unfortunately, he had spent the $3 million he'd earned. Loans to friends, poor investments, expenses, and overspending had left him broke, with a tax debt to the government. To earn money, Louis fought again. Although overweight and aging, he did win eight boxing matches in 1950 and 1951 before Rocky Marciano, who idolized Louis, had to fight him. Marciano knocked out Louis and later said he felt terrible doing so.

Still needing money, Louis fought in exhibitions and even worked as a wrestler. "It's an honest living," he said when people did not approve. He did public relations work and appeared as a nightclub host. Louis's third wife, a lawyer, went to court to settle his tax debt. In poor health, he could not attend a tribute that his friends arranged for him in 1970. At Joe Louis Appreciation Night in Detroit, people watched films of Louis's greatest moments as a boxer. An article about Louis that same year said, "Louis was the black Atlas on whose broad shoulders blacks were lifted, for in those days, there were few authentic black heroes."

Joe Louis spent his last years enjoying his family and many friends, and playing golf. At his funeral, the Reverend Jesse Jackson spoke of his contributions, saying, "We are honoring a giant who saved us in a time of trouble. He lifted us up when we were down."

Luce, Clare Boothe

(1903–1987)

AMERICAN EDITOR AND REPORTER, PLAYWRIGHT, U. S.
REPRESENTATIVE, AND AMBASSADOR TO ITALY

Clare Boothe Luce was born on March 10, 1903, in New York, the daughter of a musician and a dancer. Her father left the family when she was a small child and her mother became determined that Clare should not be deprived of any comfort or social advantage. Her mother encouraged her to become an actress and as a youngster she won several small parts in plays and silent films. After her mother remarried a wealthy man, Clare was sent to private schools in Memphis, Chicago, and France. Through friendships made at these prestigious boarding schools, she came to know many prominent writers and entertainers. During World War I, she did volunteer work for the Red Cross, and after the war she traveled extensively in Europe. In 1921, she met Alva Ertskin Belmont, a leader in the recently successful struggle to give women the right to vote, and went to work briefly for Belmont's Women's National Party. In 1923, she married George Tuttle Brokaw, a millionaire who was twenty three years her senior. They had one child, Ann, in 1924, but in 1929 the couple divorced.

Though her divorce left her with a sizable income, Clare Boothe became uncomfortable with the wealthy socialite's life she had been leading with her husband, and she decided to make her own way. In 1930, she went to work for *Vogue* magazine, and then for *Vanity Fair*, and she was soon writing satirical articles on the social elite. By 1933, she was the managing editor of *Vanity Fair*. Later in 1933, she worked briefly for President Franklin Roosevelt's National Recovery Administration, but she came to dislike Roosevelt personally, as well as the way his programs controlled business activity, and soon she was back at *Vanity Fair*. Under her direction, the magazine became highly critical of the President. In 1935, she went to work for William Randolph Hearst's newspaper chain, reporting from Europe on the alarming developments in Hitler's Germany and Mussolini's Italy. But Hearst was an isolationist who did not want to stir up American interest in these events, and he soon fired her.

When she returned to New York and in November 1935, married Henry L. Luce, publisher of *Time* and *Fortune* magazines. She became interested in playwrighting, and in December 1936 the play *The Women* opened on Broadway to rave reviews. In 1938, she wrote another hit play, *Kiss the Boys Goodbye*. These plays were comedies about the role of women in society, but in 1936 she wrote *Margin for Error*, a serious attack on German fascism. In 1940, she shifted her attentions to *Life* magazine, her husband's daring new photo-journal. She became a roving correspondent, traveling to Europe and reporting on developments there. She and her husband were in Brussels, Belgium in April 1940 when the Germans bombed the city and invaded the country, and they had to flee to Paris. Luce returned to the United States and published *Europe in the Spring*, a best-selling book about the complacency of European governments in the face of Hitler's aggression.

In late 1940, Luce campaigned for Roosevelt's opponent, Republican Wendell Wilkie, but Roosevelt was easily reelected to a third term. In 1941, Luce and her husband traveled to Asia as correspondents for *Life* magazine. Luce interviewed Indian Prime Minister Jawaharlal Nehru, the Chinese leader Chiang Kai-shek, and General Douglas MacArthur in the Philippines. After the outbreak of World War II, she ensconced herself in General Joseph Stilwell's headquarters in Burma and covered the Allied retreat as the Japanese invaded the country. Her growing knowledge of world affairs and her distaste for the Roosevelt administration turned her interests toward participating in the political process.

In 1942, Luce was elected the first United States congresswoman from Connecticut. She was pro-civil rights, but generally conservative on other issues, and her main interest was foreign affairs. She spoke out bluntly, and as the wife of one of the country's wealthiest and most influential magazine publishers, she attracted a lot of attention, which her House colleagues often resented. When her daughter was killed in a car crash in January 1944, Luce emerged from the tragedy even more combative, almost as if she now felt she had nothing to lose in fighting loud and hard for the causes she believed in. In the 1944 presidential election, she lashed out at Roosevelt, accusing him of knowing in advance of the Japanese attack on Pearl Harbor. The President's health had been failing and Luce publicly accused the Democrats of trying to elect a dying President. Roosevelt won the election, but died in April, 1944.

In 1946, Luce left Congress, shunned politics, and converted to Roman Catholicism. In 1948, she wrote the screenplay for the film *Come to the Stable*, which was nominated for an Academy Award. In 1952, she returned to politics, actively campaigning for the election of Dwight D. Eisenhower. Eisenhower appointed her ambassador to Italy, making her the first woman ever to hold a top diplomatic post. In 1954, she assisted in the complex negotiations that gave Italy the city of Trieste, which was claimed at the time by Yugoslavia. In 1956, when Soviet troops invaded Hungary to put down a revolt, Luce pleaded with Washington to send aid to the rebels. When the United States chose to remain neutral, Luce resigned her post. She returned to the United States and she and her husband settled in Phoenix, Arizona. In 1959, Eisenhower tried to appoint her ambassador to Brazil, but her enemies in Congress obstructed her appointment and she refused the post. The Luces left public life and retired to the Arizona countryside.

After her husband died in 1967, Luce moved to Hawaii. She continued to spend a good deal of her time in Washington, however, working in the 1970s for President Richard Nixon and in the 1980s for President Ronald Reagan on the Foreign Intelligence Advisory Board. She died of a brain tumor on October 9, 1987.

MacArthur, Douglas

(1880–1964)

GENERAL IN COMMAND
OF AMERICAN FORCES DURING
WORLD WAR II AND THE
KOREAN WAR

MacArthur was born on January 26, 1880, in Little Rock, Arkansas to a family with a long tradition of military service. He graduated from the West Texas Military Academy in 1897 and from the United States Military Academy at West Point in 1899. He served at various posts in the United States and in Panama and the Philippines, and in 1908 graduated from the Engineer School of Applications in Washington, D.C. In 1913, he joined the general staff of the War Department.

When the United States declared war on Germany in 1917, MacArthur was appointed chief of staff of the 42nd Infantry Division, the "Rainbow" Division, which was sent to France in November 1917. Promoted to brigadier general, he was put in command of the 84th Brigade. He distinguished himself during the major American offensives of the war. Twice wounded, he received many decorations for bravery and became division commander.

MacArthur returned to the United States in 1919 to become superintendent of West Point. He reorganized the program of studies and introduced liberal arts courses to the curriculum. In 1922, he began the first of two tours of duty in the Philippines. In 1930, President Herbert Hoover appointed him army chief of staff. Two years later, Hoover ordered him to evict by force a group of unemployed veterans camped in protest near the White House, and MacArthur's reputation was seriously damaged as a result of his participation in that incident.

In 1935, President Franklin Roosevelt appointed MacArthur military adviser to the Philippines, and he was soon in command of the Philippine army. He tried to modernize the island nation's defenses, but it was difficult to get money and equipment from Washington in peacetime. When the Japanese invaded the Philippines in December 1941, MacArthur's ill-equipped troops gradually retreated to the stronghold of Bataan. Under orders from Roosevelt, MacArthur escaped to Australia a month before the garrison at Bataan surrendered to the Japanese in April 1942. In Australia, MacArthur made his famous statement "I shall return," which came to symbolize his aggressive fighting spirit and his determination to liberate the Philippines.

MacArthur was put in command of the Southwest Pacific Area. In the last six months of 1942, he stopped a Japanese attempt to reach Australia by fighting a series of bloody battles in the mountainous jungles of New Guinea. He then began to drive the Japanese back, moving slowly up the coast of New Guinea. Friction developed between MacArthur and Admiral Chester Nimitz, who was commanding naval and marine forces in the central Pacific, as the two commands competed for men and supplies. But by 1944, MacArthur had persuaded President Roosevelt to support his campaign to retake the Philippines. In October 1944, the Sixth Army invaded the island of Leyte in the central Philippines. In January 1945, MacArthur's forces landed on the main island of Luzon and fought several bloody battles, culminating in the capture of the city of Manila. MacArthur took command of all army forces in the Pacific, and was scheduled to lead Operation Coronet, the invasion of Japan planned for 1946. But Japan surrendered in August 1945 after the dropping of atomic bombs on the cities of Hiroshima and Nagasaki. From the deck of the battleship *Missouri* in Tokyo harbor, MacArthur presided over the signing of the surrender agreement on September 2, 1945.

President Harry Truman appointed MacArthur supreme commander of the Allied powers, and he became virtual dictator of Japan during the American occupation from 1945 to 1948. His policies toward the Japanese were liberal and progressive. He persuaded Washington to send large quantities of food and fuel, as Japan's cities were in ruins and the people were starving. He purged the government of militarists, had his staff prepare a new constitution for the country that guaranteed free elections and civil liberties, and took power away from the emperor, placing it in the hands of a legislature known as the Diet. The new constitution also renounced war and limited Japan's army to a small self-defense force. MacArthur broke up the *zaibatsu*, the large corporations that had supported the military, and in the early years of the occupation he encouraged the growth of political parties and labor unions. Japan quickly evolved from a wartime military dictatorship to a postwar democracy.

When the North Koreans invaded South Korea in 1950, MacArthur was appointed chief of the United Nations Command. In a brilliantly planned counterattack, he drove the Communists back into North Korea and all the way to the Yalu River near the border of China. This situation made the Chinese nervous, and a large force of Chinese soldiers crossed the border and drove MacArthur back. The war evolved into a bloody stalemate, with neither side able to make much progress. MacArthur wanted to expand the war into China and suggested the possibility of using atomic weapons against the Chinese. But President Truman feared a wider war and wanted to negotiate an armistice. When MacArthur made his disagreements with Truman public, Truman relieved him of command.

MacArthur returned to the United States a hero, and there was talk of drafting him to run for the presidency on the Republican ticket in 1952, but General Dwight Eisenhower was chosen instead. MacArthur retired from the army and died at Walter Reed Hospital in Washington, D.C. on April 5, 1964.

Malcolm X (Malcolm Little)

(1925–1965)

AMERICAN CIVIL RIGHTS ACTIVIST

Power in defense of freedom is greater than power in behalf of tyranny and oppression.
    —Malcolm X, in a speech in New York City (1965)

The black Muslim leader Malcolm X was a powerful leader in the civil rights movement. He searched for ways to end racial oppression, and for ways to foster black identity and pride.

He was born Malcolm Little in Omaha, Nebraska on May 19, 1925. His father was a minister who preached about black pride, and encouraged blacks to remain separate from whites. The Ku Klux Klan, a secret society of whites who hated blacks, were angered by his preaching and the Little family was forced to move several times to escape their repeated threats of violence. When Malcolm was six years old and living with his family in Lansing, Michigan, his father was killed; Malcolm always believed that he had been murdered by members of the Ku Klux Klan.

With her husband gone, Malcolm's mother now had to fend for herself and seven children. The family was very poor and often did not have enough to eat. They were forced to go on welfare, which meant that government gave them money to live on and sent social workers to their house. When they saw that Mrs. Little was less and less able to cope with caring for her family, and learned that Malcolm had been caught stealing food, they decided he should be sent to live with another family.

But without parents to watch out for him, he soon got into trouble and was expelled from school. He was sent to a detention home, where boys in trouble were sent to get special help and guidance. The couple who ran the home liked Malcolm, and sent him to the public junior high school in Mason, Michigan; he was the first boy from the detention home to attend school and one of the very first blacks to attend that school.

At first, he liked it and did well in his classes. A summer trip to Boston to stay with his half-sister Ella introduced him to the ways of a larger city. Boston was a whole new world to him; there were entire African-American neighborhoods, something he hadn't seen before. When he returned to school that fall, he was dissatisfied. Malcolm began to notice that people assumed blacks were inferior to whites. He began to withdraw from his classmates, and at the end of school year, when he was released from the detention home, he boarded a Greyhound bus for Boston to live with Ella.

Malcolm lived in Boston for a time, selling sandwiches on the New York to Boston railroad. This allowed him to go to Harlem, a New York neighborhood populated by African Americans. Malcolm felt immediately at home in Harlem. When he was fired from the railway company, he moved there.

In Harlem, he began committing crimes: selling drugs and stealing. When he knew the police were looking for him, as they often were, he went back to Boston. Eventually he was caught and convicted for burglary; and in 1946, when Malcolm was twenty years old, he was sent to the Charlestown State Prison in Massachusetts.

Prison life was brutal. Malcolm Little's cell was tiny; there was no running water and the toilet was a covered pail in the corner. After three years, he was transferred to Norfolk Prison Colony, a newer and better-run prison that had an excellent library. He began taking books out of the library. He read for as long as fifteen hours a day—so much that he strained his eyes, and had to start wearing the glasses that later became his trademark.

During this time, he received a visit from his brother Reginald, who lived in Detroit. Reginald talked to him about a new religion he had joined called the Nation of Islam. Its followers were called "Black Muslims." They believed that blacks should be respected by whites, but live separately from them, with their own communities and businesses. Reginald also told him about the leader of the Black Muslims, the Honorable Elijah Muhammed. Muhammed called white people "devils" who had tried to enslave black people. Malcolm was stirred by these thoughts and began to correspond with Muhammed. He also became a convert to the Muslim religion, and changed his name to Malcolm X. Because black Americans didn't know the African name of their ancestors, the Muslims used the letter "X", which is used in mathematical equations to stand for an unknown number, to show that their true names could never be known.

Malcolm X was let out of jail in the summer of 1952. He went to Detroit to live with his brother Wilfred, who was also a Muslim. He held jobs in a furniture store and on the assembly line in a factory. He adopted the Muslim customs of wearing a neat dark suit, refusing liquor and pork, and attended a Muslim Temple. In September of that year, he went to the Nation of Islam's headquarters in Chicago. There he met Elijah Muhammed and was impressed by his powerful talk about the black man's situation in America. Now Malcolm X knew what he wanted to do with his life: he was going to work for the Nation of Islam.

By the summer of 1953, Malcolm X was the assistant minister in Detroit Temple Number One. He spent his time visiting black neighborhoods, talking and trying to convert them to the Muslim faith. For the next six years, he worked hard, establishing new temples in Philadelphia, New York and other cities. When Elijah Muhammad became ill, Malcolm X took over many of his responsibilities. It seemed that he might be the Nation of Islam's next leader, for he was known as their most important spokesperson. While many people felt Malcolm X hated whites, he tried to correct their thinking: he was angry with them because of the crimes against blacks that they had committed, not just because they were white.

During his travels, he met a woman named Betty X in a temple and fell in love with her. They were married in 1958, and went on to have four daughters. Malcolm X and his family moved to a house in Queens, New York.

In 1964, Malcolm X made two trips to Africa and the Middle East. First he made a pilgrimage, or holy trip to the holy city of Mecca in Saudi Arabia. Mecca was the birthplace of the prophet Muhammad, founder of the Muslim religion. In Mecca, he took the name El-Hajj Malik El-Shabazz, a title of honor given to Muslim who had made the trip to the holy city.

When he returned to America, he decided to leave the Nation of Islam. While in Mecca, he had noticed that blacks and whites were able to get along peacefully together, and he began rethinking some of his ideas about white people. He also saw how black Christians and Muslims worked together. Now he wanted to head such a movement in America, which he called the Organization of Afro-American Unity (OAAU).

But Malcolm X Shabazz had made enemies as well as friends: many Muslims were angry with him for leaving the Nation of Islam and many whites did not want him to lead a movement of blacks. He received threatening phone calls and one night, a firebomb was thrown through the window of his house. No one was hurt, but the house was badly damaged and many of his family's things were destroyed. A week later, on February 25, 1965, the OAAU held a meeting at the Audubon Ballroom in Harlem. Malcolm X was scheduled to speak. When he appeared on the stage, there was a burst of applause, followed by angry shouting. He tried to calm the angry voices, but suddenly, gunfire rang out. Malcolm X had been shot. He fell backward onto the floor and was dead at the age of thirty-nine.

Malraux, André

(1901–1976)

FRENCH NOVELIST, POLITICIAN,
AND ART CRITIC

André Malraux was a novelist, adventurer, soldier, and art critic. He was also France's Minister for Information from 1945 to 1946 and its Minister for Cultural Affairs from 1959 to 1969.

Georges-André Malraux was born on November 3, 1901, in Paris. His parents, who had married in 1900, separated in 1905 and divorced in 1915. Malraux was raised by his grandmother, his mother, and his aunt in Bondy, a suburb of Paris.

Malraux attended private school in Bondy and was considered very advanced for his age. Before he reached high school, he had already read the works of Victor Hugo, Honoré Balzac, and Sir Walter Scott. At seventeen, he went to work for a book dealer/publisher, who paid him to search the secondhand book stalls for rare books. In 1920, he edited two volumes of poetry for publication by his employer. The quality of his work drew the attention of another publisher, and Malraux began a career as a poetry editor.

During this period, he began attending lectures at the art museums of Paris and became acquainted with many poets and painters. In 1921, he met and married Clara Goldschmidt. The couple shared an interest in art, literature, film, and travel. In 1923, they embarked on an archaeological expedition to French Indochina. Malraux discovered an ancient temple and removed some artwork. Although at this time many people did the same thing and were not punished, Malraux was arrested and sentenced to three years in prison. With the help of his wife and the petitions of French writers, he was released after serving only a few months.

Malraux's experience with what he considered to be a corrupt government led him to begin a newspaper that would oppose the government of French Indochina. The newspaper marked the beginning of Malraux's interest in politics and his inability to choose between two different kinds of political involvement: the man of action, who commits himself to specific struggles; and the intellectual, who writes of the origins and long-term effects of those same struggles.

In the 1930s, Malraux chose to be a man of action. In the Spanish Civil War, he commanded an air force unit; and in World War II, he served as tank commander until he was captured by the Germans. He escaped and became a fighter in the resistance movement that tried to sabotage the German forces that occupied France.

From a very early age, Malraux had suffered from the death of family members and people close to him. His grandfather and his father both committed suicide; his two half-brothers were killed in World War II; his second wife was killed in a train accident; and his two sons were killed in a car crash. It is no surprise, then, that death, destiny, and the futility of action were constant themes in his work.

Like Sartre and Camus, Malraux believed that in a world where people no longer believed in God or in themselves, action and the value of individual thought and effort did not make sense. Life in such a world was at best absurd. In the novels for which he is best remembered—*La Condition Humaine* (translated as *Man's Fate* in 1934), and *L'Espoir* (translated as *Man's Hope* in 1938)—Malraux suggests that belief in the essential dignity of oneself, the brotherhood of men, and the sacrifice of individual interests in the name of a greater good could restore some meaning to life.

In the 1940s, Malraux shifted his attention to the visual arts and produced several volumes of art criticism. His last works, published in the 1970s, were autobiographies. Malraux died on November 23, 1976, of a blood clot in his lung.

Mandela, Nelson

(1918–   )

SOUTH AFRICAN POST-APARTHEID LEADER

> I have fought against white domination, and I have fought against
> black domination. I have cherished the ideal of a democratic and free
> society in which all persons will live together in harmony and with
> equal opportunities. It is an ideal which I hope to live for and achieve.
> But, if needs be, it is an ideal for which I am prepared to die.
>
> —Nelson Mandela, at his trial in 1963

One of the most courageous, and remarkably forgiving, leaders of the twentieth century, Nelson Mandela survived almost an entire lifetime of discrimination, abuse, and imprisonment because of his skin color and political beliefs to become the first president of the black-majority-ruled South Africa.

Rolihlahla Nelson Mandela was born on July 18, 1918, in Transkei, South Africa. His father, a chief in the Tembu tribe, had four wives and no formal education. Both his parents were determined that Nelson would go to school. At an early age he tended the family's livestock and was often ridiculed by other children because of his poverty.

When he began studying history in school, Nelson discovered that the books presented a very different version of the story of his people from the one his tribal leaders had described. This difficulty in reconciling the white and the black perspectives of history would be a major influence on his life. At an early age he also realized that the South African government's laws made it difficult for him to have the same opportunities of education that whites enjoyed. At the age of ten, Nelson was sent to a boarding school run by Methodist missionaries. At sixteen, after also learning about his own people's history and customs, he was initiated as an adult into his tribe.

In 1939, he began studies at Fort Hare College but was asked to leave when he organized other students into a protest against school conditions. Then, to avoid an arranged marriage, he ran away to Johannesburg, where he worked for a mining company. With the help of Walter Sisulu, who would become another black activist in South Africa, Mandela entered the University of South Africa. He graduated in 1942 and, interested in law, took a job with a white law firm and continued his studies at the University of Witwatersrand.

In 1944, Mandela joined the African National Congress (ANC), a political group committed to the achievement of equal rights for black South Africans. He, Sisulu, and another colleague, Oliver Tambo, then formed the ANC Youth League. The three men gained increasing responsibility and power within the

ANC. In 1952, as president of the Transvaal ANC (a regional division of the national group), Mandela took part in demonstrations protesting apartheid conditions. Thousands of black Africans participated, and violence erupted when the demonstration got out of hand. Mandela was arrested and then "banned," which meant he could not participate in any political activities. A year later, the ruling was extended, and he was required by the government to leave the ANC.

During these years Mandela passed the bar exams and established a law practice with Tambo. When his ban was ended, he was quickly arrested again, in 1956, this time charged with treason. The trial lasted until 1961, when the case was dismissed. In 1958 he was married for a second time (his first marriage, which produced three children, ended in divorce in 1958) to Winifred Madikizela, better known as Winnie. In 1961, Mandela, after helping organize a nationwide strike of black workers, joined the Umkhonto we Sizwe (Spear of the Nation), which was the underground faction of the black freedom movement. The group attempted to drive home the seriousness of their intentions to achieve equal rights for all races in South Africa by bombing government buildings, though every effort was made to avoid injury to people.

Mandela's activities at the time forced him to hide from South African authorities. He also traveled to other countries, including England in 1962. When he returned home the police were tipped off about his hiding place and Mandela was arrested, convicted of incitement to riot and leaving the country without a passport; he was sentenced to five years in jail. While in prison doing hard labor he was tried again for his involvement in Umkhonto and sentenced in 1963 to life in prison. Walter Sisulu also was jailed, but Oliver Tambo escaped prosecution because he was out of the country at the time.

Mandela served just over twenty-seven years as a political prisoner as the rest of the world demanded his release. His wife, Winnie, maintained his leadership role in the ANC. Finally, on February 11, 1990, President Frederik W. de Klerk released Mandela and Sisulu. The transformation of South Africa into a black-majority-ruled country began in earnest. Remarkably, Mandela expressed little bitterness toward his white oppressors; instead, he embraced the opportunity to bring about profound changes in the country that had jailed him for a third of his life. He traveled the world, was hailed as a hero wherever he went, and raised money for the ANC's efforts to achieve majority rule.

Mandela and de Klerk began a difficult process of negotiations, while at the same time increasing rivalry between the ANC and the Zulu Inkatha Party resulted in appalling violence among the country's divided black population. Mandela maintained his firm resolve and dignified control over the path toward majority rule, despite the pain of Winnie Mandela's arrest and conviction for kidnapping and assault during the violence in the black townships a few years before.

In 1993, Mandela and other black leaders came to an agreement with the white government, led by de Klerk, for a new constitution for South Africa that provided for majority rule based on suffrage (the right to vote) by all races and the elimination of the black homelands. (Homelands were created years before by the white government as a means of isolating much of the country's black population. These homelands, often located in geographically undesirable places within South Africa, were called independent by the white minority government, but no foreign government acknowledged this to be true.) In April 1994, the first universal elections in the history of South Africa were held, and the ANC, as was expected, won the majority of the vote. For blacks it was their first opportunity to vote, and many walked for days to polling places and waited patiently for hours to cast their ballots. Nelson Mandela, at the age of seventy-six, became the first black president of South Africa.

Mann, Thomas

(1875–1955)

GERMAN NOVELIST, SHORT-STORY WRITER, AND ESSAYIST

Every piece of work is in fact a realization . . . of our own nature; they are stones on that harsh road which we must learn to walk ourselves.

—Thomas Mann

Paul Thomas Mann, one of the giant figures in German literature and one of the key writers of this century, was born on June 6, 1875, in Lübeck, Germany, the second of five children. His family was quite well off, although their fortunes dwindled before he was twenty. His father, Thomas, headed the family grain business and had a record of distinguished public service, first as German consul to The Netherlands, then later as a member of Lübeck's city Parliament. His mother, Julia, was born in Brazil to a German businessman with roots in Lübeck, and a Brazilian mother.

The older Mann children (the youngest was born in 1890, the year before their father died) enjoyed the fruits of prosperity—a large house on Mengstrasse, summers at a glamorous resort on the Baltic, and doting parents. Paul Thomas admired his father's strength of character, his ambition, and his dapper dress. Julia, however, had a deeper influence on the children, instilling in them a love of music and stories, a flair for the aesthetic and a recognition of a wider world beyond the borders of Germany.

With their father's death in 1891 and the subsequent dissolution of the family firm, life changed abruptly for the Mann children. The house on Mengstrasse, so lovingly depicted by Thomas Mann in his first novel, *Buddenbrooks: The Decline of a Family* (1901), was sold. Julia moved with the three younger children to Munich, a much larger, but more cosmopolitan city. The oldest child, Heinrich, had already left home to pursue a career as a writer. Thomas, almost seventeen, was left behind in Lübeck to finish his last year of high school. Thomas dreamed of following in his big brother's footsteps and becoming a writer.

Mann's first literary efforts appeared in a short-lived school paper that he co-founded. At that time, he was reading everything he could get his hands on and listening to the new music of Richard Wagner. Both his reading in German literature and his love of Wagner's operas would mark his art and life in years to come.

Immediately after receiving his diploma in 1894, Thomas rejoined the family in Munich. It was like moving from the nineteenth century into the budding twentieth. Munich was a growing city, with a Bohemian world of artists and intellectuals, and Thomas's mother knew many of them. Thomas took an office job with an insurance company and began writing in his spare time. After an important editor published an early story and encouraged him to abandon office work, he gave notice at the firm and registered for several courses at the university.

In 1895 the two brothers, Thomas and Heinrich, traveled together to Italy. In Rome, Thomas wrote his first major story, "Little Herr Friedemann." The publisher he submitted it to was so delighted that he was asked for all his earlier pieces, as well, so that they might be published in a collection. Thus it was that when young Thomas Mann returned to Munich in the spring of 1898, he found himself the promising author of a collection of stories, *The Little Herr Freidemann and Other Stories*.

The year before, Mann had begun work on a novel chronicling the fall of a family business in a small German city and its terrible effect on the family itself. Thomas finished the book in August 1900, then was called up for his mandatory year of military service, in the Royal Bavarian Infantry. Within three months he was released as unfit for service, which allowed him to return home in time to fight with his publisher over the length of his first novel, who agreed to release the book in a two-volume edition, but only in a limited printing of one thousand copies. That first edition, published in 1901, was a slow seller, but when a one-volume edition was issued shortly thereafter, *Buddenbrooks* was a huge seller. Suddenly, Thomas Mann was a famous novelist.

In 1903, Mann met Katharine Pringsheim, nicknamed Katja, the daughter of a wealthy family of Jewish descent. Her father, a mathematician, shared

Mann's enthusiasm for Wagner and was at the center of a formidable circle of artists and intellectuals in Munich. The nineteen-year-old Katja was charming and self-assured. Mann was won over by her almost instantly, and on February 11, 1905, the couple was married. They would have six children. (Erika, the oldest, would marry the poet W.H. Auden in the 1930s after the Nazis revoked the Manns' citizenship).

Mann's 1909 novel *Royal Highness* is a rare excursion into the comic mode, a sort of lightweight tribute to his own happy marriage. Two ears later, Katja was briefly hospitalized in a Swiss sanitarium with lung problems. Mann visited regularly, storing up memories of the institution that he would use in his second massive masterpiece, *The Magic Mountain* (1924). Before that book was even conceived, however, Mann wrote one of the best of his shorter works, the novella *Death in Venice* (1912).

By the time World War I began, Thomas Mann was thirty-nine. There was no question of his serving in the military, but he felt constrained to make some contribution to the war effort. He began work on a huge essay detailing his ultraconservative and nationalist political views. Heinrich, who was a socialist and a pacifist, was outraged by the *Reflections of an Apolitical Man* (1918), and it would be several years before their rift healed. As Mann himself would tacitly acknowledge by 1930, his big brother was right. Mann was already regretting his public applause for positions that were out of date before the ink was dry on the page. Even more to his dismay, the book was an enormous seller, with the antidemocratic forces that would eventually congeal into the Third Reich embracing it with delight. In 1922, Mann publicly embraced the Weimar Republic's short-lived democracy; he was now on a tightrope between disappointed old supporters and new allies who didn't trust him.

In 1924, he brought out what many feel is his greatest book, one of the most important books of the century, *The Magic Mountain*. Another enormous novel—over seven hundred pages in its current American paperback edition—*The Magic Mountain* is set in a luxurious tuberculosis sanitarium in the Swiss Alps. The sanitarium is a microcosm of European civilization in the wake of the Great War. On the strength of this novel and *Buddenbrooks*, Mann was awarded the 1929 Nobel Prize for Literature. He followed the award with a massive four-volume cycle of novels based on the biblical story of Joseph, *Joseph and His Brethren* (1933, 1934, 1936, 1943).

By 1930, Mann was coming around to a political stance closer to his brother's than to the one he had held during the previous war. After witnessing the workings of fascism on a visit to Italy, he wrote "Mario and the Magician," one of his best short stories, an allegory about the destructive nature of that ideology. When the Nazis came to power, Mann was on a lecture tour. He chose to settle in Switzerland rather than return to Germany. He did not return home for another sixteen years. The Nazis revoked his German citizenship, confiscated his property, and banned his books.

In 1935, Mann visited the United States for the second time. When he decided to come to the United States three years later, in part to take an honorary faculty post at Princeton University, he was received more warmly than most other German refugees from Hitler. His political position had evolved to the point where he now favored an "American" solution to Germany's problems, neither fascist nor communist. His books were well known, and he was a vocal supporter of Roosevelt's policies.

After his year at Princeton, Mann moved to the West Coast, living in a beautiful home in Pacific Palisades, California, where he was a central figure of the German refugee community. He became an American citizen in 1944, and shortly afterward he began work on a new novel that he hoped would at least partly explain the tragedy of his native Germany. Published in 1946, *Doctor Faustus* is an allegory in which Germany is represented by the composer Leverkühn, who makes a pact with the devil.

In 1947, Mann returned to Europe for the first time in a decade. He visited on lectures tours several more times before settling in Switzerland in 1952. The scourge of McCarthyism in the United States and the bleak cold-war period just begun in the wake of World War II depressed and upset him. Ironically, his last two novels—*The Holy Sinner* (1951) and *The Confessions of Felix Krull, Confidence Man* (1955)—are a return to the optimistic mode that he wrote in before the world had been plunged into the flames of two world wars. Both novels are humorous and even self-parodying, the work of a great artist making a final peace with himself, his conscience, and his art.

Mantle, Mickey

(1932–1995)

AMERICAN BASEBALL PLAYER

Elvin Mantle of Commerce, Oklahoma, was determined that his son would become a star baseball player. He named him "Mickey" after Mickey Cochrane, a Detroit Tigers player he admired. It is said that he kept a baseball in his son's crib and gave him a bat at age 2. During his childhood, Mickey played Little League baseball and grew steadily better. By high school, he was also a football star. Then Mickey developed a bone disease, osteomyelitis, the result of a football injury. His bone marrow was affected, and he has had brittle bones ever since.

After spending a long time on crutches, Mickey returned to baseball. By age 19, he was an outstanding hitter and pitcher and got a contract to play for the

New York Yankees. The shy, blond, rural Oklahoman seemed quick-tempered and distant at first. But Mantle later became one of the most popular and accomplished Yankees, in the tradition of Babe Ruth and Joe DiMaggio. A "switch-hitter," he could hit well from either the left or right side. Of his 536 career home runs, 163 were hit as a righty and 373 as a lefty. Pitchers had trouble figuring out how to beat him.

In his first two years, 1951 and 1952, the Yankees reached the World Series. In 1953 Mantle was again at the Series, where he hit a home run with the bases loaded—a grand slam. It was one of eighteen World Series homers, an all-time record, that Mantle would hit during his career. Yankee fans also cheered in 1956 when Mantle hit a homer that almost left Yankee Stadium but hit the top of the third deck in right field. In 1963 he again hit almost the same spot. These hits became known as "tape-measure homers."

In 1961 Mantle and teammate Roger Maris both tried to break Babe Ruth's record of 60 home runs in one season. Mantle came close with 54, but Maris got 61. Mantle's career home run total, 536, puts him in the top ten among all players.

Besides hitting hard, Mantle was praised for his speedy running. He was also a talented center fielder, known for his dramatic running catches and strong throws. He won numerous honors—the American League Triple Crown in 1956 (for homers, runs batted in, and batting average), Most Valuable Player in the American League (three times), and four home run titles. During much of his career, Mantle suffered from painful knee joints and wore elastic bandages to support weak legs.

Three months after he retired in 1969, thousands of fans cheered him at Mickey Mantle Day in Yankee Stadium. His number 7 uniform was retired from play, like those of Yankee stars Babe Ruth and Lou Gehrig. Mantle was inducted into baseball's Hall of Fame in 1974. After receiving a liver transplant, Mantle died of cancer on August 13, 1995.

Marshall, George C.

(1880–1959)

CHIEF OF STAFF OF THE UNITED STATES ARMY DURING
WORLD WAR II, SECRETARY OF STATE, AND SECRETARY
OF DEFENSE

George Catlett Marshall was born on December 31, 1880, in Uniontown, Pennsylvania. He graduated from the prestigious Virginia Military Institute in 1901.

He joined the army and served for a time in the Philippines, which the United States had occupied after the Spanish-American War of 1898. He was transferred to Fort Reno near Oklahoma City in Cheyenne Indian territory, and in 1905 he led a mapping expedition through the Texas Badlands. In 1906, he attended the Infantry and Cavalry School for advanced officer training at Fort Leavenworth, Kansas.

When the United States went to war with Germany in 1917, Captain Marshall was sent to France with General John "Black Jack" Pershing's American Expeditionary Force. In July 1918, he was sent to work at Pershing's headquarters, where he established a reputation as a brilliant organizer and strategist. He helped plan the final Allied offensive of the war at Saint-Mihiel, and he returned from France with the rank of colonel. After the war, Pershing was made army chief of staff, and Marshall served as his aide for five years in Washington, D.C. When Pershing retired in 1924, Marshall transferred to the Fifteenth Infantry, which was protecting American commercial interests in China.

Marshall spent three years in China during one of the most turbulent periods of its history. The last emperor had been forced to abdicate in 1912, and now Dr. Sun Yat-sen struggled to protect the infant republic against the intrigues of independent local army commanders known as warlords. The Communists in the poor rural regions and in the new factories near the cities were building a base of support. And the Japanese began making demands for Chinese territory. Marshall's view of world affairs had been immeasurably broadened when he returned to the United States in 1927, first to teach at the Army War College in Washington and then to become assistant commander of the Army Infantry School at Fort Benning, Georgia. Here he brought together a group of bright, young officers—including Omar Bradley and Joseph W. Stilwell—to modernize army operations.

Marshall left Fort Benning in 1932, in the midst of the Depression. He undertook various military assignments, coming to the attention of President Franklin Roosevelt for his efforts to use the army to assist the Civilian Conservation Corps job program. In 1939, Roosevelt appointed Marshall, now a brigadier general, as army chief of staff. Marshall forcefully advised Roosevelt that the United States was not prepared to fight Germany or Japan, and he spent the years before World War II persuading the President and Congress to build up America's armed forces. He also promoted and put into key positions the officers he felt the country would need to lead its armies—Bradley, Stilwell, Dwight Eisenhower, and George Patton.

During the war, he worked closely with Roosevelt, Secretary of War Henry L. Stimson, and the chairman of the new Joint Chiefs of Staff, Admiral William D. Leahy. Marshall helped plan the invasion of North Africa in 1942 and the invasion of Italy in 1944, and hoped to get command of Operation Overlord, the invasion of France. But Roosevelt needed Marshall in Washington, and Overlord was given to General Eisenhower. After the death of Roosevelt, Marshall continued as army chief of staff under President Harry Truman, and he was among those who advised Truman to use the atomic bomb against Japan to end the war in August 1945.

After the war, Truman appointed Marshall special ambassador to China. His mission was to help the country avoid civil war by urging Chiang Kai-shek's nationalists to cooperate with Mao Zedong's Communists, but the mission was hopeless. He returned to the United States in 1947 and was appointed secretary of state. On June 5, 1947, speaking at Harvard University, he announced what came to be known as the Marshall Plan, a massive economic aid program for war-torn Europe. After the North Koreans invaded South Korea in 1950, Truman asked Marshall to become secretary of defense. When General Douglas MacArthur, the commander of American forces in Korea, defied Truman's orders and threatened to take the war into China, Marshall was given the nasty job of dismissing MacArthur.

In 1953, Marshall became the first military man ever awarded the Nobel Peace Prize, largely for his efforts to rebuild Western Europe through the Marshall Plan. He died on October 16, 1959.

Marshall, Thurgood

(1908–1993)

FIRST AFRICAN-AMERICAN JUSTICE OF THE U.S.
SUPREME COURT

> Provided it is adequately enforced, law can change things for the better; moreover, it can change the hearts of men, for law has an educational function also.
>
> —Thurgood Marshall, in a speech at Howard University, 1955

Thurgood Marshall was born in West Baltimore, Maryland. His mother was a schoolteacher and his father worked as a waiter at a private sailing club. Both parents taught Thurgood and his older brother, Aubrey, to have pride in themselves and to fight racial discrimination whenever they encountered it.

Although Thurgood's father had very little education, he was an intelligent man. He liked to debate important issues, and he taught Thurgood this skill. He also encouraged his younger son to become a lawyer when he grew up. After Thurgood Marshall graduated from high school in 1925, he enrolled at Lincoln University, an all-black institution near Philadelphia. At Lincoln, Marshall was a popular student and star debater. He also became interested in the achievements of prominent African-Americans, including scholar and civil rights activist W.E.B. Du Bois and poet Langston Hughes. Marshall's lifelong interest in the role of blacks in American society began during his college years.

Marshall graduated from Lincoln with honors in 1930 and followed his father's advice by enrolling at Howard University Law School, in Washington, D.C. He and his wife, whom he had married in his senior year at Lincoln, lived with his parents in Baltimore while he commuted daily to Washington to attend classes.

In law school Marshall was strongly influenced by two professors. One was William H. Hastie, a Harvard University graduate who later became the first black federal judge. The second was Charles H. Houston. Both professors gave legal advice to the National Association for the Advancement of Colored People (NAACP), an organization founded in 1910 to combat racial discrimination. After graduating first in his class from Howard Law School in 1933, Marshall opened a small law practice in Baltimore.

The country was in the midst of the Great Depression which had followed the stock market crash of 1929. Unemployment was high, particularly among blacks, and very few people had enough money to hire a lawyer. Marshall agreed to defend people who were too poor to pay him, and he soon earned a reputation as "the little man's lawyer." In 1934 Marshall became the lawyer for the Baltimore chapter of the NAACP. He represented the organization in many successful lawsuits against groups and individuals who practiced discrimination against black people.

In 1936 Marshall moved to the NAACP's headquarters in New York to become an assistant to Charles H. Houston, who was now the organization's full-time attorney. For several years both men worked to secure the rights of black students and teachers in the South. They filed lawsuits in numerous southern cities and towns that challenged segregation in public schools and colleges. Their first major victory occurred in 1938, when the U.S. Supreme Court ruled that a black student could enroll at the formerly all-white University of Missouri Law School.

Marshall was now one of the most prominent black lawyers in the country. In the fall of 1938 he succeeded Charles Houston as the NAACP's chief counsel. A year later he became the director of a new branch of the NAACP called the Legal Defense and Educational Fund. The organization had two purposes: it provided free legal assistance to blacks who suffered from racial injustice, and it worked to provide greater educational opportunities for black women and men.

During the 1940s Marshall led a series of successful court fights against discrimination. His many victories earned him the nickname "Mr. Civil Rights." Through his efforts, the U.S. Supreme Court struck down many state laws that denied blacks the right to vote. He also succeeded in getting the Court to overturn laws that denied blacks the right to decent housing. Continuing his fight for the education rights of black Americans, he won the right of black students to attend graduate schools at several southern universities.

Marshall won the greatest victory of his career in 1954, when the Supreme Court declared public school segregation unconstitutional in the famous case *Brown v. Board of Education of Topeka.* In earlier cases the Supreme Court had ruled that as long as black children were provided with their own schools, segregation was allowed. This became known as the "separate but equal" doctrine. In reality, schools for blacks were usually inferior to those for whites. In his argument before the Supreme Court on behalf of a group of black schoolchildren and their parents, Marshall tried to show that "separate" meant "unequal." The Court agreed with Marshall and issued its historic decision that, in the words of Chief Justice Earl Warren, "in the field of public education the doctrine of 'separate but equal' has no place."

During the late 1950s, Marshall fought a series of attempts by southern states to avoid integrating their schools. He and the NAACP also became strong supporters of the new civil rights movement led by Dr. Martin Luther King, Jr. In 1962 Marshall was appointed by President John F. Kennedy to be judge of the Second Circuit Court of Appeals. During his three years on the court, Marshall ruled in a variety of cases. All of his nearly one hundred decisions were upheld by the U.S. Supreme Court. This was a remarkable accomplishment, and led to his appointment in 1965 as the first black solicitor general of the United States by President Lyndon B. Johnson.

The position of solicitor general is the third highest legal office in the country, after attorney general and assistant attorney general. As solicitor general, Marshall argued cases on behalf of the federal government before the Supreme Court. During his two years as solicitor general he won fourteen of the nineteen cases he argued for the government. Most of them dealt with civil rights and the right to privacy.

In 1967 Marshall again made history when President Johnson named him the first African-American member of the U.S. Supreme Court. During nearly two decades as an associate justice, Thurgood Marshall defended constitutional rights and the establishment of educational and legal equality for all races. Marshall retired from the Court in 1991, at the age of eighty-three. He died two years later in Bethesda, Maryland.

Marx, Groucho

(1890–1977)

AMERICAN ACTOR, COMEDIAN,
AND TELEVISION PERSONALITY

Julius Henry Marx was born in New York, the third of five sons of Samuel and Minna Schoenberg Marx. Young Julius had originally hoped to become a physician, but he dropped out of public school in New York and followed the example of his uncle, Al Shean, who was a vaudeville comedian. When Marx returned home after an unsuccessful job as a singer in a vaudeville act, his mother assembled his three other brothers together as the Four Nightingales and arranged bookings for them as a singing act. Later the boys changed their name to the Marx Brothers and became a comedy team.

The Marx Brothers toured the vaudeville circuit for several years, perfecting their comedy style, which used elements of slapstick and farce, until 1919, when they had their first major success in a routine titled "Home Again" at the Palace Theater in New York. One night when Groucho arrived at the theater too late to paste on his false mustache, he painted one on with makeup and it became his trademark look during his act with his brothers—Chico, Harpo, and Zeppo—for the next thirty years.

Groucho collaborated with another writer for a show called *I'll Say She Is*, and the brothers toured with it around the country for a year before it came to New York in 1924 with rave reviews. That play was followed by a show called *The Coconuts* (1925), which was written for the brothers by George S. Kaufman and Irving Berlin. Their third show, *Animal Crackers* (1928), was their third straight Broadway hit comedy. Groucho got so used to ad-libbing that two shows were rarely ever alike.

When the Marx brothers got tired of performing on Broadway every night, they moved to Hollywood about the time when sound movies were being produced and made film versions of *The Coconuts* (1929) and *Animal Crackers* (1930). Then they made *Monkey Business* (1931), *Horsefeathers* (1932), and *Duck Soup* (1933), which was their only commercial failure. Zeppo left the group, and the comedy team became a trio. Two of the Marx brothers' funniest films followed: *A Night at the Opera* (1935), followed by its sequel, *A Day at the Races* (1937).

In 1934 Groucho and Chico ventured into radio with a comedy show called *Flywheel, Shyster, and Flywheel.* Later Groucho would make guest appearances on other radio shows, ad-libbing comedy with other entertainers like Bob Hope. In 1947, a radio producer developed an idea for a quiz show in which Groucho would ad-lib interviews with guests. The program was called *You Bet Your Life* and it was a showcase for Groucho's quick wit. After it ran for four years, it was turned into a television show in 1951, when it won an Emmy Award for being the funniest show on television.

You Bet Your Life ran for eleven years. Groucho wrote several humor books, such as *Many Happy Returns: An Unofficial Guide to Your Income Taxes* (1942) and *Memoirs of a Mangy Lover* (1963) . Groucho retired in the mid-1960s, but he kept returning to show business with live concert appearances and television specials. As a result of Marx's lifelong contributions to comedy and entertainment, Marx was made a Commander of the French Order of Arts and Letters in 1972.

Groucho Marx died in 1977 at the age of eighty-seven.

Matisse, Henri

(1869–1954)

FRENCH PAINTER

I have never avoided the influence of others. I would have considered this a cowardice and lack of sincerity toward myself.

—Henri Matisse, in an interview with Guillaume Apollinaire, 1907

Henri Matisse, one of the greatest and most widely acclaimed painters of the late nineteenth and twentieth centuries, was born in Le Cateau, France, on December 31, 1869. He planned to become a lawyer and passed his law exams in Paris before becoming hospitalized for an appendicitis attack. To help pass the time while recovering in bed, he began to paint with a box of paints a friend had given him. Soon afterward, he became obsessed with painting. He went on, despite his late start, to become one of the most influential painters of modern times.

Matisse wanted to go to art school but failed the entrance exam for the famous School of Fine Arts in Paris. Instead, he entered the private studio of painter Gustave Moreau to learn painting technique, while studying sculpture at night.

Matisse's studies were important to his development as a painter. He took a theoretical as well as a practical approach to his work. Although he later claimed to detest academic painting for its narrow-mindedness and resistance to new ideas, he made use of the many academic techniques and ideas he gleaned from books and associates, which he combined with new ideas, as well as with his own sense of color and form.

One of the innovations for which Matisse is best known is his bold, flat use of bright colors. Early in his career he became a leading representative of the Fauve movement, known for its bright, aggressive use of color. "Fauve" is the French word for "wild beast," a name Matisse and others were given at an exhibition that shocked critics who thought this new generation of artists painted without self-control.

Matisse was also strongly influenced by the impressionist movement. One of the more striking features of Matisse's work is his ability to suggest depth, or three-dimensional space, without shading or modulating color, but simply by making a few, well chosen lines on a flat field. This technique, combined with his use of vivid colors, has made his paintings distinctive and has helped to transform the way other artists paint.

Matisse contended with poverty and illness throughout much of his life. He was so poor at one point that his two sons went to live with relatives while he continued painting. To earn money, he painted decorations for the Paris Exposition in 1900. In 1908, he opened his own painting class, which was successful for two years.

Matisse did thirteen paintings that appeared in 1913 at the famous armory show in New York, where his simplified representation of three-dimensional space and his wildly bright colors shocked American art enthusiasts. Most Americans were then more conservative than Europeans and were unused to modernist art. Matisse, like other modernists, was rejecting many of the old conventions that governed the way pictures were painted. Later, he tried to assure Americans that he was "a normal man" despite his revolutionary work.

During the German occupation of Paris in 1940, Matisse moved to Nice, in the south, to avoid dangerous confrontations. His daughter Marguerite, however, was a member of the French resistance movement in Paris and was captured and tortured by Nazis.

Despite difficulties and a late start in the art world, Matisse had a long career. He earned a reputation for being an innovative artist early in the century and renewed his reputation in the 1950s when he began incorporating paper-cut-out shapes into his art and working on very large surfaces with brushes attached to handles several feet long. Some of the work he did during that time was stage designing for theatrical performances. During that period he drew on his interest in decorative art, while continuing to use bright colors and unusual contrasts.

Matisse felt that one of the most important features of his approach was simplicity. Throughout his career he tended to avoid elaborate blendings of shape and color in order to emphasize what he felt were more essential forms and contrasts. Despite the challenges he faced, he felt painting should be a joyous thing. He is perhaps best known for his two paintings of people dancing in a circle, entitled *The Joy of Life* and *The Dance*, exhibited originally in 1906.

Matisse's approach to art has been extremely influential to artists and designers who worked after him. He had a long and full career, remaining active as a painter until his death, in 1954. Near the end of his life, he said that he tried to conceal the effort that went into his work.

Mays, Willie Howard, Jr.

(1931–   )

AMERICAN BASEBALL PLAYER

Willie Mays was one of baseball's most popular players, and few were praised so often or so lavishly for their all-around ability. A former teammate once said of Mays's outfielding, "If a ball stayed in the park, he'd catch it." New York Giants manager Leo Durocher said, "There are only five things any ballplayer can do: hit, hit with power, field, run, and throw. Willie can do them all to perfection."

Willie had excellent coaching from the start as a child in Fairfield, Alabama.

His father had been an outfielder with the Birmingham Black Barons in the Negro National League. In school, Willie was good at several sports and played sandlot baseball on a team with his father.

By 17 he was good enough to join the Black Barons as a professional. A New York Giants scout saw him and signed him to a contract with the team. He spent only a short time in the minor leagues, showing composure and consistency despite his youth. He achieved an outstanding batting average and moved on to the major leagues at age 20.

Willie got off to a slow start, not getting a hit during eleven times at bat. Then fans began to see that Willie Mays had something special. Playing against the Boston Braves, Mays belted a home run off left-handed pitcher Warren Spahn. The Giants won the league pennant and Mays's performance that season earned him Rookie of the Year honors. He met Joe DiMaggio, one of his heroes, and the two men became friends.

Mays served in the military for two years, then returned to play in 1954. The Giants had won the pennant and faced the New York Yankees in the World Series. In the first game, Willie Mays made a catch that some experts call the best in Series history. It was the eighth inning and the score was tied 2–2. Two men were on base and nobody was out. Outfielder Mays managed to catch a 440-foot drive over his shoulder, with his back to the plate, then return it to the infield so fast that neither runner could get to the next base. His dazzling play kept the other team from scoring three runs on this potential homer, which had been hit by Vic Wertz. That year, Mays was named Most Valuable Player (MVP) in the National League and Athlete of the Year by the Associated Press.

For the next few years, Mays continued to hit well and play good defense in the outfield. He was known as the "Say Hey Kid" because of the way he greeted people. In 1961 he hit four, then three, then two homers in three different games. Playing into his thirties, Mays hit fifty-two home runs in the 1965 season, again winning the MVP award. By 1970 he had reached a career hit mark of 3,000 and had batted more than 600 career home runs. He also won eleven Gold Glove awards for his superb fielding.

His team moved to San Francisco, where Mays played for a while before being traded to the New York Mets. Although over forty now, Mays hit a home run against his former team the first time the two teams met. That same year, he was an All-Star for the twentieth time in a row.

Mays retired in 1973 after twenty-two seasons in the major leagues. He had invested his money wisely and had succeeded in public relations work. A baseball historian wrote in 1981 that if Mays's career had not been interrupted by the army he would have topped Babe Ruth's record of career home runs. He called Mays the "best, most exciting number one" player.

Mead, Margaret

(1901–1978)

AMERICAN ANTHROPOLOGIST

> Studying . . . peoples, who are living now as they have lived for cen-
> turies and who embody ways of thinking and feeling we do not know
> about, we [can] add immeasurably to our knowledge of who we our-
> selves are.
>
> —From Margaret Mead's autobiography *Blackberry Winter* (1972)

Born in Philadelphia, Pennsylvania, Margaret Mead grew up in a family that
loved ideas. Her parents were both well-educated. Her father was a business
professor, and her mother was a sociologist, particularly interested in helping
the residents of slums. She also worked to end the treatment of American
women as second-class citizens.

After high school, Mead decided she also wanted to become a sociologist.
To get the education she needed, she enrolled in Barnard College in New York
City. During her senior year, she happened to take a course in anthropology.

Mead was very excited by the course. It was taught by Franz Boas, a German-born man who had virtually created the new science. Mead was also impressed by his teaching assistant, Ruth Benedict, who would later become a
leading anthropologist.

When Mead graduated from Barnard in 1923, she decided to continue
studying anthropology at the neighboring Columbia University. While at
Columbia, she married another young student, Luther Cressman. But Mead
was far from ready to settle down. As an anthropologist, she knew she had
to do fieldwork, the term for visiting an area to study the people who lived
there.

In 1925, Mead set out to perform her first fieldwork on the islands of Samoa
in the Pacific Ocean. Soon after arriving, she settled in the village of Tau of
Manua. With a population of about a thousand, Tau was little more than a collection of huts.

Although she herself lived with the family of an American medical officer,
Mead planned to do far more than just observe the people of Tau. She wanted
to get to know them well and for them to accept her as part of their community.
Mead felt that only then could she truly understand the way Samoans lived.

Mead's plan was to study the teenage girls on the island. She was going to
test an idea of Boas's. He believed that people were more influenced by the environment in which they grew up than anything else. It was clear to Mead that
the teenage years of most American females were stressful and upsetting. She

wanted to see if Samoan girls suffered the same struggles or, as Boas assumed, had an easier time in their relatively carefree society.

To learn about Samoan teenagers, she spend hundreds of hours interviewing them. Mead also joined them in their social activities. Many evenings, Samoan singers and dancers would come to her house and have parties. Mead especially enjoyed playing on the beach at sunset with her new friends. Even so, she often found herself lonesome for home.

Mead returned to the United States in the spring of 1926. She brought with her suitcases of notes on what she had seen and heard. From them, she compiled a book titled *Coming of Age in Samoa*. Mead found that Samoan teenagers did indeed have a much simpler life than young people in America. But she also felt that young Samoans missed out on the benefits of a difficult adolescence. Mead wrote that they experienced "less intensity, less individuality, less involvement with life."

Published in 1928, Mead's book became a best-seller. Its ideas were new and fascinating to many readers. Although she was only twenty-seven, the work earned her respect as one of the country's best anthropologists.

Mead's success and her time away from her home put a strain on her marriage. She and Cressman divorced, and soon after she married a psychologist named Reo Fortune. Together they went to New Guinea, an island near Australia. Mead brought with her piles of white paper. She passed them out to the children of the Manus people in New Guinea and asked them to draw pictures. Manus children spend all their days playing. Mead wanted to test a theory that play made children more creative. She returned home with more than 35,000 drawings.

After a second trip to New Guinea in 1931, Mead and Fortune divorced. She then married Gregory Bateson, a noted anthropologist. They did research together in Bali, another island in the Pacific, in 1936. By this time, Mead had perfected her research methods. To get a complete view, she combined observing, interviewing, photographing, and sometimes filming the people she studied. She had developed these techniques herself. Anthropology was so new that, before Mead, no one had made any rules about conducting fieldwork.

When World War II (1939–45) broke out, Mead and Bateson returned to the United States. They settled in New York City and raised a daughter.

In 1953, Mead set out again for New Guinea. The children who had made drawings for her were now adults. They welcomed their old friend, but Mead could not help showing her distress at what had happened to the Manus. When she first met them, the Manus were isolated from the rest of the world. They lived in much the same way their ancestors had thousands of years before. But during World War II an American military base has been built on their territory. This exposure to the modern world disrupted the Manus's way of life. Many of traditions that had long enriched their lives were now forgotten.

When Mead returned, she realized she had also changed. In ill health, she had to abandon field work. Mead then dedicated herself to teaching. Her classes at Columbia University were always full. From them emerged the next generation of anthropologists.

In the years just before her death in 1978, Mead's work received criticism. Some anthropologists thought her research was sloppy and many of her conclusions were wrong. Others, however, revered her. They saw her as a pioneer who nearly single-handedly created modern anthropology. Anthropologists today still use her research methods to learn about people around the world.

Meir, Golda

(1898–1978)

ISRAEL'S ONLY WOMAN
PRIME MINISTER

A leader who doesn't hesitate before he sends his nation into battle is not fit to be a leader.

—Golda Meir, from
As Good as Golda

Prime Minister Golda Meir was born Golda Mabovitz in Kiev, Ukraine, on May 3, 1898, and was brought by her family to the United States when she was eight years old. Growing up in Milwaukee, Wisconsin, with a carpenter father and a shopkeeper mother, Golda went through the Milwaukee schools, attended the Teachers Seminary, and found a job teaching. Later she worked as a librarian in New York and Chicago. It was her marriage to an ardent Zionist, Morris Meyerson (the name was later changed to Meir), that motivated Golda to learn more about her religion and the idea of a Jewish state.

In 1921, after joining the American Labor Zionist Organization and taking part in its Pioneer Women of America division, Golda and her husband moved to Palestine, which, at that time, was under the control of Great Britain. For three years she worked on a kibbutz, an agricultural cooperative farm where everyone shared equally. By 1928, she was a well-known leader in the region's women's labor council and the labor federation. She also took a leadership role in Zionist activities, speaking in many parts of the world and serving as a delegate to the World Zionist Congress. In 1940, she became the labor federation's expert on foreign affairs.

In 1948, the state of Israel was created after the Jewish settlers fought a war against both the British and Arabs, including the Palestinian Arabs living in the same region. Golda Meir was one of the signers of Israel's Declaration of Independence, and the only one to have come from the United States (most other early Israeli leaders came from Europe). Very quickly, Meir also became the only woman in the country's first, temporary legislature and the first minister to the Soviet Union. In 1949, she was elected to the Knesset, Israel's parliamentary body, as a representative of the labor party, Mapai. Prime Minister David Ben-Gurion chose her as his minister of labor and, later, minister of foreign affairs.

Meir gained international attention as Israel's articulate and powerful representative to the United Nations, where she served from 1953 to 1966. Then, when her country's prime minister died suddenly in 1969, Meir became Israel's first woman leader. Already past seventy at the time, she served during a difficult period of Israel's history, one dominated by unresolved conflicts with neighboring Arab states. Golda Meir died on December 8, 1978.

Mencken, H. L.

(1880–1956)

AMERICAN JOURNALIST,
EDITOR, AND WRITER

Born in Baltimore, Maryland, Henry Louis Mencken had a relatively happy childhood. Mencken was an avid reader, and although his father wanted him to inherit the family tobacco business, Mencken wanted a career in writing and publishing.

Mencken's father died in 1899. Mencken became a reporter for the Baltimore *Herald*, and by 1906 he became the editor of the newspaper. He joined another newspaper that year, the *Sun*, and he wrote poems and short stories for magazine publication. In 1905 Mencken published a book, *George Bernard Shaw: His Plays,* and another in 1908, *Philosophy of Friedrich Nietzsche.* With Theodore Dreiser (who was then a magazine editor) and George Jean Nathan, Mencken started a magazine, the *Smart Set.* From 1908 to 1923 Mencken was editor of the magazine. He also contributed monthly articles of five thousand words.

In 1912 Mencken published another book, *The Artist, A Drama without Words.* Five years later he published a book of literary criticism, *A Book of Prefaces.* During World War I, Mencken began his largest literary achievement, a book of American lexicography entitled *The American Language.* It was published in 1919, and updated reprints of the work appeared in 1921, 1923, and 1936. Mencken also published two supplements to the original volume in 1945 and 1948.

Besides *The American Language,* Mencken published, beginning in 1919, six volumes entitled *Prejudices,* which contained articles he had previously written. During that year, Mencken also served as editorial adviser to the new publishers of the *Sun* newspapers and he contributed articles to the *Evening Sun.* In 1924, Mencken and Nathan founded another journal, *American Mercury,* from which Mencken would eventually retire in 1933.

During the 1920s Mencken began to shift his own writing from literary criticism to social and political commentary. In 1926 he published *Notes on Democracy,* a collection of previously published articles. In 1930 he published a book about politics, religion, and morals entitled, *Treatise on the Gods,* and in 1934 *Treatise on Right and Wrong* was published to poor sales and reviews.

Mencken's popularity declined during the Depression, perhaps because his concerns seemed irrelevant during such hard economic times. *American Mercury* began to show signs of faltering, and Mencken eventually left in 1933. He virtually gave up journalism and turned his attention to revising *The American Language* for the fourth edition (1936). He also published *A New Dictionary of Quotations* in 1940.

In the 1940s, Mencken wrote a series of autobiographical articles for the *New Yorker* which were collected in book form. *Happy Days* (1940) described his childhood; *Newspaper Days* (1941) gave an account of his newspaper career; and *Heathen Days* (1943) completed the author's trilogy of reminiscences. In 1948 Mencken returned to the *Sun* papers to cover the presidential conventions.

Mencken's last book, *Minority Report: H. L. Mencken's Notebooks* was published after his death in 1956. Mencken was an exacting editor who gave many writers their start in the business. He was an important voice of literary criticism as well as a valuable social critic.

Mies van der Rohe, Ludwig

(1886–1969)

GERMAN ARCHITECT

> Less is more.
>
> —Ludwig Mies van der Rohe

Ludwig Mies, one of the most famous and influential architects of the twentieth century, was born on March 27, 1886, in Aachen, Germany. The son of a mason and stonecutter whose parents could not afford to provide him with expensive schooling, Mies gained firsthand knowledge and experience with stone and other building materials by working on construction projects with his father part-time as he was growing up. He went on to become a highly acclaimed architect. He added his mother's family name, van der Rohe, to his last name when he became an architect.

After finishing trade school, Mies van der Rohe got a job with a Berlin architect before realizing he wanted to know as much about wood as he already knew about stone, so he apprenticed himself to the furniture designer Bruno Paul. He then began working with Peter Behrens, with whom the famous French architect Le Corbusier had also worked.

In 1913, Mies van der Rohe opened his own office, but he was drafted soon afterward to serve in the German army. During World War I, he was stationed in the Balkan Peninsula, where he served as an engineer designing bridges and roadways. Because he had not graduated from a university, he was ineligible to become an officer.

After the war, in an atmosphere of political, as well as artistic, uncertainty, Mies van der Rohe helped point architecture in a new direction, becoming an important spokesman for a structurally daring use of industrial materials—concrete, steel, and glass—and the elimination of unnecessary ornamentation. He became a member of the artists' collective Novembergrüppe, named for the month during 1918 when the Weimar Republic was founded. He also co-founded the magazine *G*, which stands for *Gestaltung*, or "creative force," devoted to modern art.

During the period after World War I, he designed one of the first skyscrapers to have an exterior made almost completely of glass. He compared the way this building was designed to the human body, saying that the building's structural supports, made of steel, were like a skeleton and should be located on the inside, while the glass exterior was like skin. This "skin and bones" design was a radical departure from conventional architectural practice, which used structural supports on the outside of buildings.

This revolutionary glass skyscraper was formally, as well as structurally, new. It was designed to have an irregular shape in order to create interesting reflections with its hundreds of angled glass windows. Although the building was never actually erected, it represented a radical new attitude toward architecture.

During this same period, Mies van der Rohe also designed and built villas for wealthy clients. In some ways, his villas resembled those of the American architect Frank Lloyd Wright, whom Mies van der Rohe admired. Both Mies and Wright saw architectural form as something that should result from, rather than precede, structural considerations. To use the famous words of Wright's teacher, Louis Sullivan, "form follows function." Mies van der Rohe's equally famous maxim, "less is more," also suggests the importance of structural, as opposed to formal, considerations.

In 1930, Mies van der Rohe succeeded Walter Gropius as director of the Bauhaus, the prestigious school of architecture and applied arts that helped solidify the relationship between the knowledge of new industrial capabilities and architectural design. He remained director of the Bauhaus until it was shut down in 1933 by the Nazis, who sensed that the revisionary aims of modern art contradicted the nationalist fervor of Hitler's Germany.

Eventually, Mies van der Rohe moved to the United States and became an American citizen in 1944. As an American, he designed some of his most important skyscrapers, including the 860 Lake Shore Apartments in Chicago in 1957, and the Seagram Building in New York in 1958.

In later life, Mies van der Rohe claimed to be uninterested in politics, although his interest in design sometimes took political form at various stages in his career. During the period of political uncertainty in post–World War I Germany, he not only associated with republican artists, but designed a monument for martyred leaders of German communism.

Part of Mies van der Rohe's success as an architect stemmed from the clarity of his artistic principle, to which he adhered throughout the most turbulent period in German history. His fixed creative purpose and penetrating recognition of the new possibilities of industrial building materials enabled him to relate effectively both to radical artists and conservative businessmen.

Millay, Edna St. Vincent

(1892–1950)

AMERICAN POET
AND PLAYWRIGHT

Edna St. Vincent Millay was born in Rockland, Maine. Her parents were separated but, although she lived with her mother, she kept in touch with her father. Her mother was a trained singer who worked as a nurse and wrote musical scores for a local orchestra. She taught Millay how to write poetry when she was four, and how to play piano when she was seven.

In her twenties, Millay went to Barnard College and then Vassar College, both in New York. She was an excellent student, and she liked to act in plays. She graduated in 1917 at the age of twenty-five. That year, she published her first book, *Renascence and Other Poems*.

Millay lived in Greenwich Village in New York City, a community filled with artists. She wrote and published poems in magazines and acted in plays, some of which she wrote, with the Provincetown Players. Millay also published stories in magazines and did readings of her work in public and on radio.

In 1920 she published the poetry book, *A Few Figs from Thistles,* as well as the play, *Ariada Capo*. In 1923, she won a Pulitzer Prize for *The Harp Weaver and Other Poems*. The book sold very well and launched her popularity with the public. In the same year, Millay married Eugen Boissevain, a New York importer. They settled on a farm in Austerlitz, New York, and although they experienced some financial problems, they lived a happy simple life. Besides writing, Millay enjoyed bird-watching, gardening, swimming, and music.

Millay continued to publish at a regular rate. In 1926, *Three Plays* came out, and one year later she published another play, *The King's Henchman*. In 1928 *The Buck in the Snow and Other Poems* came out, followed by *Fatal Interview* in 1931, a collection of sonnets on a failed love affair. Millay's other books include *Wine from These Grapes* (1934), *Conversation at Midnight* (1937), *Huntsman, What Quarry?* (1939), *Make Bright the Arrow* (1940), *Collected Sonnets* (1941), and *Collected Lyrics* (1943).

Millay's maturity as both a person and author during the Depression and World War II is evident in her work. Her themes explored love and hate, life and death, the psychological distance between women and men, nature, and beauty. She showed concern later in life for social injustices and war, and her poetry became more serious and militant in spirit. Millay's husband died in 1949 after a lung operation, and she followed him one year later.

Miller, Arthur

(1915–   )

AMERICAN PLAYWRIGHT AND
ESSAYIST

Born in New York, Arthur Miller grew up in Harlem and Brooklyn during the Depression. A poor student, he failed many subjects and hardly read at all. When his family began to suffer financially during the Depression, Miller went to work in an automobile parts warehouse. At the time, he read *The Brothers Karamazov* by Fyodor Dostoevsky, and he decided he wanted to become a writer.

Miller saved money in order to attend the University of Michigan. He studied journalism and worked nights as an editor at the *Michigan Daily*. When he won a prize for a play he wrote, it changed the course of his career. Miller graduated in 1938 and went to work for the Federal Writers Project, a government-sponsored program, in New York. He wrote a comedy, but because the government program lacked funds it was never produced. Miller then wrote several radio plays.

During World War II, Miller published *Situation Normal* (1944), a play about American military training. His first Broadway production was *The Man Who Had All the Luck,* which was not very successful. One year later he published his only novel, *Focus,* which was about anti-Semitism. Miller achieved national fame with *All My Sons* (1947), which ran for over a year and won the New York Drama Critics Circle Award.

Miller bought a farm in Connecticut where he lived with his wife and two children. He wrote *Death of a Salesman,* his second Broadway success which brought him international acclaim. Miller expressed his humanitarian and liberal views in his next two plays. The first, *An Enemy of the People* (1950), was an adaptation of Henrik Ibsen's play. The second, *The Crucible* (1953), was about the Salem witch trials of 1692. Some people thought that these two plays were attacks on the House Committee on Un-American Activities, which at the time was trying to root out communism and communists in America.

In 1956, Miller was subpoenaed to appear before the committee. He spoke freely about his own communist activities, but refused to give the names of other writers he had seen at a communist writers' meeting held in 1947. Miller was accused of contempt of Congress and fined. He appealed the ruling before the Supreme Court and was acquitted in 1958.

Miller experienced other personal troubles as well. In 1956 he divorced his wife and married actress Marilyn Monroe. They went to England to live in order to escape publicity. Miller worked on *A View from the Bridge.* When they returned to the United States, Miller became disappointed in the American theater which had become more conservative. He had difficulty writing plays and turned to writing a short story, *The Misfits* (1960). It was made into a film directed by John Huston and starring Marilyn Monroe. After finishing the film, Miller and Monroe divorced.

Miller remarried in 1962 and returned to playwrighting in 1964 with *After the Fall.* He wrote the play during many critical points in his life: his mother's death in 1961, his new marriage in 1962, and the death of Marilyn Monroe in 1962. Miller felt increasingly alienated from the New York theater, though he did produce several plays on Broadway. They included *Incident at Vichy* (1964), *The Price* (1968), and *The Creation of the World and Other Business* (1972).

He also sought alternate regional theaters for *Fame* and *The Reason Why* in 1970. In 1977, *The Archbishop's Ceiling* was produced at the Kennedy Center in Washington, D.C., and *The American Clock* played at the Spoleto Arts Festival in South Carolina in 1980. The Long Wharf Theater in New Haven, Connecticut, put on *Elegy for a Lady* and *Some Kind of Love Story* in 1982; the Studio Theater in Washington, D.C., did *Playing for Time* in 1985; and *I Can't Remember Anything* and *Clara* played at Lincoln Center in 1987. Miller's screenplay, *Everybody Wins,* was produced in 1990. One year later, *The Crucible* was revived simultaneously with the opening of *The Ride Down Mount Morgan,* a play about a conniving insurance executive.

Miller's plays, which explore public and private morality and politics, maintain a sense of optimism and hope in the face of adversity. He is one of the most outstanding and prolific American playwrights of the twentieth century.

Modigliani, Amedeo

(1884–1920)

ITALIAN PAINTER AND SCULPTOR

> I am the prey of great forces that surge up and then dissolve. But I
> wish instead that my life were like a fertile river, joyfully flowing over
> the earth.
>
> —Amedeo Modigliani, from an undated letter to Oscar Ghiglia

Amedeo Modigliani is remembered not only for his paintings and sculptures of
the human form that combine the influences of modernism and the Italian Renaissance, but for his unconventional attitude toward life.

Modigliani was born in Livorno, Italy, on July 12, 1884, to a family of
Sephardic (from the southern Mediterranean area) Jews. It was a time of economic depression, when his parents, once prosperous, were experiencing difficult financial circumstances. As his mother was giving birth to him in her
bedroom, creditors were busy reclaiming furniture and other possessions from
the house. Meanwhile, the rest of the family prevented their most valuable possessions from being removed by piling them up on the childbed, since Italian
law prohibited anyone from disturbing the bed of a woman in labor.

The Modiglianis were cultured people, interested in the arts. As a boy,
Modigliani studied literature and began taking drawing lessons at age fourteen.
Not long afterward, he contracted typhoid fever and was in danger of losing his
life. While in a delirious state, he revealed that he wanted to be a painter. When
he recovered, he became a full-time art student despite his young age. He was
by far the youngest student in his art school, and he became close friends with
young men several years older than himself.

Modigliani was obsessed with drawing and painting, while he continued to
be troubled by illness. He left art school for several months while he was suffering from pleurisy (a lung disorder) in order to go on a tour of Naples, Rome,
and Venice, where it was hoped the warm climate would do him some good. In
those cities, accompanied by his mother, he visited great museums and cathe-
drals, where he gazed for hours at his favorite paintings and sculptures.

Soon afterward, he began reading Friedrich Nietzsche and was inspired by
the German philosopher's ideas on the social role of the artist. He was also an
avid reader of the Hebrew Bible and of the decadent French poet Le Comte de
Lautréamont, whose verses Modigliani was known to recite out loud at night in
a graveyard.

In 1906, Modigliani moved to Paris, where he lived the life of a Bohemian
artist, getting by with little money, carousing with friends, attending séances

and other offbeat gatherings, consorting with prostitutes, and indulging in alcohol and drugs. His new lifestyle was a drastic change from the life he had lived in Italy, where, thanks to the support of a rich uncle, he enjoyed expensive food, clothing, and habitation.

When Modigliani first arrived in Paris, other artists considered him to be something of a dilettante, someone who merely dabbled in art. He continued to paint obsessively, however, despite his recurrent illnesses, his dissolute lifestyle, and in spite of the fact that he frequently changed residences in search of suitable, affordable places to paint.

Modigliani's paintings reveal his interest in Renaissance art. Indeed, he refused to join with the Italian futurist movement, which rejected traditional influences, because of his appreciation for the past. He liked to paint traditional subjects: portraits, the human body, and the human face. Many of his paintings exhibit a classical sense of form, combined with modernist, abstract influences.

In 1909, he began sculpting instead of painting, although he continued to favor the human body as a subject. He produced several graceful, elongated portraits in stone that resemble caryatids, sculptures of women done in ancient Greece that were used as pillars to support buildings. His foray into sculpture was brief, however, since he could not afford the necessary blocks of stone. He refused to work in clay or plaster, disdaining them as "mud," so he returned to painting for the rest of his brief career.

Modigliani's work is distinctive. Many of his portraits reveal a subtle sense of the characters of those he painted. He painted his fellow artists Pablo Picasso, Jacques Lipchitz, and Chaim Soutine, and poets Max Jacob and Jean Cocteau. His many portraits of nude women are frankly sensual. In fact, they caused a riot when they were exhibited in 1917 because of their bold, revealing postures.

Modigliani died at an early age from tuberculosis. His life exemplifies the romantic notion of the Bohemian artist, recklessly defying conventions in pursuit of new experiences.

Montessori, Maria

(1870–1952)

ITALIAN PSYCHOLOGIST
AND EDUCATOR

Education is a natural process which develops spontaneously in the human being.
—Maria Montessori

Long after her death, the unique educational system founded by Maria Montessori, an Italian educator who was the first woman in her country to earn a degree in medicine, was influencing schools and child development philosophy around the world.

Maria Montessori was born on August 31, 1870, in Ancona, Italy, and was educated at the University of Rome, where she studied literature as well as medicine. Her first job was teaching in a mental-health clinic and working with mentally ill children. A lecture she gave in 1898 about her work with these patients impressed Italy's minister of education, who appointed Montessori to direct a school for retarded young people. Applying her own unique techniques of therapy, Montessori was able to educate her pupils so well that they surpassed "normal" children in school examinations.

In 1900, Montessori returned to the University of Rome for further education in psychology and philosophy. In 1907, she became involved in a new school system for the poor of Rome; this was the first time she attempted to apply some of her techniques for working with retarded children to those with normal intelligence and mental health. From her earliest experience, she had observed that severely disturbed children could function if they had an object to touch and play with. Montessori tried the same approach with her new students, providing them with objects to touch, creating an environment of quiet, unhurried learning in which the children were neither punished nor rewarded. In essence, her philosophy was that children needed to be given a safe environment in which they could establish their own individual discipline.

These techniques became the basis of the Montessori school system. In 1911, Switzerland adopted her methods for its public elementary schools. After World War I, she taught her system to English educators, and in 1922 she became an inspector for the Italian schools. With the rise of Benito Mussolini and his fascist government, however, Montessori left Italy in disgust for Catalonia, a region of Spain that claimed to have no government at all. Through the 1930s and 1940s the Montessori method of teaching continued to grow in popularity, spreading throughout Europe and to the United States, where more than three thousand Montessori schools were established.

Maria Montessori died in Holland in 1952.

Moore, Henry

(1898–1986)

ENGLISH SCULPTOR

> Because a work does not aim at reproducing natural appearances it is not, therefore, an escape from life—but may be a penetration into reality, not a sedative or drug, not just the exercise of good taste, the provision of pleasant shapes and colors in a pleasing combination, not a decoration to life, but an expression of the significance of life, a stimulation to greater effort in living.
>
> —Henry Moore, from *The Modern Movement in English Architecture, Painting, and Sculpture*

Henry Moore was one of the most important sculptors of twentieth-century England, experimenting methodically with a variety of forms and materials, and thinking deeply about the relationship between art and social existence.

Born in Castleford, England, on July 30, 1898, Moore knew at an early age that he wanted to become a sculptor, but he waited some years before attempting to realize his ambitions. After becoming a grammar-school teacher, he joined the English army and served during World War I. In 1919, after the war, he took classes at the Leeds College of Art.

He did so well at Leeds that he won a scholarship to attend the Royal College of Art in London. The curriculum at the Royal College had not yet been influenced by the new modernist ideas that had been transforming art in Continental Europe. Instead, Moore's course of study was traditional and academic. He had to look beyond his course work for the revolutionary influences that he would later incorporate into his famous sculptures.

One important source of inspiration that Moore discovered outside college was the British Museum. There Moore developed a particular interest in African art and South American art of the pre-Columbian period. He further broadened his ideas about art when traveling to France in 1923 and to Italy in 1925, visiting important art centers where modernist influences were more widely recognized than in England. Yet Moore's interest in art was not limited to modernism. Instead, he cultivated his appreciation for a variety of styles and periods of art.

Moore brought together traditional, modernist, and academic influences both in his sculpture and in his writings about sculpture. He tended to work with traditional subject matter—reclining nudes and mother-and-child compositions. Moore believed those subjects best conveyed and humanized a sculptural ideal of repose, expressing both the physical quality of his materials, wood or stone, and the emotional quality of peace. He said of one of his more famous sculptures, *Madonna and Child* (1944), that he wanted to make the woman look so comfortable that she could remain in her position forever, which she would have to do, of course, since she is made of stone.

Although Moore valued centeredness and natural repose in sculpture, he also wanted to make his forms dynamic and tended toward abstraction. To do that, Moore implemented the idea of forming holes, or voids, in his sculptures. By introducing gaps in his work, empty spaces strategically enclosed by sculpted material, Moore made his work look complicated, energetic, and capable of movement, yet natural and balanced, containing its center of gravity within itself.

Moore studied nature as well as art in developing his own approach to sculpture. He noticed how natural structures exhibited the qualities of the materials that formed them. He saw bones, shells, trees, and rocks as expressions of the structural possibilities of specific physical things.

Although Moore was interested in abstraction, in the idea that art did not have to represent things that already existed, he believed sculpture should be organic rather than geometric, that shape should be expressive and suggest the responsiveness of living things. As a result, Moore made sculpture that was asymmetrical, that looked different from every angle.

Although Moore was interested in structure, he was not a constructivist like the Hungarian sculptor Laszlo Moholy-Nagy. He was not interested solely in new possibilities for abstract structure, but tried to demonstrate organic connections between structure and form.

Moore's interest in art was an aspect of his interest in humanity, and vice versa. Even his most abstract work was intended to have emotional force. He continued to do figurative work throughout his career. Moore's interest in humanity was evident in his "Shelter Drawings," done during World War II, when many Londoners were forced to take refuge in the vast Underground (subway) to escape bombing attacks from the air. Moore's own studio was destroyed in an air raid in 1940.

Moore continued to work up until the final years before his death. He is recognized as one of the most important sculptors of the century, having exhibited throughout the world and been awarded honorary academic positions by institutions in several countries.

Mother Teresa

(1910–   )

YUGOSLAVIAN HUMANITARIAN
IN INDIA

We try to pray through our work by doing
it with Jesus, for Jesus, to Jesus. That helps
us put our whole heart and soul into doing it. The dying, the crippled, the mentally
ill, the unwanted, the unloved—they are
all Jesus in disguise. We have very little, so
we have nothing to be preoccupied with.
The more you have, the more you are occupied, the less you give. But the less you
have, the more free you are. Poverty for us is a freedom. . . . I find the rich
much poorer. Sometimes they are more lonely inside. They are never satisfied.
They always need something more. . . . I find that poverty is hard to remove.
The hunger for love is much more difficult to remove than the hunger for
bread.

—Mother Teresa, on caring for society's poorest people

Agnes Gonxha Bojaxhiu, now called Mother Teresa, was born in Skopje, in
what was then Macedonia, in 1910. Her family were Albanian Christians who
lived in harmony with their Christian and Muslim neighbors. Her father was
the town's grocer. She decided to become a nun at the age of twelve, and she
took her vows in a Irish order of nuns, the Sisters of Loretto, when she was
eighteen. The Sisters of Loretto ran a mission in Calcutta, India, where she
went after completing her training in Darjeeling, India. She worked at St.
Mary's School, for wealthy girls, first as a teacher, and later as principal.

Just outside the walls of the school were the slums of Calcutta. Mother
Teresa saw thousands of homeless children, poor orphans, sick adults, and people suffering from leprosy (a medical condition that eats away at a victim's flesh
and limbs). Because it was believed (incorrectly) that leprosy was extremely
contagious, no one would help, or even go near the lepers. In 1946, Mother
Teresa heard a "call within a call," and she decided to leave the convent and
live among the poor. It took two years to get the permission of the Catholic
Church to do so, and in 1948 she left the convent and received medical training from American nuns in India. The outdoor classes attracted other volunteers, who later formed the Missionaries of Charity. They believed that by
serving the poorest people on earth, they were serving God directly. In 1957,
the Missionaries of Charity opened a treatment center for lepers in a home for

dying poor people in Calcutta. In the next few years, with increased support from the Roman Catholic Church in India, they opened leper treatment centers in other Indian cities.

In 1965, Mother Teresa received permission from the Vatican to open Missionaries of Charity centers outside India. She sent nuns to Venezuela, Ceylon (now Sri Lanka), Tanzania, Australia, Italy, Jordan, London's East End, and New York's South Bronx. More than 12,000 coworkers minister with Mother Teresa to the poor of the world. In 1979, she received the Nobel Peace Prize. In her acceptance speech, she told the world of her love and respect for the people she serves. She spoke of the beautiful things the poor have taught her. She explained that the person who gives help is really the recipient of much more than the one who receives the help. The helper must be completely humble. Mother Teresa continues to show the world that simple service can provide the richest life of all.

Mulroney, Brian

(1939–)

CANADIAN PRIME MINISTER

Martin Brian Mulroney was born in 1939 in Baie Comeau on the St. Lawrence River, north of Quebec City, Canada. In 1955, he attended St. Francis-Xavier University in Nova Scotia. He studied law for a year at Dalhousie University and then transferred to Laval University in Quebec City, where he was one of the first English-speaking students to take all his courses in French. At school he became interested in politics and associated himself with the Progressive Conservative party. In 1956, he worked for the election of Prime Minister John Diefenbaker and made many friends in the government.

After school, Mulroney went to work for a Montreal law firm and developed a reputation as a superb labor lawyer. Both businessmen and labor leaders trusted him to arbitrate disputes. In 1974, after workers building a hydroelectric dam on James Bay rioted, Mulroney was appointed to a special commission to investigate their grievances. The commission's report uncovered secret deals between government officials and union officers, and the scandal pushed Mulroney into national prominence.

In 1977, Mulroney became president of the Iron Ore Company of Canada, which was at the time a failing business. He reached an agreement with dissatisfied workers and made the company profitable. But in 1983, falling demand for steel forced him to close several of his plants and lay off more than seven hundred workers, though he offered them generous severance benefits that softened the blow. In 1983, he assumed the leadership of the Progressive Conservative party and was elected to the Canadian Parliament. A year later he was elected prime minister.

Mulroney is a moderate conservative who strongly supported Presidents Ronald Reagan and George Bush regarding most American foreign policies. Though he supports Canada's national health system and social welfare programs, he also advocates incentives for businesses and investors. In recent years, he actively promoted controversial trade agreements between his country and the United States. After nearly a decade in office, though, he stepped down as prime minister in 1993 to allow his party to regroup in the face of a strong liberal challenge in the elections. A slumping economy, a bad political climate, and nagging problems with federalism and Quebec brought Mulroney to pass on the reigns of power to Kim Campbell, Canada's first woman prime minister.

Nasser, Gamal Abdel

(1918–1970)

EGYPTIAN PRESIDENT AND
PAN-ARABIST

We're a sentimental people. We like a few kind words better than millions of dollars given in a humiliating way.

—Gamal Abdel Nasser, 1958

President Gamal Abdel Nasser, founder of the United Arab Republic, was born in Alexandria, Egypt, on January 15, 1918. By the time he was in elementary school, he was already taking part in protests against the British government, which occupied Egypt and much of the Middle East at the time. In 1938 he graduated from the military academy in Cairo as a second lieutenant. In 1943, Nasser became an instructor there.

As an army officer, Nasser took part in an unsuccessful attempt to prevent the formation of an independent Jewish state east of Egypt. The state of Israel was established in 1948 despite armed resistance from several Arab countries.

Then in 1952, Nasser was a leader in the successful coup d'état against King Farouk of Egypt. In the new government he became deputy premier, minister of the interior, and chairman of the Revolution Command Council. By 1954 he had replaced the prime minister, and two years later he became the first president of the new Republic of Egypt.

In 1954 Nasser arranged for the British government to give up control of the Suez Canal. At the time he was considered to be pro-Western in his thinking. But he quickly shifted allegiances when the U.S. and Europe did not support Arab actions against Israel and the West attempted to force Egypt to side against the Soviet bloc. Nasser allied himself with other nonaligned countries like India and developed closer ties with communist countries such as Yugoslavia and Czechoslovakia. In 1956, he moved to nationalize the Suez Canal and succeeded when the U.S. and the Soviet Union, expressing a rare common purpose, persuaded the British and French to withdraw.

In 1958, Nasser helped form the United Arab Republic (UAR), composed of Egypt and Syria, which lasted until 1961. Domestically, he instituted land and farm reforms, industrialization, and significant social change toward a more modernized country. He solicited financial and technical assistance from the Soviet Union, but he did not break relations with the U.S. First and foremost a nationalist, Nasser nevertheless abhorred violence. Until his death, he worked to create a position of leadership in the Arab world. His patriotism was most evident during the Six-Day War of 1967, in which Israel soundly defeated Egypt and other Arab countries, claiming large amounts of Egyptian land. In defeat, the people of Egypt rallied to their leader's defense. Gamal Nasser died on September 28, 1970.

Navratilova, Martina

(1956–   )

CZECH-BORN AMERICAN TENNIS
PLAYER

A *Sports Illustrated* writer once said that Martina Navratilova's tennis ability often put her in "a zone of her own." That view was echoed by the players who lost to her on days when Martina seemed incapable of making a mistake. Forceful ground strokes, a strong serve, and an aggressive net game helped to make Navratilova one of the best women players in the history of tennis.

Born in Prague, Czechoslovakia, Martina grew up in nearby Revnice. Her grandmother played amateur tennis and her mother taught skiing. Martina's mother and stepfather played tennis and encouraged her to learn. She spent hours practicing at the local tennis club. At age 8, Martina played in a tournament for children up to age 12 and was unbeaten until the semifinals. Her childhood idols included Australian Rod Laver and American Billie Jean King.

Martina went through turbulent political events when Russian tanks invaded Czechoslovakia in 1968. That day, Martina was in another town playing in a tennis tournament. At age 11, she saw Russian soldiers shooting at people in the streets. Her coach had been outside the country when the invasion occurred. He chose not to return. Martina later said how depressed Czechs were after the invasion. She visited other countries for tennis tournaments and longed for the same quality of life and more freedom.

The left-handed player steadily improved. She was Czech national 14-and-under champion, then top woman player at 16. When she played in the United States in 1973, American sports commentator Bud Collins saw promise, and he called her playing "bold, determined, and agile." Practicing in sports like soccer, skiing, and ice hockey helped muscular Martina gain even more strength. She worked on her backhand, a weak part of her game. She was also a top student in school, even though she devoted most of her time to sports.

By 1975 Navratilova was reaching the finals in major tournaments. That autumn, while on a tournament trip, she decided not to go back to Czechoslovakia. She explained, "The control was tightening. I wondered if I'd get out again." She knew her career would decline if she could not travel to tournaments.

After moving to America, Navratilova found new friends. She also began overeating, especially such favorites as hamburgers, cheesecake, pizza, and milk shakes. Her weight rose to 172 pounds, and she often felt upset and impatient. Her playing was inconsistent and she was winning no matches. Sportswriters called her "the Great Wide Hope." Martina later said, "I was lonely. I couldn't turn to my parents for help, but I did have some good friends who helped."

She found a friend and advisor in Sandra Haynie, a former golf champion who now ran a business representing athletes. The two women shared a house near Dallas, Texas. Haynie helped Martina to get through this rough period and to learn to control her emotions during matches. Navratilova lost weight and became more fit. She began winning matches, and her confidence rose.

In 1978 she won seven tournaments in a row in the Virginia Slims tennis circuit. She had long wanted to win the All-England title at Wimbledon. That year she had to play against longtime rival Chris Evert in the finals. Each won a set. Then came the third and deciding set. Evert won four games in a row. In contrast to previous years, Martina was able to control her emotions. She fought her way back with steady, hard strokes and won the set 7–5. In tears, Martina met her rival and friend to shake hands at the net after she won.

It was the first of eight Wimbledon titles for Navratilova, including six in a row. In 1980 she had a bad year and was ranked number three. Again she went to work improving her strokes and following a healthy diet and exercise program, including weight lifting. She lost the U.S. Open in 1981, but won the Australian Open. Her record in 1982 was 90 wins and only 3 losses. At both the 1983 and 1984 U.S. Open tournaments, she was victorious. By capturing the U.S. Open, Wimbledon, the French Open, and the Australian Open between 1983 and 1984, Navratilova won the Grand Slam of tennis. Her earnings in just a year were about $1.5 million.

While playing in 1984, Navratilova realized she needed glasses, and her game improved with them. With Wimbledon wins in 1985 and 1987, Navratilova tied Helen Wills Moody for the most Wimbledon singles titles in that tournament. She won a U.S. Open tournament in 1987 too. As the 1990s began, she faced younger and talented players but continued to rank among the top women players until her retirement in 1995.

Nehru, Jawaharlal

(1889–1964)

INDIAN NATIONALIST LEADER
AND PRIME MINISTER

Long ages afterwards history will judge of
this period that we have passed through . . .
—Jawaharlal Nehru, 1948

Younger colleague of Mohandas Gandhi in India's independence movement, Jawaharlal Nehru became his country's first elected leader after independence from Britain. He was a highly respected and sometimes criticized world leader during the 1940s and 1950s, and his style of dress even launched an international fashion trend.

Born on November 14, 1889, in Allahabad, India, Nehru was the son of a wealthy and politically connected lawyer. He also belonged to India's highest caste, the Brahmans, and as a boy lived a very privileged life. Nehru was first taught in India by private British tutors and then was sent to prestigious schools in England, including Harrow and Cambridge. After studying natural sciences, he gravitated toward involvement with India's independence movement.

After becoming a lawyer in London in 1912, Nehru returned to India and joined the Indian National Congress, a political group advocating reform of British laws regarding Indian citizens. In 1916 he married Kamala Kaul, a bride arranged for him to wed by his father. The couple had one daughter, Indira, who would later succeed her father as prime minister. Nehru also met Mohandas Gandhi in 1916 but did not actively join his independence movement until three years later, after almost four hundred Indians had been killed by British troops during a protest. It was through Gandhi that Nehru first came to understand and respect the lower classes of India. As a result, Nehru chose to simplify his own life as Gandhi had done.

In 1921, Nehru was jailed for three months for his part in a political protest. Then, in 1925, he took his wife, who was ill, to Europe, where he became involved in internationalism and socialism for the first time. His trip included a visit to the Soviet Union. Returning to India in 1927, Nehru began to play a more active role in the independence movement. Two years later, despite

Gandhi's worries that his protégé was too radical, he recommended Nehru as head of the Congress Party. That year, 1929, at the urging of Nehru and other younger members of the party, it established independence as its top priority.

In the years leading up to 1945, Nehru would be arrested and jailed nine times for his involvement in India's struggle for independence. In 1936 his wife died. Two years later, he returned to Europe, at which time he was appalled by the British government's caving in to Nazi Germany, and by the lack of support among liberal politicians there for Indian independence. During World War II, the movement gained momentum, and by 1946 independence was inevitable. Conflicts between Hindu and Muslim Indian leaders, however, resulted in widespread violence and civil war just as independence was granted in 1947, creating India (mostly Hindu) and Pakistan (largely Muslim).

On August 15, 1947, Jawaharlal Nehru was elected prime minister of India, its first post-independence leader. His first two challenges were to deal with the religious conflict and the millions of refugees it had created, and then to deal with the assassination of Gandhi, which caused further strife. Nehru was elected again in 1950, the year India became a republic. Using a uniquely Indian brand of socialism, Nehru made a number of contributions to the modernization of India. His economic plans provided the framework for future growth, and he succeeded in doing away with many of the antiquated social customs—many based on the caste system—that prevented India from moving forward. Nehru also insisted that India remain a democracy.

In the realm of foreign affairs, he was a world leader among the nonaligned countries, taking assistance and advice from both the Soviet Union and the United States without becoming too dependent upon or too allied with either. He was criticized by Western experts for being somewhat naïve about Soviet policies and intentions and sometimes unduly harsh about U.S. and Western European actions. And in his efforts to establish good relations with communist China, Nehru was harshly criticized for failing to condemn that country's invasion and takeover of Tibet in the late 1950s. He died of a stroke on May 27, 1964, in New Delhi.

Neruda, Pablo

(1904–1973)

CHILEAN POET, MEMOIRIST, AND ESSAYIST

I believe that poetry is an action, ephemeral or solemn, in which there join as equal partners solitude and solidarity, emotion and action, the nearness to oneself, the nearness to mankind and to the secret manifestations of nature. And no less strongly I believe that all this is sustained . . . by an ever wider sense of community, by an effort which will forever bring together the reality and the dreams in us because it is precisely in this way that poetry unites and commingles them.

—Pablo Neruda, in his 1971 Nobel Prize lecture

For Pablo Neruda, one of the twentieth century's great poets, poetry was always about the meeting of "solitude and solidarity," a means to blend his own personal brand of romanticism with a deep and abiding commitment to political action.

Pablo Neruda was born Neftali Ricardo Reyes Basoalto in Parral, Chile, on July 12, 1904. His mother died shortly after his birth. His father moved the family to Temuco, in southern Chile. He remarried two years after Neftali's birth. His job as a train conductor kept him away from home a great deal of the time.

The boy began reading and writing poems when he was only ten. At fourteen he authored an essay that appeared in the local newspaper. The editors were so impressed with his work that he was put in charge of the literary page. By 1921, he had won whatever literary awards Temuco had to offer. More important, he had made the acquaintance and won the support and friendship of Gabriela Mistral, the great Chilean poet and teacher who won the 1945 Nobel Prize for Literature.

As a young man, Neftali went to Santiago, the Chilean capital, to begin French studies at the large teachers' college there. He finished only three years of his degree, but he also finished his first book of verse, *Crepusculario* (*Twilight,* 1923). He also acquired a new name, Pablo Neruda—Pablo from Picasso, Neruda from a Czech short-story writer he admired. Neruda won several significant poetry awards in the next couple of years. In 1924, he published

Twenty Love Poems and a Song of Desperation, his first great collection, and a book that remains one of the most popular in the Spanish-speaking world.

Neruda was moving toward surrealism, combining wildly disconnected images; he tried his hand at a short novel, and produced a few more volumes of poetry before a momentous occurrence in 1927. He was appointed honorary consul to Burma (now referred to as Myanmar by the military junta that runs the Southeast Asian nation). For the first time in his life, he left Latin America for a lengthy journey.

Over the next four years, Neruda was transferred throughout south Asia, first to Ceylon, then Java, where he met and married his first wife, Maria Voglezang, and finally Singapore. In the course of his travels, he continued writing poetry, with this unfamiliar part of the world as a spur to his creativity. Upon his return to Chile in 1931, Neruda published *Residence on Earth,* a major collection of his recent poetry.

Two years later, still unable to make a living as a poet, Neruda accepted another consular post, this time in Buenos Aires. While he was there, he met and befriended Federico García Lorca and the two poets remained close friends until the fascists murdered García Lorca in 1936. Neruda was then made consul in Barcelona, Spain, in 1934.

With the outbreak of the Spanish Civil War, Neruda moved politically to the left. He had always been sympathetic to the causes of the Indians and the labor unions, but the spectacle of fascist troops trying to overthrow a duly elected democratic government enraged him further. He was dismissed from his consular post, and he spent his time organizing Poets of the World Defend the Spanish People and writing *Spain in My Heart* (1937). The often lonely Neruda now had a cause, giving himself to the struggle against fascism.

Neruda returned intermittently to Chile, working on his next long poem, the book-length *Canto General,* but he was restless now and wouldn't stay put long. He traveled throughout Latin America (once getting jumped by a group of Nazis in Cuernavaca, Mexico), writing and lecturing. When World War II ended, he came home once more, this time to be elected to the Chilean Senate as an independent in 1945. He joined the Communist Party shortly afterward. The following year, he wrote one of his most famous poems, "The Heights of Machu Picchu," which was later incorporated into a section of *Canto General.*

During the 1946 election, Neruda had supported the candidacy of González Videla. He was supposedly a leftist, but after his election, he began repressing trade union activity and instituted harsh censorship of political opposition. Neruda published an attack on the censorship laws and found himself on trial as an enemy of the state. He was forced to resign his Senate seat and went into hiding, eventually fleeing the country in 1949. The bitterness of this exile fueled the completion of *Canto General.* While in Mexico, the divorced Neruda met and fell in love with Matilde Urrutia, who inspired some of his best love poems.

The publication of *Canto General* in Mexico in 1950 merely underlined the peculiar situation facing Neruda. The book was an enormous success throughout the Spanish-speaking world, except in his native Chile, where his works were banned. He traveled and taught over the next two years. In 1952, with a change in the political situation, he was finally able to return home a hero.

With the 1957 publication of *Collected Works,* Neruda was truly a poet of the world, translated into many languages, read enthusiastically everywhere, and finally able to support a family on the royalties from his books.

In the late 1950s, Neruda turned away from political verse for a time, concentrating his writing attentions on Matilde, whom he had married. His 1958 *Extravagaria,* followed the next year by *One Hundred Love Sonnets,* and finally by 1967's *Barcarole,* were all written out of his love for her. At long last, the wanderer was ready to make a home for his family and himself. Neruda established a retreat on the island of Isla Negra and allowed himself to relax in its quiet. He wrote a five-volume autobiographical poem, *Notebooks from Isla Negra* (1970), and even tried his hand at theater, authoring a play about the famous Mexican-American "bandit" Joaquin Murieta (1967).

In 1968, Neruda began writing political poetry again. The following year, he allowed his name to be put forward as the communist candidate for president of Chile. However, when his friend Dr. Salvador Allende Gossens prepared to run as well, Neruda stepped aside in his favor. Allende, as the candidate of a broad-based coalition of progressive parties, was elected in 1970. Neruda accepted an appointment as Chile's ambassador to France, where he remained until 1972.

It was in France that he was notified on October 8, 1971, that he had won the Nobel Prize for Literature. In his Nobel lecture, he spoke hopefully and stirringly of the push toward a shining city of utopian ideals, but in Chile the political situation was growing bleak.

Emboldened by what they assumed was the tacit approval of the Nixon Administration, the Chilean military prepared for the overthrow of the Allende government. Neruda, who was by then suffering from advanced cancer, returned home in 1972. On September 11, 1973, a brutal coup d'état overthrew and murdered Allende and thousands of his supporters. Twelve days later, Neruda died of cancer. He had kept writing at a feverish pace almost to the very end.

Neruda left behind a tremendous and consistently excellent body of work. From *Twenty Love Poems* to the final eight books of poetry published posthumously, a career spanning fifty years, he produced love poems, personal confessions, politically inspired poems and more, all of them marked by his inventive imagery, clarity of vision, and commitment to humanity.

Nevelson, Louise

(1899–1988)

AMERICAN SCULPTOR AND PAINTER

> Art gives me my world, it gives me my sanity, it gives me my beauty, and it gives me my life.
>
> —Louise Nevelson, at Harvard (1977)

Leah Berliawsky was born in Russia. Russian authorities did not record Jewish births and Louise (as she was called in America) never knew the exact date of her birth. Violence against Jews in Russia was increasing and Berliawsky's father, Isaac Berliawsky, left for America in 1902 and worked to earn enough money to get the rest of his family out of Russia.

Louise Berliawsky and Charles Nevelson, a treasurer for a family-owned shipping company, were married in June 1920 and moved into an apartment in New York. Nevelson was transported from the poverty of her family into the wealthy world of her husband's successful family. In February 1922, Nevelson gave birth to a son.

In 1924, Nevelson enrolled in Saturday drawing classes at the Art Students League. She became bored and frustrated by the class and entered a period of depression that kept her in bed almost an entire year.

In 1926, the Nevelson Brothers Company was failing and Charles Nevelson left the firm and moved the family to Brooklyn. They could no longer afford a nanny and Nevelson packed her belongings and moved to Maine with her son. She enrolled in a summer art class in Boothbay Harbor; her work was so poor that the teacher offered to refund her tuition, but Nevelson continued and at the end of the six-week course she was considered the best student of the class. Nevelson returned to her husband's apartment in New York in 1928 but the tension between them still existed.

Nevelson began studying full-time at the Art Students League in the fall of 1929. Her teacher was Kenneth Miller, the most distinguished instructor at the league. Miller was impressed with Nevelson's talent and took her to museums and encouraged her pursuit as an artist.

Nevelson rented a studio in Greenwich Village and worked constantly on her painting. The Mexican artist Diego Rivera asked Nevelson to work as his assistant on his murals, and while Nevelson agreed, she did little work for the famous painter.

In 1933, Louise Nevelson met Chaim Gross, a young sculptor who taught classes at the Educational Alliance and Nevelson became his student. She began experimenting with a variety of materials—clay, wood, plaster, and stone—and in a variety of styles, including abstract, geometric shapes. She also enrolled in drawing classes at the Art Students League, but her attention was moving closer to sculpture.

During the Depression, Nevelson began working for the government-funded Federal Arts Project of the Works Project Administration (WPA) in March 1935. The WPA gave more than five-thousand needy artists financial help in return for more than one-hundred-thousand pieces of art. Established artists were hired to produce paintings, sculptures, photographs, and murals for public buildings, while lesser-known artists were hired as teachers. Nevelson began teaching at the Flatbush Boys Club in Brooklyn, but the class ended by July.

In time, she was able to join the fine-arts division, first in the painting division and then as a sculptor, where she worked until 1939, when the government began cutting its support of artists.

In January 1943, Peggy Guggenheim, who had recently opened the Art of This Century Gallery in New York held an exhibition of thirty-one women artists and included Nevelson's wooden sculpture *Column*. The sculpture contained movable parts and the viewer was invited to rearrange the pieces and create their own work of art. Many critics wondered if Nevelson's playful creation could be considered art at all.

Finally, in February 1946, Nevelson sold one of her sculptures. Her work was also included in the prestigious exhibition of new art presented every year by the Whitney Museum of American Art in New York.

Nevelson began to promote her own art, attending gallery openings and joining as many organizations, associations, and groups as would accept her. She also exhibited regularly, but continued to have difficulty earning money.

By the start of 1954, Nevelson began teaching in an adult education program in Great Neck, Long Island. She was an unconventional teacher, but she provided valuable guidance for many students and managed to emphasize the basic techniques of sculpture.

In December she was notified by the Committee of Slum Clearance that the block she lived on had been bought by New York University and she had to move. Nevelson returned constantly to her demolished block and began taking wheelbarrows full of debris to her new studio to add to her sculpture. She also began to color her sculptures black, dipping the wood into a tub of thinned oil paint.

Nevelson's black sculptures quickly gained attention and in 1958 she was given a feature in *Life* magazine. Artists and critics agreed that Nevelson's examination of shadow and form provided "a whole new way of looking at sculpture" and Nevelson predicted that she would become more famous than Picasso.

Louise Nevelson's first real financial security came from Martha Jackson, a gallery owner who offered Nevelson a set income in exchange for the artist's work. Her first show at the Martha Jackson Gallery included floor-to-ceiling black constructions that covered the entire gallery. Jackson hired a professional lighting expert to unite and dramatize the sculptures. The lights provided the sculptures with a variety of shades of black. One critic wrote that "the eye no longer knows what black is—if it ever did."

From the success of her exhibit, Nevelson began to sell her work and be recognized as an important artist. She was awarded the first prize in the ART: USA '59 exhibit and the grand prize in the First Sculpture International exhibit in Argentina in 1962. The Whitney Museum also purchased her black wall sculpture, *Young Shadows* (1959–60) for $11,000.

Nevelson then began creating sculpture in white and gold, searching for new ways to experiment with color in her work. She created an entire studio filled with gold bedposts, umbrella handles, toilet seats, and numerous other objects. The Whitney Museum also presented an all-gold exhibition that astonished the art world.

In 1961 Nevelson joined the Pace Gallery in Boston, Massachusetts, headed by the twenty-three-year-old Arnold Glimcher, who immediately sold $70,000 worth of Nevelson's work to young Boston collectors.

In June 1962, Nevelson was one of four Americans represented at the Venice Biennale, the largest and most important international exhibit of contemporary art. She was also elected as the first woman president of Artists Equity, the largest group of professional painters and sculptors in the country. In 1964, the Whitney Museum exhibited a retrospective of Nevelson's work, including more than one hundred drawings and sculptures.

In the late 1960s Nevelson began working in metal and received a number of commissions for outdoor sculptures, including the Louise Nevelson Plaza in New York. She became one of the most frequently commissioned sculptors in America and her work appeared throughout the country.

Nevelson was elected into the elite fifty-member American Academy of Arts and Letters in 1983, and two years later President Ronald Reagan awarded her the National Medal of the Arts for her lifetime achievements.

Nijinsky, Vaslav

(1890–1950)

RUSSIAN BALLET DANCER
AND CHOREOGRAPHER

One of the most famous male ballet dancers of the early part of the twentieth century, Vaslav Nijinsky, through star power and pure magnetism, had a brief and spectacular career, cut short by mental illness. He became a legend in the dance world.

Nijinsky was born in 1890 in Kiev, Russia. His parents were dancers with a Polish circus, so he came by his sense of theater and talent for makeup and characterization naturally. The young Nijinsky began his dance training as a child at the Imperial Ballet School, but he was seen as a talented dancer who didn't fit in with the company. In 1909, Nijinsky joined producer Sergei Diaghilev's Ballet Russes. It was with that company, under the personal guidance of Diaghilev that Nijinsky made a sensational impression dancing in ballets such as *Les Sylphides (The Sylphs)*, *Cleopatra*, *Scheherazade*, *Carnaval*, and the title roles in *Le Spectre de la Rose (The Ghost of the Rose)* and *Petrouchka*.

Diaghilev pushed Nijinsky to choreograph new works to new music (much of it written by modern composer Igor Stravinsky); *L'Après-Midi d'un Faune (Afternoon of a Faun)*, *Jeux (Games)*, and *The Rite of Spring* were the dazzling results. These were the first truly original and trend-setting ballets of the twentieth century. When Nijinisky married and left the company, his work was never to be the same.

After World War I, Nijinsky, who had been imprisoned during the war, worked on one last piece under Diaghilev, *Tyle Eulenspiegel*. But the tensions of the years behind bars brought about a mental instability that ended Nijinsky's career as a creator and dancer. He spent the rest of his life in a series of institutions, and eventually died in England.

Nureyev, Rudolf

(1938–1993)

RUSSIAN BALLET DANCER

The main thing is dancing, and before it withers away from my body, I will keep dancing till the last moment, the last drop.

—Rudolf Nureyev, in a 1990 interview

One of the most famous ballet stars of the twentieth century, Rudolf Hametovich Nureyev was born on a train traveling along the shores of Lake Baikal in southeastern Sibera. His father was in the Soviet army, so the family moved frequently. They lived in Moscow for part of World War II and then moved to Ufa, a city on the eastern side of the Ural Mountains. It was at the Ufa Opera that Nureyev first saw ballet performances and became excited about the possibility of dancing. Because his father wanted him to join the army or take up engineering, the teenaged Nureyev began his ballet studies in secret by working with folk dance groups at school and taking private lessons with a local teacher. Eventually, Nureyev became a member of the corps de ballet (the general group of dancers) at the Ufa Opera House.

Although his father tried to discourage young Nureyev's interest in dance, Nureyev appeared with the company in 1955 in Moscow at a festival. It was there that he tried out for and was accepted at both the Bolshoi Ballet and the Kirov Ballet schools. Nureyev chose the Kirov, even though one of the teachers there said, "You'll either become a brilliant dancer or a total failure—and most likely you'll be a failure." In 1958, after three years of study under one of the Kirov's best teachers, Aleksander Pushkin, Nureyev graduated and joined the Kirov Ballet; he was given solo roles from the beginning. He frequently partnered Natalya Dudinskaya, the company's senior ballerina and the wife of its director, Konstantin Sergeyev.

Nureyev made up for his late start in ballet by being a quick learner. He mastered as many roles as he could, and he developed a great interest in foreign dancers. Nureyev was also becoming known for his independent attitude and outspoken nature. These qualities did not make him popular with the rigid Soviet authorities. In 1961, after finishing a season with the Kirov in Paris, France, Nureyev was told that he was being sent to Moscow to dance at a gala.

He suspected that this was the Soviets' way of punishing him for his unruliness, and that once in the Soviet Union, he would no longer be allowed out. So Nureyev made the choice to leave the Soviet Union and remain in the West. He did not return there until 1987, when he received a special visa to see his dying mother.

Within a week of his famous "leap to freedom," Nureyev was dancing again, making his American debut on television on January 19, 1962, on the *Bell Telephone Hour*. He made his New York stage debut at the Brooklyn Academy of Music dancing the title role of *Don Quixote* with the Chicago Opera Ballet.

At ballerina Margot Fonteyn's invitation, Nureyev became a permanent guest artist with the Royal Ballet in London. When he was cast in the ballet *Giselle* opposite Fonteyn, ballet history was made. Nureyev and Fonteyn began a long-lasting partnership that renewed her career.

Not content to dance only the classics, Nureyev danced in such contemporary ballets as Kenneth MacMillan's *Romeo and Juliet*, Roland Petit's *Pelleas et Melisande*, Jerome Robbins's *Dances at a Gathering*, and George Balanchine's *Apollo*. As ballet's first contemporary superstar, Nureyev made the male dancer just as important as the ballerina. Dancing with almost every major ballet company in the Western world, he restaged many classics and stressed the male dancer's role.

In the 1970s, Nureyev entered the world of modern dance in works by choreographers like José Limón, Paul Taylor, and Martha Graham. In 1979, the first of several touring groups named *Nureyev and Friends,* which offered classical excerpts and contemporary works, made its New York Broadway debut and then toured the world. During the same period, Nureyev made his film debut in the title role of director Ken Russell's film *Valentino* (based on the life of the great silent film star Rudolf Valentino). In 1983, he toured America as the King of Siam in the musical *The King and I.*

From 1983 to 1989, Nureyev was the artistic director of the Paris Opera Ballet. He helped make the company a first-class troupe once again, developing a more varied program of works and giving younger dancers the chance to succeed.

During that period, Nureyev studied conducting. He began to conduct orchestras in Eastern Europe. He also conducted a single performance of *Romeo and Juliet* for the American Ballet Theatre in New York in 1992 at the Metropolitan Opera House.

By that time, he had become very ill, and on January 6, 1993, he died of AIDS.

O'Connor, Sandra Day

(1930–)

ATTORNEY, LEGISLATOR,
AND FIRST FEMALE JUSTICE
OF THE U.S. SUPREME COURT

Sandra Day O'Connor was born on March 26, 1930, in El Paso, Texas to a family with a rich history. Her grandparents had been pioneers who settled in the West and weathered Apache Indian attacks, drought, and near bankruptcy—all of which set a powerful example for young Sandra.

Unable to secure a position in a law firm because she was a woman, O'Connor started her career as a deputy to the district attorney of San Mateo County, California, eventually representing the county in civil lawsuits. In 1953, she moved with her new husband to Germany when he was drafted into the army. After four years they returned to the United States, where they started their family in the Phoenix, Arizona area.

In the late 1950s, at a time when it was still very unusual to do so, Sandra Day O'Connor managed to tend her small children and make progress in her promising career as a practicing attorney by working part-time. She became active in Republican party politics, and worked hard for Barry Goldwater's 1964 presidential campaign. When her youngest son reached school age, she took a part-time job in the state Attorney General's Office, where she quickly distinguished herself as an intelligent and hardworking attorney. As her children got older, she began to work full-time and became an expert on many government issues. In 1969, she was appointed to an open seat in the state senate. Eventually, her common sense, fairness, and compassion, combined with her shrewd intelligence, made her a driving force in Arizona government.

Never one to stick to the Republican party line just for the sake of politics, O'Connor had a wide and unexpected range of opinions on some important issues—such as the death penalty, which she supported, and abortion, which she felt should be legal, as well as school busing and gun control, both of which she opposed. She felt the government should stay out of the personal matters of citizens, though she often felt that women and minorities needed an extra bit of help and protection from government in fighting the force of history against them.

Like the suffragists who had preceded her two generations earlier, O'Connor believed women should enjoy equal rights and protection under the law, and she enthusiastically supported passage of the Equal Rights Amendment (ERA). In 1972, the ERA had been passed in the United States Congress, and thirty eight of the fifty individual state legislatures had to ratify the law before it could become an amendment to the Constitution. Despite her avid and vocal support for this law, she couldn't convince her fellow legislators of its importance to women. So she committed herself to other ways to help women, minorities, and poor people by passing new laws or terminating old ones that were unfair and obsolete.

In 1974, O'Connor left the legislature and ran for trial judge in the County Superior Court. Sporting a solid legislative record and taking a tough position on crime, she won and went on to spend the next five years overseeing civil and criminal trials. She was thought to be fair and sensitive in her rulings, which were always thoughtful and intelligent. She was a tough sentencer, but also worked to find creative punishments for defendants for whom prison or an excessive fine was not the best answer.

In 1979, when a vacancy came up on the Arizona Court of Appeals, Governor Bruce Babbitt appointed O'Connor to the spot. During her time on this court, she worked to strengthen its role in the judicial process, for she believed that state courts could handle many of the sorts of cases that federal courts were handling. She also spent these years establishing the National Association for Women Judges (NAWJ), which worked to increase the number of women judges who were appointed or elected.

By 1981, Sandra Day O'Connor had a rock-solid reputation locally, nationally, and even internationally. When President Ronald Reagan was faced with the retirement of then United States Supreme Court Justice Potter Stewart, he decided to take the opportunity to make good on his campaign promise and appoint a woman to the land's highest court for the first time in the history of the institution. He wanted someone who would be considered a "judicial conservative," or one who wouldn't use his or her position on the Court to force action on political or social issues. He looked for a candidate who believed in the "original intent" of the Constitution and Bill of Rights, meaning that these documents should not be interpreted according to modern circumstances but should be looked at as adequately clear and useful just as written by the Founding Fathers.

Among the names of candidates who seemed to fit the bill was Sandra Day O'Connor, whom Reagan nominated on September 9, 1981. She was unanimously confirmed by the Senate and sworn in as an associate justice of the United States Supreme Court—its first female member—on September 25, 1981.

O'Keeffe, Georgia

(1887–1986)

AMERICAN PAINTER

I want to paint in terms of my own thinking, and feeling the facts and things which men know. One can't paint [the object] as it is, but rather as it is felt.

—Georgia O'Keeffe, in 1926

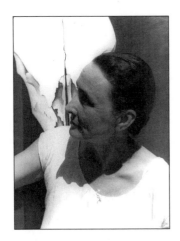

Georgia Totto O'Keeffe was born in November near Sun Prairie, Wisconsin, the second of seven children. Her father, Francis Calyxtus O'Keeffe, a farmer, married Ida Totto. O'Keeffe's mother wanted her children to be cultured and when she turned nine, Georgia was taken into Sun Prairie every Saturday for art lessons. According to her own account, O'Keeffe decided to become an artist at the age of ten.

In 1902, her family moved to Virginia, but O'Keeffe stayed in the Midwest for her education. She studied at the Art Institute of Chicago (1905–06), but her training was interrupted when she caught typhoid fever. In 1907, she attended the Art Students League in New York and earned money toward her tuition by working as a model for her fellow students. It was a general rule that women at the Art Students League at that time were training to be teachers, but O'Keeffe was convinced that she could become a famous artist.

O'Keeffe won a still-life prize that enabled her to spend the summer of 1908 at the League Outdoor School at Lake George in New York. O'Keeffe discovered that her family could no longer afford to give her any money toward her education. O'Keeffe went to Chicago, Illinois and lived with relatives while she worked as a commercial artist.

The illness of her mother in 1912 took her to Charlottesville, Virginia and she visited an art class at the University of Virginia. The teacher, Alon Bement, encouraged his students to produce their own original art instead of copying the works of the acclaimed masters. She became interested in painting again, and became friends with Bement, who invited O'Keeffe to help him teach at Columbia University's Teachers College in New York.

In 1914, O'Keeffe returned to New York City to study at Columbia University's Teachers College in order to earn a teaching degree. She also attended classes at the Art Students League, returning to the school with a strong personal style. In the fall of 1915, O'Keeffe needed to earn money to continue her education and she accepted a teaching job in South Carolina.

She began drawing in black-and-white with charcoal and sent the drawings to a friend from the Art Students League, Anita Pollitzer. Pollitzer showed the drawings to Alfred Stieglitz, who ran an influential art gallery in New York called "291." Stieglitz was impressed with the drawings and without O'Keeffe's knowledge, he displayed them in his gallery in May 1916. O'Keeffe was notified of the exhibition and she traveled to New York to make Stieglitz take her drawings off the walls of his gallery. Stieglitz refused and explained why he thought the drawings were important. Stieglitz was famous for determining what art was important; Stieglitz had been the first person to exhibit Pablo Picasso in America, and his "291" gallery exhibited many important young artists like John Marin and Paul Strand.

In the fall of 1916, O'Keeffe accepted another teaching job, in Canyon, Texas. She began painting the western landscape and Stieglitz exhibited the pictures, with O'Keeffe's approval. Her watercolors from Texas exposed visitors to "291" to a new world and caused a sensation in the art community.

In 1918, an illness forced O'Keeffe to take a leave of absence from teaching. Stieglitz offered to support her in order to allow O'Keeffe to concentrate on her painting and she accepted his offer. Paul Strand traveled to Texas and accompanied O'Keeffe back to New York, where she and Stieglitz began living together. To complicate matters, Stieglitz was married to another woman at the time.

Alfred Stieglitz exhibited 145 of his photographs in February 1921 and the pictures that caused a sensation were the forty-five nudes of Georgia O'Keeffe. O'Keeffe had appeared only briefly at the exhibit, but the photographs turned her into a much talked-about celebrity.

In 1923 Stieglitz exhibited one-hundred of O'Keeffe's paintings and the gallery was crowded with people anxious to see what the subject of Stieglitz's affection and photography would produce. O'Keeffe's paintings, however, established her as an artist, and not just Stieglitz's mistress. She sold twenty paintings from the show.

At the end of 1924, Stieglitz was granted a divorce and he and O'Keeffe were married. Being married complicated O'Keeffe's desire to be thought of independently from her famous husband, and throughout her life, O'Keeffe lived and worked apart from Stieglitz for long periods of time.

The 1925 exhibition "Alfred Stieglitz presents Seven Americans in New York" contained many of O'Keeffe's now famous paintings of flowers, which were highly praised by the writers Sherwood Anderson, Edmund Wilson, and Marianne Moore.

In 1929, she visited New Mexico and lived in a house recently vacated by the writer D.H. Lawrence. Mabel Dodge Luhan, a friend of O'Keeffe's who owned the house in Taos, New Mexico, declared that Taos was "the beating heart of the world," and O'Keeffe agreed. She returned to New York and exhibited the paintings she had produced from her trip in Stieglitz's An American Place Gallery, which established her as a leading painter in American art.

The Museum of Modern Art invited O'Keeffe and sixty-four other artist to submit drawings for a mural for the interior of the new Radio City Music Hall and O'Keeffe's proposal was accepted. O'Keeffe began to paint her mural in November, 1932.

Almost immediately, O'Keeffe encountered difficulties and when a large portion of the canvas on the wall of Radio City began to peel, O'Keeffe suffered a nervous breakdown. The mural was never completed.

O'Keeffe recovered with rest and relaxation in Bermuda, Lake George, and New Mexico. O'Keeffe became isolated from Stieglitz and preferred the solitude, which allowed her to concentrate on her painting. O'Keeffe and Stieglitz still maintained a business relationship, and in 1938 Stieglitz exhibited O'Keeffe's paintings of bleached bones suspended over the desert landscape. The show brought even more attention to the artist and she began receiving commissions from a wide source of employers.

In April 1939, O'Keeffe was selected by the New York World's Fair as one of twelve outstanding women of the past fifty years, alongside other women of distinction as Eleanor Roosevelt and Helen Keller. A month later, O'Keeffe suffered another nervous collapse. She traveled to Lake George with Stieglitz and in the late summer returned to New Mexico, alone.

The Museum of Modern Art exhibited a retrospective of O'Keeffe's work in 1946, the first woman artist to receive a retrospective. "Her art has very little inherent value," Clement Greenberg wrote in his review of the retrospective and his criticism signaled a move away from O'Keeffe's work in American art.

O'Keeffe retreated to New Mexico and in July 1946 Alfred Stieglitz died from a stroke at the age of eighty-two. O'Keeffe spent the next three years settling his estate and establishing memorials to him. O'Keeffe donated Stieglitz's finest works to numerous museums, including the Museum of Modern Art, the Metropolitan Museum of Art, and the Art Institute of Chicago. She then retired permanently to New Mexico.

In 1957, Newsweek magazine wondered what had happened to Georgia O'Keeffe, reflecting the fact that she had vanished from the public eye into the New Mexico desert. The following year saw a renewed interest in her work as the Metropolitan Museum of Art in New York devoted an entire room to O'Keeffe's paintings in its exhibition "Fourteen American Masters."

O'Keeffe's eyesight began to fail in 1964; by 1971 O'Keeffe could no longer see well enough to paint and was completely blind by the time of her death in March 1986.

Olivier, Laurence

(1907–1989)

ENGLISH ACTOR, DIRECTOR, AND PRODUCER

> I can no longer work in the theater, but the thrill will never leave me.
> The lights and the combat. The intimacy between the audience and
> me during the soliloquies in *Hamlet* and *Richard III*; we were like
> lovers. That's an actor's life. Complete freedom and versatility.
> Everything changes, as I have said. But then again, nothing
> changes. All we need is an old cigar box and someone to take
> notice.
>
> —Laurence Olivier, in a 1986 interview

Considered by most people to be the best actor of this century, Laurence Kerr
Olivier was born in 1907 in Dorking, England. When he was nine, he was sent
to All Saints, a boarding school near Oxford Circus. Almost immediately,
Olivier became interested in acting. In his second year at school, he played
Brutus in Shakespeare's *Julius Caesar.* Actress Sybil Thorndike, who saw the
performance, said, "The small boy who played Brutus is already an actor."

When he was thirteen, his mother died. His father, a clergyman who wanted
Olivier to follow in his footsteps, had always discouraged his son's acting, and
now he forbade him to act again. In 1921, when young Olivier was fourteen, he
was sent to St. Edward's school in Oxford, a training ground for clergymen.
The headmaster of the school persuaded Olivier's father to let the boy act, as it
was the one thing that he was good at. During the 1922 Easter holidays at Strat-
ford-on-Avon, Olivier appeared in Shakespeare's *The Taming of the Shrew,* and
it was then that he decided to be an actor. The next year his father remarried.
It was his new stepmother who, after seeing him play Puck in *A Midsummer
Night's Dream,* succeeded in convincing his father that Olivier should be an
actor.

Olivier entered the Central School of Speech Training and Dramatic Art in
London in 1924 and made his London stage debut in a very small role in *Byron.*
He became associated with the Birmingham Repertory Company in 1926.

For the next two years, Olivier played several interesting roles. Noticing his
good looks, as well as his abilities, critics began to predict that he would one
day be a distinguished romantic actor. After leaving the company, Olivier gave
good performances in a series of stage failures. While waiting around for a
good play, Olivier appeared in films. He had made his debut in the silent film
Too Many Crooks, and in the early 1930s he appeared in such forgotten films as
The Temporary Widow, Her Strange Desire, and *The Yellow Ticket.*

Olivier's first real stage success came in 1930, in playwright-actor-director Noël Coward's comedy *Private Lives*. Olivier was eternally grateful to Coward, who gave him a success and taught him a good deal about the stage. When the play went to Broadway in New York, Olivier went with it.

After the play closed, Olivier and his new wife, Jill Esmond (who had also been in *Private Lives*), both went to Hollywood, where they were signed to film contracts. Olivier's film career didn't really take off at that time, and he returned to the stage. In 1933, he had a great Broadway success in the play *The Green Bay Tree*. When he went back to London, he returned as a star, and he appeared in leading roles in several plays.

It was in 1935, when Olivier played Romeo in actor-director John Gielgud's production of *Romeo and Juliet*, that he had his greatest success thus far. Critic James Agate wrote: "This Romeo looked every inch a lover . . . this is the most moving Romeo I have ever seen." At that point, Olivier met Vivien Leigh, a young, beautiful actress who already adored him. When he was cast opposite her in the film *Fire Over England*, they began a passionate romance that led to marriage.

For the next year, Olivier devoted himself to Shakespearean roles as a member of the Old Vic Company. He played in *Twelfth Night, Henry V,* and *Macbeth*. Then he left the company to return to Hollywood, where, as Heathcliff, in the film *Wuthering Heights,* he became an international movie star and was nominated for his first Oscar. Olivier was establishing a career pattern. He would alternate back and forth between performing in classical theater and playing the film roles that would make him money. After shooting the film, in 1939 Olivier went to Broadway in the play *No Time for Comedy*. Then he went back to Hollywood to film *Rebecca,* which brought him another Oscar nomination, and *Pride and Prejudice*. During that time, Vivien Leigh had made the film *Gone With the Wind* (1939) and became a major star in her own right. To capitalize on their sudden fame, Leigh and Olivier opened in their own production of *Romeo and Juliet*. It was a failure and lost them a lot of money.

In 1944, Olivier was appointed codirector of the Old Vic Company. During that time he played many stage roles, but he made his greatest impression in the title role of *Oedipus Rex* (1946).

One of Olivier's great dreams had been to make great films of his favorite Shakespearean plays. In 1946, he produced, directed, and starred in the film *Henry V*. Olivier won a special Oscar for "outstanding achievement as actor, producer, and director in bringing *Henry V* to the screen," among other awards. He followed this up with the even bigger success of *Hamlet* (1948), which won him Oscars for Best Picture and Best Actor.

In the late 1950s, after making the award-winning film *Richard III* (1956), Olivier had one of his greatest stage successes in a modern play: playing the down-and-out performer in *The Entertainer*. He played in London, New York, and on film. His versatility dazzled the critics.

In 1963, the National Theater Company was established, with Olivier at its head. He gave his heart to the company and directed many of the plays and acted in many roles, including *Othello* (1964). Although his health started failing in the late 1960s, Olivier kept performing and was particularly successful playing the huge role of James Tyrone in *Long Day's Journey into Night* (1971).

By 1973, his health had deteriorated further, and he left his post at the National Theatre. He then devoted his time to television and film, appearing in such films as *Sleuth* (1972), *Marathon Man* (1976), *The Boys from Brazil* (1978), and the television mini-series *Brideshead Revisited* (1982). He played the lead role in a spectacular *King Lear* on television in 1984, and earned his fourth Emmy Award. Olivier earned many awards and nominations in his career and was knighted in 1947.

O'Neill, Eugene

(1888–1953)

AMERICAN PLAYWRIGHT

Eugene O'Neill was born in New York in a hotel room on Broadway. His father was an Irish actor, and his mother, who was from a wealthy family, was probably not well-prepared to be an actor's wife. When O'Neill was born, she began to use drugs. O'Neill grew up in the backstages of theaters until he turned seven, when he was sent to a Catholic boarding school. He then attended a secular boarding school in Connecticut, which he graduated from in 1906. By that time he knew that his mother was an addict.

O'Neill renounced his Catholic faith and he began to drink heavily, a habit he continued until 1926. At that point, he knew that he had to choose between alcohol and his work. He went to Princeton University for one year, but was expelled for not taking his final exams and for bad behavior. He did continue to read and educate himself, however.

In 1909, O'Neill married. He traveled to Honduras in search of gold, but returned to New York the following year with malaria. O'Neill recovered and went to work as an assistant manager for his father's touring company. But O'Neill loved the sea, and he landed a job as a deckhand on a Norwegian ship. He spent two months sailing from Boston to Buenos Aires, where he left the ship and worked odd jobs. He lived like a bum along the waterfront, spending most of his time eating and drinking.

O'Neill returned to New York in 1911 aboard a British ship. He lived on Fulton Street above a bar along the waterfront. Called to the sea yet again, he joined a passenger ship heading for England. All of O'Neill's experiences at sea—the characters he met, the ships he sailed on—were used in his plays.

O'Neill began to write one-act plays in 1913, and having returned to the United States, he worked as a reporter for the New London, Connecticut, *Telegraph*. In 1916 the Provincetown Players in Cape Cod performed O'Neill's *Bound East for Cardiff*, the story of a dying sailor. From 1916 to 1920, the Provincetown Players and the Washington Square Players in New York performed other one-act plays by O'Neill, including *Bound East: The Moon of the Caribees, The Long Voyage Home,* and *In the Zone.*

O'Neill had divorced his first wife, and in 1918 he married a short-story writer. They had two children, Shane and Oona, but were divorced in 1929. O'Neill's family life was racked with tragedy. His first son, Eugene, Jr., was a Yale professor who was an alcoholic until he committed suicide in 1950. His second son, Shane, was also an alcoholic. His daughter Oona, who married Charlie Chaplin when she was eighteen and he was fifty-four, also committed suicide. In 1929, O'Neill married his third wife, whom he stayed with until his death and who was a great support to him.

O'Neill achieved fame in 1920 with two important plays. *The Emperor Jones* was about the ruler of a West Indian Island who falls to the position of a savage and is killed by the local people. This short expressionist play in eight scenes featured the first major stage role for an African-American actor. It was originally played by Charles Gilpin, and later by Paul Robeson.

O'Neill's other major success was *Beyond the Horizon,* a play he wrote in 1918. His first full-length play and first Broadway success, it also won a Pulitzer Prize. The play, which portrayed the hopes, dreams, and hardships of farming families, changed American theater. Prior to this play, people went to the theater for entertainment, to escape from everyday problems. With *Beyond the Horizon,* O'Neill made it acceptable and popular to produce serious, realistic plays about American life.

O'Neill continued with a string of successes in the 1920s. His success, however, was overshadowed by yet more personal tragedy. His father died in 1929, followed by his mother two years later. His older brother, who had given up alcohol, began to drink again when their mother died, and he passed away in 1932 at the age of forty-five. O'Neill himself had a nervous disease which caused his hands to tremble, making it very difficult for him to write.

In the 1930s, most artists were concerned about social issues, the Great Depression, and the prospect of a world war. O'Neill, however, turned at this time to writing private, personal dramas. *Mourning Becomes Electra* (1931) was a realistic tragedy about death and determinism. *Ah, Wilderness!* (1933), the only comedy O'Neill ever wrote, was set in a small American town in 1906.

From 1935 to 1946, none of O'Neill's plays was produced on Broadway, but his success up until this point won him a Nobel Prize for Literature in 1936. O'Neill wanted to write serious, historical plays. Only one, A *Touch of the Poet*, was produced in 1957. He destroyed the other manuscripts when he realized he could not finish them because of his severe hand tremors.

O'Neill returned to Broadway with the production of *The Iceman Cometh* in 1946. After a long absence, the play revived interest in O'Neill. The 1946 production starred Jason Robards, and it was the longest-running O'Neill play ever. A *Moon for the Misbegotten* was produced in 1947. It depicted O'Neill's alcoholic brother's relationship with their mother. *Long Day's Journey Into the Night* reflected O'Neill's understanding of his family's dynamics and relationships. Produced in 1956 after his death, it won a Pulitzer Prize.

O'Neill was forced to stop writing when his hand tremors became too great, and he wrote nothing in the last ten years of his life. He died of bronchial pneumonia in a hotel room in Boston. Eugene O'Neill, who changed the role of American theater from escapist entertainment to realistic emotional drama, is a preeminent American playwright.

Oppenheimer, J. Robert

(1904–1967)

AMERICAN PHYSICIST

> The peoples of the world must unite, or they will perish. . . . The atomic bomb has spelled out [these words] for all men to understand.
>
> —J. Robert Oppenheimer, in a speech in 1945

Robert Oppenheimer was born in New York. Growing up in a prosperous household, Robert and his family took several trips to Europe when he was a boy. On one vacation, he visited his German grandfather, who gave the child his collection of minerals. Oppenheimer later claimed that the gift first made him want to learn about science.

At his private school, Robert developed many other interests. He liked literature, art, and language classes as much as his courses in chemistry and physics. Yet it was his talent as a science student that drew him the most attention. For instance, after writing a series of letters to the New York Mineral Society, the organization asked him to deliver a lecture to the group. The day of the lecture, the other society members were shocked to see that their special speaker was a twelve-year-old boy.

Graduating at the top of his high school class, Oppenheimer entered Harvard University in 1921. His performance as a student there was so impressive that he won a fellowship to study at the Cavendish Laboratory in Cambridge, England. The laboratory was a world-famous center for physicists. At Cavendish, Oppenheimer received still another invitation. He was asked by Max Born, a prominent scientist, to come to the University of Gottingen in Germany, from which he was awarded a Ph.D. in 1927. Born later said, "Oppenheimer seemed to me right from the beginning a very gifted man." Oppenheimer spent two more years studying in Europe. He then became so homesick that he decided to return to the United States.

Back home, Oppenheimer joined the faculties of the University of California at Berkeley and the California Institute of Technology. Oppenheimer soon earned a reputation as an excellent teacher. Science students from across the country came to California to study with him. He was known to be one of America's greatest authorities on modern physics.

In the 1930s, Oppenheimer began hearing disturbing news from his friends in Europe. Adolph Hitler was rising to power in Germany. He encouraged his followers, the Nazis, to hate Jews. Many of the European scientists Oppenheimer had worked with were Jewish, so as Hitler's influence spread their lives became endangered. Joining with other American scientists, Oppenheimer worked to raise money to help bring them to the United States where they would be safe.

In 1939, Oppenheimer heard something even more alarming. By then, World War II (1939–45) had erupted in Europe, and Germany was threatening to take over the entire continent. According to Oppenheimer's friends, German scientists had learned how to split atoms, thereby releasing a huge amount of energy. Hitler had begun taunting his enemies that these scientists were using the discovery to make a bomb of unbelievable power.

The U.S. government also heard about Hitler's bomb. After the United States entered the war in 1941, it became determined to make an atomic weapon before Germany could. The campaign to build the bomb was named the Manhattan Project.

In the fall of 1942, Oppenheimer was asked to become the project's chief scientist. He opposed war as a matter of principle. However, he saw the Nazis as such a threat to the world that he felt he had to take on the job.

Oppenheimer first had to persuade the country's best scientists to come to the Manhattan Project's headquarters in Los Alamos, New Mexico. Next he had to organize the work of his staff of 1,500 people. The task was enormous. For two and a half years, Oppenheimer worked six days a week and slept only four hours a night. But everyone involved in the Manhattan Project later maintained that his diligence and skill as a manager made a great difference. As Laura Fermi, the wife of Italian physicist Enrico Fermi, recalled, "Oppie turned out to be a marvelous director, the real soul of the project."

By July 1945, Oppenheimer and his scientists had finished their job. They had built three bombs. One contained plutonium and was nicknamed Little Boy. The other two contained uranium and were called Fat Man.

No one was sure if the bombs would actually work. The government decided to test the new weapon by exploding one of the Fat Man bombs in the New Mexican desert. For the test bombing, it chose a site named Trinity, which was about 200 miles away from Los Alamos.

At about 5:30 that morning, the first atomic bomb exploded. Oppenheimer and many of his colleagues watched at a safe distance away. The blast was amazing. It released an incredible amount of light as a cloud of smoke rose 12,000 feet in the air. Oppenheimer was at once pleased that the bomb had worked and horrified by the new invention. He later said that the blast made him think of a line from an ancient Hindu book he had read: "I am become Death, the destroyer of worlds."

By the time of the Trinity test, Germany had surrendered, but its Japanese allies were still fighting American troops. President Harry S. Truman decided to drop the remaining bombs on two Japanese cities, Hiroshima and Nagasaki. At least 180,000 people died or were injured in the blasts. Many more were injured, and cities were devastated. The bombings convinced Japan to surrender, but some Americans were angry that the U.S. government had killed so many civilians to bring a swift end to the war.

After the war, Oppenheimer supported efforts to use what was learned by the Manhattan Project scientists to create a new energy source. He worked for the U. S. Atomic Energy Commission (AEC) and made more than two hundred speeches about this peacetime use of atomic power. However, he opposed the commission's plan to build a hydrogen bomb, which would be far more deadly than the atomic weapons the United States already had.

Because many of the AEC's projects were top secret, the government investigated everyone who worked for the commission. In 1954, investigators began to question Oppenheimer's loyalty to the United States, in part because he spoke out against the hydrogen bomb. At the time, many Americans were terrified of communists. Communists ruled Soviet Russia, then the United States' greatest enemy. Oppenheimer openly criticized communism. But because some of his friends in the 1930s had been members of the communist party, he was dismissed from his job with the AEC. Many of his fellow scientists felt the government had treated Oppenheimer unfairly.

The same year, he was appointed director of the Institute of Advanced Study in Princeton, New Jersey. There he spent most of his time speaking and writing about science and its effect on the world.

In 1967, J. Robert Oppenheimer died of throat cancer at the age of sixty-two. He was remembered as one of the most influential scientists of his day. In large part because of his successful management of the Manhattan Project, the world had entered the atomic age.

Orwell, George

(1903–1950)

ENGLISH NOVELIST, ESSAYIST, AND POLITICAL AND SOCIAL COMMENTATOR

> All issues are political issues, and politics itself is a mass of lies, evasions, folly, hatred, and schizophrenia.
>
> —George Orwell, from "Politics and the English Language"

George Orwell was concerned with language as only a writer could be. Whether in satire *(Animal Farm)*, journalism *(The Road to Wigan Pier)*, or speculative fiction of terror *(1984)*, his fiction is about the destruction that political bodies can wreak on human bodies through the misuse of language.

Orwell was born Eric Blair on June 25, 1903, in Motihari, Bengal, India. His father, Richard, was a minor official in Indian customs; the family would return to England a few years after Eric's birth, and he had a conventional middle-class English upbringing for the time. After attending a fashionable prep school, he went to Eton on scholarship. For most boys that would have led to Cambridge or Oxford, but Eric failed to win a scholarship and chose a different path instead.

For the next five years, from 1922 to 1927, young Blair would serve as a member of the Indian Imperial Police in Burma. He would develop a deep ambivalence toward the experience, brilliantly portrayed in his essay, entitled "Shooting an Elephant." On the one hand, as a progressive he abhorred English imperialism and what it was doing to the Indian subcontinent; on the other, he was constantly enraged at the locals who prevented him from doing his job.

In 1927, Blair resigned from the Indian Imperial Police and, filled with guilt about his part, however small, in British imperialism, he resolved to live at the poverty level for the next few years. First in Paris, then in London, he worked at menial jobs while trying to write. Taking the pen name George Orwell (from a river in England), he published a stunning recollection of those years, *Down and Out in Paris and London* (1933), and he followed it with three novels in rapid succession.

In 1936, Orwell was commissioned by the Left Book Club to write a book about the lives of coal miners in the most depressed industrial area of England. The resulting book, *The Road to Wigan Pier* (1937), is memorable both for the extraordinarily detailed picture it presents of the hardships in the mines, and for its scathing attack on those who failed to help the men who worked in them.

The year 1936 was a watershed year for Orwell in many ways. He met and married Eileen O'Shaughnessy, and the two of them went to Spain to fight on the side of the republic in the Spanish Civil War. Rather than join the International Brigades, the Communist Party–led fighting forces that attracted most leftists, Orwell enlisted with the P.O.U.M., a Trotskyist group that opposed the Soviet Union under Joseph Stalin. Orwell would be sent home after taking a bullet in the throat in battle, but before that happened, he saw the P.O.U.M. betrayed and purged by the doctrinaire communists.

When he was recovered from his wounds—but not his disillusionment—he wrote *Homage to Catalonia* (1938), a book that still moves readers both as a portrait of men in war against tremendous odds and terrible conditions, and as a picture of political schemes that swallow up the naive and idealistic. The book was a failure at the time of its publication. Right-wingers didn't want to hear about the heroic battle to save the Spanish republic, and leftists didn't want to hear about Stalin's betrayal of that struggle. Orwell would return to this story in a 1943 essay, "Looking Back on the Spanish War," in which he would make even more explicit the connection between language used as falsehood and the terrible price that such lies inflict on the innocent.

When the war came, Orwell served in the Home Guard and worked for the Indian Overseas Service of the British Broadcasting Corporation (BBC); this latter experience may have inspired *1984*'s picture of official manipulation of the media. He also wrote and published *Animal Farm* (1945), his satire on the Russian Revolution. Again, his timing was not fortuitous. Nobody wanted to see an ally attacked during the war, and several publishers turned the book down. It would only be in later years that the book would be recognized for its incisive picture of a revolution gone haywire.

When the war ended, England continued to suffer. Rationing and food shortages would continue for some time, and the rubble of bombed-out London would take years to clear away. Orwell reflected on the state of a battered but victorious Great Britain, his unhappy battles with BBC censors, and the unremittingly brutal Stalin regime in the Soviet Union. Out of these elements he crafted one of the most famous political cautionary tales ever written, *1984*. By the time he wrote this book, in 1947, he was suffering painfully from tuberculosis. By 1950, the disease would kill him.

Orwell left behind the legacy of a profoundly skeptical leftist philosophy, one that rejected the easy terroristic solutions of a totalitarian state. He was an astute judge of intellectual dishonesty, and his vision of its role in twisting political truths is as applicable today as it was when he wrote *1984*.

Owens, James Cleveland (Jesse)

(1913–1980)

AMERICAN TRACK AND FIELD
COMPETITOR

"We all have dreams," Jesse Owens once said. Through talent and hard work, Owens fulfilled some personal dreams. He also became a lasting symbol of courage in the face of tyranny. Owens triumphed at the 1936 Olympics in Germany, where Adolf Hitler and his government were spreading hateful ideas about blacks, Jews, and other people of various religions and nationalities.

James Cleveland Owens was born on September 12, 1913, in Oakville, Alabama. His parents were poor sharecroppers, descended from slaves. James worked long hours picking cotton in the fields. He remembered, "When I got to be seven years old, I was expected to pick about a hundred pounds of cotton a day." As a child, James was often sick with pneumonia. A couple of times, he nearly died.

When he was 9, the family moved to Cleveland, Ohio. A teacher at his new school asked him his name. "J.C.," he replied, giving her his first two initials and nickname. The teacher misunderstood and wrote "Jesse" on the school records. From then on, he used that name.

Jesse began running races at age 13. One day, Olympic champion Charley Paddock, called "the world's fastest human," spoke at his school. Jesse began to dream he would compete in the Olympics someday. But he had a job after school, which meant he could not practice with the track team. So the coach began to work with him before school in the mornings.

At East Technical High School in Cleveland, he became the star sprinter. By then, Jesse had grown tall and weighed about 163 pounds. He was muscular and quick, what people call a born runner. His coach, Charlie Riley, inspired him with three guiding principles: dedication, determination, and discipline.

After high school, Owens went to Ohio State University in Columbus. Track and field athletes did not then get scholarships. To pay his expenses, he worked at night as an elevator operator and in the school library, and he waited tables by day. He practiced before work and studied whenever he could. His new coach, Larry Snyder, helped him to improve his techniques for running and jumping.

In 1935 Owens was preparing for a "Big Ten" university championship meet in Michigan. A week before the event, he was play-wrestling with a fraternity brother and injured his back. It hurt so badly Owens stopped training all week. But he competed anyway. Despite his injury, Owens won the 100-yard dash, matching the world-record time of 9.4 seconds. Ten minutes later, he broke the world record in the broad jump (now called the long jump). Then he broke the world records in the 220-yard low hurdles and the 220-yard dash. The commissioner of sports for the Big Ten universities, Kenneth Wilson, said, "He is a floating wonder, just like he had wings." It was an incredible performance.

The next year marked a triumph not only for Jesse Owens but for people around the world who valued human rights. It was 1936, just before World War II, and disturbing events were occurring. The Germans had elected Adolf Hitler, a dictator whose Nazi (National Socialist) party spread racist propaganda. The Nazis claimed that there was a superior race of white, Christian people called "Aryans" that included most Germans and some people in northern Europe. The Nazis said that people of color, Jews, Gypsies, Poles, people with physical or mental handicaps, and various others were "inferior."

With Hitler in power in Germany, many complained when Berlin was chosen as the site of the 1936 Summer Olympics. Already, the Germans had a large army. New laws there persecuted German Jews and people who spoke out against the Nazis. Some Americans wanted to boycott the Olympics, but U.S. officials decided to participate.

Owens later recalled how Hitler watched the Games each day from his private box: "When he came into the stadium, the one hundred thousand spectators would stand up and shout 'Heil Hitler' with their arms outstretched." Hitler criticized the American track team for including ten blacks and two Jews. These people could not possibly defeat the "superior" Aryans, the Nazis claimed.

Yet the black members of the U.S. team went on to win thirteen medals, including six golds. Owens was the most successful, winning gold medals for the 100-meter dash, the 200-meter dash, and the broad jump. In the 200-meter race, which included a turn, he set a world record despite the cold, windy weather. He also led the U.S. team as it set a new record to win the relay race.

As Owens darted across the red-clay track to finish the 100-meter sprint, the crowd cheered wildly. Later, sportswriters called Owens's run "perfect" from start to finish. The "Buckeye Bullet" had proven Adolf Hitler wrong, and the German leader left abruptly. Speaking about this later, Owens said, "It was all right with me. I didn't go to Berlin to shake hands with him anyway."

Married and with children to support, Owens got work as a playground instructor and did sports exhibitions in America and Europe, racing on foot against cars, motorcycles, horses, and dogs. "It was an honest living, and I had to eat," he later said of these jobs. He toured with the all-black circus basketball team and worked with youth athletic groups. He lived in Chicago for a while, then he and his family moved to Phoenix, Arizona.

Owens became a popular speaker and found he enjoyed it. He created his own public relations and marketing businesses. He often gave inspiring speeches and said he was pleased to have the opportunity to share ideas in order to help others.

Owens said that the sight of his gold medals inspired him all his life. In 1968, he helped to organize and manage the U.S. Olympic team that competed in Mexico City. He took time to write his autobiography and a book about his views on racism and civil rights.

With his wife and two of his grandchildren, Jesse Owens went back to Germany in 1972 for the Munich Olympics. Many Germans crowded around him, expressing their admiration. Owens said, "The children had read about what I had done in history books, and now they realized what it was all about." In 1976 President Gerald Ford awarded Jesse Owens the Medal of Freedom, the highest peacetime honor a citizen can receive.

In his later years, Owens exercised by swimming and walking two miles a day. But he had smoked cigarettes throughout his life and died of lung cancer in 1980 at age 66. Besides his memorable Olympic victories, Owens left a legacy of reaching out to others, especially young people. He often pointed out that sports can teach valuable lessons, such as determination, dedication, self-discipline, and effort. He said, "These things apply to everyday life. You learn not only the sport but things like respect of others, ethics in life, how you are going to live, how you treat your fellow man, how you live with your fellow man."

Paige, Leroy Robert (Satchel)

(1905–1982)

AMERICAN BASEBALL PLAYER

Like other black baseball players before 1947, Leroy "Satchel" Paige was restricted to playing in the Negro Leagues. There were many outstanding black players and sometimes exhibition matches were set up against the all-white major league teams. One of the most exciting of these games pitted Paige and his team against the St. Louis Cardinals and pitcher Dizzy Dean. For nine innings, both men pitched so well that neither team scored. The game was 0–0 as they went into extra innings. Paige remarked, "I don't know what you're going to do, Mr. Dean, but I'm not going to give up any runs if we have to stay here all night." He didn't. Paige's team finally scored in the thirteenth inning. Dean later said that he and Satchel Paige "would be worth a quarter of a million to any major league club."

Paige did not get to play in the major leagues until he was in his forties, an age by which most players have retired. Even then, his powerful arm and amazing variety of pitches allowed him to win twenty-eight games. Descriptions and records of his pitching in earlier days show he was one of the greatest pitchers of all time.

Like many children growing up poor in Mobile, Alabama, Leroy worked to help his family. At seven, he carried bags at a railroad station for a dime apiece. He designed a pole with ropes so he could carry several satchels at a time, and other boys said he was "a walking satchel tree." Satchel recalled, "Soon everybody was calling me that, you know how it is with kids and nicknames. That's when Leroy Paige became no more and Satchel Paige took over."

Later Satchel worked as a cleanup boy at a baseball park. He and his friends liked to play baseball but could not afford a ball. They used rocks instead. Satchel found he had a great throw, with unusual control over the direction. He joined the school baseball team and became the starting pitcher. After finishing school, he played on some semi-pro teams. In 1926 he began playing in the professional Negro Leagues with the Chattanooga Black Lookouts and other teams.

Paige was with the Baltimore Black Sox in 1930 when the team went around the country playing against the all-white Babe Ruth All-Stars. By then people had heard stories about Satchel Paige's remarkable "elastic arm" and ability to strike out batters. A batter on the team said it looked as if Paige was "winding up with a baseball and throwing a pea." Some people said Paige pitched with a stiff motion. A thin 6 feet, 4 inches, he had skinny legs and was told he ran "like a turkey." But Paige had superb control and seemed to never wear out. He improved his ball placement by aiming at different small targets.

Paige was a brilliant showman. He traveled around the United States and other countries, including Mexico and Puerto Rico, with his Satchel Paige All-Stars, calling himself "the world's greatest pitcher." In one famous game, Paige struck out the first batter, then waved the outfielders off the field. He struck out the second hitter and waved the infielders off the field. Then he struck out the third batter to end the inning.

Off-season, Paige was hired by teams who paid him $500 to $2,000 to pitch three innings. Batters didn't know if Paige would pitch overhand, underhand, or sidearm or if he would send them a knuckleball, curve, or one of his several styles of fastballs. Paige called one of his pitches the "be ball," saying, "It be where I want it to be." He had a "hesitation pitch," which he used to confuse batters by stopping before he followed through. He also liked pitching "thoughtful stuff"—meant to give batters "something to think about."

From 1927 to 1947 Satchel Paige pitched nearly 2,500 games. Historians believe he pitched 250 shutouts and 45 no-hitters. Once he struck out 22 batters in a single game. Star Yankee Joe DiMaggio called him "the best pitcher I ever faced."

Satchel Paige finally got his chance to play in the major leagues. Jackie Robinson signed with the Brooklyn Dodgers in 1947, breaking the color barrier. In 1948, at age forty-two, Paige joined the Cleveland Indians. People wondered if he could still pitch well. The oldest rookie ever to play baseball, Paige won 6 games and lost only 1, and helped the Indians win that year's pennant and the World Series. In his first game, he pitched two scoreless innings. In 1952 Satchel Paige, now 46, was voted to the American League All-Star team. For several years after that, he did not approach his former level. But with the Kansas City Athletics in 1965, at age fifty-nine, Paige pitched three scoreless innings. He retired in 1968, living in Kansas City with his wife and children.

He was elected to Baseball's Hall of Fame in 1971. During his long career Paige had been known for having his own remedies for sore muscles and his own particular personal philosophy of life. Among his rules for a healthy life were these: "If your stomach disputes you, lie down and pacify it with cool thoughts. Go very lightly on the vices, such as carrying on in society—the social ramble ain't restful. Don't look back; something might be gaining on you."

Palmer, Arnold

(1929–   )

AMERICAN GOLFER

People said Arnold Palmer could turn defeat into victory. He often made dramatic shots at the end of a match when the pressure was on. Attractive and friendly, "Arnie" became a celebrity on the pro golf tour. His great playing and personal appeal helped golf to become a more prestigious and high-paying sport during the 1950s and '60s. More matches were televised. Large crowds cheered "the King" on.

Arnold grew up next to a golf course in Latrobe, Pennsylvania, where his father was the greenskeeper. He often rode along on the tractor when his father cut the grass. Together they played golf, although there was a rule that they had to be done before anyone else came to use the course. Arnold could hold his own against older boys by the time he was 8. At 11, he became a caddy on the course.

Arnold was always eager to play golf after school on nice days. He learned a good grip and strong swing, honing the skills for which he became known later—power with accuracy. By 1946 he was entering tournaments, and became state junior champion three times and state amateur champion five times. He won a golf scholarship to Wake Forest University in North Carolina, but left during his senior year to spend three years in the Coast Guard.

After the service, Palmer worked as a salesman and resumed playing golf seriously. Once hot-tempered on the course, he became calm and pleasant. He had dreamed of winning a major tournament since childhood, and captured the National Amateur title in 1954. Married that year, he won a pro-amateur tournament in Florida. He and wife Winnie began traveling to tournaments in a used housetrailer they bought for $500. His decision to turn pro paid off: Arnold Palmer was the top money-winner in 1958.

Over the next few years, Palmer acquired many fans. He awed them with his robust shots and competitive style. He began to make the "miracle" shots that caused excitement during matches. His bold, all-or-nothing approach sometimes failed, but between 1958 and 1964, he dominated golf and won major tournaments. He won six individual titles in 1960, including the U.S. Open and Masters tournaments. At the Open, he hit six birdies in seven holes to win the match by just one stroke. (Birdies are two strokes below par, or the expected number of shots it would take to reach a hole). He won three more Masters and two British Opens. He also teamed with Sam Snead, Jack Nicklaus, and others to help the U.S. teams in the Ryder Cup and World Cup matches.

Palmer earned additional money from commercial endorsements and other business ventures. During the late 1960s, other players rose to challenge him. In spite of hip joint problems, he continued to play and sometimes win tournaments, often flying his own plane to get to them. In 1971 he delighted "Arnie's Army" by winning the Bob Hope Desert Classic and three other titles. He was named "Sportsman of the Decade—1960–69" by American sportswriters. Arnold Palmer said he would play "as long as I'm winning." During the 1980s and early 1990s, he was a popular player on the senior golf tour. Fans enjoy seeing him play well, and are sometimes still treated to an occasional "hole in one."

Parks, Rosa

(1913–　　)

AMERICAN CIVIL RIGHTS ACTIVIST

> We didn't have any civil rights. It was just a matter of survival . . . of existing from one day to the next. I remember going to sleep as a girl hearing the Klan ride at night and hearing a lynching and being afraid the house would burn down.
>
> —Rosa Parks, from a *Chicago Tribune* interview, recalling her childhood (1988)

On December 1, 1995, Rosa Louise McCauley Parks, an African-American seamstress, refused to give up her seat on a bus to a white man. Her arrest in Montgomery, Alabama touched off the modern civil rights movement. For more than a year, African-Americans in Montgomery refused to ride the city buses. They protested Parks' arrest and the policy of segregation that she had been charged with violating. The nonviolent protest became a model for future civil rights activists.

Rosa McCauley was born in Tuskegee, Alabama. At age two, Rosa, her younger brother, and her mother, a teacher, moved to her grandparents' farm in Pine Level, Alabama. In 1924, Rosa began attending the Montgomery Industrial School for Girls. The girls' school, founded by northern liberals, stressed the building of self-respect. The lynching and other acts of racism she experienced during her childhood would remain powerful memories throughout her life.

In 1932, Rosa McCauley married Raymond Parks, a barber who helped increase the number of African-Americans registered to vote and worked on other civil rights causes. The couple settled in Montgomery, where Rosa took classes at Alabama State College. She also did volunteer work with the Youth Council of the National Association for the Advancement of Colored People (NAACP), among other civic groups.

Parks worked as a housekeeper, a seamstress, and briefly, a life insurance agent. Every day she rode the Montgomery buses to and from work. The Montgomery buses—like most restaurants, hotels, schools, public bathrooms, and other public areas in the South at this time—were segregated. The law did not allow African-Americans to sit in the same area as white people. Whether or not the bus had any white passengers, the first ten rows of seats were reserved for whites only. African-Americans had to pay for their tickets at the front of the bus, go back outside, and reenter the bus from a rear entrance before the bus pulled away from the curb. If the white seating section was full, African-Americans had to give up their seats to allow whites to sit. The bus drivers, all white men, had the legal power to enforce these unfair seating practices. Using shouts and threats of violence, they would force African-Americans to stand or sit in the back of the bus.

Rosa Parks had her first run-in with the city's segregation policy in 1943, the same year that the Montgomery branch of the NAACP elected her secretary. When she attempted to board a bus through the front door, the bus driver kicked her off the bus. In 1955, twelve years later, she had a more famous encounter with the very same bus driver. On that day, Parks and three other African-Americans were sitting in the first row of their section of the bus. Because white passengers had filled their section, the driver told all four African-Americans to stand so that one white man could sit. After hesitating for a moment, the other three stood up. Parks, however, tired from her day's work as a seamstress in a department store, refused to stand. The driver called two police officers onto the bus to arrest her. Rosa Parks was jailed and fined $14 for breaking the segregation law.

E.D. Nixon, the former president of the Alabama and Montgomery branches of the NAACP, asked Parks to appeal the case. Despite the objections of her mother and husband, who feared for her life, Parks agreed to challenge the segregation law. The Women's Political Council, an African-American women's group, organized a protest against Parks' arrest and trial. The group handed out thousands of leaflets calling for a one-day boycott on the day of her trial. African-American church leaders, led by Martin Luther King, Jr., supported the boycott. Although normally about 70 percent of city bus passengers were African-Americans, very few rode the buses that day. That night, church leaders and the community formed the Montgomery Improvement Association (MIA), with King as its president. The group decided to continue the boycott until the bus company met their demands. At first, the MIA did not demand an end to segregation, only an end to the policy that forced African-Americans to give up their seats. The group proposed that whites take seats starting from the front of the bus, and that African-Americans take seats beginning at the back.

The seats would fill up on a first-come, first-served basis, regardless of color. The MIA also demanded more courteous drivers, and the assignment of African-American drivers on bus routes where most passengers were African-Americans.

The Montgomery bus boycott lasted for more than a year, hurting the bus companies financially. In 1956, city police began harassing drivers of carpools: pulling them over, delaying them, and sometimes issuing bogus tickets. Some African-Americans who walked to work suffered from beatings or attacks from white passengers in passing cars, who threw bricks and rotten food at them. Parks, like many of the protesters, lost her job. She also received threatening calls that she took seriously after King's house was bombed. In February 1956, Parks's lawyer filed a federal suit challenging the legality of the segregation law. Later that year, the Supreme Court, the highest court of the land, declared that the segregation law violated the U.S. Constitution's guarantee of equal rights for all. In December, a Supreme Court order ended the practice of segregated seating on Montgomery buses. Heading the boycott made Martin Luther King, Jr., a national civil rights leader. And the boycott that Rosa Parks had sparked set the standard for all civil rights protests to come.

The following year, Parks moved to Detroit, Michigan with her husband and mother. A celebrity, Parks made many appearances over the next three decades to raise funds for the NAACP. She also joined King's Southern Christian Leadership Conference (SCLC), working to foster social change through nonviolent protests like the Birmingham boycott. But life in Detroit was not easy for Parks. In 1959, the couple lost their apartment after both she and her husband were hospitalized. By taking in sewing while her husband worked as a caretaker, Parks saved enough money to move into another apartment in 1961.

In 1965, John Conyers, Jr., a member of Congress from Michigan, hired Parks to run his office—a job she would hold for over twenty-five years. She continued to make about two dozen public appearances a year, speaking on the civil rights movement on behalf of the NAACP or SCLC. In 1987, she founded the Rosa and Raymond Parks Institute for Self-Development. The institute offers guidance and career and leadership training to young African-Americans.

Pauling, Linus

(1901–1994)

AMERICAN CHEMIST AND
SOCIAL ACTIVIST

The question of peace or war has now become so important as to overshadow all other questions—it is of a far greater order of magnitude than anything else.

> —Linus Pauling, in a letter to
> scientist Leo Szilard

Linus Carl Pauling was born near Portland, Oregon. As a young boy, Linus enjoyed watching his father, a pharmacist, mix up drugs in his store. The boy soon built his own laboratory in his basement, even though he had little money to buy supplies for his experiments. Remembering these day, Pauling recently said, "I very early began to be interested in the nature of the universe."

When he graduated from high school, Pauling made plans to go on to college. His mother tried to talk him out of the idea. Since the death of Pauling's father nine years earlier, the family had been struggling to make ends meet. She wanted Linus to try to build a more secure future by finding a full-time job. In the end, Pauling ignored her advice. As he explained to his mother, "I want to learn, Mama."

While working two jobs, Pauling began studying chemistry at Oregon Agricultural College in 1917. After he earned his diploma, he continued his education at the California Institute of Technology, one of the best schools for science in the United States. In 1925, Caltech awarded him a Ph.D. with high honors.

Pauling spent several years in Europe, where many scientists were studying chemical bonds. After learning about their work, he returned to the United States and took a job on Caltech's faculty. There he wrote *The Nature of the Chemical Bond and the Structure of Molecules and Crystals* (1939). One of the most important scientific textbooks of the 20th century, it is still the best source of information on chemical bonding.

During World War II (1939–45), Pauling volunteered to help the U.S. Army. He researched explosive chemicals that improved the military's rockets and gunpowder. At the same time, Pauling began studying blood cells and their elements, particularly antibodies. He discovered that antibodies have certain shapes. They latched themselves onto viruses similar to the way a key fits a lock. The idea proved very helpful to medical researchers. They were beginning to treat diseases with antibodies made in test tubes. Because of Pauling, they learned that their artificial antibodies had to be a particular shape to kill viruses in the human body.

Soon after the war, Pauling made an even more important discovery. For many years, he had been researching protein molecules. Protein is a substance found in all living cells of plants and animals. Protein molecules are made up of thousands, or even millions, of atoms. Their structure is extremely complicated, but Pauling knew if it could be understood, scientists would know much more about the workings of many parts of the body, including muscles, blood, and bones.

Sick in bed from a cold, Pauling was thinking about the problem one day in early 1948. In his classes, he often made models out of plastic balls and string to explain the structure of molecules for his students. Pauling then did not have any plastic balls with him, so he began to draw a model on a piece of paper. Folding and twisting the paper, Pauling suddenly came to understand the basic structure of a protein molecule. His crude model made him realize that the molecules were shaped like a helix, or spiral. For this revelation, Pauling would be awarded the 1954 Nobel Prize in Chemistry.

A year after his discovery, Pauling himself applied the new knowledge to a medical problem. It help him learn the cause of sickle-cell anemia, a fatal illness that afflicts some people of African descent. Although there is still no cure for sickle-cell anemia, his work has allowed doctors to provide better treatment to its victims.

In the late 1940s and early 1950s, Pauling began devoting much of his time to a new endeavor—promoting world peace. He courageously spoke out against the atomic bomb, doing everything he could to alert the public to the dangers of this new weapon. During the war, scientists in the United States had invented the atomic bomb. Within several years, the Soviet Union also started building one. The bombs were so powerful that either of these powers had the ability to blow up the entire world.

Government officials were angry at Pauling for his stance. Claiming his ideas posed a threat to the nation's security, they would not issue him a passport. Without this document, Pauling was unable to travel to any foreign country. For many years, his research was hampered because he could not go to Europe and work with other scientists there.

Despite these hardships, Pauling believed that working to ban the atomic bomb was his duty. In 1963, his efforts earned him the Nobel Prize for Peace. He was the second person in history to win two Nobel Prizes.

Pauling's research in the 1960s and 1970s focused on the relationship between nutrition and mental illness. In the course of this work, he came to believe that vitamin-C can cure colds. He also argued that the vitamin might be a key to finding a cure for cancer. In the years before his death in 1994, Pauling studied AIDS (Acquired Immune Deficiency Syndrome) and heart disease at the Linus Pauling Institute at Palo Alto, California.

Pauling has been called one of the world's greatest scientists. Combining a keen knowledge of chemistry, physics, and biology, he made extraordinary discoveries in a variety of fields. He also inspired other scientists to openly discuss the possible effects of their work. As Pauling said, scientists have a "responsibility . . . [to explain] those problems of society in which science is involved closely."

Pavarotti, Luciano

(1 9 3 5 –   )

ITALIAN OPERA SINGER

Considered for many years to be the "new Caruso," tenor Luciano Pavarotti is one of the most famous opera singers in the world today. He was born in 1935 in the small country town of Modena in the Po River valley of Italy. Pavarotti told the *Saturday Review* in 1973: "Everybody sings. We have an old opera house seating twelve hundred where visiting companies from Bologna or Parma put on a few performances a year, and the local forces mount an annual production." Pavarotti's father, a baker, sang in the chorus of local productions and, according to Pavarotti, had a beautiful tenor voice. Despite Pavarotti's current size (he weighs well over three hundred pounds), he was an athlete and good at soccer as a youngster. But he was, as he has said, "born to be a singer. Our house was full of records, and I went to the opera a lot." He also sang in the children's choir of his local church.

Although his mother wanted him to become an accountant, Pavarotti decided to become a teacher. He taught elementary school for two years before trying out for a professional singing career. When he made the decision to pursue his singing, Pavarotti took a job selling insurance, so that he would have more freedom to study voice.

Pavarotti made his professional debut in 1961, after winning the Concorso Internationale prize, in the leading role of Rodolfo in Puccini's *La Bohème* at Teatro Municipale. During the next few years he sang in opera houses all over Italy. Then he went abroad to Holland, Austria, Switzerland, Spain, and England.

In 1965, Pavarotti toured with the great Australian soprano Joan Sutherland, and it was from her that he learned his breathing techniques. Throughout the 1960s, Pavarotti sang at the great opera houses of the world in such operas as *Rigoletto, Madama Butterfly,* and *Manon Lescaut.* When Pavarotti made his debut at New York's Metropolitan Opera in 1968, *The New York Times* wrote: "Mr. Pavarotti triumphed principally through the natural beauty of his voice—a bright, open instrument with a nice metallic ping up top that warms into an even, burnished luster in mid-range. Any tenor who can toss off high C's with such abandon, successfully negotiate delicate diminuendo effects, and attack phrases so fervently is going to win over any *La Bohème (The Bohemian)* audience, and Pavarotti had them eating out of his hand."

Forced by an attack of influenza to withdraw from his Met engagement in December 1968, Pavarotti returned to Italy and did not come back to America for three years. During that time, he sang in Rome and made several recordings, including *La Fille du Regiment (The Girl of the Regiment),* with Joan Sutherland; *Lucia di Lammermoor,* and *Rigoletto.* He also made several recital disks.

When Pavarotti returned to the United States in 1971, his American career really took off. His operatic performances onstage, on records, and on television made him a matinee idol. In the late 1970s, he was so popular that he starred in the film *Yes, Giorgio.* Critics and audiences agreed that he was better as an opera singer than as a film star. Pavarotti went back to the stage, where he can dazzle audiences with his voice.

Recently, he has joined forces with tenors Placido Domingo and José Carreras to form "The Three Tenors." Together they have performed in concert, on television, and on best-selling videos and recordings.

Pavlova, Anna

(1881–1931)

RUSSIAN BALLET DANCER

More than sixty years after her death, Anna Pavlova is still considered the ideal female ballet dancer. She is sometimes called the greatest ballerina of the first third of the twentieth century. She is what ballerinas today aspire to be.

Pavlova was born in 1881 in St. Petersburg, Russia, to poor parents. She was born prematurely. As a result, she was frail and often ill. Despite her physical weakness, Pavlova wanted to be a dancer. When she was ten years old, she was accepted into the Imperial School of Ballet. She became an outstanding student both in dancing and in academic subjects. Right from the start, Pavlova drew the attention of her teachers, Paul Gerdt and Christian Johannsen, who predicted a brilliant future for her.

Pavlova made her debut as a child, and she danced her first important role in the ballet *The Two Stars*. In 1899, after graduating from the School of Ballet, Pavlova was accepted in the Maryinsky Theatre. After several years there, she was performing solos. She went on tour with the company to Moscow and Western Europe. In 1908, she performed in Paris under the Russian producer Sergei Diaghilev in the troupe that was considered the Ballet Russe.

Pavlova danced her most famous role during that time: the dying Swan in *Swan Lake*. The image of Pavlova in that role still remains etched in ballet lovers' memories, if only from photographs and imitations. Pavlova chose not to be part of a company, but to tour on her own. Around the world, she became known as "the Dance," "the Swan," and "the Epitome of Movement." She was responsible for the choreography for fourteen ballets. The best known of these were *Snowflakes* (1915), *Dragonfly* (1915), and *Autumn Leaves* (1919).

After World War I, for the next eleven years Pavlova toured all over the world. Her image was spread worldwide through her film appearance in the silent movie *The Dumb Girl of Portici,* and through her many newspaper publicity interviews. Pavlova's views on dance, fashion, health, and physical culture fascinated newspaper readers everywhere. She also became the most imitated person in the arts. Some satire or spoof of Pavlova appeared in almost every edition of the major Broadway shows from 1910 to 1930, and in many of the musical comedies staged in London.

Peary, Robert Edwin

(1856–1920)

AMERICAN ARCTIC EXPLORER

> We were now at the end of the last long march of the upward journey. Yet with the Pole actually in sight, I was too weary to take the last few steps. The accumulated weariness of all those days and nights of forced marches and insufficient sleep, constant peril, and anxiety, seemed to roll across me all at once. I was actually too exhausted to realize at the moment that my life's purpose had been achieved.
>
> —Robert Edwin Peary, *The North Pole,* 1910

Robert Edwin Peary was born on May 6, 1856, in Cresson, Pennsylvania. He was an only child. His father died when he was three years old, and his mother moved with him to Maine, where he grew up. Peary later declared that when he was a young man, his favorite book was an account of Arctic adventures by American polar explorer Elisha Kent Kane.

Peary attended Bowdoin College in Maine and then joined the Civil Engineering Corps of the U.S. Navy. Although later he liked to be called commander Peary, he never actually held a naval rank. He remained a civilian employee of the Navy throughout his career.

Peary's work took him to Washington, where he met and became engaged to Josephine Diebitsch, the daughter of a scholar at the Smithsonian Institution. In the years to come, she would travel to the Arctic at Peary's side. In 1887, Peary was chosen to head a survey team that was supposed to find a route for a canal through the Central American country of Nicaragua. Peary was driven by an all-consuming desire to make his mark in the world. "I *must* have fame!" he wrote to his mother on another occasion.

Fame did not await Peary in Nicaragua, however. Although he surveyed a suitable route, the U.S. government decided to build the canal through Panama instead. Seeking some new endeavor in which to prove himself, Peary returned to his earlier fascination with the Arctic. Peary decided to seek his fame in the North. He would start by exploring Greenland; he wanted to be the first person to travel across the width of that huge northern island. Peary was bitterly disappointed when Norwegian explorer Fridtjof Nansen beat him to his goal by making the first crossing of Greenland. His response was to choose a new goal. He would explore northern Greenland in the hope of finding a route to the North Pole.

Peary married Jo Diebitsch in 1888 and began making plans for a trip to Greenland. In 1891, on leave from his job, he launched the first in a series of expeditions that would occupy the next twenty years of his life. He had an invaluable companion: Matthew Henson, an African-American man whom he had hired as a servant before going to Nicaragua in 1887. Henson accompanied every one of Peary's expeditions and became a noteworthy polar traveler in his own right. Jo Peary accompanied her husband and his small team of companions to Greenland on the first few expeditions.

Between 1891 and 1902, Peary made three expeditions to Greenland and nearby Ellesmere Island, the northernmost island in Arctic Canada. His and Jo's first child, Marie Anighito Peary, was born in Greenland in September of 1983, at the beginning of the long Arctic winter night. "When the earliest ray of the returning sun pierced through the window of our tiny room," wrote Peary later, "she reached for the golden bar as other children reach for a beautiful toy."

In 1895, during his second Greenland expedition, Peary made a three-month-long sled journey with Henson across northern Greenland. Their observations settled a long-standing geographical question and proved that Greenland is an island.

Peary spent part of 1896 and 1897 obtaining some prized specimens for the American Museum of Natural History. The money paid by the American Museum of Natural History for the specimens helped cover the cost of Peary's expeditions.

Peary spent most of his 1898–1902 expedition on Ellesmere Island, searching for a route to the pole. Laid up in camp after frostbite made several of his toes snap off, he fiercely scratched into the wooden wall of his bunk the words *"Inveniam viam aut faciam"*—Latin for "I shall find a way or make one." Eventually, Peary lost eight of his toes to frostbite. Yet during his years on Ellesmere, he tried twice to reach the pole. He had to turn back each time. In April 1902, after several weeks of hacking his way across the ice pack, he realized he had only advanced eighty-two miles toward the pole. He headed for home and wrote in his journal, "The game is off. My dream of sixteen years is ended." Peary had, however, reached a point farther north than anyone had gone before.

When he returned to Ellesmere Island in 1905, Peary had a new plan, which would come to be called the "Peary system." Instead of a sustained journey by a single party, he would use relays of several dogsled teams to establish supply bases in a long line stretching toward the pole. Then, from the end of the supply line, a small team could make the final dash to the pole and back.

Peary and Henson tried this system in the spring of 1906. From Cape Sheridan, their camp on the north coast of Ellesmere, they had to cover a distance of 422 miles to the pole. But weather and ice conditions were against them. Broad openings in the ice, called leads, prevented them from traveling in a straight line, and storms kept them pinned down for days at a time. Once again, Peary had to turn back short of the pole, but he was confident that he had set a new record for the farthest north reached by any explorer. On the way home, he collected letters from Jo. One of them read, "I shall not let you go away again. . . . Your children have some claim upon you also. . . . Just think, life is nearly over and we have missed most of it."

Despite this plea, Peary immediately announced plans for another attempt on the pole. He sailed for Ellesmere in the *Roosevelt* in the summer of 1908. There was a special urgency to this expedition. Peary was fifty-two years old, and he knew that he could not safely continue his battle with the Arctic much longer. In addition, Frederick Cook, now a rival explorer, had gone north earlier, and Peary believed that Cook was planning to try for the pole.

The polar team of 1908–09 consisted of Peary, Henson, and five others from the United States or Canada, together with fifty or more Inuit recruited from Greenland. They established a base camp at Cape Columbia on the Ellesmere coast, 413 miles south of the pole. At the beginning of March, the push north began. Divided into seven teams of men and dogs, the crews carried food and fuel to a series of relay bases. Plagued by soft ice and bad weather, they kept going. By April 1, Peary, Henson, and four Inuit were ready for the final run that was to take them to the pole. According to Peary's account, they found smooth ice and easy going in the final stretch, and they made remarkably good speed. They reached the pole, said Peary, on April 6, 1909. One of the last great geographic prizes had been claimed.

Peary, Henson, and the others returned to Cape Columbia, and then to Cape Sheridan and the *Roosevelt*. On September 6, the *Roosevelt* reached a harbor in Labrador, Canada, that had a telegraph station. Peary sent telegrams to Jo, to the Peary Arctic Club, to the *New York Times,* and to the Associated Press, announcing his conquest of the pole. To his dismay and fury, however, another claim had already been made. Just five days earlier, Frederick Cook had announced that he had reached the pole on April 21, 1908—almost a year before Peary. Thus began what one journalist called "the dispute of the century."

At first, public and scientific opinion tilted toward Cook, whose claim was supported by the *New York Herald.* Cook was an easygoing, likable man, while Peary seemed harsh and aloof to some. But when Cook was shown to have faked an earlier claim about climbing Alaska's Mt. McKinley, his Arctic story began to look suspicious. Although Cook continued to have some supporters, by 1910 most people regarded him as a fraud.

Now Peary emerged as the true hero of the pole. The National Geographic Society—which had been one of Peary's sponsors—supported his claim, and so did England's Royal Geographical Society (by a very close vote). There was enough doubt about the issue that the Naval Affairs Committee of the United States Congress ordered a committee to investigate Peary's report and determine whether he had really reached the North Pole. Although Peary refused to turn over his expedition journals and notes, the committee finally declared that Peary had indeed reached the pole. But some polar historians, including Canadian scholar Pierre Berton, have pointed out that the committee's decision was not based on any scientific evidence.

The dispute with Cook faded from memory, and Peary was generally accepted as the discoverer of the North Pole. His book *The North Pole,* published in 1910, established him as a public hero. He retired from public life and died in Washington, D.C., in 1920. He was buried in the National Cemetery in Arlington, Virginia.

Did Peary really reach the pole? Although no reputable scholar now believes that Cook reached the pole, the fact that Cook's claim was a fraud does not mean that Peary's was necessarily true. Some experts have questioned Peary's claim, pointing out that the distances he said he had covered appear unrealistic, and that there are curious gaps in his expedition journal, which was not released to the public until the 1980s. The verdict of most modern experts is that Peary's claim was honest, and that if he did not reach the exact spot of the pole, he certainly came very close to it. Peary unquestionably deserves recognition as one of America's greatest—and most determined—explorers.

Pei, I.M.

(1917–)

CHINESE-BORN AMERICAN ARCHITECT

> It's not just a concept, but the way that concept is executed that is important.
>
> —I.M. Pei, explaining his architecture (1979)

Ieoh Ming Pei was born in China on April 26, 1917. While attending a school run by Protestant missionaries, Pei began thinking about visiting the United States. In 1935, at the age of seventeen, he enrolled in the University of

Pennsylvania in Philadelphia. Pei began studying architecture, but he felt that he was not as advanced as his classmates, so he transferred to the Massachusetts Institute of Technology (MIT) and studied engineering. The dean of the architectural school at MIT noticed a great deal of talent in Pei's work and convinced him to resume his study in architecture.

On a summer vacation in 1938, Pei drove to Wisconsin with the hope of meeting the great architect Frank Lloyd Wright. Wright was not home, however, and Pei continued to drive across country until he arrived in Los Angeles, where he spent the rest of the summer working in a local architect's office.

Despite doubts about his own ability, Pei was an outstanding student. He earned his bachelor of architecture degree in 1940 and was awarded the American Institute of Architects Medal.

In 1942, Pei married Eileen Loo, who was planning to enroll in the landscape architecture program at Harvard University in the fall. Pei also decided to enroll in Harvard and entered the Graduate School of Design. He received his degree in 1946.

Pei became an American citizen in 1948, and traveled to New York to meet William Zeckendorf, the biggest real estate developer in America. Zeckendorf not only loved buying and selling buildings, he was also interested in building them. He was looking for young architects to work for him and immediately hired Pei.

Zeckendorf was an energetic man with big ideas and Pei soon had more work than he alone could handle. He convinced Zeckendorf to hire a larger staff of architects and they began working on larger projects, designing not just individual buildings, but whole sections of cities.

Their first large project was in Denver, Colorado, in 1952, a project that took more than fifteen years to complete. Pei and his staff designed Courthouse Square, the first structure in the United States to combine stores, hotels, offices, and parking spaces in a unified design.

By the late 1950s, Zeckendorf had tried to buy and sell too much property and Pei left the company in order to spare the real estate developer more expense.

Pei's new firm, I.M. Pei and Associates, received its first commission for the National Center for Atmospheric Research (NCAR) in Boulder, Colorado. Far from a design for a city, the NCAR buildings were located atop an isolated hill, and Pei relied upon an ancient South American tribe, the Incas, for inspiration for his modern buildings.

In 1964, Pei was selected as the architect for the President John F. Kennedy Library. His design for the building met with harsh criticism and the project was a long struggle for Pei and his staff. No one involved in the project could make up their minds, resulting in the selection of three different sites for the library. Pei was required to design a different building for each site, as he was concerned with creating a harmony between the building and the surrounding landscape. Finally, the library was dedicated in 1979 on Boston Harbor and many critics called the building a failure.

Pei's design for the East Building of the National Gallery of Art in Washington, D.C. was a triumph, however, and remains Pei's most famous work. Critic Robert Hughes wrote that the building would "take its place among the great museum buildings of the past hundred years." For his design, Pei was awarded the Gold Medal of the American Institute of Architects in 1978.

The same year, Pei finally returned to China, not to live, but to work. He had been hired to design a hotel in Beijing, in which he was able to use the garden from his childhood as an inspiration.

Upon returning to New York, Pei was commissioned to design a new convention center, named after a former Senator, Jacob K. Javits. New York was struggling to recover from financial disaster and the large-scale project again put Pei in the middle of a controversy. The main space of the convention center was large enough to hold the Statue of Liberty, or two 747 jets.

The Javits Center was the first building of I. M. Pei and Associates for which Pei was not credited for the main design, but the building's use of space and basic geometric patterns reveal Pei's influence and guidance.

Pei's next project again caused considerable controversy and debate as Pei was commissioned to design a new entrance to the famous Louvre museum in Paris, France. The seventy-one-foot glass pyramid that the architect designed angered many people around the world; the idea of doing anything to the famous building was unthinkable. The building had been changed many times over the years, however, and as the museum added more works to its collection, it had to expand and grow.

Pei studied the entire history of the Louvre and decided that the best entrance would be in the center courtyard, and the idea of the pyramid came from Pei's intense study of the history of French architecture, which often used the triangle and other simple shapes. When the new entrance was finally completed, many of the people who had criticized Pei now congratulated him. Some newspapers even recalled how many people throughout the world protested the construction of the Eiffel Tower in 1887 and called it a "pile of iron junk."

Pei's buildings have always caused criticism and controversy, but he has remained one of the most prolific modern architects. His firm has designed more than fifty buildings, including several of the largest civic and corporate constructions of the 1980s. Pei has also received a number of awards and honors, including his election as a member of the National Institute of Arts and Letters in 1961 and the American Institute of Architects in 1978.

Pelé

(1940–   )

BRAZILIAN SOCCER PLAYER

I always have a spare pair of pants under-
neath.

> —Pelé, describing adoring fans
> who mob him and tear his
> clothes off as "souvenirs"

Few athletes in history have captivated a world audience like Pelé. The soccer
player, whose full name was Edson Arantes do Nascimentos, scored 1,086
goals in his sixteen-year career, and led the Brazilian national team to three
World Cup victories. His true contribution to soccer, however, was the excitement and joy he brought to the game. His infectious enthusiasm helped to pop-
ularize the sport worldwide.

Edson Arantes do Nascimentos was born on October 23, 1940, in the village
of Tres Coracoes in the state of Minas Gerais, Brazil. His father, Dondinho, was
a professional soccer player for a small local team. Though his own career was
cut short by a knee injury, he passed on his love of the game to his son Edson.
As a child, Edson spent many hours kicking around an old ball made of rags,
learning how to control it with his nimble foot.

Edson received the nickname "Pelé" when he was about eight. Some neighborhood children gave it to him, and he never knew what it meant. At first, it
bothered Edson to be called by that name, but like a lot of childhood nicknames, this one stuck. Later it would become one of the most recognizable
names in the world.

When Pelé was ten, he left school to work on soccer full-time. He joined a
local athletic club team and began to make his mark in competition. He also attracted the attention of Waldemar de Brito, a retired player from São Paulo. De
Brito began working with Pelé to help him refine his fundamental skills and realize his potential. At age fifteen, Pelé signed on with the Santos soccer team of
São Paulo, on a trial basis at a salary of $75 a month.

In Pele's first game for Santos, he scored four goals in a 7–1 victory. "I was
scared of failing," he said later of his emotions before his debut. They were
only the first four of the 1,086 goals he would put into the nets in his career, but
they were among the most important. They announced to all of Brazil that a

major new talent had arrived. Almost overnight Pelé evolved from the rookie who bought soda for the older members of the team to someone the other players looked up to and idolized. The next year, Pelé was a starter on the Santos first team. In 1958, he scored 125 goals for the season. Soon after that, he was selected to play for Brazil's national team at the World Cup tournament.

Some soccer stars are one-dimensional talents. They can kick hard, or elude defenders, or they are expert at the passing game. Pele's genius was that he was good at all of these things. At many of them, he was the best in the world. Pele's ball-handling, for example, was so expert that he would routinely weave his way around three defenders on his way to the goal. He could do some impossible, jaw-dropping things, like rebounding his passes off his opponents and back to himself as he drove toward the net for a score. He was superior with the header (a shot using one's head) and was deadly on the penalty kick. Perhaps most exciting of all was his ability to stop a ball in midair, gain control of it, and explode toward the goal. Much like Michael Jordan in basketball, Pelé had moves that no one could defend.

Pelé saved some of his best performances for World Cup competition. In 1958, he scored six goals in the final three games after sitting out the opening rounds with an injury. The amazing feat gave Brazil its first World Cup championship and made Pelé an international superstar. Injuries prevented him from topping that performance in 1962, though Brazil won the cup for the second consecutive time. In 1966, it was constant, brutal fouling by opponents that kept Pelé out of the action. At the 1970 World Cup in Mexico, however, Pelé added some more heroics to his growing legend, as he netted four important goals, including a game-winning header against Italy in the final that gave Brazil an unprecedented third victory in soccer's most prestigious tournament.

Pelé became soccer's first legitimate international superstar. When he appeared at matches in foreign countries, fans would mob him after the game and attempt to rip off pieces of his shirt and shorts for souvenirs. He responded good-naturedly. "It happens all over the world," he said with a shrug. "It's a pleasure for me." In perhaps the most powerful example of his influence, when Pelé visited the war-torn African nation of Biafra, the two sides in the civil struggle called off fighting for two days until he left.

While an international audience watched him every four years in the World Cup, Pelé displayed his skills to Brazilian fans on a yearly basis. Unlike many soccer stars, Pelé did not drift from club to club as the lure of big-money contracts compelled him. He stuck with Santos, and was able to record his 1,000th career goal for the squad on November 19, 1969. It was one of the greatest news events in Brazil's history. One hundred thousand fans watched in adulation as Pelé—who averaged more than a goal a game over the course of his career—reached a milestone few had thought possible.

Pelé retired from Brazilian soccer after the 1974 season. It was a bittersweet moment for world soccer fans, but happily they did not have to wait long for his return. In 1975, the Brazilian legend signed a three-year contract with the New York Cosmos of the North American Soccer League (NASL). Their mutual goal was to help spread a love of soccer in America. Over the next three seasons, they accomplished that mission, as Pelé paced the Cosmos to two NASL titles. A soccer boom erupted in the U.S. in the late 1970s, as children inspired by Pelé's example rushed to the fields to learn the game.

Pelé's impact on world soccer is truly incalculable. Many people may never have given a second thought to the game if not for his electrifying example. Numbers, impressive as they are, do not do justice to a player who is universally regarded as the greatest in the history of his sport.

Perkins, Frances

(1882–1965)

UNITED STATES SECRETARY
OF LABOR

Frances Perkins was born in Boston, Massachusetts on April 10, 1882. Her father, who owned a twine factory, was a conservative New England Republican. In 1902, Perkins graduated from Mount Holyoke College, where she studied chemistry and biology. She spent two years doing social work for the Episcopal Church and then took a job teaching chemistry at a girls' school near Chicago. In Chicago, she became involved with Hull House, the famous center for social work and social activism founded by Jane Addams. During the six months she lived there, she observed the tenements and sweatshops in the surrounding neighborhood, and what she saw changed her life. She abandoned chemistry and biology and returned to the University of Pennsylvania to study sociology and economics, then received her master's degree from Columbia University in 1910.

In 1911, now living in New York, Perkins witnessed the fire at the Triangle Shirtwaist Company, in which 146 young working women were killed because there was no safe exit from the building. The experience affected her deeply, and over the next twenty years she held a series of increasingly important jobs involving worker safety, child welfare, and women's rights. In 1912, Perkins left the New York Consumers League to become executive secretary of the New York Committee on Safety. At the same time, she served as director of the New York State Factory Commission. In 1919, she joined the New York State Industrial Commission, and in 1921 she was named director of the Council on Immigrant Education. In 1929, Governor Franklin D. Roosevelt appointed her industrial commissioner of New York.

When Roosevelt became President in 1933, he appointed Perkins secretary of labor. Perkins set about to reform the department. She dismissed a group of special agents who had been hired to spy on the labor movement in search of radicals and aliens. She strengthened the Bureau of Labor Statistics so that accurate counts could be kept of unemployed workers.

Perkins's term of service had its frustrations, however. Many conservative labor leaders would not deal with a woman. Many of Roosevelt's New Deal programs, though they affected labor, were run by independent government agencies not under her control or influence. Nor was Perkins able to prevent the breakup of the largest labor organization, the American Federation of Labor (AFL), from which dissidents had split to form the rival Congress of Industrial Organizations (CIO). In 1940, her enemies in Congress called for her impeachment because she refused to support the deportation of the radical labor leader Harry Bridges. She continued to serve in the cabinet until 1945, after which she served on the Civil Service Commission until 1953. She died in May 1965.

Perón, Eva

(1919–1952)

ARGENTINIAN POLITICAL FIGURE

Eva Perón, powerful wife of leader Juan Perón, was born Maria Eva Duarte, on May 7, 1919, in the Buenos Aires province of Argentina. Her father died when she was very young, and her mother ran a boardinghouse to make a living. Eva, who was known for most of her life as Evita, decided at a young age to become an actress, and she moved to the capital, Buenos Aires, when she was sixteen.

In 1943, after gaining a modest amount of fame in radio, she met Colonel Juan D. Perón, the government's secretary of labor and a man who had ambitions to rule Argentina. In 1945, after a group of army officers attempted to imprison Perón to prevent him from gaining any further power, Evita organized demonstrations demanding his freedom. They were married a short time later. It was his second marriage; his first wife had died.

Evita played an important role in her husband's success because she understood the concerns of the people who made up his support base. Identifying with the poor because of her own background, Evita mounted ambitious efforts to gain suffrage rights for women to vote (achieved in 1947) and to solidify her husband's support among workers. With increasing power, she established controls over the labor unions designed to give Perón support. She arranged to have dismissed any officials who disagreed with his, or her, policies. She supported the workers in calling for higher pay and better working conditions, and spent hours each day meeting with their representatives. She also was put in charge of the country's ministry of health.

The result of Evita's efforts was Perón's enormous popularity among the masses of people in Argentina. (That support remained strong later through Perón's many years in exile, and it was still there when he returned to be elected president a second term in the 1970s.) There were those who opposed Perón, however, especially people from the country's upper classes, and also various elements of the military. When, in 1951, Perón wanted his wife to run for election as vice-president, she said no out of fear of the political consequences. She was also seriously ill by then with cancer. Evita Perón died on July 26, 1952, when she was thirty-three years old.

Picasso, Pablo

(1881–1973)

SPANISH PAINTER AND SCULPTOR

The individual who insists on being an original wastes his time and deceives himself; if he attains something it is but an imitation of what he likes.

> —Pablo Picasso, in a statement to Jaime Sabartes

Picasso, one of the most imaginative painters of all time, was involved with nearly every art movement of the first half of the twentieth century. He worked in a variety of styles and media, and his work in all of them is pleasing, original, and always appealing to the eye.

Pablo Picasso was born on October 25, 1881, in Málaga, Spain. His father was a painter and art teacher who taught him the rudiments of painting. When Picasso mastered the skills that his father taught him, demonstrating that he had the most talent of the two, his father gave Picasso all of his brushes and other supplies and gave up painting for good. Picasso went on to become the single most important artist of the twentieth century.

Picasso hated school as a child, preferring to be in the company of his parents. When his father dropped him off at school on his way to the museum where he would paint, Picasso would ask to keep the paintbrushes so he would be sure his father would come back for him.

Picasso was so poor a student that he did not learn to write very well when he was young. Instead of writing letters to his friends and family, he used to send them "newspapers" that he had drawn by hand, with titles, headlines, and illustrations representing things he had been seeing and doing. He signed his name as the "editor."

Starting in 1892, Picasso attended the School of Fine Arts in Caruna, Spain, where he demonstrated his unusual abilities. After four years at Caruna, he studied art for two years in Barcelona, and then spent two more in Madrid before setting up his own art studio in Barcelona, in 1898. As he realized, however, the most important city in Europe as far as art was concerned was Paris, so Picasso made several visits there. He was so impressed with the vitality of Parisian art that he moved there in 1904 after his preliminary visits, accompanied by his friend Carlos Casagemas.

Although the art of painting was thriving in Paris, Picasso found life as a painter difficult at first. He had very little money and lived in the poor sections of the city while trying to support himself with his painting. During this time, his friend Casagemas committed suicide over a broken love affair. Picasso's unhappiness was evident in the paintings he did during that time, known as his Blue Period. These paintings depict the lives of poor people and often use shades of blue to emphasize their somber mood.

The next stage of Picasso's development is often referred as his Rose Period. The paintings of this time are less sad, but only slightly. Many depict circus performers in attitudes during moments when they are not performing. There is a hopeful, dreamy quality about these works.

While much of Picasso's work is personal and reflects his own feelings and perceptions, he absorbed a great deal from other painters he met who exposed him to new attitudes about art that he did not learn in school. He made friends with other painters, such as Henri Matisse, Georges Braque, and André Derain, as well as writers, especially Guillaume Apollinaire. Following the example of these modern artists, Picasso began to experiment with his art.

Whereas Matisse's new approach to painting involved a more aggressive use of color, Picasso experimented with form. He began his experiments by making his paintings look somewhat like sculpture, exaggerating the illusion of three-dimensional mass. He used angular lines with heavy shadows to paint people with stout bodies and thick arms and legs. These paintings reflected Picasso's interest in African and ancient Greek sculpture.

Picasso continued to experiment with form by trying to unify the things he painted with the background of his paintings. He did this by depicting them from different points of view at the same time and making these different facets part of a design that included the area around them, a technique that came to be known as cubism.

One of the first cubist paintings ever made was Picasso's *Women of Avignon* (1907). The angular bodies of the women in this painting seem folded into interesting shapes, like the drapery that surrounds them. The painting includes some fruit on a table that is tipped at an angle that defies gravity, creating a striking image at the bottom center of the painting. Two of the women appear to be wearing African masks, perhaps to acknowledge the influence of African sculpture in Picasso's visual experiment.

Picasso's experiments coincided with those of another painter, Georges Braque, who had been developing his own version of cubism at the same time as Picasso. Braque and Picasso shared their ideas as they experimented further. They began incorporating collage into their work, using wallpaper, newspaper, wood, and other objects as parts of their paintings. They also did sculpture in a cubist manner.

Picasso remained in Paris until after the start of World War I. As a Spaniard, he remained neutral, although his friends Braque and Apollinaire fought for the French army and were badly wounded. At that time, Picasso's mistress, Eva Gouel, died of tuberculosis, a disease affecting the lungs. To get away from the war and his misfortunes, Picasso went to Rome, Italy, where he worked designing theatrical sets for performances by the Russian ballet. There he met the ballerina Olga Koklova, whom he married.

Picasso moved back to France after the war and continued painting. Many of the paintings he made after his cubist period were of human forms that are distorted in a variety of ways. In *Seated Bather* (1930), a woman at the beach looks like a skeleton that has been carved out of various pieces of wood that have been propped up against one another. Ridges where the teeth should be are vertical rather than horizontal. She is an artificial monster, yet she has the casual, relaxed attitude of a woman sunbathing.

Picasso painted many monster-people in the years that followed. They are playful and bizarre, yet they have the presence and bearing of figures in classical artworks. They seem perfectly composed, despite their strange shapes. Picasso's *Woman Dressing Her Hair* (1940), for example, has her nose on one side of her face and her mouth on the other. Both eyes are on the same side of her nose, and one is vertical and the other is horizontal. Her naked body similarly goes off in all different directions. Yet her manner is perfectly casual and composed.

Picasso's most famous monster-figure painting, however, represents people and animals experiencing the chaos and horrors of war. *Guernica* (1937) was painted as a memorial to the Spanish Civil War. It represents the devastation resulting from the bombing of a Basque town.

Later in life, Picasso's work took on a playful quality, very abstract, in stark contrast to his early works. For all that he created later in his brilliant career, he will always be remembered as the ultimate master of the cubist style.

Pollock, Jackson

(1912–1956)

AMERICAN PAINTER

> The modern painter cannot express this age, the airplane, the atom bomb, the radio, in the old forms of the Renaissance or of any other past culture. Each age finds its own techniques.
>
> —Jackson Pollock, in a radio interview (1950)

Jackson Pollock was born on January 28, 1912, in Cody, Wyoming. Pollock moved constantly during his childhood and performed poorly in school, eventually dropping out during his freshman year of high school.

Pollock joined the sophomore class of Manual Arts High School in Los Angeles in the fall of 1928 and began to study art. Pollock was convinced that he wanted to be an artist, though he was discouraged by his early attempts at drawing.

In September 1930, Pollock moved to New York and enrolled in the Art Students League, where his teacher was Thomas Hart Benton. Benton, who was also a rebellious and outspoken painter, was a major influence on Pollock, teaching him the methods of the great masters of art, including Michaelangelo, Rubens, and El Greco.

Benton also encouraged Pollock to exhibit his work whenever possible and to submit his paintings to a competition at the Brooklyn Museum, which resulted in his museum debut in January 1935. After twenty-three years in New York, Benton decided to return to Missouri in the spring, and Pollock was left without his closest friend and instructor.

In August, Pollock received a job from the Federal Art Project of the Works Progress Administration (WPA). Pollock was paid $100 a month to complete one painting every eight weeks, and the painting was then given to a public building. The struggling artist once told an interviewer that he "was grateful to the WPA, for keeping me alive during the thirties." While the government provided hundreds of artists with steady incomes, it did not treat their art well, destroying thousands of paintings when the WPA was dissolved.

Pollock struggled through a period of depression and was unable to paint. He began to drink heavily and was fired from the WPA due to "continued absence." Without work and without the desire to paint, Pollock suffered a nervous breakdown and was hospitalized for several months. After his release from the hospital, Pollock began seeing a psychotherapist to help him with his emotional problems and his alcoholism. The doctor encouraged Pollock to use his painting as a way to express his emotions.

In November 1941, John Graham organized an exhibition of paintings from France and America and included Pollock's work alongside Henri Matisse, Pablo Picasso, and two other young Americans, Willem de Kooning and Lee Krasner. Krasner and Pollock soon began sharing a studio and offered each other advice and encouragement on each other's paintings.

In October 1942, Peggy Guggenheim, a wealthy supporter of the arts, asked Pollock to exhibit his paintings in one of her shows, and Pollock's paintings were singled out by many art critics as the most promising of the group. Guggenheim scheduled a one-person show for Pollock in November 1943.

This show was covered by many major newspapers and magazines and helped promote Pollock as an important American artist. In March 1945, Pollock exhibited his second one-person show and the art critic Clement Greenberg wrote that Pollock was "the strongest painter of his generation."

Jackson Pollock married Lee Krasner in October and they moved to a small house on Long Island. Pollock painted in a barn next to their house and began work on his most innovative artwork. He had been painting large canvases for a while, but the barn allowed Pollock to paint on an even larger scale. He placed his canvas directly on the floor, getting rid of the easel altogether, and worked on his painting from all four sides. Instead of using a brush, Pollock began dripping paint from a stick or turkey baster in a "controlled accident" approach to creating images. Pollock was concerned with the process of painting, the action of applying paint to canvas, and this style became called abstract expressionism.

In January 1948, Pollock exhibited his most revolutionary paintings. The critical response was disappointing, except for Clement Greenberg, and the sales were worse. Pollock was once again faced with poverty and while Krasner offered to take a teaching job, Pollock refused, determined that they both should continue painting.

While Pollock was struggling at home, Peggy Guggenheim arranged to have six of his paintings exhibited at the Venice Biennale, the largest and most respected European art fair. It was his first appearance at an international exhibition and Pollock's paintings were considered to be the best of the American exhibit, which included Thomas Hart Benton.

In the fall of 1948, Pollock again sought treatment for his alcoholism and managed to remain sober for the next two years, producing sixty paintings.

Pollock exhibited another group of his "drip" paintings in January 1949 and his work began to sell. The Museum of Modern Art purchased its second Pollock and nine paintings were sold in all. The next month *Life* magazine sent a photographer to Pollock's home to take pictures of the artist at work. The story ran in August, and the publicity made him famous around the world and brought attention to other abstract expressionist painters.

In May 1950, Pollock and twenty-seven other artists boycotted the "American Painting Today" exhibition organized by the Metropolitan Museum of Modern Art in New York in protest of the museum's hostile attitude toward the modern art movement and abstract expressionism. The boycott made the front page of the *New York Times* and other newspapers, as well as appearing as another story for *Life* magazine, providing the artists and their work with more exposure than the exhibit could have offered.

Pollock began to struggle with his painting in the fall of 1950, feeling that he had taken his "drip" technique as far as he could. He became depressed and began drinking again. Pollock's struggle led to some of his most violent paintings, placing crude human figures among his trademark slashes of paint. These paintings were almost completely done in black or dark brown pigment and have come to be known as the "black" paintings, in which Pollock tried to break away from his usual style. The paintings were not well received by the critics or the public and Pollock grew even more depressed.

A retrospective of Pollock's paintings was being organized in the fall of 1956 at the Museum of Modern Art in New York when Pollock was killed in a car wreck. Pollock's death created an even higher demand for his work and helped make Jackson Pollock one of the most popular as well as one of the most important artists of the twentieth century.

Pound, Ezra

(1885–1972)

AMERICAN POET, CRITIC,
AND EDITOR

Great literature is simply language charged
with meaning to the utmost possible degree.
— Ezra Pound, from *How
to Read* (1931)

Ezra Pound was born in a mining town in Idaho. When he was three years old, the family moved to Philadelphia where his father worked at the U.S. Mint. Pound's ancestry was colorful: his paternal grandfather was a Congressional Representative from Wisconsin and his mother was related to two families of poets, the Wadsworths and the Longfellows.

Pound entered the University of Pennsylvania when he was sixteen to study poetry and languages. After graduating from Hamilton College in New York, Pound received his Master's degree from the University of Pennsylvania. He became friends with other poets, such as Hilda Doolittle and William Carlos Williams.

After spending a year in Europe, Pound taught at Wabash College in Indiana. He then moved to Philadelphia, became engaged to Hilda Doolittle, and planned to move to Europe to write poetry. Pound never married Doolittle, but he did travel to Italy. He published his first book of poems, *A Lume Spento,* by himself in 1908. Pound traveled to London, England, where he met the poet William Butler Yeats. Pound, who idolized Yeats, remained in touch with him for a long time. When Yeats was ill, Pound took care of him, read to him, threw parties at his home, and discussed Yeats' poetry with him.

Pound was beginning to gain recognition for his work in Europe, and in 1912 he published a second book of poems, *Ripostes.* In the same year, he was hired as the foreign editor of *Poetry* magazine, which was published in the United States. Yeats asked Pound to help publish some of his poems in *Poetry.* Without asking Yeats' permission, Pound revised some of the British poet's work. Yeats forgave Pound, though, and Pound worked as the poet's secretary until 1916.

While living in London, Pound associated with musicians, artists, and other writers such as Ford Madox Ford and Henry James. Ford published some of

Pound's work in the *English Review,* a literary journal, and encouraged him to modernize his poetic style. Pound took Ford's advice and founded the imagist movement in 1913. The imagists included the American poets Hilda Doolittle and William Carlos Williams, and the British writers Richard Aldington and James Joyce, among others.

Pound edited an anthology of the imagist poets' work entitled *Des Imagistes* (1914). He also became a consulting editor for *The New Freewoman* magazine, which would later become *The Egoist,* for *The Little Review,* and for the *Dial,* one of the most important avant-garde magazines. Pound promoted other writers' work in his reviews and essays. He was instrumental in helping James Joyce publish and promote *Ulysses;* he also helped T.S. Eliot publish his first book, and he often edited Eliot's work. Pound translated poetry, hoping to incorporate foreign styles into modern English poetry.

In 1920, Pound moved to Paris where he joined other American expatriates. Pound became interested in the Italian dictator Benito Mussolini, who ruled from 1922 to 1943, and he moved to Italy in 1925. By the time Italy invaded Ethiopia in 1935, most Americans were against Mussolini. Pound, however, supported the dictator, and even published a tribute to him entitled, *Jefferson and/or Mussolini.*

Pound spoke on cultural and political issues on Italian radio during 1941, and alienated himself from many Americans who disagreed with his views. When he tried to return to the United States after the attack on Pearl Harbor, he was not allowed admittance into the country. He stayed in Italy and continued to do his radio broadcasts, and in 1943 the U.S. government indicted him for treason. Pound was jailed in Italy, where he began to write *The Pisan Cantos,* which related his feelings in regard to his situation.

Pound was eventually transferred to Washington, D.C., and was declared incompetent to stand trial because of insanity. He was sent to St. Elizabeth's Hospital for the Criminally Insane, where he stayed for thirteen years. *The Pisan Cantos* was published in 1948, and the following year it won the Library of Congress Bollingen Award for Poetry. The award, which was granted by a committee of writers including Conrad Aiken, W.H. Auden, T.S. Eliot, Allen Tate, and Robert Lowell, caused much controversy given Pound's incarceration.

While he was in the hospital, Pound continued to write and translate poetry. Other writers often visited him, and in 1958, Robert Frost, Archibald MacLeish, T.S. Eliot, and Ernest Hemingway helped to get Pound released. He returned to Italy and published the last two sections of *The Cantos.* Begun in 1915, the volumes of cantos were Pound's most important work. They comprised a long epic poem that represented civilization of the Eastern and Western countries.

Pound, a very prolific author, died in Venice, Italy. Ezra Pound was an important American poet not only for his own poetry, but for his promotion of other writers.

Proust, Marcel

(1871–1922)

FRENCH NOVELIST AND CRITIC

The truth of the matter is that what happens
in a man's life is without interest so long as it
is stripped of the feelings which make that
life a poem.

—Marcel Proust

Marcel Proust was a man who spent much of the later part of his life confined
to bed by illness, yet he was able to write a stunning thirty-page introduction to
his great eight-part novel, *Remembrance of Things Past*, in which the only thing
that "happens" is a man turning in bed trying to fall asleep. By turning the ordinary into poetry and excavating the workings of memory, Marcel Proust is responsible for one of the signal literary achievements of this century. With his
innovative technique and rich, gloriously dense style, Proust brought the realistic French novel into the twentieth century and redefined it for the modern era.

Marcel Proust drew on his own life in such great detail for *Remembrance*
that sometimes it is hard to separate him from the "Marcel" who narrates the
3,100-plus pages of that book. The real Marcel Proust was born in Paris,
France, on July 10, 1871, one of two sons of a highly regarded doctor and professor of medicine, Adrien Proust. Marcel's mother, Jeanne Weil Proust, was
the daughter of a wealthy Jewish family. She remained a committed Jew, just as
her husband remained a conformist Christian, but neither imposed their beliefs on their sons. The family's wealth guaranteed that Marcel would be financially independent all his life.

Marcel was a sickly child, suffering from severe asthma from the age of nine.
After that, his school attendance was irregular, interrupted by periodic illnesses. Indeed, the only period of uninterrupted health that Proust experienced was during the time he was in the army. Asthma kept him awake at night
and the adult Proust slept days and worked nights.

He was often able to go out at night, to the theater and to parties, and to
take short vacations, but for most of his adult life, Proust was ill.

The one completely happy time of his life was his childhood, particularly the
summers he spent when very young in Illier and Auteuil, the towns that served
as the model for his fictional Combray.

Proust was educated in the Lycée Condorcet in Paris. At first a poor student due to his frequent absences, his grades improved significantly later. After his two years of military service, he took a degree in law and another in literature at the University of Paris and the Free School of Political Science. His parents were not thrilled with his interest in the arts, but they eventually accepted their son's ambitions.

From the time he was seventeen, Proust had been enthralled by the spectacle of high society. He frequented some of the most fashionable salons and drawing rooms, rubbing elbows with nobility, who later found themselves turning up in his novel, thinly disguised.

In 1896, Proust published his first book, a collection of short stories entitled *Pleasures and Regrets*. He had contributed to a variety of magazines and journals earlier in the decade, mostly as a literary critic and author of short, often satirical pieces. *Pleasures and Regrets* was published privately in an expensive deluxe edition that Proust's friends delighted in making fun of.

However, Proust seemed to be serious about his literary career, despite appearances that he was merely a wealthy dilettante. While the first book was still on press, he had begun work on a much more ambitious volume. *Jean Santeuil* would occupy him for several years before he abandoned it in 1899. He picked it up once more briefly three years later, but the novel was never finished, and Proust did not intend for it to see the light of day, except in passages that he reworked into *Remembrance*.

Jean Santeuil, which was finally published in its unfinished form in 1952, is more closely autobiographical than *Remembrance*, perhaps too much so. An exhausted and ill Proust apparently had begun the novel without having an idea of how it would be structured, and it eventually grew into a mammoth and unmanageable manuscript. (A paperback edition published in the United States in the 1960s was nearly eight hundred pages long.) The novel involves its protagonist more directly in the world of Paris in the 1890s than in the later work, with the Dreyfus affair and other topics of current interest interwoven into the narrative.

Surprisingly, given his apparent lack of political interests and his rather oblique relationship to his Jewish heritage, Proust told the story of Captain Dreyfus—who was framed for espionage and railroaded to Devil's Island by anti-Semites in the French army—with great intensity, and he was one of the signatories to a petition denouncing Dreyfus's trial and conviction.

Together with his growing illness, the events of that scandal led to Proust's gradual withdrawal from society. He was further depressed by the death of his parents: his father in 1903, and his mother two years later. Although he periodically reemerged (making frequent visits to a gay brothel of which he was reputedly a financial backer), Proust became essentially confined to his home and, most specifically, to his bedroom, from 1906. In 1910, complaining of the street noise of Paris, he had the room lined with cork paneling to insulate him from the sounds.

The death of Proust's parents left him financially independent. In 1905, he began preliminary work on the first volume of *Remembrance of Things Past*. He struggled for three years with the novel, unable to find a satisfactory form. Then one day in January 1909, he had a cup of tea and a cookie. The taste of the two together brought memories of his youth flooding back. Thus was born one of the most famous literary devices in history, Proust's use of the Madeleine cake as the trigger for his narrator's reminiscences. Now, he began work in deadly earnest, and by 1912 the first volume, *Swann's Way,* was completed.

The problem was that no one wanted to publish it. After the manuscript was rejected by a large number of editors, Proust decided to publish it himself, and it was issued in 1913. The book, which was riddled with typographical errors, was not particularly well received, although Proust managed to get some favorable reviews by friends of his, including Jean Cocteau, planted.

André Gide, who had been one of the editors who had passed on the first book, was persuaded by his boss at the important publishing house Gallimard that he had been wrong about *Swann's Way,* and Gide offered to publish the next volume. In 1919, *Within a Budding Grove* was published to critical acclaim. When the novel won the Prix Goncourt, perhaps the most important literary prize in France, Proust's fame was secured. He was made a *chevalier* of the Legion d'Honneur the following year.

He published another three installments in his lifetime, before dying of pneumonia in his famous cork-lined room on November 18, 1922. The remaining volumes were published posthumously, utilizing the extensive notes and fragments that Proust had scrupulously maintained as he wrote. It remains one of the great monuments of twentieth-century literature.

Presley, Elvis

(1935–1977)

AMERICAN SINGER AND ACTOR

Elvis Presley was born to Vernon and Gladys Presley in Tupelo, Mississippi. He had a twin brother, Jesse, who was stillborn. During the Great Depression, Elvis's parents worked at whatever jobs they could get. Elvis was brought up as part of a close family unit. While Elvis was growing up, he asked for a bicycle and a guitar. His parents bought him the guitar because they thought it was safer than a bicycle. Elvis was influenced by the popular country and western songs he heard on the radio and gospel music that he heard in church. His family moved to Memphis, Tennessee—the country music capital of the world—in 1948 when he was thirteen years old.

At Humes High School, Presley listened to blues music (which was popular among African-American musicians, such as B.B. King, and "hillbilly," or country music (that was played by folk singers who accompanied themselves on guitars or banjos). Elvis played his guitar with other musician friends from school. His early music was called "rockabilly," a combination of rock and roll and country music. Outside of school, Presley also had jobs, such as one as an usher in a local movie theater. It was there that he decided to become an entertainer, using the talents that he was developing as an amateur musician and singer.

In 1953, Presley went to the Sun recording studio in Memphis to make an inexpensive recording of two pop ballads, a birthday present for his mother. Presley formed a band with Scotty Moore on guitar and Bill Black on the string bass. Presley was brought to the attention of the owner of the studio, Sam Phillips, who later recorded the young musicians. From 1954 to 1955, Elvis's earliest "rockabilly" recordings were picked up by local radio stations. When Presley's contract was up with Sun Records, Presley's manager, Colonel Parker, signed him with the RCA label for the sum of $35,000.

Presley made his first television appearances on the Dorsey brothers' show and Milton Berle's variety show in April 1956—just as his first national hit song ("Heartbreak Hotel") sent teenagers around the country to stores to buy his records. The string of songs that would top the charts in 1957 began with "Don't Be Cruel" and "Love Me Tender." Promoters were quick to capitalize on Presley's fame by steering the teen idol into the first of a series of movies, beginning with *Love Me Tender* and *Jailhouse Rock*. Presley's brand of rock and roll music set the style for bands to imitate in America, as well as the groups that came from England in the 1960s such as the Rolling Stones and the Beatles.

In 1958, his career was interrupted when Presley was inducted into the U.S. Army. While he was serving in Germany, he only made one record, "A Big Hunk of Love," but he quickly resumed his career when he returned home. Starting in the 1960s Presley changed his focus from records to movies. He had been attracted to the glamor that Hollywood had to offer ever since he was a boy. His record sales declined when most of his new music came as the result of a released soundtrack (a music score that is made to accompany a film).

By the late 1960s, the public became less interested in Presley's output, but his career improved when he married Priscilla Beaulieu in 1967 and had a daughter the next year. His popularity rose again as he made a comeback to recordmaking and live performances, which reached a peak during his sold-out shows from large hotels in Las Vegas to New York's Madison Square Garden. Presley made a live worldwide concert telecast from Hawaii in 1973 (and also recorded it for release as an album) and donated all the profits to charity.

Throughout Presley's active career he made dozens of records that sold over a million copies each and achieved numerous gold and platinum awards. Although he appeared to be returning to his former fame in the early 1970s, his personal life was falling apart with his divorce from his wife and his widowed father's illnesses. In order to keep up with his marathon concert tours and hectic schedule, Presley started taking drugs to keep him awake and then sleeping pills to make him sleep, all of which took its toll on his deteriorating health.

Elvis Presley died at his Graceland mansion in Memphis on August 16, 1977, as the result of a drug overdose at the age of 42. The world remains fascinated by Presley, and grateful for the tremendous contribution he made to the evolution of popular music.

Price, Leontyne

(1927–   )

AMERICAN OPERA SINGER AND GRAMMY AWARD WINNER

> The voice is so special, you have to guard it with care, to let nothing disturb it, so you don't lose the bloom, don't let it fade, don't let the petals drop.
>
> —Leontyne Price, speaking about singing, *Opera News,* (1985)

Mary Violet Leontyne Price was born in Laurel, Mississippi. Her father worked in a sawmill and her mother brought in extra income as a midwife. As amateur musicians, they both encouraged their daughter to play piano and sing in their local church choir. Price graduated from high school in 1944, then attended Central State College in Wilberforce, Ohio, and studied music education with the hopes of becoming a music teacher. After she finished college in 1949, Price auditioned for the Juilliard School of Music in New York, where she was awarded a four-year scholarship.

One of the experiences that Price remembers so vividly was attending a concert in Jackson, Mississippi, in 1936 when she was nine years old. The world-renowned singer Marian Anderson performed, inspiring Price to pursue a career in music. Price received another boost of inspiration after she attended a concert given by Paul Robeson.

Price thrived at Juilliard, studying under vocal teacher Florence Page Kimball. Later, when Price appeared in a student production of Verdi's opera *Falstaff*, she caught the attention of composer Virgil Thomson. He cast her in a revival of his opera *Four Saints in Three Acts*, which was Price's professional debut in 1952. That led to a two-year job singing in a revival of George Gershwin's *Porgy and Bess*, which toured throughout the United States and Europe. During that time, Price married her co-star in that production, William C. Warfield.

In 1954, Price made her concert debut at New York's Town Hall, where she sang modern compositions with equal skill and command of voice. Price's career moved forward in 1955 when she appeared in Puccini's *Tosca* on television, becoming the first black opera singer to perform on television. Price was later invited to return with performances of Mozart's *Magic Flute* (1956), Poulenc's *Dialogues of the Carmelites* (1957), and Mozart's *Don Giovanni* (1960). One of the most fruitful associations of her career began in 1957 when Price was invited by conductor Kurt Herbert Adler to sing Poulenc's opera at the San Francisco Opera. She later returned to challenge herself with new roles to expand her repertoire (list of operas that she was able to perform).

Price became a guest soloist with such companies as the Chicago Lyric Opera and the American Opera Theater. She credits the conductor Herbert von Karajan with introducing her to European audiences, with *The Magic Flute* in 1958 and Verdi's *Aida* in 1959. After returning to the United States, Price made her debut at New York's Metropolitan Opera House, where her 1961 performance in *Il Trovatore* brought a standing ovation of forty-two minutes, the longest ever given at the Met. She appeared at the Met in 118 productions between 1961 and 1969.

When the Met moved to its new home in Lincoln Center in 1964, Price was invited by director Rudolf Bing to open the house with the world premier of Samuel Barber's *Antony and Cleopatra*. Price spoke about the experience: "*Antony and Cleopatra* was the event of the century, operatically speaking. I was there. I lived like a hermit for a year and a half so as not to have a cold. I simply did everything possible to have it be right. I accepted that responsibility with the greatest happiness. This was the greatest challenge of my life."

In the 1970s, Price cut the number of opera appearances that she made to focus on giving recitals. She enjoyed the challenge of creating several roles on stage in succession. Her career credits include dozens of recordings, thirteen Grammy Awards, the Presidential Medal of Freedom in 1965, the Kennedy Center Honors for lifetime achievement in the arts in 1980, and the first National Medal of Arts in 1985. Price has served as an inspiration to other opera soloists, including Kathleen Battle.

Puccini, Giacomo

(1858–1924)

ITALIAN COMPOSER

One of the most celebrated opera composers of all time, Giacomo Puccini was born in 1858 in Lucca, Italy. Beginning with his great-great-grandfather, all of Puccini's ancestors were musicians and composers of local renown. Although, as a child, Puccini showed no special talent or any interest in music, his mother, Michele Puccini, a music teacher, was determined that he continue the family tradition; she sent him to the Istituto Musicale of Lucca. There, her student, Carlo Angeloni, became young Puccini's teacher. After Angeloni's patient teaching had finally awakened an interest in Puccini, he soon made quick progress and became a good pianist and organist. At fourteen, he began his career as an organist in local churches and started to compose.

In 1877, Puccini submitted a cantata, *Juno,* to a local competition, but it failed to win the big prize. Nevertheless, he produced the work, which won considerable local success. Puccini's ambition became stronger, and when he saw the opera *Aïda* in Pisa, he became determined to become an operatic composer. With a scholarship, and financial support from an uncle, Puccini entered the Milan Conservatory in 1880, and studied with Antonio Bazzini and Amilcare Ponchielli for three years.

While still a student, Puccini entered a competition for a one-act opera. He and his partner, Ferdinando Fontana failed to win the big prize. However, their opera, *Le Villi (The Witch-Dancers)* came to the attention of publisher Giulio Ricordi, who arranged a successful production at the Teatro del Verme in Milan, and he commissioned a second opera. It took the team five years to come up with *Edgar.* When it was produced at La Scala in 1889, it was not successful. Puccini decided that the libretto was the cause of the failure. He became convinced that to have a really effective opera, he needed a good idea and someone with whom to write the piece. To that end, Puccini asked playwright Domenico Oliva to write the text of *Manon Lescaut.* However, Puccini and his publisher, Ricordi, rewrote the text so thoroughly that in the published score Oliva's name is not even mentioned. Produced in Turin in 1893, *Manon Lescaut* achieved a success such as Puccini had never known, and he became celebrated outside Italy.

His next opera, *La Bohème,* surpassed *Manon* in stature and fame, although it was not as successful in Turin in 1896. Together, these two works not only carried their composer's name throughout the world, but they also have found and maintained their places in every opera house to this day. With fame came wealth, and Puccini built a magnificent house for himself, where he wrote his next opera, *Tosca,* which was enthusiastically received by the Roman audience at the Teatro Costanzi in 1900. *Tosca* is Puccini's most dramatic work and contains some of his best-known tunes.

Puccini's next work, *Madama Butterfly,* was hissed at its premiere at La Scala. However, when it was revised by the composer, it was greeted with acclaim in Brescia. It was presented at New York's Metropolitan Opera House in 1907 in the presence of the composer.

Puccini became the acknowledged ruler of the Italian operatic stage, his works rivaling those of fellow Italian composer Guiseppe Verdi in number of performances given. It was at this time that someone suggested that Puccini write an opera on an American subject. After witnessing a performance of American playwright-producer David Belasco's *The Girl of the Golden West,* Puccini knew he had found his subject. *La Fanciulla del West* premiered at the Metropolitan Opera House in 1910. While it never achieved the success of *Tosca* or *Butterfly,* it returned to popularity in the 1970s.

Puccini followed this with *La Rondine* (1917); and three one-act operas—*Il Tabarro, Suor Angelica,* and *Gianni Schicchi* (1918). Puccini's last opera, *Turandot,* was left unfinished when Puccini died in 1924, but it was completed by composer Franco Alfano. *Turandot* was performed at La Scala in Milan in 1926, and at the Metropolitan Opera House in New York that same year.

When Puccini died, all of Italy went into mourning. In 1930, after his wife died, their house was turned into a museum.

Rachmaninoff, Sergei

(1873–1943)

RUSSIAN COMPOSER AND PIANIST

Among Russian composers, Sergei Rachmaninoff occupies a very important place. His broad, sweeping melody lines, mixed with melancholy moods, have kept his works alive as concert favorites in Russia, England, and the United States.

Rachmaninoff was born in 1873 on his father's estate at Oneg, in the district of Novgorod, Russia, into a musical family. His grandfather was an amateur pianist, and his father also played the piano. When the family estate had to be sold due to financial problems, Rachmaninoff was taken to St. Petersburg where he became a piano pupil at the conservatory there from 1882 to 1885.

At the advice of his cousin, the well-known pianist and conductor Alexander Siloti, Rachmaninoff went to Moscow and studied piano at the Moscow

Conservatory. Three years later, Siloti himself took Sergei as a student. At about that time, while studying composition with Taneyev and Arensky, Rachmaninoff met the composer Peter Ilich Tchaikovsky, who appreciated his talent and gave him friendly advice.

Rachmaninoff graduated from the conservatory as a pianist in 1891. The next year, he became a composer and received a gold medal for his opera in one act, *Aleko.* He also wrote the *Prelude in C-Sharp Minor,* which became one of the most celebrated piano pieces in the world.

His first symphony was performed in Moscow in 1897, but it met with little success. That failure depressed Rachmaninoff so much that he did not write again until 1901, when he composed his *Second Piano Concerto,* which became the most famous work of its kind written in the twentieth century. During that time, Rachmaninoff set out on a new career as a conductor, appearing in Moscow and London and conducting opera at the Bolshoi Theatre in Moscow for two seasons, beginning in 1904.

In 1909, Rachmaninoff made his first American tour. His fame was such that the Boston Symphony Orchestra offered him the post of permanent conductor. However, he declined the honor and returned to Moscow, where he conducted the Philharmonic Society Orchestra from 1911 to 1913.

When the Russian Revolution (1917) put an end to the world that Rachmaninoff had known and loved, he left his native land, never to return. At first he lived in Switzerland. In 1935, he decided to make the United States his home, settling first in New York and then in Los Angeles.

There was a period of creative silence until 1926 when he wrote the *Piano Concerto Number Four.* That piece was followed by a handful of works over the next fifteen years. During that period, however, he was active as a pianist in America and in Europe.

Ray, Satyajit

(1921–1992)

INDIAN FILM DIRECTOR

Satyajit Ray was an unusually gifted filmmaker and director. His body of work is very popular in India, and his films are the most well-known in the West of all those made by Indian directors.

Ray was born in Calcutta, India, on May 2, 1921. His father was a writer, illustrator, and critic. After studying economics at the University of Calcutta, Ray worked as an art director for an advertising agency, an illustrator, and a typographer. He was also a writer of novels and short stories, and a musician and composer. He even invented his own typeface, a design of print for the Roman alphabet that has an Indian style. He is most famous, however, as a film director.

Ray had been interested in film and filmmaking for several years before becoming a director. He was especially interested in Western styles of filmmaking. He met the famous French film director Jean Renoir in 1951 when Renoir was shooting his film *The River* near Calcutta. The two exchanged ideas, and Renoir encouraged Ray with his work.

At first, Ray made films in his spare time with very little equipment and very little money. Those limitations, however, were not serious drawbacks because Ray wanted to make his films in the realist manner. He wanted the scenes and acting to seem as much like real life as possible, rather than like aspects of a glamorous production, so Ray made his first film, *The Song of the Road* (1954), using ordinary daylight and amateur actors.

This film became the first part of a trilogy, or series of three films. It tells the story, based on an Indian novel, of a young boy who is abandoned by his father and fights to survive on his own. Ray earned a reputation as a creative and insightful director for making it. This made it easier for him to raise funds for making the rest of his movies.

Ray's films are remarkable for the way they portray even morally bad characters in a sympathetic light. He filmed all his characters in a way that makes viewers feel intimately acquainted with them. Ray had an understanding and appreciation for humanity that enriches the stories his films relate.

Several of them deal with tensions between tradition and modern influences. The film *Devi* (1960), for example, is about an old man who thinks his daughter is the goddess Kali, a Hindu deity of destruction. Despite her modern education and her disregard for old superstitions, she is strongly affected by her father's ancient beliefs.

Many of Ray's films have excellent musical scores. His first film included music performed by the famous Indian sitar player Ravi Shankar. Ray himself wrote the music for some of his films. His music, as well as his directing, have always received favorable critical response. He wrote musical scores not only for his own films, but for one of Ismail Merchant's, *Shakespeare Wallah* (1965).

Most of Ray's films have a hopeful quality, although some do not. Most of his movies present characters in a sympathetic light, although some have represented Indian society in a negative manner. All of his films, however, exhibit a deep interest in humanity that has made them admired by people all over the world.

Ride, Sally Kristen

(1951–   )

ASTRONAUT AND THE FIRST
AMERICAN WOMAN IN SPACE

I didn't particularly care that I was the role
model, but I thought it was important that
somebody be.

> —Sally Ride, after her first
> space flight, 1983

Sally Kristen Ride was born on May 26, 1951, in Los Angeles, California. In 1968 she graduated from Westlake Girls' High School in Los Angeles, where her physics teacher had inspired her with a love of science and logical thinking. Sally Ride was already thinking about becoming an astronaut.

At the same time, however, she was also deeply involved in sports, particularly tennis. She took lessons from a champion tennis player, and she competed in national tournaments. By the time she was in college, she was considered one of the top amateur women players in the country. She even considered a career as a professional tennis player, but she chose instead to continue her education. In 1973 she graduated from Stanford University in Palo Alto, California, with a double degree in English and physics. From then on, her education followed the scientific path. She received her master's degree in physics in 1975, followed by a doctoral degree in 1978.

Ride was working at Stanford as a teaching assistant and a researcher in laser physics when she saw a notice in a campus newspaper that the National Aeronautics and Space Administration (NASA) was looking for scientists who wanted to train as astronauts. "I don't know why I wanted to do it," she later said. "I honestly can't tell you what was going through my mind. I only know I was on my way out of the room to apply while I was still reading the notice in the newspaper."

More than eight thousand people applied to NASA that year, but only thirty-five were chosen to enter the astronaut program. Six of them were women, including Sally Ride. After completing her basic NASA training, she was qualified as a mission specialist. She then worked for several years on NASA projects related to her area of special interest: X-ray physics. (This delay was normal; all astronauts, from the early test pilots and military officers to the more recent scientific mission specialists, must perform ground-based duties for a few years before being assigned to a mission.)

Ride made history on June 27, 1983, when she became the first American woman to go into space. She insisted, however, that she be treated like any other astronaut. "I did not come to NASA to make history," she told *Newsweek* magazine. "It's important to me that people don't think that I was picked for the flight because I'm a woman and it's time for NASA to send one." The mission took Ride and five other astronauts aloft in the space shuttle *Challenger* for six days. Her most important task aboard the shuttle was operating the robot manipulator system (RMS), a mechanical arm operated from within the shuttle that can be used to launch satellites or collect them from orbit. The shuttle crew launched two satellites and retrieved another. They joked that their motto was "We Pick Up and Deliver." Upon returning to earth, Ride said, "The thing I'll remember most about the flight was that it was fun. In fact, I'm sure it was the most fun I'll ever have in my life."

In October 1984, Ride made a second journey aboard the *Challenger*. Her companions were four fellow astronauts, including another woman, Kathryn Sullivan, and two civilian scientists. During this mission, Ride launched a satellite and joined her crewmates in making photographic observations of the Earth. She was scheduled for a third mission in the summer of 1986, but that mission was canceled after the tragedy of the *Challenger* explosion in January 1986, when six astronauts and a civilian passenger were killed.

Ride was part of the presidential commission that investigated the *Challenger* tragedy. Since then she has served in NASA's administrative offices in Washington, D.C., and as a member of the Stanford University Center for International Security and Arms Control. Her book *To Space and Back* was published in 1986. Modest about her own importance, Ride gives the women's movement credit for opening doors in science and space exploration to women. She also recognizes that her achievement has made her a role model for young women everywhere. "When I go out and give talks at schools, and an eight-year-old girl in the audience raises her hand to ask me what she needs to do to become an astronaut, I like that," she has said.

Rilke, Rainer Maria

(1875–1926)

CZECH-BORN AUSTRIAN POET
AND NOVELIST

"Ask yourself in the most silent hour of your night: *Must* I write?" Thus did Rainer Maria Rilke phrase the question in one of the most famous passages from his *Letters to a Young Poet,* written between 1903 and 1904. For Rilke, there was never a doubt.

Rainer Maria Rilke was born on December 4, 1875, in Prague, Czechoslovakia, the son of an Austrian railway conductor, Josef, who had pretensions to an aristocratic background. Josef's brothers had both served in the Austrian army with distinction, but he was forced to resign from the service due to ill health. His greatest ambition for his son was that the boy should fulfill his own, thwarted military ambitions.

At the age of ten, Rainer was sent to a military academy. For five miserable years, he endured at the school until he was finally sent home on June 3, 1891, suffering from "continuous ill health." But he wasn't sent home; his father had him transferred to a business school in Linz, Austria. Surprisingly, he was much happier in his year there, especially after he began an affair with a local governess.

When he returned home to Prague, he found his parents had separated, with his mother living in Vienna. His father had, for all intents and purposes, disowned him, and would not see him. However, Jaroslav Rilke, Rainer's uncle, was sympathetic, and he hired tutors to teach Rainer. When Jaroslav died suddenly in the winter of 1892, Rainer was suicidally depressed. However, a girlfriend, Valery David-Rhonfeld, stepped in to help him. Taken under her wing, he passed his entrance exams for the University of Prague in 1895; she also encouraged him in his desire to write verse, paying for the publication of his first book in 1894.

That first book, *Life and Song,* offered no hint that his was the voice of a great poet in the making. In fact, neither did his second book, *Larenopfer*

(1896). His early verse was derivative, highly sentimental and ornate, and very much under the spell of the worst excesses of German Romanticism.

The young Rilke had a short attention span; he changed majors at the university several times before dropping out, and he dropped Valery for another girl. The following year (1896), he transferred to the University of Munich, where he studied art history, focusing particularly on Italian painting. He traveled repeatedly between Florence, Italy, and Munich for the next two years. It was while he was in Florence that he discovered a book that he would later say changed his life, *Niels Lyhne,* by the Danish novelist Jen Peter Jacobsen. Indeed, his love for that novel was so great that he learned Danish in order to reread it in its original language. All that time, he was still publishing verse, and there were signs in his early writing of someone who was beginning to grow as a poet.

A pivotal point in that growth was his contact with his cousin, the brilliant and mercurial Lou Andreas-Salomé. One of the most extraordinary women of her time, Andreas-Salomé was a lover and colleague of the German philosopher Friedrich Nietzsche, and later a protégée of psychoanalyst Sigmund Freud. She guided Rilke on a lengthy trip through Russia in 1899. He later called that country his "spiritual fatherland," and returned on his own the following year after studying Russian. On his second visit, he met, among others, Russian novelist Leo Tolstoy.

Once more back in Germany, Rilke accepted the invitation of painter Heinrich Vogeler to visit Vogeler's artists' colony at Worpswede. There he met a young sculptor, Clara Westhoff; the two fell in love and were married the following year.

Married life was hard and uncertain for two artists. They lived in a cottage in Worpswede for a time. She worked on her sculptures, he on his next book of poetry, *The Book of Images* (1902), which was perhaps his first relatively successful writing, including some of his most popular poetry. He wrote to friends asking for help finding a job. His father even offered to help him—with a job in a bank. In 1902, Rilke was offered a chance to write a monograph on the French sculptor Auguste Rodin, whose work Clara admired greatly.

Meeting Rodin had a great effect on Rilke. It was Rodin who instilled in him the idea that a creative artist must work hard, work continuously, not merely when one was in the grip of "inspiration." After a brief trip to Italy, where the sickly poet rested and recovered from a bout of illness, he returned to Meudon, Rodin's home, and the great artist took him on as a secretary. He held the position less than a year, but it became a turning point in his life.

After that job ended, Rilke then turned his attention to the final publication versions of *The Book of Images* and *The Tale of the Love and Death of Cornet Christopher Rilke,* his only popular success. He immediately followed those important books with two of his greatest volumes, *New Poems* and *New Poems: The Other Part.*

The first volume was published in December 1907. Barely eight months later, Rilke sent the second manuscript to his publisher. Rilke was writing at a white-hot pace, producing the ninety-six poems of the second book in less than a year. Rodin's advice had made an impression; Rilke was trying to suppress his initial attention to "feelings" in order to concentrate on creating forms that would express them. With those two books, Rilke emerged as a major European poet, a poet who combined a precision of imagery with an ear for musicality.

At the end of such a period of explosive creativity, Rilke was understandably wrung dry. For the next two years, he would travel once more, this time in the Mediterranean. He was recuperating from an illness that he had suffered in Cairo, Egypt, having arrived exhausted and still wobbly in Venice, Italy. There he was befriended by the Princess Marie von Thurn und Taxis-Hohenlohe, who offered him the use of her Duino Castle near Trieste, in northeastern Italy.

In January 1912, Rilke was walking outside the castle, trying to focus his mind on a business letter. Rilke suddenly heard a voice inside his head, speaking two lines of a poem. They became the first two lines of his *Duino Elegies,* a series of poems he would write over the next several years, and which possibly was his greatest poetic achievement.

Once more, Rilke took to the road, traveling to Spain and France. With the outbreak of World War I, he returned to Germany. He volunteered for the army and was mustered into the First Infantry Regiment. However, his poor health resulted in his being transferred to detached duty at the war department. Finally, he went home to Munich, where he spent the remainder of the war.

Over the last seven years of his life, from the war's end until his death, in 1926, Rilke lived in solitude in Switzerland. He felt the heat of intensive creative energy once more and on February 11, 1922, he finished the *Duino Elegies.* A few days later, he completed his cycle, *Sonnets to Orpheus.* Both were published the following year.

He spent the last three years of his life resting and trying to mend his weak body. He corresponded with a huge number of friends and acquaintances. His influence as a poet was enormous, ranging from the Russian greats Marina Tsvetaeva (a close friend) and Boris Pasternak, to W.H. Auden. He died of leukemia on December 29, 1926. Auden summed up Rilke's importance neatly: "Rilke is almost the first poet since the seventeenth century to find a fresh solution" to the perennial problem of how to express abstract ideas through concrete images in verse.

Robeson, Paul

(1898–1976)

AMERICAN ACTOR AND POLITICAL ACTIVIST

> Like every true artist, I have longed to see my talent contributing in an unmistakably clear manner to the cause of humanity. . . . The artist must take sides. He must fight for freedom or for slavery. I have made my choice.
>
> —Paul Robeson, speaking in London at a rally to aid the Basque refugee children on June 24, 1937

Paul Leroy Bustill Robeson was born in Princeton, New Jersey, the youngest of eight children born to a father who escaped from slavery at the age of fifteen. His father, who had changed the family name from Roberson (the name of the slave owner), joined the Union Army in 1861 and later became a Protestant minister in Somerville, New Jersey. When Paul was six, his mother died from burns in a household accident.

The year before Paul graduated high school in 1915, he scored the highest on an exam that earned him a four-year scholarship to attend Rutgers College in New Jersey, where he was the only black student. Robeson won prizes for speaking, collected twelve varsity letters in four sports, and was named an All-American end in 1919 on a football team that originally threatened to boycott his presence. Robeson served on the student council, spoke at his graduation in 1919, and was elected to the Phi Beta Kappa honor society.

In 1920, Robeson moved to Harlem and entered Columbia Law School. In his first year he performed in an amateur production of the play *Simon the Cyrenian* at the Harlem YMCA. The person who encouraged Robeson to take time away from school to act in a play on Broadway was Eslanda Cardozo Goode, a chemistry student at Columbia whom he later married in 1921. Robeson graduated from Columbia with a law degree in 1923 and was admitted to the New York bar and a law firm.

Because of his lack of enthusiasm for a career in law and his interest in theater, he joined a theater group called the Provincetown Players—an experimental company in New York that included the playwright Eugene O'Neill—in 1924. Robeson starred in two O'Neill plays: *All God's Chillin Got Wings* (about an interracial marriage), and *The Emperor Jones* (about a black dictator of a West Indian island). He also starred in the London production of *The Emperor Jones.*

In 1925 Robeson and the pianist and composer Lawrence Brown created a musical program singing and playing black spirituals and folk songs in several languages that was so successful that they did a concert tour in the United States, Great Britain, and Europe. During the next fifteen years Robeson made over 300 recordings and regularly toured in many countries including—the Soviet Union, which he visited for the first time in 1934.

The dramatic role that brought Robeson the highest acclaim was *Othello,* which he first played in London in 1930. When that same production opened in New York in 1943, Robeson received unanimous praise for his portrayal. It was also the first Othello on Broadway with a black leading man and a white supporting cast, and its run of 296 performances was longer than any previous Shakespearean drama on Broadway.

Two of the eleven films in which Robeson had leading parts were originally stage plays that he starred in previously: *The Emperor Jones* (1933) and *Show Boat* (1936). In *Native Land* (1942), a documentary based on a Senate investigation of discrimination in the South, he narrated the text and sang the songs in the film. Sidney Poitier once said of Robeson: "Before him, no black man or woman had been portrayed in American movies as anything but a racist stereotype."

But Robeson felt he had fallen short of his goal. After he decided to give up working in Hollywood motion pictures, he said: "The movie industry is not prepared to permit me to portray the life or express the living interests, hopes, and aspirations of the struggling people from whom I come."

Robeson became identified with many left-wing causes in his later career. When he first visited Russia in 1934, he was greatly interested in their socialism. He learned the language and said that he loved the country more than any other. He sent his only child, Paul, Jr., to school in the Soviet Union because of that country's lack of racial and class discrimination. During the 1930s, Robeson lived for a long time in England, where he gave many benefit performances for Jewish and other refugees. He met with the West African Political Union and other left-wing groups. During the Spanish Civil War, he spoke out against the Fascists, and he went to Spain to entertain the Republican troops.

By the time the Robesons returned to the United States in 1939, the country had made some improvements in the racial climate under President Roosevelt. Robeson recorded a patriotic song called "Ballad for Americans." He joined anti-Fascist groups and his reputation grew as a spokesman for the oppressed. However, after World War II when the Cold War between the Communist party and the West intensified, the House Committee on Un-American Activities often cited Robeson as a Communist sympathizer, and the public turned against him.

In 1949, Robeson reaffirmed his views on the Soviet Union, and expressed his belief in "scientific socialism," which held that "for all mankind a socialist society represents an advance to a higher stage of life." At a music festival that Robeson sang at in 1949, riots broke out among several liberal and radical groups, and scores of people were injured. In 1950, the State Department demanded that Robeson surrender his passport and refused to issue him a new one until he signed an oath that stated he was not associated with the Communist party. Robeson's unwillingness to cooperate led to eight years of court battles, which also prevented him from earning a living since few if any would hire him to perform at a concert.

By the time he regained his passport in 1958, he gave a farewell concert at Carnegie Hall, recorded an album, and went abroad to live. While in the Soviet Union in 1959, Robeson was hospitalized and later had to stay in nursing homes in Europe and England for various ailments until he and his wife returned to the United States in 1963. Robeson would not speak to the press until he announced his retirement from performing and all public affairs. He remained in seclusion until his wife died in 1965, after which he moved to Philadelphia to live with his sister.

Robeson was awarded the Stalin Peace Prize in 1952, honorary degrees from Hamilton College and Rutgers University, the Springarn Medal of the NAACP, the Whitney Young, Jr., Award of the New York Urban League, and the Donaldson Award for his role as Othello. On April 15, 1973, a seventy-fifth birthday salute was staged at Carnegie Hall by leaders in the entertainment world and the civil rights movement. Robeson was too ill to attend but he sent a tape-recorded message in which he said: "I want you to know that I am the same Paul, dedicated as ever to the worldwide cause of humanity for freedom, peace, and brotherhood."

Paul Robeson died in 1976 from double pneumonia and kidney failure in a hospital in Philadelphia.

Robinson, Jack Roosevelt

(1919–1972)

AMERICAN BASEBALL PLAYER

Jackie Robinson was a great athlete. He was also a pioneer and a courageous hero as the first black player in the modern major leagues. In his autobiography, Robinson wrote, "I had to fight hard against loneliness, abuse, and the knowledge that any mistake I made would be magnified because I was the only black man out there."

Jack Roosevelt Robinson was born in Cairo, Georgia, on January 31, 1919. His father left Jackie's mother on her own with five children when Jackie was a baby. Mallie Robinson moved her family to Pasadena, California. There they still met with racism and other problems. Jackie worked to help the family. In junior high he got involved with a street gang. A neighborhood mechanic and the minister at his church helped to steer him away from trouble. They urged him to think for himself and not follow the crowd.

Jackie's brother Mack was a fine runner. He won a silver medal (second to Jesse Owens) for the 200-meter dash at the 1936 Olympics. By his teens Jackie, too, had made a name for himself in track, as well as in baseball, football, and basketball. At Pasadena Junior College, he set a broad jump record and starred on the college's 1938 championship baseball team.

The University of California at Los Angeles offered him an athletic scholarship. Robinson became its first four-letter athlete (basketball, track, football, and baseball). He was also good at swimming and tennis. During his last year at UCLA, Jackie became engaged to nursing student Rachel Isum. He took a job at the National Youth Administration and played semipro football with the Los Angeles Bulldogs in order to send money to his mother.

World War II had raged in Europe since 1939. America entered the war in December 1941 after Japanese bombers attacked the U. S. naval base at Pearl Harbor, Hawaii. Robinson was drafted. Because he met the qualifications, he applied to Officer Candidate School (OCS) at his base, Fort Riley, Kansas, but was rejected because of racial discrimination in the armed forces. The popular heavyweight boxing champion Joe Louis was stationed at Fort Riley too. He and Robinson worked to change the OCS policy. Robinson was then accepted. He became a second lieutenant in 1943 and was honorably discharged in 1944.

After leaving the army, Robinson wanted to make his living from sports. He signed a contract to play with the Kansas City Monarchs, a Negro American League team. Larry Doby, who played in the Negro Leagues and later for the Cleveland Indians, once spoke of his experiences there, saying, "We had our good times. The Negro League players were dedicated athletes playing a game they loved. There was laughter and songs in the bus, new people, fans in every town." But black teams faced obstacles. Often they lacked access to good playing fields or locker room facilities. When playing in certain areas, they had to sleep in buses or poor hotels because some places would not admit them. They got less pay, less news coverage, and less recognition than whites.

In 1945 Brooklyn Dodgers scouts noticed Jackie Robinson's great playing with the Monarchs. Branch Rickey, the Dodgers' manager, had decided to integrate his team with talented black players. An Ohio native, Rickey had a reputation for recognizing a man's potential and developing great teams. He had spent twenty-six years with the St. Louis Cardinals before coming to New York.

Robinson recalled the day Rickey asked him to break the unofficial color line in baseball. Rickey said, "Let's say I'm a hotel clerk. You come in with the rest of your team. I look up from the register and snarl, 'We don't let niggers sleep here.' What do you do then?" Rickey then imitated an umpire waving his fist in Robinson's face and fans throwing bottles and shouting insults. Then he said, "I've been trying to give you some idea of the punishment you'll have to absorb. Can you take it?"

Robinson decided he could meet the challenge, so in 1946 he played with the Montreal Royals, the Dodgers' minor league team. Admiring fans gathered to watch him. He did so well with the Royals that he was moved up to the Dodgers the next season.

It was a difficult year. Robinson endured name-calling and taunts from the stands and sometimes from opposing players. He faced rejections on the road from hotels and restaurants. Many times Robinson felt like fighting back but had to control himself and concentrate on the game. People sent hate mail, even death threats. Quiet among his fellow players, Robinson confided in wife Rachel and Branch Rickey, whom he praised for their encouragement.

As time went on, the other Dodgers showed their support, having learned to respect Robinson as a player and as a man. When people were mean or hostile, they often defended him. Officials in the National League added their support. Robinson appreciated these efforts. His playing steadily improved. He was named Rookie of the Year.

Black Americans attended major league games in record numbers, encouraged by the presence of Robinson and a few other black players who were joining teams. By 1949 Branch Rickey told Robinson that he need no longer stay silent in the face of abuse. From then on, Robinson was more assertive. Some criticized him for this, while others pointed out that black players should be able to speak out just as white players did. That year Robinson was named Most Valuable Player in his league. His batting average was an excellent .342.

In 1950 Robinson's life story was made into a movie in which he played himself. By then he was the father of a son and daughter, with another son yet to come in 1952. He was still being harassed. That year he got letters threatening to shoot him on the field. His teammates tried to help and suggested that everyone on the whole team wear Robinson's uniform number, 42.

In the meantime, Robinson withstood the pressure. He ended the 1951 season as the third-best hitter and third in stolen bases and doubles. His work at second base gave him the best National League fielding average for the third straight year. He fielded his way to the top for a fourth year, 1952, and the Dodgers also won their league pennant. During those years Robinson spoke on television and other forums against racism. He was in his mid- thirties when the Dodgers won the pennant and their first World Series in 1955, something Robinson called "one of the greatest thrills in my life."

Looking back at a career in which he stole 197 bases (11 of them being homeplate, the most of any player of his day), Robinson said, "My value to the Dodgers was disruption—making the pitcher concentrate on me instead of on my teammate who was at bat at the time." Robinson retired at 37. He became vice-president of public relations for the large New York restaurant chain Chock Full o'Nuts.

Believing that blacks needed better jobs and a strong vote in order to advance, Robinson took part in politics. His involvement in the Freedom Bank of Harlem and the Jackie Robinson Construction Company aided black businesses. He served as special assistant of community affairs under New York Governor Nelson Rockefeller. In 1962 he was inducted into Baseball's Hall of Fame. In 1968 he campaigned for Democratic presidential candidate Hubert Humphrey.

Robinson got increasingly sick from diabetes. Heart and blood vessel problems made him frail and nearly blind. He attended a ceremony at Dodger Stadium in June 1972, the twenty-fifth anniversary of his first season with the team. Only 53, he died at his Stamford, Connecticut, home that October of a heart attack. He received a hero's funeral in New York City, where thousands of people watched as a mile-long procession took his body to Brooklyn. In his eulogy, the Reverend Jesse Jackson said, "In order for an ideal to become a reality, there must be a person, a personality, to translate it."

Basketball great Oscar Robertson once said, "He did something few of us could have done. He took a horrible beating for the sake of a principle, and all of us gained by it."

Rockwell, Norman

(1894–1978)

AMERICAN PAINTER AND
ILLUSTRATOR

Norman Rockwell was born in New York on February 3, 1894. His family moved to suburban Mamaroneck when he was nine. As a child, Rockwell had to wear corrective shoes, and began wearing glasses at the age of twelve. To gain popularity and make up for what he considered to be handicaps, Rockwell began drawing pictures to entertain his classmates.

Displaying a remarkable talent, he left high school in order to study art at the National Academy of Design. Rockwell soon began earning money designing greeting cards and teaching the actress Ethel Barrymore how to paint.

At age sixteen, Rockwell studied at the Art Students League and began illustrating books and magazines. By eighteen he was the art director for *Boy's Life* magazine.

Rockwell's early and impressive success continued and when he was twenty-two years old he sold five illustrations to George Horace Lorimer, the legendary editor of the *Saturday Evening Post.* All five illustrations were used as covers on the magazine, and Rockwell was soon contributing nearly ten covers for the magazine a year. In his forty-seven-year association with the *Saturday Evening Post,* Norman Rockwell provided 318 covers and made him one of the most popular illustrators in the history of American art.

After Rockwell's first *Post* cover, the United States entered World War I. Rockwell tried to join the navy but he was rejected because he was ten pounds under the required weight. He was determined to enlist, and ate a steady diet of bananas and doughnuts until he finally gained the needed pounds.

Rockwell was shipped to the navy yard in Charleston, South Carolina, where he painted for the navy, continued his work for the *Saturday Evening Post,* and illustrated for other magazines as well. When the war ended, Norman Rockwell was wealthy and well known; he returned to New York and built an expensive studio for himself.

As the 1920s progressed, Rockwell worked for fewer magazines, concentrating on his paintings for the *Post,* as well as a few advertising jobs. For his covers, Rockwell made a small sketch of the scene he would use, then made individual drawings of each element of the scene. He then produced a full-size charcoal drawing of the entire cover, followed by color sketches. Then he began painting. It was a long and painstaking process, but Rockwell was concerned with every detail to make his paintings more believable.

In 1935, Rockwell illustrated new editions of two Mark Twain titles: *The Adventures of Tom Sawyer* and *The Adventures of Huckleberry Finn.*

Near the end of the 1930s, Rockwell moved to Arlington, Vermont, where two other *Post* artists also lived. In 1943, his studio was destroyed by a fire; Rockwell tried to view the event as insignificant, even though he lost many of his drawings and paintings in the fire, as well as numerous objects he used for models.

The destruction of his studio led Rockwell to paint more directly from life and his paintings quickly became more specific in their depiction.

In 1963, Rockwell stopped working for the *Saturday Evening Post,* and while he continued to illustrate for other magazines, he spent most of his time traveling the world, including trips to the Soviet Union, Tibet, Mongolia, and Ethiopia.

Rogers, Will

(1879–1935)

AMERICAN ACTOR AND COMEDIAN

William Penn Adair Rogers was born in Colagah, Indian Territory (which later became the state of Oklahoma). He was reputedly of Irish and Cherokee ancestry, and he learned horseback riding and roping tricks at an early age.

After Rogers delivered mules to British troops in Johannesburg, South Africa, during the Boer War, he joined a Wild West show. He continued appearing in these types of shows until he made his way back to New York and took up performing on the vaudeville circuit. His act consisted entirely of rope tricks, and it was not until he got a laugh ad-libbing a joke to cover a failed trick that he suddenly became a humorist.

Over the next several years Rogers began making amusing remarks about politics and human nature. By 1912, he had become a well-known vaudeville performer and was able to make it on Broadway. Five years later he was a star attraction in the famous variety show *The Ziegfeld Follies.*

In 1918, Rogers went to Hollywood and made his first film, *Laughing Bill Hyde*. After making twelve more features until 1922, Rogers failed to attract an audience because his appeal was in his personality, which did not come across in silent films.

Rogers's only other film experience during the silent era was in a series of twelve shorts that he made for Hal Roach in the mid-1920s. Because of a humor column that he wrote for newspapers, his popularity continued to grow. When sound movies started in Hollywood, Will Rogers acted in *They Had to See Paris* (1929) That film was a hit, along with the next twenty movies that he made. His movies, radio performances, and newspaper columns made him a recognizable star. Rogers later was offered the nomination for governor of Oklahoma, but he declined it.

Rogers died in a plane crash in Alaska in 1935. Firmly entrenched in American cultural history, he became the subject of a hit Broadway musical in 1991 called *The Will Rogers Follies*.

The Rolling Stones

The Rolling Stones, the self-styled "greatest rock'n'roll band in the world," are considered by many to be the definitive rock and roll band. Throughout a career spanning more than thirty years, the Stones have remained consistently popular, selling many millions of recordings and packing concert halls, while successfully fine-tuning and promoting their image as the timeless "bad boys" of rock and roll.

The Rolling Stones are a product of two of rock music's preeminent talents: Mick Jagger and Keith Richards, two Englishmen from the same suburban town.

Mick Jagger, singer and songwriter, was born Michael Phillip Jagger on July 26, 1943, in Dartford, England. In 1955, when rock and roll came to England, Jagger was less influenced by the singing and gyrations of white artists such as Elvis Presley than by the harder-edged sounds of black singers like Little Richard. Later on, Jagger began listening to other American artists such as Muddy Waters and Jimmy Reed. These performers, along with Buddy Holly, were Jagger's musical heroes. It was not too long before he and some friends formed a band. Although the band (called Little Boy Blue and the Blue Boys) never played professionally, it allowed Jagger his first opportunity to experiment with the use of black performers' styles, with which he was fascinated.

As a boy at Dartford Maypole County Primary School, Mick Jagger met Keith Richards. Richards, born December 18, 1943, shared with his classmate a love of music. Indeed one of his earliest memories was of loving the guitar.

His maternal grandfather led a dance band and played several instruments, including the guitar. Young Richards used to gaze at the instrument, wishing it belonged to him. As a child, Richards was very close to his mother, who encouraged the boy to be anything he wanted to be. The two enjoyed listening to the radio together. When Richards displayed a lovely soprano voice as a child, he was entered in Inter-School competitions at London's Albert Hall. When the young Mick Jagger asked Keith Richards what he wanted to be when he grew up, Richards replied that he wanted to be a cowboy like Roy Rogers and to play a guitar. Richards' family moved away and the two boys were not to meet again for ten years.

Perhaps because of the move, Richards became a very poor student, developing discipline problems. He soon left school, entering a technical school to learn a trade. It was at this time that his mother bought him his first guitar. Richards recalls finding British rock and roll's guitar playing flat and lifeless. It was not until he heard Elvis Presley's session guitarist Scotty Moore's riffs on a Presley record that Keith Richards found the sound and style he wanted to emulate.

In 1958, Richards was expelled from technical school and began attending Sidup Art College, where future Beatle John Lennon was also enrolled. It was while he was on his way to school that Richards reencountered Mick Jagger (now attending the London School of Economics) for the first time in a decade. This chance meeting in a bus was to revolutionize the English music scene.

Jagger and Richards soon discovered that they shared a deep interest in the blues and American rhythm and blues (R&B). They also had a mutual friend in Dick Taylor, who was a classmate of Richards's at Sidup and was playing in Jagger's band, Little Boy Blue and the Blue Boys. Richards joined the band as second guitarist. But, soon after, Jagger and Richards left the band, joining with guitarist Brian Jones (b. February 28, 1942, in Cheltenham) in a new band called Blues, Inc. Richards became lead guitarist, while Jagger was the featured singer.

Richards, Jagger, and Jones began sharing a tiny, cheap London apartment. With drummer Tony Chapman, they recorded their first demonstration tape. By this time, in 1962, they had re-christened the band The Rolling Stones, taking the name from a Muddy Waters song.

On July 12, 1962, The Rolling Stones (Jagger, Richards, Jones, Dick Taylor on bass, and Mick Avory on drums) played their first show at the now-legendary Marquee. By 1963, Taylor and Avory were replaced by drummer Charlie Watts (b. June 2, 1941, North London) and bassist Bill Wyman (b. October 23, 1936, South East London). The group now contained the nucleus of its lineup for decades to come.

In contrast to the Beatles, who had established themselves as the "Fab Four," garnering international celebrity and success as well as a reputation for wit and charm, the Stones were promoted as a nasty, raunchy alternative. Their first single, "Come On," reached a respectable number twenty-one on the British charts. Their next two singles, "I Wanna Be Your Man" (written by John Lennon and Paul McCartney) and "Not Fade Away," were much bigger sellers. "Not Fade Away" reached number three on the British charts, and number forty-eight on the American.

In April 1964, their first album was released in England. Two months later, the Rolling Stones made their first American tour, which was a great triumph. Riots erupted wherever the group appeared. In England, their next five singles, including "Its All Over Now," hit number one. And by 1965 they had established themselves as second only to the Beatles as the most popular British rock group, a position they held until the Beatles split up.

The crucial factor distinguishing the Stones from their competition was their successful move from blues-rock cover band to performing their own rock material with a blues base. Jagger and Richards had developed into a songwriting team as early as 1964, and by 1965 such original Stones hits as "Satisfaction" and "The Last Time" were wildly popular on both sides of the Atlantic.

For the next several years, The Rolling Stones toured extensively, but their involvement with drugs limited their ability to perform in the U.S. after 1966. Despite their personal involvement with drugs, the Stones, unlike the Beatles, were never quite comfortable musically with psychedelia. After their 1967 "Sgt. Pepper" knock-off, "Their Satanic Majesties Request," they returned to their familiar hard-rock style, as evidenced by the single "Jumping Jack Flash" and the album "Beggars Banquet," hailed, upon its release, by critics as the group's finest achievement to date. By this time, every album that the band released automatically sold over a million copies.

In 1969 the Stones reemerged as a concert attraction after firing Brian Jones, whose drug and alcohol problems had become too much for even the other Stones to handle. (Jones was to drown in his swimming pool a few months later, amid rumors of foul play.) Guitarist Mick Taylor (b. January 17, 1948) replaced Jones. Upon releasing the single "Honky Tonk Women" and the album "Let It Bleed," the band embarked on an American tour culminating in the disastrous free concert at Altamont, in Northern California. At a performance captured in the film "Gimme shelter," "security" was provided by Hells Angels who stomped and hacked to death a young man brandishing a gun. Despite the scorching publicity, after the Beatles disbanded the following year, the Stones were undeniably the most important rock and roll band in the world.

Mick Jagger was increasingly sought after as a personality, and was soon asked to appear in the movies "Ned Kelly" and "Performance." After starring in the latter, Jagger met and married Nicaraguan fashion model and socialite Bianca Pérez Morena de Macías. The pair quickly became international celebrities. The couple had one child, Jade, but later divorced. Jagger went on to live with, and eventually marry, American model Jeri Hall.

By the 1970s, the Rolling Stones toured every three years, releasing a slew of million-selling, chart-topping records, in spite of Keith Richards's addiction to drugs. Richards was arrested in Toronto in 1977 for heroin possession. He subsequently kicked the habit by having a total blood transfusion, after once again serving no time in jail. Assuming a more active role in the band's creative projects, a rejuvenated Richards seemed to help improve the quality of the Stones's concerts and recordings in the late '70s and early '80s.

The 1981–82 Rolling Stones tour (filmed by American director Hal Ashby and released as a feature film, entitled "Let's Spend The Night Together") was the largest-grossing tour in rock and roll history. That same year, their album "Tattoo You" outsold their 1978 success, "Some Girls." But, when Jagger completed a solo album in 1985 and refused to tour with the band to promote their 1986 release, "Dirty Work," the Rolling Stones's long ride together seemed to have come to a halt. Jagger released his second solo album in 1987, touring Japan in 1988. That same year, Richards released his own solo album, "Talk is Cheap." But by the time the album appeared, the Stones were already discussing a reunion. The group released "Steel Wheels" in 1989, and toured in support of the album well into 1990.

Bill Wyman left the group after the "Steel Wheels" tour (guitarist Mick Taylor had been replaced in 1976 by former Faces guitarist Ron Wood); the Stones remained without a bassist for several years, even signing a multi-million dollar contract with Virgin Records in 1992 as a four-piece band. Finally, in 1994, the band replaced Wyman with former Miles Davis and Sting bassist Darryl Jones. That summer, the Rolling Stones released another major-seller, their most recent effort, the album "Voodoo Lounge." Though the future of the world's longest-running, consistently successful rock and roll band now seems somewhat uncertain, its bold impact upon modern music and culture remains beyond dispute.

Roosevelt, Eleanor

(1884–1962)

WIFE OF PRESIDENT FRANKLIN D.
ROOSEVELT AND SOCIAL ACTIVIST

Anna Eleanor Roosevelt was born on October 11, 1884, in New York, the daughter of a wealthy society family. She was educated at a private school in England, and in 1905 she married her distant cousin, Franklin Roosevelt, who was attending Columbia Law School at the time. The marriage was not an easy one. In the early years, she felt dominated by Franklin's mother. Later on, she developed an unusual relationship with Franklin that was both close and distant, something like that of a special companion and adviser.

Roosevelt became interested in politics as her husband rose from New York state senator in 1910 to assistant secretary of the navy in 1913. During World War 1, she worked in a canteen at Union Station in Washington, serving soup and snacks to soldiers passing through the capital. In 1920, she joined the League of Women Voters, which sought to increase the role of women in politics. A year later, she had to interrupt her political work to care for her husband, who had been stricken with polio. In 1922 she joined the Women's Trade Union League, and in 1923 she became active in the Democratic party. In 1927, she purchased the Todhunter School, a private girls' school in New York, and served as the school's vice principal and one of its teachers. By this time, she was also writing numerous articles for newspapers and magazines, and was in great demand as a speaker with women's groups.

In 1928, Franklin Roosevelt was elected governor of New York. Polio, however, had left him unable to walk, and Eleanor frequently took his place on official visits. In the wake of the Depression, her husband was elected president in 1932. Roosevelt was first lady for more than twelve years. She traveled widely throughout the country, studying the living conditions of people during the Depression, becoming her husband's eyes and ears. She held weekly press conferences, but only invited female reporters, in an effort to encourage newspapers to hire more women. She became a leading spokeswoman for her husband's New Deal policies, for women, for black Americans, and for labor, and since she had no need to please voters she could speak more freely about these issues than her husband. In 1933, she pushed her husband to appoint the first woman cabinet member, Frances Perkins, as secretary of labor. In 1934, she helped to create the National Youth Administration, a New Deal program designed to provide jobs for young people. When in 1939 the black singer Marian Anderson was denied permission to sing in a Washington auditorium by the Daughters of the American Revolution (DAR), Roosevelt resigned her membership in the DAR and helped to organize an alternate concert in front of the Lincoln Memorial.

During World War II, Roosevelt worked for the Red Cross and traveled throughout Europe and the South Pacific, visiting American troops. On April 12, 1945, a few months before the end of the war, Franklin Roosevelt died and Vice President Harry Truman became President. Though she was no longer first lady, she became, in Truman's words, "First Lady of the World." Truman asked her to serve as one of the American delegates to the newly formed United Nations. She became chairwoman of the UN Commission on Human Rights, and in 1948 she co-wrote and pushed for the adoption of the Universal Declaration of Human Rights. It established many of the basic principles that guide the activity of the United Nations, and describes the responsibilities of all governments toward their citizens. She actively worked for the election of liberal Democrat Adlai Stevenson in 1952, but Republican Dwight Eisenhower won the election.

In 1953, after Eisenhower became President, Roosevelt resigned her post at the UN. She became honorary chairwoman of Americans for Democratic Action and spoke out against Senator Eugene McCarthy of Wisconsin and his anti-Communist crusade. She traveled all over the world in support of the United Nations and world peace. In 1961, President John Kennedy reappointed her to her UN post. She also served on the National Advisory Council of the Peace Corps. She died of tuberculosis in New York on November 7, 1962.

Much loved by Americans during the Depression and the war years, by the time of her death she had achieved worldwide recognition as a spokesperson for the oppressed and downtrodden. She was a woman of intellect and compassion, and is considered the most effective first lady in the history of the American presidency.

Roosevelt, Franklin Delano

(1882–1945)

GOVERNOR OF NEW YORK AND THIRTY-SECOND PRESIDENT
OF THE UNITED STATES

Franklin Delano Roosevelt was born on January 30, 1882, in Hyde Park, New York. An only child, Roosevelt was the object of much attention and lived a life of luxury. Before he was fifteen years old, his parents had taken him to Europe eight times.

In 1896, Roosevelt was enrolled in the Groton School, a small Massachusetts prep school. He entered Harvard University in 1900, majoring in history and government. In his freshman year, his father died, leaving him a rather large sum of money. In 1904, he enrolled at Columbia University Law School. A year later, he married a distant cousin, Anna Eleanor Roosevelt. Another distant cousin, President Theodore Roosevelt, gave the bride away at the wedding. The couple eventually had five children.

In 1910, Roosevelt decided to run for the New York state senate on the Democratic ticket. He had a charming manner and great personal warmth, and he won the election. As state senator, he earned a reputation for independent thinking, and became especially interested in conservation and labor issues. A strong supporter of Woodrow Wilson, Roosevelt attended the inauguration ceremony in Washington when Wilson was elected President in 1912 and was offered the job of assistant secretary of the navy, a position he held for seven years. He inspected ships and naval bases and did much to modernize the navy during World War I.

In 1920, the Democratic party chose James M. Cox, governor of Ohio, as its candidate for President, and Roosevelt was chosen as the party's candidate for vice president. Cox and Roosevelt lost the election to Republicans Warren G. Harding and Calvin Coolidge.

In 1921, at the age of thirty-nine, Roosevelt was stricken with polio. He would never walk again. He had to wear heavy steel braces just to stand. But he did not let the disease conquer his spirit. He designed his own wheelchair and had his car rebuilt so that he could drive it without using his legs. In 1926, he purchased a health spa in Warm Springs, Georgia and turned it into a treatment center for polio victims. Those closest to Roosevelt observed that the affliction brought out his courage and strength, and his wife Eleanor encouraged him not to lose interest in politics.

In 1928, the Democrats tried to regain the White House by nominating Al Smith, governor of New York, for President. Smith needed someone to replace himself as governor of New York, someone who was popular and could rally the state's voters behind Smith's bid for the presidency. Roosevelt was chosen. Smith lost the presidential election to Republican Herbert Hoover, but by a narrow margin Roosevelt was elected governor of New York. As governor, Roosevelt began to reveal a concern for the less privileged. He worked to improve the state's criminal justice system, its hospitals and health services, and its workers' compensation laws.

In October 1929, prices on the New York Stock Exchange fell drastically, and the country was gripped by a financial panic. Banks failed, businesses and factories closed, and by 1932 twelve million Americans were unemployed. The Depression was the worst economic crisis in the country's history. Voters became pessimistic about the nation's future and blamed their difficulties on President Herbert Hoover's inaction. At the Democratic convention in Chicago in June 1932, Roosevelt was nominated for President and made a speech that included the phrase that would forever identify his administration. "I pledge you," he said, "I pledge myself, to a new deal for the American people." He won a landslide victory in the November election.

As President, Roosevelt was a pragmatist. "Do something," he said. "If it works, do it some more. And if it does not work, do something else." He believed that government had a responsibility to actively regulate the economy and to protect the interests of the less fortunate. He was influenced by the ideas of the English economist John Maynard Keynes, who argued that the capitalist system might not recover from the Depression unless government spending was used to stimulate the demand for goods. Roosevelt's first task was simply to instill confidence in the American people that the problem could be solved. He began a series of radio broadcasts that became known as "fireside chats," in which he explained his ideas and programs to the radio audience as if he were sitting in their living rooms.

The 1932 elections had also given the Democrats a majority in both houses of Congress, and Roosevelt took advantage of this by promoting a great many new laws designed to put people back to work. In 1933, he created the Federal Emergency Relief Administration to give individual states money for the poor and hungry. This was followed by the Civilian Works Administration, which hired six million people to build and maintain roads, parks, sewers, and airports. The Public Works Administration paid private companies to build bridges, hospitals, and dams. In 1935, many of these programs were reorganized and placed under the WPA, the Works Progress Administration. The WPA not only supervised public works, but provided employment for artists, writers, musicians, and actors in government-sponsored programs. The Civilian Conservation Corps employed almost three million young people in projects such as tree planting, forest-fire fighting, and park and beach improvement. The Agricultural Adjustment Act of 1933 paid farmers to grow less, thereby raising farm prices and helping many farmers to avoid bankruptcy.

The National Recovery Act set standards for minimum wages and maximum hours of work. The Tennessee Valley Authority built fifteen dams and hydro-electric power stations in the poverty-stricken Tennessee River valley, providing cheap electricity for seven states. The Federal Deposit Insurance Corporation guaranteed that savings deposits in participating banks would be protected even if those banks failed. The Securities and Exchange Commission began to regulate stock trading more closely to prevent fraud and speculation. In 1935, Congress passed the Social Security Act, which provided older workers with a pension when they retired. Workers could now count on unemployment insurance if they lost their jobs, and the Wagner Act of 1935 guaranteed the right of unions to organize and bargain collectively with employers.

Never before in American history had there been such a flood of new legislation, new programs, and new government agencies. Millions of Americans found some kind of employment; their confidence in the country's future was restored and Roosevelt's popularity soared. He easily won reelection to the presidency in 1936.

In the late 1930s, Roosevelt had to turn his attention to events overseas. Fascist political parties had taken control of governments in Germany, Italy, and Spain. Japan was waging a brutal war for control of northern and eastern China and Korea. In 1939, the German dictator Adolf Hitler invaded Poland and England's treaty commitments forced it to declare war on Germany. World War II had begun. Germany quickly conquered Belgium, France, Norway, Holland, and Denmark. Roosevelt at first tried to avoid American involvement in the war, as Woodrow Wilson had done at the beginning of World War I. But his sympathies were clearly with the European democracies and China. After winning reelection to a third term as President in 1940, Roosevelt pushed for passage of the Lend Lease Act, which allowed England, China, and other favored nations to "rent" American military equipment.

On December 7, 1941, Japanese forces attacked the American naval base at Pearl Harbor in Hawaii and the United States was forced into war in the Pacific. Roosevelt's new regulatory agencies enabled him to organize the American economy quickly for war production. The country became, in Roosevelt's words, "the great arsenal of democracy."

As the war progressed, Roosevelt traveled frequently to meet with other world leaders to plan the future peace. He met with Winston Churchill, the prime minister of England, at Casablanca, Morocco and at Cairo, Egypt in 1943. Roosevelt and Churchill met with Joseph Stalin, leader of the Soviet Union, at Tehran, Iran in 1943 and again at Yalta in the Soviet Union in 1945. Secret agreements were made to redistribute certain territories in Eastern Europe after the war, and these agreements created problems for Roosevelt's successor, Harry Truman. All these conferences and all the traveling, as well as the stress of the war itself, began to wear down Roosevelt's health.

Roosevelt was reelected to a fourth term as President in 1944. On May 7, 1945, Germany surrendered and the war in Europe was over. But Roosevelt did not live to see the final victory over Japan in August 1945. On April 12, 1945, at the age of sixty three, Roosevelt died of a cerebral hemorrhage while resting at his polio clinic in Warm Springs, Georgia. He was buried at his family home in Hyde Park, New York.

Roosevelt's bold economic policies rescued the country from the Depression and changed the way the American economy worked. Though the country became more conservative in the years to come, the economy could no longer be described as purely capitalistic. It became a "mixed" economy in which the government regulated banks, businesses, and the terms under which money could be borrowed. It was now commonly accepted that the government would use taxing and spending policies to control inflation, unemployment, and economic growth and to lift the country out of depression or recession. Certain New Deal programs—Social Security, unemployment insurance, bank deposit insurance, and price supports for farmers—became part of what Americans expected from their government.

Roosevelt, Theodore

(1858–1919)

GOVERNOR OF NEW YORK AND TWENTY-SIXTH PRESIDENT OF THE UNITED STATES

Theodore Roosevelt was born on October 27, 1858, in New York. His father, also named Theodore, was a wealthy glass importer who had helped found the Metropolitan Museum of Art and the Museum of Natural History. As a child, Roosevelt suffered from asthma and had to work hard to build up his strength. He enjoyed reading, especially adventure stories, and liked to study the animals in the woods during vacations in the Adirondack Mountains. In 1876, he went to Harvard University, where, having improved his health, he took up boxing, fencing, and football. After graduation in 1880 he married Alice Hathaway Lee of Boston.

Returning to New York, Roosevelt joined the Republican party, and in 1881 he was elected to the New York legislature. In 1884, both his mother and his wife died, and Roosevelt, deeply shaken, gave up politics and went west to the Dakota territory to become a cattle rancher. The short, bespectacled easterner quickly earned the respect of his tough western neighbors—in one instance he spent nine days in the freezing Dakota winter tracking down and bringing back to justice two outlaws who had stolen property of his. He returned to New York in 1886, ran for mayor and lost, and then married Edith Carrow. The couple took up residence in a mansion on Sagamore Hill in Oyster Bay, New York. He began to write his third and most popular book, *The Winning of the West,* and became interested in politics again.

In 1888, Roosevelt was appointed commissioner of the civil service. He worked to end the "spoils system," in which government jobs were given to friends and party loyalists, and introduced examinations to select civil servants on the basis of merit and ability. In 1885, Mayor William Strong of New York City appointed him to the Board of Police Commissioners, where he worked to eliminate bribery and corruption in the police department. Walking the streets of the city, he began to learn about the poverty of the working class. When William McKinley was elected President in 1896, Roosevelt was appointed assistant secretary of the navy. He tried to increase funding for the navy, believing that the United States would soon go to war to support Cuban revolutionaries fighting to free their country from Spain.

When war came in 1898, Roosevelt resigned his government post and joined the First Volunteer Cavalry Regiment, known as the "Rough Riders," which sailed for Cuba that summer. At the battle of San Juan Hill, Roosevelt led his men in a courageous but foolhardy charge that drove the Spanish from their positions. He returned to the United States a hero. In November 1898, he was elected governor of New York. In 1900, he was persuaded to run for vice president on a ticket with President McKinley. McKinley and Roosevelt won the election, but in September, 1901, McKinley was assassinated in Buffalo, New York; at the age of forty-two Roosevelt became President of the United States.

At the turn of the century, the economy of the United States was expanding rapidly, and great wealth had been accumulated by entrepreneurs such as John D. Rockefeller, J.P. Morgan, and Andrew Carnegie, who formed huge combinations of businesses in the oil, steel, coal, and railroad industries. These combinations were known as trusts or monopolies, and they were powerful enough to defeat all competitors and set whatever prices they desired. Roosevelt's father had taught him that wealthy people have public responsibilities and should not be motivated by greed, and Roosevelt himself had seen the poor conditions under which workers had to survive in New York City. As President, he was determined to act against the trusts. Using the Sherman Antitrust Act of 1890, Roosevelt took the monopolies to court and broke them up, restoring competition and fair prices in many areas of the economy. He earned himself the name of "Trust-Buster" and gained great popularity among the poor and working classes.

Roosevelt was equally tough in foreign affairs. His policy was expressed in the now-famous phrase "Speak softly and carry a big stick." When European governments threatened to intervene in Latin America to force repayment of money they had loaned to poor countries there, the President issued the Roosevelt Corollary to the Monroe Doctrine. It stated that the United States would use military force to prevent anyone from seizing South American territory as payment for outstanding debts. In 1902, he successfully suppressed a revolution in the Philippines, which had become a possession of the United States after the Spanish-American War.

In 1903, revolutionaries in Panama, which was then a province of Colombia, overthrew their Colombian overseers and established an independent republic with the aid of United States troops. It was part of Roosevelt's plan to build a canal across the isthmus of Panama, and he quickly negotiated with the new government to begin construction. The Panama Canal was finished in 1914, and it was one of Roosevelt's greatest achievements, for it reduced transportation costs for shipping companies and gave the United States Navy the ability to quickly shuttle back and forth between the Atlantic and Pacific oceans, instead of having to travel all the way around Cape Horn in South America.

In 1904, Roosevelt was reelected President. Under the slogan of giving Americans a "Square Deal," he continued his attack on big business. The Interstate Commerce Commission was given the right to regulate railroad rates. Congress passed a Pure Food and Drug Act to regulate abuses in the meat-packing industry. He appointed the conservationist Gifford Pinchot to head the United States Forest Service and put 230 million acres of land under federal protection from unregulated development. In 1906, he received the Nobel Peace Prize for helping to negotiate the Treaty of Portsmouth that ended the 1904–1905 war between Japan and Russia.

In 1908, Roosevelt refused to run for a third term. His secretary of war, William Howard Taft, received the Republican nomination and won the election. In 1909, he set out on an ambitious hunting and scientific expedition through Africa. He continued his travels through Europe, giving lectures at major universities. Upon his return in 1910, he found the attraction of politics irresistible. He had been unhappy with President Taft, who seemed to favor big-business interests. Along with other dissatisfied Republicans, he formed the American Progressive party, nicknamed the "Bull Moose" party, and he ran for President again in 1912. But the split in the Republican party gave the election to the Democratic candidate, Woodrow Wilson.

Out of politics again, Roosevelt undertook another scientific expedition to South America in 1913, later writing a book about his adventures, *Through the Brazilian Wilderness.* Back in New York in 1914, he began to publicly denounce Wilson's policy of neutrality toward the European powers fighting in World War 1. When the United States finally declared war on Germany in 1917, Roosevelt pleaded to be put in command of a division of American troops, but he was refused. On January 6, 1919, he died at his Sagamore Hill estate.

Rostropovich, Mstislav

(1927–   )

RUSSIAN CELLIST

> It is my aim, my destination in life, to make the cello as beloved an instrument as the violin and piano. But this cannot be until there are more and great new works for the cello.
>
> —Mstislav Rostropovich, on his love of the cello

Mstislav Rostropovich's cello playing has inspired such contemporary composers as Sergei Prokofiev, Dmitri Shostakovich, and Benjamin Britten to write specially for him. Although he can do anything he wants with the cello, Rostropovich always chooses to express the music as it was written.

Rostropovich was born in 1927 in Baku, in what was then the Soviet Republic of Azerbaijan. His father was a cellist who taught and played in symphony orchestras, and his mother was a pianist. She introduced him to the piano when he was four. He began studying the cello at age eight, and composition at age eleven. When the family moved to Moscow, where his father played in the orchestra of the All-Union Radio and taught cello at the Gnessin Institute, Rostropovich continued his lessons in his father's class. Rostropovich had the advantage of having a father who took him with him when he played with various symphony orchestras. By the time he made his public debut in 1940, he was familiar with the life of a professional musician.

In 1941, his father died and Rostropovich took his father's place as a cello teacher in the local music school, teaching students older than himself. After graduating from the Moscow Conservatory he became a teacher there. Seven years later, he became a music professor, the youngest in the Soviet Union at that time. In addition to his teaching, Rostropovich performed with the Moscow Philharmonic as a soloist, winning many prizes for his playing.

Despite the cold war, in the mid-1950s the Soviet Union sent many famous artists to America. In 1956, Rostropovich made his debut at Carnegie Hall in New York. He was hailed as a great talent. His later visits to the United States have solidified his reputation as one of the best cellists of our time. He has come to be accepted as the successor of the great Spanish cellist Pablo Casals, who died in 1973. His playing has inspired several pieces to be written for his cello. Prokofiev wrote the *Sinfonia Concertante for Cello, Opus 125* (1950–1952) for Rostropovich. Shostakovich, who considers *Opus 125* to be Prokofiev's finest work, was himself inspired to compose the *Concerto in E-Flat for Cello, Opus 107*, for Rostropovich. Benjamin Britten, who was a close friend of Rostropovich's, wrote three works for him. Over the years, his country has given him many honors, including the State Prize in 1951 and the Lenin Prize in 1964.

Rubinstein, Artur

(1887–1982)

POLISH PIANIST

Artur (or Arthur) Rubinstein had few rivals among contemporary pianists. He was considered one of the greatest pianists of the century. Rubinstein was born in 1887 in Lodz, Poland. He was the youngest of seven children. His parents had little interest in music, but they were quick to recognize the talent of their son. Rubinstein began taking lessons when he was four years old. At six, he performed at a charity concert in Warsaw. At the age of eight, young Artur was sent to Warsaw to study with Professor A. Rozychi at the Warsaw Conservatory of Music. Before too long, it was discovered that there was nothing more that Rubinstein could learn from his teacher. When his sister went to Berlin to get married, she took Rubinstein with her to perform for violinist Joseph Joachim. Joachim was so impressed with the boy that he became his part-time teacher and helped Rubinstein to make his Berlin debut at the age of eleven. Recitals in Dresden and Hamburg followed, and in 1902 he played with the Warsaw Symphony Orchestra.

Within a few years, Rubinstein was famous in Europe. With his travel expenses paid for by the Knabe Piano Company, he came to the United States in 1906 to make his New York debut as a soloist with the Philadelphia Orchestra in Carnegie Hall in New York. Although he received some good reviews, the concert was not a success. Audiences of that time were more impressed by the extravagant mannerisms of contemporary pianists and Rubinstein's direct and clear playing did not delight them. He was ahead of his time, and after seventy-five more concerts in major American cities, he returned to Europe, discouraged.

Rubinstein decided to study. He was lucky enough to meet and work with Ignace Paderewski, one of the leading pianists of his day. Not until 1910, at the age of twenty-three, did he return to the concert stage. By 1914, he was established in Europe as a top-ranking concert pianist.

During World War I, Rubinstein gave recitals for the Allied cause. He was so enraged by the German's treatment of the Belgians and the Poles that he vowed never to appear in Germany again and never did.

In 1916, Rubinstein went to Spain for a tour that became one of the turning points in his career. Originally scheduled to give four concerts, he remained for 125. His success resulted in an invitation to perform in South America, where he became beloved by Spanish-speaking audiences. The reaction to his second Carnegie Hall concert in 1919, however, was less than enthusiastic. It wasn't until 1937, when he performed at Carnegie Hall for the third time, that Rubinstein scored a hit with an American audience. After that, however,he became idolized all over the country. *The New York Times* called him "a brilliant pianist and musician who should have been heard more often in later years on this side of the ocean."

During World War II, Rubinstein brought his wife and two children from France to the United States to settle in Beverly Hills, California. In Hollywood, he was signed by a number of movie studios to play the piano for actors who were playing the roles of composers Robert Schumann, Franz Liszt, Johannes Brahms, and others in the films *I've Always Loved You* (1946), *Song of Love* (1947), and *Night Song* (1947). In the films *Carnegie Hall* (1947) and *Of Men and Music* (1951), Rubinstein appeared as himself.

Meanwhile, his tours took him to all parts of the world, including North Africa, China, Japan, Java (Indonesia), and Australia.

In 1946, Rubinstein became an American citizen. He organized and served as president of the Frédéric Chopin Fund, which raised money for needy musicians in Europe. In 1953, after moving to New York City, Rubinstein gave the first of his famous piano marathons, in which he gave five concerts in less than two weeks. In 1961, he performed in ten recitals in Carnegie Hall in one month. Rubinstein performed well into his seventies. As his performing commitments decreased, he wrote a two-volume autobiography. Over the years, Rubinstein made a great number of recordings, which have been reissued over and over again.

Rudolph, Wilma Glodean

(1940–   )

AMERICAN TRACK AND FIELD
COMPETITOR

The crowd at the 1960 Summer Olympics roared and applauded as American Wilma Rudolph broke the tape three yards ahead of her nearest competitor. She had just won the 100-meter dash, earning the first of three gold medals that year for her skill in running. No woman track athlete had ever achieved such a feat at the Games. What made Rudolph's victory more astonishing was that as a child, this graceful, smiling champion could barely walk. Wilma Rudolph's triumph in 1960 was achieved through years of hard work and her mother's loving determination that Wilma would regain the use of her leg.

Wilma Rudolph was born on June 23, 1940, in a tiny farming town in Tennessee. Her father was a porter and her mother did domestic work six days a week. Wilma was the fifth of eight children, with eleven stepbrothers and stepsisters. Born prematurely, she weighed only 4½ pounds and was sickly from the start. She had measles, mumps, flu, and many other illnesses. There were times doctors said skinny, weak Wilma would die. She later wrote, "I was the sickliest child in all of Clarksville."

At age 4, she had double pneumonia and scarlet fever. She may also have had polio, a viral disease of the spinal cord that once killed and crippled thousands every year. The muscles in her left leg and foot weakened, so that Wilma could not walk. She faced her condition bravely. "The other children came and played with her while she sat there in her chair," her mother recalled.

Medical treatment for black people in the area was poor and hard to find. The nearest hospital for blacks was fifty miles away, in Nashville. So for two years, twice a week, Blanche Rudolph took Wilma by bus to Nashville for treatments to strengthen her leg. She wore special shoes and did painful exercises. Her mother learned to massage the leg and to do some of the treatment at home. Along the way, they were forced to ride in the back of the bus with other black people; Wilma quickly became aware of racial discrimination and the disadvantages blacks suffered. She remembered thinking, "White folks got all the luxury, and we black folks got the dirty work. There's something not right about all this."

For years Wilma could not walk normally. Then, at age 11, she surprised her family by not only walking, but running and throwing balls through the peach basket her brother had set up in the yard. As a tall 13-year-old, Wilma made the girls' basketball team at Clarksville High School. A fast, skillful player, she was popular with teammates for her sense of humor and personality. Wilma became the star of the track team too. Once partly crippled, she now had long, smooth strides. She won every race in high school. Her coach called her "Skeeter" because she darted as swiftly as a mosquito.

Wilma made the 1956 U.S. Olympic team that went to Melbourne, Australia. She won a bronze medal that year when her relay team placed third. In 1957 she entered Tennessee State University in Nashville. Coach Ed Temple took a strong interest in her, but Wilma suffered from illnesses and could not train in 1958. She spent time resting in bed and reading, one of her favorite pastimes.

When Wilma began running again in 1959, she was better than ever. Temple encouraged her to eat a healthier diet. He was strict, insisting that, team members be prompt and do their best. Wilma injured a thigh muscle just before an important meet, a big disappointment, but recovered and began working hard again. She won a place on the U.S. Olympic team and headed for Rome in 1960. By then Wilma was 5 feet, 11 inches tall and weighed 130 pounds. Her maturity and stamina enabled her to withstand the 100-degree heat at the Games and intense pressure of competition.

In the 100-meter dash, Wilma outran her competitors even though she had hurt her ankle as the race began. In fact, her time of 11 seconds set an Olympic record! She excited the crowd by bursting ahead in the 200-yard dash to win by four yards. She and three teammates then won the 400-meter relay. Wilma was photographed smiling radiantly, one gold medal around her neck and one in each hand. She was a hero at the Olympics. People from other countries loved the pretty American with her ready smile and friendly manner. The Italians called her "La Gazella" and the French called her "La Perle Noir" (black pearl).

U.S. coach Payton Jordan called her "the smoothest runner I have ever seen. . . . She has those long, graceful strides. While the other runners were taking two steps, she needed only one."

After the Games, Wilma and her teammates raced in exhibitions throughout Europe. Her graciousness continued to make Wilma quite popular with fans and reporters. She signed autographs for people all over the world. Wilma returned to finish college. She ran in many indoor track meets in 1961 and set world records in the 60- and 70-yard sprints and the 100-meter dash. That year, she won the Sullivan Trophy as America's best amateur athlete, becoming one of only three women to have ever received it up to that time. She won Italy's Christopher Columbus Award as the most outstanding world sports figure. Wilma, her mother, and her coach met President Kennedy at the White House.

After a race in 1962, Wilma Rudolph stopped competing. She got her college diploma, married, and raised four children. Through the years she taught school, modeled, lectured, ran a community center and several learning institutions, coached track, worked in public relations, wrote her autobiography, and appeared on TV as a commentator. She traveled for Operation Champ, a government project to train young athletes in American inner cities. She later wrote, "I grew up in a small, segregated southern town, but the oppression there was nothing compared to the oppression I saw in the big-city black ghettos."

Rudolph raised money for the Track and Field Hall of Fame in Charleston, South Carolina. She supported the Women's Sports Foundation and Title IX, a law requiring equal treatment for women's college athletic programs. Throughout her life she had worked for underprivileged children; she started the nonprofit Wilma Rudolph Foundation for them in 1981, enabling athletes in need of training to get it free. Rudolph had once called her life "rich in opportunities." She has devoted herself to expanding opportunities for others.

Russell, Bertrand

(1872–1970)

ENGLISH PHILOSOPHER, LOGICIAN, MATHEMATICIAN, SOCIAL CRITIC, AND POLITICAL ACTIVIST

Three passions, simple but overwhelmingly strong, have governed my life: the longing for love, the search for knowledge, and unbearable pity for the suffering of mankind. These passions, like great winds, have blown me hither and thither, in a wayward course, over a deep ocean of anguish, reaching to the very verge of despair.

—Bertrand Russell, from *The Autobiography of Bertrand Russell*

Bertrand Arthur William Russell, Third Earl Russell, Viscount Amberley, was quite simply the most widely known, widely read and controversial philosopher of the twentieth century. He was also one of the most important philosophers and logicians of his era, an astonishingly prolific, long-lived writer, and fearlessly himself. Over the course of his nearly hundred years of life, Russell's philosophical and political positions evolved almost constantly; he remained active, lucid, and vocal almost to his death, one month before his ninety-eighth birthday. There were few issues he didn't address in his voluminous writings, in lucid, wittily ironic, and elegantly thought-out English prose. One of the finest English-language essayists of all time, he was the 1950 Nobel Prize winner for Literature.

Bertrand Russell was born on May 18, 1872, at Ravenscroft, his parents' home in Monmouthshire, England. His family on both sides had a distinguished history. His parents were Lord and Lady Amberley; among the family members were several members of the peerage and, Russell recalled, the Honorable Charles Elliot, K.C.B., Russell's great-uncle: "I was told that he was Rear Admiral and that there is a grander sort of admiral called Admiral of the Fleet. This rather pained me and I felt he should have done something about it."

When Bertrand was two, his mother and sister died of diphtheria; eighteen months later, his father died. Bertrand and his older brother Frank were supposed to be raised by legal guardians, both of whom were atheists, so his paternal grandparents took the matter to court and had that provision of the will set aside. Thus it was that Bertrand and Frank came to live with Lord and Lady Russell.

Lord John Russell was a member of Parliament at the time of the Battle of Waterloo, and he would twice serve as prime minister of England. His friends included most of the prominent inhabitants of the British Isles, and on at least one occasion, young Bertrand, then two, managed to silence the great poet Robert Browning, announcing in a loud voice, "I wish that man would stop talking." Lord Russell was an invalid, and would die in 1878, but his wife, Bertrand's grandmother, was more than twenty years younger, a puritanical, repressed, and irascible woman who browbeat the younger child, but also instilled in him an irretrievable sense of independence.

Ironically, given his later achievements in mathematics, Bertrand struggled at first with that subject, unable to master the multiplication tables and convinced that his algebra instructor was deliberately not telling him what x and y equaled out of sheer meanness. He also found geometry rather unsatisfying, because the proofs were based on unproven axioms, a state of affairs that appalled his orderly mind. Years later, he and Alfred North Whitehead would write *Principia Mathematica* for the express purpose of leaving no axiom unproved.

By the time Bertrand reached his teens, however, mathematics had become his chief delight, and it would, he later said, save him from suicide. In 1890, Russell went to Cambridge University, drawn by the excellence of its mathematics department. He studied mathematics for three years and philosophy for one, made many new friends, and found himself constantly challenged intellectually. He also met and married the first of his four wives, Alys Pearsall Smith.

In 1896, Russell published the first of his many books, *German Social Democracy*, a political analysis. In his 1903 *The Principles of Mathematics*, Russell offered a vigorous defense of "logicism," the claim that all mathematical concepts were definable by way of a small number of primitive logical concepts, and that all mathematical propositions were deducible from a small number of fundamental logical principles. This theory, which in this early book is loaded down with a heavy freight of Platonic idealism, is reproduced in a vastly more sophisticated way in the three-volume *Principia Mathematica* (1910–1913), perhaps the single greatest work of philosophical and mathematical logic produced in the twentieth century. In between writing volumes of the *Principia*, Russell authored a small book of essays, *The Problems of Philosophy* (1912), which is still the most accessible and clear-headed introduction to philosophy in the English language.

World War I was the most politicized period of Russell's career, although he had already run unsuccessfully for Parliament in 1907 on a women's suffrage ticket. By the outbreak of war, Russell was a firmly committed pacifist (a position he would move away from in the face of the threat of Nazism one war later). He would write in later years, "When the war came I felt as if I had heard the voice of God. I knew it was my business to protest, however futile it might be."

He opposed war with Germany, worked for an early peace, and fought against compulsory military service. At the age of forty-two, he was too old to be drafted himself. He was sent to prison in 1916 for writing a leaflet protesting the jailing of a conscientious objector; as a result, he was stripped of his teaching position at Trinity College, Cambridge. The government prevented him from going to Harvard in the United States as a guest lecturer; shortly after that, he was jailed for six more months for suggesting that the American army, about to enter the war, was better at strike-breaking than war-making. While in prison, he wrote the first parts of *Introduction to Mathematical Philosophy* (1919) and *The Analysis of Mind* (1921).

As turbulent as his political activities had made his public life, his private life was an even bigger mess. He had fallen out of love with Alys, had taken a mistress, Lady Ottoline Morrell, who refused to leave her husband, then embarked on a stormy relationship with the actress Colette O'Niel (Lady Constance Malleson). They never married because Russell wanted children, but Lady Constance did not.

He then began an equally tempestuous relationship with Dora Black. The two traveled to the Soviet Union, where they quarreled explosively over the new Bolshevik (communist) state, which Russell deplored (as he reported in his resolutely anti-Leninist *The Theory and Practice of Bolshevism*). They also went to China together, with Russell producing yet another book from that trip.

Dora shared his interest in having children, but not in marriage. This time, he got his way. The couple was married in 1921, seven weeks before the birth of John Conrad Russell.

For the first six years of his marriage to Dora, Russell led a relatively stable life, writing books of popular science, philosophy, and politics, and being financially comfortable. His daughter Katharine was born in December 1923. Then in 1927, the Russells opened Beacon Hill School on the estate that had belonged to his brother Frank, as a means to test their theories on progressive education. The school was surprisingly successful, but it wrecked the marriage and hurt the children, who couldn't understand why they had to be treated the same as any other students. In 1934, the Russells were divorced; John and Katharine went to the Dartington School and divided their vacations between the two parents. Russell married Patricia "Peter" Spence and had another son, Conrad, the following year.

Russell had been living on his writing income. He had long ago given all his inherited money to charity. With Frank's death in 1931, he inherited the title of earl, but there was no money attached to it. In fact, he was obliged to supply Frank's widow with an allowance. With two families to support, he needed to return to teaching. After being turned down by Cambridge, Princeton, and Harvard, he finally managed to get a year's appointment at the University of Chicago, and he sailed for America in September 1938.

It was during his period in the United States, which lasted six years, that Russell wrote many of his best-known essays. The essays collected in such major books as *Why I Am Not a Christian*, *Skeptical Essays*, *Unpopular Essays,* and the delightfully titled *In Praise of Idleness* are mostly drawn from this period. He was unhappy in exile, unhappy in America, unable to get steady teaching work. After he completed the year in Chicago, he went to the University of California at Los Angeles (UCLA), where he had a run-in with the university's extreme right-wing president and resigned. He was offered a position at City College of New York (CCNY).

The flap over Russell's appointment at CCNY was one of the most notorious incidents in his long and colorful career. The forces of "moral outrage" denounced Russell for the ideas that he set forth in his frank volume *Marriage and Morals*. A Mrs. Jean McKay filed suit to prevent city-run CCNY from using tax dollars to hire "an alien atheist and exponent of free love." A right-wing judge upheld the suit, and Mayor Fiorello LaGuardia, under intense political pressure, threatened to withhold the CCNY budget if the offer to Russell were not rescinded. When the offer was officially withdrawn, Harvard invited Russell to come up to Cambridge, Massachusetts, and deliver the annual William James lecture. He was invited to teach for the coming year at Pennsylvania's Bryn Mawr College, and, while there, he continued to work on a book growing out of the aborted lecture series.

The result of that project was his biggest financial success, *The History of*

Western Philosophy (1945), which probably introduced more people to philosophy for the first time than almost any other volume of its kind. Russell, then back at Trinity, also became a panelist on a high-rated British Broadcasting Corporation (BBC) talk show. Suddenly, he was a heralded and popular figure at home once again. In 1948, he published his last philosophical work, *Human Knowledge*; essentially a restatement of previous work, it was not particularly well received.

In the period following World War II, Russell focused his attention on the threat of nuclear weapons. By the early 1950s, he would be a vigorous opponent of nuclear proliferation. He spoke on the subject at every opportunity, served as president of the Campaign for Nuclear Disarmament, and was arrested in civil disobedience campaigns.

In 1960, Russell took on a young American from the London School of Economics as an assistant. Ralph Schoenman was an avid fan of Russell's and a relentless self-promoter who was supposed to help organize a War Crimes Tribunal that Russell and Jean-Paul Sartre had called in protest against United States conduct in Vietnam. The tribunal was less than successful, and Schoenman began issuing statements on political issues in Russell's name. Finally, in 1969, Russell disowned the younger man's actions and published an account of their dealings. On February 2, 1970, Lord Russell died at his home, Plas Penrhyn, Wales.

He left behind a legacy of concern for human rights and human dignity, and a skeptic's creed, stated many times in many ways, most of them brilliant and effective.

Ruth, George Herman (Babe)

(1895–1948)

AMERICAN BASEBALL PLAYER

As 1920 began, baseball, regarded as America's favorite sport, was under a dark cloud. There had been a scandal at the 1919 World Series: Some members of the White Sox had been suspended for trying to deliberately lose to the Cincinnati Reds.

Then a new player arrived to wear the number 3 uniform of the New York Yankees. His name was George, but everyone called him Babe. He was a large, round-faced, outgoing man who batted left-handed. During that unforgettable season, Babe Ruth hit a record-shattering 54 home runs. Spectators flocked to the ballparks. That summer marked the beginning of a baseball legend. The name Babe Ruth was forever linked with baseball, and the sport enjoyed a new surge of popularity.

George Herman Ruth was born in the poor waterfront area of Baltimore, Maryland, on February 6, 1895. There were eight children in all. George's father worked long hours in a saloon and his mother was often sick. George took to roaming the streets with other boys rather than attending school. Speaking of these years, Ruth later said, "I was a bum when I was a kid."

Unable to care for their son or control his behavior, the Ruths sent him to St. Mary's Industrial School, a reform school run by a religious group of Catholic brothers. Between ages 7 and 18, George spent most of his life at the school. There, George received more attention, got a good education, and ate regular meals. He took up sports, which were strongly emphasized at the school. Like the eight hundred other boys, he played handball, volleyball, and soccer, and tried track and wrestling. But his favorite was baseball, and he excelled at it.

By age 18, "Big George," as they called Ruth, was 6 feet, 2 inches tall and weighed over 200 pounds. He was the best ball player at the school, usually serving as pitcher. With his large, muscular frame he could be counted on to hit at least one homer every game. Jack Dunn, owner of the Baltimore Orioles, saw him play and signed him to a contract with his team. The older players on the Orioles called him "Dunn's newest babe," and that soon became his nickname.

Babe played well with the Orioles, but the team had to sell him and some other players to the Boston Red Sox in 1914. Within two years, Babe was an acclaimed pitcher—some said the best left-handed pitcher in the leagues. But he was a great hitter, too, and could not bat in every game unless he stopped pitching. The team management moved him to the outfield so he could be in the batting order more often. The Red Sox and their star player got a lot of publicity, and fans crowded stadiums to watch the "Sultan of Swat." In 1919, he broke the previous home run record by hitting 29 in one season. By year's end, he had hit a home run in every city.

In 1920, the Red Sox needed money and sold Ruth's contract to the New York Yankees, where he broke his own season record for homers, with 54. The Yankees became the first team to sell more than a million tickets in a season. People cheered when the lively, potbellied Babe whacked the ball and took off on what sportswriters called his "matchstick" legs.

Ruth was known for his exuberance off the field too. A heavy drinker, he also had a huge appetite. People claimed he once ate a dozen hot dogs, washed down with several bottles of soda pop. Between the games of a doubleheader, he might snack on pickled eels and chocolate ice cream. A warmhearted man, Ruth especially loved his young fans. He took time to sign autographs and visit children in hospitals. Ruth was unassuming and saw no need to treat an official better than a newsboy or janitor. He once greeted President Calvin Coolidge by saying, "Geez, it's hot, ain't it, Prez?"

In 1921, his second season with the Yanks, Ruth set a new record for career home runs, passing the 136 mark set by Roger Connor in the 1800s. When the Yankees moved from the old Polo Grounds in New York to the new Yankee Stadium in 1923, they called it "The House that Ruth Built."

A strong team, the Yankees continued to thrill fans. The great Lou Gehrig batted right after Ruth for nine years; people called them the "one-two punch." The Yankees won the 1928 World Series, where Ruth achieved a phenomenal 10 hits in 16 times at bat—a batting average of .625. This statistic was one of the most remarkable of his career.

Babe Ruth hit his 700th home run in 1934. Only two other players had even surpassed 300. His career homer total was 714 when he retired. He also had the highest career slugging average (total bases reached on hits, divided by the official number of times at bat). No player had broken this record, although Roger Maris hit 61 homers in 1961 to break Ruth's season record, until Hank Aaron hit the 715 career homer mark in 1973.

In 1935 Ruth became a player-manager of the Boston Braves. He hit his last homer in the last game he played, in May of that year. In that game against the Pittsburgh Pirates, at the age of 40, he hit three home runs. Thousands of fans stood to give him a tremendous ovation. Ruth went on to coach the Brooklyn

Dodgers in 1938. After leaving the Dodgers, he appeared in the movie *Pride of the Yankees,* about the life of former teammate Lou Gehrig. He hosted a radio show. He did bowling and golf exhibitions to raise money for the Allies and promoted U.S. war bonds during World War II.

Then, in 1946, Babe Ruth discovered he had cancer of the throat. Several operations did not stop the disease. Although ill, he worked to promote American Legion junior baseball that year. He appeared in his number 3 uniform in 1947 for Babe Ruth Appreciation Day at Yankee Stadium. He talked about the importance of baseball programs for young people, then said, "I'm glad I had the opportunity to thank everybody." Later that year he started the Babe Ruth Foundation for underprivileged children. In June 1948, for the twenty-fifth anniversary of Yankee Stadium, "The Babe" donned his uniform once again and joined the Yankees who had won the team's first world crown in 1923 and the newer members of the club. He was so weak he leaned against a baseball bat. When it was his turn to speak, his voice cracked as he described the day he got the first home run ever hit at the Stadium and how proud he had been to play with the Yankees. Many people in the stands wept.

Babe Ruth died two months later at age 53.

Saarinen, Eero

(1910–1961)

FINNISH-BORN AMERICAN ARCHITECT

Eero Saarinen was born in Finland on August 20, 1910. His father, Eliel Saarinen, was a famous architect who sailed for the United States in February 1923 to work on the redevelopment of the lakefront in Chicago, Illinois. The following year, the elder Saarinen accepted a teaching position at the University of Michigan in Ann Arbor.

By 1930, Eero Saarinen began studying sculpture in Paris, France and later studied architecture at Yale University. He practiced architecture in Finland from 1934 to 1936, which gave him distance from his father's influence and allowed him to study the modern architecture of Europe.

On his return to Michigan in 1937, Eero Saarinen joined his father's firm, which became known as Saarinen, Swanson, and Saarinen and included a brother-in-law, J. Robert F. Swanson. The most widely acclaimed design of the firm at this time was the first-prize entry for the Smithsonian Art Gallery (1939) in Washington, D.C. The Gallery included an enclosed courtyard, a reflecting pool, and sculpture used as an architectural element.

During the 1930s and 1940s, Eero Saarinen accepted a number of independent projects, and worked with Charles Eames on a remarkable series of furniture designs for the Organic Design in Home Furnishings Competition (1940–41) at the Museum of Modern Art in New York. Saarinen became an American citizen in 1940 and established himself as one of the most important furniture designers and architects of the twentieth century.

Father and son worked on the General Motors Technical Center (1945–55) in Warren, Michigan, but Eliel Saarinen's death in 1950 left the revisions and final design in the younger man's hands. Eero Saarinen's finished building moved away from his father's affection for nineteenth century architecture and revealed a modern influence, especially the work of Mies Van der Rohe. The General Motors complex is regarded as one of the finest designs for a corporation after World War II, and the international recognition made Saarinen one of the most important architects in America. Saarinen is best remembered, however, for a series of sculptures in the 1950s. His arch for the Jefferson National Expansion Memorial competition in St. Louis, Missouri was accepted in 1948, but the silver arch on the shores of the Mississippi River was not completed until 1964.

The Trans World Airways terminal (1956–62) at Kennedy International Airport is considered to be Saarinen's masterpiece. His use of concrete arches and tilted glass suggests a bird in flight, and revealed how sculpture and architecture could be united in the modern style.

Shortly before his death, Saarinen began the sketches for a skyscraper for the Columbia Broadcasting System (CBS) in New York. His design for a black tower of granite was an obvious contrast to the glass and steel skyscrapers of the period, and was the last work of Saarinen's to be built. The CBS building was completed in 1964, and helped Eero Saarinen's reputation as one of the finest architects in American history.

Sadat, Anwar el-

(1918–1981)

EGYPTIAN PRESIDENT

I come to you today on solid ground to shape a new life and to establish peace. We all love this land, the land of God; we all, Moslems, Christians, and Jews, worship God.

> —Anwar el-Sadat, speaking before Israel's Knesset

President Mohammed Anwar el-Sadat was born in the Nile Delta in Egypt in 1918. He spent his early years with his grandmother while his parents were living in the Sudan, where his father worked as a lower-level bureaucrat. In 1925 his parents returned home and Anwar was sent to schools in Cairo, Egypt's capital. Even as a boy he joined protests against the British control over his country. In 1938 he graduated from Egypt's military academy, where he had become friends with Gamal Abdel Nasser, soon to become the country's leader.

Sadat joined the army's signal corps in 1939 and continued his subversive activities against the British. In 1942 he was arrested for aiding German spies who had infiltrated Egypt and were collecting intelligence against the British. Two years later he escaped from prison. However, in 1946 he was implicated in the assassination of a rival politician and he was arrested again. He was acquitted during the turmoil that surrounded Egypt's participation in war against the new state of Israel in 1948.

After renewing connections with Gamal Nasser, who was plotting the overthrow of the Egyptian government under King Farouk, Sadat was called to Cairo on July 22, 1952, by the revolutionary leader and discovered that the king's government had, indeed, already been toppled. Sadat delivered the news to the public. In the new government, however, he was given only marginal positions of power. In the 1960s he became the speaker of Egypt's National Assembly, but it was not until 1969 when, in failing health, Nasser appointed Sadat his vice-president. Rivals referred to the younger man as "Major Yes-Yes" because of his loyalty to Nasser.

Sadat became leader of Egypt when Nasser died in 1970. Considered initially to be a pushover by political opposition leaders, he proved to be surprisingly tough. What he called the "corrective revolution" eliminated opposition by sending all rivals to jail. Then, in 1971, Sadat surprised the world by initiating peace overtures to Israel, Egypt's traditional enemy. In 1972 he asked the Soviet advisors to his government to leave the country, hoping to win American approval. When that did not happen, he reversed course and ordered his army to attack Israel in 1973. Egypt was defeated, but Sadat had finally attracted the attention of the Americans. He developed a good relationship with President Richard M. Nixon and was cooperative when the U.S. made a concerted effort to bring about peace in the Mideast.

In November 1977, Sadat again surprised the world by traveling to Israel and talking peace with the Israeli legislature. This was followed by further talks, mediated by U.S. President Jimmy Carter. The Camp David Accords of 1978 resulted in an agreement for an Egypt-Israel peace treaty and the eventual realization of a self-governing Arab Palestine in the Israeli-occupied areas of the Gaza Strip and the West Bank (this was just coming to fruition in the late 1990s). For his efforts, Sadat shared the 1978 Nobel Peace Prize with Menachem Begin, the leader of Israel.

Meanwhile, at home, Sadat's fortunes were not so positive. His economic measures, aimed at increasing foreign investment and economic development, had served mainly to enrich the Egyptian upper classes. In 1977, riots instigated by students and workers erupted over government reductions in food allotments to the poor. At the same time, Sadat's rather indulgent lifestyle with his fashionable, Westernized wife, Jihan, caused resentment among his people, and the Muslim religious conservatives grew increasingly angry over his peace overtures with Israel. Sadat responded with harsh crackdowns on civil liberties and arrested opposition politicians.

On October 6, 1981, while reviewing a military parade, Anwar Sadat was assassinated by Muslim fundamentalists. Although he was mourned by Western diplomats as a leader in Middle East peace initiatives and a political friend in the Cold War against the Soviet Union, a high percentage of the people of Egypt were largely indifferent to his death.

Saint-Exupéry, Antoine de

(1900–1944)

FRENCH NOVELIST, MEMOIRIST

One must learn not to write but to see.
—Antoine de Saint-Exupéry

French novelist Antoine de Saint-Exupéry was born on June 29, 1900, to a family of minor nobility. His father, Jean, worked for an insurance company, but he died before Antoine was four. Antoine was the third of five children. When their father died, they were brought up by their mother, Marie, a loving and attentive woman, in the homes of a great-aunt and Marie's parents.

"This world of childhood memories will always seem to me hopelessly more real than the other," Saint-Ex would write as an adult, and his recollections of his childhood are of a period of unalloyed joy. Led by Antoine, a mischievous child with a head full of golden curls, the Saint-Exupéry children were holy terrors. He also read voraciously and began writing poetry while still a boy. He wrote at night, and he thought nothing of waking his brothers and sisters, dragging them into their mother's room, and reading his latest offering to the assembled (and sleepy) family gathering. (This habit never died; he called friends at all hours of the night to test passages of his work-in-progress.)

Saint-Ex's (as his friends called him) first education took place at home. He then went through a series of Catholic schools before finishing up in Paris. He was good at math, bad at French composition, and failed the entrance exams for the naval academy at the École Bossuet. He enrolled briefly in architecture classes, but he had absolutely no aptitude for the field.

What he did have an aptitude for, and a lifelong obsession with, was flying. Aviation was still a new phenomenon; Saint-Ex was born three years before the Wright Brothers' first flight at Kitty Hawk, North Carolina. But as a boy, Antoine was fascinated by planes and was determined to fly them someday. After his laughable attempts to study architecture, he was drafted. While doing his national service as a mechanic in the air force, he paid for private flying lessons.

It was not until 1926 that he was able to secure a flying job, but when he did, he knew he had found a world as congenial as that of his childhood. For the first time in his adult life, Saint-Ex had found an all-male world, and the once-pampered mama's boy fit into it almost immediately.

He had taken a position with the air-mail company that would eventually become Aéropostale, and his first assignment placed him at the airfield at Toulouse, France. His boss was Dider Daurat. By 1927, Saint-Exupéry was a pilot for the company, handling the mail route from Toulouse, France, to Dakar, Senegal, with stops in Western Africa. It was the perfect job for him. He had a boss he respected, work he enjoyed, and the solitude of the desert in which to write when he wasn't flying. The work itself was demanding and dangerous, flying the Breguet 14—an open-cockpit plane with a wooden propeller, no radio, and no brakes—over the desolate and hostile Sahara Desert.

After a year, Saint-Ex was promoted; he was made chief of an airfield at Cape Juby, in the western Sahara. It probably was the most isolated airstrip in the world, in the middle of a desert full of hostile tribesmen. Saint-Ex was delighted. He made friends with the children of the nomad tribesmen and thrived on the comradeship of his small staff of fliers and mechanics. All of this worked its way into *Southern Mail* (1929), which he was in the process of writing.

By March 1928, Saint-Ex was back in France, taking classes in aerial navigation as preparation for a new post: Aéropostale had promoted him to head of its operations in Argentina. There he was reunited with Daurat and many other old friends. By April 1930, he had established weekly mail service from Patagonia, the frigid southern tip of South America, to Buenos Aires, Argentina. After eighteen months, he returned to France with the manuscript of his second book, *Night Flight* (1931).

Night Flight was the book that made his reputation in France, winner of the Prix Fémina, recipient of a preface from André Gide, a virtual poem on male heroism combined with an exotic locale, a book so successful that the perfume company Guerlain manufactured a perfume inspired by it. In addition to suddenly being a best-selling author, Saint-Ex was now a married man, as well. His wife, Consuelo, was Salvadorean and beautiful, but she was also a pathological liar, quarrelsome, chronically late, and unfaithful. It was a stormy marriage, compounded by Saint-Ex's own foibles; he, too, was unfaithful, reckless, and hard-living.

Saint-Ex's reputation was built on the idea that he was a great pilot. In fact, nothing could have been further from the truth. As his colleagues often observed, he was more famous for his crashes than for his flights. Marcel Migeo, an ex-comrade who wrote a memoir of his friendship with Saint-Exupéry, said that he was a talented pilot but was too easily distracted, too inattentive in the cockpit. At any rate, it is fortunate that *Night Flight* made Saint-Exupéry a successful writer in 1931, because the airline he worked for was liquidated shortly thereafter, subsumed into the growing Air France. Saint-Ex was through as a commercial pilot. He began to earn his living as a writer, alternating between journalism, more books about flying, and public relations work for the new national airline.

When France fell to the Germans in 1940, Saint-Ex was in New York for what was to have been a four-week promotional tour for the French war effort. He was stuck there for two years, isolated, ill, unable or unwilling to learn English. He dallied with numerous young ladies until Consuelo arrived in New York.

What Saint-Exupéry really wanted to do was to get back into the air, flying for the Free French. In 1943, he left America for Algeria, where he joined a French squadron. He was at once the hero of the other fliers in the unit, the most experienced pilot and the least disciplined soldier. He was in constant pain from old injuries, so he drank heavily. He was too old and set in his ways to adjust to the vastly more sophisticated U.S. Army Air Corps P-38 pursuit planes, and he crashed them repeatedly. In one of the most famous anecdotes about Saint-Ex, he was grounded after a particularly awful crash during his stint with the U.S. Army Air Corps during World War II. He told his American operations officer, "Sir, I want to die for France." The officer replied, "I don't give a damn if you die for France or not, but you're not going to do it in one of our planes."

In May 1944, he was reassigned to the Mediterranean island of Sardinia and was allowed to resume flying. He took off on a reconnaissance mission over southern France and disappeared. He left behind a half-dozen books written in his lifetime, including the perennial favorite, *The Little Prince* (1943), and a legacy of heroism.

Salinger, Jerome David

(1919–   )

AMERICAN NOVELIST AND SHORT-STORY WRITER

J.D. Salinger was born and raised in New York. His father, an importer, was Jewish, and his mother was of Scotch and Irish descent. Salinger had one sister.

Salinger went to a prep school, the Valley Forge Military Academy. He attended Ursinus College and Columbia University, but he never graduated. While in college, Salinger wrote reviews of movies and worked on the literary magazines. He took a short-story class at Columbia that was taught by Whit Burnett, the founder of *Story Magazine*. Known for publishing new authors, the magazine printed some of Salinger's work.

From 1941 to 1948, Salinger wrote numerous stories that were published in magazines such as *Collier's, Saturday Evening Post, Esquire, Cosmopolitan, Good Housekeeping,* and the *New Yorker.* Most of them were very short, sentimental and colloquial stories, and some were about the army. Salinger served in the Army Signal Corps and Counter-Intelligence Corps during World War II.

After World War II, Salinger published two stories in the *New Yorker* which became very popular: "Slight Rebellion Off Madison" and "A Perfect Day for Bananafish." He then published his first novel, *The Catcher in the Rye,* in 1951. The novel initially received fair reviews and sales, but as more and more teachers and students began to talk about it, its popularity grew.

Nevertheless, Salinger did not receive wide recognition until he published a collection, *Nine Stories,* in 1953. All of the stories were originally printed in the *New Yorker,* and they introduced characters that would appear in more of Salinger's later work. Many of the stories were about bright but disturbed children in conflict with their parents. In "A Perfect Day for Bananafish," an older brother, Seymour Glass, commits suicide. The Glass family is involved in other stories, and they would later be used in *Franny and Zooey* (1961), *Raise High the Roof Beam, Carpenters,* and *Seymour: An Introduction* (1963).

As a writer, Salinger was not very interested in politics or issues of reform, and his main characters tended to be passive and escapist. For this reason his work was not as appealing to the 1960s generations as it had been to 1950s readers, though interest in Salinger was renewed in the 1970s. In contrast to protest fiction that called for the reforming of society, Salinger viewed "escape" from the mainstream as good. Believing in Eastern philosophies such as Hindu-Buddhism, Salinger felt that, rather than fight the system, people could develop their spirituality to transcend the phoniness and material corruption of society.

Salinger lives somewhat reclusively in New Hampshire. Although he was not particularly prolific, he was the subject of extensive scholarly criticism and analysis. Often read and studied by students today, Salinger, in his own way, has become an important voice in American literature of revolt against shallow and corrupt society.

Salk, Jonas

(1914–1995)

AMERICAN MEDICAL RESEARCHER

My job . . . is to help people see what I see.
If it's of value, fine. And if it's not of value,
then at least I've done what I can do.

— Jonas Salk, in a 1992 interview

The son of a garment worker, Jonas Edward Salk was born in New York. He was a studious boy who worked hard to make good grades. When he was sixteen, he graduated from high school and went on to the College of the City of New York. During the summers, Salk held a job as a technician in a research laboratory. He liked the work so much that he decided to go to medical school so that he could become a medical researcher.

After graduating from the New York University College of Medicine, Salk joined the staff of the University of Pittsburgh. He soon headed its new laboratory for research into viruses.

In 1949, Salk began researching the virus that produces poliomyelitis, also known as polio. By 1952, Salk had created a vaccine from dead polio cells. He first tested it on monkeys. When the trial was successful, he was so convinced that it was safe and effective that he injected it into his wife, his children, and himself.

With funding from the March of Dimes, Salk tested the vaccine on two million first, second, and third graders in 1954. The children were called Polio Pioneers. Newspapers praised them for their courage in participating in the experiment.

The test was a great success. The Salk vaccine protected the Polio Pioneers from poliomyelitis. Salk was called a genius and celebrated as a hero around the world.

Yet Salk and his work were not without their critics. Some scientists resented his fame, claiming that his research was unoriginal. Others thought that Salk's vaccination of the Polio Pioneers was irresponsible. They believed that he should have tested his vaccine more thoroughly before giving it to so many children.

Salk himself did not enjoy the publicity he received. He feared that it would destroy his credibility among his colleagues. Years later, Salk said, "The worst tragedy that could have befallen me was my success. I knew right away that I was through, cast out [by my fellow scientists]."

To escape the public eye, Salk retreated into his laboratory. He continued working on other vaccines until the early 1960s, when he decided to create his own research center. The universities that funded most centers usually told scientists what problems they should research. Feeling that this hampered researchers' creativity, Salk wanted scientists at his center to be free to study whatever they chose. With funding from the March of Dimes and many other foundations, he founded the Salk Institute for Biological Studies in La Jolla, California, in 1963.

Working at the institute, Salk spent the next twenty years researching cancer. He also tried to find a cure for multiple sclerosis, a disease that like polio often leaves its victims paralyzed.

In the early 1980s, Salk turned his attention to a new medical crisis—Acquired Immune Deficiency Syndrome, or AIDS. AIDS is caused by the HIV virus, which attacks its victim's natural resistance to disease. For a person with AIDS, exposure to almost any germ can prove fatal.

Drawing from his research on polio, Salk started work on an AIDS vaccine. In 1987, he began performing experiments on monkeys. After infecting them with the HIV virus, he injected them with a vaccine made from dead HIV cells. The monkeys developed such high levels of HIV antibodies that the virus had disappeared. Salk was encouraged by the results, but, as many of his colleagues pointed out, monkeys were not ideal test subjects. No monkey had been known to contract AIDS outside of a laboratory. Many researchers believed that the animals may be so resistant to the HIV virus that it disappeared naturally from Salk's monkeys.

In the summer of 1992, Salk began another test with the approval of the U.S. government. His vaccine was given to 650 people who have the HIV virus. Their health will be monitored for three years to see whether the Salk vaccine can kill HIV in humans. If the test is successful, Salk will be hailed as the man who ended not just one, but two, of the deadliest plagues of modern times. Jonas Salk died on June 23, 1995.

Sandburg, Carl

(1878–1967)

AMERICAN POET

Carl Sandburg's parents emigrated to the United States from Sweden. Sandburg was born in Galesburg, Illinois. He attended public schools until the age of thirteen when he had to go to work. He drove a milk truck, worked in a barber shop, changed sets in a theater, operated a brick kiln, and worked as a carpenter, dishwasher, and housepainter.

During the Spanish-American War, Sandburg served eight months in Puerto Rico. He then began attending Lombard College, and his first book, *In Reckless Ecstasy,* was a thirty-nine-page pamphlet printed on a hand press in his professor's basement. Of the fifty copies printed in 1904, only a few still exist today.

From 1907 to 1908, Sandburg worked as an organizer of the Wisconsin Social-Democratic party. He wrote for a Milwaukee newspaper, *Leader,* and he married that year. From 1910 to 1912, Sandburg served as the secretary to the first socialist mayor of Milwaukee, Emil Seidel.

Sandburg moved to Chicago where he wrote for the *Daily News* and *Daybook.* Some of his poems were printed in magazines, and in 1916 he published *Chicago Poems.* This book was followed by *Cornhuskers* in 1918. Both books were praised by the general public as well as by other poets.

As Sandburg gained popularity in the 1920s, he left journalism to focus on writing and lecturing full-time. A real performer, he toured the country reading his poems, playing guitar, and singing folk songs. Sandburg's songs were collected in *The American Songbag* (1927) and *The New American Songbag* (1950).

Sandburg enjoyed writing about American themes, especially the values of democracy and freedom. He was interested in Abraham Lincoln, and his studies led to the publication *Abraham Lincoln: The Prairie Years,* two volumes published in 1926, and *Abraham Lincoln: The War Years,* four volumes published in 1939. The series won a Pulitzer Prize. The first twenty-six chapters of the biography were published as a separate volume, *Abraham Lincoln Grows Up,* in 1931, and all six volumes were condensed into *Abraham Lincoln,* published in 1954.

Sandburg wrote a book about his brother-in-law, Edward Steichen, entitled *Steichen the Photographer* (1929). He also published *The Chicago Race Riots* (1919) and *Mary Lincoln, Wife and Widow* (1932). His children's books are *Rootabaga Stories* (1922), *Rootabaga Pigeons* (1923), *The Rootabaga Country* (1929), and *Potato Face* (1930). He published a novel, *Remembrance Rock,* in 1948, and two autobiographical works, *Always the Young Strangers* (1952) and *Prairie Town Boy* (1955).

Sandburg was a prolific author who is best recognized as an American poet. In addition to his Pulitzer Prizes, Lyndon B. Johnson awarded him the Presidential Medal of Freedom.

Sanger, Margaret

(1879–1966)

AMERICAN FEMINIST AND BIRTH-CONTROL ACTIVIST

I resolved that women should have knowledge of contraception [methods of birth control]. They have every right to know about their own bodies. . . . I would scream from the house tops. I would tell the world what was going on in the lives of these poor women. . . . *I would be heard.*

—Margaret Sanger (1931)

Margaret Louise Higgins Sanger pioneered the birth-control movement in the United States. A feminist, Sanger was committed to the cause of enabling women to control their own bodies. She opened the first birth-control clinic in the United States. Sanger also founded and served as president of both the American Birth Control League and the Birth Control Clinical Research Bureau. These two organizations would later merge to form the Planned Parenthood Federation of America.

The sixth of eleven children, Margaret Higgins grew up in poverty in Corning, New York. Her father, owner of a monument shop, supported a variety of reform causes: women's voting rights, tax reform, and socialism. He encouraged his children to join in discussing these issues as his equals. Although her father did not believe in God, her mother was a devout Irish Catholic. Margaret blamed her family's poverty on the teachings of the Catholic church. She was angry that the church encouraged couples to have as many children as possible, whether or not they could support them.

After graduating from Claverack College, a private prep school in Hudson, New York, Higgins for a short time taught first grade among immigrants in Little Falls, New Jersey. In 1896, she returned to Corning to care for her mother, who died of tuberculosis. Higgins blamed her mother's illness and death on her exhaustion at having to bear and rear eleven children. Although she objected to her father's demand that she take his wife's place, Higgins ran the household for the next three years.

In 1899, she began attending nursing school at a hospital in White Plains, New York. After completing two years of training as a practical nurse, however, she quit to marry William Sanger, a socialist, architect, and artist. Margaret Sanger gave birth to three children between 1903 and 1910. But she was not content with her life as a housewife and mother in Hastings-on-Hudson, New York. In 1912, the family moved to Manhattan, where Sanger joined the Socialist Party and organized women workers for the radical labor group, the International Workers of the World (IWW). Sanger helped organize the withdrawal of strikers' children from Lawrence, Massachusetts, where IWW was leading textile workers in a strike. Through her organizing activities, Sanger met Emma Goldman and other labor leaders. Goldman helped Sanger develop the idea that in order to free themselves from male control, women had to seize control over childbearing. The right of women to control their own bodies, they insisted, must take priority over the struggle for higher wages and other labor reforms.

In 1912, Sanger also worked as a visiting nurse in a New York slum. The high rate of venereal (sexually transmitted) diseases and poor women's ignorance about childbirth and abortion shocked Sanger. Sanger was infuriated that women were being denied information they needed to know. Witnessing the horrors suffered by poor women, Sanger became committed to teaching women about sex education, venereal disease, and contraception. That year, she wrote "What Every Girl Should Know," a series of articles on female sexuality for *The Call,* a socialist newspaper. When she wrote about a venereal disease, the government—acting on an 1873 law that defined birth control, abortion, and other subjects related to sex as "obscene"—banned the issue containing her article.

In 1913, she traveled to Paris, France, to learn more about contraceptive methods. Returning to the U.S the following year, she began editing and publishing *Woman Rebel,* a radical feminist journal. She urged lawmakers to make "birth control"—a term that she invented—legal. That year, Sanger wrote *Family Limitation.* This pamphlet insisted that women had a right to sexual fulfillment and called for an end to all laws opposed to birth control. It also included information on how to use a variety of contraceptive methods. In 1914, Sanger fled the country to escape charges of sending obscene materials through the mail. But even in exile, she continued to promote sex education at home. She sent instructions to send thousands of secretly stored copies of her pamphlet to labor leaders across the nation.

When, in 1915, her husband was arrested and jailed for thirty days for handing out *Family Limitation,* Sanger returned to the U.S. The following year, the government dropped the charges against her. Later in 1916, Sanger and one of her sisters opened the nation's first birth control clinic in Brooklyn.

Sanger was sentenced to thirty days in jail during a 1917 trial. She challenged the law in an appeal to a higher court, arguing that the law forced women to risk death in pregnancy. The Court of Appeals upheld her conviction and sentence, but Sanger also achieved an important victory. The judge ruled that doctors had the right to provide married patients with birth-control information in order to cure or prevent venereal disease.

Sanger founded and served as the first president of the American Birth Control League, which promoted the reform of national birth-control laws. Two years later, in 1923, with funds provided by her new husband, a wealthy oil executive, Sanger opened the Birth Control Clinical Research Bureau in New York. The nation's first birth-control clinic with a staff of medical doctors offered women access to reliable advice about contraceptives. The success of the Clinical Research Bureau served as a model for the three-hundred more birth-control clinics that Sanger would open during the next fifteen years.

In 1926, Sanger organized the first World Population Conference, held in Geneva, Switzerland. The conference addressed the problem of overpopulation, which was just then recognized as a threat to the future of the world. In a dispute with its board of directors, Sanger resigned from both the presidency of the American Birth Control League and her position as editor of *The Birth Control Review* in 1928. The next year, following a police raid of the Clinical Research Bureau, the court ruled that the bureau's work prevented disease and promoted the health of mothers and infants. A 1936 court ruling allowed contraceptive materials to be imported into the United States in order to save lives and promote patients' well-being. This ruling marked the greatest victory of Sanger's birth-control movement: birth control was no longer regarded as obscene. The following year, the American Medical Association accepted birth control as a medical service and recommended teaching contraceptive methods in medical schools.

In 1938, the American Birth Control League and the Birth Control Clinical Research Bureau merged. Sanger was named honorary chair of the new Birth Control Federation of America. As the birth-control movement began to shift its emphasis to the concept of family planning, this organization became the Planned Parenthood Federation of America in 1942. Ten years later, in Bombay, India, Sanger helped found the International Planned Parenthood Federation, serving as the organization's president for the next six years. Also in 1952, Sanger helped obtain funds for research to develop the birth-control pill, which first appeared on the market in 1960.

Sartre, Jean-Paul

(1905–1980)

FRENCH PHILOSOPHER, NOVELIST, PLAYWRIGHT, ESSAYIST, LITERARY CRITIC, AND POLITICAL ACTIVIST

Dostoevsky said, "If God did not exist, everything would be possible." That is the very starting point of existentialism. Indeed, everything is permissible if God does not exist, and as a result man is forlorn, because neither within him or without does he find anything to cling to.

—Jean-Paul Sartre, from *Existentialism and Humanism*

Jean-Paul Sartre is one of the central figures of philosophy since World War II. He didn't "invent" existentialism, but he was its best-known champion. An entire generation, shaped by the war and its aftermath, looked to him as its leader. He responded with a body of work that is astonishing in its quality, if not always consistent in its ideas.

Sartre was born on June 21, 1905, in Paris, France, to a middle-class family. His father died when he was only two, and he grew up alongside his young widowed mother and her father, Carl Schweitzer (uncle of Albert Schweitzer, and a professor of German at the Sorbonne university). He led a quiet and protected life as a child, raised mainly by women who pampered him free from a father's discipline. Grandfather Schweitzer taught him a love of books and intellectual activity.

When Jean-Paul was twelve, his mother remarried and the family moved to La Rochelle, on France's Atlantic coast. Suddenly, his mother was no longer like an older sister to him, and a new authority figure entered his life. In fact, as he would later recall, his stepfather was good to him, and tried to teach him about mathematics and the sciences, with rather dismal results. La Rochelle was a port city, "a tough town," as Sartre remembered it. The kids in his school were quite different from the ones he knew in Paris. As events occurred, he was somewhat ostracized as a Parisian, and out of that solitude grew his need to write, to explain and justify himself.

In 1920, Sartre moved back to Paris. By 1924, he was a student of philosophy at the prestigious École Normale Supérieure. It was there that he became friends with some of the key figures in postwar French culture: Maurice Merleau-Ponty, Paul Nizan, Raymond Aron, and Claude Lévi-Strauss.

He also met a young woman, Simone de Beauvoir. She would later recall that among his friends "he was the dirtiest, the most poorly dressed, and I also think the ugliest." Sartre impressed Beauvoir with the wide sweep of his mind—he seemed to be interested in everything—and by his firm conviction that he would be a successful writer. It was the beginning of a relationship that, despite some rocky periods, would last the rest of their lives.

Sartre and Beauvoir had decided almost from the outset of their relationship that they would neither marry nor have children. Their relationship to each other would be the principle one in both their lives, but they agreed that each would have "contingent" relationships. When their teaching assignments came through, placing them at opposite ends of France, he in Le Havre, she in Marseilles, Sartre changed his mind and proposed. Beauvoir refused, feeling that it would be wrong to get married for the sole purpose of getting their assignments changed so that they could live together. She didn't want to become dependent on him and didn't want to change a freely chosen and designed relationship into a legally binding torment. Luckily, after a year, she was transferred to Rouen, much nearer to Le Havre.

Although Sartre spent a year at the French Institute in Berlin in 1933, studying Martin Heidegger and Edmund Husserl, neither he nor Beauvoir saw the storm clouds of war approaching; they would tour Austria and Germany together the following year, still convinced that Nazism was a passing trend. Although they would become the leading socialist activists of their generation in the years after World War II, in the 1930s neither Beauvoir nor Sartre was particularly political, so events in Europe caught them as much by surprise as they did many others.

Sartre had begun to publish philosophical works in the mid-1930s. His first books, *Psychology and Imagination* (1936) and *The Transcendence of the Ego* (1937), attracted little attention outside the academic world. But his 1938 novel, *Nausea*, was a huge and controversial success. The book represented the first—and in some ways the most forceful—statement of Sartre's version of existentialism, and it was a departure from the kind of book that French readers were getting in the years just before the war broke out.

Written in the form of a diary, *Nausea* is the story of Roquentin, who is living alone in a city very much like Le Havre, while trying to write a biography of an eighteenth-century marquis. He begins to feel oppressed by objects and overwhelmed by a sense of repulsion for his environment. Finally, sitting under a chestnut tree in the park, he has a vision of apocalyptic intensity and immensity that will lead him to a kind of clarity. The world cannot be either justified or explained, he realizes; nor can existence, even his own. It follows no rules, it is absurd, but therefore also free.

At the center of *Nausea*, as it will be in Sartre's philosophical works of the next decade, is the question of how to achieve salvation in a universe without God, a universe without "meaning." As Sartre would write in 1946: "Existence precedes essence." Man must decide what he is, what his essence is. Man is free to make that choice, must make the choice; hence the existentialist formulation, "condemned to be free."

When war was declared in September 1939, Sartre was called up for military service; he had been in the army for sixteen months back in 1932. His military career was a brief one; in June 1940 the French army surrendered and he was declared a prisoner of war. By 1941, he was back in Paris.

As the world learned from Sartre's *War Diaries* (which were published in 1983), he spent much of his spare time in uniform working on his next book, a massive and—for the moment—definitive statement of his philosophy, *Being and Nothingness* (1943). Like Martin Heidegger in his epochal *Being and Time*, to which Sartre's title is an obvious homage, Sartre is concerned with the problems of being in the world, of "facticity." Unlike Heidegger, Sartre does not deduce from this reality a destiny for man, only the notion of a radical freedom that cannot be evaded. *Being and Nothingness* is a difficult book, one that systematizes and expands on the notions explored in *Nausea*. It is with this book that Sartre emerges as a key voice of existentialism as technical philosophy, much as *Nausea* introduced him to a wider readership as a guide for the perplexed.

Out of the army and back in Paris, Sartre was reunited with Beauvoir. The two began working for the resistance, helping put out underground newspapers. Sartre, who had always been interested in theater, turned his hand to playwriting. His first effort, the three-character drama *No Exit* (1943), presents another variation on the themes of his other writings. When his three characters, trapped together in a drawing room that is located in Hell, realize that "Hell is other people," they are merely offering a dramatized version of the idea that in one's own consciousness, it is impossible to escape the judgment of others.

With the end of the war, Sartre found himself juggling four kinds of writing. He continued to write plays, encouraged by the director-producer Charles Dullin, whom he had known since the mid-1920s. He was writing philosophical essays on existentialism. In 1945, he began publishing a tetralogy of novels, only three of which were completed, called *Roads to Freedom* (consisting of 1945's *Age of Reason* and *The Reprieve,* and 1949's *Troubled Sleep*). And in the immediate aftermath of the war, Sartre, Beauvoir, and Merleau-Ponty co-founded *Les Temps Modernes* (Modern Times), a monthly periodical that would be the principle mouthpiece for the existentialists. Although it began life as a literary magazine, it increasingly came to reflect Sartre's growing engagement with current events and his gradual shift toward Marxism.

In the 1950s, Sartre and Beauvoir eased into a political status that could be called an amalgam of existentialism and Marxism. Sartre wrote favorably of the Soviet Union in the early part of the decade, but never joined the Communist Party. When the Soviets invaded Hungary in 1956, Sartre angrily denounced the action and, in his book *The Ghost of Stalin,* broke publicly with the French communists.

However, he and Beauvoir remained committed to Marxist philosophy, and they would flirt with several different movements on the left over the rest of their lives. By the time of the student uprisings of 1968, they would be affiliated with small Maoist groups. Sartre even attempted a major work synthesizing existentialism with Marx in order to, in his words, "make history intelligible." The resulting book, *Critique of Dialectical Reason*, is as enormous as *Being and Nothingness*; one critic has called it "the greatest Kantian work of the twentieth century."

Sartre decided quite deliberately not to join the communists because of the message that his membership would send to others. He chose his political battles with great care for the same reason. And he refused numerous public rewards for his work, including the Legion of Honor and, most famously, the 1964 Nobel Prize for Literature. He did not want to become "an institution," he commented at the time.

Until the last decade of his life, he continued to be a prolific writer. From a brief memoir of his childhood, *The Words* (1964), to a major volume on the novelist and playwright Jean Genet, from a steady stream of collections of his essays on politics, literature, and philosophy, published semiregularly under the title *Situations*, to a stunning three-volume assessment of the life, times, and writings of the nineteenth-century French novelist Gustave Flaubert, Sartre was an imposing fixture on the French intellectual scene.

In the last decade of his life, however, Sartre's health problems began to catch up with him. He was virtually blind and could no longer read or write, except by dictation, which limited his output severely. He gradually became enfeebled and, on April 15, 1980, he died. Beauvoir wrote movingly of the painful last year of his life in her book *Adieux* (Goodbye) (1980). Although at the time of his death Sartre had supposedly been marginalized by the stridently anticommunist rhetoric of the then-fashionable "new *philosophes*," tens of thousands of Parisians attended his funeral. Since his death, numerous posthumous publications—ranging from the obligatory collections of letters (quite fascinating) to his war diaries (still being published in France) and unfinished projects like his monumental collection of notes for a second volume of *Being and Nothingness* to focus on a theory of ethics—have been received with enthusiasm by critics, scholars and readers alike.

Schweitzer, Albert

(1875–1965)

GERMAN-BORN PHILOSOPHER,
THEOLOGIAN, MUSICOLOGIST,
MUSICIAN, HUMANITARIAN, AND
PHYSICIAN

Albert Schweitzer was a man of many faces. There was the Albert Schweitzer who was a pioneer in historical theology, author of *The Quest for the Historical Jesus* (1906). There was the Albert Schweitzer who wrote a massive philosophical study, the two-volume *Philosophy of Civilization* (1923). Then there was the Albert Schweitzer who was a world-class classical organist and organ builder, the one who wrote several important studies of the famous composer Johann Sebastian Bach and edited his music. Also, there was the Albert Schweitzer known to the public as a self-sacrificing doctor who ran a clinic in the heart of Africa, the one who received the Nobel Peace Prize in 1952.

Albert Schweitzer was born in a Lutheran parsonage in Kayersberg, Upper Alsace, on January 14, 1875. At the time, Alsace was in German hands; it would later become part of France. Schweitzer received a doctorate in philosophy in 1899, and another in theology the following year, both from the University of Strasbourg. Between 1905 and 1911, he began making an intensive study of the music of Johann Sebastian Bach, and he wrote a definitive two-volume study of Bach that was published in 1905 and 1908. He was also a superb organist and, not surprisingly, a renowned Bach interpreter. Later in his life, he would only play concerts occasionally as a fund-raiser for his African clinic. At the clinic he owned a zinc-lined organ (to protect it from the extreme heat and humidity) that he would play for his own pleasure.

In 1906, Schweitzer shook up the world of religious history with his book on the "historical Jesus." Schweitzer argued that the previous lives written reflected less the historical record and more the theological biases of the authors. The actual facts about Jesus, as found in the Gospels, are tantalizingly few. But based on what historic record there is, Schweitzer argued, Jesus cannot be understood except in light of Jewish eschatology—that is, the imminent, supernatural transformation of the world. Schweitzer followed this volume with acclaimed studies of the Apostle Paul.

At some point after that, Schweitzer encountered a statue of a suffering African. He was moved by this image and vowed to become a doctor to alleviate suffering in a concrete, immediate way. In 1913, he received his M.D. degree; he and his wife, Hélène Bresslau, also a doctor, established a clinic called Lambaréné in Gabon in French Equatorial Africa. Schweitzer's encounters with the real suffering Africans were somewhat less idyllic than the image of the statue; his condescending attitude, typical of his class and time, toward his patients bordered on racism, but his work was generally beneficial, his sacrifice real. It has been observed that the image of Lambaréné probably reached more people and affected them more deeply than any of Schweitzer's many writings on theology or philosophy. On the other hand, the phrase at the heart of his philosophy, "reverence for life," still reverberates long after his death in 1965.

Selassie, Haile

(1892–1975)

EMPEROR OF ETHIOPIA

Apart from the Kingdom of the Lord there is not on this earth any nation that is superior to any other. Should it happen that a strong government finds it may, with impunity, destroy a weak people . . . God and history will remember your judgment.

> —Emperor Haile Selassie, asking
> for the help of the League
> of Nations, 1936

Emperor Haile Selassie was born Tafari Makonnen in the Harar region of Ethiopia, in eastern Africa, on July 23, 1892. His family claimed direct lineage to King Solomon of the Bible and the Queen of Sheba. Tafari was taught by French priests as a boy, and by the age of fourteen he held the title of Commander of the Door at the Emperor Menelik's palace. In 1910, he became governor of the Harar province.

In 1916, upset by Emperor Lij Yasu (who succeeded Menelik) and his anti-Christian policies, Tafari led a rebellion that took control of Ethiopia and installed Menelik's daughter, Zauditu, as empress, although Tafari actually ran the country.

Tafari's power increased with strengthened military support, and he embarked on a program of modernization inspired by Western European countries. He built schools and instituted a program for young Ethiopian men to study in foreign countries. He also abolished slavery in 1924. In 1928, Tafari took the title of king, and in 1930 he was sworn in as emperor, taking the name Haile Selassie, which means "Might of the Trinity." Pursuing his goal of modernizing his country, Selassie instituted a new constitution that called for a two-part legislature, much like Western models, and a cabinet. He did not relinquish much political control, however.

In 1935, Benito Mussolini and the Italian army invaded Ethiopia, and Selassie was forced to flee the country. The following year he spoke before the League of Nations, which his country had joined in 1923, and called for support in driving the Italians out. He failed and Ethiopia did not return to his control until the defeat of Mussolini during World War II. In the meantime, however, Selassie joined with the British to help lead the military campaign in Africa that defeated the Italians.

In 1941, Selassie returned to Ethiopia and began a program of land reform and further modernization efforts. In 1950 he succeeded in having the United Nations agree to his incorporating Eritrea, a neighboring territory and former Italian colony, into Ethiopia (this arrangement lasted until 1993, when Eritrea became independent). In 1955, Selassie revised the constitution and granted universal suffrage to all adults. In the 1960s he played a prominent role in creating the Organization of African Unity.

Selassie ruled Ethiopia until 1974, when, fueled by rising discontent about inflation, unemployment, and severe hunger, a group of army officers seized control of the government. Haile Selassie, under house arrest, died on August 27, 1975.

Shaw, George Bernard

(1856–1950)

IRISH PLAYWRIGHT, NOVELIST,
CRITIC, AND ESSAYIST

After he won the 1925 Nobel Prize for Literature, George Bernard Shaw turned down the money that accompanied the honor, complaining that he had been besieged with requests for loans from every bankrupt writer he had ever known. His comment was typical Shaw: "I can forgive Alfred Nobel for having invented dynamite. But only a fiend in human form could have invented the Nobel Prize."

He was a witty rebel who defied convention, a man with an opinion on everything from socialism (for) to English spelling (against). He was a successful drama and music critic and a failed novelist who didn't write his first play until he was thirty-six; he went on to become the most celebrated playwright of his age. Yet he was as famous for the lengthy essays that preceded his plays in print as for the plays themselves.

Bernard Shaw was born on July 26, 1856, in Dublin, Ireland, into a family of the Irish aristocracy. He would later say of his family history, "I am pure Dublin. . . . We are a family of Pooh Bahs—snobs to the backbone. Drink and lunacy are minor specialties." Shaw's father was an unsuccessful merchant, and his mother was a singer who left her husband to teach voice in London. At fourteen, young George left school to work as a clerk in a real estate office. At twenty, wishing to be a painter or novelist, he left Ireland for London, not to return for another twenty-nine years. Unfortunately, as he would later admit, he was limited in those pursuits by a distinct lack of talent in either one.

Between 1876 and 1883, Shaw wrote five novels, none of which would be published in book form until their author was famous for other endeavors. However, some of them were serialized in small socialist magazines, as Shaw became involved with the Fabian movement, a group of writers and thinkers who expounded a brand of democratic socialism by evolution rather than revolution.

Shaw quickly became a spokesman for the movement, a compelling public speaker and natural wit, even getting elected as a vestryman and a city councilor on several occasions. After he became famous as a playwright, he used the pulpit that that renown afforded him to discuss his political and social ideas. As he once said in response to a question about using his comic writing to advance serious positions, "If you're going to tell people the truth, make them laugh or they'll kill you."

Shaw may not have been a novelist, after all, but his failures offered him a good grounding in the craft of writing. He began working as a journalist in the late 1880s. He became friends with William Archer, a playwright, drama critic, and champion of the works of Henrik Ibsen, the Norwegian playwright whose stark dramas represented a considerable contrast to the melodramatic rubbish that was then ruling the English stage. Archer helped Shaw secure steady work as a music and drama critic, and he introduced Shaw to Ibsen's plays, which thrilled the younger writer. (Ibsen also exerted a powerful influence on another transplanted Irishman, James Joyce.)

Shaw soon made a name for himself as a music and drama critic of considerable honesty, wit, and knowledge. Shaw's first play, *Widower's Houses* (first performed in 1892), was a stunning denunciation of slum landlords. He would follow it immediately with two more social dramas: *The Philanderer* (first produced in 1905), about the double standard in marriage; and *Mrs. Warren's Profession*, a play about prostitution that was considered quite shocking in 1893. Indeed, the latter was banned from public performance until 1925, although it had a privately produced debut in 1902. The trio would be published in book form as *Plays Unpleasant*, in a volume with three *Plays Pleasant* (*Candida*, *Arms and the Man*, and *You Never Can Tell*, three satirical comedies written shortly after) in 1898.

Like his esteemed Ibsen, Shaw wrote serious plays on serious topics, often scandalizing the bourgeois theatergoer, even when his writing was comic. He was quickly establishing himself as a public personality—acerbic, clever, verbose, cynical, and brilliant. "I have advertised myself so well that I find myself, whilst still in middle life, almost as legendary a person as the Flying Dutchman," he quipped.

Shaw followed these successes with his 1896 *The Devil's Disciple*, *Caesar and Cleopatra*, and *Captain Brassbound's Conversion*—his *Three Plays for Puritans* (1901). From 1904 to 1907, the Court Theatre ran repertory seasons of his complete output to great commercial and critical success. A great playwright, he was congratulated in print for his originality; he dismissed the praise as "nonsense." But no one before Shaw had used the nineteenth-century forms— drawing-room comedy, melodrama, farce—to present serious ideas, or such articulate and highly literate discussion of them.

In the first decade of the twentieth century, he wrote several of his greatest plays: *Man and Superman*, a dramatization of German philosopher Friedrich

Nietzsche's ideas of the "superior man"; *Major Barbara*, a satire on the Salvation Army and arms manufacturers; and *The Doctor's Dilemma*, a denunciation of modern medicine. Those works were followed shortly thereafter by *Androcles and the Lion* and *Pygmalion* (which would achieve a second life when it was turned into the musical *My Fair Lady*, a notion that Shaw detested).

One of Shaw's more peculiar but memorable campaigns was his battle for simplified spelling. Beginning with *Pygmalion*, with its droll Henry Higgins expounding on the irrationality of the English language, Shaw argued for the rest of his life that the illogical nature of the English language could be cured only by applying some logic to the language's spelling and usage. In the preface to *Pygmalion*, he argued for the inclusion of the schwa (an inverted letter *e*) in the English alphabet, "for, though it is one of the commonest sounds in English speech, our wretched alphabet has no letter" to express it.

With the outbreak of World War I, Shaw sacrificed popularity for principle, arguing vehemently against the conflict. He suffered for that position. By 1919, however, when the British looked back and saw a generation of young men killed or maimed, they realized the truth of his warnings. *Arms and the Man* enjoyed a successful revival. That was followed by a huge success, *Heartbreak House*, a play in which Shaw condemned the moral bankruptcy of the society that had permitted the war to happen. Two years later, his five-play cycle, *Back to Methuselah*, continued his attacks on war.

Shaw continued writing plays through the 1930s and authored many essays and books on political and other topics up to his death. He wrote only one more great play, perhaps his greatest—*Saint Joan* (1923). His iconoclasm in full display, Shaw argues in this play that Joan's devotion led to her death because the world was not yet ready for her message. The world, Shaw slyly implies, cannot stand idealism in an age of cynical "realism." The success of the play, which Shaw considered his best, spurred the Nobel Prize committee into selecting him to receive the 1925 award.

Shaw's impact on the theater is almost incalculable. A list of playwrights he influenced would cover dozens of countries, from the Germany of Bertolt Brecht and Peter Weiss to the France of Jean Anouilh, the America of Eugene O'Neill, and, of course, his own England.

Sinatra, Frank

(1915–   )

AMERICAN SINGER, ACTOR, AND ACADEMY AWARD WINNER

Francis Albert Sinatra was born in Hoboken, New Jersey. Originally he had hoped to be a sportswriter, and worked briefly as a copy boy for a local newspaper. After hearing the music of Billie Holiday and Bing Crosby, however, he decided to pursue a singing career. He started a band with a few local musicians called the Hoboken Four, and when they eventually broke up, he toured the vaudeville circuit as a singer. Sinatra took a job as a singing master of ceremonies at the Rustic Cabin, a roadhouse in Englewood, New Jersey. It was there that band leader Harry James heard him sing and hired him as a vocalist for his band in 1939. A year later he joined Tommy Dorsey's vocal group called the Pied Pipers.

Sinatra went out on his own and appeared on radio's "Your Hit Parade," and then his own show, "Songs by Sinatra." The turning point came in 1942 when he performed at the Paramount Theater in New York. Bobby-soxers swooned over his smooth musical style, and he soon became his generation's most popular entertainer.

While still a band singer, Sinatra appeared in several Hollywood films. The musicals he appeared in with the dancer Gene Kelly, such as *Anchors Aweigh* (1945), *Take Me Out to the Ball Game* (1949), and *On the Town* (1949), were very popular. Sinatra did several movies that failed at the box office and resulted in a considerable drop in his popularity. When he found himself suffering from severe vocal chord problems in 1952, it appeared as if his career was over.

Sinatra pleaded for a part in the film version of *From Here to Eternity* (1953). The movie became a hit and won Sinatra an Academy Award for best supporting actor. Sinatra made some of the best movies of his career during the 1950s: the musicals *Guys and Dolls* (1955) and *High Society* (1956); the dramas *The Man with the Golden Arm* (1955) and *The Joker Is Wild* (1957); and the espionage thriller *The Manchurian Candidate* (1962). In the early 1970s Sinatra announced his retirement from show business, but he kept returning to recording and concert tours. His last movie was the leading role in *The First Deadly Sin* (1980).

Snow, C(harles). P(ercy).

(1905–1980)

ENGLISH NOVELIST, ESSAYIST, AND SCIENTIST

English novelist and scientist Charles Percy Snow was born in Leicester, England, on October 15, 1905, the son of a working-class family that had an almost religious faith in the ability of education to raise its children to another level of life. As a boy, Snow dreamed of being a man of letters, but his local school was weak in the humanities and strong in the sciences, so he directed his energies accordingly. He won a scholarship to University College, Leicester, and graduated in 1927 with honors in chemistry. He stayed on for another year, receiving a master's degree (M.A.) in physics, again with honors. As a result of his outstanding work as an undergraduate and graduate student, Snow received a scholarship to the University of Cambridge to do research in physics.

While still an undergraduate at Leicester, Charles had tried his hand at writing a novel, *Youth Searching,* but he destroyed the manuscript without submitting it to publishers. Thus, his first published work was his doctoral dissertation. As a young scientist, he was regarded as a man of promise, and in 1930 he went to work with Sir Ernest Rutherford, England's greatest living physicist. Rutherford was a great believer in science as a potential cure-all for humanity's problems, a powerful optimist who passed his beliefs on to his young associate.

For all his involvement in science, Snow was still interested in a second career as a writer. In 1932, he published his first book, a shipboard murder mystery, *Death Under Sail.* He followed it with an anonymous science fantasy, *New Lives for Old* (1933). The next year he published another novel, *The Search,* about a struggling young scientist at Cambridge. With three novels in three years (and three genres), Snow was on his way to success in his second profession, as well.

It was on a vacation shortly after the publication of the last of these three books that Snow conceived the idea for a series of novels that kept him occupied through most of the rest of his life. The cycle, which bore the title of its first novel, *Strangers and Brothers* (1940; republished in 1970 as *George Passant*), would finally include eleven novels. It is intensely autobiographical, following the career of a lawyer, Lewis Eliot. Although uneven in quality, these books, at their best, capture nicely the atmosphere of England between the outbreak of World War I and the 1950s, from the highest levels of government to the halls of the academy. To a large extent, Snow's reputation as a fiction writer rests on them.

Snow continued to practice science, as well. During World War II, he held several science-related government posts and was made a Commander of the British Empire in 1943 in recognition of his contribution to the war effort. In 1950, he married fellow novelist Pamela Hansford Johnson, and his play *View Over the Park* was produced successfully in London. The following year, *The Masters*, generally considered the best of his novels and the standout of the *Strangers and Brothers* series, was published to considerable critical and popular acclaim. The year after that, his only son, Philip Hansford Snow, was born. In 1957, Snow was knighted, and two years later he entered the most spectacular controversy of his career.

The so-called Two Cultures controversy actually had its roots in the 1920s. At the same time that Rutherford and Snow were expounding their science-based optimism, poets like T.S. Eliot and critics like Snow's Cambridge colleague F.R. Leavis were proclaiming the collapse of Western civilization in works like Eliot's *The Waste Land*. The decay of the West was an accepted belief in the works of the great literary modernists of the period, and in 1956 Snow challenged that belief in an essay, "The Two Cultures." Snow argued that literate modern society was breaking down into two cultures—the scientific community and the literary community. He said that the two cultures were finding it increasingly difficult to communicate with each other. The battle royal broke out, however, when he expanded that thesis into a lecture delivered at Cambridge in May 1959, entitled "The Two Cultures and the Scientific Revolution," which *Encounter* magazine reprinted shortly thereafter. For months, letters and articles flew back and forth in *Encounter* and other publications. Just as the heat was dying down, Leavis started the pot boiling again with a 1962 attack on Snow in a lecture at Cambridge. The debate continued for several more years in England, although Snow seemed to be offering something of a hand of peace in a speech calling for magnanimity in human relations in spring 1962.

Snow also dabbled in politics. A staunch supporter of the Labour Party, he served as parliamentary secretary in the Ministry of Technology for two years in the early 1960s. He reflected on his political experiences in *Corridors of Power* (1966), another novel in the *Strangers and Brothers* series.

In the last decade of his life, Snow—now Baron Snow, having been elevated to the peerage in 1964—continued to produce books, although he often told interviewers that he now found writing a tiresome chore. He had completed the *Strangers and Brothers* series with *Last Things* (1970). He was struggling with eye problems, but he was still able to produce several volumes of essays about famous men he had known, plus a few more novels. He even managed to write another mystery story, *A Coat of Varnish* (1979), shortly before illness claimed his life on July 1, 1980.

Solzhenitsyn, Alexander

(1918–)

RUSSIAN NOVELIST

To reach this chair from which the Nobel lecture is delivered. . . . I have mounted not three or four temporary steps, but hundreds or even thousands, fixed, steep, covered with ice, out of the dark and the cold where I was fated to survive; but others, perhaps more talented, stronger than I, perished.

> —Alexander Solzhenitsyn, accepting the 1970 Nobel Prize for Literature

Alexander Solzhenitsyn was born on December 11, 1918, in Kislovodsk, a resort town in the south of Russia. His father, a self-made man who had served as an officer in the czarist (royal rule) army, had been killed in a hunting accident, six months before his son's birth. His mother, Taisia, who came from a wealthy family, had lost everything in the Russian Revolution. Shortly after his birth, Solzhenitsyn's mother took him and moved to the larger city of Rostov, where she hoped to find work. Because of the family's background as well-to-do landlords and czarist officers, Taisia was unable to find a steady job or get an affordable apartment. She worked overtime just to make enough to buy food and clothing for herself and Alexander.

A product of the indoctrination that he received in school, Alexander grew up a devout believer in the Bolshevik system. Early in his life, he developed an interest in writing; he tried his hand at science-fiction stories when he was only nine.

When he graduated from secondary school, still intent on a writing career, he was unimpressed by the literature faculty at the University of Rostov, but he was unwilling to abandon his mother, who had developed tuberculosis (a disease of the lungs). Consequently, he became a student at the university as a math major. He also enrolled in a correspondence course with Moscow University, hoping to do some academic work that would be closer to his heart. In 1940, he married Natalya Reshetovskaya, a fellow student. The following year, he graduated with honors.

But that was also the year that the Germans invaded the Soviet Union. Solzhenitsyn, wanting to follow his father's example, went to officers' training school to become an artillery man. From there he was sent to the front, where he served with distinction and was promoted to the rank of captain. While he was fighting the Nazis, his mother died in 1944.

Solzhenitsyn had been growing disillusioned with Joseph Stalin and the Soviet system, and in the course of a letter that he wrote home from the front to a friend, he made a joke about Stalin's moustache. The letter was intercepted by the NKVD (the forerunners of the KGB; the Soviet secret police) and in February 1945, Solzhenitsyn was sentenced to eight years of hard labor for disseminating anti-Soviet propaganda. There was no trial.

For the next ten years, he was either a prisoner in the Gulag or lived in internal exile. Those ten years utterly transformed his ideas and his understanding of what he was destined to do with his life. Throughout this period, he continued writing. He began writing in verse because it was easier to memorize, and he dared not commit anything to paper.

The year before he was supposed to be released, Solzhenitsyn was diagnosed with stomach cancer. Under crude camp conditions, he was operated on. Miraculously, he seemed to experience a full recovery and was back at work in two weeks. In March 1953, his term at hard labor expired and he was sent to his place of internal exile, a rural town in Kazakhstan, located in South Central Asia. By then a hardened thirty-four years old, Solzhenitsyn began work teaching math and science at the local school. To his surprise, he enjoyed teaching and liked his students, who returned his feelings. But at night, he was secretly writing down the thousands of verses he had committed to memory over eight years in the camps. He was also writing new material. He was free for the first time to write in privacy since he had entered the nightmare world of the Gulag. And, in 1957 an amnesty for political prisoners freed him to go home.

Solzhenitsyn relocated in central Russia, eventually settling in Ryazan, about a hundred miles from Moscow. Reunited with Natalya, he was teaching again. In this period he turned out two of his most famous works, *One Day in the Life of Ivan Denisovich* and *The First Circle,* both of which drew on his experiences in the camps and the research institute. When the so-called Khrushchev thaw began, he was actually able to publish the first of these two novels, with the premier's personal approval, in 1962. He had also submitted *The First Circle* to magazine for publication.

In May 1964, the Communist Party was prevented by Nikita Khrushchev from interfering with the awarding of the Lenin Prize for literature; it went to *One Day*.

Solzhenitsyn began working on *The Gulag Archipelago*, a massive three-volume history of the work camps. He hid the manuscript of that work-in-progress and his two novels with friends, but the KGB seized them. He now waited for the repercussions that he knew must surely follow. Solzhenitsyn rushed to finish *The Cancer Ward*.

It had become impossible for him to publish in the Soviet Union. However, in open defiance of the KGB, he began a series of readings. He also arranged for the publication of *The First Circle* in the United States. It appeared in Russian in England and France in 1968. Solzhenitsyn had burned his last bridges in the Soviet Union. He was expelled from the writers' union in 1969. He received the Nobel Prize for Literature the following year, as much as a symbolic gesture of solidarity with an embattled opponent of repression as for the body of writing he had produced thus far. His marriage was also breaking up, and he became involved with his secretary, Natalia Svetlova, shortly after.

In 1971, a French publisher brought out a Russian-language edition of *August 1914*, the first volume in a projected multi-volume novelistic re-creation of the rise and fall of the Bolshevik system, to be entitled *The Red Wheel*. At the end of December 1973, the first volume of *The Gulag Archipelago* was published in Paris. Within weeks, a meeting of the leadership of the Communist Party was held in the Kremlin (the center of Soviet political activity). After a heated discussion in which such options as imprisonment and even assassination were talked about, it was decided that Solzhenitsyn would be stripped of his Soviet citizenship and expelled from the country.

On February 12, 1974, the KGB picked up Alexander Solzhenitsyn and transported him to Lefortovo Prison; from there he was flown to West Germany, where he was warmly received by writer Heinrich Böll. For the next year and a half, he stayed in Zurich, Switzerland. Finally, in 1976, Solzhenitsyn and his family relocated to the United States, in the small town of Cavendish, Vermont.

Over the next nineteen years, Solzhenitsyn seldom deviated from his daily routine. He rose early, ate breakfast with his wife and sons, then went to the study, in a separate building from the house, where he would write in his tiny script for several hours. He would break for lunch, then continue again until dinner time. He would often write for as many as fourteen hours a day.

On those rare occasions when he did emerge for a public appearance, he often outraged his American hosts by telling them that their own culture was decadent and morally corrupt, and that the West was not doing enough to bring about the fall of the communist system.

In the early summer of 1989, Alexander Solzhenitsyn was readmitted to the Soviet Writers' Union. The board of the union urged the government to restore his citizenship. His books were to appear in government-sponsored editions. His Nobel lecture was printed on the front page of *Novy Mir*. Successive volumes of *The Red Wheel* were published in the United States and Russia. And the Soviet government collapsed.

Recently, after nearly two decades of exile, Alexander Solzhenitsyn and his family returned to the former Soviet Union. Years before, in a BBC (British Broadcasting Company) interview, Solzhenitsyn had said, "I am inwardly convinced that I shall go back. I live with that conviction—I mean my physical return, not just my books." He had survived the Gulag, in which some thirty million prisoners had died. He had survived stomach cancer, despite the doctors' estimate of only a one-in-three chance of recovery. Now he had outlived his enemies and was returning home.

Spielberg, Steven

(1947–　　)

AMERICAN FILMMAKER AND ACADEMY AWARD WINNER

Steven Spielberg was born in Cincinnati, Ohio, on December 18, 1947. He was the oldest of four children of Arnold Spielberg, an electrical engineer and computer expert, and Leah Posner Spielberg, a concert pianist. During Spielberg's childhood, the family moved from Ohio to New Jersey and then to Phoenix, Arizona.

When Spielberg saw Cecil B. DeMille's film *The Greatest Show on Earth* (1952) at the age of five, he fell in love with the movies. While he was still in grade school, Spielberg borrowed his father's 8mm movie camera and made a three-and-a-half minute film with his friends. He went on to make short Westerns and horror films, and by the time he entered high school, he had become skilled in many of the basic techniques of Hollywood filmmaking.

As a teenager, Spielberg organized a tree-planting business to pay for his film and equipment. He won his first filmmaking contest at the age of fourteen with a forty-minute war movie called *Escape to Nowhere*. Three years later, Spielberg made a two- and-a-half hour science fiction film, *Firelight*. His father was so impressed with the movie, that he rented the local movie theater and sold tickets for a one-night showing.

The family then moved to San Francisco, California. Because of poor grades, Spielberg was not accepted into the University of Southern California (USC) film department. He entered the California State College in Long Beach and studied English, graduating in 1970. He continued to make his own films, and won film festival awards with *Amblin'* (1969). Sidney Sheinberg, the head of the Universal-MCA television division, saw the twenty-minute film and hired Spielberg to a seven-year contract.

Steven Spielberg's first TV assignment was for Rod Serling's "Night Gallery" horror series, which led to directing jobs for "Marcus Welby, MD" and "Columbo." His breakthrough opportunity came in 1971 with *"Duel,"* a "Movie of the Week" for ABC television, which many critics regard as the best made-for-TV movie ever made.

The first film Spielberg made for theaters was *The Sugarland Express* (1974), an action picture written by Hal Barwood and Matthew Robbins, who had both graduated from the USC film school Spielberg had wanted to attend.

Universal then assigned the twenty-six-year-old director the film version of Peter Benchley's best-selling novel *Jaws.* Spielberg almost rejected the job due to his lack of experience and the fact that the story was similar to *"Duel."* He finally agreed to the project and *Jaws* (1975) went on to become the biggest moneymaking film to that time, earning $60 million dollars in its first month of release.

By the time *Jaws* was completed, Spielberg was already at work on his next film, *Close Encounters of the Third Kind* (1977). Costing over $20 million to make, the film was predicted to be a financial disaster. It was, in fact, a huge success and earned Spielberg his first Academy Award nomination for Best Director.

Spielberg's next film was even more costly to make, and *1941* (1979) was a complete disaster at the box office. Many critics have even called it one of the worst films ever made. Spielberg followed this failure with a succession of hits, including *Raiders of the Lost Ark* (1981), in which he joined forces with his friend George Lucas, and *E.T., The Extra-Terrestrial* (1982), which set box-office records. The director was honored by Academy Award nominations for both films.

In 1983 Spielberg returned to his beginnings, in a sense, as he released *Twilight Zone—The Movie,* based upon the Rod Serling television series. The movie remade four episodes, with Spielberg acting as producer of the film and directing one episode. It was not one of the filmmaker's best efforts, and the film was marred by the tragic deaths of Vic Morrow and two Vietnamese children in the episode directed by John Landis, who became involved in a lengthy lawsuit over the question of the director's negligence.

Spielberg produced a number of other films before directing the screen version of Alice Walker's *The Color Purple* (1985). The film caused a controversy as many people thought that Spielberg had made an almost Disneylike version of the difficult and powerful novel. The film was nominated for eleven Academy Awards, but failed to earn a single Oscar.

The same year, Spielberg returned to television and produced the series *"Amazing Stories,"* which was quickly canceled due to poor ratings. Spielberg also produced *An American Tail* (1986), his first animated feature, which starred a mouse name Fievel Mouskewitz.

Spielberg's biggest successes then came from the films he produced, rather than directed. He produced the hits *Back to the Future* (1985), and its sequels, and *Who Framed Roger Rabbit?* (1988), while directing the commercial failures *Empire of the Sun* (1987) and *Always* (1989).

He continued to produce, achieving his old success as a director with *Indiana Jones and the Temple of Doom* (1989). His expensive follow-up *Hook* (1992), his version of the story of Peter Pan, was another disappointment. Spielberg, however, broke box-office records with *Jurassic Park* (1993). His 1994 film, *Schindler's List,* won Spielberg an Academy Award as best director.

Spock, Benjamin

(1903–   )

AMERICAN PACIFIST, PEDIATRICIAN, AND AUTHOR

What is the use of physicians like myself trying to help parents to bring up children healthy and happy, to have them killed in such numbers for a cause that is ignoble?

  —from Benjamin Spock's trial testimony (1968)

The world's most well-known pediatrician, Benjamin McLane Spock, became a leader of the peace movement in the 1960s. The author of *Baby and Child Care,* which has sold more copies than any other original book produced in the United States, Spock offered advice on child rearing to two generations of parents.

Spock, born in New Haven, Connecticut, learned from his strict parents a commitment to high moral principles that would later inform his activism. Benjamin was educated in private schools in Hamden, Connecticut and Andover, Massachusetts. When he enrolled at Yale University in 1921, Spock planned on a career as an architect. A summer job as a counselor at a camp run by the Newington Crippled Children's Home, however, changed the direction of Spock's life. He decided to become a doctor.

Graduating from Yale University in 1925, he studied medicine at Yale Medical School and at the Columbia University College of Physicians and Surgeons. After receiving his medical degree from Columbia in 1929, Spock worked as an intern and a resident (in pediatrics and in psychiatry) at several New York hospitals over the next four years. He also received six years of training in psychoanalysis. From 1933 to 1944, Spock had a private practice as a pediatrician (a children's doctor). Near the end of World War II, he served as a psychiatrist in New York and California naval hospitals run by the U.S. Naval Reserve Medical Corps.

The Common Sense Book of Baby and Child Care (in later editions, simply called *Baby and Child Care*) first appeared in 1946. This comprehensive, supportive guide for parents stood apart from other books on child care. Rather than simply telling readers what to do, Spock focused on explaining child development. While setting out general guidelines, Spock stressed that every baby was unique. He called on parents to remain flexible and supportive of their child's individual talents and abilities. Spock advocated feeding infants on demand: whenever the baby wants to eat, feed her or him. He encouraged parents not to worry about spoiling the baby. This advice marked a departure from the strict child rearing practices recommended in the past. The book, in its original and revised versions, has sold well over forty-million copies and has been translated into more than thirty languages.

For the next twenty years, Spock taught psychiatry and child development at universities in Minneapolis, Minnesota, Pittsburgh, Pennsylvania, and Cleveland, Ohio. From 1955 to 1967, he also served as supervising pediatrician at Western Reserve University's Family Clinic in Cleveland. He also continued to advise parents on child rearing. Beginning in 1954, he wrote a regular column on the problems of parenting for *Ladies Home Journal* and then *Redbook*. He cowrote *A Baby's First Year* in 1954 and *Feeding Your Baby and Child* in 1955. Two collections of his magazine columns—*Dr. Spock Talks with Mothers* and *Problems of Parents*—were published in 1961 and 1962.

Spock increased his political activism in the 1960s. He endorsed Presidential candidate John Kennedy's proposal for Medicare—a federal program providing medical care to the aged—in 1960. Two years later, President Kennedy announced that the U.S. would resume above-ground testing of nuclear weapons. Spock quickly joined the growing peace movement, committing himself to the cause of world peace. He criticized the nuclear arms race between the United States and the Soviet Union as a futile and never-ending attempt to catch up or stay ahead of each other. That year, he joined the board of the National Committee for a Sane Nuclear Policy (SANE). His first public statement on the nuclear arms race appeared in a paid advertisement in the *New York Times* later that year. Spock warned that nuclear testing contaminates milk and other food. He then described how radioactive contamination affects a child's growing body. In 1963, he was elected co-chair of SANE.

When President Lyndon Johnson massively increased U.S. military involvement in Vietnam in 1965, Spock wrote a series of letters urging the President to reverse his policies on the war. His letters ignored, the angry pediatrician joined in antiwar demonstrations. By 1967, Spock had retired from Western Reserve's clinic in order to devote all of his time and energy to ending the war. He attended antiwar rallies in Washington and New York. Later that year, he was elected co-chair of the National Conference for a New Politics. The conference brought together militant African-Americans, pacifists, and other radicals. When the more conservative SANE board members objected to his growing association with radicals, Spock resigned as co-chair, but remained a SANE member.

Spock also actively opposed the military draft. In 1967, he joined poet Allen Ginsberg and others in collecting nearly one-thousand draft cards from young men who refused to serve with the armed forces in Vietnam. He then turned them over to the Justice Department. Later that year, he was arrested for crossing a police line during a protest in front of a New York draft board. At Johnson's urging, the Justice Department began to take action against draft resisters and those who promoted resistance. With four others, including Yale University chaplain William Sloane Coffin, Jr., Spock was charged with conspiring to aid and abet illegal resistance of the draft.

Four of the five men were found guilty and sentenced to two years in prison in 1968. Spock and Coffin were also fined $5,000 each. Yet at a news conference after he had been sentenced, Spock vowed to continue to work against a war he considered illegal. Later that year, he coauthored *Dr. Spock on Vietnam,* detailing his opposition to the war. In 1969, an appeals court overturned the four convictions. The court ruled that the trial judge had denied the defendants' right to a fair trial by issuing improper instructions to the jury. Spock continued to speak out against the war until American involvement ended in 1974. He ran for president in 1972 as the candidate of the pacifist People's Party. In 1974, tying together his concern for child care and his opposition to U.S. policies, he published *Raising Children in a Difficult Time.* Spock has continued to provide comforting advice to parents as a columnist for *Redbook,* and as a contributing editor of *Parenting* magazine beginning in 1992. He supported movements to overcome the lack of quality daycare facilities and to improve the government's financial support of schools, especially those serving poor communities. In the 1980s, he was arrested several times for taking part in peaceful demonstrations to protest cuts in the government's housing budget and to support more aid to the homeless. His autobiography, *Spock on Spock: A Memoir of Growing Up with the Century,* was published in 1989.

Steichen, Edward Jean

(1879–1973)

AMERICAN PAINTER AND PHOTOGRAPHER

Edward Jean Steichen was born on March 27, 1879, in Luxembourg. Steichen's mother, Marie Kemp Steichen, decided that her son would grow up in America and the family moved to Hancock, Michigan, in 1882. Steichen's father worked in the copper mines, but when he became ill, Marie Steichen supported the family, working in a hat shop.

Steichen was apprenticed as a designer to a commercial lithographic company in Milwaukee, Wisconsin, in 1894. He won a prize for an envelope he designed in 1897. He then studied painting and organized the Milwaukee Art Students League; he learned photography from a local photographer and took his first photograph in 1896. Steichen became a naturalized American citizen in 1900.

On his way to Paris in the spring of 1900, Steichen stopped in New York to visit Alfred Stieglitz at the New York Camera Club. Stieglitz was the leader in the struggle for the recognition of photography as art. Stieglitz purchased three of Steichen's prints and urged the young artist to continue his work with the camera.

Shortly before his return to the United States in 1902, Steichen had a one-person exhibit in Paris that featured both paintings and photography. Back in New York, Steichen joined the New York Camera Club and became close friends with Stieglitz. He opened a studio at 291 Fifth Avenue and began photographing portraits of prominent people, including J.P. Morgan.

Steichen convinced Stieglitz to open an art gallery at the 291 studio in order to exhibit the photographs of Stieglitz and his followers, known as the Photo-Secession group. "291" quickly became a gallery known not only for its photography, but for its new paintings and sculpture, introducing modern art into American culture.

By 1906, Steichen was becoming a popular photographer, but he felt that people were more interested in his conventional photographs. He wanted to pursue more creative styles in his work and returned to France. The Lumiere Company had just introduced color photography and Steichen began experimenting with the new process. He traveled to London and photographed a color portrait of the writer George Bernard Shaw, which Stieglitz immediately reproduced in his influential magazine *Camera Work*. Steichen also photographed his friend, the sculptor Auguste Rodin, along with Rodin's work. Stieglitz purchased the photographs and presented them to the Metropolitan Museum of Art in New York, along with many other prints he had acquired.

These prints remain the only surviving work from Steichen's early years. His early photographs are characterized by a soft-focus, which created a kind of haze around the subject. This style was favored by the Photo-Secessionists in an attempt to make photographs appear more like paintings.

With the help of Gertrude Stein, an American writer in Paris who was friends with many artists, Steichen arranged to have the first exhibitions of Henri Matisse's and Pablo Picasso's paintings in America at "291." Steichen also became friends with many American painters in France and helped organize the Society of Younger American Painters, which included John Marin and Max Weber. The Society also exhibited at "291."

At the outbreak of World War I, Steichen returned to New York and when the United States enter the war, Stieglitz and Steichen closed the "291" gallery. Steichen enlisted in the Signal Corps and commanded the Photographic Division of Aerial Photography. He retired with the rank of lieutenant colonel in 1918.

"The wartime problem of making sharp, clear pictures from a vibrating, speeding airplane ten to twenty thousand feet in the air had brought me a new kind of technical interest," Steichen wrote. He turned away from his soft-focus technique and began photographing objects with painstaking precision and clarity. Steichen also destroyed his paintings, determined to commit himself to photography.

He then operated a commercial studio in New York from 1923 to 1938. He worked frequently for *Vogue* and *Vanity Fair* magazines. For both magazines Steichen created a remarkable series of fashion photographs and celebrity portraits, including the dancer Martha Graham, and the actors Charlie Chaplin and Greta Garbo.

In 1942, Steichen was commissioned in the U.S. Navy to photograph the war at sea. Lieutenant Commander Steichen, with the help of his brother-in-law, the poet Carl Sandburg, directed an exhibition of his war photographs, Road to Victory, for the Museum of Modern Art in New York.

Steichen then served as the director of photography at the Museum of Modern Art from 1947 until 1962, directing more than fifty important photographic exhibitions. The most influential exhibit was Family of Man in 1955, in which Steichen and his staff selected 503 prints from over two million submissions, representing 273 photographers from sixty-eight different countries. Family of Man was called the greatest photography exhibition ever and was seen by millions of people in more than seventy countries throughout the world. Steichen was awarded the Presidential Medal of Freedom in 1963.

Steinbeck, John

(1902–1968)

AMERICAN SHORT-STORY WRITER
AND NOVELIST

John Steinbeck was born and raised in Salinas Valley, California. His family owned lots of books, and he educated himself by reading them. Steinbeck's father was an official in the city government, and his mother was a teacher who encouraged him to read.

Steinbeck went to Stanford University where he studied marine biology. Although he attended the school on and off for approximately five years, he did not earn a degree. When he was not in school, Steinbeck worked as a rancher, road worker, deck hand on a boat, and a cotton picker.

In 1925 Steinbeck traveled to New York, where he worked as a newspaper reporter. Four years later he published his first novel, *Cup of Gold.* When Steinbeck returned to California he lived alone for two years, working a variety of jobs. He was a painter, chemist, fruit rancher, and he worked in a trout hatchery. During this time he continued to write, and his stories were mostly about the blue-collar workers with whom he lived and worked.

Steinbeck published a collection of his work, *God Unknown,* in 1932. The characters in these stories led simple lives and were connected to the land on which they lived. Steinbeck's next two books established his reputation as an author. *Tortilla Flat,* published in 1935, was about Mexican-Americans living in Monterey, California. *In Dubious Battled,* published the following year, dealt with the strike of California fruit pickers.

Steinbeck's next book, *Of Mice and Men,* is one of his best- known novels. Published in 1937, the story is about a mentally retarded man. Steinbeck originally had conceived the story as play, and when it was dramatized in 1937 it won the Drama Critics Circle Award.

Steinbeck followed *Of Mice and Men* with a collection of stories, *The Long Valley* (1938). His next major novel, *The Grapes of Wrath,* was published in 1939. It depicted the despair of the 1930s as farmers fled the Dust Bowl for work opportunities in the West. *The Grapes of Wrath* won a Pulitzer Prize and was made into a motion picture in 1940.

Steinbeck wrote two novels about life at sea called *Sea of Cortez* (1941) and *The Log from the Sea of Cortez* (1951). His novella, *The Red Pony* (1945), depicted the life of a boy living on a ranch in California. *The Pearl,* published in 1947, was about a Mexican-American fisherman who finds a pearl that brings him bad luck. Steinbeck portrayed three generations of the Trask family in *East of Eden,* published in 1952. In 1961 he published *Winter of Our Discontent,* and the following year he won the Nobel Prize for literature.

Although Steinbeck was not a political activist, he became disillusioned with materialism and authority as he watched the struggle of ordinary people to survive. In depicting the unity and dignity of all human life, his books stirred American readers' consciousness. Steinbeck's work is valuable today for its portrayal of both American history and the triumph of the human spirit.

Stravinsky, Igor

(1882–1971)

RUSSIAN COMPOSER
AND CONDUCTOR

Throughout a long creative career, Igor Stravinsky and his music were linked closely with the ballet world, changing how the world thinks about music's relationship to dance. His music helped to alter the way in which dance was created, as well as bringing a new awareness of music's function as an vital ingredient in dance.

Igor Fyodorovich Stravinsky was born in 1882 in Lomonosov, Russia. His father was a famous bass singer at the Marinsky Theatre in St. Petersburg, so Stravinsky came to music naturally. At the same time that he studied law at St. Petersburg University, Stravinsky was taught the piano with Leokadia Kashperova, and harmony with Vassily Kalafaty. From 1902 to 1908, he became a friend and pupil of the great Russian composer Nikolai Rimsky-Korsakov.

Rimsky-Korsakov's music had a great influence on Stravinsky's early compositions. He was also influenced by the music of other Russian contemporaries, such as Tchaikovsky, Borodin, Glazunov, and, from 1907 to 1908, French composers Debussy and Dukas.

This colorful mixture of inspirations produced his first ballet score, *The Firebird,* winning him international acclaim when it was produced in 1910 by Sergei Diaghilev for his Ballet Russes dance company, with choreography by Michel Fokine. It became the single work of Stravinsky's that was most often performed, to the extent that he was once addressed in public by a stranger as "Mr. Fireberg."

Stravinsky went with the Ballet Russes company to Paris, France, and spent much of his time in France from then onward, composing *Petrouchka* in 1911 and *The Rite of Spring* in 1913 for the company. These scores showed an extraordinary development in his work. Both used folk tunes. The driving rhythm and energy of *The Rite of Spring* proclaimed an important change in Western music, which had none of these qualities before. *Petrouchka* was first written as a concert work with solo piano, but was turned into a ballet by choreographer Fokine.

Of *The Rite of Spring,* the composer was later to write: "I was guided by no system whatever. I heard, and I wrote what I heard. I am the vessel through which *The Rite of Spring* passed." This ballet was choreographed by the great dancer Vaslav Nijinsky. Stravinsky revised *The Rite of Spring* in 1921 and in 1943. The masterwork has continued to challenge choreographers to this day.

When World War I disturbed the activities of the Ballet Russes, Stravinsky moved to Switzerland, where he composed the choral ballet *Les Noces (The Wedding);* a short play to be read, played, and danced, called *The Soldier's Tale;* and several groups of songs. When the war was over, Stravinsky continued to write for the Ballet Russes, touring with them as conductor and pianist until 1923. During that period, Diaghilev produced Stravinsky's *Le Renard (The Fox), Les Noces (The Wedding Festivities),* and finally *Apollon Musagète* in 1928.

All this time, Stravinsky was living in France, and his music was beginning to sound more French than Russian. However, his Russian roots were not completely gone. He orchestrated pieces by Tchaikovsky to make the ballet *Baiser de la Fée (Kiss of the Fairy),* which was choreographed by Nijinsky for Ida Rubinstein's company in Paris.

In the 1930s, Stravinsky concentrated on instrumental works that included the *Violin Concerto,* the *Concerto for Two Pianos,* and the *Symphony in C.* It was during the composition of this symphonic work, in 1939, after his wife and mother both died, that Stravinsky moved to the United States, settling in Hollywood in 1940 and marrying his second wife. Film projects followed, but none of his works reached the screen. His music seemed more suited to dance than to background for drama. Some of the music that was intended for movies wound up as orchestral pieces, including the *Symphony in Three Movements* (1945).

In America, Stravinsky found a suitable collaborator in choreographer George Balanchine, whom he had worked with before, on the ballet *Jeu de Cartes (The Card Party)*, in 1937. For Balanchine, he composed *Orpheus* (1948) and *Agon* (1957). Stravinsky devoted the late 1940s to the composition of the opera *The Rake's Progress,* which was produced in 1951. Stravinsky had written operas before (*The Nightingale, Mavra*), but this was his most successful effort.

Throughout the 1950s and 1960s, Stravinsky continued to compose religious pieces, such as *Canticum Sacrum, Threni,* and *Requiem Canticles.* He also composed memorial works, such as *In Memoriam Dylan Thomas* and *Elegy for J.F.K.* All of these were written after his seventieth birthday, and he continued to write and conduct his music (recording all of his works) well into his mid-eighties. During the later part of his career, many of his orchestral pieces were turned into ballets by Balanchine, Jerome Robbins, and others.

Sun Yat-sen

(1866–1925)

REVOLUTIONARY AND FOUNDER OF MODERN CHINA

> ... the rest of mankind is the carving knife and the serving dish, while we are the fish and the meat ... if we do not earnestly promote nationalism and weld together our four hundred millions into a strong nation, we face a tragedy.
>
> —Sun Yat-sen, 1924

Sun Yat-sen holds the distinctive position of being honored in both communist and nationalist Chinese histories of the twentieth century. To the former he is a founder of the revolution that created Communist China; to the latter he is the founder of the Republic of China.

He was born in the Kwangtung province of China on November 12, 1866, to a peasant family. At the age of twelve he moved to Hawaii, where he studied English and Western history before returning to China in 1882. His schooling in China did not last long, thanks to his rebellious spirit, and he moved to Hong Kong, where he became a Christian and, in 1892, a doctor. In 1894 Sun returned to Hawaii, where he formed the Revive China Society, whose purpose was to rally supporters in an attempt to overthrow and reform Chinese society. After a failed attempt at rebellion in Canton in 1895, he was exiled for the next sixteen years. After an attempt by his political enemies to kidnap him in London failed in 1896, Sun became known around the world for his efforts to revolutionize China.

From outside the country, Sun directed several failed attempts to overthrow China's government between 1900 and 1911. That year the Wuchang Revolt succeeded and Sun was named provisional president of the Republic of China in 1912, but he resigned quickly in an attempt to avoid further civil war. He was made chairman of the Kuomintang, or national party, and in 1913, when his presidential successor attempted to make himself emperor, Sun again tried to overthrow the government. Failing, he fled to Japan, where he enlisted additional support before returning in 1916 to set up a rival government in Canton.

Creating a republic in Canton, Sun turned to the communists, both in China and in the Soviet Union, for support in maintaining power. Acceptance of their financial and military aid in 1923–1924 helped create an alliance between Sun and the Chinese communists that resulted in a reorganization of the Kuomintang Party and the creation of its army (which would prove essential in the eventual victory by the communists in their struggle to unite China). Sun, however, did not live to see his dream of a modern China, free of backward traditions, become a reality either on the mainland, where the communists established themselves, or on Taiwan (originally known as Formosa), where his republican successors, under the leadership of Chiang Kai-shek, created Nationalist China. Sun died on March 12, 1925, before either of the states became a reality

Thorpe, James Francis

(1888–1953)

AMERICAN DECATHLON AND
PENTATHLON COMPETITOR,
FOOTBALL PLAYER, AND BASEBALL
PLAYER

Jim Thorpe was named the "Best Athlete of the Half-Century" in 1950 and some sports experts still consider him the greatest all-around athlete in history. The versatile Thorpe showed uncanny ability at a young age.

Jim Thorpe was born on May 28, 1888, near Prague, Oklahoma. He had Chippewa and Sac and Fox Indian heritage. His tribal name was Wa-Tho-Huch, or "Bright Path."

His father wanted Jim and his twin brother, Charles, to get an education. The boys went to a training school in Kansas, but Charles died there from pneumonia. Jim ran away and returned home.

At age 16, Jim was sent to the government-run Carlisle Indian School in Pennsylvania, to study tailoring. Since Carlisle was a trade school as well as a high school, many of its students were older than 18. The school's football team played successfully against top-rated college and university football teams with bigger players.

At age 18, Thorpe was about 6 feet tall and weighed 155 pounds. He was a substitute halfback in 1907 and showed talent in running, kicking, passing, and tackling. When the regular halfback was injured, Thorpe showed he could fill his shoes. That year Carlisle beat every team it played except Princeton. By 1908 Jim had added fifteen pounds and was starring on the varsity team.

In 1909 Thorpe joined other young athletes who played in semipro baseball leagues during the summer. The North Carolina team paid him and the others some money to cover their expenses, about $25 a week. He did not return to Carlisle for two years, working instead on an Oklahoma ranch. When he went back, he was 185 pounds and stronger than ever. His superb playing helped his team defeat the previously unbeaten Harvard team. He stood out in every game, leading Harvard coach Perry Haughton to call him "the theoretical 'superplayer' in flesh and blood."

When it was time to enter the Olympics, Thorpe decided to compete in both the pentathlon (made up of five events) and decathlon (made up of ten events).

What followed has been called one of the greatest athletic feats of the twentieth century. Thorpe did so well in the pentathlon that his score was twice as high as that of the second-place finisher. He proceeded to win the decathlon, too, with four first place wins. He became the only person ever to win both events. Since 1928, the pentathlon has not been part of the Olympics, so his record was never broken. When the King of Sweden gave Thorpe his awards, the king said, "You, sir, are the greatest athlete in the world."

Jim Thorpe returned to America as a hero. He was honored at a New York City parade and received a congratulatory letter from President William H. Taft. Instead of accepting offers to make money as a professional athlete, he went back to Carlisle. In a football game that fall, a newspaper article read, "He went through the West Point line as if it was an open door; his defensive play was on a par with his attack and his every move was that of a past master." Thorpe was twice named an All-American football player.

Shortly after the West Point game, a Boston newspaper ran a story saying that Thorpe was not truly an amateur athlete because he had received money for playing baseball a few years earlier. Thorpe admitted what had happened but insisted he had not realized that what he did was wrong. Many other athletes had done the same thing, lying about their names, and he asked the Amateur Athletic Union (AAU) to forgive the mistake. Instead it enforced the rule strictly and said he could not compete in the Olympics if he had been a professional. Thorpe was ordered to return his gold medals, which were offered to the second-place finishers. Those men refused, saying that Thorpe had won even if some rule had been broken. Still, Thorpe's name and scores were removed from the official Olympic records.

Upset but unable to change things, Thorpe left college to play pro baseball. He started with the New York Giants, then played with the Cincinnati Reds and the Boston Braves. But he was not as good at baseball as he had been at football. In 1915, while continuing to play baseball, he joined the Canton Bulldogs football team. The pro football teams decided to organize into a league (the American Professional Football Association) in 1920. Thorpe was named president and held that office for a year as he continued to play. The league became the National Football League in 1922.

Throughout the 1920s Thorpe was losing speed and strength. In 1929 he was 41 years old. A newspaper sports story called him "a shadow of his former self." He quit playing and tried to find other work. Those were rough years. The nation was going through the Great Depression of the 1930s. Thorpe drank too much alcohol. He and his wife, Iva, were divorced. He found jobs as a painter, carpenter, movie extra, then digging with a pick and shovel. When it became known that he was struggling, people were shocked. The U.S. vice-president, Charles Curtis, invited Thorpe to sit in his special box at the 1932 Olympic Games in Los Angeles. The crowd cheered his arrival.

During World War II, Jim Thorpe served with the merchant marine. Afterwards, in 1945, his second marriage broke up. He remarried again and lived a quiet life in a trailer in California. In 1950, sports experts named Jim Thorpe as the greatest male athlete of the first half of the twentieth century. They also agreed he was the greatest football player of the last fifty years.

People had tried for years to get the Amateur Athletic Union to reverse its decision and return Thorpe's medals and restore his Olympic records, but it refused. Thorpe died of a heart attack in 1953 at age 64.

His third wife, Patricia, his friends, and his seven children kept asking that Thorpe's medals and titles be restored. They finally succeeded in convincing both the AAU and the International Olympic Committee. In January 1983, new medals were given to Thorpe's children. A statue of Jim Thorpe stands near the entrance to the Pro Football Hall of Fame in Canton, Ohio.

Tito, Josip Broz

(1892–1980)

NATIONALIST COMMUNIST LEADER OF YUGOSLAVIA

I thought of the day when Kumrovec and thousands of other towns and villages all over Yugoslavia would rouse themselves from backwardness, when young people would at last have a chance in life . . .

—Marshal Tito, speaking about Yugoslavia in the 1930s

In the history of communism in the twentieth century, few figures are as interesting as Josip Broz. Known to the world as Tito, the man who reunited the many ethnic groups of Yugoslavia into a stubbornly independent communist state after World War II probably came closer to achieving the "pure" goals of Marxism-Leninism than any other leader.

Josip Broz, born on May 25, 1892, was one of fifteen children of a peasant family in the village of Kumrovec, Croatia. After studying to be a locksmith, he worked in several neighboring countries as a mechanic before World War I. Drafted into the Austro-Hungarian army at that time, he was captured and sent to prison in Russia. After the war he joined the Red Army following the Russian Revolution of 1917, which marked the beginning of the communist Soviet Union.

The ethnic regions of Serbia, Croatia, Bosnia, and other smaller areas were first united as Yugoslavia in 1918. However, strong rivalries and ethnic and religious hatreds persisted (as evidenced by events in the region during the 1990s), making any Yugoslavian government fragile. It was in this atmosphere that competing political philosophies flourished, ranging from communism and fascism to monarchism. Not until 1944 was Tito able to establish firm control and lasting power.

Tito (his alias during years of guerrilla fighting and hiding from political authorities) returned from Russia to Croatia in 1920 and joined the Yugoslav Communist Party. In 1928 he was sent to prison for five years for his illegal political activities in Zagreb, Croatia's capital. This prompted him to return to the Soviet Union, a communist state, where he rose in the ranks of the outlawed Yugoslav Communist Party. Tito was the only Yugoslav leader to survive the massive purges of the Soviet leader Joseph Stalin in the early 1930s, which were designed to eliminate any officials who might disagree with him.

As head of the party in 1937, Tito was successful in building it into a powerful military and political force by uniting the people in the cause of preserving the unity of Yugoslavia. During World War II, Yugoslavia again threatened to fall apart over the issue of which side to fight on. A resistance movement led by a General Mihajlovic, which favored the return of the monarchy to Yugoslavia, sided with Germany and the Axis countries. Tito, on the other hand, mounted one of the most remarkable resistance warfare movements in history in battling the Germans. This won him support from the Allies, including the United States, where Tito was viewed by many as a nationalist rather than as a puppet of the Soviet Union.

In 1941, Tito expanded his military operations against the Axis powers by establishing the National Liberation Army. He also spent the war years preparing the country for a change to communism by attempting to remove class structures and force changes in the economic system. By 1943, he was the leader of the Committee for the National Liberation of Yugoslavia, which, in effect, was the country's only legitimate government. At the end of that year, the Allies gave further support by recognizing Tito's forces as the Allied army in Yugoslavia. In October 1944, his troops entered Belgrade, the capital of Serbia, and drove the German army out. On November 29, the Federated Republic of Yugoslavia was established.

There is no doubt that Tito used totalitarian means to solidify his power. From 1945 to 1953 he served as prime minister; he was then named president, and in 1963 he was declared president for life. In the mid-1950s, however, Tito began to implement changes that increased individual freedoms, liberalized the court system, and diminished government control over many areas, including the economy. He also maintained an independence from Soviet leaders that was unusual among communist countries after World War II. He tried to unite a group of nonaligned countries that would support neither the Soviet Union nor the United States, and he condemned the Soviets for their invasions of Hungary (1956) and Czechoslovakia (1968). Tito also was an active participant in the United Nations.

Tito's goal—never attained, but attempted—was to create a democracy based on socialism, by passing through the step of communism, as described by Karl Marx and Vladimir Lenin. In his attempts to use governmental control to reform society and his fierce refusal to follow the road, or the demands, of the Soviet Union, Tito was more successful in going further toward Lenin's goals than any other communist leader. He died on May 4, 1980, in Ljubljana.

Trilling, Lionel

(1905–1975)

AMERICAN LITERARY CRITIC AND SCHOLAR

Lionel Trilling was born in New York City. He was educated at Columbia University and taught at the University of Wisconsin and Hunter College during the 1920s. Trilling returned to Columbia to do graduate work in English literature and began teaching there in 1931. Trilling received his Ph.D. from the university in 1938 and eventually became a professor of English there. He was associated with Columbia throughout his life.

Trilling's first book was *Matthew Arnold.* Published in 1939, it was a study of the nineteenth-century poet and critic. Four years later he published a literary biography of the twentieth-century English novelist E.M. Forster. In these and other books, Trilling borrowed research methods from psychology, cultural anthropology, and sociology to explain literature and its creators.

During the 1940s Trilling became one of the leading literary critics in the United States. Throughout his life he contributed many important book reviews to national periodicals, including the *Nation,* the *New Republic,* the *Kenyon Review,* and *Partisan Review.* He also served for many years as an editorial adviser to both the *Kenyon Review* and *Partisan Review,* and was responsible for their becoming excellent literary journals.

Several collections of Trilling's essays were published as books. They include *The Liberal Imagination* (1950) and *Beyond Culture: Essays on Literature and Learning* (1965), as well as *Sincerity and Authenticity* and *Mind in the Modern World* (both 1972).

Trilling's other books of criticism include *The Opposing Self* (1955) and *A Gathering of Fugitives* (1956). Trilling also wrote two books about Sigmund Freud (1856–1939), the Austrian physician who created psychoanalysis: *Freud and the Crisis of Our Culture* (1955) and *The Life and Work of Sigmund Freud* (1962).

In addition to his critical writings, Trilling published several highly praised short stories and a novel, *The Middle of the Journey* (1947). He also edited a number of works, including *The Portable Matthew Arnold* (1949). Trilling was married for many years to Diana Trilling (1905–1995), also a noted critic and writer. He died in New York in 1975.

Trotsky, Leon

(1879–1940)

RUSSIAN REVOLUTIONARY LEADER

> The working masses of the whole world are joining the flag of the Soviet authority, and the world robbers of imperialism are being betrayed . . .
>
> —Leon Trotsky, 1919

Socialist revolutionary Lev Davidovich Bronstein (Leon Trotsky was an alias he adopted to avoid arrest) was born near Kirovograd, Russia, on October 26, 1879. His family were Jewish farmers who, though successful, lived a very basic, rural life. As a young boy, Lev was taken to Odessa by an older cousin who provided much of his education.

It was in the small port city of Nikolaev that Lev had his introduction to radicalism, at the hands of a group of elderly exiles who had formed a group called The People's Will. He also met his future first wife, Alexandra Sokolovskaya, another revolutionary. By age seventeen, Lev had established a reputation for himself as an eloquent, powerful speaker, even when talking about political philosophies he knew little about. As his involvement in radical groups increased, he joined the South Russian Workers Union, was arrested, and was banished to Siberia (a vast area in the east of the country known for its inhospitable landscape and harsh extremes of climate) for four years. His new wife persuaded him to escape, and they fled to Western Europe.

Using false identity papers naming himself Leon Trotsky, the young radical arrived in London around 1902. There he met Vladimir Lenin, the man who would become the first leader of the Soviet Union. By 1903, with strong ideas of his own, Trotsky had emerged as Lenin's top rival at a time when the Russian revolutionaries were splitting into two groups, the Bolsheviks and the Mensheviks. Trotsky allied himself with the latter, but only temporarily. It was his ideas on the necessity of socialist revolution, however, that would eventually bring Lenin and Trotsky together again, however tenuously. Trotsky also warned that there was a danger that revolution could merely create another despotic bureaucracy, which was what eventually happened in the Soviet Union after his and Lenin's death.

In 1905, Trotsky was involved in the general strikes and violence that erupted in St. Petersburg, Russia, and he was again exiled two years later. He remained out of the country until the Russian Revolution broke out in 1917. During those ten years Trotsky lived in Europe and attempted to unite the Bolsheviks and Mensheviks, but he was not successful. When he was thrown out of France for his revolutionary activities, he traveled to the United States and was there when the rebellion in Russia began. Joining Lenin back in Russia, the two leaders urged the Russian people to revolt, and Trotsky was put in charge of the armed forces. With the success of the revolution, he was named people's commissar for foreign affairs and the commissar for war. In this capacity he enlarged the new Soviet army from ten thousand men to more than five million in less than three years.

During the civil war between Lenin's supporters and enemies that erupted after the revolution, Trotsky remained powerful. In 1920, as the war was resolved, he suggested using the same methods he had applied so successfully to the army to create a new economy. With Lenin's approval, he called for the organization of labor along military lines, in effect almost removing the distinction between the army and the civilian work force. But Lenin died in 1924 and Trotsky was left without his primary support. Joseph Stalin, another Lenin assistant, proved to be far more politically powerful during the struggle for leadership that followed.

In 1928, after being banished from the Communist Party, Leon Trotsky was exiled to a remote region of the Soviet Union, and once again he fled the country. This time he went to Turkey, France, and Norway before finally settling in Mexico. He lived long enough to witness Stalin's emergence as the very bureaucratic despot ("dictator" would not be too strong a word) he had warned against. Trotsky was killed by a Soviet assassin on August 20, 1940.

Truman, Harry S.

(1884–1972)

UNITED STATES SENATOR, VICE PRESIDENT, AND
THIRTY-THIRD PRESIDENT OF THE UNITED STATES

Harry S. Truman was born in Lamar, Missouri on May 8, 1884, the son of John and Martha Ellen Truman. His father worked at many trades, including farming and buying and trading in livestock. In 1890, the family moved to Independence, Missouri, where it was thought that the boy would get a better education at a larger city school. Truman did not like sports, but he loved to read. He claimed that by the age of twelve he had read every book in the Independence public library. It was in Independence that Truman met Elizabeth "Bess" Wallace, his childhood sweetheart and the woman he eventually married.

In 1903, the family moved to Kansas City, where Truman, now a high school graduate, worked as a bank clerk. In 1905, he joined the Missouri National Guard, but soon left to help his family with the farm they had purchased in Grandview, Missouri. In Grandview, Truman began to take an interest in Democratic party politics, and also served as the town's postmaster and a member of the local school board. The family farm did not prosper, however, and in 1914 Truman's father died, a few months after the start of World War I.

In April 1917, President Woodrow Wilson declared war on Germany and allied the United States with Britain and France. Captain Harry Truman arrived with his men in France in February 1918, and in September distinguished himself at the Battle of Argonne Wood. The war ended in November, and by May 1919 Truman was back in Missouri, discharged from the army. He married Elizabeth Wallace and the couple moved into the home of Elizabeth's parents in Independence. They had one daughter, Margaret, born in 1924. He and another army friend opened a clothing store in Kansas City, but by 1922 the store went out of business and Truman was left with heavy debts.

Truman now decided to take advantage of political connections he had made both locally and in the army. He had come to the attention of Tom Prendergast, a powerful political boss of the Missouri Democratic party. In 1922, Truman was elected a county judge, even though he was not even a lawyer. As a judge, Truman acquired a reputation for hard work and honesty, but he was also often accused of being too close to the corrupt Prendergast political machine. In 1929, the Depression struck and millions of Americans lost their jobs. Desperate for new economic ideas, in 1932 the voters abandoned President Herbert Hoover and the Republicans and elected Democrat Franklin D. Roosevelt to the presidency. Sensing that the political tide was now with the Democrats, in 1934 Prendergast picked Truman, who was still not well known, to run for the United States Senate. At the age of fifty one, Truman was elected a United States senator.

In 1940, Truman had to run for reelection to the Senate. The year before, Prendergast had been convicted of tax evasion, and Truman could no longer count on his powerful friend. But he had made himself popular by supporting reform legislation, and he earned the support of many black Americans by speaking out against Jim Crow state laws that denied blacks equal employment and educational opportunities, as well as voting rights. He won reelection by a narrow margin.

The main concern of the Senate in 1940 was the war in Europe. In September 1939, Germany, under the leadership of Adolf Hitler, had invaded Poland, and both England and France had then declared war on Germany. Germany invaded and conquered France in June 1940. President Roosevelt publicly tried to remain neutral, but he quietly began to build up America's defense industries to supply war materiel to England. On December 7, 1941, the Japanese attacked the American naval base at Pearl Harbor in Hawaii, and the United States was forced into the war.

Senator Truman worked hard to make the country's defense industries strong. This work earned him the respect of his political colleagues, and they began to pressure Roosevelt to consider him for vice president in the 1944 election. Roosevelt's health was failing. He suffered from polio, and the problems of fighting a world war had exhausted him. The Democrats regarded the current vice president, Henry Wallace, as too liberal, and did not want him to become President if anything happened to Roosevelt. Wallace was discarded, and Truman became Roosevelt's running mate. The Democrats easily won the election.

Truman was vice president for only eleven weeks when, on April 12, 1945, Franklin Roosevelt died of a brain hemorrhage. Truman was the new President, but he was ill prepared. Roosevelt had never talked to Truman about his war strategy or his private agreements with allied nations. Nor had Roosevelt told Truman about the Manhattan Project, the secret program to develop an atomic bomb.

By the spring of 1945, German cities were in ruins from allied bombing and its borders were overrun by English, American, and Russian armies, and on May 8, 1945, Germany finally surrendered. In June 1945, United States Marines captured the outlying Japanese island of Okinawa. Truman was faced with a fateful decision.Could the war be ended by using the destructive power of the atomic bomb? Believing that American lives would be saved, Truman ordered the use of the bomb.

On August 6, 1945, an atomic bomb was dropped on the Japanese city of Hiroshima, and on August 9 a second bomb was dropped on the city of Nagasaki. Both cities were leveled. In each city more than seventy thousand people died instantly and tens of thousands more eventually died of burns and radiation poisoning. On August 14, 1945, Japan surrendered. Truman's decision had produced the desired result, but it was a decision that is criticized to this day. A new type of weapon of mass destruction had been used against civilians, and there was no defense against it. A country that possessed such weapons and was willing to use them posed an intolerable threat to other countries. By this one act, Truman had pushed the world into the nuclear age, and there was no turning back from the suspicions and rivalries of the resulting arms race that began between world powers.

The major problem facing Truman after the war was the worsening relationship between the United States and its wartime ally, the Soviet Union. Soviet dictator Joseph Stalin insisted on controlling the future governments of the countries of Eastern Europe. This seemed to go against agreements worked out between Roosevelt and Stalin at a conference at Yalta in the Soviet Union in February 1945. At a conference in Potsdam, Germany in the summer of 1945, Truman took a hard line with Stalin, demanding, for instance, a freely elected, democratic government for Poland. But there was little Truman could do after the war to enforce this or other measures, as Soviet troops were occupying Eastern Europe.

These were the opening events of the Cold War, and Truman responded in several ways. With his new secretary of state, George C. Marshall, Truman prepared a $22 billion aid program for Europe to repair war-torn economies and to bolster them against the influence of the Communists. In March 1947, he announced the Truman Doctrine, which implied that the United States would rush to the defense of any democracy anywhere in the world. American foreign policy would be to contain communism. This direct challenge to Soviet expansionism meant that the United States would become involved in new, expensive commitments to other nations all around the globe. Complicated political events came to be interpreted simply as elements of the struggle between the Western and Communist alliances.

In 1948, Stalin cut off Western access to Berlin, the capital of Germany, which was within the territory occupied by Soviet armies. Here, the Truman Doctrine received its first test. Truman organized an airlift of food and supplies to the beleaguered city, skillfully avoiding a confrontation with Soviet ground troops.

Truman faced mounting problems at home as well. Harry Truman had made enemies. He had angered the left by abandoning Roosevelt's liberal policies. He had angered the right by failing to stop the threat of communism. There seemed good reason to believe that in 1948 Truman would not win election to the presidency against the popular governor of New York, Thomas Dewey.

In a stunning upset that proved the predictions and the newspaper headlines wrong, Truman was elected President again. He had held together a coalition of working people, urban and black voters, and many Americans who simply preferred his tough, plain-spoken, midwestern manner to that of Dewey, the cultured easterner.

Truman's second term was eventful and controversial. On April 4, 1949, the United States joined with European countries in forming the North Atlantic Treaty Organization (NATO). Its purpose was mutual defense against possible Soviet aggression in Europe. Eventually, Stalin ended the blockade of Berlin, but in September 1949, Truman learned that the Soviets had developed their own atomic bomb. On October 1, 1949, with the nationalists defeated and retreating to the island of Taiwan, Mao Zedong established the People's Republic of China. Soon afterward Truman's critics were accusing the Democrats of "losing" China. Americans became very fearful of the Soviet Union and China, and anti-Communist feelings in the country became very strong.

In 1950, an ambitious senator from Wisconsin, Joseph McCarthy, accused the Truman administration of being "soft" on communism. He claimed that the State Department was full of Communist sympathizers and spies. McCarthy organized a Senate committee to investigate the loyalty of Americans working in the government, the army, the schools, and the entertainment industry. Before he was discredited, many innocent citizens had lost their jobs and had their whole lives destroyed by McCarthy's accusations. The new conservative mood also made it difficult for Truman to persuade Congress to pass the laws he wanted in the areas of health insurance, aid to education, and civil rights.

In June 1950, war broke out in Korea. The country had been occupied by Japan during World War II, and when Japan was defeated, the Soviet Union and the United States had agreed to divide the country in two. North Korea had a Communist government and South Korea had a government struggling to create a democracy. Now a North Korean army had invaded South Korea. With the approval of the United Nations, Truman sent American troops under General Douglas MacArthur to stop the invasion. Instead of just driving the North Koreans back across the border, MacArthur invaded their country. As American forces pushed north, the Chinese entered the war, sending a million troops into Korea to oppose the Americans. MacArthur wanted to extend the war into China and publicly disagreed with Truman, who was more cautious. Truman decided to remove MacArthur from command. Finally the armies in Korea could not defeat each other, and peace negotiations dragged on for months. The war began to erode Truman's support, and he decided not to run for reelection in 1952. The Democrats nominated Adlai Stevenson, but the Republican candidate, Dwight Eisenhower, won the election. Truman returned to Missouri and lived a quiet life with his family until he died in Kansas City on December 26, 1972.

Tuchman, Barbara

(1912–1989)

AMERICAN HISTORIAN
AND WRITER

I am a seeker of the small facts, not the big
explanation; a narrator, not a philosopher.
> —Barbara Tuchman, in a
> 1963 interview

Barbara Tuchman was born Barbara Wertheim in New York City. Her father was a prominent banker. She became interested in history at a very young age when she read a famous series of children's books by Lucy Fitch Perkins, beginning with *The Dutch Twins* (first published in 1911). These were known as the "Twin" books because they were stories about the lives of twins in countries around the world. Some of them were set in different historical periods, including *The Puritan Twins* (1921) and *The Colonial Twins of Virginia* (1924).

Barbara Wertheim was educated at private schools in New York and spent summers in Europe with her parents. In 1929 she entered Radcliffe College. She graduated in 1933 with honors in history after writing a senior paper on the British Empire. Later that year, Barbara Wertheim accompanied her grandfather, a diplomat, to the World Economic Conference in London. This trip increased her interest in world affairs.

In 1934 Barbara Wertheim began working at the Institute of Pacific Relations in New York as a research assistant. A year later she was sent to the institute's branch office in Tokyo, Japan. After her return to New York in 1935 she became a staff writer at the *Nation,* a journal that was owned by her father. She wrote articles for the *Nation* for several years, and traveled to Spain as a correspondent for the journal in 1937, during the Spanish Civil War.

Barbara Wertheim then moved to London, where she wrote magazine articles and worked on her first book, *The Lost British Policy: Britain and Spain Since 1700.* It was published in England in 1938. She returned to New York in September of that year. For the next two years she worked as a freelance writer for the *Nation* and later as a correspondent for a leading British journal, the *New Statesman and Nation.*

In 1940 Barbara Wertheim married Dr. Lester Tuchman, a New York physician. The couple later had three children. During World War II, Barbara

Wertheim Tuchman worked for a while as an editor at the Office of War Information. However, for many years she devoted most of her time to her family, although she continued to read widely.

In the early 1950s Tuchman began work on a second book, a history of England's political activities in the Middle East. This was published in 1956 as *Bible and Sword: England and Palestine from the Bronze Age to Balfour.* Two years later she published *The Zimmerman Telegram,* a book about diplomatic relations between Germany and Mexico just before World War I.

In 1959 Tuchman began research for her next book, a study of the first month of World War I (August 4–September 4, 1914). During the summer she visited the European battlefields of that war. She also traveled the routes that the German armies had followed as they marched through Luxembourg, Belgium, and France. During the next two-and-a-half years, Tuchman did extensive research on the war at the New York Public Library. She was especially interested in letters, diaries, and other personal documents because she wanted her book to reflect the human side of events.

In 1962 her fourth book, entitled *The Guns of August,* was published. The book was an immediate success and was praised by critics as well as the general public. It became a best seller and was translated into a number of different languages. The book was later made into a movie. The following spring Tuchman was awarded the 1963 Pulitzer Prize for general nonfiction for *The Guns of August.*

Tuchman's next book was *The Proud Tower* (1966), a study of European and American society in the years before World War I. This was also a best seller. In 1971 she published *Stilwell and the American Experience in China, 1911–45.* This was an account of the longtime relations between the United States and the Chinese Republic, with special emphasis on the experiences of an American army general named Joseph Stilwell. Stilwell had been the head of the U.S. armed forces in China, Burma, and India during World War II. In 1972, *Stilwell and the American Experience in China* won a second Pulitzer Prize for Tuchman in the category of general nonfiction.

Tuchman spent seven years doing research for and writing her next book, *A Distant Mirror: The Calamitous 14th Century.* This was an examination of events in fourteenth-century France. It was told from the point of view of a typical knight and nobleman of the period. *A Distant Mirror* was published in 1978 and was also a popular success.

During the 1980s Tuchman completed three more books before her death: *Practicing History* (1981), a collection of essays about the writing of history; *The March of Folly: From Troy to Vietnam* (1984), a study of warfare throughout human history; and *The First Salute* (1988), a book about the American Revolution. She died suddenly at her home in Greenwich, Connecticut in February 1989.

Veblen, Thorstein

(1857–1929)

AMERICAN ECONOMIST AND SOCIAL PHILOSOPHER

Thorstein Veblen was born in Manitowoc County, Wisconsin. His parents had emigrated from Norway in 1847 and settled on the Wisconsin frontier, where they lived under great hardship. When Thorstein was eight, the family moved to a farm in Minnesota. There were other Norwegian immigrants in the area, and they formed a small but active community. Thorstein grew up speaking mostly Norwegian and trained in Norwegian social customs.

At the age of seventeen, Thorstein Veblen was enrolled in college preparatory courses at Carleton College in Northfield, Minnesota. Several years later he entered the college. Veblen had a difficult time at Carleton. He was unfamiliar with American social customs and had very little money. Other students often teased Veblen, calling him "Norskie." However, he managed to do well in his classes and graduated in 1880.

Veblen taught for a year in a Wisconsin high school. Then he moved to Baltimore, Maryland, to do graduate work in philosophy and economics at the new Johns Hopkins University. After a semester he transferred to Yale University in New Haven, Connecticut. Although Veblen was a brilliant student, he was once again a social outsider at Yale. He received a doctorate in philosophy in 1884 but could find no teaching job. He therefore returned to the family farm in Minnesota.

For the next seven years Veblen tried to make himself into a farmer. However, he was miserable and longed to be associated with a university. Finally, in 1891, at the age of thirty-four, Veblen abandoned farming and moved to Cornell University in Ithaca, New York, with his wife. He talked the chair of the economics department, Lawrence Laughlin, into giving him a special fellowship so that he could do additional graduate work in economics. A year later, Laughlin became chair of the economics department at the University of Chicago and he brought Veblen along with him on another fellowship.

During the 1890s Veblen did research and taught at the University of Chicago. He also published a number of papers in professional journals and became managing editor of the *Journal of Political Economy,* which was published at the university. Veblen attracted wide attention with his articles, which were based on research in cultural anthropology and sociology as well as economics.

Veblen published his first book, *The Theory of the Leisure Class,* in 1899. This was a savage attack on the upper and middle classes in American society. Veblen accused them of being interested only in making and spending money.

At the turn of the century a number of social reformers were making headlines with their attacks on the wealthy and their call for help for the poorest classes. Therefore, Veblen's book was published at a time when many people were as critical as he was of wealth and privilege. *The Theory of the Leisure Class* was read widely, and Veblen became a nationally known celebrity.

Five years later Veblen published his second book, a critical examination of American business called *The Theory of Business Enterprise.* He left the University of Chicago in 1905 and later taught at Stanford University in California and at the University of Missouri. During this time he published three more books. The first, *The Instinct of Workmanship* (1914), is a book based on his most popular course, "Economic Factors in Civilization." The second was an economic history called *Imperial Germany and the Industrial Revolution* (1915). The third, *An Inquiry into the Nature of Peace* (1917), criticized the business community for being an obstacle to lasting world peace.

In 1918 Veblen moved to New York, where he briefly edited the *Dial,* one of the leading magazines of the day. A year later he joined the faculty of the New School for Social Research. Veblen continued to criticize the business community in his later books. These included *The Higher Learning in America* (1918), an attack on the control of universities by businessmen. His other books were *The Vested Interests and the State of the Industrial Arts* (1919), *The Engineers and the Price System* (1921), and *Absentee Ownership and Business Enterprise in Recent Times* (1923).

In 1925 Veblen was elected president of the American Economic Association but he declined, saying, "They didn't offer it to me when I needed it." A year later Veblen moved back to California, where he lived until his death in a cabin near Palo Alto.

Wallenberg, Raoul

(1 9 1 2 – ?)

SWEDISH DIPLOMAT AND HUMANITARIAN

A businessman and diplomat, Raoul Wallenberg became a legendary figure through his efforts to rescue Hungarian Jews during World War II. Personally credited with saving over 100,000 Hungarian Jews from deportation to Nazi death camps by German occupation authorities, the near-mythic status of Wallenberg, the "Righteous Gentile," grew tragically even stronger after his mysterious disappearance while a Soviet prisoner.

Born in Kappsta, near Stockholm, on August 4, 1912, Wallenberg, a member of a distinguished family of bankers, industrialists, and diplomats, enjoyed a youth of privilege and wealth. He traveled widely, becoming proficient in a number of languages. Pursuing his interest in architecture and city planning, Wallenberg studied at the University of Michigan in the United States. Upon graduation in 1935 he began work with a business firm in South Africa and for a Dutch bank in Haifa (Palestine), where he came in contact with Jewish refugees from Nazi Germany.

In 1936 Wallenberg became the foreign representative of a central European trading company, the president of which was a Hungarian Jew. Throughout the 1930's, as he continued his career as a manager of an export-import business in Stockholm, Wallenberg found himself increasingly disturbed by the growing brutality and belligerence of the Nazi régime. And, in September of 1939, when the Germans invaded Poland and the World War began, Wallenberg, a citizen of neutral Sweden, began to seek out ways in which he could be of help to the threatened communities of European Jews.

After visiting Hungary in the early 1940's, Wallenberg, convinced that Adolf Hitler's campaign to destroy the Jews of Europe must be resisted by whatever methods possible, began to work actively to alleviate the misery and suffering the Nazi occupation of Europe had brought about.

Raoul Wallenberg's actions soon came to the attention of the World Jewish Congress and the American War Refugee Board. He was offered and accepted their invitation to direct a program in Hungary to save remaining Jews there. After the Nazis sent troops and S.S. units into Hungary in March of 1944 to round up Jews and other "subversives," Wallenberg, with the help of various Swedish and U.S. Jewish and refugee organizations, persuaded the Swedish Foreign Ministry to send him to Budapest on a diplomatic passport. On July 9, 1944 Wallenberg arrived in Budapest, amply funded by his backers. He immediately began distributing fabricated passports and identification papers to thousands of Jews assigned for deportation to death camps, while placing other Jews in buildings under the protection of the Swedish government. Thus thousands of Jews—perhaps as many as 20 to 35 thousand—were given shelter by Wallenberg in "safe houses" flying the flags of Sweden and other neutral countries.

Adolf Eichmann, the infamous Nazi official who directed the sending of Jews to concentration camps, ordered Wallenberg to cease interfering with German plans for "The Final Solution" of the Jews. Raoul Wallenberg refused. Eichmann attempted to have Wallenberg assassinated, but the attempt was unsuccessful. Wallenberg continued interceding on behalf of the Jews. Indeed, in the final days before the liberation of Budapest by the Soviet army, he persuaded the Nazis of the wisdom of canceling a plan to wipe out an entire ghetto, effectively saving some 70,000 Jews. By the end of the war in Hungary, in early 1945, Raoul Wallenberg had prevented the murder of 100,000 Hungarian Jews. This achievement, for which he often risked his own life, would later earn him worldwide admiration, fame, and honors. Yet, on January 17, 1945, he was arrested by the newly occupying Soviet authorities who reportedly believed him to be an American agent. The Cold War was just commencing; Raoul Wallenberg became one of its first and most famous casualties.

After leaving Budapest by car accompanied by his driver and two Soviet officers, ostensibly for a meeting with Soviet officials in Debrecen, Hungary, Wallenberg and his driver vanished. According to Swedish authorities, the Soviets later admitted privately that his arrest had been a mistake arising from the confusion of the war's end; they later alleged that Wallenberg had died on July 17, 1947, of a heart attack in a Moscow prison cell. Indeed, in 1957 the Soviet government officially confirmed Wallenberg's death as occurring ten years before. There were a number of unconfirmed reports from released Soviet prisoners, however, that he was subsequently seen alive in prison. Such reports continued to surface, notably in 1951, 1959, and as recently as 1976, leading an international committee to conclude that as of January 1971 he was still alive.

On October 5, 1981, President Ronald Reagan approved a special act of the U.S. Congress granting Raoul Wallenberg honorary American citizenship, a distinction awarded to only one other person—Sir Winston Churchill. This tribute to the long-vanished hero enabled the U.S. State Department to pursue more vigorously the truth concerning the mystery of Raoul Wallenberg's disappearance—a mystery which remains unsolved still.

Waller, Fats

(1904–1943)

AMERICAN PIANIST AND SINGER

Fats Waller was born Thomas Wright Waller in New York, the son of a Baptist preacher. As a child, Waller played the reed organ at open-air services that his father gave in Harlem, and he played the piano at his public school. At age fifteen he became the organist at the Lincoln Theatre in Harlem. When his mother died in 1920, Waller moved in with the family of the pianist Russell Brooks, who introduced him to the musician James Johnson. Waller later studied piano with Leopold Godowsky and music composition with Carl Bohm at the Juilliard School.

In 1922, Waller made his recording debut as a soloist with "Muscle Shoals Blues" and "Birmingham Blues." In 1923 he made his broadcasting debut for a Newark radio station, and he continued to perform as a singer and pianist throughout his life. In 1927 Waller recorded his musical work "Whiteman Stomp" with Fletcher Henderson's orchestra, who performed many pieces written by Waller in later years. Waller collaborated with the lyricist Andy Razaf for the all-black Broadway musical *Keep Shufflin'* (1928), and then later for *Load of Coal* and *Hot Chocolates* (1929).

In 1934, Waller began recording the first of a series records with a six-piece band known as Fats Waller and his Rhythm. Later in the mid 1930s Waller performed on the West Coast with Les Hite at Frank Sebastian's New Cotton Club. Waller also appeared in two Hollywood films in 1935: *Hooray for Love* and *King of Burlesque.* Also in 1935 Waller formed and led his own big band under the direction of Don Redman, touring in the United States and Europe and recording albums.

The last few years of Waller's life were spent making several recordings and touring in America. In 1943 he returned to Hollywood to make the film *Stormy Weather* with Lena Horne and Bill Robinson. While he was performing as a soloist at the Zanzibar Room in Hollywood, he died of pneumonia in 1943.

Warhol, Andy

(1928?–1987)

AMERICAN PAINTER, PHOTOGRAPHER, AND FILMMAKER

By most accounts, Andrew Warhol was born in Pittsburgh, Pennsylvania, on August 6. Throughout his adult life, however, Andy Warhol confused people by changing the time and place of his birth, as well as many details of his childhood. He was constantly creating his own history and his own image.

His parents had come to the United States from Russia in 1921; his father worked as a coalminer and died when Warhol was a child. His mother was often sick, and the family lived in poverty.

Warhol began studying art in high school and graduated from Carnegie-Mellon University in 1949. While a student, he worked at a department store in Pittsburgh, painting window displays. He also submitted a painting to the annual Pittsburgh Associated Artists exhibition, a portrait of himself with a finger up his nose, titled *The Broad Gave Me My Face, but I Can Pick My Own Nose* (1949). The painting was rejected from the exhibit, even though many of the jurors felt that it was an excellent work.

Warhol came to New York in the summer of 1949, and soon became a successful illustrator for fashion magazines and department stores. In 1957, he established Andy Warhol Enterprises.

He was a successful commercial artist until 1960, when he began to paint comic strips and labels of cans. His large comic strip paintings of Dick Tracy was used a 1961 window display from Lord & Taylor's department store in New York. Warhol began his famous Campbell's Soup can paintings because he claimed to have the soup everyday for lunch.

In 1962 Warhol began silkscreening photographs, a technique of mechanical image transfer, which made his work seem more impersonal and allowed for a faster and easier way to repeat images.

In *Marilyn* (1962), the colors of the famous actor's pink flesh and yellow hair are deliberately mismatched so that the color spills over the dark outline of her face. The painting explores the similarities between beauty and ugliness.

Warhol's use of repeated images in his paintings, resembling a film strip, led him to make movies, starting in 1963. His early film *Sleep,* which recorded a person sleeping for six hours, rejected the traditional stories of popular movies. The same year, Warhol moved to the loft that became known as "The Factory."

In 1964, Warhol had a disagreement with the architect Philip Johnson, who had commissioned the artist to do a mural for the World's Fair in New York. Warhol had created a twenty-foot black-and-white painting called *The Thirteen Most Wanted Men,* based on mug shots of criminals. Johnson informed Warhol that he had to replace the painting within twenty-four hours, so Warhol painted the entire canvas silver. A year later, Warhol produced the first record by the band The Velvet Underground, and when they played on stage, he showed his films behind them.

As a founder of American Pop art, Warhol's subject matter and techniques were borrowed from commercial art, comic strips, television, movies, and advertising. As a whole, Pop art reacted against the emphasis on the individual found in abstract expressionism: the popular style of the day characterized by an individual and personal technique of applying paint onto the canvas.

After Warhol survived a murder attempt on his life in 1968, his art and lifestyle changed. His early and controversial paintings were replaced by slick portraits of such celebrities as Elizabeth Taylor and Mick Jagger. His films became more commercial and he launched the celebrity-profile magazine *Interview.*

In the late 1970s, Andy Warhol spent his time attending parties and the disco nightclub, Studio 54, where he mingled with other celebrities. He returned to art in the early 1980s, collaborating with the young artist Jean-Michel Basquiat. It was the first time Warhol had painted since the 1960s.

Warhol's return to the art scene was brief, however, as he became involved in television. He appeared on "The Love Boat" series as himself and produced a number of music videos. He also produced a short television show for MTV, "Fifteen Minutes with Andy Warhol." The title was taken from his famous 1967 statement, "In the future everyone will be famous for fifteen minutes." Warhol's own fame, however, seems to be longer lasting. His paintings appear in almost every major museum and a large retrospective of his work was exhibited at the Art Institute of Chicago and the Museum of Modern Art in New York in 1989. Warhol died in 1987 after undergoing routine surgery.

Warren, Earl

(1891–1974)

GOVERNOR OF CALIFORNIA AND CHIEF JUSTICE OF THE UNITED STATES SUPREME COURT

Earl Warren was born on March 19, 1891, in Los Angeles, California. He grew up in Bakersfield, California, where he attended public schools. He also worked to help earn money for his family. He graduated from the University of California in 1912 and from its law school in 1914. He served in the army in World War I, after which he set up a law practice in Oakland, California. He held a variety of local offices, eventually becoming district attorney of Alameda County, California, where he served from 1925 to 1938. During this time, he developed a reputation as a tough, racketbusting prosecutor. He was not known as a brilliant attorney, but as a very thorough one. His cases were so solidly argued and so flawless in their legal presentation that not a single conviction he obtained was overturned on appeal.

Warren ran for state attorney general in 1938 and won, having been active in the Republican party for some time. He served ably, but clearly had his eye on higher office. In 1942, he ran for governor and beat the popular incumbent Democrat, Culbert Olson. Warren wasn't an extraordinary governor but he was capable and well liked, and won reelection in 1942, and again in 1950, this time beating James Roosevelt, son of the late President Franklin D. Roosevelt. In 1948, he was drafted to run for vice president with Governor Thomas Dewey of New York, but the team lost to Harry Truman and his running mate, Alben Barkley. In 1952, Warren vied for the Republican nomination for president himself, but lost to the popular Dwight D. Eisenhower, who went on to win the presidency in the general election.

It was at the 1952 Republican National Convention, when Warren finally threw in his support with Eisenhower over Senator Robert Taft of Ohio, that he established the relationship with Eisenhower that would lead to his nomination to the Supreme Court. Warren was a typical California Republican—conservative, individualistic, friendly—with a law-and-order reputation. In 1953, a Supreme Court seat became vacant and Eisenhower nominated Earl Warren. The seat happened to be the chief justice's seat, and instead of elevating another justice to chief and letting Warren take the associate's seat, Eisenhower made him chief justice. Although he had no judicial experience, he was confirmed easily by the Senate in March 1954.

Eisenhower must have thought he was taking the safe route, appointing a conservative Republican to the seat. But Warren proved to be an unpredictable jurist who presided over a number of momentous, distinctly liberal decisions. The most important decision was Brown v. Board of Education in 1954, which ended segregation in the nation's schools. This decision led to many other decisions that struck down racial inequalities in most areas of public life. Another important ruling involved the "one man, one vote" doctrine, which determined that voters must be equally represented in state legislatures, not according to geographic or other considerations.

The Warren Court variously ruled to extend the boundaries of free speech; to eliminate required religious exercises in public schools; to allow the receiving and sharing of birth control information; and to guarantee accused criminals the right to an attorney and to protection from police abuses. While serving as chief justice, Warren also headed the now-famous commission that investigated the assassination of President John F. Kennedy in 1963. The Warren Commission, as it was known, determined that no conspiracy had played a role in the event, and that the assassin, Lee Harvey Oswald, had acted alone.

Earl Warren died in 1974. He had served as chief justice of the Supreme Court from 1953 to 1969. He is remembered for many traits and accomplishments. For instance, unlike most other jurists, he used plain language in his arguments and written decisions, claiming that it was important to represent the Constitution's concepts in simple terms to support his notion that the Supreme Court was really "a people's Court."

Though many of his decisions were controversial, he led the court toward landmark decisions in the areas of civil rights and individual liberties.

Weil, Simone

(1909–1943)

FRENCH PHILOSOPHER, EDUCATOR, POLITICAL THEORIST, AND RELIGIOUS MYSTIC

> What a country calls its vital economic interests are not the things that enable its citizens to live, but the things that enable it to make war. Gasoline is much more likely than wheat to be a cause of international conflict.
>
> —Simone Weil, from *The Need for Roots*

Since her death in 1943, Simone Weil has been regarded as everything from a revolutionary Christian reformer to a heretic, from a brilliant philosopher to an impractical dreamer. Her life and writings have attracted a veritable cult, and her detractors are almost as numerous and no less vociferous.

Simone Weil was born on February 3, 1909, in Paris, France, to a comfortable bourgeois Jewish family. Her mother was a strong-willed intelligent woman who supervised her children's education almost obsessively. Simone's older brother, André, would become a famous mathematician, and she always felt at a severe disadvantage next to his precocious genius. Even in childhood there were signs of the self-destructive, self-depriving behavior that would eventually turn into anorexia nervosa and kill her. As a five-year-old, she would give up sugar as a sacrifice for the soldiers at the front during World War I. By the time she was fifteen, she had turned from an attractive and charming girl into a somber eccentric, still plagued by feelings of inferiority to André.

At the Lycée Henri VI, she studied under the prominent philosophy teacher Alain (Émile Chartier). A Cartesian, he exerted an influence on her, and she would often resort to René Descartes's method of systematic doubt in the years to come. The importance of looking at every side of an argument would stay with her throughout her writing. She went on to the École Normale Supérieure, where she thrived intellectually on the intense competition. (Although she and Simone de Beauvoir were students at the ENS at the same time, they reportedly met only once.) She received her degree in 1931, then began a career teaching philosophy at the high-school level.

As a high-school teacher, her teaching methods came in for praise, but many of her students failed. She developed a reputation for political militancy that would repeatedly cause her trouble. She was thought to be a communist and did nothing to discourage that rumor, but she never joined the Communist Party and quickly became disillusioned with it. Her final break with communism was reputed to have come after a 1933 visit to Germany, where she decided that the communists weren't strong enough to stem the rising tide of Nazism.

Weil took a year off in 1934 to work in a factory, in order to experience "the universal enslavement of the human spirit." She firmly believed that one's social action should be as rooted as possible in direct experience. She kept a journal of the experience that would only be published after her death. The year of factory work would change her life in many ways, and inspire her book *The Need for Roots.*

On the other hand, Weil's health, always precarious and always neglected, finally snapped under the strain of mental and physical exhaustion. That summer, she would take a vacation with her parents in Portugal to recuperate.

In Portugal, Weil had the first of many mystical experiences; suddenly she felt that she understood the connection between Christianity and affliction, and that she was at heart a Christian. After the summer, she returned to teaching, using her spare time to help a family of local peasants.

With the outbreak of the Spanish Civil War, Weil felt that although she was a self-proclaimed pacifist, she had to do something to contribute to a noble cause. She decided to join one of the Spanish anarchist groups that were in combat. On her second day at the front, she spilled boiling oil on her leg in a field kitchen, burning herself so severely that she was sent home immediately. However, her brief experience of the war convinced her that no side had a monopoly on right or justice; it was a decision that fueled her growing pessimism.

In the fall of 1937, she took a new teaching post, but by the end of the first term had to leave due to ill health. She was still writing on social questions, but was increasingly preoccupied with spiritual matters. During her attendance at an Easter service, she had another mystical experience, and when she had yet another while reading George Herbert's poem "Love," she decided that she had encountered the presence of Christ.

Becoming a Christian exacerbated Weil's tendency toward asceticism to the point of self-destruction. She began to sleep on the floor or a table so that she could deprive herself of sleep, and she ate even less than ever. Her reading began to focus on theology and scripture, while she began writing her theological defense of humility and suffering. In her principal theological work, *Gravity and Grace,* she depicted a transcendent God who has tied His hands in the face of evil.

The outbreak of World War II in September 1939 caused her further anguish. She decided that since war had been declared, she must oppose the evil of Nazism with all her being, even though she was still an avowed pacifist. She tried to hook up with the French resistance, then decided that she could do more from England. After a brief stay in New York with her family, she went to London to offer her services to the Free French. She went to General Charles de Gaulle with a series of increasingly bizarre plans and repeatedly demanded that he give her secret assignments behind German lines; he was convinced that she was insane.

In April 1943 Simone Weil was admitted to Middlesex Hospital, suffering from tuberculosis, extreme exhaustion, and the effects of undernourishment. By that time, she had found it virtually impossible to eat; when she did, she experienced excruciating stomach pains. She was moved to Grosvenor Sanitorium, where she died on August 17. The coroner would rule her death a suicide by starvation.

After her death, her manuscripts were collected, edited, and published by friends, particularly Father Gustave Thibbon, whose work with agricultural laborers Weil had aided. Until he published the first book drawn from her private notebooks, none of her friends (except for Thibbon and the poet Joe Bosanquet) knew about her mystical experiences or her spiritual concerns.

Welles, Orson

(1915–1985)

AMERICAN ACTOR, DIRECTOR, AND ACADEMY AWARD WINNER

Orson Welles was born to a wealthy Wisconsin couple. He was an enormously gifted child who could read Shakespeare as a five-year-old. His mother died when he was eight, and four years later his father died. Dr. Maurice Bernstein, a physician friend of the family, became Welles's guardian.

Welles never attended college. He was offered many scholarships, but instead he set off to Ireland to make drawings. While in Ireland, he faked his way into an acting career by pretending to be a famous New York theater star, making his professional debut in a leading role at the Gate Theater. Welles got excellent reviews and planned to continue his acting career but failed to get roles in either London or New York. Instead, he continued to travel in Europe.

Back in America, Welles tried the theater again, this time making it to

Broadway in the 1934 production of *Romeo and Juliet.* In the same year he married actress Virginia Nicholson. Welles codirected and appeared in a four-minute short film entitled *The Hearts of Age.* During the rest of the 1930s, Welles was very active, performing on radio, coproducing and directing the Phoenix Theater Group, the Federal Theater Project, and the innovative Mercury Theater. Welles and actor John Houseman created a radio show called the *Mercury Theater on the Air,* which was responsible for the stunning Halloween broadcast of H.G. Wells's *The War of the Worlds.* The program offered fake news reports of a Martian invasion, causing widespread panic throughout the country. Welles directed the program and played the leading role.

In Hollywood, the struggling RKO studio was in desperate need of making money from a hit movie. They saw Welles as a showy, theatrical personality who could provide them with exactly what they needed. The studio gave him permission to make a film with complete freedom just as long as he stayed within a tight budget. After several false starts, Welles settled on *Citizen Kane* (1941), a thinly-veiled biography of newspaper owner William Randolph Hearst. Hearst's attempts to stop the distribution of the film failed. It received critical raves but did not do very well at the box office upon release. *Citizen Kane,* however, was recognized as a superb film and it was honored with nine Oscar nominations. It only won one award—for best original screenplay.

Citizen Kane represented a step forward in filmmaking, both in its style and its subject matter. The dramatic story of lost innocence was much better than those offered in other superficial Hollywood movies of the time. Welles's brilliant work was not appreciated by RKO. His second film, *The Magnificent Ambersons,* was drastically cut in his absence while he was away making a film in South America. The movie was dismissed by both the critics and the public.

After only halfway directing his thriller *Journey into Fear* (1943), Welles gave his control over to Norman Foster, and he did not direct again until he made *The Stranger* (1946). It was a rather conventional suspense film to which Welles brought his flair as director and actor. The commercial success of that film led to his opportunity to write and direct *The Lady from Shanghai* (1948), starring his second wife, Rita Hayworth. The film is best remembered for its clever climax in which the characters have a shoot-out in a hall of mirrors, shattering the multiple images. Unfortunately, the movie did not make much money.

Welles went on to make movies wherever he could. In order to raise money to make them, he acted in almost anything that came along, usually improving them just by his presence. In the 1940s and 1950s he directed *Macbeth* (1948), *Othello* (1952), *Mr. Arkadin* (1955), and the low-budget gem *Touch of Evil* (1958), which many consider among Welles's best films after *Citizen Kane.*

Welles spent much of his time where he was most appreciated, living and working in Europe. He made only a few other films there. Meanwhile as an actor, he appeared in *Jane Eyre* (1944), *The Third Man* (1949), *Moby Dick*

(1956), *Compulsion* (1959), *A Man for All Seasons* (1956), *Catch-22* (1970), *Voyage of the Damned* (1976), and *Butterfly* (1982).

In 1975, Welles received the American Film Institute's Life Achievement Award. He later settled in Las Vegas, became a frequent TV talk-show guest, and made commercials.

Welles died of a heart attack in his home in Las Vegas in 1985. His remarkable body of work has inspired countless directors to take artistic risks in their attempts to tell stories on film.

Williams, Tennessee

(1911–1983)

AMERICAN PLAYWRIGHT, POET, AND FICTION WRITER

Tennessee Williams was born Thomas Lanier Williams III in Mississippi. His father was a traveling salesman and he looked down upon Williams' desire to write. Williams, who was a sickly child, was closest to his older sister Rose. He liked to read, and when he turned eleven his mother gave him a typewriter for his birthday. It was then that Williams really began his lifelong passion for writing.

Williams attended the University of Missouri for three years. He won many prizes for his fiction and poetry, and he tried his hand at writing plays. Since his father objected to his career choice, he refused to continue supporting his son. Williams went to business school in St. Louis, and worked in a shoe warehouse. At night, he returned home to write. The strain of studying, working, and writing took its toll on Williams, and in 1935 he suffered an emotional breakdown. It took him several months to recover fully.

Determined to be a writer, Williams went to the University of Iowa to participate in their playwriting program. He received his B.A. in 1938. While he was at Iowa, his sister Rose, who had also experienced emotional problems, had a frontal lobotomy. This was an operation that removed the part of the brain that doctors believed caused mental illness. It was later discovered that this was not a cure at all, and in fact the operation destroyed many lives. Rose Williams had to spend the rest of her life committed to an institution.

In 1939 Williams moved to New York and found a literary agent to represent him. He began to sign his plays, which depicted American life, as "Tennessee Williams." Williams hit success on Broadway in 1945 with the production of *The Glass Menagerie.* This was a "memory" play, in which one character Tom, looks back at life in a tenement with his mother and lame sister.

All of the characters in the play escape the hardships of the Depression by delving into their fantasy worlds. The play secured both Williams' reputation and his financial position.

He followed *The Glass Menagerie* with other hit plays, including *A Streetcar Named Desire* (1947), *Cat on a Hot Tin Roof* (1955), and *The Night of the Iguana* (1961). Williams won four New York Drama Critics Circle Awards for these plays.

In the 1960s, the American theater changed. Serious, realistic drama was not popular, and the avant-garde work of the absurdists came into vogue. Although Williams tried to accommodate his earlier audience's desire for realism, he persisted in creating his own style of art despite the public trends.

During the last decades of his life, Williams relied on alcohol and drugs, although he continued to write. His brother committed him to a rehabilitation hospital (for which Williams never forgave him) but the program did not help. As soon as he was released, Williams started using drugs again. He died in a hotel in New York when he choked on the plastic top of a nasal spray. He was seventy-two years old.

In the course of his life and career, Tennessee Williams endured criticism and trends in drama that did not necessarily agree with his style. He never gave up his craft, however, and today his plays are classics of American literature and theater.

Wilson, Edmund

(1895–1972)

AMERICAN LITERARY CRITIC AND WRITER

Edmund Wilson was born in Red Bank, New Jersey. He was educated at Princeton University and after graduation became a newspaper reporter in New York. During World War I he worked in a French hospital and later served in the U.S. Army.

After the war Wilson began his career as a critic. He wrote reviews and essays for a number of publications. He also served as managing editor of the magazine *Vanity Fair* (1920–21) and associate editor of the *The New Republic* (1926–31). During the late 1940s Wilson was the regular book reviewer for the *New Yorker.* After he left that post in 1948, he contributed long reviews and essays to the magazine for the rest of his life.

In addition to his many contributions to magazines, Wilson wrote a number of books of literary criticism. He also published plays, short stories, poetry, and a novel. However, Wilson is chiefly remembered as one of the leading critics of the twentieth century. His best-known works include *Axel's Castle* (1931), a study of Symbolist poetry; and *The Wound and the Bow* (1941), which discusses the relationship of art and illness.

Another widely read work of Wilson's was *To the Finland Station* (1940), which discusses events leading up to the Russian Revolution of 1917. Wilson is also remembered as the author of *The Scrolls from the Dead Sea* (1955), a highly praised, scholarly account of biblical-era scrolls found in the Middle East. Wilson taught himself Hebrew to help him with his research for this book.

Many collections of Wilson's reviews and essays were published during his lifetime. They include *Classics and Commercials* (1950), *The Shores of Light* (1952), and *The Bit Between My Teeth* (1965). After the death of his friend the novelist F. Scott Fitzgerald, Wilson edited Fitzgerald's unfinished novel, *The Last Tycoon,* and published it in 1941. He also edited Fitzgerald's notebooks, which he published in book form in 1945 as *The Crack-Up.*

During the 1930s Wilson was married to the writer Mary McCarthy and they had a son. They later divorced. Wilson died at his home in Talcottville, New York, in 1972.

Wilson, Woodrow

(1856–1924)

TWENTY-EIGHTH PRESIDENT OF THE UNITED STATES

Thomas Woodrow Wilson was born in Staunton, Virginia on December 28, 1856. His father, Joseph Wilson, was a teacher and a Presbyterian minister who encouraged his son's interest in religion, politics, writing, and speaking. The young Wilson was a slow learner, and modern historians believe he suffered from dyslexia, a visual problem in which letters, words, and objects appear reversed. The family moved often, and Wilson was raised in Georgia, South Carolina, and North Carolina. One of his earliest memories was of standing by the gate to his house in Augusta, Georgia and hearing a passerby say that Abraham Lincoln had been elected and that there would soon be war.

In 1873, Wilson enrolled in Davidson College in North Carolina. But in 1875 he switched to a small college in New Jersey that was soon to become Princeton University. He did well in history and government studies, and became editor of the student newspaper. Upon graduation in 1879, he enrolled at the University of Virginia Law School. In 1882, he worked as a lawyer in Atlanta, Georgia for a short time, but he came to hate the practice of law. He went back to graduate school at Johns Hopkins University in Baltimore, Maryland to continue his studies of history and government. In 1885, he wrote the first of many books, *Congressional Government.* In the same year, he married Ellen Louise Axson of Savannah, Georgia.

In September 1885, Wilson began teaching history and political economy at Bryn Mawr College near Philadelphia, Pennsylvania. In 1888, Wilson accepted another teaching position, at Wesleyan University in Middletown, Connecticut. In 1890, he moved to Princeton University. At Princeton, Wilson published nine more books, including a five volume *History of the American People* and a biography of George Washington. His nationwide reputation as a scholar was significant. In 1902, he was named president of Princeton, and he worked hard to improve and expand the university.

In 1910, Wilson accepted the nomination of the Democratic party for governor of New Jersey. Wilson surprised his supporters by campaigning as a progressive. He was elected governor and began to undertake certain reforms. Wilson became very popular, and was widely thought to be a good choice as the Democratic party's next presidential candidate.

In 1912, the Democrats indeed chose Wilson to run for President. His campaign was aided by a similar split in the Republican party between progressives and conservatives. Republican Theodore Roosevelt, who had served as President from 1901 to 1909, refused to support the current Republican President, William Howard Taft, a conservative, for reelection. Roosevelt formed a new political party, the Progressive or "Bull Moose" party, and ran for president again himself. The split between Republicans gave Wilson a landslide victory, and he assumed the presidency in 1913.

The people had elected Wilson on a program of reform, and he proved to be an effective leader who could work well with Congress. He pushed for a law to reduce tariffs, the taxes the government placed on foreign-made goods. To make up for lost revenues from the lower tariffs, Wilson introduced the first-ever federal income tax on everyone who earned more than $3,000 per year. Wilson also created the Federal Reserve banking system, in which the U.S. government controlled the interest rates at which people could borrow money. This gave the government a great deal of power to affect business conditions in the country.

In 1914, Wilson created the Federal Trade Commission, which was charged with preventing unfair competition. In the same year, the Clayton Act made it illegal for companies to secretly agree to fix prices, or for one company to own shares of a competing company. The Clayton Act also legalized unions and the right to strike. Wilson persuaded Congress to pass laws against child labor, laws granting credit to farmers, and laws providing compensation to injured workers.

In August 1914, Germany invaded France through the neutral country of Belgium. Soon England, France, and Russia were allied with each other in a great world war against Germany, Austria-Hungary, and Turkey. At first, Wilson wanted to keep the United States out of the war, and he practiced a policy of neutrality. As he was trying to steer the country clear of war, Wilson suffered a personal tragedy. In August 1914, his wife Ellen died of tuberculosis. In December 1915, he married Edith Galt, a Washington, D.C. jeweler and a distant descendant of the Indian princess Pocahantas.

Avoiding war was becoming more difficult. On May 7, 1915, a German submarine sunk the passenger ship *Lusitania.* It was a British ship and it was carrying war materiel to England, but many American passengers died when the ship sank. American opinion began to turn against Germany. In March 1916, a German submarine sank the *Sussex,* a French ship also carrying American passengers. Wilson warned the Germans that such actions must stop. In spite of the worsening diplomatic situation, in 1916 Wilson campaigned for reelection on his record of keeping the country out of war.

On January 31, 1917, Germany officially proclaimed its right to sink all ships, including those of the neutral United States, that approached the coasts of England or France. On March 1, 1917, Wilson announced that British intelligence had decoded a secret telegram from the German Foreign Secretary Arthur Zimmermann to the German embassy in Mexico. In the telegram, the foreign secretary suggested that if the United States declared war on Germany, Mexico should attack the United States and recover its lost territories in Texas, New Mexico, and Arizona. U.S.- Mexican relations were already strained, so Wilson sent an American army under General John J. Pershing into Mexico to track down the Mexican guerrilla leader Pancho Villa, who had led raids into American territory. Finally, in March 1917, German submarines sunk four American ships, and on April 6, 1917, the United States declared war on Germany.

Wilson recalled General Pershing from Mexico and made him commander in chief of the American Expeditionary Force. On May 18, 1917, Congress passed the Selective Service Act, "drafting" eligible men to serve in the war. The first American soldiers arrived in France in June 1917. By the end of the war, more than a year later, two million Americans had served in Europe.

As America produced more and more supplies for its own army and the armies of the Allies, the economy prospered. The government, under Wilson's powerful War Industries Board, closely controlled business activities and regulated prices. The government raised taxes and sold Liberty Bonds to help pay for the war. Wilson also supported Congress's passage of the Espionage and Sedition Acts. Under these laws, fifteen hundred Americans, including the Socialist leader Eugene V. Debs, were sent to jail for opposing the war. The government also officially encouraged anti-German feeling among the American people through propaganda posters and other announcements.

Eventually, the Americans learned to sail their ships to Europe in large convoys protected by fast destroyers with antisubmarine weapons. The German submarine threat was neutralized and American shipping losses declined. On January 8, 1918, Wilson put forward another peace plan known as "the Fourteen Points." It was a bold plan that called for peace with fair and equal treatment for both sides. There would be no secret treaties to divide and take control of conquered territory. There would be free trade and freedom of the seas and an agreement to disarm. And there would be a League of Nations, an international organization where states could meet and resolve their differences peacefully. The governments of Europe were suspicious of Wilson's plan because it challenged the very reasons they had gone to war, but to the war-weary people of the world, Wilson became a hero. Finally, on November 11, 1918, an exhausted Germany surrendered.

When Wilson attended the peace conference held at Versailles Palace near Paris, France through June of 1919, he had high hopes that his Fourteen Points would be the basis for a peace treaty. But his own advisers were not committed to his plan, and he faced skillful European statesmen—Prime Minister David Lloyd George of England and Premier Georges M. Clemenceau of France—who wanted harsh terms for the defeated Germans. The harsh terms eventually imposed on Germany at Versailles, along with the worldwide Depression of the 1930s, are now widely thought to be a major cause of the growth of German fascism. The Treaty of Versailles, signed in June 1919, ended the war and dismantled the Austro-Hungarian empire and created three new independent states—Poland, Czechoslovakia, and Yugoslavia.

When Wilson returned from France in September 1919, he undertook a nationwide tour to get public support for Senate ratification of the peace treaty and the League of Nations. The trip was exhausting, and on October 2 Wilson suffered a stroke that left the left side of his body and face paralyzed. His political enemies took advantage of his incapacity, and the Senate approved neither the Treaty of Versailles nor the League of Nations.

But Wilson carried on from his bedroom in the White House. His wife Edith prepared his letters and documents and held them up for Wilson to sign. But it was clear he was weakening and losing control of the government. Wilson's ambitious attorney general, A. Mitchell Palmer, taking advantage of public fears about the growth of labor unions and Socialist sentiment, began to arrest thousands of innocent people as "subversive aliens." Intolerance spread throughout the nation. African-Americans had migrated from the South to the northern states to work in the country's war industries. With the war over and unemployment increasing, there was racial tension between white and black workers. The Ku Klux Klan grew in strength during this period.

Not all the news during this period was negative, however. Women's groups had been pressuring Wilson to grant women the right to votes As men went into the army during the war, women took their places in the factories. Their new life-style as wage earners encouraged their demands for political rights. In

August 1920, a constitutional amendment was ratified that gave women the right to vote.

Wilson grew more and more isolated from politics. In 1920, the Democratic party refused to nominate him for another term. Republican candidate Warren G. Harding won the presidential election. In December 1920, Wilson was awarded the Nobel Peace Prize, but he knew his efforts for a just peace had been blocked. After leaving the White House, Wilson made few public appearances, and he died on February 3, 1924.

Woolf, Virginia

(1882–1941)

ENGLISH NOVELIST, ESSAYIST, AND LITERARY CRITIC

Surely it was time someone invented a new plot or that the author came out from behind the bushes.

> —Virginia Woolf, *Between the Acts* (1941)

Virginia Woolf was a new voice writing a new kind of novel. Women had written novels before, even great ones, but none had written a novel that reflected a woman's consciousness in quite the same way as Woolf would.

Virginia Stephen was born on January 25, 1882, in London, England, the daughter of the writer and critic Sir Leslie Stephen. Stephen was a notable example of the Victorian man of letters, the author who was responsible for the creation of the first of the great biographical reference books, *The Dictionary of National Biography*. She and her sister Vanessa (who became famous as a painter), had little formal education, but they were given the free run of their father's extraordinary library. As Virginia later said of his influence, "To read what one liked because one liked it, never to pretend to admire what one did not—that was his only lesson in the art of reading." It was advice that would stand her in good stead in later years, when she became one of the most discerning and readable of literary critics.

The family was a large one. Virginia was the third of four children, Vanessa being the oldest. In addition, three children from Julia Stephen's first marriage lived in the house, as well as Laura Stephen, Leslie's mentally retarded daughter by his first marriage. In 1895, when Virginia was only thirteen, her mother died. Virginia had her first nervous breakdown, the first of many. The only cure that seemed to work was an extended period of rest, walks, and reading.

Sir Leslie died in 1904. The family moved to Bloomsbury, then an unfashionable but pleasant neighborhood near the British Museum. In November 1906, Thoby, Virginia's beloved older brother, died of typhoid. Two days later, Vanessa agreed to marry Clive Bell, an event that served as another blow to Virginia. Finally, Virginia and her younger brother, Adrian, were alone in the Bloomsbury house. For the next five years, Virginia struggled with her health, while trying to write her first novel.

In 1912, Virginia announced her engagement to one of Thoby's old friends, Leonard Woolf, "a penniless Jew," as she jokingly described him in the formal announcement. A member of the original circle of Cambridge students who had formed the core of the Bloomsbury literary group, he had been abroad for several years in government service in Ceylon (now Sri Lanka; at that time, Ceylon was under colonial British rule) and was now, not unlike Virginia's departed father, a freelance man of letters.

Theirs was a marriage of great and enduring mutual respect, but little sex. Their most important offspring was the Hogarth Press, the publishing firm that they founded and ran. In 1917, they had bought a small handpress, which came with a book of instructions, and they set it up on the dining room table in their home, Hogarth House (hence the firm's name). Leonard hoped that the manual labor of running a printing press might provide some relaxation for his emotionally overtaxed wife. They planned on occasionally issuing some of their friends' writings. They did not expect to be publishers in the commercial sense.

The Woolfs were better judges of good writing than they gave themselves credit for. Within a short time, Hogarth Press was self-supporting. More than that, it became an important outlet for writers and topics that a more conventional, profit-driven publisher wouldn't have touched. They became among the first to publish works by Sigmund Freud, John Maynard Keynes, T.S. Eliot, E.M. Forster, Katherine Mansfield, and many others.

Perhaps most important, they published the novels and essays of Virginia Woolf. With the Hogarth Press, Virginia had unlimited access to print. As the publisher and the author, she could follow her books from manuscript to final bound book, a luxury afforded to few authors. Most of all, she didn't have to adjust her writing for the exigencies of the marketplace. She had hated taking her earlier novels—*The Voyage Out* (1915) and *Night and Day* (1919)—to a conventional publisher (her half-brother's firm, Duckworth and Company). She could never have published her later ground-breaking work there.

Her work was becoming increasingly experimental in nature. Her first two books only hinted at the poetic techniques and radical approach to plot and theme that would emerge later. Her first breakthrough occurred with *Jacob's Room* (1922), a novel about a young man of promise who is failed by society.

The subject is not out of the ordinary, but the treatment of a coming-of-age novel in reverse—that is, the story of the destruction rather than the growth of a young man—most certainly is.

With her next book, *Mrs. Dalloway* (1925), Woolf joined the ranks of the great writers of High Modernism. Like James Joyce's *Ulysses,* the book's action takes place in a twenty-four-hour period. Her Clarissa Dalloway is struggling with a madness not unlike her own problems, and the novel is as much about her feelings and state of mind as it is about the tragic events surrounding her.

To the Lighthouse (1927), Woolf's next novel, is another inversion of genre, a family novel about how a family disintegrates. The book has three distinct sections, including a lengthy passage, central to the book, of the decay of the house in which the action takes place, a passage in which none of the human characters even appears.

By contrast, *Orlando* (1928) is a romp, a satirical biography of a young Elizabethan nobleman and his life over several centuries and two genders. Conceived as a tribute to her friend and lover, Vita Sackville-West, the novel is a lively, funny gem.

The Waves (1931) is probably Woolf's most accomplished novel, her masterpiece. By that time, as she herself readily acknowledged, she was "writing to a rhythm and not to a plot." Like *To the Lighthouse,* it is a novel that explores the question of what endures from a life.

After *The Waves,* it was hard to imagine how Woolf could push her poetic techniques any further. Not surprisingly, her next book headed in a different direction. *The Years* (1937) was originally conceived by the author as an "essay-novel," a multigenerational family saga that allowed Woolf to explore the events of the past century.

For all the seeming detachment of the Bloomsbury circle, Woolf was keenly aware of the darkening trends in the world. A pacifist married to a Jew, she could not ignore what was happening around her. And, indeed, it was taking a terrible toll on her emotional balance. Her nephew, Julian Bell, was killed in the Spanish Civil War in the mid-1930s. The Woolfs' house was destroyed by a German bomb during the blitz. Virginia was exhausted from writing the first version of her latest novel, *Between the Acts.* She began to hear the birdsong that had always preceded one of her breakdowns. She couldn't bear the thought of putting Leonard through another of her bouts of "the madness," as she called it. On March 28, 1941, she drowned herself in the River Ouse, near their country home in Sussex.

Woolf left behind an extraordinary legacy of writing. Her essays and criticism, influenced many writers. Her essays on feminist topics, particularly as they relate to literature, hold up very well a half-century after their original publication, and the novels are among the most important written in the twentieth century.

Wyeth, Andrew

(1917–   )

AMERICAN PAINTER

Andrew Wyeth was born in Chadds Ford, Pennsylvania, on July 17, 1917. He was the son of the gifted and successful illustrator and painter, N.C. Wyeth. Andrew Wyeth was educated at home and trained by his father, who was a stern and often severe teacher.

His primary activity as a child, besides drawing, was to take long walks in the countryside and talk with the farmers who lived nearby.

At the age of twelve, Wyeth provided illustrations for an edition of *Robin Hood*. Wyeth first exhibited his paintings in Philadelphia at the age of nineteen, and had his first one-person exhibit a year later in New York. His bright watercolors of the Maine landscape were so popular, that Wyeth sold all of his paintings within the first twenty-four hours of the exhibition.

Wyeth's work and life were divided between two farms: the Kuerners's farm in Chadds Ford, Pennsylvania, and the Olsons's farm in Maine. It was important to the artist that he paint only what he knew—the people and places that were close to him.

Wyeth's father died in 1945 and Andrew Wyeth's paintings became more serious and bleak, using darker colors and images. He depicted a scene realistically but used images to give the painting a symbolic, meaningful aspect. *A Crow Flew By* (1950), depicts a man in tattered clothes with a crow (a symbol of death in the painting) flying overhead.

Some critics used Wyeth's use of symbols to call him a "magic realist" and Wyeth admits that he is interested in more than just presenting a scene with photographlike precision. "If you can combine realism and abstraction, you've got something terrific," he has said.

Christina's World (1948), which depicted a crippled girl crawling toward a farmhouse in the distance, is one of the best- known American paintings of the twentieth century, contributing to Wyeth's standing as one of America's most popular artists.

In 1987, the National Gallery in Washington, D.C., exhibited its first one-person show of a living artist, Andrew Wyeth. Many critics suspected that the show was due not to the quality of the artist's work, but to the media coverage that had surfaced the previous year over Wyeth's paintings of Helga Testorf, a German immigrant who worked on the farm of Wyeth's neighbor. For fifteen years, Wyeth had sketched and painted Testorf, clothed and naked—awake, asleep, or working near his home.

Yeats, W(illiam). B(utler).

(1865–1939)

IRISH POET, PLAYWRIGHT, AND ESSAYIST

Of course I know quite well that this honor is not given to me as an individual, but as a representative of a literary movement and of a nation, and I am glad to have it so.

> —William Butler Yeats, upon receiving the 1923 Nobel Prize for Literature

Irish poet William Butler Yeats, born in Dublin, Ireland, on June 13, 1865, grew up as a member of the Protestant Irish Ascendancy, the son of a famous painter, J.B. Yeats, and a daughter of shipbuilders, Susan Pollexfen Yeats. Jack Yeats was a legendary figure, eloquent and elegant, verbose and moody. His son would be the same.

At first, William thought he would follow in his father's footsteps as a painter. He went to school in London, England, and spent his summer in Sligo, Ireland. At nineteen, he returned to Dublin to attend the Metropolitan School of Art and, after, the Royal Hibernian Academy School. Unfortunately, he lacked his father's talent. With that realization, he put aside paint and palette for poetry. He published his first poems in 1885.

Once more in London, Yeats organized the Rhymers' Club, a group of literary figures who met to talk about art and poetry. Under the spell of the old Irish folk legends, he also became involved with the Hermetic Students of the Golden Dawn, a group interested in esoteric (little known) texts and practices. He began to write and compile folk materials; he soon became one of the leading figures in the loosely configured movement called the "Celtic Twilight."

Yeats had dabbled briefly in Oriental themes in his poetry and verse drama, but he quickly realized that his heart was with the Irish tales. He began writing about the heroic and mystical Irish past. In 1893, he gathered the work of a group of like-minded poets in an anthology, *The Celtic Twilight,* exploring fairy stories and supernatural themes.

The Celtic Twilight writers, Yeats chief among them, were trying to reclaim and reconstruct an Irish culture that had been long neglected. Their writing focused on the local, their mood on the ethereal; they were deeply concerned with restoring if not the Gaelic language, then at least some of its feeling.

Yeats, who was now writing not only verse, but also poetic drama based on old Irish legends (beginning with his 1892 play, *The Countess Cathleen*), sought a vehicle for a truly Irish theater. He was fortunate enough to meet Lady Augusta Gregory, who helped him found what eventually became the Abbey Theatre. For Gregory, the creation of an indigenous theater was just another step on the road toward Irish Home Rule, which she supported strongly. At first, she provided encouragement and support for Yeats and the others who were trying to get the Abbey Theatre off the ground.

In the first decade of the new century, a new tone was heard in Yeats's writing. His poetry grew sharper, more focused, the language less ornate and more thoughtful. Many critics attribute the shift to his work with Lady Gregory, John Millington Synge, and the Abbey. Although Yeats wrote several plays for the Abbey, they survive more as examples of his poetry than as working dramatic texts; his contributions were more practical. As a theater manager, he certainly found himself dealing with more down-to-earth problems than fairy life. He struggled to make sure bills were paid, rehearsals scheduled, and plays chosen. He also wrote essays on his theories of drama and he defended Synge and company from the Philistines (people who have no respect for intellectual or artistic values) who drove James Joyce out of the country under similar circumstances.

Yeats was now under suspicion by the British authorities of harboring Irish nationalist sentiments. The Abbey performed several plays with strong anti-English, pro-Home Rule sympathies (mostly written by Gregory); many of his fellow Anglo-Irish Protestants were beginning to consider him a traitor to his class. Ironically, Yeats had endeavored to remain above the political fray. He had been wooing the writer and Irish nationalist Maude Gonne for years, and his lukewarm attitude toward "the cause" was one of the reasons that she resisted his advances.

Yeats was now in his most productive period. His verse reflected a new clarity of thought and a musicality that adapted the natural rhythms of speech to poetry. His style was continuing to evolve and grow. (So was his life: In 1917, a fifty-two-year-old W.B. Yeats married George Hyde-Lees.) His poetry took on an introspective, somber cast, conversational but musical. The outcome of the Irish Troubles, the terrible toll of World War I, the Bolshevik triumph in Russia—all these added to the feelings of despair, of a world spinning out of control, that he wrote of in "The Second Coming," which was undoubtedly his best-known poem, with its dire prediction: "The center cannot hold/Mere anarchy is loosed on the world." He received the 1923 Nobel Prize at least in part as a recognition of his ongoing achievements.

But he was far from done. For the remaining fifteen years of his life, Yeats was still a major poetic voice. In theater, he discovered and championed Sean O'Casey, whose plays at the Abbey were quite controversial, until the two writers had a falling-out in 1928. He also served in the Irish Parliament from 1922 until 1928.

That was the year of the first of his brilliant books of late verse, *The Tower,* the beginning of a series of final books of great stature. It was followed by *The Winding Stair and Other Poems* (1933); *New Poems* (1938); and a posthumously published collection, *Last Poems and Two Plays.* All this activity went on despite Yeats's worsening health.

What carried him through his last years was his personal philosophy, compounded of the mysticism and spirituality he had acquired when younger, and a surprising serenity that came with age. As he wrote to a friend in this period, "How strange is the subconscious gaiety that leaps up before danger or difficulty." It is a philosophy that is reflected in the late poems, as well.

On January 28, 1939, Yeats died in France and was buried in the cemetery of the medieval Riviera town of Roquebrune. In September 1948, his body was exhumed and returned to Ireland. He was buried with full honors in the Drumcliff churchyard, Sligo. It was as he requested in his poem "Under Ben Bulben": "Under bare Ben Bulben's head/In Drumcliff Churchyard Yeats is laid."

Zaharias, Mildred (Babe) Didrikson

(1913–1956)

AMERICAN BASKETBALL PLAYER, GOLFER, AND TRACK AND FIELD COMPETITOR

Babe Didrikson Zaharias once said, "I never wanted to be as good as somebody else. I always wanted to be better." The woman who would be voted Woman Athlete of the Half-Century by the Associated Press in 1950 was born in Texas in 1914. Her Norwegian immigrant parents worked hard to support seven children, of whom Mildred was the sixth. Her father loved sports but could not afford much equipment. He made bars from broom handles so his family could practice jumps and hurdles in the backyard. The Didriksons used barbells weighted on each side with flatirons.

Young Mildred was a natural athlete. The neighbors nicknamed her "Babe" because she hit so many home runs, like the legendary Yankee slugger Babe Ruth. And at Beaumont High School, she was the star of the girls' basketball team. An athletic director at the Employers Casualty Company read about her in the Texas newspapers and came to watch her remarkable playing. When Mildred finished school, she was invited to work there and to continue playing on its basketball team and start a track squad. When she wasn't working, Babe practiced running to increase her speed.

Babe Didrikson was 18 years old and just over 5 feet tall when she competed in the 1932 Olympics. She placed first in five of the eight track and field events she tried out for, easily making the team. Because of her age and size, she was only allowed to enter three events at the Los Angeles Games. Even so, Didrikson won two gold medals and one silver. She broke two of her own world records—in the javelin throw (143 feet, 4 inches) and 80-meter hurdles (11.9 seconds). In the high jump, she placed second.

After the Olympics, Didrikson was in the news again. Sportswriter Grantland Rice had invited her to play an 18-hole game of golf. Afterwards, he wrote about her skillful shots and predicted that she would be a champion. Didrikson learned golf with the determination she had shown in her other undertakings. "Weekends I put in twelve and sixteen hours a day. . . . I'd hit balls until my hands were bloody and sore," she later wrote in her autobiography, *This Life I've Lived*. In 1935, Didrikson won her first amateur golf tournament. But her title was taken away two days later on the grounds that she was a professional, not amateur, athlete, since she had earned some money at sports exhibitions.

Didrikson entered professional golf tournaments and continued to do exhibitions. She welcomed a chance to earn money so she could help her parents, describing the "hard times Momma and Poppa had gone through to raise us seven Didrikson kids." At exhibitions, Babe Didrikson ice-skated, rode horses, swam and dove, bowled, and played tennis and baseball. She set high goals and mastered any sport she tried. Spectators cheered as she drove golf balls more than 300 yards and pitched a baseball an amazing 296 feet.

At age 23, Babe Didrikson was playing in a golf exhibition in Los Angeles. There she met an outgoing, talented wrestler named George Zaharias. They were married that same year, 1938.

In 1943 Didrikson regained her status as an amateur golfer and was allowed to enter the major tournaments. From 1946 to 47, she won several major titles, including the U.S. Women's Amateur, the British Women's Amateur, and three U.S. Women's Opens. During these years, Didrikson set an all-time record by winning seventeen major tournaments in a row. Author and sportswriter Paul Gallico called her "probably the most talented athlete, male or female, ever developed in our country." In *This Life I've Lived,* Didrikson said that she "was always determined to be the greatest athlete that ever lived."

Didrikson was only 39 years old when she found out that she had cancer. In 1953, surgeons removed part of her colon (a part of the large intestine). Fans from around the world sent get-well letters, telegrams, and gifts to the popular athlete. With courage and her husband's helps Didrikson returned to golfing. Three and a half months after her operation, she played at the All-American Golf Tournament. Although tired and in pain, Didrikson placed fifteenth. Two days later, she came in third in the world championship. These achievements helped her win the Ben Hogan Trophy for the year's greatest comeback.

In 1954, Babe Didrikson won the U.S. Women's Open. Her remarkable victory inspired other people facing cancer. She said, "Every time I get out and play well in a tournament, it seems to encourage people with the same trouble I had." When she won the All-American that year and was voted Woman Athlete of 1954, she said it would "show people not to be afraid of cancer. I'll go on golfing for years."

Sadly, Babe Didrikson Zaharias died two years later. Her many fans mourned the loss of this great sportswoman and courageous person, one of the finest all-around athletes the world has ever known.